PUEBLO INDIAN RELIGION

Volume II

Elsie Clews Parsons

*Introduction to the Bison Books Edition
by Ramón A. Gutiérrez*

University of Nebraska Press
Lincoln and London

∞ The paper in this book meets the minimum requirements of American
National Standard for Information Sciences—Permanence of Paper for
Printed Library Materials, ANSI Z39.48-1984.

First Bison Books printing: 1996
Most recent printing indicated by the last digit below:
10 9   8   7   6   5   4   3   2   1

Library of Congress Cataloging-in-Publication Data
Parsons, Elsie Worthington Clews, 1875–1941.
Pueblo Indian religion / Elsie Clews Parsons; introduction to the Bison
Books edition by Pauline Turner Strong.—Bison Books ed.
p. cm.
Vol. 2: Introd. to the Bison Books ed. by Ramón A. Gutiérrez.
Includes bibliographical references and index.
ISBN 0-8032-8735-6 (v. 1: pbk.: alk. paper).—ISBN 0-8032-8736-4 (v. 2:
pbk.: alk. paper)
1. Pueblo Indians—Religion.   2. Pueblo mythology.   3. Pueblo Indi-
ans—Rites and ceremonies.   I. Title.
E99.P9P32   1996
299′.784—dc20
95-47046   CIP

INTRODUCTION TO THE BISON BOOKS EDITION

Ramón A. Gutiérrez

Back in 1969, as I began my own education on the archaeology, history, and anthropology of my birthplace, New Mexico, a teacher at the University of New Mexico sent me packing to the library with a "must read" list. Dutifully, I began to read the classics: the Spanish chronicles of exploration, conquest and settlement, the memorials of the Franciscan friars, the archaeological site studies. When finally I entered the library's stacks looking for Elsie Clews Parsons's *Pueblo Indian Religion*, the shelf was bare. Zimmermann Library had once owned multiple circulating copies of the work, the circulation clerk informed. All of them had disappeared. The library had one copy of *Pueblo Indian Religion* under lock and key. Access was limited. Privileges to copy anything out of the 1275-page tome were restricted. I soon discovered that at other New Mexican libraries the fate of *Pueblo Indian Religion* had been quite similar.

The missing books. Why? Why had so many copies of *Pueblo Indian Religion* disappeared from New Mexican libraries? Into what political vortex had this book been drawn? As the months passed by and my dogged determination to see a copy of Elsie Clews Parsons's most celebrated work increased, some of the complicated reasons for the missing books emerged. Librarians told me that *Pueblo Indian Religion* was controversial. It has been since its first publication in 1939. Some Pueblo Indians were angry that Elsie Parsons had published secret, sacred knowledge about the relationship between the Pueblos and their gods. Pueblo priests believed that words had power. To utter or print sacred words outside their religious context was to desecrate them. Destroying copies of *Pueblo Indian Religion*, thus denying "outsiders" access to "insider" information, was deemed by some a tactic for the preservation of culture.

Since 1598, when the Spaniards first conquered the Pueblo Indians and imposed Christianity on them, the Puebloans have resisted "outsiders" and tried to maintain the integrity of their religious and ceremonial life by practicing a strict code of silence about it. Ritual knowledge in every pueblo was always highly restricted knowledge gained only very slowly and only fragmentarily after decades of gift exchange between elders and aspirants. Into this warp of knowledge/power the Franciscan friars entered violently, prohibiting native religious practices. At those pueblos that became most visibly Christianized, Pueblo religion went underground and knowledge of its intricacies became even more secretive and restricted. Today as one travels from west to east, from the Hopi pueblos in Arizona to the pueblos of the Rio Grande drainage in New Mexico—from the desert villages where Spanish culture and institutions were marginally imposed to the villages situated around lush mountains and irrigated river valleys where the Spanish colonial project was centered and most transformative of Pueblo ways—one finds a west to east continuum that goes from "liberal" to "conservative" regarding "outsiders" and attitudes toward religious secrecy. The pueblos most studied by nineteenth- and twentieth-century ethnographers were the Western Pueblos—Hopi, Zuni, Acoma, Laguna. The Eastern Pueblos have been the least studied, the most Christianized, the most secretive, and also the most suspicious of "outsiders."

Elsie Clews Parsons first seriously entered the world of Pueblo Indian ethnography through the Western Pueblos, visiting Zuni on 20 August 1915. Interested in anthropology, she collaborated with Franz Boas at Columbia University and from there decided to follow his aspirants into the field. Alfred Kroeber, a Boas student, was then conducting research at Zuni. He served as Parsons's entré to the village, gained her hospitality in the home of Zuni's governor, where she befriended the governor's wife, Margaret Lewis, an Oklahoma Cherokee schoolteacher who had married into the tribe. Lewis quickly became Parsons's confidant, a relationship that was absolutely crucial for the anthropologist's work (Panday 1972:321–37). Lewis acted as her interpreter, secured her informants, and kept her constantly informed by letter and journal of events at Zuni (Hare 1985:133).

When her first visit to Zuni ended, Parsons was absolutely ecstatic about what she had seen and learned. "In Zuni, I shall have a great opportunity for brief periods of fieldwork, the thing I've been hankering for for years," she wrote her husband, Herbert. "The glory of this place . . . I do wish you could see and feel it" (Zumwalt 1992:

155, 152) Thus began Parsons's roughly twenty-five years of work among the Pueblo Indians. In that time she resided at Zuni, Laguna, Acoma, Jemez, Isleta, and among the Hopi. Her field trips to New Mexico and Arizona were short and intensive. They usually never lasted more than a month.

What most fascinated Parsons about Zuni was the power women enjoyed there. Women owned the houses in which they lived. They continued to reside in them even after marriage. A man joined the household of his wife and there, at her pleasure, worked and lived (Hare 1985:141). For Elsie Clews Parsons, and for the countless women anthropologists who would follow her into the Southwest, the area became an important site to escape the patriarchal conventions of industrial society in the eastern United States. In the expansive, unsettled, and open landscape of the Southwest, they could break the shackles of bourgeois Victorian conventions.[1] Among the matrilineal Western Pueblos, women were as highly valued as men.

As an ardent feminist, Elsie Clews Parsons had long detested the social restrictions women endured. At a young age she rebelled against traditional women's roles and highly structured relations with men.[2] Deeply committed to giving every individual the utmost freedom of self-expression, she determined to "set personality free from the overbearing rule of age-class, of sex division, of economic and political class, of family and nation" (Spier 1943:245). In her first book, *The Family* (1906), Parsons examined the ways patriarchs encroached on the self. She urged couples to live together in trial marriages before embarking on a lifelong commitment and children. So heterodox was the idea of trial marriage, so public the furor, that it almost cost her husband, Herbert Parsons, a Republican congressman from New York, his career (Friedlander 1988:284–85). But Elsie Clews Parsons continued to revolt against social conventions that perpetuated women's subordination, seeking through her writing to liberate the individual from societal constraints.[3]

Desley Deacon, a recent biographer of Elsie Clews Parsons, maintains that she was an outsider in her own society and an even greater outsider among the Pueblo Indians. "She never identified herself with the people she wrote about; nor did she establish close relationships with informants that went beyond the courtesy due, in her system of ethics, to any other individual," writes Deacon (1992:12–38). What

Parsons learned about Pueblo culture she learned almost exclusively from a very small number of paid informants and from her host families at different pueblos. At pueblos like Isleta, which were particularly secretive, she took no notes during her interviews and only wrote up what she had learned when back in her hotel room (cf. Lamphere 1989:523). She relied heavily on the published and unpublished notes of other ethnographers who had worked among the Pueblos. Frank Hamilton Cushing's reports on Zuni and John Stephen's journal from the Hopi First Mesa, were particularly important. In 1936, after close to nine years of editorial work on it, she published *The Hopi Journal of Alexander M. Stephen* (Parsons 1936a).

Throughout Parsons's fieldwork among the Pueblo Indians, access to information constantly bedeviled her. At Acoma in 1917, for example, she was received cordially, but coolly. When they learned that she intended to stay to see one of their important ritual dances performed, they rapidly rescheduled it. In 1921 when she arrived at Jemez Pueblo to witness the deer dance, the village governor ordered a guard to keep her indoors. He even had her room window covered with sacks so that she would not be able to see the dancers as they went by (Hare 1985:145, 147).

When Parsons visited the Hopi villages for the second time in 1920, news was circulating that she was writing books about their secret ceremonies. Hoping to blunt the criticism and to become an "insider," a member of the tribe, in June 1920 she sought ritual adoption into a family, incorporation into a household, and a Hopi name. The Hopi elder Sixtaine and his sister Chii obliged. Chii performed the hair washing ritual that transformed her into a family member. Later that year when Parsons returned to Hopi, hoping now as an "insider," as a member of the pueblo, to observe a kiva ceremonial, she learned that women were not permitted to witness this male ritual (Hare 1985:143–45).

As a scientist working among the secretive Pueblos, Parsons wrote that to do her work she had become "the most ruthless of detectives." Heeding the advice of previous ethnographers in the area, she quickly realized that it was often easier to obtain information from Puebloans when they were alone, off the pueblo, and out of the direct line of sight of their war captains, who were also known as "outside chiefs" because they protected the pueblo from outsiders. Such a technique served her well in learning Keres kinship terminology. Eager for information on Santo Domingo Pueblo, one of the most secretive of the pueblos, she coaxed a pottery vendor at Lamy's train station, by promising him a dollar an hour. Parsons explained that this amount was "more than you can make all day selling those bowls." When the session was over, she asked for the man's name and promised to write him. He refused. "It would get me into trouble," he replied (Hare 1985:146).

For twenty-five years Parsons labored under the constant surveillance of "outside chiefs" and their threats to punish anyone who revealed esoteric knowledge. Nonetheless, she was always able to obtain informants. She offered relatively large amounts of money for information. And this money undoubtedly lubricated conversation and tempered how threatening sanctions might appear from afar. With gifts, cash, and undoubtedly some "ruthlessness," Parsons got several Puebloans to talk. Did they divulge "secrets"? Let us return to this question. For the moment, suffice it to say that Parsons's Isleta artist/informant, for example, produced more than 140 paintings depicting many aspects of the relationship between the ritual cycle and the life cycle, knowledge that some deemed "secret." These paintings are the only pictorial record of Pueblo rituals created entirely by a native informant (Goldfrank 1978; Zumwalt 1992:244, 247).

In the early 1920s, while working on her 1925 monograph *The Pueblo of Jemez*, Parsons obtained numerous drawings of ceremonial masks. "They would put me in jail for this. . . . It is our life. They say if we tell about it, we are going to die," explained her informant. As another informant handed her similar drawings, he too said that the village authorities will "kill me for this" (Hare 1985:147–48).

Shortly after the book's appearance she received letters from Jemez residents reporting how people were being "persecuted," falsely suspected as her informants. They begged her to divulge the names of the true informants so that the terror could end. One of the falsely accused told Parsons that he had been called before the pueblo's governor several times and had had his water rights severely cut. But Elsie Parsons refused to divulge their names. She maintained that *The Pueblo of Jemez* would only be read by a "few wise white people."

The book, which she paid to be printed privately, was her gift to the Jemez Indians. It was, she said, a gift from a close friend that would one day help children and grandchildren remember their ancient customs (Hare 1985:146–47).

Elsie Clews Parsons was no stranger to controversy. Her work angered and enraged. She was snubbed and banished. Numerous times she was even threatened with death. Her 1936 book, *Taos Pueblo*, begins with this dedication.

> To: My best friend in Taos, the most scrupulous Pueblo Indian of my acquaintance, who told me nothing about the pueblo and who never will tell any white person anything his people would not have him tell, which is nothing.

Once the book appeared, it was instantly apparent that a member of the Big Earrings Kiva had revealed much too much. Parsons was immediately considered by some as the town's archenemy and informed that if she visited Taos Pueblo again, she would be killed. When asked about the death threats the book had provoked, Elsie Parsons allegedly replied, "Why do you think I have not set foot in Taos Pueblo again?" Parsons maintained that no secret knowledge had been revealed in *Taos Pueblo*. She had not be been able to secure "secrets." What information she reported was open knowledge. Consciously, she had written it in such a way that no one faction of the town could use it against another (Hare 1985:162). The controversy continued (Bodine 1967:18). Parsons tried to defuse it by writing to the Taos Pueblo Governor and Council: "Anyone reading the book would see that I like and admire Taos people and do not wish to hurt their feelings or disturb them in any way" (Hare 1985:162).

Did Elsie Clews Parsons and her informants divulge "secrets"? This issue cannot be addressed adequately without first exploring how social inequalities in the pueblos are politically articulated. The relationship between Puebloans and their gods is solely the province of men. More specifically, this is knowledge that senior men, organized into esoteric associations known as kivas, control. When junior men seek the knowledge and power to hunt successfully, to make war, to cure, to make rain, or when they simply seek blessings, they or their ritual sponsors offer gifts to priests of a particular kiva in return for what they need. Knowledge obtained with gifts is always exchanged slowly, over a long course of time. This maximizes the dependence of the young on the old, of aspirants on ritual specialists, and perpetuates the material inequality on which the gifting calculus is based. Without secrecy, the value of knowledge in the calculus evaporates.[4]

No kiva knows it all. No group of priests controls all knowledge or the sacred power that stems from it. Factionalism and conflict are endemic to many Pueblo towns precisely because of competing knowledge/power claims. The origin myths of different kivas, the specific songs and prayers that only certain priests can recite, the genealogies that only a few are empowered to tell are "secret" knowledge. But this knowledge when uttered or printed becomes profoundly political narrative. For when the priests of one kiva outline the organization of society in mythic times, detailing the order of creation, who helped whom emerge from the underworld when and where, these men assert that their spatial claims in the village, their rights, and their precedence in relationships with other men, with women, and with the members of various households, moieties, and clans are of divine and supernatural origin. These are always highly contested claims. Records that date back to the sixteenth century illustrate that contestation of this sort is not new, but quite antique. Indeed, the origin myths of every pueblo tell of fights, of communities splintering around lineage and household lines, of intense kiva rivalries, of fragmentation, dispersal, and reaggregation when such contests were lost or won.[5]

When Pueblo informants spoke up out of turn, out of place, to the wrong sorts, when Pueblo artists drew paintings for Elsie Parsons, they offered in their texts narratives that contested what kiva priests knew and controlled (cf. Yava 1978; Talayesava 1942). When Parsons spoke with Pueblo women who were outsiders to the world of the gods and men, they too offered a different vision and version of the very order of things (Parsons 1991). When Parsons befriended male transvestites, outsiders in the political world of men, she found situated knowledge of a different sort (cf. Gutiérrez 1989). The Pueblos have never been a unitary people, nor have their villages been hermetically sealed. Pueblos and non-Pueblos have married out and in. Children assimilated, first Spanish, Mexican, and eventually

American ways. Christianity had a profound effect, both Catholic and Protestant strains. Material innovations have been adopted, accommodated, and resisted. The social fractions produced by such alternative ways, the ebb and flow of Pueblo life, this is what Elsie Clews Parsons discovered from her informants. This is the political context within which the rhetoric of "secrets" must be placed. These were the historical tensions within which Parsons herself worked. These are still very much the politics within which any scholar, Puebloan or not, writes.

The impetus for the production of Parsons's monumental tome, *Pueblo Indian Religion*, began in 1924. This is how she then formulated the task:

> The Pueblo Indians of New Mexico and Arizona have the most complex culture, it is generally agreed, of any of the Indians of North America, and their culture has been one of the most resistant to disintegrating influence. Surrounded by predatory Indian tribes, and subject to the White race for three centuries, first to the Spanish Conquistadores and friars, then to American traders and Washington agents and school teachers, this population of ten thousand Indians, living in thirty towns scattered through a very large territory, have held their own to an amazing degree. Contrasted with their alien neighbors, Indian or white, whether economically as farmers, house builders, or craftsmen, or from the point of view of family, government, or religion, the Pueblos have appeared homogeneous; yet from within the population presents wide variations. . . . Such differentiations raise a twofold problem in historic reconstruction; from what outside sources may have come these varying cultural elements, and what have been the inter-pueblo processes of communication and imitation or of resistance to imitation? (Parsons 1924:140)

In the years that preceded the 1939 appearance of *Pueblo Indian Religion*, Parsons read and observed, compared and contrasted the patterns she found dispersed throughout the Pueblos and the rest of Spanish America. Confident of the Boasian idea of the multiplicity of historical factors that accounted for particular cultural situations, she traveled to Mallorca, to Oaxaca, in southern Mexico, and to Ecuador to study the impact of Spanish Catholicism on indigenous peoples (Spier 1943:246; Reichard 1943:45–56). As a result of these larger concerns, in 1927 she openly wondered whether witchcraft beliefs among the Pueblos were indigenous or Spanish. Known sources of affliction and the way to cure them were certainly Pueblo and pre-Spanish. But "all these beliefs . . . were enriched by Spanish witchcraft theory, which also spread, if it did not introduce the idea that anybody might practice witchcraft" (Parsons 1927:106–12, 125–28).

Parsons advanced the theory that certain fundamental elements of the Pueblo Kachina Cult—clown performances, masked imper-sonation, flagellation—were of Spanish origin. She believed that a Pueblo ritual nucleus had been augmented by Spanish influences (Parsons 1930). She found and reported "Ritual Parallels in Pueblo and Plains Culture" (1929), "Some Aztec and Pueblo Parallels" (1933), and similarities between "The Sacred Clowns of the Pueblo and Mayo-Yaqui Indians" (1934). Indeed, her monographic study of an Oaxacan town, *Mitla, Town of the Souls* (1936b), was researched in an effort to trace the connections between central Mexican pat-terns and development and those found among the Pueblos, which Parsons considered better preserved.

Pueblo Indian Religion appeared in 1939, the culmination of Elsie Clews Parsons's extensive data collection and comparison of Pueblo cultural traits, their diffusion, and change over time. Broad in scope, encyclopedic in its detail, *Pueblo Indian Religion* was the first com-prehensive survey of Pueblo social organization, religious beliefs, and practice. Every major study of the Pueblos since has relied on it extensively. Fred Eggan's *The Social Organization of the Western Pueblos* (1950), Robin Fox's *The Keresan Bridge* (1967), Edward Dozier's *The Pueblo Indians of North America* (1970), Alfonso Ortiz's *The Tewa World* (1969) and *New Perspectives on the Pueblos* (1972), were fundamentally framed by Parsons's groundwork in *Pueblo In-dian Religion*. By today's standards Elsie Clews Parsons certainly typified the excesses of colonial anthropology—the exploitation and abuse of informants, the condescension toward her hosts, grandiose generalizations based, at best, on shards. Nevertheless, a fundamen-tal fact remains. *Pueblo Indian Religion* has yet to be superseded by any other work.

In the preface to *Pueblo Indian Religion,* Elsie Clew Parsons wrote that a white woman once asked a Taos Pueblo resident, "What is

Indian religion?" "Life," he responded. By which he meant that "religion was a means to life, that it covered life as a whole, and, . . . that . . . everything was alive and a part of religion. Life, in Zuni terms *tekohana*, light, life, well-being, and . . . how to ask for it—that is indeed Pueblo religion" (vol. 1, xxxiv). Today, we usually think of religion as a subjective differentiation of the supernatural from the natural. But for Parsons, religion was a kind of instrumentalism, a systematic utilitarianism by which individuals got what they wanted and needed. Pueblo religion was:

> a form of instrumentalism controlling the natural through the supernatural, usually, of course, as a flow of interest, not as planned enterprise. The technique of control is largely magical, that is, ritual acts are automatically effectual: prayer or song or dance, color or line are formulistic or compulsive; but there is more here than magic—there is conceptual control. . . . Pueblos have classified and interpreted their world the better to control it. Other peoples have done likewise. Religion is less antithesis to science than it is science gone astray. (xxxii–xxxiii)

In volume 1 of *Pueblo Indian Religion* Parsons sketched the dimensions of Pueblo ceremonial organization, cosmology, and calendar, and then moved on to a town-by-town review of rituals and ceremonies. All of the evidence gathered culminates in volume 2 with chapters on "Variation and Borrowing" and "Other Processes of Change," which are supremely historical in scope. Having sifted through considerable contextual detail here, Parsons pulled together the theoretical strands, illustrating the syncretisms, the cultural convergences wrought by colonialism. She saw mixing. She saw blending. She saw hybridities which were the product of adaptation, of acculturation, way before 1492, and long after it. "Pueblos are or were Spanish Indians," Parsons boldly asserted, "although we rarely think of them as such, and their history should be compared with that of Hispanicized Indians elsewhere, the better to analyze out the Spanish and the Indian, and understand early cultural changes" (xxx). By looking at the foreign influences that had shaped the Pueblos in prehistoric and historic times, one might best predict the likely course of change.

Parsons proposed that the proliferation of ceremonialism among the Western Pueblos was due to cultural involution, that process whereby one cultural aspect is developed into a complex whole. The high value placed on this complex engenders involution, and the continued interest in ceremonialism accounts for the success of Western Pueblo life against alien impact: "as long as people are working at or playing with their cultural patterns, their way of life appears integrated, sincere, and vital" (vol. 2, p. 1150). Pueblo culture had a certain elasticity, a "mobility within steadfast design," which had enabled it to remain dynamic even during the most adverse conditions: "Once the urge to involute is arrested, the desire to elaborate design or to reapply it, decadence of a sort sets in. . . . That is why Pueblos still show a greater cultural vitality than other North American Indians" (pp. 1149, 1150).

Parsons believed that any change in the basic pattern of material life would undoubtedly change the ideological integrity of Pueblo culture. What might begin as innovations in irrigation, wasteland clearing, house construction, might quickly lead to the disintegration of indigenous life. "Any irrigation system independent of rainfall will be fatal to the prestige of the kachina" (p. 1143). "If individual male ownership emerges from current practices in clearing wasteland or building houses off the mesa, the clan will break down, and, . . . a good deal of Hopi ceremonial will lapse" (p. 1159). "Pueblo arts are ritual arts, their motivation is religious. If this motivation lapses, the arts will lapse; for the only substitute motivation in sight is commercial gain" (p. 1142). Had Elsie Clews Parsons witnessed the development of Pueblo gaming, she undoubtedly would have made similar predictions.

Elsie Clews Parsons greatly loved and admired the Pueblo Indians for their "kindly live-and-let-live attitudes." Harking back to the social preoccupations that had brought her to the Southwest, Parsons noted in *Pueblo Indian Religion* that among the Pueblos one found "Social responsibility combined with individual tolerance—here perhaps is an American lead to that working substitute for the glorification of God or of State or of Mankind other Americans are seeking" (vol. 1, xxxvi).

Toward the end of her life Elsie Clews Parsons confided to Gladys E. Reichard, her student, that "she thought of her work as a mosaic and that she hated to omit any detail, even if at the time it might seem irrelevant, for she believed and often had had proved to her satisfaction, that the record of an apparently trivial detail might after many years furnish an invaluable clue to someone with a different point of view" (Reichard 1943:47).

Parsons's concern for detail is what will long make her *Pueblo Indian Religion* necessary for students of the Southwest. Long after psychological, symbolic, and interpretive anthropology have been forgotten, Elsie Clews Parsons will be remembered for the myths, the folktales, the calendar of ceremonies, the names of clans, moieties, and deities, which are quickly being forgotten and which young and old Puebloans want to remember and never to forget.

NOTES

1. For a feminist interpretation of Elsie Clews Parsons's career in anthropology, see Lamphere and Babcock and Parezo (1988).

2. Parsons was apparently greatly influenced by Theodore Roosevelt's ideal of a strenuous life of outdoor activity and contact with primitives as a route to personal and national salvation. On this point see Deacon (1992).

3. On these points, refer to Parsons (1913, 1914, 1915, 1916).

4. On Pueblo gifting calculus, see Gutiérrez (1991:3–36).

5. On Pueblo factionalism, see this volume (1137–38, 1094–97), French (1966), Pandey (1977), Whitely (1988).

BIBLIOGRAPHY

Babcock, Barbara A. and Nancy J. Parezo
    1988 *Daughters of the Desert: Women Anthropologists of the Native American Southwest, 1880–1980.* Albuquerque: University of New Mexico Press.
Bodine, John James
    1967 Attitudes and Institutions of Taos, New Mexico: Variables for Value System Expression. Ph.D. diss., Tulane University.
Brandt, Elizabeth
    1977 The Role of Secrecy in Pueblo Society. In *Flowers of the Wind: Papers on Ritual, Myth and Symbolism in California and the Southwest*, ed. Thomas C. Blackburn, pp. 11–28. Socorro NM: Ballena Press.

1980 On Secrecy and the Control of Knowledge: Taos Pueblo. In *Secrecy: A Cross-Cultural Perspective*, ed. Stanton K. Tefft, pp. 123–46. New York: Human Sciences Press.

Deacon, Desley
1992 The Republic of the Spirit: Fieldwork in Elsie Clews Parsons's Turn to Anthropology. *Frontiers* 12, no. 3:12–38.

Dozier, Edward P.
1970 *The Pueblo Indians of North America*. New York: Holt, Rinehart and Winston, Inc.

Eggan, Fred
1950 *Social Organization of Western Pueblos*. Chicago: University of Chicago Press.

Fox, Robin
1967 *The Keresan Bridge*. London School of Economics Monographs in Social Anthropology, no. 35. London: The Athlone Press; New York: Humanities Press.

French, David H.
1966 *Factionalism in Isleta Pueblo*. Seattle: University of Washington Press.

Friedlander, Judith
1988 Elsie Clews Parsons (1874–1941). *Women Anthropologists: A Biographical Dictionary*, ed. Ute Gacs, et. al., pp. 284–85. New York: Greenwood Press.

Goldfrank, Esther
1978 Notes on an Undirected Life: As One Anthropologist Tells It. *Queens College Publications in Anthropology* no. 3: 21–34.

Gutiérrez Ramón
1989 Deracinating Indians in Search of Gay Roots: A Response to Will Roscoe's "The Zuni Man-Woman." *Out/Look* 4 (spring): 61–67.
1991 *When Jesus Came, the Corn Mothers Went Away: Marriage, Sexuality and Power in New Mexico 1500–1846*. Stanford: Stanford University Press.

Hare, Peter H.
1985 *A Woman's Quest for Science: Portrait of Anthropologist Elsie Clews Parsons*. Buffalo NY: Prometheus Books.

Lamphere, Louise
1989 Feminist Anthropology: The Legacy of Elsie Clews Parsons. *American Ethnologist* 16, no. 3 (August): 523.

Ortiz, Alfonso
1969 *The Tewa World*. Chicago: University of Chicago Press.
1972 (ed.) *New Perspectives on the Pueblos*. Albuquerque: University of New Mexico Press.

Pandey, Triloki Nath

    1972 Anthropologists at Zuni. *Proceedings of the American Philosophical Society* 116, no. 4:321–37.

    1977 Images of Power in a Southwestern Pueblo. In *The Anthropology of Power*, eds. Raymond D. Fogelson and Richard N. Adams, pp. 195–216. New York: Columbia University Press.

Parsons, Elsie Clews

    1913 *The Old-Fashioned Woman: Primitive Fancies about the Sex.* New York: G. P. Putnam's Sons.

    1914 *Fear and Conventionality.* New York: G. P. Putnam's Sons.

    1915 *Social Freedom: A Study of Conflicts between Social Classifications and Personality.* New York: G. P. Putnam's Sons.

    1916 *Social Rule: A Study of the Will to Power.* New York: G. P. Putnam's Sons.

    1924 The Religion of the Pueblo Indians. In *XXI Congres International des Americanistes.*

    1925 *The Pueblo of Jemez.* New Haven: pub. for the Department of Archaeology, Phillips Academy, Andover MA, by the Yale University Press.

    1927 Witchcraft among the Pueblos: Indian or Spanish? *Man* 27:106–12, 125–28.

    1929 Ritual Parallels in Pueblo and Plains Culture. *American Anthropologist* 51:642–45.

    1930 Spanish Elements in the Kachina Cult. In *XXIII International Congress of Americanists, Proceedings*, 582–603.

    1933 "Some Aztec and Pueblo Parallels," *American Anthropologist* 35:611–31.

    1934 The Sacred Clowns of the Pueblo and Mayo-Yaqui Indians. *American Anthropologist* 36:491–514.

    1936a (ed.) *The Hopi Journal of Alexander M. Stephen.* New York: Columbia University Press.

    1936b *Mitla, Town of the Souls.* Chicago: University of Chicago Publications in Anthropology.

    1936c *Taos Pueblo.* Menasha WI: George Banta Publishing Co.

    1991 *Pueblo Mothers and Children.* Comp. Barbara Babcock. Albuquerque: University of New Mexico Press.

Reichard, Gladys E.

    1943 Elsie Clews Parsons: Obituary. *Journal of American Folklore* 56:45–56.

Spier, Leslie

    1943 Elsie Clews Parsons: Obituary. *American Anthropologist* 45:244ff.

Talayesva, Don C.
   1942 *Sun Chief: The Autobiography of a Hopi Indian*. New Haven: Yale
        University Press.
Whitely, Peter M.
   1988 *Deliberate Acts: Changing Hopi Culture through the Oraibi Split*.
        Tucson: University of Arizona Press.
Yava, Albert
   1978 *Little Falling Snow: A Tewa-Hopi Indian's Life and Times, and
        the History and Traditions of His People*. New York: Crown.
Zumwalt, Rosemary Levy
   1992 *Wealth and Rebellion: Elsie Clews Parsons, Anthropologist and
        Folklorist*. Urbana: University of Illinois Press.

CHAPTER VI
CEREMONIES

Offering the Spirits what they like, in pay for what is asked of them—favorable weather, fertility, health and longevity; control of conditions through mimetic magic, including foreknowledge; cleansing or secularizing—these are the major religious and magical categories the rites fall into. A ceremony is a congery of such rites, and the ends or purposes of all ceremonial are more or less similar: rainfall or snowfall, stilling the wind, prediction of the coming season, abundance of crops, animals, or children, cure of disease whether from the dead, the kachina, or the animals, longevity. Social assurance, gratification of desire for stability and order, these are implicit in this notably utilitarian or instrumental version of the same desire for spiritual law in the natural world which motivates other forms of religion.

More or less esoteric techniques by the chiefs or doctors, techniques of restraint and concentration, of offerings, of mimetic behavior, of prayer and song are followed by spectacular procession, race, or dance, in which the co-operation of other groups is solicited, often with a cigarette of invitation.

Sun's arrival at his house, the winter solstice, is celebrated variously in the different Pueblo tribes, but in general all the ceremonial groups function, and lay people take part in a way not usual in other ceremonies. Almost all the Spirits are represented, although more particularly the Sun and, in the West, the War gods. One common feature is ritual for increase, through prayer-images or through seed corn. It is the time when everybody plans or prays for the new year. Every group is more or less self-expressive or participant, so that there are many rituals or ceremonials, at least in the West.

Between the Hopi and Zuni celebrations there are several parallels. In both tribes there is a general offering by everybody of prayer-sticks made by the men. And there is a special Sun prayer-stick-making, at Zuni by Pekwin, on First Mesa by the Sun chief or watcher with his maternal group. Incorporated into the ceremony or following closely upon it is a War god ceremony. Certain kachina appear, and at the ceremony, or shortly after, the way is "opened" for the return of the kachina who have been prescriptively absent from Zuni since their departure after Shalako and from the Hopi towns since they "went home" (Nima'n) the July preceding.[1] As at Acoma certain cosmic personages and Whipper kachina appear, performing dramatic rituals in Chief kiva at night (Walpi). There are council meetings. Ceremonial plans for the year are made by the paramount chiefs or submitted to them. Kachina impersonators are appointed and kachina dances by kiva arranged. At Oraibi an expedition for wafer-bread stone or for salt would be announced at this time. "Everything branches out from the Soyal."[2]

Ceremonial organization in the East differs so much from that of the West that the solstice ceremony is necessarily very different. Solar observation is made by the Town chief, if made at all. Celebration begins about December 1, the date reckoned, apparently, by the Julian calendar. There is no general prayer-stick offering, but laymen may be invited to join in the preliminary "fast" or emesis (Santo Domingo, also Isleta) by society or Corn group. For four mornings the Keresan societies vomit;

they hold a day and all-night ceremony which is called Haniko, Southeast, referring to the position of "Sun's house." At Santo Domingo the shamans make prayer-sticks and miniature bows and arrows and net shields; lay visitors make prayer-feathers and prayer-images—ears of corn, melons, horses, or cattle; a silversmith would make a little wooden hammer. After lying on the altar, all these things, also seeds and bits of turquoise, are bundled together and the bundle which is called "Sun" is taken out to be offered,[3] undoubtedly to Sun;[*] there is a night dance in kiva. At Acoma the Town chief presents Sun with a miniature suit, and Sun together with the Chiefs of the Seasons and other supernaturals come in as kachina. At Jemez the Town chief observes the sun and the societies conduct ceremonial. Seed corn lies on the altars overnight. Among Tewa the moiety Town chiefs observe the sun. "The sun rests" in his "house" for four days, during which various taboos are observed by all the people; no smoking outdoors, no ashes or refuse taken out (San Juan, Nambé). At San Ildefonso after the four-day solstice re-treats by the Town chiefs, kachina exhibit. There is no informa-tion about solstice observance by Tewa medicine societies. At Isleta there are synchronous four-day ceremonies by all the Corn groups and the medicine societies. Infants get their "Corn names." The Town chief receives reports, but holds no cere-mony. The winter solstice is observed at Taos by the Cacique who is accounted a semi-Spanish official, but whatever ritual there may be is a minor part of the forty-day celebration of "staying still" by all the townspeople, and of ceremonies for getting power by all the kiva societies.

The summer solstice, "when the sun turns back to winter," is observed, but ceremonial celebration is everywhere less im-portant than at the winter turning. At Oraibi the group in charge of the Sun changes, but no transfer ritual has been re-ported. The Walpi Sun chieftaincy make prayer-sticks for the

[*] As at Cochiti, where included in the bundle are miniature kick-sticks and hunting-sticks. Sun is prayed to for success in fighting, and to protect the harvests (Dumarest, 203). See Parsons 48 for account of a Keresan winter solstice shrine in a volcanic pit.

Sun which are deposited in his mountain shrine, the "house" where he rests four days before "turning."[4] At Zuni Pekwin announces prayer-stick-making by all, and he performs a one-night rain-making ceremony. The solstice ritual dates the summer rain retreats and starts the series of summer rain dances. In the East the Town chief or chiefs observe or once observed the sun, but little or no ritual is reported. In some towns the solstice initiates the rain retreats; in other towns the rain retreats are quite independent of solstice observance.

SOYALA AT ORAIBI[5]

The day after the conclusion of the Wüwüchim ceremony the Soyal kachina goes around impersonated by the Soyala chief.[6] Sixteen days after his advent the smoke talk and initial prayer-feather-making occur (in 1900, on December 15).* In the morning in Poñovi or Chief kiva Soyal chief makes sixteen prayer-feathers and four feathered-string "road-markers" to deposit in shrines on the four sides of town, also four prayer-feathers to give to the Crier. About an hour after sundown seven men assemble in kiva—the chief who is Shokhungyoma of the Bear clan, a Parrot clansman, Tobacco chief of the Rabbit-Tobacco clan, Crier of the Reed clan, Star Man of the Sun clan, War chief of the Badger clan, and Yeshiwa of the Young Corn Ear (Pikyas-Patki) clan who represents his absentee uncle, assistant, almost joint, chief in the ceremony.† The men sit in a semicircle around the fireplace, the chief having before himself on the floor a tray

---

* At Oraibi, curiously enough, the sun is watched not for the solstice but for the performance of the Wüwüchim ceremony. Horn society chief (Soyal chief, according to Voth 2:152, n. 4) watches the progress of the sun from its summer to its winter house. When the sun reaches Dingapi, Horn chief announces that it is time to hold the Wüwüchim ceremony. Dingapi is so located in relation to the solstice point or Sun's house that enough time will intervene so that the climax of the Soyal will occur on December 21 (Titiev 3).

† Shokhungyoma is brother of the Town chief; Soyal chieftaincy is in their Bear clan. The Parrot clansman is chief of Singers; the Young Corn Ear man impersonates Aholi kachina (he also represents the Town chief at the Moenkopi colony), and his corn fetish stands on a secondary small altar associated with the Hawk dance. Star Man is chief of the Sun clan and happens to be brother-in-law to Town chief and Soyal chief. The seven chiefs mentioned correspond more or less to the Council (Titiev 3; Parsons 55:54–55).

of the prayer-feathers made for the Crier, and prayer-meal. All the men but Star Man and War chief are nude. The chief fills a pipe with native tobacco and in anti-sunwise circuit it is smoked and passed on, terms of relationship being exchanged as it is passed from one to another, until it returns to the chief who again smokes, cleans out the pipe, and lays it on the floor. He picks up the tray, holding it in both hands and over it says a prayer; then he takes a pinch of meal from the tray, holds it to his lips, and, waving it in the six directions, places it in the center of the tray. The tray circulates to the same ritual by each man. Again the smoking circuit. Finally the tray is handed to the Crier, who the following morning will deposit the prayer-feathers in the roof shrine of the house whence he calls out that the ceremony has begun.

On this day, at sunrise, Soyal chief takes to the kiva his prayer-stick-making outfit—the boxes in which he keeps his feathers, his sticks, corn meal, cotton string, and various herbs, likewise the Soyal standard, which he brings from his sister's house, the house of the maternal family of the Bear clan in charge of the ceremony. Shokhungyoma sets the standard of four sticks with alternate side feathers of flicker tail and bluebird against the wall of the kiva hatchway. He sprinkles meal on the standard and casts some toward the rising sun. Then he erects the standards at the three other kivas where the Wüwüchim societies assemble. Returning to Chief kiva, Shokhungyoma falls to smoking, together with others who have come in. Smoking is kept up by one or more almost without interruption during the entire day, in fact during the entire ceremony. All the eight leaders of the ceremony are expected to present themselves in kiva some time during the day, likewise during the following three days of preparation, and they usually eat in kiva in the morning. Other members sometimes participate in the ceremony, from the first day. They are expected to remain, however, on the elevated part of the kiva.

The three following days are spent similarly, in smoking or preparing prayer-sticks or other paraphernalia, in spinning, in repairing moccasins, or in other work of a personal, nonceremonial nature. The standard is put out in the morning and taken in at night. On the morning of the so-called third day (actually the fourth day) there is an additional standard, that of the War chief, a long stick to the top of which are fastened twelve flint arrow- and spearheads. Today for the first time the War chief is to appear as a representative of Pöokon, elder brother War god, with the function of guarding the kiva from intruders.

This morning before leaving home all the Soyal members have had their heads washed. Additional members visit the kiva. War chief descends to Flute spring where at the side of the spring he deposits with prayer four prayer-feathers, sprinkling them with meal and casting meal on the water. He fills his gourd bottle, and starting up the trail, at a short distance from the spring, he deposits a long feathered string "road-marker," a trail from the spring to the altar he is to make. Returning to kiva, he puts down the gourd bottle, smokes, chews a piece of root, and, spitting into his hands, rubs them over his body.

Shokhungyoma and his assistant make prayer-sticks over which they smoke, pray, and spit honey. These prayer-sticks a messenger will bury in a place where he is to collect white clay for ritual use. Shokhungyoma and his assistant themselves deposit prayer-feathers in three places, in a kachina shrine, in the shrine of Spider Woman, a patron of their clan, and in a cavity in the face of the rock wall south of town.

In the afternoon the War chief's ceremony is in order. War chief Koyongainiwa sprinkles meal on the kiva floor from the six directions and at the center places a cornhusk ring and on it a basket tray containing prayer-feathers, into which he sprinkles from the six directions. He sprinkles meal on the floor on the six sides of the tray and on the meal places stones, among them stone mountain-lion fetishes. From the contents of his bag which he has emptied on the floor he adds to each object a number of stones, bones, spearpoints and arrowpoints, some of which he also throws into the tray, sprinkling meal. Into each pile he thrusts a long black eagle-wing feather. He pours the water he brought from the spring into a watertight Havasupai basket, pouring from the six directions. He chews certain roots, dipping water from the basket and spraying it back on the basket. A powder of human hearts taken from slain enemies is said to be a component of this medicine water.

Now Koyongainiwa is to be painted by the Screen man of the Coyote clan. He is painted on the forehead with red, and on cheeks, chest, back, legs, and arms with Pöokon's mark, two short parallel lines, in white. Handed to Koyongainiwa, after being waved toward him from the six directions, are: a white corn ear, a pair of moccasins, a pair of ankle bands, knee bands, a buckskin bandoleer containing the dried entrails of slain enemies, stone tomahawk, a shield, two caps, bow and arrows, and his standard. After he is arrayed, across the bridge of his nose is painted Kachinalike a streak of black in specular iron.

The second cap Koyongainiwa puts on the head of Yeshiwa, assistant Soyal chief. Koyongainiwa also hands Yeshiwa the standard, after waving it from the six directions, and Yeshiwa places it in the tray, the arrowpoints up, holding it so with both hands throughout the ceremony.

Now all present strip and sit around the tray, all but Soyala chief, who remains aloof, carding cotton. Koyongainiwa, holding in his left hand the bow, arrows, and ear of corn, sprinkles a line of meal over the standard toward and up the ladder, returns and again throws a pinch toward the ladder. Along this meal road he sprinkles some specular iron, and also rubs some on the face and under the right eye of Yeshiwa.

Tobacco chief hands a cigarette to Koyongainiwa, who puffs four times, and puts the cigarette into Yeshiwa's mouth. Yeshiwa also puffs four times. Koyongainiwa puffs again four times, blowing the smoke toward the standard. All sing. Koyongainiwa marks four lines of meal on the four kiva walls and throws a little meal four times to the kiva roof, and on the floor.

During or after the second song, Koyongainiwa sprinkles meal from the six sides into the tray and on the stones around it. Third song. Koyongainiwa casts meal into the tray from the north side, takes the long black eagle feather from that side, thrusts it into the tray, uttering in a high pitched voice the word *pooh*. He repeats with the other five feathers. He withdraws the six feathers from the tray, hands them to the Screen man who ties them into a bundle and returns them to Koyongainiwa. With them he beats time during the remainder of the ceremony.

Fourth song. Koyongainiwa pours some water into the tray. He dips the feathers into the water and sprinkles. He calls very loudly into the tray: "Haih, aih, aih, hai, hai!" The stones and water in the tray he stirs with his right hand and sprinkles with his fingers. All this he does six times, each time putting some corn meal into the tray before stirring.

Fifth song. Screen man dips water from the tray with a shell and wets some clay which had been placed near by. He smears the clay on the chest and back of each present and on his own body makes additional marks on the upper and lower arms and legs.

Sixth song. Tobacco chief lights the cloud-blower and hands it to Koyongainiwa who blows smoke over the tray. He asperses from time to time, and he mounts the ladder to spray honey out of the hatchway and to asperse.

Seventh song. Koyongainiwa and the Screen man stand up, on either side of the tray. Koyongainiwa puts the corn ear which he has been holding in his hand behind his belt, fastens the shield to his left arm, and takes the tomahawk in his right hand. Screen man takes a spear point from the tray, holding in his left hand a bunch of feathers. Both step with a wagging motion from foot to foot. Screen man feigns to stab Koyongainiwa, who protects himself with his shield. The song grows wilder and wilder, both actors stoop down, and Koyongainiwa beats the floor with the edge of the shield, striking tomahawk against shield, and Screen man strikes the shield with his spear point. All present yell vociferously. All this, including the final war cry, is repeated six times. Tobacco chief hands a cigarette to Koyongainiwa, who smokes it and holds it to the mouth of Yeshiwa, who is still holding the standard in the tray.

Eighth song. Koyongainiwa beats time with the feathers and asperses occasionally. Some smoke, exchanging terms of relationship. Koyongainiwa calls Yeshiwa "my elder brother," Yeshiwa replying, "my younger brother." Ninth song. Koyongainiwa asperses repeatedly. The song concluded, all say *kwakwai*, thanks. Koyongainiwa and Yeshiwa smoke a third cigarette alternately. Each man in the first row smokes four puffs, blowing the smoke toward the standard.

Koyongainiwa prays, takes off Yeshiwa's cap, and relieves him of the standard and with water from the tray rubs the standard and Yeshiwa's arms and shoulders. He takes off his own cap, dips water to his lips from the tray with various stones, bones, and shells, holding them to his heart before replacing them. All the others do likewise, in each case holding the dipper or thing sucked from to their heart, "to make their heart strong." Each retains a little water in his mouth, takes a pinch of the clay remaining on the floor, and goes to his house, where he wets the clay and rubs a little on each member of his family, on breast, back, arms, and legs.

Supper is eaten in kiva, and the early evening is spent by most of the men practicing kachina songs.

An evening ceremony is to be conducted by the Town chief, Lolulomai, brother of Soyal chief. Lolulomai wears his ceremonial kilt and has daubed with white clay his shoulders, forearms, lower legs, and above the knees with a small band, hands, feet, and hair. Koyongainiwa is wearing his war costume. Two Agaves and one Horn are on guard outside the kiva, each holding his chief stick.

All present chew a piece of an herb, spit it into their hands, and rub it over the body. Lolulomai lays a weasel skin on a pile of moist sand, saying a prayer, and draws diagonally a line of meal from the pile in the southeast part of the kiva across toward the northwest corner and from there southward toward the elevated part of the floor, where he put down a little befeathered wooden cone "mountain." Thence he runs the meal line eastward to the diagonal line, putting down another cone at the junction. Tobacco chief hands a cigarette to Lolulomai, another to Koyongainiwa, and another he takes out to the guards. All smoke and then sing several songs. Again all smoke. Lolulomai removes the skin and the cones. He picks up two pointed sticks with hawk feathers erect and pendent, which are

called "wings." He goes to the east side of the ladder and waves
the sticks up and down to a song hummed by all present. He
then goes from right to left along the line of singers, touching
with the sticks the feet of each singer. He steps to the west side
of the ladder, waves the sticks up and down to the same song
and, passing along the line of singers from left to right, draws the
sticks across their knees. Similarly, he touches the shoulders of
each singer, his face, and the top of his head. All spit into their
hands and rub themselves. The floor is swept up, and the
standard taken in for the night.

Fifth day: About an hour before sunrise all the men in kiva
go to a rock halfway down the mesa southeast of town. Here
each sprinkles meal toward the east. The War chief touches the
breast of every man starting back, with his standard, and the
Screen man touches each with the hawk wings. This rite is to
be repeated the three succeeding mornings.

Fasting for four days begins on this day in all the kivas except
Agave kiva. No meat or salted food. The leaders in Chief kiva
fast all day, eating only one meal late in the evening. Soyal chief
makes the kiva rounds early in the morning, putting up a
standard at every participating kiva. On this day the men begin to assemble in the participating kivas except in Agave,
Nashabe, and Singers kivas, where they are supposed to assemble
on the same day as in Chief kiva. Prayer-sticks and altar
paraphernalia are made, cotton carded, or moccasins repaired.

After kachina song and dance practice in the evening, the
ceremony is performed of which the performance the night before was a rehearsal. From the personnel engaged this ceremony
appears to belong to the maternal family of the Bear clan in
charge of both the Soyal ceremony and the Town chieftaincy.
Town chief and a kinsman, the Bear clansman who is to succeed
him in his Soyal functions, conduct it, War chief and others also
officiating, among them the woman who is serving her four years
as Soyal Maid and two former Soyal Maids, all of the same Bear
family or connection.

These three women are led into kiva by the Bear clansman
who is to impersonate Hawk. The women wear ceremonial

blankets and carry each an ear of white corn. They sprinkle meal on the sand pile, are given a piece of the medicine sprig, and into each woman's mouth War chief puts a piece of root from the medicine tray. Hawk Man repeats the arrangement of meal lines, cones, and sand pile of the preceding night. Cigarettes are passed and smoked.

Hawk Man leaves the kiva. Suddenly a screech is heard outside, made by Hawk Man from a bone whistle concealed in his mouth. The sound is answered by a like screech from Lolulomai (Town chief) inside the kiva. The three women say, "Come in!" In a few minutes the screech is repeated closer by and again answered. Hawk Man throws down four meal balls and then comes down. He is dressed in kilt and dance belt; his hair flowing, with a bunch of feathers on top; around his left leg below the knee a string of small bells. He carries the two hawk wings made up prayer-stick fashion which figured the night before. Squatting down and facing northward, Hawk Man takes a hawk-wing stick in each hand, screeches, and, to the singing and rattling of the others, waves the wings vigorously backward and forward, often slowly raising them with a quivering movement after a forcible thrust forward. These movements are repeated as Hawk faces in turn each of the other three directions. The song ceases, the women say, "Thanks!" Again the song begins, Hawk Man steps slowly along the diagonal line of corn meal, waving the hawk wings in time with the song. At the end of the line he lays down the wings and leaves the kiva. From a point about ten yards north of the kiva he sprinkles a line of meal to the hatchway, and he lays a like line from the other five directions, including points at the southwest (zenith) and at the southeast (nadir, a variant for the northeast). Standing at the end of the southeast line he screeches, and he is answered from within, the women saying, "Come in!" Approaching near the hatchway he screeches again and is answered. He enters and is sprinkled with meal by the women. He sprinkles meal on the hawk wings on the ground and begins to dance, raising and lowering his feet very rapidly, jangling the bells on his leg. After screeching he picks up the hawk wings and changes the dance step, he forcibly puts down one foot, raises the other very slowly, then puts it down forcibly, and at the same time he slowly raises the hawk wings from about his knees to above his head, with a quivering motion. Then he advances along the meal line, screeching. He lays down the hawk wings, the singing ceases, the women say, "Thanks!" The hawk dance is repeated with variations, then Hawk Man leaves the kiva.

It is Lolulomai's turn to perform a hawk dance.* Close to his heels follows Soyal Maiden; she imitates all his motions but instead of hawk wings she holds an ear of white corn.

After this dance, during another song, Lolulomai performs other ritual. In a squatting posture, waving the hawk wings vigorously backward and forward, he moves toward the sand pile, screeching at short intervals and keeping his eyes fixed on the pile. He thrusts the hawk wings into the pile, then he squats down before Soyal Maiden and on either side of her works the hawk wings up and down, touching her with them on feet, knees, shoulders, and head. In reverse order he touches the wings to his own person and then works his way back to the sand pile. All this, four times. Now Yeshiwa and Soyal Maiden perform a dance variant, and in conclusion the hawk wings are touched to the knees, shoulders, back, and head of all present. All spit into their hands and rub their limbs and bodies.

This ceremony is to be repeated the following night. During the day the making of ceremonial paraphernalia has gone forward. All in Chief kiva are very devotional and serious throughout the day, talking mostly in a whisper only.

Seventh day: This is the great prayer-stick-making day in Chief kiva. The men, after loosening their hair and undressing, some putting on kilts, arrange themselves in rows and set to making the prayer offerings—paired sticks of the most common type (corn sticks, which are to be placed in the fields), now and then a crook stick which is the first stick to be made for a little

---

* Compare the dance by Hawk Youth and Maiden at Walpi (Stephen 4:17–19). The maiden is not called Soyal Maiden but she is, as at Oraibi, the prospective clan mother in the clan in charge of Soyala, not the Bear clan, but the Water-Corn clan.

boy, hunt sticks, sticks for Sun and Moon, and by the hundred the long willow stick which is the characteristic Soyal stick to which the prayer-feathers are to be attached. Many prayer-feathers are made, and now and then a man hands some of them to another, saying: This is for your boy, burro, peach trees, house, or chicken-house. On the finished sticks a little honey is spat and smoke is blown.

Eighth day: About sunrise Soyal chief takes to each of the participating kivas a special prayer-stick on which the *hihik-wispi*, "objects to breathe on," are to be hung. These objects of cornhusks, cotton string, and prayer-feathers with some corn meal and pollen are now carried outside by the kiva members who made them. The *hihikwispi* is held up toward the rising sun. "Breathe on this!" says the holder, who then runs home, to his wife's house, if he is married, if unmarried, to his mother's house, and stands outside, saying, "Come!" The woman comes out, he hands her the *hihikwispi*, saying, "You breathe on this!" She takes it into the house, all breathe on it, then she returns it to the bringer. Now he goes on to the houses of his ceremonial father and aunts. In each house after the breathing rite, the runner is given food, usually a roll of wafer-bread. This gift is omitted at the houses of his own clanspeople, the next visited. When two runners pass each other outdoors, each breathes from the *hihikwispi* of the other. When all these objects have been returned after use to their respective kiva, they are taken with the prayer-stick they hang on to Chief kiva. This breath rite is prophylaxis against respiratory disease [which is inferably from the beings of the spring (see below), i.e., from the kachina].

On this day the altars are set out in Chief kiva, "and so the day may properly be called the most important of the nine cere-monial days." The large altar of Soyal chief has a simple frame reredos of uprights and crosspieces under which seed corn is stacked. Artificial squash blossoms are placed on the frame and on the stacks. There is a line of two corn fetishes and chief sticks, and *in the center a quartz crystal fetish* from which leads out a meal road set with crook prayer-sticks. Meal-painting of four semicircular clouds and "rain" falling on the fetishes. The small altar set by Yeshiwa of the Young Corn clan, assistant Soyal chief, consists of Yeshiwa's corn fetish, and various types of prayer-sticks or staffs thrust into a sand pile, and on either side a wooden cone "mountain." Bow and arrow used in Hawk dance, four animal skins.

All the leaders have had their heads washed in the early morning. Altar clay is sent for, the messenger carrying with him prayer-feathers and some prayer-meal.

Throughout the day the bowl which contains water to mix paints is whistled into with a bone whistle, in imitation of bird warble, one whistler relieving another. In the sand field in front of the sand ridge at the back of the altar the Town chief makes about twenty-five holes, blows smoke into each and closes it up, a "planting" of smoke.

Corn ears of various colors, the bunches tied with yucca blade, are brought in by the participants and stacked at the rear of the altar. Four messengers to collect corn ears from all the households are sent out, arrayed in kachina kilt and belt, foxskin, yarn around legs, ankle bands, feathers in hair. Their arms up to the elbow, hands, lower legs, feet, shoulders, and hair, are daubed in white; and abdomen and knees are banded in white. Before ascending the ladder, each one, holding to a round, lies down on the ladder and goes through the motions of coition. Each carries a tray and picks up to take with him on his rounds one of the four standards outside the kiva.

Later in the afternoon these four messengers carry each to deposit at the spring west of the mesa, four black prayer-sticks set into corn meal in a basket tray together with cornhusk packages and the bunches of *hihikwispi*. These trays were sprinkled with meal during singing and gourd-rattling at the small altar. Reaching the spring, in single file the messengers encircle it anti-sunwise four times, descend to a terrace halfway into the spring, go around the terrace four times, and thrust *hihikwispi* and prayer-sticks into the wall of the north side of the spring. Removing a stone from the wall on the west side, into the opening they throw the cornhusk packages and the black prayer-sticks. The corn meal they have thrown, by small pinches, against the walls as they have encircled the spring. On returning to kiva, they are hailed with *kwakwai*, thanks.

Meanwhile two Mastop kachina have appeared outside the kiva, where they run around among the spectators, talking a lot in a disguised voice, and sometimes taking hold of a woman from behind and going through the motion of copulation. They enter the kiva where they are sprinkled with meal and given meal and prayer-feathers for rain. These they put into a sack and go on to the other kivas to repeat their performances. In conclusion they carry all the offerings to the Maski or house of Masauwü, a shrine to the north.

On the masks of these kachina are represented Pleiades and Dipper, and on the back, frogs; over their blackened bodies are white imprints of hands. The impersonators have come from Agave kiva. From this kiva also have come into Chief kiva two Agaves arrayed in dance kilt, belt, and foxskin, and carrying in the left hand their horizontal chief's stick to which three bells are fastened. Sprinkling meal toward the altar, they sit down on either side. With the War chief who is also ceremonially arrayed these Agaves are serving as kiva guards.

Toward sundown the singing at the small altar, Yeshiwa's altar, ceases, the War chief and those at the altar smoke, Yeshiwa rubs his hands in corn meal, keeping a little in his left hand into which he puts his corn-ear fetish, steps to the north side of the trays left empty by the four messengers to the spring, waves the *tiponi* to the southeast and prays, all responding with "thanks." The meal in his hand he sprinkles on the prayer-sticks on the altar. All present spit on their hands, rubbing their bodies.

In the evening the War chief's ceremony is repeated. Four Agaves sit on guard oustide.

Later in the evening the mimetic Hawk dance is performed as before, first by the Bear clansman and then by Lolulomai and Soyal Maiden. At the conclusion, the performers, together with Lolulomai's sister withdraw into her house, i.e., the house of the maternal family holding the ceremony.

Here Soyal Maiden and Yeshiwa are now arrayed ceremonially for ritual to be conducted by the Coyote clansman Voth has called from this ritual the Screen man (priest). The screen or panel picture he has made and is in charge of is a picture of Müy'ingwa, the god of germination, and is referred to as the "house" of Müy'ingwa. Before this picture, which has been made in Wikolopi kiva, is taken into Chief kiva, several of the leaders visit the maternal house of the Bear kin and deposit prayer-sticks in a shrine under the ladder leading into the room where Soyal Maiden and Yeshiwa are being arrayed. These two go to the kiva, Yeshiwa, holding the hawk wings and screeching outside, to the rejoining screech from within. As before, Yeshiwa throws down four balls of meal. Then he and Soyal Maiden do the Hawk dance around the panel picture. Lolulomai hands to Soyal chief a tray containing two corn ears, corn meal, and prayer-sticks. Over these Soyal chief and the leaders with him pray. All smoke, and Tobacco chief blows smoke from the cloud-blower against the back of the panel picture. With a corn ear from the tray Soyal chief scrapes all the seeds from the picture into the tray, seeds of corn, watermelon, muskmelon, squash, cotton, etc.; he also runs the corn ear over the artificial blossoms on the edges of the panel, as if scraping them also.

It is about three in the morning and the final, and, Voth thinks, most significant ritual, is in order. The War chief goes over to Wikolopi kiva and from his medicine bowl sprinkles the Star Man. They return to Chief kiva, Yeshiwa sprinkling corn meal in front of them, and at the kiva, lines of meal from the six directions. Inside, Star Man begins to dance backward and forward, to a drum. He half-sings, half-talks. In his right hand he holds a long crook, a black corn ear fastened at the middle [the kachina staff]; in his left hand he carries seven ears of corn, a chief's stick, and a gourd water bottle. He wears the kachina dance costume, his body painted with lines of white dots, on his forehead a large four-pointed star. Of a sudden he makes a leap toward Soyala chief, handing him what he carries and receiving from Yeshiwa a sun shield. Twirling this very fast, Star or Sun Man dances from east to west, aspersed by the War chief. The song is about Water Serpent. At the close

Soyala chief gives a prayer-stick to Star Man who, I think, is T'aiowa.

Now in turn all the participating kivas send for their trays of prayer-sticks which were taken to Chief kiva the preceding day. After the prayer-sticks are smoked over in the respective kivas, a messenger is dispatched with them, a prayer-stick and prayer-feather from every man in each kiva, to Sun house, a shrine on a mesa about three miles southeast of Oraibi. From Chief kiva the messenger also carries four small cakes, two wheels, two cylinders, and the grass from the altar.

Soyala chief, Crier, and War chief now have to bury the crook stick from the altar halfway down the east side of the mesa. The War chief digs a hole about two and a half feet deep, and from it a trench about eight inches deep. After sprinkling meal, Soyala chief puts in the crook stick and along the trench the fifteen-foot feathered string or "road-marker." All sprinkle meal, and the earth is replaced. All walk along the covered "road-marker," and return to kiva. To it now come in successive groups men from the participating kivas, to sing and dance, kachina fashion, hair loose, and naked but for kilt or breechcloth. They are sprinkled with meal before they dance.

Toward morning the men from the different kivas carry their prayer-sticks to their houses. At sunrise out come the women and children carrying handfuls or armfuls of prayer-sticks to thrust into the ground at the east edge of the mesa.* Members of the Sand clan plant theirs together, about fifteen yards from the others at a place called Awatobi, whence the clan is said to have come. To Antelope house or shrine south of town run men and boys at top speed, carrying hunt prayer-sticks and hallooing as they run; some have bells at the waist; their hair hangs loose. Everybody has had a hair wash. "This early morning rite is a picture never to be forgotten."[7]

Later, in various ways prayer-feathers will be offered: tied to ladders to prevent falling; put into chicken-houses that the hens may lay; into cattle and sheep corrals, and tied to horses'

* Some women, including recent brides in their wedding robes, deposit prayer-sticks near the shrine of Sowika, patron of offspring (Titiev 3).

tails or to the necks of dogs, goats, or sheep, for increase; to peach trees for large crops; in springs for an abundant water supply. Prayer-feathers were once tied to Voth's watch as it hung on the wall.

Of prayer-sticks there are three kinds, the bent stick made for a little boy by his father, hunt "sticks" which are prayer-feathers tied to a stem of grass, and for the dead prayer-feathers tied to long sticks [or willow twigs] each bunch of feathers for a deceased individual, and short double sticks for the dead in general or for the Cloud people.

Later in the morning the altars in Chief kiva are dismantled: four messengers carry through town the corn ears which have lain on the altar during the night ceremony, and each woman picks out her own parcel. This is seed corn.[8]

In the afternoon of the eighth or ninth day appear the Qööqö-qlöm kachina: from fifteen to twenty males and from five to seven females who are like those with Hümis kachina. The kachina rub meal on the four sides of the hatchway of each kiva —"opening the kivas." Powamu chief sprinkles the kachina with meal.

The next three days are spent rabbit-hunting. Men sleep in kiva but eat at home. On the fourth day in the afternoon the men of Chief kiva go in single file to the house of Soyal Maiden. They are arrayed in kilt and sash, and daubed over in white. The Screen man goes first, carrying a pot of roasted rabbit for Soyal Maiden. The others carry small trays of mush. From the roof of Soyal Maiden's house the men now throw out to the people presents of meal in cornhusks which have been prepared by Soyal Maiden, and squash, watermelons, etc. As they throw, water is tossed over them by four girls, until their paint has been thoroughly washed off. A feast, particularly on rabbit meat, follows in all the kivas.

ITIWANA* AT ZUNI[9]

Pekwin watches the sunrise from a petrified stump in a field on the east side of town; and, when the sun rises over a certain

* The Middle, referring to the sun reaching the middle, meaning both the town, the middle place, as Zuni is called, and the middle of the ceremonial year,

point of Corn Mountain, he informs War chief elder brother who summons the paramount Rain chiefs to a meeting that night in the house of the Town chief, Rain chief of the North.

The following morning Pekwin deposits in his shrine on Corn Mountain two pairs of prayer-sticks, blue and yellow in each pair, for Sun and his sister, Moon. Four days later Pekwin deposits in a field four prayer-sticks to his deceased predecessors and every four days hereafter for sixteen days* he deposits in alternation prayer-sticks to Sun and Moon or to deceased predecessors. The four days following the offering to Sun and Moon he fasts from meat; and during the whole period, including four days before the first offering and four days after the last, he has to remain continent.

The day following his final prayer-stick offering Pekwin announces from the housetop that in ten days, when the Sun will reach the Middle, everybody is to offer prayer-sticks. Meanwhile Rain societies and curing societies meet each in its ceremonial room to make prayer-sticks, laymen working at home.

War god images are made in the house of the Deer clansman who is the image-maker of War god elder brother. A Bear clansman is the image-maker of War god younger brother. Offerings of prayer-sticks and of miniature gaming implements are also made by Deer and Bear clansmen to whose clans the War gods belong. The War chiefs make other altar paraphernalia, also prayer-sticks to be placed in the girdles of the images. The images are made of cottonwood, which is always associated with water; the War gods at this season are addressed for rain. After the images are set out, many come in to sprinkle them with meal and to say a prayer (Fig. 2).

---

the central point for all the cults (Bunzel 2:534). And yet Dr. Bunzel always translates *itiwana* as "New Year," which I think is somewhat misleading. There is no Zuni term for new year, so Bunzel may have derived her usage from our own culture or specifically from Cushing who writes: "New Year is called the 'Midjourney of the sun,' that is, the middle of the solar trip between one summer solstice and another" (Cushing 6:154).

* This in theory; but there is dissent. Once my copy of Stevenson was borrowed as an authority. Desire to have the solstice observed at the full moon is one cause of dissension (Bunzel 2:534).

On the ninth day, the Badger clansman who has been appointed fire-maker* by the Town chief makes domiciliary rounds, collecting a fagot of cedar from each house, the woodgiver saying a prayer for the year's crops. The wood is taken into He'iwa kiva, and there in the fireplace under the ladder some kindling is laid in a square, crisscross, to a height of about a foot and a half. At sunset the sacred fire, *matke teshkwi*, is lighted. At sunset Pekwin makes his meal-painting on the floor at the west end of the kiva [i.e., the meal road is to the east]. The paramount Rain chiefs assemble in the kiva, whence this tenth night they go to bring in the War god images from the house of the Deer clansman. After meal is sprinkled on the images to prayer, the War chiefs whirling their whizzers, the procession departs for the kiva, first, Pekwin sprinkling meal as he goes, then the keeper of the *pa'eto·ne* (Navaho fetish) who carries it, and the keeper of the Big Shell who carries it, then the Town chief with his *eto·ne*, the Deer man with the image of the elder War god and two more Deer men with the god's paraphernalia, the Bear man with the image of the younger War god and two Bear men with paraphernalia. War chief elder brother walks to the right of Pekwin and War chief younger brother to the right of the last man in file, each chief whirling his whizzer. After all enter He'iwa kiva, Pekwin places images and fetishes on the meal altar. The War chiefs sing the War gods' Shomatowe songs for the eve of fight or raid. This tenth night all the curing societies are holding Cloud or Rain ceremonies.

At sunrise the images are carried by the War chiefs to the Deer and Bear clan houses. Food is set before the images, and many in the household and from outside sprinkle meal on them and offer beads. Now the War chiefs carry the images and their paraphernalia to the mesa-top shrines, Elder Brother is carried to Uhana mesa by War chief elder brother and the paraphernalia are carried by War chief younger brother and his assistant to Corn Mountain. There the War chief kindles a fire which can be

---

* Fire is associated with the Badger clan because the fire is drilled from a dry piece of soft root, and the badger best knows how to find roots (Cushing 6:31), a typical Zuni explanation! See p. 516.

seen from the town and is the signal for the beginning of the fire taboo of ten days. No light may be made outdoors and no ashes or sweepings taken from any house lest the family fields suffer from drought. As the house is full of ashes so will it be full of corn. The sacred fire is kept burning in He'iwa kiva where the fire-maker sleeps, going out only to collect cedar or to eat; food may not be taken into the kiva.

This day, the Town chief deposits the prayer-stick bundle of the Rain chiefs, which has rested on the War gods' altar in He'iwa kiva, at the foot of Matsakya, the hillock ruin near Corn Mesa; the curing societies deposit prayer-sticks in their shrines. Laymen, including women and children, plant prayer-sticks in their fields, where the next day they are to be completely covered over. Before planting, everyone has had his hair washed.

This day of general prayer-stick offering is the beginning of a *teshkwi* period of ten days. Meat and grease may not be eaten or touched for four days—children and members of the Hunters' society and of the Shi'wanakwe society being exempt. No trading* for four days; continence for eight days. By the chiefs all the taboos are observed for ten days. This is the second ten days' count. The first ten days were counted by the Pekwin for the Sun, the second ten days are counted by the chief of the Kachina society for Pa'utiwa, chief of the kachina.

The eleventh to the fourteenth nights are given over to the retreats and ceremonies of the curing societies, with an all-night ceremony ending at dawn on the fourteenth day. On this afternoon occurs the second general planting of prayer-sticks to the kachina, to the animals (beast gods), and to the dead for wealth.

On the following day the Rain chiefs again make prayer-sticks for the Uwanami and have the prayer-sticks deposited in a spring before the chiefs "go in" for their night ceremony. On the altar meal-painting are placed the fetishes, also corn ears and

---

* Or rather barter; there may be buying from the store on credit. Dr. Bunzel interprets this barter taboo, which is peculiar to Zuni, as based on the feeling that the whole follows a part (see p. 93), in a time of ceremonial potency (Bunzel 2: 501).

clay images of animals, peach trees, and money. Prayers are for increase or fertility and for rain.

Prayer-sticks are made by the paramount Rain chiefs and the officers of the Kachina society for Pa'utiwa, kachina chief. The Corn clan and the "children of the clan" assemble to choose an impersonator for Pa'utiwa who is to appear as the kachina witch. In the house of the impersonator of Pa'utiwa, Sun clansmen and Corn clansmen meet to make kachina prayer-sticks which all will carry to the riverbank. The sixteenth night, very late, about two or three o'clock, Pa'utiwa or kachina witch comes in to town, dodging about as would a witch. He is wrapped in a blanket, probably without a mask. He ascends the ladder of each kiva, going first to Chupawa kiva, throws a ball of meal* down the hatchway, and marks the crossbar with four lines of meal. Each day a line of meal is rubbed off by the kiva dance chief. With the rubbing-off of the last line the *teshkwi* period is to close.

On some night during the ten days of the fire taboo, generally the night of the Rain chiefs' retreats, each family that owns sacred possessions of any kind employs them in rites of fertility magic.† Clay objects, similar to those used on the altars of the Rain chiefs, are modeled by the women of the house. These are set out at night along with ears of corn and the sacred possessions: mask, rain fetish, sacred medicine, or personal fetishes such as pebbles to which are imputed magical properties. For one night the family are in retreat. They remain awake until day and repeat prayers and songs for fertility of crops and flocks, and for the fecundity of women. The corn is for spring seeding. The clay objects are later buried in the floor of the house, or thrown out on the twentieth day with the sweepings. They are the seed from which the real objects will grow.

On one of these days pregnant women, especially those who have been unfortunate with previous babies, visit phallic shrines on the west side of Corn Mountain. The woman is accompanied

---

* See p. 293.

† *Itsuma·wa*, the ritualistic term for planting (Bunzel). This I have paraphrased in early publications as rite of magical increase.

by her husband and a Rain chief. They deposit prayer-sticks, and the woman scrapes dust from the rock and swallows it, from one side if she desires a boy, from the other if she desires a girl. A pregnant woman may have made for her at this season a kachina doll. The doll is made by anyone who "knows how," that is, who has the supernatural power to make it effective. It insures a safe delivery and a healthy child.

On the nineteenth day the paramount Rain chiefs, the Kachina society chief, and the fire-maker are engaged in He'iwa kiva making the crook sticks of appointment for the impersonators of the kachina chiefs and for Bitsitsi of the Ne'wekwe. The paramount Rain chiefs and the Kachina society chiefs have been consulting over impersonators and over the houses in which the Shalako are to be entertained.

The Big Firebrand society is also meeting in the kiva. The society chief and the Kachina society chief send each two men to fill netted gourds with spring water for their medicine bowls. Before sunset, a meal altar with corn-ear fetishes is laid down by the crier chief of the Kachina society. Just at sunset, from the East, from Shipapolima, "bringing the new year" come in Shitsukya and Kwelele, kachina of the Big Firebrand society. These kachina and the four exorcising Sayathlia,* the Blue Horn kachina, dance all night to the songs of the Big Firebrand society. The Blue Horns dance for the old year. Pa'utiwa appears and unmasks; his mask† is placed on the altar. The im-

---

* Turquoise-colored mask, two blue horns, ball eyes, large mouth with long, sharp teeth made of folded cornhusk, white horsehair on top and back with eagle-tail and owl feathers, coyote fur collar, body painted black with crescents of red, blue, white; fringe of black hair around waist, foxskin at back; turtle shell rattle under each knee; yucca in right hand, staff with black goat's hair carried horizontally. Impersonators chosen by kiva chief from general membership, *men who are "never unhappy"* (Bunzel 5:919–20, Pl. 21*b*).

† Turquoise colored, on top black hair and macaw breast feathers, erect behind eight macaw tail feathers; projecting snout; ears of twigs covered with black hair, large so he can hear everything his people ask for. "If anyone has very sharp ears, we say, 'You are a regular Pa'utiwa.'" White shirt and usual kachina array, with an additional embroidered blanket "because he wants his people to have plenty of fine clothing."
The mask is kept in the house of the Town chief. The impersonator is alter-

personator sits behind the mask between lines of Dogwood and Sun clansmen. Late at night the Blue Horns visit all the kivas "to send out the old year." No one is in the kivas, but they think the old year is in there and they want to hurry him out (Bunzel). At the rising of the Morning star, Kwelele and a chief in the Big Firebrand society kindle a fire by fire-stick, so does the Badger clan fire-maker. Now in this order they leave the kiva for Kushilowa, on the east edge of town: Shitsukya carrying a whizzer in his right hand and an ear of yellow corn in his left; the crier chief of the Kachina society with a basket of meal and his corn fetish in left hand, while with right hand he casts meal ahead; Pekwin with meal basket and ear of blue corn; the Badger fire-maker carrying in his blanket over his left arm four ears of corn set around prayer-sticks, and in his right hand his firebrand; the Kachina society chief with corn fetish and meal basket; Pa'utiwa carrying prayer-sticks and sprinkling meal; the four Blue Horns, carrying out the sweepings which they call corn; four Sun clansmen, and, a little in the rear, Kwelele with his firebrand, cedar fiber, and fire-stick.

At Kushilowa the two firebrands are laid on the ground, and the crier chief of the Kachina society runs a line of meal between them. All face east. They sprinkle the kachina with meal and breathe in. The prayer-sticks are buried in the hole made for them by the ceremonial father of the impersonator of Pa'utiwa. The prayer-sticks are for Sun, for the kachina including Blue Horns, Shitsukya, and Kwelele, for the deceased rain-maker chiefs, for Kupishtaya* or lightning-makers, and for Poshai-yanki, giver of raiment.

The exit of this group from the kiva has been the signal to the townspeople to carry out their sweepings and ashes, embers, and live coals. The households go out to their fields, everyone carrying a bowl or basket. On depositing the sweepings, a

---

nately Dogwood clan or child of Dogwood, chosen by former impersonators, a cult group (Bunzel 5:908, 910).

* This Keresan term among Keres, we recall, includes most of the cosmic beings, but at Acoma it refers to a special winter solstice group.

woman says, "In one year you will return to me as corn." To the ashes she says, "I now deposit you as ashes, but in one year you will return to me as meal." On sweepings and ashes, meal is sprinkled and prayer-sticks are deposited.

The procession has now returned to kiva, where the kachina dance to a choir from Big Firebrand society. The Blue Horns depart swinging their goat-hair sticks, "to sweep away what is left of the old year" (Bunzel). After sunrise all but the kachina impersonators go home to breakfast. A paternal aunt calls through the kiva hatchway to the Badger fire-maker to summon him to her house where she is to wash his head and give him breakfast.

After breakfast Pekwin hands to the War chief the feather-sticks of office he is to take to the newly chosen impersonators of the kachina—Shulawitsi, Sayatasha, two Yamuhakto, Hututu, Pa'utiwa, their father Koyemshi, and Bitsitsi, and on years of kachina society initiation or Ky'anakwe ceremonial, Kiaklo and the chiefs of the Ky'anakwe. The War chief returns to the kiva followed by the appointees. Now in kiva they are installed by Pekwin who presents them with more prayer-sticks, clasping in his the hands of the recipient and praying. The stick is passed in front of the mouth of its recipient to be breathed from, just as are the canes of secular office.

During the day Shitsukya and Kwelele dance on the roof of the kiva. To the kiva ladder is attached a horizontal bar with pendent black goat's wool, a squirrel skin, and at each end downy eagle feathers. Below in kiva the Big Firebrand society is singing. Toward the late afternoon Shitsukya and Kwelele walk about hooting on the kiva roof and throw down to the people cooked ears of sweet corn strung horizontally with yucca.

Now Pa'utiwa comes into town* carrying prayer-sticks and befeathered miniature implements of the hoop and stick game, also in his left hand a twig with crow and owl feathers, repre-

* His mask and paraphernalia have been carried out to him by Sun clansmen. This impersonation of Pa'utiwa belongs to the Dogwood clan, and the mask is kept in a Dogwood house; the office of ceremonial father with the function of arraying Pa'utiwa belongs in the Sun clan (Bunzel 2:522). All this is Hopi-like.

senting a Navaho scalp.* Pa'utiwa encircles town four times, each time closing in. After the fourth circuit he goes to a house on the east side of town to deposit in a wall excavation some of the prayer-sticks he carries. They are for Sun and Moon. He proceeds to houses on the other sides of town, north, west, and south and for zenith and nadir to houses on inner streets to make like wall deposits of his prayer-sticks.† At the foot of the ladder up to He'iwa kiva Pa'utiwa is met by Kwelele, Shitsukya, and Pekwin. The latter two sprinkle meal on the ladder, and, as he ascends the ladder, Pa'utiwa throws meal up ahead. Inside kiva, Big Firebrand society start their song for Pa'utiwa. Reaching the kiva roof, Pa'utiwa throws the "Navaho scalp" down the hatchway. He lays down sticks of office for the impersonators and hosts of the Shalako, and he draws four lines of meal on the hatchway log, to represent the four visits that are to be paid by the Salimobia kachina. The "scalp" has been thrown back on the roof, and Pa'utiwa kicks it four times with his left foot. [Circles it around his head (Bunzel).] All this ritual Pa'utiwa repeats at the five other kivas, accompanied by Kwelele, Shitsukya, and Pekwin. With the crooks Pa'utiwa brings in *itiwana*, "the new year."

At the northwest corner as the kachina are about leaving town Pa'utiwa is met by a Dogwood clanswoman who gives him a *hakwani*, a knotted cotton fringe, and says to him a long prayer for food and raiment. The kachina move on westward to the river. There Pa'utiwa takes off his mask, giving it to the Sun clansmen waiting for him. The impersonator now goes to the house of the Town chief to report to all the assembled chiefs and to Dog clansmen the omens of his "babies" and town circuits.[10]

After dark Chakwena kachina woman‡ comes into town and

* Navaho are believed to transform into crows.

† And to inspect the images, "his babies," in these wall shrines. In his third circuit he has deposited prayer-sticks in permanent excavations on the four sides of town (Bunzel 5:912–13).

‡ Black face mask with round yellow eyes and mouth, hair done up behind like a Zuni woman's (*not* wheeled on one side, and hanging on the other like the

enters He'iwa kiva, to be received there by the Blue Horns, and visited by her people, the Ky'anakwe group of Chupawa kiva. She makes an anti-sunwise circuit of town with the Blue Horns and then leaves by the southwest. When Chakwena Woman came in, pregnant women stationed themselves where they could see her, as an aid in labor.

Now Atoshle kachina are going about town, frightening the children and scolding. In He'iwa kiva the Blue Horns are whipping those who come to be cured of headache or nightmare. About eleven at night the Thlelele, maskless nude figures covered with sheepskin or wagon canvas, go through town to be pelted from every house with embers. There is dancing by the kachina from kiva to kiva. The Salimobia bring in baskets of seed to distribute to all present, seed which is sure to yield bountifully. About midnight the Blue Horns are sprinkled with meal by the two warriors of the Kachina society, and then with the Thlelele they depart toward the west. The altar in He'iwa kiva is dismantled, and the crier chief of the Kachina society deposits the meal from the painting in the *sipapu* of the kiva.

Every fourth night until their four visits are completed the Salimobia return to dance and distribute seeds.

NAPE'I* AT ISLETA[11]

White Corn chief summons his helpers to his house to talk about beginning their ceremony, saying, "Our father Sun is going south (winter solstice), or north (summer solstice)." One assistant goes to the Town chief to tell him they are going to begin their ceremony in four days (December 4 or June 4), for during

---

Hopi Chakwena Grandmother), red society feather, archaic women's black dress with dark-blue embroidered border and fastened on both shoulders, gourd rattle which she rattles as she goes.

The mask is kept in a Badger clan house and worn by a Badger man who owns the ritual.

Chakwena Woman blesses the houses with babies (Bunzel 5:931 ff.). See p. 526.

* *Pe'* means bed for planting. This ceremony is performed separately by each of the seven Corn groups, the White Corn going in one day ahead, and the Shichu going in last.

the ceremony the Town chief will remain in his ceremonial house. The evening of the third day a Corn group helper goes to the houses of all the men of the group, of all "his sons," to summon them to a meeting at the chief's house, at which he will tell them that he is going to begin to fast the following morning, for four days. If anyone wish to fast for this time or for a shorter period, one, two, or three days, he is to prepare for it. The following morning three men are chosen to go to all the houses of the group to tell the people that their Father is going to fast and to say that if they wish they can help by fasting for a day or half a day. A rabbit hunt is managed by the War captains for the Fathers, probably on the second day of the retreat as the rabbits are for the festive supper at the close of the ceremony.

First day: The chief takes a seat by the fireplace with his helpers. Of the attendants, the men are on one side, the women on the other. The chief sings one song; then he gives permission to his helpers and to any attendants to sing. The chief summons his woman helpers (*keide*, mother) who stand in front of him. He gives them permission to work with him, to get water and have their bowls ready for vomiting and head-washing. (He has sent a man out the day before to get soapweed.) The women set out three bowls. Three by three the helpers kneel in front of a bowl, the chief helper taking the middle bowl. Each sprinkles pollen to one side of the bowl and from the dipper drops some water to the east, north, west, and south (south by east, according to a recent picture) and, at the south point, up and down. Then he drinks, his hair having been unbelted by the mother as he knelt, since he may not drink without loose hair. After drinking, each withdraws back of the fireplace and in the bowl set there vomits the warm water he has drunk. The chief is the last to perform the rite. There is a song for this vomiting. Head-washing follows.

Now the chief stands in the middle of the room and throws pollen toward the east. Prayer-feather-making follows. The chief bids a mother to set out the basket, and a male helper to bring down the box of ritual feathers from where it hangs to a beam. A feather is placed in front of each helper; there are to be twelve feathers, the turkey feather, "the oldest one," being in front of the chief. All sing the song that belongs to working on the feathers. The mother begins to grind the ritual black paint, with a duck feather dropping some water from her little bowl on to her stone for grinding. A song for this grinding. A helper carries the paint to the others, each putting some of it on his index finger. Then each paints the mid-rib of his feather, all singing the song of the black paint and the feather. The chief helper gathers up the feathers, taking first the turkey feather of the chief and placing the feathers one on top of the other. Another song for this. The helper tells a mother to take to the chief some cotton string which he will measure off by holding the end between the tips of his middle and fourth fingers and stretching the string to his wrist, doubling this measure three times and then cutting the string with his flint knife, leaving twelve ends. The chief helper brings him the grinding-stone of black paint of which he takes some on his index finger and thumb. Holding one end of the string in his left hand, he rubs the paint from his index finger and thumb on to the other end of the string and on the middle. Turning the string he then paints the other end—thus in three places he has painted the string. For this painting of the string there has been a special song. And now, again, as he ties the feathers there is a tying song.

A mother takes a basket of meal of the color characterizing the group to the chief. Facing the east, he breathes out on the meal three times and then waves it in the anti-sunwise circuit. This rite, to which there is a song, is repeated in turn by the chief helper, the other helpers, and any others present. Then the mother returns the basket to the chief. On it he lays the prayer-feathers, to song, and sprinkles the feathers with meal.

Follows the rite of drawing down the Sun by the power the chief has asked from the Town chief. In the roof of the ceremonial room there is a hole through which at noon the sun shines on a spot on the floor near where the chief now stands. In front of the chief stand his helpers, then a row of other men, and then a row of women. All turn to face the east, singing to call the Sun. This is repeated in anti-sunwise circuit, before each song each sprinkling meal from the meal basket or pollen received from the chief helper. All return to their places, except the chief who makes drawing-in motions from all the directions from the Corn Mothers, throws pollen up toward the roof hole and points upward with his stone knife. All sing the song of "pulling down the Sun," while the chief makes the motions of drawing something toward himself. Now the Sun drops down on the spot of sunlight on the floor. It is a round object, white as cotton, which opens and closes.* To this the chief ties the prayer feathers, as all sing. All stand and throw pollen toward the "Sun." The chief waves the "Sun" which shines so brightly you can hardly look at it. (The room has been darkened by closing windows.) All breathe on their clasped hands. As the chief waves the Sun around his head, the Sun goes back through the roof hole. This is noontime when for a little while the Sun stands still. Elsewhere in the town at this time, knowing the work that is going on (in the ceremonial houses) people withdraw indoors or stay in, and ask the Sun to help.

After the Sun leaves, the chief takes his place by the fireside, and his chief helper comes and presses him all over, restoratively. The chief is tired from holding the Sun and all he has been doing. His helper gives the chief a cigarette to smoke, first in the directions for the help he has had from all the Corn Mothers, then to the Sun. Now the chief gives permission to all to stand up and walk about and rest. After a while the chief makes a speech, advising the people to be good to their parents and wives, and to help one another. He tells them about old times. He tells them not to think about food and drink, to think only about their ceremony. Then he tells his helpers to see that all resume their regular positions and practice their songs. The mothers who care to go out to attend to their own work may go now. They are not fasting, they may eat at home, returning toward sunset.

Now the chief sends out a mother to call in the first boy or man belonging to their group whom she may encounter. At the

* Possibly a ray of light has been refracted with a crystal into the chamber, as is done in Hopi altar ritual.

door the one summoned takes off his shoes. *Aukuwa'm!** Greetings! he says, as is usual on coming to a house. He helps himself to meal from the basket, unless he happens to have meal with him; he breathes on it, waves it in the directions; throws it toward the Sun. He approaches the chief, saying "Do you need me?" The chief answers that the last ceremony of the year is coming; as one of their sons he asks him to help them and go out into the hills and get some yucca in order that they can wash their heads on the fourth morning. He will say, "All right"; he is glad to help his fathers. Now they resume their places and start song practice.

After dark, about seven or eight, the chief helper says, "All right, my sons, it is time to go out." All take meal from the basket. The chief starts out, his chief helper follows, all follow. They stand in line, facing east. The chief says, "Ready!" Then all breathe out on their meal, wave it in the directions, throw it to the east, throwing it to the Moon and Stars, praying and giving thanks for their first day. They return indoors to their set positions, from which to receive permission to move about. Now is the time they will sit around, telling tales. If anyone is sleepy, the chief gives him permission to sleep.

The following days and nights are passed similarly. Each morning at sunrise, the women will fetch water from the river, the chief giving to the senior mother a prayer-stick to cast into the water when she asks the Water People for their water. On the return of the mother the water jar is placed in the center of the floor, and from his usual seat by the fireplace the chief thanks the woman, also the Water People. Then one of the male helpers gives the chief a cigarette to smoke in circuit and toward the river, thanking the Water People with smoke. The chief concludes with breathing on his own clasped hands and with them making the ritual circuit, saying that the Water People are sending all present long life and health.

The third evening the messenger returns with yucca. The chief makes a road of meal for him from the door to the meal basket and over it the messenger follows the chief to the basket

* You are well, *qk'uwa'm*, is also the Taos greeting.

where he gets meal, waves it in the directions, throws it toward the Sun. The chief takes his seat by the fireplace, beside him the messenger. The chief thanks him, and the chief helper gives each a cigarette. Both smoke in the directions and to the Sun. All present are now given permission to walk about and smoke.

Fourth day: In the morning between four and five the chief starts for the river, the others following in line. In line they stand on the river bank. Each breathes on the meal he has taken with him and throws some of it to the Sun; the rest he moves in the directions and throws into the running water. This rite is to ask the Sun when he turns southward "that they will be living" (? to let them go on living). They wash face and hands and return in line to their house.

Now the mothers are to go for water. The chief leads the others out of the house, sprinkling meal, as the helpers sing. At the river the senior mother stands in the middle and throws meal into the water. Then she places in the water the prayer-feathers the chief has given her for the Water People. Returning to the house, they step into the center of the room, and the senior mother relates to the chief helper the whole episode, from the time she received the prayer-feathers from the chief to their return. The chief helper gives thanks. Two water bowls are placed in the center of the room, the third in a corner. Then the mothers wash the heads of all present, including themselves. The rite of emesis is performed.

Prayer-feather-making. Five bunches of prayer-feathers are to be made. The turkey feathers are put down first, in front of the chief and four helpers, next a duck feather, next a goose feather, next a red feather, next a yellow bird feather. All this to a song. Follows the rite of painting the string. This time red paint is used.

Follows the ritual of medicine-water-making. A mother places the water jar in front of the line of helpers. The chief helper takes meal from the basket and sprinkles in the directions. From the water jar, with a shell, he sprinkles a few drops of water in the directions. He bids the mother pour water from the jar into the medicine bowl. All this to singing. He bids the mother fetch the *wahtainin* (all the people)* from the buffalo-skin bag which hangs from the beam to which the ceremonial properties or supplies are hung. As the chief helper takes out the *ke'chu tainin,* he breathes on his own hand, as does everyone present. He drops the *ke'chu* people into the bowl, beginning with one on the east side and so on in circuit, the one for the fifth direction of up and down being dropped in the middle of the bowl. The Mother takes up the lightning stone, dips it into the water jar, rubs it on her small grinding-stone, letting the drip from it fall into the medicine bowl. The chief helper tells the Mother to fetch the *thleachi tainin,* rain people. Wetting this stone, she again grinds, letting the drip fall into the bowl. And this grinding and dripping is repeated with the stone called *weryu tainin,* all the animals, wild and tame; also with the stone called *tör'ju tainin, tör'ju* meaning in between or in the center between top and bottom, but what "people" these may be I do not know. Now grinding and dripping are repeated with stone points white, black, yellow, blue, spotted, each ground in all the directions, for this rite refers to all the Corn Mothers, who are mutually helpful. Any one of their "children" may drink of the water.

The chief helper smokes in all the directions, reverses the cane cigarette, holding the lit end in his mouth, and blows the smoke into the bowl. He passes the cigarette on, and so it circulates, each helper smoking in the directions and swallowing the smoke.† From the helpers the cigarette passes to the other men who may be present and from them, if anything of the cigarette is left, to the women present (who always hope that none of the cigarette will be left over for them to smoke).

The chief helper drops two duck feathers into the medicine bowl. He takes up an ear of corn of the color of the group, holds it in both hands by butt and tip, blows on the butt as he circles the bowl with it three times. Then he dips the tip in the water and sprinkles with it in circuit, everybody breathing in from their clasped hands. The helper passes his hand over the bowl as

---

* Referring to the fetish animals and birds.
† A favorite incident in Pueblo folk tales to test a person's power.

if gathering something in, which he gives to himself and then waves in circuit as if bestowing it upon those present. This rite is called by a ceremonial term meaning imparting understanding or virtue.

Now the meal design of the altar is to be made. The chief helper bids the Mother fetch the meal basket. As the chief helper sprinkles meal for the *nake'e* (village), as the design proper is called, the others sing. The meal is of the color which characterizes the group. (For the Corn groups of all colors meal of any color is used.) The arrowpoint or blade on the altar is of corresponding color. The fetish stones are placed around the "village," and the prayer-feathers laid down. On each side of the "village" several ears of corn are stacked (for the name-getting infants), and at the foot of the "village" is placed the medicine bowl. Now the chief assistant chews the ritual root and sprays over the "village." Chewing another piece, he sprays over those to the left in the room, beginning with the chief, then over those to the right. A mother gives him some water to rinse his mouth, since he may not swallow any of this root, only the chief may swallow it. With the two duck-wing feathers from the bowl the chief helper sprinkles the "village," tapping one feather against the other. Similarly he thrice sprinkles the chief, who responds *ka'a*, father. He sprinkles all present in one circuit saying, "Your life arrowpoint may you grow old." All respond, "Father, father, father!"

Now the chief takes the place of his helper, sprinkling the altar with meal and, with water from the duck feathers, sprinkling his helper who says, "Father," to which he responds, "My son." The chief chews the root which he has to swallow. He picks up the arrowpoint with his left hand, and in his right holds some pollen. Facing the east, he begins to dance, the others singing. To help him, the mothers dance also. At a certain word in the song the chief sprinkles the pollen on the altar, saying *ha'i, ha'i, truhi, truhi*. Then in turn facing the north, west, and south, he repeats his rite. Finally, for the fifth repetition he faces toward where the Sun is shining through the roof hole—it is noon. The chief puts the prayer-feathers in the basket, breathes from them, and passes the basket on for each to breathe from as was described before. If there is not time for all to do this while the Sun is shining through, from their seats they will merely throw meal toward the prayer-feathers. Now the Mother ties back the hair of the chief with cornhusk. With basket in left hand and arrowpoint in right he dances, pointing the arrowpoint up toward the Sun and calling out *ha'i, ha'i, truhi, truhi.*

The ritual of solar advent is repeated. Everybody rests. About one, the errand man arrives, at the door removing his moccasins and knocking. A mother opens the door. "Greetings!" The chief helper bids the errand man approach the medicine bowl and gives him a mouthful which he spurts over himself. There is general talk except on the part of the chief who is silent because he still has his power in him. The errand man reports that he went around town among the members of the group to tell them to come in and get the water of their Corn Mother and to bring their infants. The chief helper gives a cigarette to the chief. Smoking ritual.

Now the people begin to come in, at the door removing shoes or moccasins. Each woman brings a basket of bread and a dish of beans or stew, setting the food in a corner of the outside room. This is the time they sing the song about the Emergence, giving the names of all the springs, beginning with those "from which we were born," Shipapu and Kaithlirebe'ai, and the names of the mountains. About four they begin to bring in the infants. [The name-giving ritual appears to be omitted.] The chief tells his helper to lay on their side all the fetish stones. All the men present smoke, in the directions and on the altar, giving thanks to the fetish stones. A mother restores the fetish stones to the bag. With duck feathers the chief helper sweeps up the meal of the "village" of which everyone has to get some to wrap in a cornhusk. The chief helper says they are to take it home to their corn storerooms to bury in their field in the springtime or, if a person has no field, to throw into the river. Then everyone receives a drink from the medicine bowl and puts some of its contents in a small bowl to take home. The chief addresses them all, thanking them and releasing them.

The mothers bring in the presents of food, including the large bowlfuls from the women of the house. The largest baskets with a bowl of stew in front of it are placed where the chief had stood in front of the altar. Then a basket and bowl are set out for each helper, and behind these are rows of baskets all edged around with bowls of stew. The chief helper and the helper next to him start from different sides to go around these baskets and dishes, each carrying a tortilla into which he puts bits of the food, the first man carrying the tortilla in his left hand and picking up the bits with his right hand, the second man reversing this, carrying with his right and gathering with his left. Both men go up to the chief, who puts some tobacco on each food collection. The first or right-hand man takes some meal from the basket with his right hand, the second or left-hand man, with his left hand. They return to the farther end of the baskets and wave their food collection in circuit. All present perform the exorcising slicing motion. Then the two helpers go out to the ash pile where they pray, the right-hand man feeding Weide, the left-hand man feeding the Dead. They return and tell the others what they have done and that Weide and the Dead have sent them their *washiha*, they have got their food, what is left "their sons" may eat. The chief goes to the basket and bowl of the first helper, takes a little, prays to Weide for permission to feed "his son," and puts the food in his mouth. This he does for each helper. Then he takes his own seat, and the chief helper in turn feeds him, while the others give thanks to Weide and to the people and ask that all may get more food, for themselves and for all the town. Then the chief gives permission to all to eat. After eating, the last helper divides all that is left between attendants, appropriating one basket and dish for the people of the house, another basket and dish, as is usual, for the Town chief to be taken to him the following morning by a mother, and another basket and dish for the Stillborn. Now the chief gives permission to all to go home and take their food with them, after joining their relatives who have been waiting outside in another room for them.

The last helper will have told one of the attendants to return early in the morning, before sunrise. When this man returns, he finds the chief and his helpers sitting around the fireplace where they have been making for the Stillborn a prayer-stick which consists of an unpainted piece of willow, measured on the last two joints of the middle finger, and tied to the end several hummingbird feathers. The chief sprinkles meal in the directions and then a "road" to the door, over which the last helper and the outside helper pass and leave the house, the one carrying the food offering, the other the prayer-stick. The last helper tells his companion not to turn back or look to one side. When the two arrive at Nam'pekötöade', they find there a bank with a hole in it through which the last helper throws meal, then goes in a little way, extending his hand with the prayer-stick, praying, and waiting for the Stillborn to take the prayer-stick from him. This they do. Then he withdraws and calls to the outside helper who has been casting his meal and burying his crumbs under a near-by bush. Both men run for a little way and then walk back to the ceremonial house. "Greetings!" and the last helper tells the story of the whole affair, from the time they made the prayer-stick to their return, what they met on their way, how the Stillborn took the prayer-stick, how they ran and then walked back.

By this time the sun has risen. All go out and throw pollen to the sun and give thanks. When they re-enter the house, they dismiss the outside helper, who carries with him as pay the basket and bowl from which he had taken the crumbs. Now the chief and his chief helper go to the ceremonial house of the Town chief* to tell him all about the ceremony they have accomplished. Returning from the Town chief, they tell the waiting helpers of how they made their report. All thank one another. The chief gives permission to all to leave.

Pesa at Jemez[12]

Sun work, Pesa, is the reference both to winter solstice, "winter middle," and to summer solstice, "sun middle." The Town

* During the days of the ceremony the Town chief has remained in his house to receive reports, but he has not himself engaged in ceremonial.

chief's solar observations are said to determine June 1 for the summer ceremony, and the first days of December or the last of November for the winter ceremony. The Town chief watches the sunrise from the ruin mound of the old church for a few days in advance and then sends his two helpers to summon "all those who have Mothers," i.e., the society heads to meet in his house to talk over their "work for the Sun."

It is an eight-day ceremony. Four days the ceremonialists live at home, taking a daily emetic; they make prayer-sticks "to dress up the Sun," and prepare the altar which they are to place on the fourth night, each society in its respective house. The fourth-night ceremonials are public, and, in accordance with the Pueblo circulatory dance pattern, society members visit and dance in the houses of other societies. They dance kachina, and side dancers or kachina chiefs visit from one society room to another and are "made to dance" by the society. Ears of seed corn, five or six, from "every woman" have been placed on the altar. The all-night ceremonials conclude with a drink of medicine to all visitors. Follows for each society a four-day retreat with fasting from meat and salt.

At the solstice season any man may put down prayer-sticks, made for him by any one of the societies, in the middle of his field. A woman who wants a child may also offer society-made sticks. Prayer-sticks are offered to the rabbits by the Hunters' society. For domestic animals, men may put down feather-strings in the hills.

INSTALLATION CEREMONIAL

Possibly in accordance with the general Pueblo attitude that trusteeship of sacrosanct things or holding office is dangerous, exacting, and onerous, to be avoided if possible, little ceremonial attaches, as a rule, to installation into office. Fetishes or sticks of office, official regalia, are passed on or "handed," breathed on or from with prayer, counsels are given, and that as a rule seems to be all there is to installation. Accounts, however, are meager, excepting accounts of the installations of an associate Town chief at Zuni and of the annual war captains at Acoma which is initiation-like ritual, and sketches from Nambé of the installation of a Town chief, and from Cochiti of the investiture of the War chief. An account of the handing of the canes of the secular officers at Zuni may be included, for the canes are sacrosanct and are probably "handed" like fetishes. Stephen was on First Mesa when a new Town chief was installed, but he says merely that at night during the Winter solstice ceremony in Chief kiva in the presence of the chiefs the corn-ear fetish was handed to the new Town chief by his mother's brother.[13] A Zuni woman has told briefly of her own installation in the Zuni Rain chieftaincy of the South: "My grandmother grew old. My two uncles said, 'You will succeed your grandmother.' During the winter solstice, my uncle gathered sticks. Next day they all met together to cut prayer-sticks, my three grandfathers and two uncles and grandmother; and for me also they cut prayer-sticks. So they laid hold of me, they took me by the hand.* 'Into a person such as we are, right here, we shall make you. You will have care of all your world. All your children you will hold fast. Carefully you will watch over your fathers, the Ones-Who-First-Had-Being. This sort of person you shall be.† Do not be lazy!' "[14]

OF NAMBÉ TOWN CHIEF,[15] AT TESUQUE

In 1917 about the middle of December, he who had been left-hand man to the Winter Town chief of Nambé was installed as the Winter Town chief. A year before, a preliminary ceremony had been held to initiate the waiting period which is referred to as "egg-setting." The installation took place at Tesuque because there were no Winter chiefs at Nambé to officiate.

The installation is a twelve-day ceremony‡ about which little was known to the informant who was a kinswoman of the Nambé man except that he had to bathe every midnight in the river

---

* Probably the breathing rite is meant. See p. 596.

† Compare how the first Town chiefs of San Juan were "caught hold of" and given counsel, p. 250. See pp. 597 ff.

‡ This is highly questionable. I surmise that the installation merely took place in the course of a prolonged Tesuque ceremony, perhaps the winter solstice ceremony.

through the ice, to make himself hard since he was to be an Ice man, and except that two by two the Nambé man's kinswomen took food to the Winter chiefs in their house of retreat. Two War captains would receive the bowl of food. One captain carried a bowl of medicine water from which the other gave a drink to the women. When one of them was pregnant (pregnant women liked to volunteer), the other woman would spray the water over her saying, "Expect a baby boy!"

The public performance on the last night was held in the kiva of the Winter People. From the altar in the ceremonial room of the Winter chief a cactus fetish was carried to the kiva and to song was passed from hand to hand in the circle of Winter men. Were the cactus dropped, it were a sign of misfortune. Three more trips from the altar were made with Cactus Grandmother, the plant appearing smaller each time. The third time the Nambé man brought it into the circle, and his ceremonial father brought it in the fourth time. In the last dance the cactus became so small that it disappeared, "going back where they brought her from."

Corn meal was dropped into a jar of boiling water for the Winter men to stir around four times with their fingers. They do not burn themselves, they are Ice men. The dough was given to the women present to take home as medicine for burns.

At dawn the kachina arrived, and in their presence the Winter chief handed to the new Town chief the white ice-like stone which was to be his Mother. It was to be wrapped with parrot and chaparral cock feathers and kept covered in a willow mat.

The next day there was an exchange of meals and of presents between the families of the new Town chief and his ceremonial father, a Winter man of the Tesuque chieftaincy. All day long Summer People were invited to eat in the houses of Winter People.

Of War Captains of Acoma[16]

The newly appointed War captain (chief) chooses a place for his headquarters for the coming year. This is usually located in his own home, but whatever rooms are set aside for the War captains are cleaned and replastered. The outgoing War captain passes to his successor a permanent prayer-stick-like image. Just before leaving office, he also orders every family in the village to bring a load of wood for the new War captain.

The day after the War captain and his two lieutenants and their two cooks move in, the lieutenants set out for Spider spring to the southwest to get wood for prayer-sticks. They wear the official buckskin shirts and carry quivers made of mountain-lion skin. Each carries two *ya'Bi* or sticks of office. One is the usual cane of office; the other smaller stick is kept permanently in the lionskin quiver. On their return, when they approach close to their house, their chief comes out to meet them, singing. He makes two lines or "roads" of corn meal on the ground along which they walk to enter the house, just as Spirits are welcomed; are they not impersonating the War Brothers?

The next day is spent making prayer-sticks. In the evening the three captains visit three springs to deposit their prayer-sticks and to fill a small water jar at each spring.

It is about three o'clock in the morning when they get back to town. The War captain goes to the chief kiva and calls: "Greetings, Fathers, Mothers, Chiefs, may I come down?" The Antelope clansmen and shamans respond: "Yes, it is yourself, come down!" In the kiva pit which is the opening to Shipap, the War captain deposits four prayer-feathers, with prayer. As he leaves, those present give him words of encouragement.

The War captain goes to the shrine of Ma'sewi on the east side of the mesa and prays. Then at the very edge of the mesa he prays to the Sun, that is about to rise. Now he walks up and down the streets calling to the people that Sun, the Father, is coming and that they should get up and pray to him. Everyone comes outdoors and prays to the Sun, sprinkling corn meal toward him. At sunrise the two lieutenants take out the three jars of spring water to empty into the reservoir pools of the town.

The next day the War captains make more prayer-sticks. That night they go west, as two nights before they went north, with their prayer-sticks and water jars. This time it is the first lieutenant who goes to the kiva, and to arouse the people. On their third trip to the springs the War captains go south, and the second lieutenant goes to the kiva upon their return. The fourth trip is to the east, and the head War captain goes to the kiva.

Formal initiation of the War captains is to take place four days after the above circuit is completed. The Town chief requests the War captain to inform Kaвina society chief who being the only surviving member of the society will get a Flint society member as helper. The day before initiation, Kaвina chief lays down his altar in the chief kiva. On the altar are two fetishes made of buckskin* with feathers at the top and called Tsamai'ye and Tsamahi'a.[17] In front are arrowpoints, stone fetishes, and in the middle a large stone lion.

Kaвina chief and his helper go to the chief kiva early in the morning of the initiation day and begin to sing. Food is brought into kiva and placed before the altar. Anyone may attend, even women. Many people wish to be whipped at this time, believing that the whipping will give them strength, or luck in hunting, racing, and gambling.

The War captains come in wearing only a breechcloth, and barefoot. Each ties prayer-feathers to the fetishes Tsamai'ye and Tsamahi'a. Then each in turn steps onto the *sipapu* plank. Kaвina chief and his helper are standing on opposite ends. They begin to sing and dance. Then the shaman at the east end strikes the captain forcibly on the shins with his yucca whip; the one on the other end strikes him on the shoulders. They sing and dance again, and strike the captain again. This is done four times. The shaman on the east end whips upward, striking first the shins, then the thighs, then the belly, and last the chest. The other shaman whips downward, first the shoulders, then the middle of the back, the back of the thighs, and last the calves of the legs. The three outgoing captains are whipped in this way, together with their two cooks; the three incoming captains are whipped, but not the incoming cooks. Now, after one night, the former

---

* Should not this read "covered with buckskin"? For are these not the stone implements called elsewhere by the same name?

captains and cooks may again sleep with their wives, with whom they have not slept during their whole year in office.

Toward evening everyone leaves the kiva except the new War captains, the Кавina chief, and his helper, and, perhaps, a few other shamans. Кавina chief grinds some droppings of a snake, puts it into his medicine bowl, and pours in water. Then he sings six songs, moving the bowl toward each of the cardinal points and up and down. The chief asks the two lieutenants if they wish to take this medicine. They have the privilege of refusing, but the head captain *must* drink it. If the lieutenants refuse, then Кавina chief and one or two of the other medicine men will probably drink some "to keep the War captain company." This medicine gives great strength and also the ability to foretell events through dreams. The captains remain in kiva four days and four nights. No one may touch them during this time, nor do they touch each other or even each other's blanket; "they are so powerful." Food is brought to the captains, by their wives. The altar remains in place, and Tsamai'ye and Tsamahi'ye are given food at each meal, and a cigarette afterward.

After the War captains have rested for a few days, they again make the circuit of the springs of the four directions. A rest interval of eight days follows.* From then on to the end of the year the War captains take turns going singly to the springs. They do not bring water back to the pueblo, but on their return they do go to the kiva to pray, and then to summon all the people to pray to the rising sun.

INVESTITURE OF WAR CHIEF OF COCHITI[18]

In the house of the Town chief before an altar the War captains directed the Town chief to array the new War chief (Nahia, ? Under chief). He was dressed from the feet upward: moccasins and leggings, buckskin belt, bandoleer, armlets; face painted red;

* Some such routine may have been observed at one time by Laguna War captains who in 1917 were depositing prayer-sticks in each quarter of the moon (Parsons 14:185-86).

white paint and eagle down over his hair. Then they gave him a bow, arrow, quiver, and stone club.*

The Town chief said to the War captains, representatives of the War gods: "Father Ma'sewi and Oyoyewi, here is Father Ompi'† Nahia. Everything is ready. You should be the ones to start Nahia Ompi'. If you give him permission, he will start; if you do not give him permission, he will not start." When "Ma'sewi" told him to start, Nahia took office.

Into Town Chieftaincy of Zuni, December 13, 1896‡

In the ceremonial chamber of the Town chieftaincy, from midday on for six hours, all the Rain chiefs are present, also the officers of the following societies: Shi'wanakwe, Ne'wekwe, Hunters, Wood, Ant, Cactus, also the four officers of the Kachina society—almost all the chiefs.§

Formal greetings. Moccasins and head kerchiefs are removed. War chief younger brother looks to the seating. The junior Town chief spreads a blanket and over it a buckskin on which he sprinkles a line of pollen and on this lays bead necklaces.‖ The appointee stands on the buckskin, a foot on either side of the pollen line. Pekwin clasps the appointee's hands, breathes on them, and four times moves the two pairs before the mouth of the appointee to breath from, the familiar breathing rite. He prays. Everyone present in turn, excepting the woman member of the Town chieftaincy,¶ performs this rite, nobody loosening his hold on the hands of the appointee until the next man takes

* Compare the investiture of White Wildcat Man, the War chief, in Tewa myth, p. 250; also the investiture of the War chief during the winter solstice ceremony of Oraibi (p. 559)

† Opi, the scalp-taker.

‡ Stevenson 2:168–71. The group is referred to by Stevenson as the Rain chieftaincy of the North which is also the Town chieftaincy. But the representative assemblage was present, I surmise, because a Town chief was being installed.

§ Absent: Shuma'kwe, Big Firebrand, Little Firebrand, Bedbug, Snake Medicine, Uhuhukwe.

‖ The straight road of life (Stevenson).

¶ All she does is to supply cornhusks to smokers.

hold. (This seems to be an important point.)* In conclusion
Town chief and War chief say long prayers. At the next assemblage of the Town chieftaincy the new member will be presented
with the water and seed fetishes to breathe from.

OF GOVERNOR, ZUNI, JANUARY 16, 1917[19]

The installation of Zuni officers usually takes place in Big
court, before all the people, a sort of assembly or, in Spanish,
junta, to ratify the appointments which were made by the
chiefs during the winter solstice ceremony when kachina impersonators also were appointed; but in 1917, owing to friction between the high chiefs, the installation was held privately in the
house of the Town chief. The uncle of the outgoing Governor
and I were the only outsiders. All the major Rain chiefs were
present except the junior Town chiefs, one being out of town, the
other staying away to express disapproval. The outgoing Governor and the "Mexican chief" (*sipaloa shiwanni*) referred to in
English as Lieutenant-Governor had been notified by Ts'awele,
the War chief. Also, I presume, the two incoming officers.

As we waited for Ts'awele, the chiefs talked and smoked, except in sign of disapproval the two who were against changing
the officers. When Ts'awele arrived, he reported that Owelisio,
the outgoing *teniente tsanna* (little lieutenant), refused to give
up his cane as it was personal property received from his uncle.
After telling this story, Ts'awele folded his blanket and placed it
on the box he had been sitting on; on the floor in front he placed
a folded blanket belonging to the house. The Governor-Elect
sat down on the box, and on the blanket in front the outgoing
Governor knelt on his right knee, holding his cane nearly vertical
in both hands. He had dropped his blanket, as did the others
who also removed their headbands. We all stood as the kneeling
Governor prayed:† "This day, our Sun father, now that you

---

* Compare the recurrent prayer phrase "hold fast." The reference to installing the Pekwin is "hold by the back," *onanyatenakya*. For "embrace" (and
breath rite) on installing into Town chieftaincy see Cushing 6:122.

† In several instances for my own rough translations I have substituted Dr.
Bunzel's smooth and correct translations of the stereotyped phrases of Zuni
prayer.

have come out standing to your sacred place, you have passed me on the road. Our fathers, our mothers, the ones who first had being, water beings, seed beings, with their prayers I take hold of you. All my people I give you. My country I give you. Look out for my people carefully! Look out for my country carefully! The breath of my fathers their breath my breath behind I add to your breath. Where the life-giving road of your Sun father comes out may you arrive, may your road be fulfilled. Whenever you talk of work, if any of the children of the Corn chiefs do not listen, twice, thrice, four times strike them. For that you will not be blamed. Thus [my] prayer for you is finished. Therefore may you be blessed with life, my elder brother." Concluding his prayer, the Governor moved the cane forward four times to the mouth of the seated man to breathe on, and then handed him the cane.

The Town chief took the place of the outgoing Governor, kneeling also. With the cane in his left hand he made the sign of the cross with his right hand, his lips moving inaudibly in the usual "Mexican prayer." "My child!" said Town chief. "My father," rejoined Governor-Elect. The Town chief prayed: "This day you, our Sun father, have come out standing to your sacred place. You have passed me on my road. My fathers, the ones who first had being, with their hands, with their hearts, I shall hold you fast. My fathers, my mothers, with their prayers I add to your breath. Your fathers, all those whose sacred places are round about, I ask for light (life), north chief, west chief, south chief, east chief, above chief, below chief, their breath of old age, their breath of seeds, their breath of waters, their breath of strong spirit, for their breath I ask. Asking for their breath, into my warm body inhaling their breath I add to your breath. Do not despise the breath of your fathers! Where the life-giving road of your Sun father comes out, may your road reach, may your road be fulfilled. Thus for you I finish my prayer. My child, make good your spirit! Make good your heart! My fathers, my mothers, the ones who first had being, with their prayers may you be blessed with life. My child, I give you my country. I give you my people. Love my backs, my hands!

With light talk do not scold my people. Love my country, my people! For you, my child, I have finished the prayer. May you be blessed with light!" During this prayer the others would rejoin, "That is so" (amen). At the close the Town chief moved the cane to be breathed on as before. The ritual was repeated for the incoming Lieutenant-Governor, as it would have been for all the other officers had they been present, in each case the outgoing officer and the Town chief installing the incoming officer.

After this ritual the outgoing Governor left at once, saying, "I am going," to which the others responded with the formula customary in the house of a chief, "Go, may the sun set well for you!"

Ts'awele and the new officers made speeches, the Governor about leasing some grazing land, the Lieutenant-Governor to the effect that if the men did not obey the order to work on the ditch the officers would resign. The new Governor was interrupted by one of the chiefs telling Ts'awele to treat the new officers better than he treated the old ones, and, when Ts'awele was in the middle of a second speech, the new officers said the usual goodbye, "I am going," and went out.—I have the impression that the ability to listen closely is not developed in Zuni or other Pueblo circles. There may be some connection between a tendency to inattention and the habit of repetitious or formulary speech.

INITIATION CEREMONIAL

To the Pueblos, as to us, initiation is distinguishable from installation. Initiation sets up new familial relationships between the family of the initiate and the family of his sponsors or godparents; place or official power is acquired, a new name, and the duty or right to dance or cure or hunt or fight in special ways, and these obligations or "privileges," as they would be called on the Northwest Coast, together with being "saved" entail heavy expenditure for feasting and present-giving; the family connection will contribute and so they are consulted in advance.

Between dedication and initiation a considerable interval may elapse. Dedication may appear to be a kind of preliminary initiation so that a double initiation appears to take place, notably in

the kachina cult (Zuni-Hopi) and in the Flute and Snake-Antelope societies, perhaps in other Hopi societies. In other terms,
the Hopi who has been dedicated or initiated in infancy before
participating in ceremony will be reinitiated.[20]

Anyone who has been dangerously exposed to the contagious
influence of the society, i.e., a trespasser, or anyone gravely
harassed or sickened by the spirit patrons of the society, in order
to be saved should be initiated. A cure of bewitchment does not
necessitate initiation; the ideology is quite different.

In initiatory ceremonial the initiate is brought into close contact with any fear-inspiring object like yucca switches or with
any fearful being the group is associated with, with Bear or
Mountain Lion or Snake or the Dead. He is frightened so he will
no longer be afraid, a kind of inoculation against fear.* He receives the paraphernalia proper to membership. He goes through
the indispensable rite of head-washing and naming. He may be
treated ritually as an infant, for he is "reborn," into another circle, a world-wide theory or initiation. At Zuni the annual ceremony at which the initiation takes place will be held in a
waxing moon, a time propitious to rebirth; the preliminary retreat will be held four days before the full moon.[21] When the
Fathers of Isleta initiate, they dramatize the birth by covering
the novice and his "mother," the senior woman of the society,
with the same blanket. From under the blanket as they sit near
the altar the "mother" draws the corn-ear fetish which "through
the power of the chief has been born from her." The chief em-
braces "mother" and novice under this blanket from which the
novice emerges as a bear. "That is the way they are born, in the

---

* For example, the Keresan initiate is cuffed around by society members
wearing bear paws, "so that he wont be afraid of witches" (White). The Isletan
scalper is struck with the scalp; the youthful Hopi hunter who goes through
initiatory forms is switched or scraped with his dead jackrabbit (see p. 602).
The prototype of the San Juan Hunt (War) chief was scratched by the supernatural prey animals (Parsons 42:10). The medicine order of the Zuni society
imitate mountain lions, wildcats, and bears, slapping and clawing at the initiate,
growling and snarling (Benedict 3:II, 39). All this is inoculation for power as
well as against fear, giving a "strong heart," a "new heart." It is getting power
in accordance with familiar Indian ideas, but, in accordance with Pueblo pattern,
always through a group, not on your own.

form of a bear."[22] The initiates into the Hopi Wüwüchim societies are carried like infants on their godfathers' backs, sleeping
with their godfathers under the same blanket and being shielded
from the sun.* For six days they are below the lake in the underworld, with their Mother, Dawn Woman.† Then they are born.[23]
"The Wüwüchim is the beginning of life."[24]

Just so at Acoma: the same Emergence song, sung by the
Mothers when they came up, is sung in naming an initiate as in
naming an infant, for birth and rebirth.

> I am going to pray, am I not
> I am going to pray.
> Lake in the east
> For life I am going to pray,
> Going to pray.
>
> I am going to pray, am I not
> I am going to pray.
> Lake in the east
> For luck I am going to pray,
> Going to pray.
>
> I am going to pray, am I not
> I am going to pray.
> Lake in the east
> To grow, to get old, I am going to pray,
> Going to pray.

In the initiation into the Walpi Snake society Mountain Lion
and Bear are impersonated; Lion carries a snake and puts it into
the mouth of the novice, Bear puts a cornstalk into the novice's

---

* At her adolescence retreat the Mishongnovi girl is also kept in the shade;
she fasts from salt and meat; she is "like a baby." She wears a prayer-feather in
her hair, and offers a prayer-feather early every morning to the Sun. After four
days, at her head-washing she is given new names by her "aunts" (Beaglehole
1:44–45).

† Dawn Woman is to be identified with Iyatiku, the Keresan Mother from
whom the unborn are to come and to whom the dead return. The Wüwüchim
initiation ritual has not been witnessed, but there are hints that the initiates are
brought into contact with death: possibly Skeleton or Death is impersonated by
the Agave society who have a separate initiation. The initiate into the Zuni
Big Firebrand society has to behave like one who has been in contact with the
dead (see p. 724, n.*). A kachina-like or whipping initiation would be expected in
connection with Dawn Woman. See p. 246.

mouth, and the Snake society chief moves his corn-ear fetish up and down in front of the novice. These three, Lion, Bear, and the Chief, are called endowers; contact with the snake is to free the novice from fear of snakes, to introduce the novice to the snakes so they will not bite him, and to insure long life to the novice. The cornstalk is also to endow with longevity and to produce quick and vigorous growth like that of a cornstalk. The corn-ear fetishes (Antelope chief waves his also) are motioned with prayer that the novice may be strong and brave, that he may not fall sick, and may live long.[25]

Impersonation is a marked trait at initiations. At Oraibi, Müy'ingwa, god of vegetation, is impersonated at the Powamu society initiation. Keresan and Zuni curing societies introduce kachina at their initiations. The impersonation seems planned to impress the novice. For example, when the Müy'ingwa and Seed goddess impersonators are to be arrayed at Oraibi Oaqöl society initiation, the novices are sent home, they are "too young" to look on.[26]

Flagellation is a characteristic rite of initiation, but it does not always occur, even in initiation into the kachina, the supernaturals the rite is most closely associated with. Initiates into the kachina Powamu society (Oraibi) are not whipped, nor are kachina novices at San Felipe. Possibly the "whipping of the children" is primarily a general rite of purification and only secondarily a specific rite of initiation (see pp. 470–71). The way a boy is "whipped" with the first jackrabbit he kills (Second Mesa) supports this interpretation, for the boy is not being initiated into a hunt society; there is none. After the kill the hunt is stopped, and all gather around the boy. His father or other kinsman chooses the best hunter on the field as "hunt father" to the boy "because he wants the boy to be as good a hunter as this man." The boy is stripped. The men form a circle around him, holding each other's wrist (Huichol-like). The kinsman bends the boy forward with his back to the north, while the hunt father swings the dead rabbit across the boy's back from left to right leaving a blood mark on the flesh. This is repeated for the other three directions.

I will give the rest of the account as it brings out familiar initiatory features. During the following three days the boy fasts from salt and meat. Each morning at dawn his "father" takes him to a spring to deposit prayer-sticks, to bathe in the spring and to drink from it. On the fourth morning the boy's head is washed in the maternal house of his father, and he is given a name, also food presents and two painted throwing-sticks. A hunt has been called for this morning, and the "father" makes the ritual fire. He and the boy are arrayed and painted ceremonially: kilt, hair plumes, two red vertical lines on each cheek and two yellow lines on various parts of the body. *The boy's name is announced,** and he is chosen to lead one of the two surround wings. The first rabbits he kills he gives to his "father" to pay for the throwing-sticks. In later hunts he may give rabbits to his hunt "aunts."[27]

The following account of initiation into the Hopi Flute society[28] brings out other typical initiatory features.

When a young person is brought to look on the Flute altar for the first time, he gives a handful of prayer-meal to the man he has chosen for a "father." The "father" casts the meal on the altar. The "father" loops three hawk prayer-feathers on a twig of sumac, the fourth one he ties to the novice's scalp lock. On the fourth night of the ceremony the novice† is admitted to the chamber and is given the ritual corn ear, his "mother," which he holds throughout the song. The fifth morning he deposits in the shrine the uppermost prayer-feather and the other prayer-feathers on the sixth and seventh mornings. The eighth morning he deposits his hair feather. The corn ear he places in his mother's house. It insures good flesh and bodily health, and this is why a symmetric ear is always chosen.

Initiation is sporadic, "every four years," i.e., when there are enough novices, but it is always performed at the regular annual or biennial ceremony which is thereby prolonged or in various ways amplified. Altars, for example, are more elaborate; indeed the full altar may be laid only at initiations (Hopi).[29] Was the initiation the fundamental ceremony and the annual ceremony

---

* Compare p. 1031, n. ‡.

† Lā'n-vana, Flute put in, or Oa'qöl-vana, Chū'-vana, Oa'qöl-put in, Snake-put in (Voth 4:11, n. 2).

merely a commemorative abbreviation? Certain Zuni curing societies do not hold a quite independent ceremony unless there is to be an initiation, i.e., the initiation is the ceremony. Fuller information about the Keresan type of curing society ceremony elsewhere, at Isleta and Jemez, among Tiwa and Keres themselves, might reveal a parallel situation. (We are reminded of the Californian shaman dance to instruct novices and show off shamanistic powers.)

A War Captain Visits Sia To Assist at an Initiation into the Hunt Society*

When we set out from our pueblo to go to Sia, our Hunt chief took his corn-ear fetish, his eagle-wing feathers, and his mountain-lion image. As a War captain helper I took a mountain-lion skin quiver and bow and arrows. When we neared Sia, the Hunt chief and a War captain met us, relieved us of what we carried, and took us to the house of the Hunt chief. We were given corn-husk cigarettes, and, when we finished smoking, the visiting Hunt chiefs told how they had received the invitation meal and how they had come. All shook hands.

This was about sunset. The following day we go to the house of the War captain who tells us to watch outside the house of the Hunt society. In the evening we go inside and eat supper and then we are given permission to visit about in the pueblo. The third day two Hunt society members go to the mountains to gather yucca for whips, different kinds of grass, and oak. The others set out their altar. In the afternoon we see them sitting behind it. In the evening the society sing. The next morning on the ground around the house the society put a line of corn meal which is called a trap. The War captains on guard stay outside of it. Indoors, the society is putting feathers on the things they

* Related to Dr. White by a War captain invited from another Keresan pueblo. I have taken the liberty of citing the account as if given in the first person. It is of course not verbatim. Pueblo English is quite different.

The other pueblo is inferably Santo Domingo. See White 4:178. Because the people had all been together at the Emergence and afterward, town had budded from town, "that is why the Shikame of Santo Domingo goes to Santa Ana to initiate new men into Shikame, and why Shaiyak (Hunt Chief) goes to Sia and San Felipe to make new Shaiyak."

are going to use, and getting ready the grass to put on the initiate. At sunset the meal line is brushed away from the house. This evening the War captains are summoned to the house of the Hunt society. The parents of the initiate come in. The Hunt chief says the initiate is "going to be born again just like a little baby, he is going to become a new person." They sing. Two come out from those sitting behind the altar and begin to whip the disease away with their eagle feathers, motioning as if cutting and discarding. With a corn-ear fetish in each hand the chief dances in front of the altar, the others sing, asking the Mother to sit down, i.e., to be present for the sake of the game animals.

Outside, a shaman asks if they will allow him to come in, if the War captains are there, if they want to have "the new born boy" brought in, if they will "believe in him." The shaman leads in the initiate by two eagle-wing feathers which he holds backward over his shoulder, a feather in each hand. A shaman walks behind the initiate. Both have rings of grass around each arm, a red spot on the navel incircled by bird down, the same on the back; buckskin kilt, moccasins, and a bear-claw necklace. The three follow the meal road and stand in front of the medicine bowl until the song ends. The society chief crosses his eagle-wing feathers on the meal road, and the initiate steps on them and stoops forward. The shaman who has followed him in—he is called Ro'hona [weasel, jaguar, possibly badger, from Sp. *tejón*]—whips the initiate four times with his yucca whip. Again the chief crosses his feathers on the road and the initiate is whipped again *hard*. In a song the initate is given a new name. Ro'hona whips the chief and all the other members and is in turn whipped by the chief. All stand on the feathers while being whipped. After everything is removed from the person of the initiate and of Ro'hona, a shaman and a War captain take them to the river to bathe. Whips and grass bands are thrown into the river.

The parents of the initiate have brought in food, and the father says that he gives everything, food, baskets, pottery, etc., to the society whom he thanks for initiating his son. The chief gives the initiate a corn-ear fetish, a rattle, eagle-wing feathers, the mountain-lion image, and the image of Paiyatyamo, Sun Youth. All these the initiate's mother puts into a basket to take home. Everyone leaves but the society and the War captains. The food is divided. It is almost sunrise when we War captains return to the room we have been given.

The next day the War captains of Sia get us our horses. All the visitors from Santo Domingo, San Felipe, and Sant' Ana set forth together accompanied by the Sia society for about half a mile where the roads separate for the visitors and where the Sia men leave us.

Wüwüchim Ceremony with Initiation, at Walpi, 1891[30]

FIRST DAY

At sunrise standards are set up in all four kivas, Chief (Singers), Wikwalobi (Wüwüchimtü), Horn (Horns), and Goat (Agaves).* At Agave kiva the standard consists of crane-wing feathers and eight strips of cornhusk bound on the end of a round stick, forty inches long. I watch the chief sprinkle meal on the standard and toward the sun.

The women began heating their cooking pits at from one to two hours before daylight this morning, and by half-past eight they have their meal-pudding jars in and baking.

The meal altar of the directions is placed in Chief kiva soon after sunrise. It is also placed in the other kivas, at a little after noon in Agave kiva. Here Anawita of the Water-Corn clan, Agave chief, also War chief in the Masauwü cult, strips off and, over the *sipapu*, sifts brown valley sand in an irregular circle about two feet in diameter; he makes three intersecting lines with white prayer-meal and sets the crenellate bowl on the intersection, pouring water into the bowl and sprinkling pollen. Masaiumtiwah, Spread Eagle Wings, Badger clansman and Medicine chief, comes in and strips and sits down on the north side of the bowl, Anawita sitting close beside on his right. Anawita produces six ears of corn and a box of feathers. In the tray

* From now on each kiva will be referred to by the name of the society using it.

of prayer-meal he sticks six sprigs of pine needles to each of which he has fastened short cotton strings. Both men begin to sing, and Anawita beats time by tapping on the floor with the end of a feathered rod, holding it vertical. Masi lays the feathers down on the meal lines, then the ears of corn, yellow at the northwest first as usual. With the ears of corn he lays down stones, pebbles, etc. As the song proceeds, Masi lays the pebbles in the bowl, sprinkles, asperses, then lays the yellow corn ear in, and the others. At each cardinal point Anawita lays down another set of bird skins or feathers; these skins and feathers, during the song, are also taken up by Masi and the tip or distinctive colored end of each is dipped in the water in the bowl and then replaced.

After the long song Masi takes out a lump of clear quartz crystal, sucks it and gives it to a younger man who sits near stitching a kilt. This younger man goes up the ladder and deflects a ray of sunlight into the bowl and then comes down and gives back the crystal to Masi who puts it in the bowl. During the song Masi also sprinkles pollen into the bowl.

About 4.15 P.M. the Agaves, led by Anawita carrying his tray of meal, move in an informal procession to Chief kiva, Singers' kiva. They are followed by the Horns from Horn kiva, led by Winüta of the Reed clan;* then by the Wüwüchimtü from Wikwalobi kiva, led by Singoïtïwa of the Mustard-Chakwena clan. These leaders all carry a tray of prayer-meal; others carry a feathered rod; the novices, prayer-sticks. Arriving at the hatchway, each casts a handful of meal down upon the fireplace, throws it down strongly before he steps on the ladder.

No one is in costume, but the Horns have a spot of white on each cheek, zigzagged with a wet finger. They and the Singers sit facing the hatchway. The other societies stand around the walls on both the main floor and the upraise. I could not count, but there must be at least one hundred and forty in kiva, about equally divided. Hani, Wiki of the Snake clan and Antelope

* The chieftaincy is in the Bear clan, but, when Mi'le the Bear man died, his sister's grandson Kotka was too young to act as Horn society chief, so for many years Winüta, son of Mi'le and so child of Bear, acted as regent. Regency of this kind is an important adjustment in Hopi-Zuni clanship.

society chief, Anawita, Singoïtïwa, and perhaps three others stand up quite naked save for breechcloth, each holding a feathered rod. They stand on the north side of the fireplace facing east; in a small clear space on the south side of the fireplace, the Horn fire-maker sits with a helper. He has a straight line of white from shoulder to wrist and from ilium to ankle, these lines down the outside of arms and legs. He holds his fire rod vertical. It is about thirty inches long, the lower end resting in the fire board. Another pair of fire makers, Agaves, sit on the north side of the fireplace.

They wait five minutes, then at a signal from Hani,* chief of Singers society and of the entire ceremony, all four societies burst forth each in its own vigorous song and time. Some beat time with cowbells, a tremendous potpourri, no disorder, not displeasing. They sing for about ten minutes. In about three minutes fire is made by the Horns. They light up the cedar bark, then the Agaves do the same, and a good large bark fire blazes up. Short prayers by six of the principal men. Hani plucks up his pine-needle strings from the tray and casts all six, one after another, in the fire. Singoïtïwa follows him, cast by cast. Before the blaze dies out, a young lad, Avaiyo of the Agaves, is sent to carry lighted wisps of cedar bark to the kivas. Prayers by four or five old men. This ceremonial is called "the placing of all the chiefs' Masauwü sacrifices."

Just before sunset, Kakaptï of the Horn society,† wearing horn headdress and a large buckskin mantle, comes up the stair trail bearing in a tray a figurine about twenty inches high with yellow face and black hair, Talatümsi, Dawn Young Woman. In the girdle around the middle are thrust two sets of blue-green prayer-sticks. Kakaptï has on his ordinary clothes, but he has a turtle shell rattle on each leg and a deer horn in his left hand.

---

* Hani was a famous warrior and possibly for that reason was chosen chief of ceremony, for there is no evidence that the paramount chieftaincy of the four societies belonged in his clan, the Tobacco-Rabbit clan.

† As Sand-Lizard clansman he fetched sand for the altars of the societies he belonged to. He knew about the Sand Altar Young Woman figurine, he and his uncle, Yellow Bear, who was a Pobosh society doctor (see p. 715). Figurines and curing society all seem Keresan.

Another man, Talahoya, a Horn and chief of the Stick-swallowers, stands wrapped in buckskin at the foot of the ladder and facing it with a deer horn in his hand. He has a pair of small horns on the front and top of his head and a smear of white clay down nose and mouth. Kakaptï sets down the figurine at the hatchway and stands beside it.

Just at sunset elderly men come up leading nine young lads, the youngest at least twelve or thirteen, the oldest perhaps seventeen. All these novices are quite naked, save for white embroidered kilt tied with string, their hair loose, and they take off their moccasins before stepping on the kiva hatchway. They give up moccasins and blankets to the elderly men who bring them. Each novice then casts a handful of meal down on the fire before he steps on the ladder; as he steps down one rung, one of the Singers comes up the ladder and the lad clings around the Singer's neck and takes his feet off the ladder. The Singer bears him down and passes him into the arms of another. Some lads are set down in a blanket on the south side of the kiva, others on the north side. Vigorous songs, different words and tunes by each society. All the novices have woodpecker wing and tail feathers tied to their scalp lock.

Short prayers. Then Talahoya starts up the ladder followed by the principal men. The novices come up and put on their clothes. Nearly every man of the village is here. I do not see any Tewa men, however. When all have gathered, Talahoya strikes off followed by the long procession in file out through the passageway and down over the point of mesa. Kakaptï leaves his figurine sitting on the hatch and closes the procession. They say they go down the Mishongnovi trail, circle around in the valley* and return.

At 8:15 two Horns with wicker headpieces and horns and two without headpiece, all naked, with turtle rattle on right leg, go along the mesa and through the villages. At 8:25 five Agaves, all wearing their gourd horns and each carrying a long

* Probably to the old site of Walpi.

white baton in left arm and a cowbell at right garter, also pass up the mesa toward Tewa. Such coming and going of Horns and Agaves and moving hither and yon!

At midnight the Agaves don their horns, take off their clothes, and sitting around the crenellate bowl as in the morning sing for an hour and a half. The Horns sing for an hour, all naked with their horns on. All the novices are in Singers' kiva. They are rubbed with yellow mud about as wide as the palm around the top part of the calves and have two black finger marks vertical and parallel down each cheek, and Hani and Singoïtïwa each takes a hand. The three Agave novices are good lumps of boys from twelve to fourteen years old.

SECOND DAY

The Singers come out to dance about half an hour after sunrise. They are not in costume, but the novices are naked and carry deer horns. It is an unearthly kind of an act [it is indeed and different from any other Pueblo dance]; the song is in stentorian voices, and they move sideways, oval fashion, sometimes in crooked line, almost an oval at times. They sidle down to the space in front of Wikyatïwa's house, dance and sing about fifteen minutes, and then sidle off through the village to Chief kiva, singing all the time; two Horns, one in front, the other behind, as escort. They leave the novices at Singers' kiva.

At 11:40 P.M. the Singers wrapped in blankets all crowd around the Agave hatchway and sing a fine solemn chant. Their novices wrapped in blanket, each with a member, stand on the west end of the kiva roof. The chief of the Horns and the old fire-maker, Singoïtïwa, and another Wüwüchimtü come down to the hatch and stand beside Hani who is close beside the figurine, looking down. These chiefs all have trays of meal which they sprinkle on the figurine and on the Agave fire, also during the song they cast meal. The two groups of novices, six Singers, three Agaves, are taken separately to shrines. The Singers sing at the hatchway until 1:00 A.M., when they return to Chief kiva.

FOURTH DAY

The watchmen of the Horns, carrying elk horn, go out as sentinels on the trails before sunrise. About 8:30 A.M. all except Agaves join the Singers in their oblique dance through the village to my front door (Wikyatïwa's house), there they turn and then the Horns drop out at their own kiva, the other societies continuing the song to their kivas. They are in strong force, in curious transition costume, all arrayed in their best garments and as these are now almost wholly civilized they are, one may say, wholly arrayed in shop suits of shiny black, white and print shirts, and straw hats. Oddly enough, however, all bear a hunting weapon and a bundle of food, melon in blanket, etc., rabbit stick, bow and arrows, and there are many repeating rifles. All wear moccasins.

Agave sentinels go in pairs. White-clay smear on shoulders, elbows and hands and knees, black about two fingers width from temple to temple across the eyes, red moccasins, yarn anklets, short blue leggings, blue hank of yarn gartering each leg, white embroidered kilt supported by white brocaded girdle, gray foxskin hanging from loins, blue yarn hank on right wrist, wealth of beads around neck, turquoise bead strings in ears, hair hanging down and large tuft of parroquet plumes on top of head, large bells at leg garter and girdle, chief's stick, the club, on left arm. They make the round outside the walled springs of all the trails and on their return report what tracks they have seen, etc., to Chief Anawita. Horn sentinels go singly and each carries an elk horn.

This morning after the procession of the three societies, all but a few members take the Singers' novices and march off in procession over the point of the mesa, from fifteen to twenty miles to the southwest. They are going to hunt,* to collect white clay for pigment, and to dig yucca root for head-washing. The three Agave novices still hold their vigil in Agave kiva. Today

---

* On the sixth morning all the societies will sally forth to hunt and collect greasewood. Some of the rabbits will be given to the women by men jesting in falsetto as kachina impersonators. (Possibly this is reminiscent of a rabbit hunt with the girls.)

at noon they are stretched out and given a good rubbing and massage. Several Agaves relieve each other in making the rounds.

A slab or frame altar is put up in Horn kiva, by Tüwasmi, uncle of Winüta and joint chief, and one helper. On the altar are two corn-ear fetishes and three stacks of corn ears. The meal-painting suggests the terrace design. The upright frame at the back has three openings and is surmounted by lightning sticks and knobbed sticks, all very old and in very dingy colors— green, yellow, red, and black. [Strikingly like an Acoma altar! This is the only frame altar in the ceremony, and it probably was used in the night initiation.] It takes forty-five minutes to set up the altar. The two men do not speak while thus engaged, and frown at my attempts to question. They make a meal trail along the floor and up the ladder and toward the east, then both sit down by the fireplace and smoke, puffing toward the altar semiformally.

The burros are all corralled on the summit of the mesa. The sheep are taken out. Where are the horses sent to? Püche and Anawita had me write a notice to stick up on the trail near Polaka's to the effect that this day no one would be permitted to approach the mesa. No person nor any animal even. They all warn me to keep indoors tonight, not to look at Agaves and Horns who perambulate the village at a swift pace back and forth, always anti-sunwise. If any profane should look at them tonight, no snow would come. When the Pleiades come over-head the patrolling ceases, at least so I understand. No women look out,* no one stirs abroad save Agaves and Horns. They are in separate patrols, two, three, five, and six of a kind together, bells and empty coal oil cans beaten with sticks, by Agaves; hoofs and tortoise rattles used by Horns. The size of the bands increase to twenty-five or thirty in each, and at 8:15 both socie-ties go up the mesa toward Tewa, leaving some small patrols here. They return at 8:35. Grim challenge and greeting, hollow

---

* In 1927 it was reported that Walpi women had to remove to Sichomovi or Tewa (Steward 2:58). Even in Sichomovi and even in the ceremony without initiation the windows of my room were covered.

responses, clanking and jangling, the dogs barking, and swift scuffling tread of bare feet.

As the night grows later, the pace waxes swifter until as the Pleiades reach the zenith both Horns and Agaves are encircling Walpi at a furious run and this they maintain until Pleiades and Orion are in the place they occupied when the Singers and Wüwüchimtü finished their songs on the previous nights at the hatch, or about 12:30, then these racing horned ones go into their kivas. But all through the night the regular sentinels of Agaves and Horn march around the village and do not cease until sunrise. I was barred out from the kiva ceremony [in Singers kiva] through the inadvertence of some of the Horns [barred from the initiation ceremonial].* [The Agaves had their initiation in their own kiva, and this too was missed by Stephen who was not told about it until the next day. Undoubtedly he was deliberately overlooked at both initiations. As we have seen, he got in bad earlier in the day with the Horn chief.]

FIFTH DAY

About an hour before sunrise the Singers march down wrapped in blankets and stand around the Agave hatchway singing their solemn chants. The chiefs of Wüwüchimtü and Horn and certain of their elders stand close to the figurine also, meal trays in hands. Wüwüchim and Horn societies squat around on Horn kiva roof, the great snow pipes are passed around, everyone smoking. Two Horn sentries stand on the west end of Agave kiva roof, in front of the Singer novices. About twelve Agaves take the Singer novices to the shrine beyond the Break, returning with them. Singers and Wüwüchimtü, about twelve in all, take the three Agave novices to the same place and return with them to kiva, shortly before sunrise. Just as the sun comes up, the

* At which, we make a guess, Masauwü is impersonated or some terrifying death array is presented to the novices. The night patrols, I infer, are against ghosts or witches, corresponding to the sortie of Eastern shamans and War captains against witches during an initiation or curing ceremony.

Or perhaps, as Steward was told, it is a kachina-like whipping or a whipping like that at the installation of the War chiefs of Acoma. This would explain why until the youths have been initiated at Wüwüchim they may not dance kachina. It would correspond to the second whipping at Zuni, during Shalako.

Singers finish their song. Kakaptï takes the Dawn Young Woman figurine in his arms to place her in her "house" in the rocks below. All go in procession. First the Singers file off, then the Wüwüchimtü, and most of the Horns wearing their helmet and buckskin, and fifteen or twenty of the Agaves wearing their helmets. On the lowest terrace the three groups, Singers, Wüwüchimtü, and Agaves, keep apart, and Wüwüchimtü and Singers sing for perhaps fifteen minutes, the others, the Horns, move back and forth constantly along the face of the cliffs. A great feast is served as soon as the men return to the kivas, about 8 :oo A.M. The novices break their fast, they do not seem very ravenous. Now they sit down with the others as full-fledged members.

About 1 :oo P.M. the Singers, about thirty, come up out of their kiva, naked save for breechcloth, bodies entirely covered with chrome-colored clay pigment, these phallic designs ⊔ ⌣ rudely done in bright-red ocher on back, breast, and arms; several have this ⊓⊔ on back, covering from shoulders to loins; some have it reversed ⌒⌒ also in front, covering the entire breast; mostly, however, each has several designs, from four to six inches square. On the face are two red ocher stripes about two fingers wide, one across mouth from jaw to jaw, the other across eyes from temple to temple. Round their necks and from their ears they wear curious tufts of rabbit fur red stained and fastened to yucca strands. The hair is drawn in front of the head and done up in conical coil trimmed with vertical corn-husks; all barefoot, and in right hand an ear of corn. One carries and beats a drum of small hollow cottonwood. Hani and another elder carry each a feathered rod.

As soon as they emerge, they begin singing and drum-beating. They gather in a huddled group of three or four irregular lines,[31] and use the ears to point their gesticulations to the women clustered on the terrace. All the women are gathered on the roof terrace and shout back at them in assumed anger, throw water on them from small basins, and some elder women run in among them and pour water on individuals from a gourd. From one house the women, after throwing water and scolding, flouting, and vituperating, pelt them with melon rinds and refuse. The novices are in the ranks. The same two Horns, each with antler in his hand, guard and escort the Singers as on the other days, but these Horns do not wear their helmet today. They dance and sing before each house group along the east front around the end of the village to the dance court back to their kiva, in a little less than an hour. As they pass Agave kiva, Masi asperses them from his crenellate bowl, as did Winüta from Horn kiva.

A little after four, the Wüwüchimtü come up singing, beating their drum. They are divided in two groups: eighteen in one group cluster around the drum as choir and sing a good lively air. There are twelve dancers who do not sing. The eighteen are naked, save for breechcloth. The greater part of the hair is gathered up on top and bound with cornhusks around the ears next the scalp, the rest of it is loosely gathered at the sides. A large lock is also bound with husk, ends hanging. Across eyes and mouth a streak of dull yellowish clay; annular streaks broad as the hand around chest, loins, and above and below knee, around fore and upper arm; and three short horizontal stripes on each side in front and below chest. Of the twelve, six are arrayed thus, and six wear old tunic gowns, these alternating with the naked six. These "women" have yellow feet, and a band around the calf. Singoïtïwa, naked, leads these twelve, and Süyükü closes it disguised as a woman. Each has a feathered rod. All the Wüwüchimtü carry an ear of corn in the right hand and the "vulva" symbol in the left. It is made of sumac wrapped with cotton string and pubic hair. The handle is called "its leg." A young lad carries the red fringed goatskin Sun tablet on his back.

After reaching the dance court, led by Singoïtïwa, the twelve move backward in stiff-legged sliding jerks without lifting the feet from the ground, describe about a circle, and then about-face and revolve backward again, always backward. They move around and back this way for an hour. It is almost dark before they stop. Women drench them with water and some old urine. They go among them and pour water over them individually from a gourd, mostly old women, a few younger, and one or two maidens. Women scream back to their bawdy taunts and thump several of them with the emptied gourds, throw ashes on them also. Winüta asperses them from his crenellate bowl as they dance. Three Horns guard them and two of them move with the dancers, backward motion, the other stands by the choir. The Horns wear their small antelope horns and carry elk horns in their hand. They check runaways from dousing.

At the end of the dance after the others move to the kiva, two Wüwüchimtü continue to taunt the women and gesticulate and are unmercifully drenched, with water mostly but also with some foul filth. The Horn sentries pull the breechcloth from these two, and still they continue their jests until almost quite dark. The Horns throw them down with violence and women rush down and dash water and urine over them. At dark the Horns take them back to kiva. It is cloudy, bitter cold, and windy.

At 6:20 ten Agaves in helmets and with chief sticks go north to the Break, go around the entire village, and return to kiva at 6:40. Five Horns follow in the same round at 6:50. Patrols during the night.

EIGHTH DAY

Forty-four Horns in full rig file into Chief court at 4 P.M., led by Hani, Winüta next, file on the north side of Singers' kiva and around it; two with fancy horn helmets, stand at right and left, about three paces from the line and facing it. Hani clanks a hoof rattle. The Singers file out, each carrying a tray of corn ears, and place themselves alternating between the Horns. Hani and Winüta take the meal trays from the two aids and each sprinkles meal along the front of the line. They leave a lump of meal in the hands of the Heyapauwüh or Black Cloud aids, who throw the lump along the ground toward each other and start after it as fast as they can fly sideways, and at once upon reaching opposite ends of the line begin a leaping step in front of it, as the men in line break out in a fine solemn song.

Women come out and get ears of corn from the Singers' trays; men also take up some kernels and cast meal on the procession. It is very fine.

The Singers wear white embroidered kilt, an embroidered

blanket or a white blanket with scarlet borders, their hair loose, and a decoration in white pigment on legs and feet from knees down, above knee two narrow bands, band over shoulders, two stripes down breast to waist, two down back, two down arm to elbow, from elbow down all white. All the Horns have horn in left hand and ear of corn in right. The two Black Clouds have also a short chief stick in left hand, holding it dangling by string. How they spring and maintain their spring!

Singoïtïwa from his kiva, Winüta and Masi from theirs, asperse the procession and the six cardinal points, as usual. At the end of every stanza the line stops singing for a moment. The Black Clouds change.

Two Singers in kilts, two Horns in helmet and breechcloth, and two Agaves with back tablets go around in couples this afternoon, each bearing a tray and two sets of blue-green prayer-sticks. From every house a woman or girl brings a double hand-ful of prayer-meal of which she casts a handful in each large Havasupai tray.

At midnight in Singers' kiva we hear clanking, and as foot-steps halt at the hatchway two wads of prayer-meal are thrown down, striking the center of the main floor. These are thrown by Tüwasmi and Winüta. These two are bareheaded, wearing cere-monial mantle, each carrying in right hand an ear of corn, in left, the *tiponi*. Winüta has also a chief stick. Following these two, a white-haired old Alosaka.* These three file on the right side of the ladder and stand in the center of the floor facing the ladder. Then enter all the Horns and file around, standing on the main floor as three sides of a square; double and treble rank. Alosaka spreads a Navaho blanket in the center on the floor just in front of where the three stand, and on it spreads a large ceremonial mantle. Winüta asks the godfathers to bring in the three Agave novices. They are brought in and set squatting on their heels, first joint of toe on mantle, with great care. They are completely nude and hold a corn ear in their hand. Song by Horns, very fine and solemn, stamp time; at certain phrases the asperser sprinkles the novices. Winüta presses each novice with

---

* One who wears the horned helmet and acts as scout (War captain).

tiponi and corn ear, on feet, knees, breast, and back, head and shoulders and arms. The song ceases, and all the Horns except the chiefs file out. Tüwasmi prays, he and Winüta pass each his *tiponi* vertical in front of the novices with horizontal circular motion. Winüta prays, each waves his *tiponi* again. Winüta calls on the godfathers to come and take the novices away. [The ritual with the fetishes of the Horn society was the last act in their initiation.] Alosaka folds up the blankets and the three go out.

NINTH DAY

In Agave kiva. All form on main floor to sing. Much care in sizing rank, tallest in center. Link arms and sing to curious knee bending, foot lifting step from 1:15 to 1:45 A.M. Wikyatïwa is fugleman. Avaiyo takes elk horn and blanket and goes up to the top of the hatchway as tiler. Assemble at 1:50 and sing thirty-two songs, ceasing at 3:30. Anawita makes a short prayer, the members thanking him. Anawita takes his feathered rod, the others take the chief stick and bells and to an undistinguishable song beat time, very tedious. A few words of prayer at close by Anawita. Charlie fills pipe and tallies songs with corn kernels.

As soon as they finish they begin decorating. From below knee and from below elbows, white, a band around knee. This on the novice. Others have knees blackened with corn smut; elbows blackened; face all white. Some have broad black stain over left shoulder to right loin in front. Some only a broad band above waist all around and a broad vertical stripe from navel to neck, the fingernails of first and second finger drawn through black band as ornament. Those with black elbows have the sash decoration, the others have legs black from calf to above knee and arms from below elbow to shoulder. All wear all the necklaces and ear turquoise they can raise. Black knees defined above and below with narrow bands made by whitened string, the pigments the consistency of cream. Elbows and sash band also thus defined with white. Three white annulets are made on each black knee by the whitened flaring base of a gourd stem two inches in diameter, also on elbows, and three on breast on sash. White embroidered kilt and girdle; foxskin from loins; garters a hank of blue yarn; parroquet plume on top of head. Anawita and all the godfathers are impressing the novices as to grip and hooking of arm in going up ladder. They all rub the white clay off the face and rub the face with powdered corn from the corn obtained from the Singers' tray today. This wonderfully brightens the complexion, lending to these old grizzled faces the smoothness and dainty soft glow of a maiden.

All being ready, Anawita puts on his helmet and a large white ceremonial mantle, and takes up his *tiponi* and feathered rod, and goes up the ladder, all the rest following, the lame one coming last after the novices and taking up the feathered rod from the kiva hatchway. All have the chief stick in hand, and thus they file out, Tüwasmi stepping in front of Anawita when they reach Horn kiva and Winüta bringing up the rear.

They go out to the dance court where three large bonfires have been made some time before by four of the Horns, these four wearing their helmets reversed, that is the horns pointed in front, and have rabbit-skin rugs wrapped around their bodies, but girded close to the waist with ends tucked in girdle, leaving their legs free. Each has as usual a tortoise rattle on each leg. They mimic very excellently the actions of mountain sheep, never still a moment, nor ever walking in ordinary gait, constantly bucking and jumping, first on the watch at the west side, then bucking across the court to look out in a huddle westward. There are large piles of wood between the fires, and they buck and jump over the fires when they go down to trim and mend them. The Wüwüchimtü wrapped in their blankets but displaying each the green sun disk on his head, and the Singers without insignia, all file in and sit down against the house side of the court, facing toward the fires. Other people, women and children, also occupy that side, and the terraces are covered with folks.

About 5:00 A.M. the Agaves file in, pass around the court toward the house side and around dance rock and back toward their kiva. Halting close to the edge of the cliff and facing the fires, all link arms with each other, the man next Anawita taking hold of his mantle, Tüwasmi and Winüta not touching any of the Agaves. Masi bears a tablet on his back and carries a crenellate bowl and a feather aspergill, aspersing frequently during certain phrases of song. Wikyatïwa also bears a tablet on his back and dances in front as he did in kiva; capital fugleman, he lifts his feet high and sings a solemn impressive song. At certain phrases the lame one (Hayi of the Town chieftaincy), who carries a bag of meal, sprinkles a broad streak in front of the line, ten inches or a foot wide, and then sprinkles back on the same line. He does this four times and at the concluding stanza he takes his feathered rod and brushes along the line he has made to right and left as if to obliterate it. The song finished, the Agaves return to their kiva and the other societies to theirs, and the people to their homes. It is piercing cold and still quite dark. It must still lack an hour of sunrise, the first streak of dawn just faintly beginning to show.

An hour after sunrise Wüwüchimtü dance through the village in costume, as do also the Singers, but Agaves and Horns make no more public appearances. The Agaves go to their homes about 9:00 A.M. and eat there. Broad trails of meal, scattered yesterday and this morning, lead to the main shrines.

Thus Hopi youths are initiated into tribal status and, we may add, into the status of warrior. Wüwüchim might well be considered a war ceremony; it incorporates so many ceremonial war traits: patrol, hunt, burlesque, phallicism, and peculiar secretiveness. And consistently with this interpretation, Horn society, which is conspicuously a war society, is in charge of altar and fetishes.

WAR CEREMONIES

Scalps are kept in several towns, but the organization of scalp-takers has lapsed almost everywhere, and ceremony has lapsed with organization. Possibly, except for feeding the scalps as any fetishes are fed, there is little ritual in connection with them. The Zuni scalp ceremony and in part the Acoman and Isletan are dramatizations or near-dramatizations of the arrival of the victorious war party and of subsequent practices. The

Isletan ceremony is so involved with race ceremonial, as reported, that I have not attempted any separation.

The Zuni ceremony is concerned with cleansing or exorcising the scalper from danger from the slain enemy and, "to save his life," initiating him into the War society. Dramatization of War god myth, in fact of two distinguishable myths, is suggested.[32] In the Isletan ceremony, except for a rite of hitting the scalptakers with the scalps which suggests initiation, no initiation is recorded, nor any purification. After the abusive rite of kicking the scalp, the Zuni initiate or adopt the scalp into the tribe, through washing and feeding it. It is to become a potent rainmaker.

Owinahaiye was the annual autumn ceremony of the Zuni War society.[33] As in the Scalp dance, there is dancing by changing sets of girls planned by the Scalp chiefs, and the Warriors go dancing into the plaza. Affiliation is with the Rain chieftaincies and kiva organization, not with the curing societies, Ant society excepted, or with the clown groups, a final exorcism by a Ne'wekwe excepted. But burlesque is presented. Burlesque is characteristic of warrior ceremonial. Throw-away and sexual license are features, as in war dances of Papago and other tribes. Conceptually it is rather surprising to find the kachina appearing; there may be a historical explanation. At Acoma, where the scalps have been buried and the Koshare are extinct, the dance is given as an installation dance for the annual War captains in an abbreviated form; "we don't know how to dance it any more."

The winter ceremony of the Wood society of Zuni is held jointly with the War society and with the stick-swallowing order of the Big Firebrand society which has war traits, so I am including this ceremony as a quasi-war ceremony. The Hopi Stickswallowers were an order at Oraibi of the Momchit war society. They assembled in the same kiva, but if any Momchit stepped down from the raised part of the floor he had to join the stickswallowing order, "initiation by trespass." The two groups held a joint or synchronous two-day ceremony in the autumn (Oraibi) or following upon the winter solstice ceremony (Walpi).

The Oraibi stick-swallowing ceremony is like that of the Zuni stick-swallowers in several particulars—a rough cedar stick is swallowed the first day; and subsequently an ornate swordlike stick; the sticks are swallowed facing the directions; fingers are imbricated; the step is high or prancing; and the body is painted yellow.[34]

The Hopi Snake-Antelope ceremony is today associated with weather control or with curing, and prayer-sticks are offered for "many children,"[35] but the ceremony has many out-and-out war or warrior features; Snakes and Antelopes were sometime warriors, the tradition being that the old Antelope men made war medicine at home for the Snake warriors on the war trail. Today, in theory, the Antelopes sing to make the snakes peaceable. Ants are said to obscure the tracks of Zuni warriors; in a vague way the relation of the Ant society to Zuni warriors may be compared with that of the Antelope society to the Snake warriors.

Scalp Ceremony at Zuni, 1921 *

About sunrise three men come into town to call out that a Navaho has been killed. They call it into an anthill. "Come up, hurry up, the Navaho is coming!" one of them calls in.† The man in town who hears the call first is to be the first to have his name called out when they throw the arrows the last day. (A faint echo indeed of counting coup!)

The Scalp chief comes out to meet them. They cleanse with cedar, waving cedar in the left hand around their heads, spitting on it and casting it down. "You left your family," says the Scalp

---

* From Parsons 36. Based on observation of the final night and day performances and on information from participants. Consistently with origin myths of the Scalp ceremony (pp. 227, n. *, 233) the scalp was said to be that of a Navaho girl found dead under brush. Nick, the cynic, said the hair came from a barber shop in Gallup.

† To the Raw people (Bunzel 6:133). Acoma warriors left the scalps out four nights on an anthill, asking the Ants to whip, kill, and eat the scalps (Stirling). (Tortoise shells are cleaned on First Mesa in this way.) According to another account the scalp is merely drawn across the anthill, in the cardinal directions, and the scalp-taker and the "brother" at whom he has cast the scalp are thrown upon the anthill to be stung and made strong and enduring (White 2:96).

chief, "and went to the Navaho country. What happened there?" This in secular terms; actually in ritualistic language the Scalp chief says:

> Now, neglecting your children,
> Neglecting your wives,
> Yonder into the country of the enemy
> You made your road go forth.
> Perhaps one of the enemy,
> Even one who thought himself virile,
> Under a shower of arrows,
> A shower of war clubs,
> With bloody head,
> One of the enemy,
> Reached the end of his life.
> Our fathers,
> Beast bow priests,
> Took from the enemy,
> His water-filled covering.
> Now you will tell us of that,
> And knowing that we shall live.
> Is it not so?[36]

The announcers report also formally on the war trip, camping places and all. In this talk they should name an aunt (senior paternal kinswoman) for each man, for the scalper and his "older brother," to kick the scalp, and, for each, two kinsmen of the "aunt" to wash the scalp. This time they name only one aunt, the other aunt does not want to do it. Perhaps she is afraid and thinks her husband would not like it because for four nights she (as scalp-kicker) could not sleep with him. Nor for this period may the scalp-kicker eat meat or salt or any hot food.

The scalper does not come into town with the others; he stays out about a mile, and his family takes the midday meal out to him. Late in the afternoon others go out to where he is, the woman scalp-kicker, the two men scalp-washers, men on horseback, and boys. At this time parents tell their boys that if they go out to this place they must stay through—they tell them four times—otherwise the scalp will come after them. For the youths to smoke, Pekwin has six cane cigarettes, one colored for each direction. Four times the youth smokes,* the remains of the cigarette being given to the Scalp chief.

Pekwin has made two sand hills covered with corn meal, and running to them a corn-meal road with four lines across to step on. The scalper and his "elder brother" step along the line, the "aunt" holding them behind. They sing as they go, and they are followed by the men and boys.

Now the "aunt" stands out in a good place, "elder brother" sets the scalp on her left toe, and four times she throws it forward with her toe, everybody singing the while.† (In her moccasin, at the little toe, has been placed a chaparral cock feather.) Then she picks up the scalp with her left hand and goes running around the town, by the south road, around the cemetery, around Big plaza, four circuits. Everybody acts as if they were at war, they rush about, knock down the dogs, just as if fighting.

The Scalp chief has put a pole up in Big plaza; and now he takes the scalp from the "aunt" and puts it up on the pole. Pekwin addresses the people, referring to the scalp as a water being, a seed being:

> Desiring the enemy's waters
> Desiring his seeds
> Desiring his wealth
> Eagerly you shall await his day.

And Pekwin bids the people to procreate during these coming nights.

> To some little corner
> Where the dust lies thick
> (You will steal away)

---

* This is a sort of initiation into smoker or warrior status. The Pueblo boy was told he might not smoke until he killed his first coyote (Havasupai also [Spier 2:324]), which meant at Zuni and Isleta his first Navaho. Even boys in the Snake war society (Oraibi) smoked very little (Voth 3:294). Forgotten rules! Old Tsatiselu of Zuni would give a cigarette to little Jim, his grandson, as he sat interpreting for us.

† Songs taught by the War gods, as are the songs of the scalp-washers (see below) (Bunzel 6:134).

In order to procreate sturdy men
And sturdy women,
Tirelessly you will live.*

The War chief follows with similar oratory. Then Scalp chief who has already fed the scalp offers another handful of bread.[37]

The "aunt" takes the scalper and his "older brother" to her house, where on the roof or *outside* (inside it would be too dangerous) she and her relatives wash the two men, afterward throwing the bowl into the air to break it so that none can use it. The lookers-on shout. The two men go to their homes, eat, collect their bedding, and go to the house of the War chiefs. Here the two men and the "aunt" stay four nights. They sleep little, do not speak, sit away from the fire, eat no meat or grease or hot food, drink emetics, and go out each morning to pray for deliverance from the scalp.†

On the fifth day, in the afternoon, the two scalp-washers go to Big plaza and get the scalp from the Scalp chief. They go singing along the south road. The scalp-washers are supposed to fast from meat and salt, but, if they do not wish to fast, as they carry the scalp they may pretend to be dangerous or prey animals, a lion or wolf, and bite at the scalp.‡ With them the scalp-washers carry bread, an arrow, two bowls, soapweed, and a hairbrush broom, all in a Hopi blanket, the white with blue and red border. They go to the river to wash the scalp. They must be careful not to have the water they use flow back into the river from which

* Bunzel 4:679. Children thus conceived are thought of as protégés of the War gods, just as children conceived promiscuously Christmas night at Laguna are the "Saint's children," at least a Zuni visitor to Laguna so reported.

† Bunzel 4:675; Cushing 6:619. Cushing was allowed not even a cigarette and was thoroughly wretched.

‡ The Navaho youth was enjoined to take care of his teeth by abstaining from salt and from warm and sweet foods, until he had chewed his first scalp. Scalp-chewing made the teeth last for life (Haile, 38, 51–52). We recall that the scalps at Isleta cure toothache. Inferably they cause it. The scalp is chewed too at Isleta. See p. 351, n. §.

Ritual cannibalism elsewhere has been interpreted as medicine against disaster from the victim.

the people use water.* After making suds with soapweed and washing the scalp, they throw up the bowls to break them. They brush the hair of the scalp. The bread they wave around their heads and throw down. Anyone who comes there to look on may pick it up. (Inferably it is medicine, see p. 351).

They take the scalp to the house of the War chiefs. There they dance, the two scalp-washers, the War chiefs, the "aunt," and any men who want to join. This time there were also two women who wanted to join. They stand in two rows to dance, and then they make a dance circuit of the town.

The Scalp chief takes the scalp and puts it up on the pole for all to dance around it. The two scalp-washers and the women who have danced are taken home by their "aunt" to be washed. From this day of washing the scalp they count again, in eight days they will have the big dance.

On the fifth day (scalp-washing day) they begin to work on the prayer-sticks of appointment to office. War chief elder brother and War chief younger brother go, respectively, to the houses of the Deer clansman and the Bear clansman who make Ahaiyuta, the wooden War god images, to give these image-makers the prayer-sticks for getting the wood. In giving the sticks they pray for rain. The next day the image-makers go to the house of the Navaho fetish to get some black "from the beginning" paint to put on one of their prayer-sticks. Now the image-makers put down their prayer-sticks in the fields; it is their pay to the War gods in order to get easily the wood for their images. This wood must be from a lightning-struck tree, and it may be hard to find. Lightning has killed the tree, just as there is killing in war. That is why they take the wood of a riven tree. The next day the image-makers start out to look for this wood. They pray to find it. After finding it, they leave it in a field outside of town for four days. "They don't like to bring it into town at once, something might happen." After they do bring the wood in, they pray in working on it; they say to it, "You will be

---

* This bit of sympathetic magic is paralleled by the Zuni practice of sprinkling on the floor, i.e., not throwing out indifferently the water any precious thing has been washed in, such as a turquoise bracelet (Benedict 3:I, 156, 157).

Ahaiyuta. You must help me to do just as we have always done." ("Ahaiyuta are wise men.") The night they bring in the wood they make the head of the image, the day following they work on the face and body, in one day they finish. They paint them and then, after all the household has sprinkled meal on them, they take them to the house of the Navaho bundle, *pa'e·tone*, for "from the beginning" paint which has to be put on them. From the Navaho bundle house they take them to the house of the chief of the Kachina society.

This was the tenth day. On the eleventh day, in the morning, they work on the prayer-sticks for Ahaiyuta in the houses of the image-makers. The women work on the cotton fringes representing clothes. To the house of the image-maker of the Deer clan go the Deer people and their "children," the Bear people and their "children." They dress the images. The wives of the men bring in the supper bowls. The images are stood to face the east. Whoever brings food in takes a bit from the bowl and places it before the images. All sprinkle meal on the images. They eat; they go home a while to rest. All this is just as at the winter solstice when the War god images are made and dressed, except that then lightning-struck wood is not used.

To the house of the Kachina society chief come Pekwin, the War chiefs, the scalper, and his "elder brother." Thence the War chiefs go to fetch the Navaho fetish and Big Shell from the houses where they are kept. Now all go to the house of the War chiefs, the image-makers carrying their images. There they go around the altar four times. The meal terrace altar has been made by Pekwin. Pekwin puts down the things on the altar, the sacred things of the Rain chiefs he first puts down, then Navaho bundle which belongs to younger brother Ahaiyuta, then Big Shell which belongs to Elder Brother, then the images. All sit down. The War chiefs sing. Around the scalper they put the bandoleer which has been made in the house of the War chiefs, "it *has* to be made there," on the sixth and seventh days. In the bandoleer there is some Navaho hair, also scrapings from inside the moccasin of the Navaho as well as some of the medulla oblongata of the Navaho. The scalper and his "elder brother" dance. At sunrise the singing finishes; all go home. The new War chief has been initiated or installed.*

This is the last night of the dancing around the pole. In the dance circle there are women as well as men; all stand very close, shuffling sidewise, in anti-sunwise circuit, the ring widening or narrowing according to the number participating. Men sing the unbroken refrain, and now and again a man smokes. Much joking and a spirit of hilarity, no solemnity whatsoever; the women quiet as ever, although it is the nearest approach to a petting party Zuni can make. About midnight small groups of youths, from three or four to seven or eight, begin to go about from house to house, singing to a drum, to ask for food, bits of which they will give to the scalp. This is the only night all houses may be visited; other nights they may solicit only at the houses of War chiefs and image-makers.

At sunrise, this twelfth and last day, Pekwin is in Big plaza to prepare the ground for the altar to be laid out on the north side. First with his crowbar, Mexican style, he digs a hole, to the northwest where War god younger brother is to stand, then a hole to the northeast for War god elder brother. Out in front quite a large hole is dug, for the three war fetishes combined— Navaho bundle, Big Shell, and the War chief's feather bundle. He sprinkles white corn meal thickly to form the cloud terrace or step pattern from which leads a line of meal to the foremost excavation. Off in the northeast corner of the plaza stands a short pole, about four feet and a half high, the scalp on top. The dancing this day is *for the Scalp*. As the scalp-washer prayed:

> When in the corn priests' water-filled court,
> He [scalp] has been set up
> All the corn priests' children
> With the song sequences of the fathers
> Will be dancing for him.
> And whenever all his days are past,
> Then a good day

* I was allowed to look in through the window of the house of the Deer clan image-maker and saw the images. The altar ceremony in the War chief's house occurs after 1 A.M. and is completely exclusive; my Zuni acquaintances did not even mention it.

A beautiful day,
A day filled with great shouting,
With great laughter,
A good day
With us, your children,
You will pass.
Thus the corn priests' children
Winning your power,
Winning your strong spirit,
Will come to evening.[38]

A short time before midday people begin to gather; at dawn chairs were set out on the housetops to pre-empt good places. About midday the major part of the Zuni hierarchy begin to advance into the plaza by dance step. They come in three files, Pekwin leading the middle file, and the chief of the Coyote society well in the rear. He may be recognized by his hair feather, the eagle-wing feather tied curving up concavely which is always worn by Coyote society members. Their chief was invited into the ceremonial by Pekwin, with the cigarette of invitation. Whenever a prey animal is to be mentioned in song it will be the part of the Coyote society chief to growl, acting like wolf or mountain lion.

Behind Pekwin file the other high chiefs, first the three Town chiefs, then the Rain chief of the West, the Rain chief of the South, the Rain chief of the East; follow the chiefs of the Big Shell, the chief of the Navaho bundle, a boy of the Corn clan who is water-carrier for Younger Brother, the scalper carrying the image of Younger Brother, a man of the Dogwood clan who is water-carrier for Elder Brother, and Hompikya, a War chief, carrying the image of Elder Brother.

In the file to the right of Pekwin are: at the head, Ts'awele, older brother War chief, Sisiwah, the Deer clansman image-maker, and seven Ant society* members. In the file to the left are: at the head, Wayeku, younger brother War chief, Aku, the Bear clansman image-maker, and four Ant society members.

* Wherever an enemy falls, "adding to the flesh of our mother earth" is formed an anthill (cf. p. 622). Therefore prayer-sticks are planted in anthills, and the Ant society figures in the Scalp ceremony (Bunzel 4:687).

The Ant society members and the War chiefs carry bow and arrows or guns. They and the Rain chiefs are wearing white cotton shirt and trousers. The Ant society members wear a bunch of hawk feathers in their cap or hat. The chiefs wear prayer-feathers in their hair, as do also the water-carriers. The water-carriers are kilted, with a white buckskin over their shoulders. The scalper and his "elder brother" are wearing the War chief hood of buckskin, and their faces are painted, below the mouth black, the black of "from the beginning" paint, and above, yellow, from pollen. (Deceased War chiefs are painted in this way.) The chiefs carry wrapped up the fetishes or prayer-sticks that are to be laid out on the altar.

After repeating several times an advancing dance step and with a turn about-face a withdrawing step, singing to their dancing, the three files merge into a single file and make an anti-sunwise circuit four times around the altar, each person sprinkling meal four times in his circuit from each of the four directions. Then the line stands along the north wall, and Pekwin takes from each man whatever object he may be carrying to furnish the altar. The first object to be laid down is the bundle of the Town chiefs, then the Big Shell, the Navaho bundle, and the feather bundle of the War chiefs are made into one large bundle and placed in the excavation at the end of the meal line where they appear merely like a big bunch of eagle-wing feathers. Eight corn-ear fetishes are set in line at the back of the altar. In front of them at the west side the image of Younger Brother is set in the excavation made for him, and then, at the east side, the image of Elder Brother. A line of prayer-sticks is set out in front of each image. Two very long stone knives have been laid down, also the two gourds of water.*

This dressing of the altar has been done very deliberately and reverently by Pekwin, the only hitch being in making the prayer-sticks stand up, the ground is hard. Ts'awele takes a hand, sending for some earth, and planting the sticks himself. Clay-hold-

* The water will be poured into the bowl at the shrine Hepatina after the altar is dismantled.

ers, such as are used by Hopi, or a sand ridge would have been a convenience.

Pekwin proceeds to seat the chiefs where they have been standing behind the altar. With his hands on their shoulders he gently presses them down into their wall seat. Chairs are brought out for the War chiefs, the image-makers, and the Ant society members; two men carrying spears take position out in front of the altar and facing in. At significant times in the cere-monial, at the time of exorcism, for example, this position of guard is taken by the War chiefs, Ts'awele and Wayeku, who at other times are relieved by another War chief or by one or an-other of the Ant society men. At times the War chiefs swing a whizzer.

The entrance dance and the dressing of the altar took about three-quarters of an hour. Now the dancing groups appear, first the two Shake girls, the Scalp chief, and a choir of three including the drummer. In the northwest corner of the court two planks have been set into the ground and covered over for the girls to dance on. Meal and shell were sprinkled in the excavation for the planks, "so people will come, it draws their hearts." The planks are the door for the people inside the earth, dead Apache, Navaho, Sioux, Hopi, Acomans, and Mexicans (not for people of Laguna or Americans).* "It makes their hearts tremble and shake." The dance or the dancer is called Hashiya, Shake. Prob-ably the girls represent the ghost girl who pursued the War Brothers (see p. 650, n.†).

The two girls first face the choir, but soon turn and face the court. The girls' knees are flexed and they start dancing by a gentle movement up and down. Their left arms are extended sideways, their right arms bent and forearms raised. After a few moments this position of the arms is reversed. Both feet are off the ground at the same time; the step is a jump.

The girls wear an embroidered Hopi blanket draped so as to leave the arms bare. A bunch of bells is fastened to one side of the woven belt. A fan of eagle-wing feathers fastened to a black

* Compare stomping on planks in dance court by Hopi Snakes and Antelopes. See pp. 382–83 and note use of *sipapu* in war cult as in Kachina cult.

wig tops the head. At the base of the fan is a bunch of parrot feathers from which stream red and yellow ribbons. The girls' own hair is flowing and their bang falls over the face to the tip of the nose. Legs and feet bare; nothing in hands.

This dance is referred to as ground cleansing. It continues throughout the day, danced by a series of girls, couple succeeding couple at brief intervals. But of the Shake girls proper there are but two, the two who have been appointed by the Rain chiefs, and who have black stripes on lower cheeks and chin, put on by Pekwin. At the conclusion of the day's ceremonial, the wives of the Rain chiefs (custodians of from-the-beginning paint) wash off this paint, keeping the water to sprinkle on their own corn store. For four successive ceremonials the two girls will hold their positions.

There should have been another set of girls, to dance in the southeast corner of the court, with the Scalp chief woman to stand alongside. But the office of Scalp chief woman is vacant. Besides, girls had proved backward about dancing. The Scalp chief had difficulty in getting enough girls for his own dance set. This was his fault, a critic alleged. The man had been chosen just for this dance by the War chiefs. He was ignorant of much, for example, instead of putting down the *sipapu* planks at early dawn with none about to see, he put them down at midday.

Besides these girls, there are other dancers. About thirty men with three or four women compose each of two alternating dance sets. One set dances in singing from the northeast entrance, dances forward and backward several times, and as it withdraws the other set dances in from the southwest entrance to perform the same maneuvers. The set is bunched together in a more or less irregular oval formation, the women dancing mostly in the middle, whence presumably the name of the dance set, Otulah-shonakwe, dance within. Much shouting and flourishing of bows or guns. The women carry each in her right hand an arrow painted black and red, the point up. Women wear moccasins and their ordinary black blanket dress, with a man's dance kilt draped as bodice. To the top of the head is fastened a bunch of parrot feathers with pendant ribbons. The bang falls over the face. Hands and forearms are painted yellow, with hanks of yarn tied around the wrist. Men are togged out in bits of finery, with no attempt at uniformity, wearing *bandas* or beribboned caps or befeathered hats, silver Navaho belts or woven dance belts; some in moccasins, some in shoes, two wore high russet leather riding boots.

The women are "gathered up" by two men in each set, the men serving for this function for four ceremonials. The men in each set belong to the same kiva.

As soon as a set arrives, all those seated around the altar arise to remain standing to the conclusion of the dance. In conclusion each of the dancers approaches the altar and sprinkles meal.

Between those around the altar and the choir of the dancing girls there was also some degree of recognition. The choir in its song would mention persons by name, and anyone mentioned sitting about the altar would then with his left hand point an arrow toward the sky, "showing it to the Sun," wave it around his head, and throw it on the ground in front of the foremost fetish bundle. A member of the choir would leave his seat and pick up the arrow. The man first to hear the returning war party is, we recall, the first to be mentioned. That it is proper to mention the name of the impersonator of Sayatasha, the foremost figure in the Shalako ceremonial, I learned from being told that on this occasion he was forgotten. The names of the War god image-makers are mentioned. I happened to have been earlier in the morning in the house of one of them when a kinsman who had "helped on the feathers" came in to ask if his name would be called out. "No, only mine," said his senior kinsman, the image-maker, "only the chief of us, and I am the chief." The young man was almost as plainly dissatisfied over this as the older man was proud of his distinction.*

At one time Pekwin leaves his seat to blow smoke on the altar, placing the rest of the cane cigarette back of the image of Elder Brother. At another time, at a certain part of the song, the water-carriers in turn carry prayer-sticks to the choir. Now the

* Such unusual vanity surprised me as it once surprised observers of the Hopi Snakes (Dorsey and Voth 2:236). Warrior vanity!

choir sing or call out for the first time the new name of the scalp-taker, the initiate. The dancers hear and acclaim by shooting off their guns.

On the fourth appearance of the dancers the scalper appears with one set, his "elder brother" with the other, scalper and "elder brother" carrying each on his head a basket of red wafer-bread which he tosses into the air. The Scalp chief takes the empty baskets and refills them with the bread he picks up from the ground, setting the baskets under the scalp pole. This wafer-bread has been made by the "aunts" of the two men. In the bread-making they have used the left hand, just as in weaving the baskets of willow which scalper or "elder brother" has gathered they have used this hand.

It is dinner time for all. Two lines of women come in, carrying on their heads bowls or bundles of food. One line is led by the scalper, the other by his "elder brother." They stand in single file, each file facing a member of the girls' choir who says a longish prayer and then clasps in prayer the hand of each woman, her bowl or bundle having been set down on the ground. The women face about, and each is sprinkled on her shoulder with corn meal by the Scalp chief. Meanwhile the women of the chiefs' households come in and each places food in front of her respective husband or father. Before leaving, each woman sprinkles meal toward the altar.

It is four in the afternoon before the dancing resumes. Dancing with the large groups are now many women, they are the paternal aunts of the men dancers. A young man who is child of the Coyote clan stands with his hands clasping the scalp pole which he gently rocks. In his hair he wears a downy eagle feather, over his shoulders, a large bucksin of which a tail piece is held by a girl of the Coyote clan. This girl or woman is known as "Scalp-Fall-Down." Like the Shake girls and others, she holds her position for four successive ceremonies.

On the second and last appearance of the dancers in the afternoon the two groups come into the court at the same time and mingle together. The dancers throw arrows into the air to be picked up by the onlookers and kept by them. The Coyote chief emits his wild-animal growls. The shouting and shrieking grow more and more boisterous. Again the new name of the scalp-taker is mentioned by the girls' choir, and the clamor reaches a climax. All sprinkle the altar, and withdraw.

During the final dance of the girls, onlookers pick up from the ground bits of cedar bark, then at a point in the song all stand and with the left hand wave the bark around the head, once, twice or more, spitting on the bark in waving it and at the close before throwing it to the ground. At the same time Ts'awele is rocking the foremost group of fetishes, and the image-makers, the War god images, laying them down together with the prayer-sticks at the close. And the man at the scalp pole rocks it, also throwing it down at the close. Pekwin proceeds to dismantle the altar, each object being wrapped up and returned to its guardian.

Now the Arrow button* ceremony is in order. The pottery drum is carried out into the center of the court and placed on a chair. Standing with his arms encircling the drum, the drummer says a longish prayer and sprinkles meal on the drum. He asks it to sound as loudly as the water star when it falls into the river. Five men take seats around the drum. They are Ts'awele, two sons of his older sister, all Coyote clansmen, a very old man on crutches, Sepo, Turkey clansman and child of Coyote, he is the son of Ts'awele's mother's brother, and a Badger clansman who is also child of Coyote.† Back of the drummer is placed the pole

* Referring to an arrow which buttons in, cannot be taken out, inferably an arrowpoint with down-raking barbs, characteristic of early Pueblo (Roberts 1:159).

† For Coyote clan census, Kroeber 2:126–29. Ts'awele, the War chief, is close to Jesús, the adoptive Yaqui. (Note "Yakki" in clan census. Jesús Iriarte [Bourke 2:117] and a girl, both aged about fifteen, were captured by Apache and sold to Zuni. Jesús and the girl had a son, Henry Gasper, who is this year [1937] the Governor, a full-blood Yaqui governor of Zuni!) About forty miles south of Zuni at the "Mexican" town of Atarque there lived another Yaqui (reports Mrs. Kluckhohn) who may have been captured along with Jesús and the girl. Possibly Jesús and Henry Gasper and Jesús' son Leopold by a Zuni wife were on visiting terms at Atarque.

The prayer to the drum in this ceremony is paralleled in the Coyote dance of the Yaqui. The Zuni explanation of the relation between the Coyote clan and the ceremony is not convincing (Stevenson 2:604–5); but there is not enough evidence for more than a tentative suggestion of historic connection between Yaqui and Zuni performances.

with the child of Coyote holding it, and the Coyote girl holding him by the end of his buckskin mantle.

Formerly the singers were all War chiefs, only the drummer was a Coyote man (after the people came up, at Hanthlipinkya, the War gods gave the drum and the loop drumstick to the Coyote people),* but with the diminution of the War chiefs, the Coyote men took their places as choir. These Shomatowe War society songs refer to beings in the fourth lower world—Whirlwind, Wool-Wrapped-Up, and others (see p. 226). (Are they being pierced down with arrows as in the equivalent Navaho ritual the alien dead are being clubbed down? See p. 1047.)†

Now the Rain chiefs advance and form a circle around pole and choir. This circle is joined by their "aunts"‡ of whom each, like the Coyote girl, holds her relative by a piece of his garment, "to save him from the scalp." In anti-sunwise circuit the circle side-steps slowly around. In conclusion a shout is raised by the on-lookers, all wave cedar and spit again, and again the scalp pole is thrown down.

The Scalp chief unfastens the scalp from the pole and places it on top of the two baskets of wafer-bread. Holding all in extended arms, he begins to walk out slowly, very slowly, from the court, by the southwest passage. He will secrete himself on the northwest edge of town until late at night when he will place the scalp in the jar in the scalp house, an irregular conical mound of earth and stone slabs. Concluding a long prayer, the Scalp chief asks the scalps to add to themselves, much as dead deer or rabbits are asked to send their children to the hunters,

> So that your people you may waft hither only,
> So that you may speed them hither,
> On this do not fail to fix your thoughts.[39]

---

* That is, to a maternal family within the Coyote clan. At Oraibi the Coyote clan or lineage was in charge of scalp-takers and sang "magic songs" at the initiation (Titiev 3). In Zuni and Navaho mythology war songs are from Coyote. See p. 226.

† Possibly they were summoned on the eve of war (Stevenson 2:36, 39) and are now being sent down again.

‡ Now called elder sisters (Stevenson).

Entering town, the Scalp chief will dodge in and out of four houses "to fool the scalp." At each house he leaves a grain of black corn, "to make his road dark." He has also been carrying some black grains under his tongue, to preclude ghost pursuit. At his own house the ladder has been turned upside down. As soon as he mounts it, it is righted so that the ghost cannot follow him up. He prays and waves his black corn around his head in exorcism. His "aunts" wash his head and bathe him.[40]

The heads of all the participants in the ceremony have to be washed. When the final dance circle was broken up,* several women came into the court to take the men in the circle to their houses; these were their "aunts," and at home they were to wash the heads of the participants. That evening I happened to be in a house where a youth had his head washed. For a reason not explained the "aunt," accompanied by a girl, a junior "aunt," came to the youth's house. A bowl of water was set out for them. Bending over it stood the boy, while first the older woman and then the younger dipped one handful of water first to the boy's head, and then over his hands: a highly formalized and curtailed ablution. Neither before nor after the rite was there any conversation between the visitors and members of the household.

The day following, images and prayer-sticks have to be deposited. The image of Elder Brother is taken to one mesa, that of Younger Brother, to another. Prayer-sticks are put down by the man who calls into the anthill, by the Shake girls proper, and by the Scalp chief, black sticks to the "old ones" by ant-summoner and girls, black and purple sticks, like those of the War chiefs, by the Scalp chief.

The new War chief and his "elder brother" have each to have intercourse with a woman other than his wife before he may have conjugal intercourse again.† "Even if he is an old man he *has* to get a woman outside." The new War chief has still to receive his warrior hair badge, his "great feather" (p. 398), his equivalent for the curing society's corn fetish.[41] The Ant society is

---

* Now the initiation proper will take place (Bunzel 6:134–35), presumably in the house of the War chief, but there is no account of it.

† On the Northwest Coast this rule applied to the returned hunter (Boas).

to be maker of the "great feather," and it is to be conferred at
the ceremony of Owinahaiye which the new War chief will announce, some time before the November ceremonial of Shalako.
Obviously, the Owinahaiye is held to be a return ceremonial; just
as at Acoma its counterpart[42] is the ceremony given by the War
captains after their installation.

Scalp Ceremonial and Relay Racing at Isleta[43]

About the middle of March or early in April on three Sundays
there are races, "Town chief races," for the Sun—"the Town
chief is going to clothe* the Sun and help him run; that is why
they run east and west." The War chief talks over the first race
date with his helpers and notifies the Town chief who has summoned Kumpa war chief and Shichu, a Corn group chief. All
perform ceremonial the night before the race in the Black Eyes
kiva, the Round house. They make "pay" or offerings to bury
at midnight in the middle of the race track. Medicine water is
also made, and anyone may go to the Town chief's ceremonial
house the next morning and get a drink.

In the morning from eight to ten there is dancing in the plaza
—racing dance, a dance open to all. It is after this that people
go for their drink of medicine water. Also, at this time, the
babies that are to belong to the Shichu Corn group may get
their name.

Meanwhile this morning Black cane War chief in the plaza has
called out for those who want to race to go to the Black Eyes
Round house, it is a "free race" for anybody. As the men come
in, the War chief sings and drums. Town chief and Shichu bring
in their medicine water and sprinkle it on the four posts of the
kiva, also on the pit shrine where the fetish animals are kept.
All stand and sing a song for the Sun during which whenever the
Sun is mentioned Town chief sprinkles meal in a line from east to
south. ("This is like calling the Sun.") After they finish singing,
one by one the men pass in front of Town chief who sprays them
with medicine water. As each withdraws, he takes off his clothes
to prepare for the race. Each passes in front of Kumpa and

* Give him prayer-feathers.

Shichu who paint, Kumpa a streak of red, Shichu, a streak of white, across each cheek. Then Shichu gives permission to all to paint themselves on their hands and body. All the elder men smoke in the directions and to the Sun, asking Sun to help them in the race. The Town chief is watching the sun hole in the roof and when the sun shines in he sprinkles the sun spot with pollen. Then, after the sun has moved a little, they divide up the runners, Kumpa on one side, and Black cane War chief on the other, choosing the fastest runners, regardless of moiety.* The runners stand in four rows, two to the west, two to the east, with Kumpa in the middle to pray and sing, the runners joining in the song. Kumpa holds his bow and arrow and is wearing his sacrosanct bandoleer.

Town chief, Kumpa, and Black cane War chief go out to the starting-point at the east end of the track. One race director, an appointee, leads the two eastern rows of runners to the east end, the other race director leads the western rows to the west end. Town chief and Black cane War chief sing while Kumpa takes out the first two runners, one from each row. At the close of the song, Kumpa with his bow and arrow pushes the two runners from behind to start them. At the west end of the track the runners who are to relay are placed in position by the race directors.

At the close of the race all return to kiva whence with a drum they make a circuit of the town, singing. All but Town chief, Kumpa, and Black cane War chief, who remain in kiva. The last runner of the losing side who has been overtaken and had his queue caught by the last runner of the winning side has also to remain in kiva to pick up all the husk refuse from rolled cigarettes which he will give to Kumpa to burn. When the runners return from going around the town, they stand on the kiva roof and sing. The kinswomen of the runner who caught the queue of the loser carry to the kiva baskets of meal and bread with

* But the sides represent Sun and Moon (Parsons 52:387), as in the Jicarilla Apache relay race which Jicarilla have borrowed from Taos. As Jicarilla associate the Sun with game animals and the Moon with crops or fruits (Opler), possibly Taos does likewise. If Sun (the white side) wins, the season will be better for the animals; if Moon (the red side) wins, it will be better for the fruits.

packages of sugar and coffee. From these Kumpa takes bits to sprinkle below the wall niche of the Scalps. Then Black cane War chief presents all the baskets to the man whose queue was caught, the loser let us call him.* The loser presents a basket to Town chief, another to Kumpa, another to Black cane War chief. The bread is distributed among all the runners. Whatever is left over the loser keeps, his relatives helping him carry it home. Black cane War chief addresses all and dismisses them. The chiefs remain to give thanks to one another.

Every three, four, or five years a race is held in connection with the Scalp ceremony which the Town chief decides upon performing, "making up his mind to wash the Scalps, to give them fresh air." This race is the fourth race in the spring series, but the Scalp ceremony begins before the first race is run off.

Toward evening the Scalp-takers leave town with some young men ("to show them," and the youths vary from time to time) and a burro packed with camp supplies and wood. With them they are taking the Scalps, "to give them fresh air." The party shoots off guns; people come out on the housetops to see them off or follow as far as the railway station. The war party goes on to the west to camp overnight, building a fire. In the morning Town chief, Kumpa, Black cane War chief and others go out to meet the campers, shouting *é——o! é——o!* All return singing, through the orchards to the north and into the plaza, which they go around five times, the Town chief, Kumpa, and Black cane War chief in the lead, sprinkling meal and pollen, making the road. In the plaza Town chief buries something known only to himself, Kumpa, and Black cane War chief. All shout *é——o! é——o!* Town chief addresses the people. The party proceeds to the Round houses to replace the Scalps, and to be dismissed by the Town chief.

During the next four weeks—the racing period—the Scalp-takers have to take care of the scalps, taking them out of their wall niches several times to comb and wash their hair. With the

---

* May it be that he is thought of as having been beheaded as are the losers in folk tales and is therefore "fed" as would be a scalp? Compare the Hopi kachina racer who overtaking a runner will cut off his hair.

water from the washings they make mud balls, "Navaho mud," medicine which may be dispensed by Town chief to anyone sick from worry or longing.

Before the fourth race Town chief summons all the chiefs including the Scalp-takers to talk about the ceremonial. There follows a four-day fast, for the chiefs, "outside fasting," i.e., the men live at home, taking a daily emetic, and living continent. During this period people will not go abroad at night, especially women, because the Navaho dead are about. The Saturday afternoon before the Sunday race, the war party, including the Scalp-takers and their young men arrayed with lance and bow and arrows, start forth with their pack horses and burros to stay out overnight. The following morning the chiefs meet at the Town chief's to go forth to meet the war party with the Scalps. After all return singing, they enter the churchyard to kneel and pray, giving thanks for their safe return. A dance follows in the plaza. Two dance lines of men with the Scalp-takers between, led by Kumpa; the women stand on the other side of the lines of men, protected by them against contact with the Scalp-takers. The women wear their *manta*. The hair of the men must hang loose like that of warriors, and they wear beaded buckskin clothes. The scalp is carried on a lance, bound with red, and surrounded by feathers.* The Scalp-takers wear buckskin and a bandoleer, and carry bow and arrows, club, gun, lance, and shield. Their faces are striped across with various colors. The dance is started on the east side of the plaza and continued in a circuit. The Scalp-takers "sing in Navaho"† which sometimes angers Navaho visitors. There is shooting into the air, and yelling. After the scalps are taken to the Round house‡ and restored to their wall niche, the Scalp-takers offer them crumbs of food and blow smoke on them. The rest of the day the Scalp-takers remain in the Round house.

* Formerly, if not today, the scalps were carried in a buckskin on the back of their woman custodian (Lummis 2:241). See p. 351, n. §.

† Which probably means merely using one or two Navaho words.

‡ In another connection it was said that there were scalps in *both* Round houses.

That night, at the request of the Town chief, the chiefs of the Corn groups assemble their members and tell them to prepare for the race next day. In the morning the men meet at the respective houses of the Corn group chiefs to be led to the Round house where are met together the other chiefs. Black cane War chief asks the moiety chiefs for their drums and Town chief tells Black cane War chief to give the drums to the boys. The Day (White Corn) People and Earth (Yellow Corn) People receive one drum; the other Peoples, the other drum. Both sets begin to drum and sing at the same time, different songs, while in the hubbub so the boys cannot hear what he says Kumpa addresses the seniors. In the midst of his "preaching" he gets out the Scalps, and moving them up and down, he sings. He moves the Scalps in the directions, calling thrice *é——u*! *é——u*! to the Navaho dead. Twining his fingers in the hair of the scalp he hits the Scalp-takers, each of them, three times with the scalp, calling out at each blow *é——u*! *eu*! Then he returns the scalp to the Scalp-takers. (The runners would not approach the Scalps lest they dream of them.)

Town chief begins to "preach," watching for the Sun. At noon, when the Sun shines in, everybody stands and dances. Everybody sprinkles meal on the prayer-feathers of Town chief who sends them up to the Sun. The medicine society chiefs exorcise with their feathers. They may remove strings from the runners' legs, sent in by witches. Two War captains are sitting on the roof alongside the ladder to keep out intruders. The chief of the Laguna Fathers holds up the crystal and the chief of the Town Fathers gazes into it, to see what day high winds are coming, or hail. By way of the crystal the race track is examined for tacks (!) or anything injurious to runners, and the War captains are directed to clear the track. This is the time the medicine men know who will be caught in the race; but they do not tell. They do tell if they see that some boy has applied to one of their helpers for power to win in the race and, having asked with a cigarette, been given the power. Through Kumpa or the War chief the boy will be sent for and then deprived of his power, "cleaned out," by the curing chiefs. For this power which consists of inducing cramps in the runner opposed to you should not be used against a townsman.*

The runners divide into the usual four rows, but by Corn groups, the Town chief having in charge the Day People and the Earth People, Kumpa having the remaining groups to form his two rows. Each runner has a stripe of white on the left cheek. They undress. As Town chief and Kumpa lead them out, each runner makes with his clasped hands the gathering or drawing-in motion, asking help from the Scalps, and on top of the kiva repeats the ritual motion, asking help from Sun. Town chief and Kumpa stand at the east end of the track, where on this occasion the former will push forth, i.e., start, the first two runners. At the east end also stands the Town Fathers' chief, with the Laguna Fathers' chief at the west end, both safeguarding the track. The Corn group chiefs are distributed along the track to keep the onlookers back. Under their blankets the curing chiefs have their exorcising things so that each runner as he comes in approaches one chief or the other to be "cleaned up," the chief moving his things circlewise, always under the blanket.

Each runner may be called upon to race several times. If a man does not want to race again, he may run directly from the race track to the Round house. In the Round house the Scalp-takers have remained, not going to the race track because there are too many persons around, especially women. Sometimes the racing is so even that nobody is caught. Then they have to run again the following day. After the runner is caught, the routine is as usual after a race except that after supper there is a fire dance or circle dance in which anybody may join, men, women, and children. They first dance in front of Town chief's house, then around the big fire in the plaza, dancing in anti-sunwise circuit. The scalp is borne aloft near the fire. Town chief and Kumpa are out. Town chief is spotted over head and body with cotton. His face is striped horizontally with various colors. He wears a mountain-lion hide. Kumpa wears a lion or wolf hide and carries a bow and quiver of arrows. Black cane War chief is

* There are several stories of its successful use against Navaho and White; also against their race horses.

there with his helpers who from time to time shoot off their guns. The defeated runners have to drum for the dance, and fetch wood for the fire. About midnight the wives or daughters of all the chiefs and of the Scalp-takers carry food to the chiefs in the plaza. The women of the Scalp-takers' households carry a big bowl of syrup from sprouted wheat for all the chiefs to drink. At this time the chiefs withdraw to the Round house, others staying to dance until sunrise, under the charge of Black cane War chief.

Scalp Dance at Taos[44]

Scalper and those first to run up and shoot at the slain enemy formed a temporary group called Talana, to celebrate the scalp dance. If a solitary man happened to take a scalp, the townsmen who ran out to meet him and were first to touch him became Talana. Scalpers hollered when they approached the town. Everyone came out "making fun, shooting at the scalp. The young women were bashful, but the old women kicked the scalp, spit or pissed on it, calling it bad names. They bared their buttocks to it. They said it was their second or third husband and lay down on it as if having intercourse. All this was to take power away from the enemy."

The scalper and all the warriors reported to the War chief who was also Scalp chief, Talat'unena. As chief of the Bear society he stayed in Water kiva while the war party was away and sang his songs to help them.

The War chief painted the inside of the scalp red, to a special song, and stretched the scalp on a stick. Other things from the slain enemy were given the War chief and stored in a secret bundle.

The scalper had to compose "a brave song" about the affair and sing it through town about ten o'clock at night and three o'clock in the morning, for four days.

The War chief appointed ten men to gather medicine plants, a couple going each day in one of the cardinal directions, beginning and ending in the east. They had to go early and return before the scalp or mocking dance began. It lasted four days during which the War chief remained in kiva praying to Earth Mother and Sun.

The scalp on its pole was brought out from Water kiva by the Talana. Save for breechcloth and moccasins they were naked, painted black all over, hair loose, a turkey feather on the crown of the head. They carried bow and arrow, quiver, club and shield. They danced until about nine o'clock. When they withdrew to kiva for their midday meal or for the night (they had to remain continent), they carried the scalp pole with them.* Before eating the native food they were restricted to, they crumbled a pinch from each dish on the ground behind, as offering to Earth Mother and to deceased warriors. Also they threw corn meal and pollen and red paint on the scalp.

After the warrior dance all the townspeople danced around the pole, men and women, but only the men were compelled to dance. A shirker would be thrown into the river by the P'iülenöma, the Red Painted people, and made to dance all day or all night unless he were ransomed with food.

During the early morning warrior dance the old women acted as obscenely toward the warriors as they had acted toward the scalp.†

Whenever the Talana returned to kiva with the scalp, the War chief sprinkled them all with plant medicine, "killing the noise" of the scalp. In conclusion a plant medicine drink was given by the War chief to all the dancers or to anyone who wanted it, and the War chief appointed two men to asperse from the highest point of each of the two house clusters "to make everything quiet." The War chief removed feathers, the yucca strand necklaces and bracelets, and their paint from the Talana, giving all to two men to place in rocks in the mountains "for those who did the same work," deceased predecessors.

* According to another account the scalp pole was left out all night to be danced around.

† Was this to deprive them of war power, no longer needed? Compare the behavior of Hopi women toward the Wüwüchim and Singers society, in their early morning dancing.

Owinahaiye of Zuni[45]

At any time after the harvest the War chief may summon a meeting of the paramount Rain chiefs and the Scalp chief and his assistant, in the house of the woman in the Town chieftaincy. Here the chiefs make cigarettes of invitation which are given to the Scalp chiefs to give eight days later to a man in each kiva* asking them to collect girls for the dance. Four days after getting the cigarettes, the men invite the girls. During these days the young men have been practicing or composing songs, and the War society have been making the warrior feather badges that are worn on the crown of the head.

On the afternoon of the twelfth day the warriors dance in their room, then with two girls, each holding an arrow, outside their house. Two files of warriors and women move on to dance in Big plaza, youths and little boys joining the dance processional. On the way the files halt and dance vis-à-vis. "After the first song the dancers advance westward sidewise."†

This night the Ant society assembles in its ceremonial chamber. A man and woman dance to the choir, the man impersonating Bear. In come the War society members, their bodies zigzagged in white lightnings. Naiuchi, their chief, holds a live coal in his mouth and swallows an arrow as he dances. The society dance in an ellipse. Navaho impersonations (without mask) enter and dance. The War society dances again. Another Navaho dance by two lines of black mustached dancers who sing and by a man and a girl impersonated by a man doing a very lively step between the lines. With these is a clown wearing a bushy wig and an ash-colored mask with prominent nose. He has on shabby American trousers and coat and carries a pistol. Later in kiva this Hopi-like "grotesque" carries on a comic dialogue with Nannahe, a Hopi married into Zuni. He burlesques the Navaho dancers and in a squeaky voice he speaks a few words in Hopi. "Why you are a Hopi!" someone calls out.

---

* Compare the initiation of ceremonial at Isleta.

† This is not clear, but it suggests a sidewise movement like that of the Hopi Wüwüchim dancers.

Two kivas are used; some of the Rain chiefs of the Council sit in one; some, in the other with the chiefs of the Kachina society. The two Navaho dance sets go from one to the other. The kiva choir of young men sing, and the leader selects girls from the audience to dance, set after set. Now three young men select others, and lead them over to the girls. If a girl accepts a youth, he sits down at her feet and is handed a bowl of water which he passes on to her and she bathes her face, hands, and legs. A second youth is led over to her, and with both she leaves the kiva (leaving Mrs. Stevenson in no doubt about what they are up to).

Thirteenth day. Prayer exchange in the house of the woman in the Town chieftaincy between the Town chief and the Scalp chief; a cigarette is first puffed and then carried by the Scalp chief to the medicine chief of the Ant society (White Bear, cf. p. 232), inferably a request for the Ant society to paint and array the Warriors. While the Ant men do the hair* and paint the face of the two War chiefs and two warriors, the other warriors sing. Bear grease is rubbed on the face and then black and red pigments. Chin, upper lip, tip of nose, eyebrows, and a circle on the crown are whitened with kaolin and hawk down stuck to the paste. "White Bear" puts an arrowpoint under the tongue of each of the four warriors (cf. p. 332) and then gives medicine from a shell to each, also a reed cigarette. Each warrior picks up a bow and arrow and feather wand. Two go to Uptsanawa kiva, which represents Elder Brother War god and two to Chupawa kiva, representing Younger Brother. Scalp chief is in Uptsanawa, his assistant in Chupawa.

The men of the two kivas have been arraying two girls in each kiva with the warriors' feather wand erect at the back of the head and a leather *banda*, on one side a wooden horn and on the other an artificial squash blossom. Bang over eyes to nose. A red foxskin hangs from the right wrist, a tassel of blue yarn from the left. A spread turkey tail is attached to the back of the waist. In right hand, an arrow. The two kiva parties go to Big plaza,

* See pp. 637–38 for the making of the hair plumes by the Ant society.

the two warriors, the two girls, the choir, and there the girls dance [? Hashiya, Shake]. Group follows group until *all the warriors* have taken part. In the last performance the four girls form in two rows, about ten feet apart. A burlesque Buffalo appears and dances between the rows. He is painted black and wears an enormous wig of black sheepskin. He shakes his rattles and clasps one of the girls "in an obscene manner," all this to the "enthusiasm of the spectators." Another Hopi innovation.

Night dance: In the room of the Ant society after the members paint themselves in white, they form in an elipse to dance, men and women alternating and the men singing. Thence they move on to Chupawa kiva to dance. The girls here are urged to dance between the lines formed by the Ant society. The Navaho dance is repeated. Three young men appear as grotesque old Zuni, hobbling with a staff, their clothing ragged, their hair unkempt. One carries a stone ax. The warriors dance. Girls and young men act the same way as on the night before.

This night kachina dance groups circulate from dwelling to dwelling (the dwellings presumably as in Shalako representing kivas).

Fourteenth day. Both indoor and outdoor dance by the War society as on preceding day. The warriors are "painted white to represent animals, snakes, and the heavens." They wear white embroidered or buckskin kilts and pendent foxskin, also war pouch and bandoleer. As each set of warriors appears clanswomen and women of their wives' clans deposit baskets of food or yards of calico and ribbon behind the warriors and *sprinkle the warriors with meal*. As soon as each warrior couple is through, they put on their ordinary apparel and then throw away to the crowd the contents of their baskets. (Naiuchi is described as returning to the plaza, after he has thrown away his baskets of food, dressed in black cloth trousers and vest and a long scarf, all of which he takes off and throws to the crowd.)

After the last dance the two kiva choirs and all the warriors form in two lines, each set in front of its kiva, and a Ne'wekwe doctor passes between the lines brushing the warriors with his eagle feathers. People on the housetops cleanse with cedar bark, spitting on it and waving it around their head. The warriors scatter to various houses to have their heads washed.

War Dance* at Acoma,[46] January 27–28, 1917

About seven in the morning the church bells ring, and the drummer begins his rounds. An hour later the officers—Governor and two lieutenants, and the three War captains—have gathered about the church portal, their canes in hand. With some of these officers men and women coming to church shake hands. My Pueblo host had instructed me "to shake hands with the Governor." The women line up one behind the other along the left or south wall, the men along the right or north wall, small groups standing near the portal. On entering, the sign of the cross has been made by everyone and a prayer said, by some on their knees. Men with hats remove them, *bandas* are not removed. One woman who is dressed entirely in American style reads a prayer-book and remains kneeling. She is the sister of one of the Lieutenant-Governors.

A long prayer is said by a man standing at the candle-lit altar. It is followed by an address made by one of the officers at the portal which is assented to every few seconds by one or another of the other officers. Then the church empties, and in a few minutes the officers disperse.†

About 10:00 a.m. the War captains make the rounds of town, calling out the order to come to the kivas to prepare for the dance. Two hours later appears a dance group on the terrace of Daut'kori·ts kiva. The first to descend the ladder is the drummer. After he has drummed a couple of minutes, the men of the choir descend and form into three or four lines, eight or ten to the line. Next to descend are four women. And after them an elderly man, who carries in his arms certain feather and worsted paraphernalia. On the ground he proceeds to fasten to the back of two of the women feather pieces for their flowing hair and to

* Fiesta del Rey, or Montezuma dance. Compare the extinct Scalp dance (White 2:98–101); also the Laguna Scalp dance (Boas 2:289–90).

† Compare Parsons 62:172–73 for a like Mexican picture of the "salute" by the officers after their installation.

distribute to all four the feathers they are to carry upright in their hands. Meanwhile the choir has been reinforced from the street by two lines of about twenty boys of all ages from eight to sixteen, and all have begun to sing and to move forward in dance step. The women led single file by the old man, the two head-befeathered women in the lead, catch up with the choir and with the woman's shorter dance step begin to pass along from one line of the choir to the other.* The group proceeds singing up the street, one or another dancer whooping or shouting now and then, until they come to the dance court or rather floor, *kakati*, the middle. Here the choir form into a group of concentric rings, the boys on the outside and the women weaving slowly in and out except in the outermost ring of boys. All continue to dance and all the males, some of the boys excepted, to sing, in one song using Navaho words. After about fifteen minutes the song ceases, and the two women without the feather ornament in the hair are led out by one of the men of the group and down the street and back to the kiva. Now the other two women take a position on the north side of the choir, i.e., between the choir and the house wall. Facing them is the elderly man who has been taking the director's part. The choir closes up into a more compact group as it is now merely to sing and not to dance. The drummer leaves his position on the outside to stand in the center. The two women face each other and, as they step from foot to foot in the same place, they move their bent arms up and down, right arms or left arms up or down together. After a minute or two of this they turn and, facing the choir, they side-step away from each other a few feet, holding out both arms in the direction of the movement. Then they move back into the first position.† The man who faces the women stands the whole

---

* The girls and the way they circulate among the warriors are noted in Navaho myth, two girls were sent out to meet each returning warrior (Haile, 21, 227). Girls were also sent out at Acoma and probably these are being represented in the dance.

† Compare the dance (Zuni, Hashiya; Acoma, Ăshi'ă) by the girls in the Zuni Scalp dance. In Acoma tradition these girls represent the mother of the War Brothers who in the pristine performance of the ceremony represented the ghost girl. In Apache (Jicarilla) warfare the home-staying woman (mother, sister, or

time on the same spot, beating time with his feet rather than dancing, and moving his arms like the women only less so. His movements are those of a conductor rather than a participator. After the last repetition the man relieves the women of their hand pieces and leads them down the street to their kiva. The choir follows. The whole performance has taken about half an hour.

Now it is the turn of the companion kiva, Mauharots. Mauharots, Chief kiva, is the kiva which usually initiates the dance, but this year its dancers were not ready, so word was sent to Daut′kori·ts to begin. The only notable variation in the performance by Mauharots is the presence of the three War chiefs or captains in the rear of the group, in a separate line. During the preceding dance they were sitting with the other officers on their rock ledge.

From now on until sunset the two groups perform alternately, the drummer summoning his group from the kiva about the time the other group quits the dance floor. Each group comes out five times. Each is supposed to come out ten times, I am told, but it is never done because they start so late. The only variation in the performances is caused by the appearance of women, during the first part of the general dance, one, two, three, or more at a time, with pans or bowls of bread or meat which they throw into the dancing group. The men scramble for the things without interrupting their song or dance. On the appearance of the women throwers, the women dancers withdraw to the outskirts of the group, to preclude being hit by the flying objects.

The men of the choir wear the usual miscellany of American or Indian things, hat or *banda*, boots or moccasins, overcoat or blanket. The three War chiefs are conspicuous for their red *bandas* and red blankets. The dance director wears two downy eagle feathers in his hair, and across his cheekbones is a line of red paint. The women wear the usual wrapped moccasins—the toes of one pair stained magenta—and the usual combination of

---

wife of the warrior) was subject to many restrictions (Opler 2:209–10) having as much influence on the success of the warrior as in Pueblo-Apache hunt techniques has the wife of the hunter.

silk kerchief across the back, black dress fastened over the right shoulder and under the left, and American white petticoat and calico shirt. The black cloth dress is fastened along the side with silver buttons or bits of tin. On the crown of the head is a circlet of white, whether of paint or cotton or downy feather I could not distinguish. In the forelock are two downy eagle feathers. A round spot of red paint almost covers each cheek. Hands are painted white, the fingers laden with turquoise and silver rings. The head ornament of the two dancers consists of a large bunch of parrot feathers and a few peacock feathers held upright in place at the back of the head. From the feathers fall two twists of reddish yarn to the ends of which at the waistline a smaller bunch of the same feathers is attached. The two stiff eagle feathers and the two bells the dancers hold in each hand and, in the case of the Mauharots women, a large yellow artificial flower, are bunched with red yarn.

The evening of this day two sets of dancers are going about town, dancing in several houses. The two houses to which we follow them are the house of Miller, the dance director from Daut'kori'ts, and a house where the Governor is sitting. In both houses the audiences appear to consist only of the households and their usual visitors. The first set of dancers consists of eight young or middle-aged men performing a Navaho dance. They dance in line, stepping vigorously and singing to the drum. They wear American clothes but for a silk kerchief tied around the waist and pendant to it at the back a foxskin. They wear a *banda* and, erect on one side or the other, two stiff eagle feathers. Bells are attached below right knee, and in right hand each dancer carries a gourd rattle. During this dance and the next, in pauses of song, the audience utter encouragement. A few minutes after the Navaho dancers leave and after the Governor has asked me questions about Zuni Shalako—for example, how tall the Shalako mask is—a group of about fifteen boys come in to give a Comanche dance or to watch it. Three boys about seventeen sing, and another carries a bag for the gift expected from the household on leaving. In both houses the woman of the household drops a roll of bread into the bag. There is but one dancer, a little fellow about ten years old. Hanging from his head is one of the gay silk kerchiefs worn on the back by women. On the crown rises a crest of several eagle wing feathers. In his right hand a toy bow. Now and then someone in the audience smiles a bit at the boy's agile performance, but on the whole the audience take the boys quite seriously, giving them exactly the same verbal encouragement as they gave the older performers.

The next morning early the church bell begins to toll. Soon a few persons straggle in to say a short prayer; but there is no general service. During the following hour I notice men with bundles under their blankets ascending the ladder of Mauharots. At 8:30 the drummer descends and beats his drum. The men descend, forming in two lines single file, with the three War captains and their three "cooks" in the rear and back of them all a solitary figure, the feeble old deaf "cacique," the Town chief. All but the cacique begin to sing as they dance forward. After advancing about one hundred feet to the west, the head of one line turns in and back, the head of the other line keeping on the outside and also turning back. Meeting each other the two heads dance forward again, leading their lines to the middle. On the fourth repetition they throw out to the crowd of on-lookers, from underneath their blankets, ears of corn, turnips, boxes of crackers, and packages of tobacco. The boys and women scramble for the things and, closing in, begin good-naturedly to mob the throwers. They persist, however, in their dancing and singing and proceed back to their kiva. The Town chief has on an American overcoat and carries nothing to throw; but all the other men are blanketed, their blankets mostly red. Some of the men have irregular blotches of red, red and white, or white paint on their cheeks.

On the withdrawal of the Mauharots group the other kiva group performs. The performance of both groups lasts not more than a half-hour. All the people in town, or at least the greater part of them, have turned out to look on.

This morning the dancers come out about eleven. They follow the same routine as the day before. With one exception the women's parts are filled by different women. On both days the women from Mauharots are middle-aged to old. Among the women of the other kiva some are young.

The dance concludes, I was told, with the coming-together of the groups from the two kivas. Unfortunately, I did not see it. So anxious was my host to have me descend the mesa and so tricky about getting me off, that I suspect the dance concludes with ritual. At San Felipe the scalps are brought out at this time.

SNAKE-ANTELOPE CEREMONY AT SHIPAULOVI
AUGUST 17–26, 1892[47]

FIRST DAY

This morning, shortly after dawn, Hümimüi'nïwa, the Antelope chief, sets up his standard on the hatchway of his kiva, Spider kiva, and goes down and, after stripping naked save for breechcloth, sweeps the floor carefully and carries off the debris in his blanket. Returning with some pipes and tobacco, he sits down and smokes. Hümimüi'nïwa is a very deft smoker, and emits rings of smoke with much readiness and gives them direction with precision.

The stalks of the standard are newly painted with red, and new prayer-feathers were added yesterday. At sunrise Hümimüi'nïwa goes to the northwest corner, where are the two fetish bundles he brought down, and, taking a pinch of meal from a pouch, prays upon it in a whisper, motions as if casting to the cardinal points but without sprinkling it; he then sprinkles at the base of the longer bundle, which I fancy contains his *tiponi*, and casts the pinch along the floor toward the southwest. He says he will not make the altar for four days yet, a striking variation from Walpi. It is a good while after sunrise, and no one yet come to kiva except the chief. There seems to be no equivalent for the morning ceremony of the Walpi altar of the directions.

Sikyapiki, Yellow Wafer-bread, the Snake chief, comes in to my house to see me and says I must come down to his kiva, Low kiva. I must divide my time, now with the Antelopes, now with him. Before breakfast I did go to his kiva. There was a standard quite similar to the Antelope on the hatchway, but there was no one then in kiva.

Now Sikyapiki brings down twenty-one snake whips, sets them on end leaning against the northwest end ledge, whispers a prayer on a pinch of meal, sprinkles them, and casts meal along the floor toward the southwest. The whip consists of two wooden stems and two eagle feathers with two small feathers tied to their tips. Stems, thongs, and the feathers at the tips are stained red. All have the journey-food prayer-stick-like package tied on.

There has been no one in either of the two kivas today except the two chiefs. Püh'tabi, Road-marker, one of the old men, not a chief, has been asked by Sikyapiki to proclaim from the house-top, which he does just after dark, after all the people have got in from the fields, to this effect: Tomorrow all of the Snake members to go down to Low kiva and then go out to hunt snakes toward the northwest, that the gathering of the snakes will make all things good.

SECOND DAY

Antelope chief sets the standard at his kiva and then goes to his house. Snake chief sets his standard, then begins making prayer-feathers of eagle-breast feather, called Snake prayer-feathers. He has made a new snake whip as his old one (which is dismantled and lying by the fireplace) has grown too dilapidated. I ask him why he does not keep the wood stems of the old one. He does not answer specifically, but says the whole is worthless, that he made it a long while ago and has now made a good new one. The old one he will take with him on the hunt today and bury at the northwest. He prays on a pinch of meal and sprinkles it on the new whip and lays it on a small tray and then smokes over it.

He makes Snake prayer-feathers for all the members and smokes over them. In the little tray are two bundles of the small slender root of the plant called *hoho'yoûña* (beetle), and Sikyapiki says each man carries some of this while hunting snakes. If one bites him, he eats a little of the root, chews it a little, and lays it on the wound, and no harm ensues. An infusion of the same root is drunk as an emetic, a purification, at the end of the ceremony.

The stillness of these kivas is remarkable in contrast with the Walpi kivas. About 8:00 A.M., in Antelope kiva the chief tells me to cease talking and to sit down. He then takes some valley sand from a bag and makes a little mound in the northwest corner, sprinkles meal over it in the customary six lines, then unwraps his *tiponi* and sets it very firmly in the heap. He pats and smooths the heap, then adds the meal lines on the smooth surface. Before placing the *tiponi*, he makes passes with it in the six directions. He then smokes over it. The *tiponi* is two feet high, wholly of eagle-wing feathers with eagle feathers tied to the tips; it is wrapped with red-stained buckskin thongs. Hümi seems quite proud of his smoking accomplishment, sending forth countless rings. After setting up the *tiponi*, Hümi puts on his moccasins and goes to breakfast. He warns me not to enter the kiva in his absence; when he is here, he will be glad to welcome me.

In Snake kiva Sikyapiki is still alone smoking. He again smokes over the tray containing the prayer-feathers and root medicine. He has tied a Snake prayer-feather to the center of his head.

One man comes down and smokes tobacco, semiformally, with Sikyapiki. The Snake whips, the root, all these things I see, are medicine of great value, worth many dollars, and Sikyapiki expects me to give him some.

Another old member comes down, is greeted, and smoked with. He also takes up the tray and smokes over prayer-feathers and root; after which he says "My son" to Sikyapiki, who gives him the pipe, Sikya responding, "My father." When the pipe is given back, Sikya says, "My father," and the old man responds, "My son." They pass the pipe back and forth frequently while it lasts, and every time the same terms of relationship are exchanged. The pipe is passed as close to the floor as possible.

Some showers fall in the valley toward the southeast today, only a few clouds, this about 11:00 A.M. There seems to be a heavy storm over at the Canyon, but the "bad wind" comes up and drives it away from the mesas.

About noon, Sikyapiki and the other two old fellows quietly slip off to the northwest carrying Snake whips, a hoe, and sticks. They put red on the face, but not on the body, and each ties a feather on the head. They return at sunset, only these three, each carrying a snake bag. They lay the three bags down at the northwest end, then each takes a mouthful of water and a sprig of sage and goes upon the kiva roof and washes his hands, rubbing them with the sage. Then they come down again and sit by the fireplace and smoke, puffing the smoke over their shoulders toward the snake bag. They smoke until some twenty minutes or half-hour after sunset, then get up and put on their clothes and go home to eat.

THIRD DAY

In Snake kiva, after setting up the standard, the two Snake men, other than the chief, transfer the snakes from the bags to two large water bottles. They spread valley sand around the bottles. Then, taking up the bag which contains a very large rattlesnake, the little-eyed man unties it, and laying it down, pinches the bottom end, causing the snake to crawl out, rattling fiercely. When he is quite disengaged from the bag, but before he gets into coil, Little Eyes takes him up in a very unconcerned way, just as if he was handling the fag end of an old rope. He holds the snake about ten inches from the head and, removing the corncob plug from the hole near the top of the large bottle, thrusts the snake head first through the hole, and, after it has crawled in, replaces the stopper. The other two are put in the other bottle in the same manner. The men then go up and wash their hands.

There are two others here this morning. All bring their breakfast here, four members and the chief eating together. Another old man comes down. Sikya fills and smokes the pipe a while and hands it to the elder who after a puff or two says, "My younger brother," Sikya responding, "My elder brother." The elder, after smoking a while, hands to a younger man who says, "My father," the elder responding, "My son."

After smoking, Sikya says a prayer, while yet squatted at the fireplace, the other two responding. Three others in kiva lying down take no part.

Sikya brings down a small basket of prayer-meal and lays it on the northwest side of the fireplace beside the other basket containing herb roots and prayer-feathers. This is the first prayer-meal introduced, other than the pinch brought down by Sikya in his fingers. They idle about until about ten, then strip save for moccasins and breechcloth, rub the whole of the face with red, and those who are new today, loop the red prayer-feather, Snake prayer-feather, to a small lock of the hair about in the center of the top of the head. They put a little of the meal from the tray into the individual meal pouches, select their whip and snake pouch, and Sikya carries a small bundle of wafer-bread. They go up the ladder; each takes a hoe or a throwing-stick, some carry both, and then, Sikya in the lead, the six others follow, silently, in a single file. They go down the trail leading to Toriva spring and thence out in the valley to the southwest. They have the same objection as the Snakes in Walpi to anyone not of the society accompanying them from the village.

Between four and five this afternoon, after all these hot, dry weeks and months, a good thundercloud came overhead and gave us a rattling shower and some hail. It remained cloudy until sunset, with occasional showers.

The seven Snake men returned at about sunset, in single file and in the same order as they set out. They were not very successful, as only three of them brought back each a snake in his snake bag, the chief, no snake, but a jackrabbit. They laid the bags containing the snakes on the sand spread around the water bottles.

Old Sikyapiki has just come up this evening and lays an embargo on my going down into Antelope kiva. That is, he gives me my choice to observe the ceremony either in his Snake kiva or the other, whichever I choose I must abide by and not enter the other. As I can talk with Sikya and as the Snake chamber is really the more recondite, I choose it. He then tells me I must take down a handful of meal tomorrow and choose a godfather.

On the day of the final ceremony, he cautions me, I may not eat until after the dance.

FOURTH DAY

Several Snake men are pounding rawhide this morning preparatory to making new moccasins for the dance. All the six members and the chief slept in kiva. During the morning five or six additional members come down to kiva and eat their breakfast. As at Walpi, members go to their homes for food and bring it to kiva to eat.

About 10:00 A.M., while four or five are seated with the Snake chief around the fireplace smoking on the prayer-feathers, the chief makes a short prayer, the others responding. He then tells me to take a handful of meal from the tray and choose a father. I take a handful and give it to Sikya, thus choosing him.* He thanks me, and rising up goes to the northwest end of the kiva, carries his right hand containing the meal to his mouth, prays in low tones upon it and sprinkles it over the snake jars, over the whips and then along the side of the floor toward the southwest. Some of the members chew some sprigs of their root medicine, spitting the secreted saliva on their hands and rubbing their breasts and limbs. They also give me a sprig to chew, telling me it is "good medicine," pointing to the snake jars. Some of them also rub red on the head at the parting of the hair, and on body and limbs, not at all thoroughly, but they all carefully rub the face completely with red. Those who have not before got their prayer-feathers now loop them on, and about 11:00 A.M., thirteen, that is, twelve in file, silently follow Sikyapiki to the southeast. Antelope kiva is left quite tenantless through the day, and no one goes near it.

The reason for surrounding the vessels with sand and making the surface smooth is made apparent this evening. On their return two Snakes, kneeling beside the sand, examine the surface closely and at once say a snake has escaped. Sure enough, the young house snake brought in this morning has escaped through the interstices between the cobs stopping the mouth of the

* This is initial or partial initiation. Compare Voth 3:297.

bottle. They poke their fingers in the wall crevices, but can find no trace of it. As on former evenings the two men empty the bags, laying them flat on the sand, untying the mouth and gently urging the reluctant snakes. One of the bags holds two rattlers. The young man picks up both of them in the same hand; the wonderful unconcern displayed in handling the snakes constantly astonishes me. He holds them nearer the tail than the head and while trying to make them go in the small orifice takes the head between finger and thumb, pressing the head in with his finger. About a dozen snakes in all were brought in, mostly rattlesnakes.

Sikyapiki brought in no snake pouch, but in his left hand carried three cottontails. I noted another man with a prairie dog. These animals were cleaned on the upraise and the little carcasses carried home.

Old Hümimüï'nïwa made the Antelope altar in his kiva today, but as I must preserve my taboo, I have been unable to go near that kiva.

FIFTH DAY

Same standards at both kivas. All the Snake men except two have gone out to their fields. The taboo prevails here preventing Snake men speaking to anyone during the ceremony, but perhaps it is not quite so rigidly observed as at Walpi. I noted yesterday a woman who wanted to speak to a member in the kiva. She did not even venture on the terrace where the kiva is but came along on the cliff above it and called the man she wanted. He came up the ladder and received the message.

Sikyapiki says he is going over to Antelope kiva,* but he will not permit me to go with him; he says it would be bad. He shortly returns with three red-stained and three unstained prayer-feathers, short string, lays them in the small tray, and smokes upon them.

Sikya takes down his feather box and taking out his pollen pouch takes a pinch, and at his prompting I do the same. We then go over to the inverted jar containing the rattlesnakes and

* At Oraibi throughout the ceremony Snake chief visits Antelope chief every morning and evening and smokes with him.

he withdraws the plug, and I thrust my fingers in and sprinkle the pollen on the snakes. (I do not like this part of the exercises much.) He then thrusts his fingers in and sprinkles them, then across the hole sprinkles the three intersecting lines of the directions. We both pray for clouds and rain, on the pinches before sprinkling. He whispers that in four days I shall know much.

An old fellow now brings down a robust rattlesnake, loose in his hand, that he has just found in his cornfield. He first casts it on the floor and then in a jocose spirit picks it up and throws it upon Lodge's head who is lying on the banquette beside me. Lodge and the others laugh as the snake crawls over him, and presently Lodge gets up and, taking it about in the middle—it is about forty inches long and just as thick as the corncob stopper —after considerable difficulty, thrusts it into the newly inverted jar. He has to take the head in the fingers of the left hand and thrust it into the hole and has to use considerable force with his right hand pushing the snake through. It is a very close fit.

I thought I would risk breaking my taboo and so I have come down to Antelope kiva at the urgent request of old Hümi-müïniwa, and I am glad I did, for I found that what I was "told" was, as usual, an error. They are just about beginning to make the altar now. The old chief does not make the altar, but, like the Navaho shaman, directs an assistant constantly. They first sweep the floor, then from a blanket of valley sand the Sand chief, using the sieve and prompted by the chiefs, sifts sand over the region of the *sipapu*, about five feet square, pressing the crevices close and full but not using "whips" as at Walpi.

Another member comes in, takes a pinch of meal and goes to the *tiponi*, sprinkles and prays, unlooses his hair and takes off his clothes, then, prompted by the chief, assists the other at the altar. Now the Sand chief gets the white sand lying in a broken basin on the upraise (all the colored sands sit there in small vessels) and sifts it across the surface. The lines inclose a square of about four feet on each side, and this is sifted entirely with white sand, very lightly, but over the whole surface from the outside lines. I note that several others of this kiva have the chief's art of making rings of smoke.

After the white is sifted, one of the helpers takes a fragment of basin containing black sand and between finger and thumb pours it along the inner line on the northwest side, then along the next outer line on the same side, making lines about three-eighths of an inch wide. Another takes a hand, and now three are engaged in making the lines, all pouring from between thumb and finger under the direction of the chief who thus far has not touched the sand. One is finishing lines on the northwest side, another on the southwest side, and another on the southeast side. The lines are very even. They are "rainbow house."

The chief brings down a small basin with fragments of dull-green sandstone and gives it to another to grind, he himself then takes a bundle of peeled willow wands which have been prepared since the first day, and cuts a prayer-stick length from the edge of the palm next the wrist to the tip of the middle finger. He cuts off two more from the center of the palm to the middle fingertip.

The three have much measuring to space off for the clouds. Hümi does not interfere, gives no heed to them, but continues at his prayer-sticks. Another old man advises the makers. They then begin to pour from thumb and finger, yellow sand, forming the cloud line next the inner northwest side. They are not very expert and work slowly.

A small crenellate bowl with handle on the side is nearly filled with water from a small netted gourd by the old lame man who prays upon a pinch of pollen and sprinkles it on the surface of the water, to the six directions.

Four small clay cones called "cloud mountains," yellow, black, red, and white, each with a small hawk-breast feather thrust at the apex are made and set at the four corners by the chief. They are made of mud and stained with sands as used at the altar. On these the clouds perch, at the four corners of space and the four chiefs live in them.

It is now about 5:30. The women have brought wafer-bread, stewed peaches, and beans and all sit down to eat, as they tell me the altar is finished, although the chief is still making pedestals for some old long black prayer-sticks that were bundled next the *tiponi* bundle. But I must go and meet my Snake people;

they will be coming home before long. About 11:30 this morning fourteen set out for the northeast.

Just about sunset the Snakes return. It is cloudy, and almost dark in kiva. There are four house snakes, two sinew snakes, and three rattlesnakes. Four of the elder men remain squatted around the fireplace smoking, the other ten squat in a semicircle around the snake pouches. From a fetish bag they produce two small tambour-shaped rattles, one is mute, and give them to one chosen to lead the songs by reason of his good strong voice. A vigorous song of very rapid measure is rolled out, in excellent unison, the leader shaking both rattles, although the one in the left hand produces no sound, the others shaking their whips over the pouches containing the snakes with the same motion as used when compelling a snake to uncoil. Now they untie the bags and produce three house snakes, each nearly five feet. The three who had captured them hold them up together at arm's length and straighten them out so as to determine which is the longest. All go up and wash and then bring down their suppers.

SIXTH DAY

It is now late in the afternoon, and here in Antelope kiva nothing has taken place today. The old chief has his spindle and is spinning cotton string for prayer-sticks.

Few members in Snake kiva today. I fancy they are all down in their fields.

SEVENTH DAY

In Snake kiva, about half an hour after sunrise, Sikyapiki, the same as on the two preceding days, withdraws the plugs from the snake jars and sprinkles the snakes within with pollen. The three pinches are, I fancy, the three directions lines, although he calls them snake food; he also says when the snakes are liberated after the dance they will go to the house of the Sun in the west and will be recognized there by these pollen marks on their backs.

In Antelope kiva, in evidence of the efficacy of his song-prayers, Hümi cites the heavy rain showers that have fallen since his ceremonies began. Hümi is making seven sets of standard blue-green prayer-sticks—one set for Sun, one for vegetation, one for medicine, one for each of the four cardinal points in the usual sequence. Those for the cardinal points are for the Cloud chiefs who sit at those far places. Black is the color emblem of the above; when I ask him as to color emblem of the Below, he says never mind it. Spider Woman* and Müy'ingwa are together there, are the man and woman chiefs there. Spider Woman, he says, is my mother, is all mother, the mother of all.

There is no Sand chief here, nor at Shuñopovi, but Hümi says there is one at Oraibi and one at Mishongnovi. No Sand chief here because there is none of the Sand clan either here or at Shuñopovi, but there is at the other two villages.

After the seven sets of prayer-stick stems are made, Hümi makes another set for Moon, the same size. Each female stem is marked with a flat facet or blunt end. Also he makes a prayer-stick set for a spring on the west side of the mesa. The old man tells me to wait until tomorrow, when he will have all these prayer-sticks finished. I suppose I harass the old chap with my questioning while he is making them.

I go to Snake kiva, but there is only one man lying asleep in it.

EIGHTH DAY

As soon as it becomes light enough, Sikyapiki and Hümi, each at his own kiva, sprinkle bands of sand, radiating from the hatchway, across the roof of the kiva in every direction.† Over each band of sand, a narrow line of prayer-meal is sprinkled. This is called the All Directions altar, also cloud road-marker, since over these numerous roads they pray the clouds to travel this way from the far corners and converge right over these kivas.

The Snake costume seems to be the same as at Walpi, but the decoration differs somewhat, and not all the kilts show the serpent head. The Snake hair feather is the same as Walpi, red-stained eagle feathers, the small wing feathers of the bluebird

---

* A notable reference in the identification of the Antelope society with the Keresan Spider-Kaвina society. See p. 976.

† No mention of the customary Antelope race.

fastened to the tips. Armlets of cottonwood scraped thin, tied in annulet with red-stained deerskin string; the bandoleer; a stem of reed five inches long, fastened at the lower curve of the bandoleer and wrapped with red-stained deerskin. Fastened close to the end of the reed, on the bandoleer, are two oliva shells which came from Great Water in the southwest and a fine rimmer of quartz about three inches long, this is the rain knife and came on the fingers of the lightning from Cloud. A scallop shell is fastened at the opposite end of the reed. One man pats himself on the breast saying, "It is mine, it is me, I am the shell. I am a warrior." That is, the shell is the warrior token.

In Antelope kiva are Hümi and seven others, all preparing prayer-sticks. None seems to prepare just exactly the same number or kind.* An old fellow at my elbow prepares three sets of blue-green prayer-sticks (male and female); two of these sets are painted red at the butts. These he calls corn prayer-sticks. The other set is black at the butts, and this is Sun prayer-stick. All the Sun prayer-sticks are blue-green with black butts. He makes four single blue-green stems, red butts, with two prayer-feathers attached equidistant. These are plant prayer-sticks, for all plants, and will be planted in different places tomorrow. He also makes four perched prayer-sticks.

I forgot to note that yesterday I had occasion to sharpen my pencil and, in deference to the speckless condition of the floor, I stooped over the fireplace to let my shavings fall in the pit. Old Hümi promptly stopped me, telling me to put my shavings on the floor under the ladder, because when a fire was made the wood shavings would make a bad smell. He assured me that the odor of red cedar was offensive, not for ritual reasons† but personally he disliked it. And yet the horrible stinks they generate in the kiva, he seems not only to tolerate but relish.

The journey-food packet for the prayer-sticks is prayer-meal

---

* Apart from prescriptive prayer-sticks made by chiefs in every reoccurring ceremony, a good deal of scope is left to the personal inclination of the prayer-stick-maker. If he happens to think about a special spirit, he will make an extra prayer-stick or even more commonly prayer-feather (Voth 3:320, n.1).

† Cedar charcoal, however, is associated with Masauwü, Death. (See p. 72.)

and pollen, honey taken in the mouth and the saliva generated spat in the mixture and mixed into a moist compound. The feathers used are turkey for wrappers; hawk, duck, and yellow-bird for the various prayer-feathers. The Sun prayer-stick has for prayer-feathers eagle-breast feather and small yellowbird. All the blue-green prayer-sticks made by Hümi are identical, except that the Sun prayer-stick has a black butt.

It is now about 5:00 P.M., and the Snakes are getting their costume in order. The face is rubbed with red. There is a smear of white clay on the hair over the right eye. A few add some touches on the body. With palm of hand dipped in white clay, they lay on the smear outside of calf, mid-thigh, forearm and upper arm, on each breast, and on stomach. The decorator takes a drink of water to generate saliva, no seed; he takes a pinch of clay and spits on his hands and rubs the clay to a thin white paste.

The kilt is girded on with long fringed deerskin girdle. Tortoise on right leg behind knee. Deerskin garter on left leg. Fringed anklets over moccasins. All red-stained as at Walpi. Bandoleer over right shoulder, fringed armlets on upper arm. Necklace of shell, turquoise, and coral. Gray foxskin at the small of the back. Fringed meal pouch in left hand. Snake whip in right hand.

The Antelopes decorate at about the same time as the Snakes. From foot to knee, and wrist to elbow, solid white; zigzag on upper leg, "clouds" over shoulders and zigzag down outside of arm, all in white. White kilt with embroidery at right and white brocaded girdle, gray foxskin depending from girdle. The chief leads, carrying the *tiponi* on the left arm, flat rattle in right hand; followed by one carrying gourd and prayersticks in left hand, rattle in right; the next one with two rattles, the one in left hand mute; next the asperser with cottonwood-wreathed chaplet, rattle in right hand, medicine bowl in left; the next seven and a little boy (about twelve) have two rattles; all the left-hand rattles are mute.

On entering the court, the Antelopes pass around the shrine

and in front of the bower which was erected in the afternoon. The Snakes follow and pass in the same route four times, the chief casting meal on the plank in front of the bower, and stamping vigorously; others do the same; also the chief casts meal to the shrine (Pl. VIII).

After perhaps six short songs [as the two lines face each other], a Snake takes an Antelope up between the lines. The Snake has a whip in his left hand, and this arm is laid over the Antelope's shoulder; the couple go up and down twice, then the Antelope stoops to the bower and withdraws with a bunch of cornstalks, the end held fast in his mouth. The Snake, as companion, leads him up and down between the lines many times, the Antelopes singing, not the Snakes. The Snakes link arms but do not imbricate the fingers. So do the Antelopes. The Snakes do not sing. Both lines maintain the swinging "mark time" step. The Snake and the Antelope couple also dance up and down in time. This is very long and monotonous, although the Antelopes sing very well.

The Snake chief carries the bow standard in his left hand, a whip in the right. They now circle wide around the shrine and in front of the bower, stamping on the plank as when they first came in, four times, and then out through the passageway to the kiva.

The Antelope now circle in a small radius, within the bower and the shrine. They circle four times and out. The dance ends a little before sunset.

This evening Sikyapiki tells me that tomorrow I must fast until after the dance; that I must not pass through the part of Joshua's house occupied by the women. I must avoid all women tomorrow because their smell is offensive. He says that tomorrow I will see the snakes' heads washed, after which my own head will be washed and a Hopi name given me.

About 10:00 P.M. a Snake passes to different points around Antelope kiva whirling the whizzer. He also whirls around Snake kiva.

In kiva this morning at early cockcrow, the Antelopes sing the same songs as they sing at Walpi. An uncostumed girl,* hair loose, face rubbed with white meal, ordinary blue tunic gown and barefooted, sits on the north side of kiva on the banquette. The chief's position at the altar is next the fireplace, instead of, as one would expect, next his *tiponi*.

As daylight approaches, the chief anoints two to carry out the prayer-sticks for distribution, and begins dispatching them. These two wear the white kilt girded with string, otherwise they are naked, with hair flowing. They do not go together, although each in turn makes distributions to all four points, and they are simultaneously engaged in this office while the songs are yet in progress. There must be at least seventy-five or eighty prayer-sticks of different kinds to distribute. Members make at discretion, no prescribed number.

Long before daylight the Crier arouses the young men to go out to the southwest to race. Just after sunrise girls and children, the little boys costumed very prettily, stand on the edge of the cliff at the trail leading down to Toriva spring, holding cornstalks and melon and squash vines in their hands, awaiting the coming of the runners. Six or seven young men from Mishongnovi take part in the race.

Shortly after daylight, and while the songs are yet in progress, Hümi takes up his *tiponi*, gives the girl a large number of prayer-sticks and prayer-feathers, and goes up the ladder, the girl following. They go down to the extreme southeast point of the detached mesa on which the village stands. The chief takes the prayer-sticks from her and sets them in a shrine which is merely a shallow depression with two or three stones laid on its west side. About sunrise, two Snakes come to the roof of Antelope kiva. One carries the whizzer, the other, the lightning lattice.

* Snake Maid. No Antelope Youth is mentioned. At Oraibi these elaborately arrayed impersonations stand near the altar, the Youth holding a rattlesnake and a *tiponi*, the Maid a water bowl. Two Snake warriors stand alongside also, with lightning frame and whizzer.

At the four directions they whizz and shoot the lattice, and then, returning to Snake kiva, do the same there.

The songs cease, and Hümi receives a buzzard feather from a member who just brought it down. He takes a handful of sandy ashes from the fireplace and lays it beside the edge. All present take a pinch of the ashes in the left hand. Hümi holds the ashes in his right hand, the feather in left. He sprinkles ashes along the feather surface and begins to sing, waving the feather horizontally over the heads of all, and at certain strains, knocking or flicking the ashes upward through the hatchway, at which time all present also wave the left hand containing the ashes over their own heads and spit upon the ashes violently and cast some of the ashes up the hatchway also. Finally Hümi touches the head of each person and makes the circuit of the altar and makes a final upcast of the ashes from his feather through the hatchway. Everyone spits violently on the ashes in his left hand for final purification and casts them from his hand up the hatchway. Several unloose the single red prayer-feather from their hair and fasten it to the tip of the *tiponi*, where a large mass of former prayer-feathers are already attached. A bundle of the root medicine is passed around, and each one helps himself to a single fiber of the root, the girl also, chewing the root. They spit upon their hands and rub head, limbs, and body; the chief cries, "Finished," and all or nearly all leave the kiva.

Shortly after sunrise the racers come in. All are feasting except Snakes and Antelopes. Several women and men from Mishongnovi feast here also.

At noon I go down to Snake kiva. On the roof are four large bottles of water brought by women, from Toriva. In kiva, all members are present, several are renewing their kilt decorations, others are sleeping, loitering, or smoking. Thus far this Snake kiva has not contained the offensive air and odors of that at Walpi, though the weather has been hot enough too. But there are only a few in this kiva, fifteen here as compared with forty or more at Walpi. The snakes too have not been disturbed since they were first put in the tight jars. Each of them, except the smaller bottle, has a small drilled air hole.

A little after noon Sikya says, in an undertone to a young man, "Let us go for some sand." Wrapping their blankets around them, they go up the ladder. Close by the snake jars two men are busy redecorating their kilts. A man brings in a snake pouch containing a large snake he found in his field; he lays it down on the sand in front of the jars. I am sitting pretty close to the northwest end of the banquette opposite the jars, but I fancy not remaining here to have these snakes dumped around my feet; evidently the washing is about to begin.

Now Sikya brings down in his blanket about two pecks of valley sand, which he casts over the banquette, on the snake side, with his hands, also spreads sand on the floor, only on the snake side. He takes a large fragment of water bottle, makes a little heap of sand and intersecting lines with meal, prays on meal first, then passes the fragment in wavy motion to the cardinal points and sets it firmly in the sand at the intersection of the meal lines. He then pours water from the gourd from the four sides.

A man takes a long wand and pokes in the upper hole in the large bottle, compelling the house snakes and sinew snakes to come out. Lodge is given them to hold, which he does, heads all one way. Another man does the same at the other bottle. They put them all in a buckskin bag. Lodge is bitten on the legs and arms several times, he rubs the wounds with sand, and no one gives it any heed. There is much difficulty in getting the last snakes out of the water bottles; they are the large five-foot fellows. They crawl out of the bag. God, how they make me creep! Lodge grabs them in a bundle half a dozen at a time and folds and doubles and bundles them up and rams them down into the bag at arm's length. An old man holds the bag. Lodge handles the snakes, two other men poke and drag them out of the bottles. The two rattlesnake jars are not yet touched. There are more of these large snakes than I thought, there must be fifteen or twenty, besides sinew snakes. They next tie the bag and get another one for the rattlers. One lifts the jar, and the mass of coiled rattlers is exposed; and, before they have time to move, two men grab them up and jam them in the bag, and an elder holds it without tying.

As the song begins, the bag of rattlesnakes is opened by Sikya, who thrusts his arm in, and brings out two snakes; these he holds in both hands and dips their heads in the water in the fragment, two or three times. He then casts them on the sanded banquette in front of him. As he dips the heads, the song rises loud and vigorous, then falling, systole and diastole throughout. He continues until twenty-five rattlers are crawling on the floor and banquette. They are restrained by members using both hands and whip, and they have to be very lively in their movements too, for the snakes do not seem to be at all benumbed by their confinement; nor do these people hesitate to pick a snake up while in coil; on the other hand, scarcely a snake rattles or offers to strike.*

The rattlers being disposed of, that is, all crawling over ledge and floor, Sikya proceeds with the other bag. I lose my count, the position they make me occupy is too close to the snakes to admit of counting those which Sikya is handling and watch the snakes at my feet and before my face. Those sinew snakes and the large dark stripe constrictors stiffen themselves and rear up from the ledge nearly their full length. It is a monstrous sight, and they fall right in my lap.

Sikya ties a red prayer-feather in my hair at the center of the scalp and a warrior feather badge at the back of my head, and sets a stone seat for me at the end of the ledge. The reptiles are altogether too close, and I confess to flinching back once or twice when half a dozen rattlesnakes chance close at my knee. None, however, offers to strike.

I think six songs are sung, occupying perhaps twenty minutes, and toward the end of the songs the snakes quiet down very

* Voth gives the same description for the behavior of the snakes, but he says he never saw a Snake man try to take a snake entirely coiled up, the only time a rattler will strike. The snake is induced to uncoil by waving the Snake whip over it. Voth discredits hypotheses of snake drugging or fang extraction. The snakes are "tamed," as Hopi say, by careful handling. The movement of the hand in taking a snake is slow and gentle but sure and unhesitating (Voth 3: 340 ff.).

perceptibly. At the close of the songs every man unties his warrior badge, and these are laid on the long undulating mass of
snakes, each man laying his plume on any snake or coil he
chooses. Each man loosens his hair prayer-feather and fastens
it to the tip of his snake whip.

The snakes by this time are all perfectly still or nearly so,
and they tell me that the virtue of the songs just sung and those
of yesterday makes all these snakes peaceable and wise.

Sikya tells me it is now time to follow him for head-washing.
I follow him up to his sister's house, and there his sister cleans
out a large basin and gets some yucca, bruises it with a stone,
pours about a quart of water upon it, and rubs it up into a full
basin of lather. She spreads a sheepskin beside the basin. I kneel
and have my head washed thoroughly by her. Meanwhile all the
females of the Sun clan to which my godfather belongs gather in
the house, about twenty. Sikya's sister brings a small ear of corn
and lays it beside the basin, and the women then in succession
rub my head four times with the corn, then wash my head with
suds and pour a little water on it. Some are old wrinkled bel-
dames, some are mere infants whose hands have to be guided by
their mothers, an albino girl among the rest. After all have taken
a turn at my head, Sikya's sister gives it a final rinse and tells me
to hold out my hands, and on these she also pours water. I then
sit down against the side of the room and Sikya's sister brings
me a handful of prayer-meal. She takes up the corn ear and,
holding it vertical, passes it up and down four times before my
face. Then she rubs my face all over with part of the meal, my
neck and the upper part of my chest. She puts the ear and the
remainder of the corn in my right hand and says, "Your name
is now Ta'wakúyiva (Sun emerges, Sunrise)." At Sikya's
prompting I go to the door and standing in the doorway pray
that the four rain clouds hasten upon my corn ear and meal, and
I cast the meal upward to the Sun.

Sikya tells me to return to the kiva, and he follows me after his
own head has been washed by himself. All the Snakes have had
their heads washed, washed by themselves.

The snakes are still lying on the ledge where I left them, but the sinew snakes are restless creatures and are beginning to set the whole mass in motion. In fact, all the other varieties are much more restless than the rattlesnake. Sikya directs two of the younger men to pick out the sinew snakes and put them in a bag and thus let the rattlesnakes rest. This ticklish job is performed by these naked fellows with the usual unconcern for the rattlers, in fact the sinew snakes are the most vicious of any and bite repeatedly, but the bitten ones merely laugh.

The house snakes are also getting restless, and Sikya tells them to bag those also. I think there are eight sinew and twelve, perhaps fifteen, house snakes. The rattlers, now left to themselves, although of three or four different varieties, colors at least, all lie in knotted groups perfectly still. Occasionally one or two wander off from the ledge to the floor, but two Snake men, one at each end of the ledge, take them in keeping with their Snake whips. These naked men step in among them with their bare feet when having occasion to reach for some object from the wall. Of course, they exercise some little care not to step on them, but they set their feet quite against their heads.

About five o'clock Lodge gathers up all the rattlesnakes and drops them into the cloth bag, four or five at a time. He picks them up by the head this time, regardless of whether they are in coil or not, holds them in his left hand by the neck, sizing them up and handling them exactly as if they were eels. The two bags are tied at the neck, the rattlers in one and the nonvenomous in the other, and are laid on the floor where the jars stood. In my absence these jars were carried off to their cache in the cliffs. The sand in which the snakes are dried and crawled upon on the banquette and floor is now swept up by Sikya and put in his blanket.

At about 6 P.M. the Antelopes, eleven men and one boy, enter the court. All have annulets of cottonwood leaf on head. The asperser has the medicine bowl in his left hand and rattle in right. Antelope chief has *tiponi* on his left arm and rattle in right hand (Pl. II). They have corn smut on body as also have the Snakes. The Antelopes have black chin, white line across upper lip. (Hands and feet black, Oraibi.) The Snake chief carries the

bow standard in his left hand and whip in his right. White Cap*
carries the bow standard of the Antelope in his left hand and a
whip in his right. All the Snakes carry a whip in the right hand
and snake pouch and meal pouch in left hand and prayer-stick
in left, the black perched prayer-stick. There is a pink clay
where white was yesterday; charcoal over the entire face, white
on neck, and under chin, no white on face. Solid pink from ankle
to garter, specular iron on cheeks.† Women stand by the court
shrine sprinkling the dancers.

I am waiting the return of the men who have all gone to
distribute the snakes, except White Cap, who is all too infirm for
scampering. The water bottles on the kiva roof contain only
water, but a very old white-haired woman and a girl about
sixteen came down together, each carrying a large basin of snake
medicine water.‡ It is nearly dark as coffee and bitter as gall.
The returning ones drink a little of this brown fluid and then
some water, and then go over to the cliff edge and vomit.

TENTH DAY

Shortly after daylight they called me to come down to the
Snake kiva. There is no standard of course, but the foxskins are
hanging on the ladder where they have been all night. All the
Snake men are washing their heads with yucca suds in large
basins on the kiva roof.

After washing heads, next they wash necklaces and hairband,
planting-stick and rabbit-stick, and they sprinkle some of the
suds on their blankets. After all have got heads washed and
have got all their things bundled up, each one takes a pinch of

* He is the Snake warrior and the cap represents the War god's "head cover."
[That is, he is impersonating the War god, as does the "bow-priest" of Zuni or
the Keresan War captain.—Ed.]

† Now the notorious dance in which a Snake man carrying a snake in his
mouth dances with a Snake man on either side up and down between the lines
of Snakes and Antelopes. The snakes are thrown into a circle of meal made by
the Snake chief. From this circle the snakes are grabbed up by Snake men and
carried off to the Snake shrines. Compare pp. 512–13.

‡ This consists of two insects, a blind beetle and the stinking tumblebug, a
great double handful, and the root medicine. If the Snake men did not take
this emetic, their bellies would swell up and burst.

ashes with the left hand. Sikya then takes his Snake whip in his left hand and a pinch of ashes in the right, sprinkles the ashes on his whip, and begins to sing a sad monotone very like the song of the Antelope chief at the purification yesterday. All are seated except Sikya, who stands and waves his whip. At strains of his song all spirally wave their left hands overhead and toward the hatchway. After the sixth repetition of the song, Sikya passes around and touches every head with the whip and then tosses up the ladder, all, as he does so, spitting violently, and tossing toward the hatchway. Each now takes a fiber of the root medicine and, chewing it, spit on their hands and then rub themselves, and spit or spurt upon every article in the kiva. This is the final purification, about forty minutes after sunrise. Now breakfast is eaten in kiva.

CEREMONIES OF WOMEN'S SOCIETIES

These are of two types, associated with war and characterized by burlesque of warriors or associated with harvest and characterized by a so-called basket dance. Fertility ritual is notable in both; likewise throwing or giving away food or baskets.

As women's societies occur only among Hopi, Tewa, and Jemez, from these peoples only are these war or harvest ceremonies reported. At San Felipe, however, there is a circle basket dance, by women and men; and at Zuni the Thla'hewe ceremony, which belongs to Pekwin, may well be considered a growth celebration. It is a woman's dance; but the dancers are appointed by the paramount Rain chiefs.[48] Marau (Hopi) and Puwęre (Santa Clara) present war ritual or burlesque; the Flute dance of Jemez, harvest or basket ritual, and see pages 869–70 for a summary of the Hopi Lakon ceremony and basket dance. Several kinds of basket dances are performed by Tewa; Tembishare of San Juan resembles the Flute dance of Jemez.[49]

MARAU CEREMONY AT WALPI, 1891[50]

In the September moon after the evening smoke talk* in the house of Shalïko, chief of the ceremony and Snake clan mother,

* At Oraibi, where the ceremony was observed over a decade, 1893–1903, there is no smoke talk. Instead, the day before the standard is placed, the

Crier chief (Shalïko's nephew) announces the ceremony from the housetop, in eight days.

On the first day of the ceremony Shalïko places the standard, a rod with a bunch of hawk* feathers, on Horn kiva and with the other ceremony chiefs makes a sand ridge for their ritual sticks, including Twister Man, thus beginning the altar which will not be completed until the fourth day. Two wrapped, befeathered *tiponi*, each with a basket of prayer-sticks, lie in front. One belongs to Shalïko, the other to Sakabenka, Coyote clanswoman and fire chief. Shalïko fetches in two novices, Tewa girls, and has them jump from the banquette into a circle of meal overlaid by a ring of yucca and bluebird feathers which Shalïko moves up and down the girl's body.† The girls and Shalïko and Sakabenka sleep in kiva.

On the second day Shalïko lays the meal altar‡ of the Directions in the usual way, and the usual ritual of song, of dipping the corn ears and pebbles of the Directions into the medicine bowl, of whistling into the bowl, and of aspersing and smoking is performed. Walls and floor are marked with four parallel lines

---

chiefs meet in kiva to make prayer-sticks and prayer-feathers. The man chief of the Lizard maternal family in charge of the ceremony makes prayer-sticks and prayer-feathers for the Chiefs of the Directions, for Sun, and for Sotu-kunangwuu (Thunder or Lightning); the women chiefs of the Lizard clan make prayer-feathers for the Chiefs of the Directions, for Sun, and for Moon. There is only one *tiponi;* but several women participants own prayer-stick bundles called *tiponi* mothers (Voth 8:35, 43).

* Sparrow-hawk (Oraibi), and two sparrow-hawk feathers are worn in the hair. In the East, sparrow-hawk is distinctive of the Keresan Kurena society and its homologues.

† At Oraibi children are thus initiated, some so small that they have to be held up, in the meal and yucca circle. The two women who raise and lower the yucca ring say: "We cause you to grow up" (Voth 8:45, 52; Voth 4:11). Compare the ring used by witches for transforming themselves or a victim into an animal, a technique without any hitherto noted medicine society parallel unless it be the Acoma-Zuni practice of spilling disease out of the yucca rectangle (see p. 364), or, let me add, the practice of the Northern Paiute of lowering a ring of meat over a boy when he first kills a deer (Kelly, Steward).

‡ At Oraibi there is no separate Directions altar. The main altar which includes a Directions altar is made on the first day, by the men chiefs (Voth 8:44). There is no sand-painting.

of meal by Napionsi, the meal chief, who is also the one to smear meal on the left cheek of every participant. The novices have a hawk feather tied in the scalp lock, are exorcised with ashes, and have two black lines drawn on each cheek. Four girls distribute prayer-feathers, as from now on they will do each day; later three of the girls and an older member whitewash the kiva walls.

On the fourth day additional women members come in, the novices are re-marked and taken to the house of the woman marking them to grind corn to take to Shalïko, who will cook it to be eaten in kiva. With the help of men members the frame altar is made, also a cloud and lightning sand-painting which reproduces designs painted on a cotton curtain. Shalïko places prayer-feathers on the sand clouds. On the altar slabs are painted Müy'ingwa Man and Maid. Two figurines are similarly called. Girls bring in cornstalks and melon and bean vines for the altar. The novices return and, holding Shalïko's crook, are led over the meal trail to the altar to cast meal on the figurines of Marau Maiden. Now girls are dispatched to Sun spring to deposit prayer-sticks and fill gourds with water. Many members arrive, and there is a night ceremonial of song, followed by the making of a Directions altar and its regular ritual, this conducted by Shalïko's husband who must therefore be considered the male chief of the ceremony. During the early singing, infants are brought in to be adopted, the mother giving a handful of meal to the godmother who casts the meal on the altar. Women also select a godmother for themselves. After the altar ritual the novices and adopted ones, adult and infant, perhaps thirty in all, have their heads washed ritually and are given a name. All members then wash their hair. At daylight Shalïko leads the novices to a shrine west of Tewa to deposit prayer-sticks. For the first time they go home and thence bring food to eat in kiva. The standard in the kiva mat has been changed.

The night of the fifth day and the morning following, members practice dancing, a burlesque of Heheya kachina which they perform in the court in the afternoon. At night in kiva the women sing, gossip, and skylark. On seventh day, kiva rehearsal and in court burlesque of Buffalo dance. The burlesques of these two days vary from year to year.

Eighth day, prayer-stick-making by women chiefs and men members. Sand-painting renewed. About sunset the women make up with red and yellow streaks on face, and hair in poke with cornhusk, Singers fashion, and outside, like Singers, they sing taunting songs and point with corn ears, and have water and urine thrown on them and ordure rubbed on. They dance and sing to the drum, just like the Singers.* This night in kiva they sing the songs that have been sung every night, addressed to Cloud, to Lightning, etc. Also they sing about particular men, "song-tying." These men have to make the women presents, usually food presents. The women also practice their public, last-day dance, circling about the kiva, singing and bowing, as they step sidewise, and moving their ears of corn up and down. Before daylight the Directions altar is placed and ritual is performed, as on the fourth night.

Now the main altar is dismantled. The women chiefs pick up each her *tiponi* and prayer-stick bundle, the third chief, the meal chief, picking up the two aspergills, and all these things they press on everybody's head, one after the other, and then, on reaching the altar, they press them on each other's heads and lay all the things down flat. In conclusion several wash their heads.

Ninth day, exhibition or dance day. At daybreak the Marau society man, who is a Wüwüchim society man and with another man is inferably a link between the two affiliated societies, carries the fire prayer-sticks made by the woman fire chief, and a firebrand to the kiva roof. He sprinkles meal on the prayer-sticks and toward the east; the firebrand he has placed on the edge of the cliff. This is a fire offering to Masauwü, performed by the man as proxy for the woman fire chief who stands alongside.†

---

* The following year the dance of Horns and Singers was imitated by the women.

† At Oraibi the man fire-tender sprinkles meal on the firebrand, and some sweet-corn meal into the kiva fireplace. Ashes and embers are deposited outside with a prayer-feather. A new fire is made in the kiva fireplace (Voth 8:64).

At sunrise the society members go into the dance court, sing, and distribute corn-ear-bearing stalks which the women have brought in at dawn from the fields. Later in the day the women form a circle in the court. As they sing, they bow and bend, and each waves a prayer-stick up and down to the rhythm of the body. Facing the chief in front, an impersonation called Chatü-maka moves backward; the others face into the circle and move sidewise. Chatümaka wears a hair mask, Zuni-like, i.e., the bang falls to her nose, a huge plume of variegated feathers, a kilt, belts, and knit jacket, foxskin pendent from the belt at the back, a bell to her left garter, and her feet, legs, and arms are particolored, yellow and green; in her right hand, a prayer-stick, in her left, a foxskin; and on her back, a skin frame or shield. Two other women called Wauhitaka who are similarly painted and habited but without back shield or hair mask and wearing a coronet shoot arrows at a cornhusk package each casts in front, repeating this maneuver from kiva to dance circle. Thence they return to kiva and bring out trays of sweet-corn nodules which from within the dance circle they toss to the spectators. These three roles are refilled, and the act repeated six or seven times.*

On this day rain should fall; then on the day following all the women should go to the fields and wash legs and arms and face in the rain pools, and with prayer deposit their prayer-sticks in the field shrine.

On the altar are two pain-makers, the Chatü bundle, referring to the small white ant which if it bites a woman causes swellings and pain, and Twister Man ("very strong lightning") who is very bad. The society member who neglects ceremonials will become twisted and her mouth distorted; her pains will kill her unless she

* At Oraibi there are five impersonations, two Archers, two Lancers, and the one with the back shield and a horsehair wand who is sometimes arrayed with vines and cornstalks and rabbit-ear effigies as "Rabbit Mother." (Is this an impersonation of Childbirth Water Woman, Mother of Game, wife of Müy'ing-wa?) The Archers shoot into a bundle of vines, the Lancers throw wheels at which they cast sticks. The late performances are not as elaborate or serious as the early ones. In the last performance all will participate although that performance, too, is for the entertainment of the crowd.

goes to kiva and throws meal on the altar; then she will recover. Marau is both a rain-making and a curing society.*

More speculative is the hypothesis, my own, that the performances by Archers or Lancers are dramatizations of killing the enemy, head or scalp ritual, and that the dough balls thrown to the lookers-on correspond to the scalp cakes made at Isleta by the Mafornin Scalp women against sickness from the dead. Throw-away is a war trait, and, among Plains tribes, so is dressing up in warrior toggery. I would suggest that all Hopi Women's societies are genetically war societies, and such perhaps are all Pueblo women's societies.

PUWĘRE AT SANTA CLARA†

This is a two-day initiation war dance which is performed nowadays only at Santa Clara, where it is in charge of the women's war society. The four men who dance are appointed by the Tse'oke kwiyo, war society old woman, i.e., chief. Women dress as men, and men as women, some of them making up as pregnant women,‡ and these sing, "Some of those boys made me pregnant." The men in masquerade do women's work, fetching water, baking bread outdoors in the ovens on street or roof, and carrying dinner to the dancers. The women masqueraders with cloths in their hands to clean the ovens go from door to door and sing, "I am scared, let's run away!" People give them bread. "You are lazy. You don't bring us wood, you don't hunt deer,

---

* At Oraibi, no curing aspect is suggested except the dough balls made by the Archers in the court and thrown to the crowd; but there are war and fertility aspects. Wrist guards of the Marau men or warriors are made of deer, elk, or buffalo hide, and of bone plates from the scapula of a bear or slain enemy; the rings into which lances are cast are covered with buckskin taken from the enemy; the arrows used in the trail ritual are finally deposited in the War god shrine. There has been made for the altar a cone of soft clay inset with corn kernels. The last procedure is breaking up the cone and distributing the pieces with the kernels to the participating women, undoubtedly for seed corn (Voth 8:58, 66, 69).

† Parsons 49:212–13. Puwęre is danced in other Tewa towns, and compare San Ildefonso women's burlesque at which the men talk at the dancers and disconcert the girls (*ibid.*, p. 211).

‡ Compare Hopi Wüwüchim makeup.

you bring nothing to us," men say to the women. In the dance, women sing for the men, taunting songs referring to such things as earrings of cotton, full of lice. Other women carry a basket of bread on their head and say, "My *pare* (elder brother or sister) is dancing and I throw this bread." They throw other things, too, "corn, dishes, everything." According to Santa Clara tale, Puwẹre was danced after the return of warrior women bringing back scalps.

Puwẹre is performed in November, but only when there are girls to initiate. It was performed in November, 1923, after an interval of about fifteen years, the girl babies that had been "given to them" having grown up and being just old enough to dance. The ceremony is for fertility, to have a good year in crops, children, horses, and cattle.

The society women bathe and go into retreat for four days, observing continence. They have stone fetishes, inferably an altar.

FLUTE DANCE AT JEMEZ, SEPTEMBER 17, 1921[51]

This was danced as usual after the autumn retreat of the Clown society (Tabö'sh) by the two Women's societies, with the Sun society to sing and the clowns to play. The Women's societies are invited to dance by the Town chief.

About 11:30 A.M. the dance procession enters town led by the flutist, playing as he walks, and another man who carries a basket from which he sprinkles meal ahead. A standard-bearer and three choristers follow, two by two, then in single file, two groups, the first consisting of eleven women and five or six little girls—these together with the meal-sprinkler are the Jemez Women's society; the second consisting of a man leader, fourteen women and several children, a little boy* among the girls, these the Keresan Women's society. Flutist and choristers are members of the Sun society. (One of the membership of five has stayed away because his grandson has just died.) The procession encircles, anti-sunwise, the spruce tree near Turquoise kiva.

* He is not a member of the Society. Several of the children, if not all, are not members; this first morning dance is for the children, for any who want to dance.

Then the standard-bearer takes position north of the tree, the flutist beside him, the choir sitting behind. A drum has been brought out for them.

The standard has been made by the Sun society. It is similar to that which is carried in the saint's-day dancing in Keresan towns. At the top of the standard is a gourd, painted turquoise with an encircling block pattern of white and black. Above and below are fringes of horsehair stained red; on the very top, a bunch of parrot feathers, to one of which is fastened a downy eagle feather. Below the gourd are a short kilt of Hopi cloth and a dance belt, and extending halfway down the pole are two long strips of Hopi cloth, each finished off with a tassel. The pole is painted light blue. The whole is curiously suggestive of a kachina dancer.*

Standard-bearer and choristers are dressed in white cotton shirt and trousers, wearing moccasins and *banda* and in their forelocks downy eagle feathers. The flutist and men leaders of the two groups and the little boy are more ceremonially arrayed, in dance costume—white shirt, embroidered white dance kilt, pendent foxskin and long fringed dance belt, moccasins with skunk fur heel-bands, and cotton net leggings. Under each knee is tied with yarn a leglet of brass bells. The hair of the dancers is in queue, and in the forelock is a bunch of parrot feathers. The hair of the flutist is flowing. To his shoulders are fastened two large fans of eagle feathers.† His richly embroidered shirt is poncho cut, but with sleeves which are slit in the medieval fashion from wrist to elbow. Save for the flutist, all the men carry tall stalks of ear-laden corn.

Several of the women wear a dress of the embroidered white Hopi blanket, and across the shoulders, the white Hopi blanket with red and blue border. The other women wear their ordinary black dress, but to their single shoulder-kerchief they have added another. One woman displays three superimposed silk kerchiefs. All wear puttee moccasins, their hair flowing and

* The similar standard of the Keres is called Sun Youth. See p. 542.

† Is the flutist impersonating Sun Youth who fluted for the Sun Father or for the Corn Maidens (Stephen 4:154; Stevenson 2:192)?

fastened to their forelock two downy eagle feathers and a jay-wing feather. On cheeks, daubs of white and black paint.

From the dance ring the children are withdrawn by one of the men leaders and placed in line, the little boy in the middle of the line of girls. The women in the ring put down on the ground the baskets of bread, melons, and grapes which they have carried on their left arm, and take in either hand the bunches of corn leaf they have carried in their right hand, to wave them either up and down or from side to side in time to the song. They, as well as the children in line, dance on the same spot, the line dancers turning, to face east, and then back to face west. After dancing for about fifteen minutes, the circle forms in single file and proceeds to encircle the second spruce tree, one of the men leaders picking up and carrying with him the first tree. Another drum is supplied from the kiva, and the dance is repeated, this time, not the children but three of the women stepping out of the circle to form with two of the men the dance line on the north.

Every three or four minutes during the dance, the figure of a clown has emerged, waist-high, above the kiva hatch, to call out something that amuses the spectators, a nude figure garlanded with yellow flowers.

Now the second little spruce is uprooted, and the dancers move on into the plaza, the Middle. A circuit is made around the spruce-tree bower almost in front of Squash kiva. Against the bower are propped the two little trees which have been brought from the other plaza. In front of the bower the standard is planted firmly in an excavation, already made, and alongside are planted a spruce branch and the prayer-sticks which eventually are to be thrown into the river. The choir sit down within the bower, and to the right of the standard stands the flutist. The line dancers, three women alternating with two men, take position again in front of the flutist. During the dance which follows appear six clowns, three at the east end of the plaza, three at the west end, first to hoot and chatter and then, standing in line, their bodies inclining forward, to dance down toward the central dance group, singing as they prance.

A line of Fathers advances toward the spruce-tree bower, each man in succession to sprinkle meal on or toward the flutist and the standard, and, moving on a step or two, in each of the directions. Now another group of four clowns appear on the west side. These too wear a wreath of yellow flowers; in the forelock, instead of a feather, all the clowns wear a cornhusk. Garlands of clematis and verbesina encircle shoulders and waist and ankles. There are streaks of white paint under eyes and across lips and cheeks, and broad white bands across shoulders and back and around waist, and around arms and legs, at ankles, below knees, and across thighs. All wear a clout of shabby cloth.

The ten clowns bunch together, back to back, rubbing against each other, rather violently, disheveling garlands and wreaths. Breaking up, they form a circle holding hands around the bower, facing the circle dancers. They sing four times, revolving a few steps in between, as if to sing toward the four cardinal points. On the shoulders of the flutist and on the flaring tip of his flute-trumpet each clown sprinkles meal. One of the clowns says a ten-minute prayer, and the dancers disperse.

During the prayer and before, from all the houses women have been bringing baskets of breadstuffs and of melons and grapes and bowls of stew to place on the ground near the circle dancers. All this together with the dancers' baskets the clowns now collect, emptying and sorting the contents on blankets which have been laid on the ground. The clowns eat the while, greedily, taking a visible satisfaction in their presents.

The afternoon dancing is comparatively complicated, for the dance circle revolves. There are two quite definite parts or steps. In the first, the forearms, held at right angles to the body, are moved up and down; and, keeping their feet close together, the women side-step, left foot following right, or make little jumps sidewise with both feet. The line dancers single-step in place, with a turn, from east to west, by way of the north. They, too, wave their forearms up and down. In the second step or movement the forearms of the circle dancers are waved sidewise and the side step is longer. The line dancers raise one arm and then the other to the level of the forehead, raising the arm on the side of the direction they are turning in.

All the women dancers hold in each hand an ear of corn, the men dancers hold spruce twigs. The men leaders still wear their ceremonial dance costume, but several men in ordinary dress join the dance circle. Fewer women are wearing the embroidered blanket dress, most wearing their black dress. The line dancers have discarded or tucked in the calico underslip, leaving neck and arms bare. Each woman line dancer has a short line of red paint on the upper forearm, and some a black line on the lower cheeks, parallel to the line of the jaw. The hair is worn in queue, with forelock feathers. To the queue is fastened, in the case of the women line dancers, an eagle-feather fan.

Within a quarter of an hour the dancers, or most of them, ascend the ladder to Squash kiva, whence, after an interval of five minutes or so, they descend to dance for another quarter of an hour. These withdrawals and returns continue throughout the afternoon, into the dusk, changes of personnel taking place, from appearance to appearance. The dance circle is much larger than in the morning, varying from sixty to seventy. Anyone may join the dance circle, and anyone may also dance in the line after all the society members have had their turn.

The clowns have been sitting still, some alongside the bower, others on the wall bench where sit the *principales*. But in the last two dance appearances a clown joins the line dancers as one of the two male dancers. And now, as the last circuit is danced, the clowns bunch up before the standard where their leader recites a long prayer. At its close the Fathers come forward one after the other to throw meal toward each dancer. The dancers disperse, and the clowns with noisy chatter begin to uproot the trees, dragging them to their houses. Meanwhile the standard has been raised, and with it in their midst the flutist and choir proceed very slowly, singing in hushed measures, toward the end of the plaza, where in the dark they are lost to sight. It is an extremely reverent progress rendered nonetheless impressive by the clattering and raucous clowns or by the little boys rushing up to break off twigs from the trees sacred to the Cloud people.

The so-called curing societies of Zuni and Isleta and the Snake-Antelope and Flute societies of Hopi are of the Keresan type of undifferentiated curing and weather society, conducting private cures and initiations but also performing weather ritual for the benefit of all, at the winter solstice ceremony (Zuni, Keres) or in a series of rain retreats. The society "go in" or "count their days," four or eight days devoted to prayer-stick- or prayer-feather-making and to mimetic altar rites, "acting like Clouds" or "calling the Clouds."

Rain retreats are performed serially by the societies of Keres and Tewa, of Jemez and Taos, and by the Rain chieftaincies of Zuni. The Isletan Fathers are in retreat for rain two days in April and twelve days in July. Hopi ceremonies involve a retreat and are for rain; but they are complicated with other rituals and they are timed by lunations. The one-day winter ceremonies of some of the Hopi societies, however, might well be called retreats. They consist only of altar ritual, which may be followed, like retreats elsewhere, by a kachina dance.

Except for Stevenson's Sia and Zuni accounts* there are no firsthand reports of rain retreats. Keresan retreats, and probably those of Jemez and of the Tewa, are said to be much alike. The society retires to its ceremonial rooms where it remains for four days and four nights; nonsociety members are not admitted. While in seclusion members eat no salt or fat, and abstain from Mexican and American foods. Each morning for four days before the society "goes in," each member takes an emetic for purification. On the day immediately preceding the retreat members bathe in the river and have their heads washed in yucca suds. In retreat the shamans make prayer-sticks, lay down a sand-painting or meal-painting, erect the slat altar, and place an array of fetishes before the altar and on and near the sand painting: stone figurines of bears, lions, badgers, wolves, snakes, and of anthropomorphic supernaturals, Ma'sewi and Oyoyewi or warriors of the six directions; medicine bowls, honey jugs, stuffed

* Compared with accounts of Hopi altar ritual by Stephen and by Voth, Stevenson's data are in details uncertain and questionable.

parrots, deer horns, bear-leg skins, bear-claw necklaces, eagle plumes, flint knives, and, most sacred of all, the corn-ear fetishes representing the Corn Mother. The final evening ceremony lasts from about eight o'clock until midnight or later, say three o'clock in the morning, with singing, smoking, mixing of medicine water, and sprinkling of altar, fetishes, and shamans with pollen, meal, medicine water, and ashes. The flute is played; there is some dancing. Clouds are made from yucca suds and put upon the heads of the shamans, on the altar, or on the fetishes. At the close, all members drink from the medicine bowl, prayer-sticks are taken out and deposited, and sand from the painting is rubbed on the body. Supper is eaten, and the altar fetishes and sand-painting are cleared away.[52]

The altar of the Zuni Rain chieftaincies is somewhat different, no wooden pieces or sand-painting, only a meal cloud design; and what corn fetishes there are have been borrowed or belong to the chiefs as members of curing societies. Pots of precious black paint and the two supreme fetishes, the water and seed bundles, are set on the altar, also arrowpoints and thunder stones. The altar is laid at night after a day of prayer-stick-making and after the chief and an assistant have fetched water from the spring associated with their group.[53]

The summer series of retreats begin four days after the summer solstice, the four paramount Rain chieftaincies going in for eight days, Pekwin, the War chiefs and then all the minor Rain chieftaincies going in for four days. The major Rain chieftaincies also observe overnight retreats or ceremonies in winter.

Rain Ceremonial of the Snake and Kapina Societies of Sia[54]

Snake chief and his assistant make prayer-sticks in the morning and set up the slat part of the altar in the ceremonial room. Toward the close of afternoon they make the sand-painting and set out three corn fetishes (*yaya*), upon a parallelogram of meal representing, as usual, seats for the fetishes; also a small image of Yellow Woman, the images of Wolf and Bear, and to right and left of altar an image of Mountain Lion. A medicine bowl

stands in front of the Corn Mothers and, either side, two stone
adzes and two stone knives. Two more Corn Mothers stand in
front of the bowl, before each a snake's rattle. The sixth corn
fetish stands on the tail of the sand-painted mountain lion. A
miniature bow and arrow are laid before each corn fetish, and in
front of the two corn fetishes is a line of eight stone images
representing the War gods, Ma'sewi and Uyuuyewĕ, and their
warrior deputies of the mountains. A necklace of bear claws encircles the carved image of Ma'sewi as well as the stone hatchet
which represents Uyuuyewĕ. Around most of these eight images
is a fringe of white wool [their dress]. In front of these figures are
three small images of Koshairi; in front of them a shell, and on
either side of the shell a wand of turkey feathers standing in a
pedestal, a clay ball with a hole pressed into it. In front is a cross
prayer-stick. Images of a bear and cub and of a wolf are on
either side of the cross. And on either side toward the front of
the altar are massive carvings of coiled snakes.* Bear-leg skins
with the claws are piled on either side of the altar, and near these,
gourd rattles and eagle plumes in sets of two. A necklace of bear
claws with a whistle pendant hangs together with two downy
eagle feathers over a slat of the altar. The necklace is for the
chief to wear [and the feathers are presumably for his scalp lock].
A gourd of honey, a basket of meal, a shell of corn pollen, a buckskin medicine bag, an arrowpoint, and a square bowl are grouped
in front of the snake fetishes. There are other medicine bags and
turkey-feather wands with bunches of downy eagle feathers,
dyed yellow, attached to them with cotton cord. These are
wands for the women to hold. A Hopi basket of prayer-sticks
and bunches of feathers from birds of the six directions is in front
of the other snake fetish, together with another line of wands.
A stone bear is in front of the altar, and attached to the top of
the central slat a stuffed parrot. A line of meal has been laid from
door to altar for the Spirits to come in by.

In the evening members are joined by Kapina society members. All sit in line behind the altar, the chief sitting behind the

---

* Possibly natural stone formations such as are placed in Hopi shrines.

central slat figure, the chief of the Cloud People. Members carry gourd rattles in their right hand and two eagle plumes in the left. The head *banda* is off.

All sing, the assistant chief standing before the altar and waving his rattle in a circle, six times, to summon the Cloud People. At the third stanza all rise, the chief taking a corn fetish in each hand. The men sway their bodies, they wave their wands, moving their arms from the elbow. At the close the chief gives a call to the Cloud People, and all breathe from their feathers.

A woman places a bowl of water and a gourd in front of the altar. All sing. The maker of medicine water dances in front of the altar, raising first one heel, then the other, with knees slightly bent. Three times he extends his feathers toward the altar, striking them near the quill end with his rattle as he shakes them over the medicine bowl. He waves his feathers to the north and breathes from them. The Snakes put on their necklaces of bear claws and whistle. The medicine-maker dips a gourd of water from the bowl, raises it with a hoot, and empties it into the medicine bowl. He empties another gourdful into the cloud bowl standing on the sand-painted clouds. Several gourdfuls are emptied into both bowls. The medicine-maker drinks from the medicine bowl, and in an abalone shell gives a drink to each member, except the chief who after the medicine-maker takes his seat in the line passes in front of the altar to the medicine bowl and drinks from it directly.

The chief waves his feathers over the medicine bowl and calls out four times to the Cloud People to water the earth, at each call sprinkling meal into the medicine bowl. Each member does this, using buckskin bags of meal or pollen, taken from the bear-skin legs. The medicine-maker dances in front of the altar to the singing of the choir. In each hand he holds six pebble fetishes. With his right hand he touches the two front corn fetishes and then drops a pebble fetish into the medicine bowl with a cry to the Snake chief of the North to ask the Cloud chief of the North to send his people to water the earth. This is repeated for each bowl four times, the Snake chief of each Direction being called upon. Four times with the two stone knives on the altar he sprinkles the fluid from the medicine bowl upon the altar, and twice he sprinkles to the east.

The chief dips his feathers into the medicine bowl and four times sprinkles the altar by striking the feathers on top with his rattle. All gather around the tobacco by the fireplace, roll cigarettes, and sit down to smoke. The first whiff is blown toward the altar and the cigarette is extended toward the altar and waved in a circle.

The women gather before the altar and each, taking a pinch of meal from the meal bowl, sprinkles the altar. The medicine-maker picks up the shell of pollen on the altar, waves his rattle along the line of meal and out of the door which he opens, and sprinkles pollen. The chief, striking his feathers with his gourd, sprinkles the altar with water from the medicine bowl. The cloud-maker picks up the reed lying across the cloud bowl and holds it vertical together with his feathers, while he prays. The assistant chief dips ashes from the fireplace with his feathers, holding one in each hand, and sprinkles the ashes on the cloud-maker, throwing the remainder toward the choir. After his prayer, the cloud-maker drops into the cloud bowl a quantity of a root which produces suds, and sprinkles with corn pollen the surface of the water. With the reed he stirs the water into a froth which rises above the rim of the bowl and cascades to the floor. The song which has been raised during the suds-making ceases. The cloud-maker takes his eagle feathers, one in each hand, and begins dancing before the altar to song. Then with his feathers he dips the suds from the bowl and throws them to the north, calling the Cloud People, and repeating for the other directions. Two of the choir dip their feathers into the medicine bowl and sprinkle the altar, striking the upper side of the feathers with their rattle. The cloud-maker dips the feathers and, facing the east, throws them to the zenith. He dips suds into the middle of the prayer-stick basket. He throws suds toward the women on the north side of the room, and then toward those on the south side. The men sprinkle the altar from the medicine bowl. The cloud-maker throws suds to the west, to the zenith, to the altar, and then on to the corn fetishes in front. He dances and throws suds on the man at the north end of the line, then on the chief, and on the medicine-maker, again to the west and to the zenith. From the medicine bowl the chief sprinkles the altar and then all the members. The cloud-maker throws suds to the west and to the zenith. A woman dips her wand into the medicine bowl, with a call to the Cloud People. The cloud-maker throws to the west; the chief sprinkles the members; the cloud-maker places suds on the heads of the white-bear image and the parrot.

A cigarette is handed to the cloud-maker who puffs on the suds and then after smoking a little lays about one-third of the cigarette alongside the cloud bowl. The singing which has continued almost incessantly for three hours ceases, and the cloud-maker returns to his seat in the line behind the altar.

Now the women dance, first facing the east and then the west, sprinkling the altar when they reverse, and calling to the Cloud People. A man and a boy join the dance. All sprinkle the altar.

The medicine-maker places the medicine bowl before the prayer-stick basket. Taking a corn fetish in his left hand, he gives a drink from the shell to all, beginning with the women and including an infant in arms. After they sit, each touches wand or eagle feathers to the corn fetishes and from them breathes in. The chief is the last to be served, he in turn serving the medicine-maker. The medicine-maker leaves the room with the corn fetish and medicine bowl, and outside he sprays the medicine water to the different directions.

The chief picks up the prayer-stick baskets, and two members advance to hold it with him as over it he prays a long time. Then the chief gives a bundle of prayer-sticks and a cluster of feathers to each man. Each helps himself to a pinch of shell mixture and leaves to deposit the offerings at a shrine. As they leave the room, the chief plays upon the flute. On their return he receives them standing by the altar and prays.

Smoking and feasting follow. Then the chief picks up the corn fetish from the mountain-lion sand-painting and presses his palm to the sand lion and breathes from it; from the corn fetish he also breathes. He places the corn fetish among the others at the back of the altar. All in turn press their hand to the sand lion, breathe from their hand, and pass it over their body.

The sand remaining on the altar is brushed together from the cardinal points by a woman with an eagle feather; with the feather she lifts it into her left hand to carry home and rub over her sons.

The corn fetishes are collected by their individual owners who blow the meal from their feathers and inclose them in their three wrappings. Remaining are the four wands of turkey feathers in the clay holders which conceal prayer-sticks for Spider from the chief of the Kapina (Spider) society, to be deposited at sunrise on the four sides of town.

Winter Ceremony of Zuni Rain Society,* 1896†

At night‡ the altar is laid in the east end of a room in the house where the supreme fetish of the society is kept. There are eight corn-ear fetishes§ at the back, resting on a corn-meal terrace design, from which lead eight disks of corn meal edged with corn pollen and charred corncob terminating in two forking lines tipped with arrowheads. In line along the disks are a considerable number of stone fetishes, and over the cloud terrace a number of arrowheads. At either side of the corn ear fetishes are turtle shells. On two crosses of meal, formed by running four lines inward to the center, inclosed in a circle, representing the cardi-

---

* Described as of the Nadir; but Naiuchi was Rain chief only of the North; he represented the Nadir only as a War chief. The War chiefs or Bow priests have no altar, at least in the summer rain retreats. Instead, the chief, Elder Brother, visits the four shrines of the War gods, one each day (Bunzel 4:663). I conclude that the following ceremony is a ceremony of the Rain society of the North, i.e., of the Town chieftaincy. The reference to the recent installation of an assistant in the chieftaincy supports this construction.

† From Stevenson 2:173–78. The summer retreat as far as it is described is like the winter retreat, plus the rite of rolling the thunder stones (*ibid.*, 179).

‡ This is a day and night ceremonial; but the day time appears to be merely one of general preparation, which was not observed by Stevenson.

§ Of these, four belong to the kinsmen of the society members, the other four, presumably, to the members themselves, not as Rain society members, but as members of curing societies.

nal points and the world, and covered with strings of beads, rest two medicine bowls.

After bathing his hands in meal, Naiuchi, the chief, removes the supreme fetishes of rain and seed from their bowl, and with the greatest reverence places them on the cloud terrace in front of the corn fetish. Later he picks up the fetishes and, holding them together with the clasped hands of the assistant lately installed in the chieftaincy (see p. 596), makes a long prayer which is repeated by the other two assistants. This completes the installation.

The woman assistant brings a bowl of water from which six gourdfuls are dipped into each bowl. Into one of the bowls Naiuchi sprinkles meal, dropping six stone fetishes, one by one, into the water, and praying to the rain beings of the six directions (Uwanami). An assistant sprinkles a powdered root on the water in the other bowl. Naiuchi whirls the whizzer, while the assistant whips the powder into suds. An assistant plays the flute. Naiuchi dips his two eagle feathers into the water and asperses the altar. Again he whirls the whizzer while the flute is played, and a rattle is shaken, a rattle of shells hung to a befeathered crook stick. An assistant constantly sprinkles meal over the meal line, praying to the rain beings to enter and pass up the line. The following invocation is from the summer rain priest prayer recorded by Bunzel.[55]

> This day
> With the flesh of the white corn,
> Prayer-meal, commissioned with our prayer,
> This day with prayer-meal
> Four times we shall spread out the mist blanket.*
> We shall fashion the house of massed clouds,
> We shall fashion the life-giving road,
> Four times we shall fashion your spring.†
> This day,
> My father,
> My mother,‡

* The meal painting on the altar.—R. L. B.

† Terrace cloud design, meal road, medicine bowl.—E. C. P.

‡ Rain fetish and seed fetish possessed by every rain society.

Four times I shall set you down quietly.
Four times you will sit down quietly.
Holding all your world,
Holding all your people,
Perpetuating your rite had since the first beginning,
You will sit down quietly among us.
When you have sat down,
At your back,
At your feet,
We shall sit down beside you.
Desiring your waters,
Keeping your days for this
We shall pass our days.
Our fathers,
Rain-maker priests,
Rain-maker pekwins,
From wherever you abide permanently
You will make your roads come forth.
To the one whom you call father,
To the one whom you call mother,
Four times with all your waters
To us your mother,
Your fathers,
You will come.
In order that you may thus come to us,
Our father,
Our mother,
Perpetuating your rite had since the first beginning,
This one* sits quietly here.

At the rising of the Morning star a prayer-stick bundle is carried by an assistant to a field belonging to Naiuchi. Another assistant goes along to whirl the whizzer. Each carries a netted gourd bottle with prayer-feathers attached. Meal is sprinkled in an excavation for the prayer-sticks which are placed facing the east. From a spring the two gourds are filled to be emptied into bowls on the altar.

Officiating there have been four men and one woman. The families of all these have been present. Now there is singing by all, including the women present. The women have contributed to the altar corn on the ear and grains of corn in bowls, neck-

* The sacred bundle, rain fetish and seed fetish.

laces and bangles made of meal, and shoots of peach trees with balls of meal to imitate peaches. All these are now waved up and down to song, after which Naiuchi prays, and the various contributions are removed to another part of the room.*

The suds-maker pushes his bowl forward to a group of women, and each takes a handful of suds and rubs it first on her chest, then over arms and legs. Then the bowl is carried around the room for all to perform the rite. Now the medicine bowl is carried around and from a shell a drink is given to all present, concluding with the society members.

The altar is dismantled. The corn-ear fetishes are replaced in their basket and the supreme fetishes, in their bowl, each first wrapped in a piece of cotton cloth, then in buckskin, then carefully tied. From each fetish particles of meal have been carefully blown off. The meal and pollen of the altar-painting are swept up, and an assistant carries it to the river. Heads are washed by the woman member, "their sister." Food is served to all present, bits being thrown into the fire as an offering.

Ceremony for Snow, also Initiation, by the Thle'wekwe or Wood Society† of Zuni‡

Each morning at dawn the members sprinkle meal and pray on the society housetop. The men go to the river to bathe, the women and children bathe on the housetop. After the bath the first four mornings an emetic is taken, medicine boiled by two old women members. The members eat breakfast, abstaining from sweets—peaches, squash, and beans—and from coffee. During the day women members go to their homes to cook for the society, men members make prayer-sticks. Members may

* The contributions are said by Stevenson to be given to the society members. The significance of their display on the altar she fails to appreciate. It is undoubtedly a rite for increase, similar to that performed at Rain society altars during the winter solstice ceremonial.

† From Stevenson 2:452–82. She observed parts of this ceremony, early in January, 1892.

‡ Participated in also by the War chiefs, the stick-swallowers of the Big Firebrand society, by the clan mothers, by one of the paramount Rain chiefs, by kiva choirs, and by kachina burlesques.

not be touched by nonmembers, contact involves initiation into the society. On the first day each man makes six prayer-sticks, one for each of the two fetishes of the society, *thleetone* and *muetone* for snow (Crane clan), three for deceased members, and one for the kachina.

The first four days besides prayer-stick-making, there are early morning dancing and stick-swallowing on the housetop, and dancing again at sunset and at night. On the third day toward sunset the warrior of the society visits the Big Firebrand society and, accompanied by members of that society, returns to the house of the Thle'wekwe, where the Big Firebrand people dance and swallow their sticks. A Thle'wekwe man visits the house of the Rain chief of the West to receive a prayer-stick. The chief and the warrior of the Thle'wekwe and six members, all of the Crane clan, go to the Crane clan house where the *thleetone* of the society is kept,[56] and each man makes eight prayer-sticks for the Cloud people and each woman the cotton loops which represent a blanket. All these they carry to their society room together with the *thleetone* and two small bows and arrows kept with it and two stone fetishes. Now the altar is set up. A prayer-stick bundle is made, including the cotton loops and the Rain chief's prayer-stick, and carried to the society's spring, by a member who also carries a gourd bottle. He is led out for a short distance by the society chief. The chief's face is whitened with meal, in his hair are a downy eagle feather and a towhee-wing feather, he wears a black cloth kilt, and he carries a corn-ear fetish and a bowl from which he sprinkles meal on the trail. There follow in single file four members, representing Mountain Lion, Bear, Badger, and Wolf. Each carries his swallowing-stick and eight prayer-sticks. (Downy feathers are attached to the tips of the stiff feathers.) Bear and Badger are impersonated by a Bear clansman and a Badger clansman.

At the spring, the prayer-stick bundle is laid down on a rock and sprinkled with meal. The gourd carrier "smokes" the bundle, praying for cold rains and snows. What is left of a cane cigarette is stuck in the bundle, which is sunk in the middle of the spring. Thence it will be fetched by the deceased members of the society, the society ghosts. The gourd bottle is filled.

This afternoon six War society members carry prayer-stick standards to the room of the Thle'wekwe society. There is a feast for which corn has been ground in the houses of the godfathers and of the initiates.

This night as well as the next, the society goes to dance in the houses where the Muwaiye dance is being rehearsed.

On the fourth evening the initiates are taken by their godfathers to the society's room, where the emetic is given. During the first song all remain seated, the women members and the initiates sitting with fingers imbricated. A bit of medicine root is placed in the mouth of the godfather and, taking the ancient stick of the first chief of the society, he leads the initiate into the middle of the room where they dance, the godfather swallowing the stick. Then he spits the medicine into the mouth of the initiate and gives him the stick to swallow. At daylight the initiate goes to the house of his godfather to have his head washed; he is given food. The woman who does the washing accompanies the initiate to his house, bearing the wash bowl, as a gift.

At daylight on the fifth morning the prayer-stick standards are placed on the roof of the society room by the chief, and a line of meal is laid around the roof. The chief takes a position in front of the altar. In his left hand he holds his swallowing-stick, with his right hand he drops fetish stones into the medicine bowl. The men members sing. From several small medicine bags the chief drops pinches of plant medicine into the bowl. From the gourd bottle he pours water into the bowl, six times. Eight eagle feathers are laid across the bowl, their tips to the east, and sprinkled with corn pollen. All take a drink of medicine-water. The chief places the *thleetone* in the hands of a girl, her hands having been rubbed with meal. The girl goes to the court, walking in single file between two men each carrying a bow and arrows. The three are joined by four girls, each carrying the *muetone* or snow fetish of her clan, Crane, Corn (Ky'anakwe), Badger, or Mustard.

In the court are two ornate boxes, with six notched sticks and deer-leg bones. At one corner a piece of spruce is placed by the medicine chief of the Thle'wekwe, prayed over and sprinkled with meal. The fetish-bearers stand in line before the boxes, facing east, the men with bows and arrows standing on either side of the society fetish-bearer. These men and the girl fetish-bearers throw meal before them as they take up their positions. Behind the boxes sit three members of Ohewa kiva to play on the notched sticks and sing the songs which are known only to Ohewa kiva members. Each musician wears on both hands high lion or bear paw mittens. The girl fetish-bearers and the men with bows and arrows move the fetishes and the bows and arrows up and down in time with the music. At the close the singers breathe from the deer bones, and a basket of meal is passed to them to breathe from. The fetish-bearers leave the court, to be replaced by a fresh set who repeat the dance.

Now the Thle'wekwe enter the court. The men are nude, their breasts streaked with yellow, and their forearms, hands, feet, and legs halfway to the calf, yellow. They wear a black kilt, a yucca headband, and in their hair a downy eagle feather, red for members of the medicine order. The drummer proceeds, followed by the leader, a woman, who carries the corn fetish and a basket of meal which she sprinkles before her. She is followed by the society chief and his "speaker," by the retired chief, and by the warrior of the society. The members hold a rattle in the right hand and their swallowing-stick in the left. In single file they make a circuit around the boxes, singing and stepping high. The chief leaves the lines as he passes south of the boxes, and dancing face to the east he swallows his stick. Then he returns to the line, his position taken by the next to swallow the stick. Some members run two sticks down their throat at the same time. Each godfather is followed by his children and if a "child" fails to get the stick down, his father substitutes.

Returning to their room, the society members stand about the altar sand-painting of Knife-Wing and breathe from their thumbs. A woman member brushes up the sand of the picture and places it in a blanket thrown over the left arm of a male member for him to take to the society spring. The society's root medicine and a prayer-feather are also deposited in the spring. "Go to your home above!" says the depositor, addressing Knife-Wing.

The society breakfasts. About half-past nine the chief goes alone to the court to swallow his stick. He makes a circuit, faces north and swallows the stick, repeating as he faces west, south, and east. Facing east, he swallows also for the zenith and nadir. Each time before swallowing he stamps repeatedly. He repeats the ritual for the six directions, sprinkles meal to the east with prayer, and leaves the court. The musicians breathe from the deer bones.

Now the prayer-stick standards on the roof of the society room are gathered up and taken to the War society. The War chief, carrying his stick of office, and six warriors, each carrying one of the prayer-stick standards, enter the court to form a dance circle. As they move around with slow even step they wave the standards up and down. Their circle is joined by people at large who clasp hands, persons next to a standard-bearer clasping the standard below the hand of the bearer. Two men dance chiefs and two women dance chiefs have collected the dancers.

Now the Thle'wekwe enter to dance in circuit and swallow their sticks as they pass by the sacrosanct boxes. They make six circuits. After the last the chief steps in front of the boxes and prays. During his prayer the others hold their sticks point upward, and at the close all breathe from their stick.

The stick-swallowing order of the Big Firebrand society enters, as the Thle'wekwe withdraw. Two women members of Thle'wekwe return to collect the basket of meal under the box, which is to be deposited as an offering at Matsakya.

The Big Firebrand society dance, leave the court, and return to dance again. This time as they dance, the chief and the warrior of the Thle'wekwe pass within the dance circle and pray. The chief proceeds to face north and swallow his stick and then to face west and swallow the stick of the first chief of the society. The warrior is carrying six other swords in a quiver. In turn he hands them to the chief who runs to each of the cardinal points, stamps and hoots and swallows a stick. The Big Firebrand society dance concludes, their place to be taken, even before the Thle'wekwe chief and warrior have concluded their ritual, by the circling dancers of the War society and others.

The warrior of the Thle'wekwe reappears in the court, wearing a grotesque mask and acting the buffoon.

Six Thle'wekwe members appear carrying willow switches. The initiates who have been sitting in the court start away on a run, after waving a prayer-feather around their head and throwing it on the ground. The initiates are followed by the "catchers" and then by those with switches who use their switches on spectators as well as on initiates.

In the society room stand the society members and the members of the clan of each ceremonial father or sponsor as well as members of his paternal clan. The gifts of the sponsors are now presented to the initiates, a ceremonial kilt to the man, a ceremonial blanket to the woman, after the society chief and the retired chief have removed the prayer-feathers tied to the gifts and fastened them in the hair of the initiates. Prayer-sticks and four ears of corn are also presented to each initiate. The chief passes first the society fetish and then his swallowing-stick four times before the lips, heart, right shoulder, head, and left shoulder of each initiate. In turn each member swallows his stick and then passes it over the initiate. A feast follows.

Meanwhile the Big Firebrand society is dancing in the court, four times, the circle dancers filling in the intervals. At the close the chiefs of the circle dance carry the prayer-stick standards to the roof of the Thle'wekwe room. A member now goes to the court, and in the northwest corner makes two crosses in meal, a disk of meal on each cross. The two boxes are turned bottom up. Two society members who are Bear clansmen sprinkle meal upon the notched sticks and deer bones, now lying inside the boxes. Stooping before the meal crosses, each man places the small round basket he carries on the meal disk. Resting the notched sticks on the basket he runs the deer bone over the sticks outward thirty-two times, then toward himself thirty-two times. Back of these men stand the male members of the society together with the initiates holding their prayer-sticks and ears of corn. The society members begin to sing, the Bear clansmen standing in front of them, notched sticks and deer bones and basket in their hands moved to the rhythm of the song. In come the girl fetish-bearers in line with Muchailihänona, a man of the Dogwood clan, as their meal-sprinkling leader. His face is whitened with meal, a downy eagle feather and parrot feathers are in his hair, and he wears a kilt. He carries a black bowl-shaped basket, hung by three strings to a slender stick, to which a prayer-feather is tied. The basket is heaped with corn meal, over the top a cross in corn pollen, within a circle of pollen. The line advances, halts, faces west, advances to the north, halts, and faces south.

In come the Muwaiye,* dancing sidewise. The man carries his corn-ear fetish, the two girls carry feathered wands, the base wrapped with cotton and containing seeds. The sticks are painted white, the feathers are duck. (As pictured, see Stevenson 2: Pl. CXII, these look much like Hopi winter solstice prayer-sticks.)† The Muwaiye are followed by a choir of about one hundred men from Chupawa kiva.

The fetish-bearers encircle the boxes, four times, sprinkling meal. They leave the court, carrying the fetishes to a Badger clan house where the old women trustees of the fetishes receive them. The fetishes are placed in baskets in the middle of the room. Muchailihänona and the girls each carries a pinch of meal in the left hand four times around the head and sprinkles it over the fetishes. Failure to sprinkle would cause one trouble from excrescences and swellings. (A discharming rite, and presumably swelling is the infliction cured, as caused, by these fetishes.)

---

* Two girls and a boy, *all virgins*, appointed by the Town chief. Named from bending movements of the dance which reminds us of that of the Shake girls in the Scalp ceremony.

† There are other Hopi-like features in this ceremony: close relationship with clans; use of prayer-feathers; medicine-making comparable with that in Hopi war ceremony, and discharming against the sickness caused and cured by the society, sore throat or, by the snow fetishes, swellings or growths, all characteristic war society ailments. Knife-Wing is to be identified of course with Kwatoko, and the Stars (Pleiades and Orion) are addressed, as by the Hopi War chief.

Now with the right hand the fetishes are sprinkled with a prayer for rains (? winter rains or snow).

In the court the Muwaiye encircle the boxes, four times, to the singing of the kiva choir. Thence they dance to the house where the fetishes are. The bluebird prayer-feathers in the hair of the Muwaiye are tied to the society wands. They perform the discharming meal-sprinkling rite and the rite of sprinkling for rain. People from outside come in to perform the two rites.

This evening a small group of burlesque Hemishikwe kachina come in to dance in the society room and in the room of the fetishes. In the society room there is a woman's dance. First the women, three at a time, stand by the initiates, clasping their hands, the forearms held upward. Behind the initiates stand the "catchers," their hands on the shoulders of the initiates which they move slightly to right and left. The successive groups of women stand dancing in two lines, the upper arms extended, the forearms upward. They dance to the east, and then to the west. Between the lines dance the society members swallowing their sticks. At the rise of the Morning star the dancing concludes.

The society proceeds to the room of the fetishes. The four fetishes are lifted from their baskets by their guardians, the old women, and handed to their bearers, and the society chief hands the society fetish to a woman society member. Two men with bows and arrows join the line of women. The initiates face the line, the wives of their ceremonial fathers standing behind them and shoving them slightly to right or left by a hand on the shoulder. The notched sticks are played, and the fetishes waved downward, as snow and rain would fall. At sunrise the singing ceases. The fetishes are handed to their trustees and placed on the floor for the society chief to pray over. Then their trustees take them to the houses where they are kept, the Muwaiye carrying the feathered sticks, two sticks being kept with each fetish. The society chief carries the society fetish to the society room. He removes the eagle feathers from across the medicine bowl and with a shell gives a drink to all the household. Everyone performs the discharming rite with meal, and then sprinkles meal on the fetish. Clanswomen of the initiates and women of their paternal clans bring in bowls of food. To the deceased members of the society food is offered. All eat.

The society chief carries the society fetish to the Crane clan house where it is kept. The blades of the swallowing-sticks he carries in a mountain-lion skin sack to his own house; the basket and stick of Muchailihänona, the bear-feet skins, the stone fetishes, and the stick handles are kept in a storage room of the society's house. The standards are deposited at the four War god shrines of the cardinal points by the Warrior society members who are members of the Thle'wekwe society. The prayer-feathers worn by the chiefs acting for the Warrior society and for the Muwaiye are made into prayer-sticks and planted in the fields, those of the Warrior society for deceased members of the society, those of the Muwaiye for the fetish.

Four days later each godfather dresses a sheep for a feast for his "child," and the family of the initiate grind meal, etc., for the godfather. The initiate accompanies his "father" east of town and deposits his prayer-sticks to the deceased members of the society. On his return his head is washed by the women of the household of his godfather and a feast is given by the household. The ears of corn given to the initiate are kept for seed corn.

FLUTE CEREMONY OF WALPI, AUGUST 5–13, 1892[57]

At sunrise the standard which is composed of two prayer-sticks, male and female, each painted with a lightning design, is tied to the ladder of the maternal house of the Horn clan, by the Flute society chief.* He casts prayer-meal on the standard and toward the Sun. At sunset he will bring in the standard. A daily ritual.

In the "Flute house" chamber the Directions altar is laid: on the sand-covered floor, the six meal lines, the bowl at the center, and radiating from it the ears of corn, each colored ear laid in its proper color-direction, also at each direction an aspergill or cotton-bound, pollen-filled reed, a bird skin of the proper color, and

---

* He is also by birth and by right of his ceremony Horn clan chief and by selection Town chief.

a pebble supposedly of the proper color. Flute chief fills the
bowl with water, pouring it with a gourd which is lowered from
each direction.

Four chiefs—Horn clan, Crier chief of the Snake clan, Bear
clan, Patki clan—gather around the altar, their hair flowing, and
naked save for breechcloth. They smoke, exchanging terms of
relationship. As meal is sprinkled and pollen from the reed is
shaken into the water bowl, and stones, skins, and aspergills are
dipped, the chiefs sing and shake their rattles, gourd rattles and
a special "moisture rattle" of disks representing the four lower
worlds and of olivella shells to sound like the commotion of the
waters at the place of Emergence.

The corn ears are laid across the water bowl. The water is
aspersed in the directions; then whistled into, the bird call. With
a quartz crystal a sun ray is refracted into the bowl.

After this altar is dismantled the chiefs make prayer-feathers
and set up part of the main altar consisting of the three corn-ear
fetishes, the Horn, Snake, and Bear *tiponi*, which are bedded in
prayer-meal on a sand ridge, in line, with a road prayer-feather
leading from the Snake *tiponi* to the southeast. Behind the
tiponi is a large store of blue corn ears. The basket of prayer-
feathers is set in front. Follow smoking, prayers, songs, and
about noon the depositor, the Sand chief, anoints himself with
honey, has a prayer-feather fastened in his forelock, and sets
forth on a directional circuit to put down the prayer-feathers.
Like prayer-feathers are made, consecrated, and deposited each
day, in narrowing circuits, as the Clouds approach the mesa.

About 9:00 P.M. the evening or night ceremonial begins before
the *tiponi* altar: smoking, prayers, songs; the flute is played, and
on the kiva roof the whizzer is swung; meal is sprinkled on the
altar. The morning Directions altar ritual is performed but once,
but the night ceremonial is repeated for six nights. During this
time the six chiefs (a Patki clan chief and the Sand chief have
joined them) observe continence and taboos on salt and meat;
they fetch food from home and eat it in kiva, after noon and at
sunset. They also sleep in kiva.

On the fourth day the altar is renewed or completed. In a new sand ridge are set Horn, Snake, Bear, and Water-Corn (Patki) *tiponi*. The wooden figurines of Müy'ingwa, god of vegetation and of the nether world, and of Flute Youth and Flute Maid are set out together with clay effigies of the Mountains of the Directions and with painted wooden slabs and painted stone slabs or tiles, two of Locust playing a flute and four of Clouds, these latter brought by the Bear clan chief from a cache in the cliffs. In front of the altar is hung horizontally from the roof a white cotton blanket to which long string prayer-feathers are attached. In front of the blanket hang two sets of crossed sticks which look like prayer-sticks. The sticks represent the sky; the blanket, clouds; the pendent feathers, rain. In front of the altar stretches a parti-colored zone of blue and yellow pollen. On this pollen zone stand four wooden bird figurines, and between them are short lines of dark-blue sand, "footsteps." Guarding the head of the zone is a horned helmet. [Inferably this represents Sho'to-kününgwa, god of lightning; it is his usual headdress. The zone is a cornfield. This interpretation is based on the picture of the Drab Flute society altar at Oraibi figured by Fewkes.[58] Below a large figurine of Lightning spreads a parti-colored field of corn kernels, blue and yellow.*]

This night, during the ceremonial, novices are shown the altar; their initiation begins.[59] At cockcrow two couriers are dispatched to springs by Bear clan chief and Snake clan chief, and return with water-filled gourds which are set in front of the altar. At dawn the Tobacco clan chief who has been filling the pipes rubs meal on the left cheek of everyone present, beginning with the Chief.

At sunrise, fifth day, a new standard is set up, in a clay pedestal on the roof. On sand and pollen trail from altar to roof a series of meal cloud signs are made, and prayer-sticks, cloud tiles, and standard are placed in turn upon them to song and flute. The standard represents the sun (gray foxskin for gray dawn, yellow fox for yellow dawn, and red hair for red light or rays), and this ritual, I surmise, dramatizes either the placing of

---

* Compare the picture of the Aztec Lightning god striking the corn field, head on, in the Nuttall Codex.

the new sun in the sky or the emergence from the sunless lower worlds into the sunlight.

On the afternoon of the seventh day the Chief and most of the male members of the society leave town for an overnight visit to several springs where they deposit the prayer-sticks that have been made the preceding two days. The party halts for an early supper, breaking their fast from meat and salt. At sunset they make camp under a projecting rock called Flute dance house. At the rise of the Morning star the party proceeds to the last spring, listening for omens on the way, deposits prayer-sticks at the edge of the cave or in the center of the water, and fills water gourds, all to song, flute-playing, and whizzing. After being marked with smears of white clay on face and body all put on ceremonial kilts and blankets. The Chief sets down his *tiponi*, makes a long meal trail and spaces on it four cloud designs and prayer-sticks. The party moves from one design to the other, singing and shaking their rattles. Momi, a war functionary, whizzes in the rear. On the return to Walpi this ritual is repeated, four times.*

Meanwhile the war chief or scout of the other party which includes the chiefs of Bear clan, Snake clan, and Patki clan, sallies forth to observe the progress of the incoming party and to report four times to the others in the ceremonial chamber. All smear with white and don ceremonial kilt and blanket. The two groups are to meet at the Break, the narrow cliff-bound entrance into Walpi. A line or bar of meal has been drawn across the trail, closing it. The Flute chief sprinkles meal as he approaches, and, as they reach the meal bar, the party shouts and breaks forth into the same stirring song they have sung at all the halts. From the baskets carried by two maidens Bear chief and Snake chief take up their *tiponi* and Bear chief challenges the newcomers. "Why do you come to my house?"—"I come to live with you."— "I do not want you. You may bring famine or disease to my

---

* In all of this the return of a war party is suggested. Circuits were made around a spring, into which the scalps were cast to wash them and to take omens. If the hair floated toward the east and town, this meant rain, also long life to the scalper, the reverse for hair floating toward the west (Beaglehole 1 : 23).

children."—"No, I bring no disease. I shall get on all right with you."—"If I let you in, you will have to take my place tomorrow in my ceremony."—"All right. I will take your place. I will act as Town chief." After the War chief passes his chief stick along the meal bar, Bear chief rubs the bar away with his foot.

A procession forms to the ceremonial chamber: Flute chief in advance, then a line of the other chiefs, the two maidens and a little boy who has been arrayed like the Snake Youth by the Snake chief, in white kilt with blackened chin, hands, and feet, and lightning-snake in black on limbs and body. Boy and girls have been given prayer-sticks by Flute chief. Within the town the ritual of cloud marks and meal bar is repeated. Women pluck sunflowers from the heads of the Flutes and give the flowers to their children. The rushes and cornstalks carried in the procession are laid on the altar or thrust into the rafters.

Tonight about 2:00 A.M., smoking, prayers, and songs. The positions of Pleiades and Orion are observed, and about 3:00 A.M. all go out to the court to sing or play the flute while a cottonwood bower is erected near the stone-covered cavity which is the place of Emergence in charge of the Bear clan chief. The Bear chief pours water from the medicine bowl into the cavity, and all give him prayer-sticks to deposit. These are addressed to Masauwü to keep him, the god of death, out of the town. It was the Bear clan chief who originally overcame Masauwü.

Early this ninth morning there is a foot race. Late in the afternoon a procession forms for Sun spring. All are decorated with white clay and wear the ceremonial kilt, prayer-feathers in scalp lock. At the spring there is repetition of previous spring and trail ritual, besides the flute is blown into the water at the cardinal points, and the maidens and boy cast the ritual cylinder and annulets on the cloud designs. This trail ritual is repeated before the bower in the court. At the end of the songs all cast prayer-meal over the top of the blanket before the bower where Bear chief is hidden to impersonate Masauwü.

On the tenth morning the altar is dismantled. For four days the boys and girls wrangle for pottery.

Wrangling and racing are for rain; the whole Flute ceremony

is for rain and, through lightning, for fertility. The society also cures for lightning shock and formerly, it may be inferred, for arrow or gunshot wounds, Locust being the patron or medicine.* In theory the ceremony dramatizes the admission of the Horn clan and the passing of the Town chieftaincy from Bear clan to Horn clan; more esoterically or more archaically it dramatizes the Emergence, and still more esoterically or archaically the fertilization of maize by Lightning: a beautiful illustration of the a posteriori character of dramatic interpretation of ceremony typical in North America.[60]

CURING CEREMONIAL

Stephen was himself treated by a Hopi doctor, otherwise it is doubtful if any white person has ever been present throughout a Pueblo cure. All accounts are fragmentary; the most authentic account given me was in 1920 by the sister of the chief of the Shikani society of Laguna, who often assisted at her brother's cures. Accounts from Sia, Cochiti, Isleta, Walpi, and Zuni amplify various techniques—crystal-gazing, witch-fighting, sucking-out, brushing-out, retrieving the "heart." From the condition of the "heart," a grain or grains of corn, the fate of the patient is divined. The "heart" is retrieved at Zuni as elsewhere, and in spite of the highly formalized prayer-language characteristic of Zuni the ritual is probably not very different from that of the typical Keresan society. Among the Keres as at Zuni the kachina of the curing society appear when the patient is to be initiated on the spot, which is done only in very grave sickness.

Dr. White's generalized account for Sia cures describes Keresan society cures everywhere: If a sick person or his family wishes to have a medicine society cure him, his father or near kinsman takes a handful of corn meal to the chief, placing it in his left hand.[61] The chief calls the society together and distributes the meal. The doctors go out and pray with the meal. Unless the patient is critically ill, the society will spend four days, after receiving the meal request, in preparing for the cere-

* The gray or immature locust was associated with the Gray or Drab Flute society (Eggan). Hopi bows were called gray or blue (Beaglehole).

mony. They withdraw to their ceremonial room where they spend most of the time. Each morning they drink herb brew and vomit. They observe continence.

The family of the patient will be preparing, too. They vomit every morning and they observe continence. They spend considerable time getting food ready to feed the doctors and relatives on the night of the cure and to give to the doctors as payment for their services: they grind corn and wheat, bake bread, and butcher a cow or sheep.

On the evening of the fourth day the patient is taken into the chamber of the curing society. The doctors have their sand-painting made, and laid on or near it are their animal and anthropomorphic fetishes, flint knives, bear paws, medicine bowls, and corn-ear fetishes. A War captain armed with bow and arrow stands guard outside the door to keep out witches. The doctors are sitting behind the altar singing when the patient is brought in, walking, or being carried, over a road of meal. The patient is placed next the wall, on the side, but a little to the front, of the sand-painting. The two head War captains sit one on each side of the patient. Close relatives sit at the end of the room opposite the sand-painting.

The doctors sing for a while in order to induce the spirits of the curing animals (mountain lion, bear, badger, wolf, eagle, shrew) to enter the chamber, traveling over the road of meal, and to enter the animal figurines on the sand-painting. Since the doctors work only with supernatural power received from these animal doctors, it is absolutely essential that their spirits be present. A woman society member brings in a bowl of water. It is now time to mix the medicine. A doctor comes out from behind the altar and pours six dipperfuls of water into the bowl, one for each of the six directions, and songs are sung to the spirits of the cardinal points. Then each doctor puts his medicines, powdered herbs from his buckskin bag, into the medicine bowl. The doctors return to their places behind the altar and sing again. After a few songs they request the relatives to go outside for a while.

After a half-hour the relatives return, and the medicine men begin their treatment. They go to the fireplace, rub ashes on their heads, then feel the patient all over: "They are looking for the sickness," i.e., the objects which the witches have "shot" into him. Whenever they find anything, they suck it out: sticks, pebbles, thorns, or rags. After a doctor sucks something out, he spits it into his hand, holds it up so people can see it, then deposits it in a bowl.

After all the doctors have "cured" the patient, they turn their attention to witches. If they discover that they have stolen the patient's heart, they must go out and find it and bring it back. Sometimes they look into the medicine bowl to see if there are any witches around. The doctors who are to go out draw a bear's foreleg on their left arm, put on a necklace of bear claws, hang a reed whistle from their neck by a cord, and pick up a flint knife. They run out looking for witches. Sometimes they fight them: "You can hear them fighting in the dark, hollering." Sometimes a doctor is rendered unconscious; sometimes a witch [image] is captured and brought back into the curing chamber where he is "killed."* Invariably the doctors return with the stolen heart. The "heart" is a ball of rags, in the center of which is a kernel of corn; the corn is the real heart. The doctors unwrap the rags and examine the corn closely. If they find it "burned or moldy," the patient will remain sick or even die. If the corn is unblemished, the patient will get well promptly. In either case he is given the corn to swallow, and a draught from the medicine bowl. All his relatives are given this medicine. Now the patient is taken home, and his mother or close female relative and her "helpers" bring out stews, beans, chili, and bread, and everyone eats. Baskets of flour are brought in, too, and given to the doctors in payment.†

* "They grappled and fought [the Kapina shamans with the witches]. Violently they fought. Then mountain lion, bear, cat and wolf fought [i.e., the shamans as animals or with their power]. Then they killed them all" (Boas 2:67).

† In Laguna tale the pay consists of 24 baskets of meal, 24 pieces of wafer-bread, venison, 4 buckskins, and 4 blankets (Boas 2:68).

The altar is set up in the house of the patient, preferably facing east toward the Sun's house. At the back there is a ridge of moist clay, about two inches high, in which a row of prayer-sticks is set. Parallel is a line of meal on which the corn fetishes stand. Up to them leads a line of meal with four cross-lines, the "road." Near by are the medicine bowl and a bear's paw, and farther out lie four eagle-wing feathers on a piece of buckskin.

Giwire, the doctor, is nude save for breechcloth. Across his nose are two lines of red and two more across his lips. There are four vertical lines on each side of his face. He is painted like Ma·sewi, "because it is through Ma·sewi he hopes for success."† His hair is tied in a top knot, and over the fontanelle is painted a red cross "to keep away witches."

An assistant holds a crystal to the light, and Giwire goes about the room as in a daze, as if searching for the patient's heart which has been stolen by a witch animal. The ceremony itself is called "going after" [the patient's heart]. As his assistant sings, Giwire sucks the patient in different places. Then, having rubbed ashes on his body against the witches, and on the calves of his legs so as not to tire, with the bear paw on the left hand and a flint knife in the right, Giwire rushes outdoors, slashing in the air with his flint, against the witches. To protect him, two War captains with bows and arrows follow, also a kinsman with a gun. Giwire is an old man, but he runs so fast that his companions can hardly keep up with him. He may go to the river for the heart—a stolen heart is usually found in the riverbank, or he may dig somewhere else, with his bear paw. In one notable case Giwire dug up his patient's heart under a cedar.

Returning to the house of the patient, Giwire creeps in on hands and knees, clasping the "heart" in the bear paw. The

---

* From Parsons 20:118–22. Compare Boas 2:64–68. In this text account the stolen heart is retrieved by the Kapina society. For Acoma, compare White 2:121.

† That is, his patron or power is Ma·sewi. Giwire's sister, the informant, always referred to Ma·sewi as the son of Earth Mother and as a single personage, not one of the War Brothers.

War captains take the "heart" from him, his behavior being so violent that they have to hold him down. Then he stiffens into a kind of catalepsy, and his kinswomen have to massage him back to consciousness. They rub him with ashes. No matter how distressing his condition, his people may not cry; if they cry he might die.*

After Giwire comes to, he is given warm water to drink, and he goes out and vomits. Returning, he takes from the altar the eagle feathers and with them rolls up to the patient the "heart," three or four grains of corn† wrapped, one by one, in red cloth, bound with cotton. He undoes the tangle, searching out the thickly wrapped grains. If there are three grains only, the patient will die, if four, the patient will recover. In the latter case Giwire would say, "There are enough." He places the four grains on the palm of his right hand and blows as if blowing them back into the body of the patient. He blows toward the left arm of the patient, then toward the right arm, toward the left knee, and the right knee. After this, in a shell, he gives the patient the four grains of corn to swallow together with medicine from the bowl on the altar. In conclusion, the kinswomen of Giwire wash the head of the patient.‡

AT COCHITI[62]

A relative of the patient invites a doctor to cure by carrying him shell or corn meal or corn pollen wrapped in cornhusk, saying, "We come to summon you, Father, because the sick man believes that you and your Mother [Corn mother] will give him good health and long life. In four days we shall expect you. We hope that our Mother will work well the night you come to cure the sick man whose name is Mitch of the Corn clan."

On the fourth night the patient is carried to the room of the doctors where their corn fetishes (altar) are set out. The patient

---

* "If you should cry, there would be trouble," says the Kapina chief to the brother of the patient. Nobody may cry (Boas 2:58, 67).

† Yellow, blue, red, and white (Boas 2:68).

‡ And give him or her a shirt or dress (Boas 2:68) as is customary for sponsors or godparents.

is carried in over the meal line or road to the altar. The doctors asperse their corn fetishes from their medicine bowl. They brush the patient with their eagle feathers, and, striking the feather in the left hand with the feather in the right, they throw the evil they have caught to the north, west, south, east, above, and below.

"His father" looks into a translucent stone, to discover the witches. He goes out in pursuit, searching for the witch-stolen heart of the patient. He runs and hits out as he runs, he goes to the river where witches are wont to hide. The witches may appear as giants, their hands and arms black, or hands and legs dark red. The doctors fight with averted faces; for the witch giants try to make them breathe in their breath. War captains and Fiscales, holding images of mountain lion and bear for protection, will go forth to look for the doctors, and find them somewhere, perhaps in the church, exhausted.

The doctors return, "his father" having secured from the witches the rag doll which represents the patient and on which the witches had practiced the torments they desired their victim to experience. The doctor tears off from the doll a piece of the cloth, burns it, and envelops the patient in the smoke. He repeats this, throwing the ashes into a bowl, until a grain of white corn is discovered. This is the witch-stolen heart of the patient. Looking at the grain, the doctor may say, "It is still good."— "Good! Good!" exclaim the others. The patient is given the corn kernel in a drink of medicine water.

The doctor approaches the patient and sucks at the affected part of his body. Suddenly the doctor will fall down, unconscious. The assistants, drawing on their left forearm a bear's leg, will massage the doctor back to consciousness and support him while he vomits the stones, bones, cactus or thistle points, the ants or snakes sent into the patient's body.

The doctor picks up his corn-ear fetish, and those present breathe from it. He prays, "Take the breath of our Mother, receive life and health! It is true that my breath is without power, but the Mothers give me theirs, and I send it to you. Our Mother holds us in her heart," he says as he moves the fetish from his heart toward those present. With his cane the War captain or representative of Masewa makes the same motion or "benediction," as Father Dumarest, the Franciscan, describes it, not altogether improperly.

All feast on what the kinswomen of the patient contribute, the officers and doctors taking away with them what is left, and "his father" getting a double portion.

THE GIANT SOCIETY OF SIA CURES FOR ANT SICKNESS[63]

This four-day ceremony is being conducted to cure a little boy of sore throat, an ant-caused sickness; the boy urinated over the ants' house, and they entered his body and settled in his throat. The first night of the treatment a Hopi blanket is spread in front of the altar sand-painting, and from the edge nearest the painting the assistant chief sprinkles a line of meal to the white-bear image standing foremost on the painting, thence across the blanket and along the floor to the door, a road for patient and for White Bear.

After the child has been carried in and seated upon a stool on the blanket, the meal basket is passed, and he throws a pinch from it toward the altar. The singing begins, the doctors holding eagle feathers and a bundle of straws in their left hand and a rattle in their right. At the close of the first song each breathes in from feathers and straws. The song is broken by an animal call, to Mountain Lion, to give them power over the angry ants. After the second song the chief blows first on the right side of the patient, then on his back, his left side, and his breast. Two shamans breathe from their eagle feathers and straws, and, dipping them into the medicine water, each extends his feathers to the patient to breathe from. The chief dips his feathers and passes the tips through the mouth of each shaman, dipping each time. Now all but the chief begin to dance near the altar, gesticulating in great excitement and blowing upon the reed whistles of their bear-claw necklaces. With their feathers they asperse the altar, touching the animal images with their feathers and then breathing from their feathers. All stand around the patient; with their left hand they wave their feathers and straws around him and pass them down his body, striking the feathers and straws with the rattle in their right hand. As the feathers and straws are passed down, ants are supposed to be thereby brushed off. Actually tiny pebbles drop to the ground. This brushing-down is repeated six times. Then the patient is backed off the blankets over the line of meal, and given a pinch of meal to sprinkle on the extracted ants. All sprinkle meal on the blanket, the chief gathers it up by the corners, waves it around the head of the patient, and with it leaves the room. On his return, he waves the folded blanket twice toward the fetishes and toward himself, passes it twice around the patient's head and lays it upon the bear-leg on the altar. The patient is led up to the fetishes to sprinkle them with meal, and is then carried to the entrance where his mother awaits him. Supper follows.

A TREATMENT BY YELLOW BEAR OF THE HOPI POBOSHWĬMKYA, IN 1894[64]

Yellow Bear came in to see me, saying he had heard I had been ill for some time, and expressed kindly sympathy. Wĕ'hĕ and Tanshi were also in my quarters at the time, and Yellow Bear sat down and smoked and in a friendly way inquired concerning my illness. As well as my hoarseness permitted, I told him, and in response to his inquiries told him that I had taken some American medicine, and some herb drinks that Ma'shai had brought me. He then asked if I would not like him to look and see what ailed me; this not at all in a solicitous manner, but rather as a friendly suggestion. Wĕ'hĕ urged me to make the request, and as it occurred to me that I might thus have an opportunity of seeing a new phase of the Poboshtü methods, I complied, but I was in a listless, half-torpid condition, not at all in good plight for observing with accuracy.

As a preliminary, a gift of nominal value must always be made to the Hopi mediciner before he begins, usually followed by more substantial gifts after he has finished; but, differing from the Navaho, the Hopi mediciner assumes the utmost indifference on this point, and it is considered ill mannered to discuss gifts or their values before him. In very marked contrast to the Navaho, the Hopi mediciner takes whatever gifts are offered him without a single comment. A piece of cloth or calico stuff is usually the first gift, and, as I had none in my quarters, Wĕ'hĕ ran to his own house and returned with a few yards of calico which I then gave to Yellow Bear.

To begin with, he got one of my bowls and, filling it nearly full of water, placed it between me and the fire before which I was lying on a pallet, and then sat down beside me. Opening a small pouch that he constantly wears, he took out four small quartz and other pebbles, typical of the emblematic cardinal colors; although I could not perceive much difference between them, they represented yellow for the northwest, blue for the southwest, red for the southeast, and white for the northeast. Beginning with the yellow pebble, he dropped them into the bowl, one at a time, with low muttered prayers to Bear, Badger, Porcupine—these three are called brothers—and to Horned Toad and Broad Star (Aldebaran).

The prayers were to this effect: "Steve, our friend, lies here ill and speechless, maybe you will show me what the ill is, maybe you will show me what has cut off his voice." He then crushed a small fragment of dry herb root between his fingers and sprinkled it upon the surface of the water in the bowl, and this he told me made the charm water.

He now took from his pouch a beautiful willow-leaf-shaped knife, about three inches long, made of a pale green stone of compact texture, and laid it on the pallet close to my left side. He then drew from his pouch an irregular shaped lump of quartz crystal, about the size of a walnut, retaining it in his hand. "Now," said he to me, "take off your shirt and sit up and I will try to see what makes you ill." Taking the crystal between finger and thumb, sometimes one hand sometimes the other, he placed it close to his eye and looked intently at me. Then he would hold the crystal at arm's length toward me. Then he would bend over so as to bring the crystal close up to me, and thus he swayed back and forth, in silence, occasionally making passes with his arms to and fro and toward me, for about four or five minutes. Suddenly he reached over me and pressed the crystal against my right breast, and just upon the region of a quite severe pain, which I had probably described to him, but, whether or no, he located the seat of the pain exactly.

He at once put the crystal in his pouch without a word, and told me to lie down again, and, after I had done so, he took up the pretty green knife and began sawing the skin up and down, i.e., lengthwise, over the spot where he had set the crystal. It was a mere scarification, just enough to draw blood,* which, being effected, he put the knife back in his pouch and sipped a little of the charm water. He then bent over me, and, placing his lips against the wound, he exhaled twice upon it, and the effect was to send an icy chill through me from head to foot. After each exhalation he raised himself on his knees and breathed ostentatiously away from me; he again bent over me, and, placing his lips again on the wound, he inhaled twice, no marked sensation following these inhalations. But after the second time he carried my left hand to his mouth and spat into my palm an abominable-looking, arrow-shaped, headless sort of a centipede. It was about an inch and a quarter long; it was of a dark-brown color and seemed to be covered with a viscid substance; it had no head that I could make out, but its legs certainly moved, and it seemed to be a living insect. "This," said Yellow Bear, "is the sorcerer's arrow." As I understood him, it may come to one through mishap, but usually it is sent (shot) by a sorcerer; it bores through the flesh until it reaches the heart, which it also bores and causes death.

Yellow Bear only permitted me to look at it briefly because it must instantly be carried forth to the cliff edge and there exorcised. On coming in again, he made me drink part of the charm water and gave the rest to my two friends, who sat awe-struck, and, as they afterward confessed, rather badly scared. He then munched between his teeth the dried roots of four herbs,† spitting them into a bowl of cold water, and the com-

---

* "To let out the bad blood," said David of Zuni, about a similar practice of scarification, for fright sickness (Parsons 18:272).

† The fragrant herb root to which Yellow Bear attaches the most importance, and which seems to be a universal panacea, entering into almost all their herb infusions, is called the Bear charm. It is *Aster ericæfolius* (Rothrock).

pound was very fragrant, and somewhat mucilaginous. This he told me to drink from time to time for four days, which I did, and I really received much benefit, but whether from the cold infusion or the sacrification I am still in doubt; at any rate, the pain in my chest ceased from that day.

JUAN OF ISLETA IS CURED AFTER KILLING A BEAR[65]

I was out deer-hunting. I saw a bush, and the leaves were moving. I shot at it. It was a bear. My sister asked the Town Fathers to work for me. They put me alone in my own house for four days. No relation could come in, only a woman assistant brought me food. She never came close to me. On the fourth evening Tutude (Elder Sister, as the chief of the Town Feathers is called) came for me to take me to their house. He spat on me what he was chewing, from my forehead down. His two eagle feathers he waved [anti-sunwise] in front of me three times and then rubbed one feather against the other [slicing motion of discard], cleaning me. He gave me the tips of the two feathers to hold. His hands holding the feathers were crossed, so he unfolded them behind his head, and I was left behind him, still holding the tips of the feathers. This way I followed him to their house. The other people in my house followed us, first my sister, then my father and daughter, then the rest of my relations, in single file. An assistant opened the door and threw a line of pollen from the door through into the next room to the altar. All my relations stayed in the first room as well as the other people who came to see, many of them. We went on into the next room, Father (the chief) set me down in front of the altar. Then he dipped his feathers in the medicine bowl and sprinkled me, and then he circled me with the feathers three times, calling out *truhi'! truhi'! truhi'!* Then he spoke to the others (twelve of them) sitting behind the corn fetishes, and they stood up and came around me. They began to sing and to circle around me three times, each time each passed me, he circled with his feathers and said, *Hae'!* Father gave me the tips of the feathers again and set me by the fireplace. He waved his two feathers to the Mothers (the corn fetishes), and then gave me their breath, moving

the feathers in front of me three times. When he went back to
his seat, the last helper gave him a cigarette. He smoked it in
the directions, then waved it toward the Mothers. Then he said
to his helpers that they were to do all they could for their son,
not to be afraid of anything. He dipped the tips of his feathers
and sprinkled me and said, "My son, do not be afraid! You will
see with your eyes that the bear you killed is still alive and will
come to you. Do not be afraid! He will not do anything to you.
Try to be strong!" From the tips of his feathers he gave me a
taste of the medicine water. He said, "Do not be afraid of anything. That bear was sent by someone who was envious of you
in order to kill you. Where you got scared killing him, there in
that place is half your heart. Do not worry! You will get well.
Just have good thoughts! Ask Weide and Iema'paru (the Corn
Mothers) to get well!"

The doctors came out and stood in a half-circle around the
medicine bowl into which Father was looking to see the place
where I had killed the bear. Then his chief helper picked up the
crystal from the altar, and all the helpers looked into it to find
the envious person, and they got mad and said, A'a'! Father
picked up the flint and made as if to shoot in the direction of the
mountain and toward me. A helper made a meal road for Father
to the door. Outside, Father called the eagle, whistling like an
eagle; and so he got the power of the eagle and flew away.

The War chief called all the people into the room, leaving just
a line to pass through. My father and sister and aunt they gave
a seat near me. The chief helper looked into the medicine bowl.
He looked toward the mountain; he was watching Father as he
traveled, in case he needed help, so he could send him help.
The War chief was advising all the people to wish and hope that
I get good luck and be restored to health. The chief helper took
up from the altar the "sun"* and waved it three times in front
of me. Then he covered me with the sun. He told me not to be
afraid, just to make myself strong. I felt faint, when the sun
covered me, and he shook me. My sister began to cry, and some
of my relations. One of the helpers stood up and advised the
people not to cry, only to wish and hope that I get well.

* This very sacred representation of the Sun was never described.

Within three-quarters of an hour Father was to come back as a bear. (The mountain was twenty-five miles away.) Soon then the bear knocked three times on the door with his paw. The chief helper opened the door and sprinkled pollen from the door to the arrowpoint and on to the altar. The bear followed the pollen line and looked around at the people. Some got scared and covered their face with their hands. I was trying to make myself strong, but I could not stand it; I was feeling faint. I tried to look at him, but my eyes swam, and I felt faint. The bear hit the post of the house, and hit the floor, and stopped and growled. He smelt around the altar and acted as if he was going to spring on me, opening his mouth and growling. I was not afraid of him, but I was feeling faint. The closer he came to me, the madder he acted. When he came up to me he struck at me with his paws, and held my head—the sun was still covering me —and shook me. Then he went back to the altar, and the chief helper sprinkled medicine water on him and then on me. All the time the helpers were singing. Then the bear sat down in front of the stone point, swinging his head, and then three times he did like that [expelled forcibly his breath]. The last time, I saw he threw something out. The chief helper picked it up and looked at it. The bear lay there. The chief helper dipped up some medicine water and brought it to me, and in his hand was something white [? corn]. He said to me, "Do not be afraid! Be strong! I give you this, and you swallow it." I swallowed it, and he gave me the drink. It was that half of my heart. After a little while I felt well, strong.

He smoked in the directions and over the altar. He smoked over the bear. He gave me the cigarette and told me first to smoke in the directions, next to the Mother, next to puff the smoke toward the bear, lastly to swallow the smoke. My father and aunt and sister sprinkled pollen on the bear and thanked him. Also my daughter, who was crying. Now other people might go and sprinkle. Some went, but others were afraid. Two helpers gave me pollen and meal and took me over to the bear. They pushed me toward him, so I would not be afraid. I gave him meal and pollen and thanks for saving me. I took my seat. Then all the helpers stood around the bear, calling *ai! ai!* and cleansing with the feathers and singing. The bear got up, smelling. He came up to me, clapping his paws and growling. The chief helper sprinkled pollen in front of him to the door where he went out. Then the chief helper told all those present what had happened to me, and advised them not to do such a thing to anybody. Some began to cry. The chief helper looked into the bowl, watching for the return of Father. Then he came in. He went up to the altar, drawing in with the feathers, then waving the feathers out to me. He gave me a drink from the medicine bowl with the shell. He asked me how I felt. I felt all right. "Do not worry, do not recall what has happened to you!" He took the sun off my head and the sun closed, and he waved it in front of me. He went to the altar and waved the sun to the people, and everybody waved it in to themselves. He told the people they might go. Now they took apart the altar, and my relations brought food into the room, lots of food; it filled up the house. We gave it to Father, and he, to his helpers, and he told us all to eat together. When we eat together, everything is washed out, clean. After eating, they divided up all the food between the helpers to take home. Then my relations took me home.

PRAYERS AND KACHINA IN ZUNI CURING SOCIETY CEREMONIAL

Since most of the Zuni medicine societies are of the Keresan type, it is probable that their curing ceremonials are like Keresan ceremonials, but there is no complete account of any Zuni cure. We know only that doctors suck out witch-sent objects and that they retrieve a stolen heart. The prayer said by the kinsman of the patient in taking request meal to the doctor expresses belief in bewitchment.

> This day,
> Because of the ill will of the foolish ones,
> Our child wears out his spirit. . . . .
> Our child who has been bewitched
> Because the heart of someone became angry. . . . .
> The power* of the two-hearted one,
> The one who has bewitched our child,

---

* Sawanikä, weapons, also, abstractly, power. There is a double meaning to these lines. The shaman will actually remove from the patient's body foreign

> The foolish one,
> His power they will cause to stand out
> In the daylight of our Sun father.
> Then our child's breath will become well.
> His spirit will become well.[66]

The following initiation prayer-speech recorded by Bunzel and Stevenson's account of ritual performed by kachina are from the ceremonial of the Big Firebrand society whose songs are said to be borrowed from the Navaho.[67] The prayer is probably quite Zuni in character; the kachina performance appears Navaho.

When the patient's sponsor or ceremonial father summons the patient to the society's chamber, he sits down, removing his headband and moccasins, and prays:[68]

> This many are the days
> Since some evil thing
> Made our child sick.
> His breath failed.
> Because of this from among all our fathers,
> Life-giving priests,
> Life-giving pekwins,
> Life-giving bow priests;
> All the society priests,
> Society pekwins,
> Society bow priests,
> Unexpectedly
> The divine ones chose me.
> Their daylight children
> Revealed themselves to you,
> And choosing me,
> You let me know.*
> Taking prayer-meal,
> Far off to the east,†

---

matter which the witch has injected, and which is the direct cause of the sickness. Also, by revealing the means the witch has employed, he strips him of his power. For this reason torture formerly was used to extract confessions from those suspected of witchcraft. If a witch once reveals the source of his power, he becomes helpless. Any prayer or ritual loses its potency when it is told, the power passing to the new owner (Bunzel).

* Referring to the meal request of the patient's kinsman.

† The animal curers, the Beast gods, dwell at Shipapolima, in the east. All curing rituals are oriented toward the east (Bunzel).

With prayers, I made my road go forth.
Where our fathers' road comes in
I passed them on their road. . . . .
Thus anxiously waiting,
We have passed our days.*
Then when all their days were past,†
After our Moon Mother,
At her sacred place,
Still small, appeared,
And now yonder in the east
Standing fully grown makes her days,‡
Now our spring§ children,
Whoever truly desires in his heart to grow old,
Taking prayer-meal,
Taking shell,
Taking corn pollen,
Yonder with prayers
One by one shall make their roads go forth.
Yonder where they have stood since the first beginning
Our fathers,
The forest,
The brush,
Those who have been given domain
Yonder on all the mossy mountains,
There we passed them on their roads.
At the feet of some lucky one,
Offering prayer-meal,
Shells,
Corn pollen,
Even among their sharp fingers
We looked about.
Breaking off the straight green shoots of some lucky one,

* The four days during which the society holds its ceremonies of curing in the home of the patient. The sacred paraphernalia of the society is set up, songs are sung, the Beast gods are invoked, and finally the agency of sickness is withdrawn from the patient. The ceremonies are held for four consecutive nights and last from midnight until dawn (Bunzel).

† The days between the cure and the initiation.

‡ The time is now approaching the full moon. The ceremonies of initiation will begin with the making of prayer-sticks by all members of the society on the day following the visit of the father to the home of the novice (Bunzel).

§ Referring to the bowl of water on the altar which represents the sacred spring and is so called.

We drew them toward us.
Even those standing there quietly,
Holding their long life,
Their old age,
Their waters,
Their seeds,
The divine ones made their roads come hither.
Near by into the house of our fathers,
Our mothers,
The clan of the sun,
Into their house the divine ones brought their road
And there sat down quietly.
This many days,
Anxiously waiting
With us, their children, they passed their days.
And now that their appointed time had come,
Next day,
After our fathers,
Our ancestors,
Those who here had belonged to societies,
The divine ones,
After they first had taken hold of their plume wands,
We of the daylight,
Meeting one another,
With our warm human hands,
Embraced them.
For our fathers,
Our children,
Those who here belonged to societies,
For their ceremony
We shall give our plume wands human form. . . . .
Saying, let it be now,
Taking our child's prayer-meal,
Wherever we think let it be here,
Our Earth Mother
We shall pass on her road.
Offering our plume wands,
We shall make their days.*

* The four-day retreat, which begins when the prayer-sticks are planted shortly before sunset on the day following this speech. The novice has prayer-sticks made for him by his ceremonial father. In the afternoon he is summoned to the ceremonial house of the society to receive them. He then goes with his father and officers of the society to plant in a shrine at Badger place, about two miles southeast of Zuni. From the time of the planting until the conclusion

When there remains a little space,
Ere our Sun Father goes in to sit down at his sacred place
Then our father*
Will spread out his fathers' mist blanket,
Their perfect cloud house he will prepare,
Their rainbow bow he will lay down,
Their lightning arrow he will lay down,
And there will sit down quietly.
Far off from all directions
Our fathers will make their roads come forth.
Making their roads come hither
They will sit down quietly.
Sitting behind them
This many days,
Anxiously waiting
We shall pass our days.
When we reach their appointed time,†
Yonder from all directions
The ones who are our fathers,
Life-giving priests,
Life-giving pekwins,
Life-giving bow priests,
All the Beast priests,
The divine ones,
With no exceptions,
All will make their roads come hither. . . . .
Into a being like themselves
They will transform him.‡
Then sitting among his fathers,
Even at their valuable place,
Throughout a blessed night,

---

of the ceremonies he must do no work, especially lift no heavy weights. He eats and sleeps very little and is untouchable, like one who has had contact with the dead. At the same time other members of the society plant in their fields or at Red Earth and after their supper return with their bedding to the society house for a four nights' retreat. The days are spent in preparation for the great ceremony of the last night (Bunzel).

* The pekwin of the society, who sets up the altar and makes the meal-painting. This is done before the novice is summoned to plant his prayer-sticks (Bunzel).

† The fourth night of the retreat, when the ceremony of initiation takes place.

‡ By painting the face and the body of the novice. There is power inherent in body paint (Bunzel).

With us, their children,
They will come to day.
Next day, when yet a little space remains
Ere our Sun Father
Comes out standing to his sacred place,
Then with that through which our roads are fulfilled,
With clear water,
We shall add to the breath of our child.*
For since our breath is valuable,
Our child
Into his body
Will inhale our breath.
At the very place where he sees our spring
He will sit down as one of us.

In 1891 the Big Firebrand society conducted a cure which Stevenson says she attended.[69] The patient is a man with a swollen throat. Near sunset the kachina patrons of the society, Big Kachina, Shitsu'kĭa, and Kwe'lele, ascend to the roof of the house of the patient. This is the signal for placing the patient on a pallet in the middle of the floor. The kachina stomp and dance on the roof until dusk. The warrior Shitsu'kĭa carries yucca blades in the left hand and a whizzer in the right. Kwe'lele carries yucca in the right hand and fire-making sticks and cedar brand in the left. A woman member of the society makes the road of meal into the chamber and leads down the kachina. In anti-sunwise circuit the kachina circle the patient four times, as the society choir sings. Shitsu'kĭa, taking meal from his belt, runs a line with his four fingers across the patient's body to the waist, beginning at the left shoulder; and Big Kachina, standing before the patient, places his hands to the middle of his own forehead, as he clasps the yucca in both hands and then runs the blades over the meal lines on the patient. The kachina again encircle the patient, Shitsu'kĭa draws the meal lines from the right shoulder across to the waist, and Big Kachina strokes with the yucca. Again they encircle the patient, the lines are drawn from left to right across the knees, which are close together, and

---

* Referring to his ceremonial rebirth at dawn, when his head is washed and he receives his society name.

Big Kachina strokes with the yucca. Marking and stroking are repeated for back, arms, and palms. Big Kachina removes his mask, and the ceremonial father places it on the head of the patient who spits through the small mouth hole. After supper society members take turns impersonating the three kachina. The women members impersonate without mask. All dance. At dawn Kwe'lele makes fire. The burning brand is dipped into the medicine bowl, out of which the patient is given a drink.

The kachina and their woman leader leave the chamber and go to the eastward. On their return they encircle the patient, and Kwe'lele stands with a foot each side of the patient's head. He motions some yucca-tied cakes of bread down the body and makes various passes over the patient with his fire sticks and bread, and finally lays the bread over the heart. The kachina file out of town on to the eastern road, as if going to Shipapolima. The patient eats three pieces of bread and throws a fourth piece to a dog that thus absorbs the sickness.

Each member of the society dips suds on the head of the new member whose head is then thoroughly washed by the wife of his godfather and who receives from his godfather four ears of corn, two prayer-feathers, one for the Sun and one for the Moon, likewise a shirt. A feast follows supplied by the patient's wife or kinswomen who also send gifts of meal to the house of the godparents.

Communal Curing

Sia[70]

Preparations for the communal curing ceremony are quite similar to preparations for the cure of an individual patient: the societies retire to their houses for four days, vomit every morning, observe sexual continence, and get their medicines and paraphernalia ready. On the fourth evening, the night of the ceremony, all the curing societies gather together in one large house. A sand-painting is made and the fetishes laid out. The Town chief sits in the place which would be occupied by the patient if it were an individual curing ceremony. The War captains Ma'sewi and Oyoyewi sit on either side of him. Townspeople crowd into the chamber.

The ceremony opens with songs, invoking the spirits of the animal supernaturals to come in and invest their images. Medicine is mixed in the bowl, water being poured in from the six directions; there is much sprinkling of altar, doctors, and paraphernalia, with medicine water and with meal. Now the doctors come out, one or two at a time, from behind the altar where they have been sitting singing, and go over and "cure" the Town chief; they suck things out of his body and toss them into a bowl. Then the doctors go about among the other people and similarly cure them. Then the doctors look into the medicine bowl "to see if they can see any witches." If witches are seen, some of the doctors arm themselves with their bear paws, bear-claw necklaces, reed whistles, and flint knives and go out to fight. Sometimes they capture a "witch" and bring him back into the chamber where the War captain shoots him with an arrow.*

ISLETA [71]

Were sickness general in town, epidemic, the War chief would call a meeting of all the chiefs and "ask their thoughts"; then he would ask for the power of the Town Fathers and the Laguna Fathers. These would go into their ceremonial houses to stay four days, taking an emetic each morning and fasting from food completely. On the fourth morning in the same house the two groups set their ground altars, the Town Fathers setting theirs first. Each chief has chewed the root which gives power. Moved by this, with his power, the chief calls in from all the directions the fetish animals. A meal road leads from the door to the altar. Over the bowl of water from the river the chief makes a cross with his eagle-wing feathers, stirring the water. Sounds of bear, mountain lion, coyote, snake, eagle, come from the bowl. Duck feathers are put into the bowl, and sounds of ducks playing and flapping their wings are heard. Meanwhile, the assistant shamans or doctors are sitting in line behind the altar, behind the

---

* The witches that are caught and killed similarly at Santo Domingo, San Felipe, and Cochiti are large rag dolls painted and gotten up to look like Koshaire (Dumarest, Pl. 7; White 3:48; White 4:126). Informants refer to the images as if they were living human beings. The Flint shamans at San Felipe are said to eat these witches raw.

Mothers, shaking their gourd rattles and singing. With his stone arrowpoint in his right hand, in his left, his whistle, the chief now whistles into the bowl to call all the powerful animals—Mountain Lion, Bear, Rattlesnake, Eagle, and Badger.

Now the chief will call Lightning and Thunder. He tells the people present to cover their heads lest they be frightened. Thunder is heard, and flashes of lightning may be seen. The chief takes his seat in the middle of the line of doctors, and the War chief gives him a lighted cigarette to smoke in all five directions and on the line of the Mothers. With his power the chief calls Moon and Morning star. All the doctors circulate among those present and with two eagle feathers each brushes out from everybody whatever noxious thing may be inside his body— stick, rag, stone. The chief presents his crystal to the doctors who stand in a half-circle facing him. As they look into the crystal, they see all over the world, whence wind or rain will come, and on what day, what sickness may be imminent, how long the sickness will last, and how to get rid of it. Now the chief starts to call the witch who is the cause of the sickness and who is in hiding at the ends of the world. The chief calls him by singing his song. Every time he sings the witch's song, the witch draws closer to town. Some of the doctors together with the War chief and Kumpa go out to search for the witch while the chief sits near the Mothers, singing to help those who have gone on the witch quest. These spread out in a circle, as on any hunt, and close in on the witch who is so afraid of Kumpa "he does not even move." Sometimes the witch is so strong they cannot move him, and they tell the War chief to shoot him with his bow and arrow. He will shoot him through the body. His power broken, they carry him in. Everybody spits at him. They place him near the meal basket of the altar. The chief tells those present what bad things the witch has been doing, sending sickness or starving the animals. The chief will ask the witch if he is going to stop his bad ways. He will say, "Yes," and that he will keep back the bad and suffer it himself. The chief takes the stone blade from the altar and sticks it into the body of the witch, killing him. Two doctors carry him out and burn him on a pile of wood, i.e., burn his body; his spirit leaves the village to die outside. Outside the ceremonial house he looks like a grown man, inside like a little boy, with feathers in his hair, Comanche fashion. The chief addresses those present, telling them not to worry any more. The sooner they forget the sickness, the sooner it will go. The doctors again brush the people, putting everything they take out of their bodies in a large bowl by the door. The bowl is carried out by two doctors to the ash pile, where they sprinkle its contents with water taken in a shell from the medicine bowl and bury them in a hole (cf. Pl. IX).

KACHINA CEREMONIES AND DANCES

A mask makes a kachina, but a kachina does not make a kachina ceremony, for kachina appear at the winter solstice ceremony or at the ceremony of a curing society, in fact on almost any ceremonial occasion, and almost any impersonation can be converted into a kachina.* It is only when the kachina organization dominates the scene that we may consider the celebration a kachina performance. When the performance stands wholly by itself we account it a "ceremony"; when it is in honor of non-kachina groups such as a Zuni Rain chieftaincy or a Keresan or Hopi society, we account it a "dance," a somewhat arbitrary distinction, which is not native except among Hopi.

Hopi have two kachina ceremonies, Powamu and Nima'n, which include dramatization, group dancing, and altar ritual. At Zuni the curing societies lend their altars, their slab or frame altar, to the kachina, and sing for single dancers. They do this even at the greatest of Zuni kachina celebrations, the Kachina Advent or Shalako. There is no Kachina society altar at Shalako or on any other occasion. Nor is there any kachina altar in the Acoma dramatizations, Kachina attack or Shuracha. In the East the kachina come regularly to dance for the societies after their retreats; at Zuni the kachina dance after the summer solstice pilgrimage to the kachina lake and the first summer rain retreat;

---

* Hopi Buffalo dancers, for example, are given a mask in addition to their great headdress, and become Buffalo kachina. Mishongnovi's Drink Water Girl dancers figure as kachina at Oraibi.

PLATE IX

COMMUNAL CLEANSING, ISLETA

Town Father opening witch bundle with stone point from altar; War chief and helper. (Drawn by towns nan.)

among Hopi a kachina dance follows the abbreviated winter ceremonies of the societies that celebrate in full in summer and early autumn.

Several curing societies have one or more kachina who appear at initiations, at the winter solstice ceremony or at kachina dances (pp. 135, 575). Then several kachina wear the society red feather because conceptually they are associated with a society (Zuni); for example, Coyote kachina who as a hunter is naturally a member of the Hunt or Coyote society.[72] Of course Bear, the curer *par excellence*, when he comes as a kachina in the Mixed dance must wear a red feather.[73] Chakwena Woman wears one, in view of her phallic functions.

In preparation for a kachina dance impersonators may withdraw into kiva or appointed house, four days in advance, to practice songs and dance steps, to prepare masks and costumes, and by emesis and fasting to get into condition, physical and psychical. Generally impersonators sleep at home but remain continent. The night before the dance they may sleep in their ceremonial house. Evening dance practice may begin as much as two or three weeks in advance. The day before the dance, spruce boughs or small trees are fetched from mountain or mesa for dance array or to plant in the dance court.

Sometimes the kachina come out to dance very early in the morning; but usually they dance late in the morning, once or four times before dinner; and then several times in the afternoon. The file of dancers is led into the dance court or to the dance station by warrior (Zuni) or War captain, by clown society chief or member, by a Kachina Father from Powamu society (Hopi), or by any society member (Zuni); in Zuni terms he is their shepherd, making their road, sprinkling meal. Frequently the party comes in from a shrine on the outskirts of town as if coming from a distance. Their "shepherd" or "father" carries his corn fetish in his left hand, his bowl of meal in his right hand. He wears no mask, but under the eyes across his nose runs a line of black paint, kachina way. Around his head a band of yucca and to his scalp lock downy feathers red-stained, as he is a society man. Generally, back and right shoulder are covered by a buck-skin mantle (Pl. X).

The kachina stand in line; with one exception, the Ky'anakwe, there are no circle kachina dances. The dance director in the middle of the line starts the rhythmic stamp by shaking his gourd rattle, and the movement continues a short time without song. During the song, at rhythmic intervals, the dance line or file makes a half or a complete face-about; the song-dance may be repeated on different sides of the dance court. If there are individualized kachinas in the group, they stand out in front of the line or toward one end, dancing a distinctive step. Dance steps or paces of kachina chiefs are still more distinctive; the Salimobia and Ololowi of Zuni prance, the Long Horn group tread ponderously, perhaps it is a bear tread, Long Horn has the bear call. Other kachina chiefs do not dance at all (Zuni, Hopi); they are processional figures. Most kachina groups sing; a few are accompanied by a choir and drummer, or only by a drummer who may be masked. Kachina have characteristic calls but, ex-cepting clowning or burlesque kachina and apart from song or ritual narrative, no speech. They may use pantomime and con-ventionalized gestures expressive of falling rain, of clouds loom-ing, or of plants growing up, whenever these are mentioned in the dance-song.[74]

The characteristic kachina array consists of mask, kilt of embroidered cotton or of buckskin, cotton belt or white belt deeply fringed, fox pelt pendent from belt at the back, elaborate moccasins, fringed, with porcupine quill or skunk fur anklets, or spruce anklets and bare feet, spruce twigs in turquoise-colored leather armbands or pendent from belt. Spruce as trimming or held in hand is "to make the world green" (Zuni).[75] Fringes from armbands with turkey feather or painted buckskin tabs to represent the yellow butterfly which makes people "crazy."[76] The upper body may be nude and painted or shirt or mantle is worn. Bandoleer of buckskin, yucca, cedar berry, beadwork, or ribbon. Arms, hands, legs, and torso may be painted in various designs or colors appropriate to the character of the kachina. From navel to knees is painted white, for the Sun (Zuni).[77] Un-

PLATE X

GOOD KACHINA AND THEIR SOCIETY LEADER, ZUNI

PLATE XI

Kachina Maidens Ascending Hekiapawa Kiva, Zuni

der the eyes and across the nose of every Zuni kachina there is a line of the iridescent black paint[78] called *tsuhapa*, sometimes two lines of black or sometimes two lines of red or smudges of black or red on chin or cheek. (In this way the kachina were painted before they took to wearing masks.)[79] Under the cylindrical mask is a collar or ruff of spruce, fur, or feathers; feathers are worn on top of the head or at the back or in the ears; the more feathers, the more important the kachina.[80] The downy breast feather of the eagle and feathers of parrot or macaw are especially associated with the kachina; the downy eagle feather is the breath of the rain, and the parrot or macaw of the south will bring southerly rains.[81] With the bearded false face or mask to the chin are worn flowing hair, beplumed on top or lengthwise, and necklaces of silver, turquoise, or white bead. "Valuable" kachina wear a great many necklaces, as well as bracelets on both wrists. A turtle shell and antelope- or goat-hoof rattle is gartered below the right knee; there are also worsted garters, sometimes with little bells, falcon bells. In right hand, a gourd rattle.

Kachina "maidens" carry spruce instead of rattle; their hands and bare feet are painted white; their hair is put up on the sides in the huge whorls of the Hopi maiden or in the smaller yarn-bound bunch which was Zuni style. Kachina Maidens or, in Keresan terms, Yellow Women, with rare exceptions (Zuni, Hopi, Jemez),[82] are impersonated by men. They generally form a separate dance line, behind the male impersonations or between them and the wall. Notched-stick players are usually female impersonations (the parts often taken by younger boys) because the rasping is associated with grinding (see Pl. XI).

In his belt, sometimes in his yucca switch, the kachina carries his "heart," a small package of corn kernels of all colors, squash, melon, and sometimes wild seeds.* The impersonator gets the seed from his mother or wife. When a person asks that a dance be repeated, as he sprinkles the dancers with meal he takes from them or usually from the first two or three in line their seed packages.† Before dancing again they must get new "hearts,"

* Seeds of foreign plants, wheat, pumpkin, and cucumber, are not included.
† Acoma kachina carry a seed pouch (? in their belt) (Stirling).

for these give them their "power." Kachina dance visits to the
Hopi were discontinued about 1900* because, they said at Zuni,
it was learned that the exchange Hopi visitors carried no seeds
in their belts, as did the Zuni visitors to the Hopi. It was a one-
sided deal.[83]

In addition to their regular dance, kachina will put on little
dramatic acts or will engage in farces with the clowns who attend
on them, valeting them, smoothing their dancing ground, also
mimicking or burlesquing them, sometimes dancing with them
in line. Usually the kachina pay no attention to the clowns; the
most sacrosanct kachina never do; but others, light-weight
kachina like the Hopi Navaho kachina or even the Mixed
kachina, will carry on pantomime or roughhouse with the
clowns,[84] drenching or flogging them or, as Rabbit or Dog, carrying on a mock hunt or baiting a real dog. At Zuni He'he'a will
play a kind of hide-and-seek with the Koyemshi, and throw
pepper to make them sneeze.[85] O'wiwi, the grandfather of the
Mahedinasha kachina, will perform a little hunt ritual in the
court after the dancers have left. He sets out his prey-animal
fetishes on a line of meal; asking them which way to go, he
searches for deer tracks. He pretends he has caught a deer, skins
it, and rubs blood on the noses of his animals.[86] In the recently
introduced Sioux dance the buffalo impersonation is killed by a
warrior kachina.[87] In his rabbit-skin mask Masauwü plays various comedies of death with laborers in the fields or burlesquers in
the court.

Gift-bringing kachina will distribute their gifts of corn,
melons, peaches, and bread, or of little bows and arrows and
"dolls" after their first dance or before their last dance. Individual kachina may go around town, from house to house, making or receiving gifts. Woleashe kachina of Zuni looks down
chimneys and, if she sees a stew on, she asks for it. As they go
around, bogey or exorcising kachina will whip adults or scare the
children. In the West a kachina dance group will visit colonies
or other towns within the tribe, to dance and bring blessings, and

* Renewed in 1931. For the Zuni visit to First Mesa in 1892 see Stephen
4:558 ff.

to be paid with presents of food and other things. Between Zuni and Laguna[88] as between Zuni and Hopi there have also been kachina dance visits.* To Hopi dances run couriers from the other mesa towns, young men in fine ceremonial array, but maskless, who are entertained with food by friends and pluck a twig or two of spruce from the kachina to place in their field shrines.[89] A rather beautiful form of pilgrimage!

After sprinkling meal on the kachina as they stand still in line, anybody may help himself to bits of spruce or, if the kachina are wearing peach branches on their head, people will pick up the peaches that fall.[90] Peaches or spruce are for orchard or field shrine or storeroom. Spruce is also good for emesis (Acoma). Chiefs or elders frequently sprinkle the dance line, particularly toward the close of the performance. At this time at Zuni a sprinkler may request the kachina to come again the day following. In Hopi towns during the final dance the kachina will be given prayer-sticks or feathers in their left hand, to carry to the shrine near which they unmask and secularize themselves, thence to scatter homeward, separately, so as not to attract the attention of the children. At Zuni, kachina chiefs may start forth on their western road, but a kachina group here, as in the East, usually withdraws to kiva or ceremonial chamber where they perform a final dance before unmasking and exorcising. Then they go home to be bathed or head-washed by wife or mother or in the case of chiefly kachina by their father's sister in her house. The "aunt" meets the impersonator as he leaves the kiva or returns from his shrine and takes him home where paternal clanswomen perform the head-washing rite, or for Shalako participants bathe the body.

* In 1893 about fifty Oraibi came to Walpi and presented a Powamu kachina dance, a return visit for one paid by Walpi men two years before. They came in the afternoon, danced that night (or rather early morning), and left the next day. They went down into Wikwalobi and Goat kivas, and kiva chiefs accompanied them to different houses to see them properly billeted (Stephen 4:231, 235; see also 374-77, 473). For Zuni visits, see Stephen 4:558 ff., 942 ff. In 1892 the Zuni dance came off in the middle of the Home-going kachina ceremony, lasted four days, and was upsetting to the hosts. There was another Zuni party of sixty in October to dance at Sichomovi and on Second Mesa.

In the East kachina dances are often performed without mask, in particular Good Kachina* which is referred to as Turtle dance at Taos and at San Juan and other Tewa towns,[91] and is described without a name at Santo Domingo;[92] or Hemishikwe (Zuni) or Hemish (Laguna) or Hümis kachina (Hopi), the notched-bone dance which is called Spruce dance at Isleta and Hopi dance at Jemez[93] and Cochiti.† It is also danced at Santa Clara, San Ildefonso, and Santo Domingo. In mask at Santo Domingo it is called Tsaiyadyuwitsa and is considered the oldest kachina dance; they were the first kachina to emerge from Shipap.[94] Chakwena is danced maskless at Cochiti, and Su'n^yi with or without mask.[95] Indoors at night Zuni kachina often dance without mask; perhaps the dancing is considered merely a rehearsal. But the Hopi dance Powamu without masks on the last night of the ceremony, that is, as a formal dance. On Second Mesa kachina invited to a corn-planting party, almost always Navaho kachina, will go maskless. Starting in the middle of the field "because this part belongs to the kachina," each kachina will plant a few holes with mixed seeds, seeds of all the crops. While the rest of the field is being planted, the kachina will sit together and smoke and later run races with the planters and dance on the edge of the field and again finally in the court.[96]

It is a striking fact that in the East where outsiders are completely excluded from kachina masked dances maskless kachina dances are not exclusive; the whole performance may be conducted exactly like a masked performance, yet onlookers, even Mexicans, are tolerated. Looking upon the mask itself constitutes the sacrilege. *"No white person will ever see Bear Old Man,"* said Crow-Wing of Hano after he had drawn me a picture of the mask.

---

* Kok'okshi (Zuni) or Añakchina, (Long) Hair kachina (Hopi).

† Hemish is danced with and without mask at Laguna. Without mask it is called, I infer, Talawaiye and is danced at Christmastide (Parsons 20:99, n. 7, Figs. 7, 8, 9; Parsons 33:236–37, 257). Hemish was danced without mask by Acomans until they learned from Zuni sojourners how "to make a good Hemushikwe dance" (Benedict 3:II, 199, 201).

A few weeks after winter solstice ceremonial, during a period of five or six weeks, each of the six Zuni kivas presents a dance, the other kivas likewise sending out or not, as each may wish, a group of dancers. When a kiva does not wish to participate fully, it may send out a single figure to dance with another kiva group. As the series of dances progresses, an increasing number of kivas participate fully until in the final dance of the series it is usual for all the kivas to present sets of dancers.

The chief and speaker of the Kachina society determine the order of presentation by the kivas, which is theoretically the same in the summer series as in the winter series. Formally, the kiva presenting the dance gives to the kiva next in order a cigarette, sending it by the two impersonators who appear in a rite of announcement of the coming dance, performed two, three, or four days in advance.

In both the afternoon rite of announcement and the evening dances, houses and not kivas are in use. Into the house used by the Muhewa kiva members I went at 7:30, on February 17, to see the fourth dance in the series. During the following hour three-fourths of the floor space filled up with the usual audience of women, babies, and little children, and at last a dozen or more members of the Little Firebrand society take up their position around the pottery drum to the left of the slat altar. Close to the altar, on either side, sits a society official, the medicine chief on the right, and on the left the fire chief, each with a red-stained feather in his hair and in his right hand the two eagle feathers called "hands."

The society choir begins to sing, and soon there come dancing in one yellow Salimobia kachina and two Nahalisho, boys of fourteen or sixteen, followed in a few minutes by three or four more Salimobia, one Wood-Ears, and three Hatashuk, boys of ten, twelve, or fourteen. The first time a kachina comes in, he goes straight to the altar, where medicine chief and fire chief rise and, in turn, after dipping the tips of their eagle feathers into the medicine bowl on the altar, asperse the dancer by striking the left-hand feather smartly four or five times with the right-hand feather.

The caperers who come and go at pleasure between the appearances of the regular sets of dancers do not sing—the society choir always sings for them—but each impersonator from time to time utters his characteristic call. In the group there may be as many as eight Salimobia at one time or sometimes only one. All but one, a shiny black Salimobia, are yellow Salimobia. The black Salimobia and one of the yellow carry in the right hand two prayer-sticks, indicating that these impersonators are wearing the real Salimobia masks and will therefore after the dance plant prayer-sticks, the prayer-sticks they carry. They will plant them immediately after the close of the night's dancing and after they have taken their masks to the house where they belong. (The windstorm the next day, wind when rain or snow is wanted, will be explained as caused by taking out the permanent Salimobia masks. "It always blows after they take them out.")*

At 9:45 the Upikyaiupona dance set from Muhewa kiva come in, making their first appearance, according to rule, in their own house. They are met at the door by the host, who sprinkles the usual line of meal to the altar, "opening" the road. Subsequently the host meets and in the same way leads in the other sets of dancers. There are twenty-seven men impersonations and seventeen women, Kokw'e'le, Kachina Girls. The line of women figures stand, as is usual, next to the wall with the line of men between them and the audience. Each wears the black-and-red bordered Hopi blanket, the women's dress and moccasins, white false face, black-bearded, the hair in large side bunches. The men wear a turquoise-colored mask like that of the Good Kachina with its long black eye slits and black beard. Three feather-tipped cords hang down the beard, and from this variation they get their name, Hair-flowing; a bunch of parrakeet feathers on the crown; gourd rattle in right hand. In the middle of the line two impersonators carry each a large bundle of prayer-sticks. During

---

* The Salimobia are kachina warriors of the cardinal directions; wind is associated with warriors.

the dancing, for seven or eight minutes, these two impersonators, praying aloud, kneel on the right knee before the two kiva officials sitting in the middle of the room in front of the audience. In connection with the prayer the impersonators give each official a cigarette and move the clasped hands of the recipients in the six directions—north, west, south, east, up, down. These cigarettes will be buried with the prayer-stick bundles. At the close of the prayers, the kiva officials give the two prayer-stick bundles to the society officials to place behind the altar. These prayer-sticks are those of two of the kivas that are not themselves presenting dances but sending representatives to dance with the Muhekwe and to give them the prayer-sticks cut for them. The next morning the Muhekwe chief will send out six men to plant the prayer-sticks made by the kiva members and the members of the two other kivas.

While the Upikyaiupona are dancing and singing—like most kiva dance sets they sing for themselves—the medicine chief and the fire chief pass down the line of dancers, sprinkling them with their eagle feathers. The subsequent sets of dancers they sprinkle similarly. Likewise during each of the dances, the two society heads rise and, facing each other, quietly almost languidly dance-step in place, moving the feathers in time, now and then one of them giving a turn to the crossed sky sticks hanging over the altar. After this they will dip the feathers in their medicine bowls and asperse. Such aspersing is called "we live to be old," and is done to keep away bad influences. Rotating the cross is an invitation to the clouds, "clouds calling." The fire chief plays a flute.

As the Upikyaiupona are going out, after dancing about twenty minutes, four or five women among the audience give one dancer or another packages of bread, and the son of the house hands five of the women impersonators a sack filled with seed corn to be distributed at the close of the program among the audiences in the five other houses to be danced in. From their fawnskin bags the kachina maidens will pour the seeds into baskets on the altar, and at the close of the night's dancing the kiva manager will give a handful to everybody, including the little children. "So everyone always comes to the winter dances, and no matter how sleepy the little children are, they always stay up all night to get their seeds. . . . . And if their fathers are poor, the little boys run out as soon as the seeds have been distributed and go to the next 'kiva' to get seeds there too. And so they get seeds from all five 'kivas.' "[98] A Zuni way of going to Sunday school to get a pair of shoes at Christmas!

After a brief intermission of dancing by members of the Salimobia group, the Upikyaiupona Tamayakwe (Keresan) come in, led by one of the Ne'wekwe, the Keresanlike clown society. With the seventeen male and two female Upikyaiupona are two Keresan Mixed Kachina and one He'he'a. Distinguishing features of the Keresan Upikyaiupona are triangular designs in the corner of the mask, and forearms painted dark blue. The hair of the Ne'wekwe leader is bunched up on top with cornhusks a foot high. The face is blackened except for the usual Ne'wekwe line across the cheekbones and curving around the eyes, which is white. A bit of fur is around his neck, and he wears an old blue coat with brass buttons—a grotesque figure indeed.

Ohewa kiva is presenting this dance. This is only its second production. Last year it was introduced at Zuni by the impersonator of He'he'a, a San Felipe man who has lived at Zuni six years. Five years ago he was initiated, before his first dance, into Muhewa kiva. Apparently his own kiva made no claim to his Keresan dance variant.

After dancing and singing about forty-five minutes, Keresan Upikyaiupona are followed for another forty-five minutes by the Upts'anakwa kiva presenting the Wilatsukwe (White Mountain Apache) dance. There are about forty male figures. With them is a Ne'wekwe—the Ne'mosi or chief himself—to beat the bundle or, to one of their songs, a wooden drum. The Ne'mosi wears a pair of flannel trousers, flaps of calico back and front, and a dotted pink and white shirt (made for the occasion from a window curtain, he tells us later). He wears the Ne'wekwe cap with its side and top bunches of cornhusks; his face is whitened but for the black lines under the eyes and around the mouth like a drooping moustache. He carries his Ne'wekwe stick. The

Apache mask is a small, straight profile, white, false face covered with arrow and geometric designs; no two masks quite alike. The hair is flowing, with twists of yarn or fur across the forehead and hanging sidewise like braids. At the sides of the head are rosettes of ribbons, artificial flowers, and bunches of feathers of all kinds. Over the shoulders are capes of all sorts, velvet, skin, or cloth, decorated with a garish miscellany of beads, small mirrors, silver buttons, and tinsel. Under the skin kilt are flaps of calico. At the back, a flat basket is attached to the silver Navaho belt or to the rope twisted around the waist, and, to the side, a pair of spurs or a quoit may be fastened. High moccasins or fringed leggings. In right hand, a gourd rattle; in left, a lance. The Apache chief stalks in front of the irregular double line of dancers, and between songs says a few words, ejaculating *Hup! Hup!* In his left hand he carries a large bow, in his right, an arrow. A large skin quiver hangs over his back and a skin bandoleer at his side. Several large white feathers are fastened to a cord down his hair and to another cord along his right forearm.

A bundle of prayer-sticks is carried by a dancer in both dance groups, and the bundle is presented with prayer to the kiva official in the middle of the room. At the conclusion of each dance, the leader sprinkles meal on the dancers and on the corn-ear fetishes on the altar. He is then given from a shell a drink from each of the two medicine bowls on the altar.

After another hour of dancing by the Salimobia group, and a second and final dance by the returning Upikyaiupona, each member of the choir sprinkles meal upon each Upikyaiupona and again upon the corn-ear fetishes. Thereupon the dancers begin to take off their masks and their tortoise shells, not waiting for what is left of the audience to be well out of the room. It is one o'clock in the morning. As I pass through town, in two other houses I see groups still dancing, concluding their rounds of the six houses.

During the Apache dance I noticed one member of the choir leave his place, speak to the midmost figure in the dance, and then proceed to sprinkle the dancers. He was asking the dance director, whose place is in the middle of the line, to dance the next day outside; and so, the following afternoon, the Apache, twenty-nine of them, together with a society leader and the Ne'mosi to beat the bundle, are out dancing in the court. Led by their solemn "holder of the road (*awilona*)," wearing as usual a buckskin across his shoulder, and crowned with a yucca circlet and a red-stained downy feather, the dancers come in two by two; then they form a single dance line. The Apache chief as before dances out in front; likewise, at times, a very little boy dancer. The dancers perform for a half-hour and then withdraw for a half-hour. Later in the afternoon they bring with them strings of apples and bags of nuts to throw to the spectators. The dance step varies quite a little from the usual dance stomp. In one song, the right foot is brought down three times before the shift to the left foot. As the dancers go in and out of the court they sing, as well as in the dance, and, as individual dancers linger to throw their gifts, they, too, sing on leaving. It is a beautiful "going-out" song, and the Ne'mosi sings it so gaily as he passes through town that the debonair fellow is smiled at by the women in their doorways. Before the Ne'mosi and the dancers withdraw finally from the court the dance director as usual sprinkles meal on the heads of the attendant Koyemshi clowns.

The Koyemshi, in one of the intervals they fill out between dances, played bean bag or tumbled about, playing tricks with a wheelbarrow. The Koyemshi were invited to come out by the Apache kachina. The night before, i.e., the same night the repetition was asked for, the Apache dance chief took the request, with a cigarette, to Father Koyemshi. This was the first appearance of the true Koyemshi, i.e., the Koyemshi impersonators appointed during the winter solstice ceremonial; for at the preceding dance in this series they had not yet planted their monthly prayer- sticks, and the rule is that they may not come out to play before this planting.

At the conclusion of the dance in the court, Hompikya, Bow chief younger brother, sprinkles meal on the Apache and asks for a repetition next day. So this evening the Apache will dance, according to custom, in the house of their Father Koyemshi.

Good Kachina Visit Zuni after the Summer Solstice Ceremony[99]

Pekwin has watched the sunsets from the Sun shrine on Matsakya, the town ruin on a hill about three miles east of Zuni. When the sun sets behind a certain point on the mesa to the northwest, the last day or so of May, Pekwin calls out for all to cut prayer-sticks for Sun, Moon, the Dead, and the Kachina in fourteen (?) days. He himself plants prayer-sticks four days after his announcement, and the curing societies plant two days later. After an all-night altar ceremony for rain, Pekwin tells the Rain chieftaincy of the North, the Town chieftaincy, to count their days, and four days after the general prayer-stick-planting which should occur on June 22 the Town chieftaincy goes into retreat for eight days, starting the summer rain retreats. On the Town chiefs' "middle day" the kachina will come to dance.

The kachina will be fetched from Hot springs, the home of the Shalako, near ancient Hawikuh, seventeen miles southwest of Zuni, or, every fourth year, from the sacred lake, the Lake of Whispering Waters. When the Kachina society officers and the impersonators of kachina chiefs* put their prayer-sticks into the water, they say, "Hurry, come with us when we start back!" The prayer-sticks of the kiva impersonators of the Kok'okshi, the Good Kachina, have been made by Deer clansmen and "children" of the clan, clan or rather lineage relatives of the Kachina society chief. The prayer-sticks of the Koyemshi clown impersonators have been made by Badger clansmen and "children" of the clan, relatives of the crier chief of the Kachina society. The gourd of water each officer of the Kachina society brings back he gives to the Town chief to pour on his field after his retreat. Reeds brought back are given to the children to eat—something sweet (? honey dew). "We tell them they grow in the yard of the kachina who live in the water."

* This is the regular monthly planting of certain impersonators, Shalako, etc. (Bunzel 2:538).

In the afternoon the dance paraphernalia are taken by the kiva manager to Pinawa, a ruin two or three miles to the west, where the dance director deposits prayer-sticks, and the thirty or more impersonators put on their masks.* Kachina society chief, "making the road," leads in the procession in single file, Koyemshi and others swinging a whizzer. At Hepatina they stop, dance, and deposit prayer-sticks. Hepatina, the shrine of the Emergence, the Middle of old Zuni, was where formerly they put on their masks. Nowadays there are too many white residents or visitors in the neighborhood. The procession moves on into town, and the Good Kachina dance in each of the four dance courts or sites. From their ceremonial house the Town chiefs come down to receive plants and spring water.

Now they withdraw into Ohewa kiva and dance again, about 9:00 P.M. The women and children associated with the kiva through some man in the family may watch this dance through an upper window cut into an adjacent room. At the close before the dancers remove their masks and turtle-shell rattles the window is shuttered, at least it was shuttered the time I saw the dance because from ignorance I did not turn away when the other women turned away, from their proscenium seats. From one or two exclamations and the hasty shuttering of the window I realized my breach of etiquette.

In kiva, behind the two lines of dancers stand the Shalako and other impersonators of the kachina chiefs, swinging the whizzer. They are dressed in the usual white cottons, and wear the usual black or crimson silk *banda* around their heads. They also wear a prayer-meal pouch and bandoleer and carry on their

---

* Turquoise-colored face mask; black beard; hair flowing, with three downy feathers down the back, "to make the clouds come"; bunch of parrot feathers on top. Body painted with pink clay from the sacred lake; embroidered kilt; large white fringed belt; foxskin; spruce in belt and carried in both hands; spruce anklets, bare feet; turtle-shell rattle.

Slight variants are the Upikyaiapona and the Red Paint kachina. With all three groups appear a few kachina maidens impersonated by males. White face mask with beard; over the forehead a fringe of goat's hair; hair wrapped over wood and bound with yarn at sides of head, something like Hopi girl's whorls. Black dress and white Hopi blanket with red and blue or black border. Hands white, feet yellow, spruce in both hands (Bunzel 5:1012–13, Pls. 34, 35a, b).

backs long-stalked greens from the Lake. The altar of the Ant society is laid at one end of the chamber; a member plays continuously on the flute. Sitting near the altar are the nine high Rain chiefs, a group of Dogwood clansmen belonging to the cult society of Kiaklo, Deer clansmen, and "children" of the clan.

After the kiva dance all eat supper and are given a drink from the medicine bowl, after which none may eat or drink until noon of the following day. They are to dance all night alternately in kiva or in the house of the crier chief of the Kachina society where the Koyemshi clowns are dancing. Here the altar of the Snake Medicine society is laid and here sit other Shalako or Sayatasha impersonators and managers, also Badger clansmen and "children" of the clan. Throughout this night and the following morning all these men sit quietly and gravely, although now and then one would smoke or talk to his neighbor or even make a joke about a clown.

From the door to the altar is the usual "road" of meal. Over it enter Good Kachina, led by Kachina society chief, with Hompikya, War chief younger brother, swinging the whizzer. The dancers are maskless and in undress, wearing merely a breechcloth and under their knee the turtle shell rattle; around the head is a band of yucca. Before the twenty-minute dance concludes, the War chief stands before the altar and says a prayer. As each dancer approaches the door to pass out, he is given in a shell a drink from the medicine bowl. Now the Koyemshi dance. They too will dance all night, in their house or in the kiva.

Early in the morning about 6:30, the Good Kachina start to make the rounds of the four courts, on an empty stomach. Only if it rains may they have a bite of breakfast before going out to dance. Toward noon the final morning dance concludes in kiva, and the fast is broken. Women from the households of the Kachina managers and of the Deer clansmen or the Badger clansmen carry great bowls of food on their heads to kiva or house.

Early in the afternoon the Good Kachina go to dance in the house of the crier chief of the Kachina society and then outside the house. In the main court they dance four times; a repetition

is called for, and they dance again. Meanwhile the impersonators of Sayatasha, etc., are dancing in a circle in their house, nude
and carrying characteristic rattle, firebrand, or bow and arrows,
but without masks. The Koyemshi attend, some on the indoor
dancers and some on the Good Kachina in the court (Pls. XII,
XIII).

The chief of the Kachina society sprinkles the Koyemshi with
meal and leads the dancers back to kiva. At the foot of the ladder, each is meal-sprinkled by the men present. After the final
kiva dance our window is again shuttered for the dancers to unmask and to have their heads washed by the women of the Deer
clan, washed ritually by drip from an ear of corn.

KACHINA ADVENT OR SHALAKO, ZUNI[100]

This ceremony is annual and almost yearlong. On the ninth
day of the winter solstice ceremony the paramount Rain chiefs
make the crooks of appointment for the impersonators and for
the eight households in which they will be entertained. Those
for Shulawitsi, the Sayatasha or Long Horn party, and Father
Koyemshi are brought to He'iwa kiva that evening by the impersonator of Pa'utiwa, and are distributed by Pekwin next
morning to the men whom the chiefs have chosen for these
offices.

The same afternoon Pa'utiwa leaves on the roof of each of the
six kivas the crook of appointment for the Shalako from that
kiva. The kiva Shalako managers choose two impersonators for
each Shalako, inducting them into office by the presentation of
the crook. That evening, after making offerings in the river to
the dead, impersonators meet in various houses to learn prayers
and other details of office. These meetings will continue throughout the year. The Long Horn group and the Koyemshi meet
every night, with brief intermissions at the seasons of lambing,
sheep-shearing, and harvest at the outlying colonies. The Shalako meet formally only on the four nights following each prayer-
stick-planting, but may meet informally on intervening nights,
especially as the time for the public ceremonies approaches.
Trustees and managers of the cults (wo'we), are present to in-

PLATE XII

ZUNI AUDIENCES AT A KACHINA DANCE

Ts'ia'awa court, women are standing in the narrow exit; men are sitting on top of He'iwa kiva, Koyemshi below.

PLATE XIII

Good Kachina of Zuni
Koyemshi and Ne'wekwe in attendance (Stevenson 2: Pl. XXXI)

struct. The Long Horn group meets in the house of the impersonator of Long Horn, Koyemshi in the house of "their Father," and each Shalako couple in the house of "elder brother." Meetings begin shortly after dark, the early evening being spent in talk. After the family has retired, prayers and the chants which are ritualized travelers' tales are rehearsed until about one o'clock.

All the impersonators must arise before day, summer and winter, and offer prayer-meal to the rising sun in a field east of town. At nightfall they must take a portion of food from the evening meal and offer it with prayer in the river at a point west of town, Wide River. Each month at the full moon prayer-sticks are to be offered to kachina chiefs at distant shrines. The first ten plantings are at springs in the mountains south of Zuni.

On these days they gather early in the morning in their ceremonial houses to make their prayer-sticks. Long prayers are recited at the conclusion of their work. Then after a feast they leave for the shrines which lie to the south at distances of from four to eight miles. The prayer-sticks are planted in the ground near the spring, and long prayers are offered. The impersonator of Sayatasha (Long Horn) recites the prayers, the others joining in as well as they can. Toward sunset the party approaches town, marching in regular order across the plain, singing kachina songs.

Throughout the year each group of impersonators must work for the household which is to entertain them at the public festival. The Koyemshi work also individually for their "aunts," the women of their fathers' clans. They bring in wood; they do all the work of the fields; they build the new room in which the kachina are to be received. Of course, the days they work they are fed. Clanspeople are also expected to help, and, when they call, the crook of appointment or the permanent prayer-stick is brought out to be breathed from.

On the morning of the tenth prayer-stick-planting, early in October, the impersonators of Long Horn and Molanhakto (Father Koyemshi) receives each from Pekwin a day count or tally, a cotton string containing forty-nine knots. One knot is to be untied each morning. Into the twenty-fifth knot are put some ground down shell and turquoise. During this period there are plantings at intervals of ten days at White Rocks, shrines southwest of town.

The public ceremony starts on the fortieth day, with the arrival of the Koyemshi in the evening. They come masked,* visiting each of the four courts to make ridiculous or obscene remarks and to announce the coming of the kachina in eight days. They are sprinkled liberally with meal and proceed to the house of "their Father" for their eight-day retreat. Four days later the Long Horn party come in in the evening and, after eating supper provided by the people of the house where their masks are kept,† carry their masks to the house of the imper-

* Each Koyemshi has a personal name, and his mask and behavior are somewhat individualized; but they always come out together, and in most ways may be described as a unit. The mask is of Hopi cotton cloth with knobs filled with cotton wool and seeds and dust from the footprints of townspeople rendering the mask very dangerous, the most dangerous of all kachina (see p. 105, also Parsons 29:204). Downy turkey feathers are tied to the knobs or to the small hornlike appendages of some of the masks. The rings around eyes and mouth vary in shape. Mask and body are colored pink with the sacred lake kachina clay. ("If anyone touches a Koyemshi while he has his paint on, he will surely go crazy." This paint may not be washed off by their wives [Bunzel 5:947].) Around the neck is a piece of black native cloth under which is the packet of "heart" seeds, each Koyemshi having his own kind of corn (Bunzel 5:946. The youngest carries the kind that is puffed out, the kernels broken open, so that the people may ever be happy. A woman who wants her baby to laugh all the time will eat corn of this kind). Black cotton kilt, no breechcloth. The penis is tied up with a cotton string, and the kilt may at any time be removed before people. The Koyemshi are sexually immature, "just like children." Yet in their drum they carry the butterfly which makes people follow them and go "crazy" (sexually).

† In a Dogwood clan house (the people here are witch suspects). Long Horn's turquoise-colored mask has the one long horn "because he brings long life to all his people." Right eye small, "for the witch people, so that they may not live long," left eye long "for the people of one heart, so that they may have long life." Black goat's hair hangs from the horn and over forehead. Fawnskin quiver over right shoulder; bow and arrow in left hand, deer-scapula rattle in right. Many bead necklaces and bracelets "because he is very valuable."

The impersonator is chosen by the Council while the societies are holding their winter retreat. Impersonators for Hututu, Long Horn's war chief, and for the two Yamuhakto are chosen from the same society, "so as to get men who will work together." If they do well, they will be returned to office, after four years. There is a lifelong manager for the Long Horn group who teaches the prayers and chant.

Long Horn comes to make the days warm. Every morning before sunrise and sonator of Long Horn. Then with the officers of the Kachina society the Long Horn party go to White Rocks to plant prayer-sticks. There, earlier in the day, the Long Horn manager has made the two divinatory mounds of sand spread thick with meal, representing Koyemshi and Kok'okshi mountains, in which a crack will betoken disaster.

At White Rocks a woodpile has been built by the ceremonial father of Shulawitsi who now lights it with his cedar-bark torch. In two other places on the approach to town there are more bon-fires. The Long Horn party give their calls and pound out their quadrille to their scapula rattles at the last bonfire, where the torch is laid down and sprinkled with meal. This bonfire scene will be described by Long Horn in prayer as follows:

> I made the sound of the water-filled breath of the
> rain-maker priest of the north.
> Taking four steps,
> Four times striding forward,
> The water-filled woodpile
> Of my daylight father
> I stood beside.
> My father
> Four times sprinkled my head with prayer-meal.
> His rain-filled woodpile
> He sprinkled with meal.
> After him,
> I sprinkled my prayer-meal on it.[101]

The water-filled, i.e., smoky, woodpile is said to be for the clouds, mimetic magic; actually the flames are a signal to the Shalako managers and impersonators to go to the houses where the Shalako masks are kept. Hence after a feast, contributed by

---

every evening he goes out and prays to the Sun, especially early in summer and early in fall when frosts are feared. *He also sends the deer* (Bunzel 5:962 ff., 1048).

The impersonator throughout year of office is referred to by title. He lives under restrictions; he may not leave town for more than a day or two, or engage in quarrel or unseemly conduct; "his heart must be good." He has the prestige of a major Rain chief. He observes the moon and regulates the monthly Shalako plantings, conferring with Pekwin in determining the date for Shalako so it will not conflict with the winter solstice ceremony.

all the connections of the house, the impersonators carry the masks to the houses where they are making their retreats.

On the forty-eighth day Shulawitsi and his "father,"* Long Horn, Hututu (named from his call), two Yamuhakto (Stick-on-Top or Carrying-Wood),† and two Salimobia enter town in mid-afternoon. After planting prayer-sticks in six permanent excavations or shrines, Long Horn's party performing their heavy-step quadrille[102] at the same time, the kachina go to the house where they are to be entertained for the night. This is always a new or at least a renovated house, and the visit of the kachina is a blessing—a dedication. Prayer-sticks are planted inside the threshold (formerly under the outside ladder) and in an ornate box suspended from the center of the ceiling. The kachina walk into the room on the meal trail to the altar. They take their seeds from their belts and place them in a basket on the altar, for their host. They mark the walls of the house with corn meal. They deposit seeds of all kinds in an excavation in the center of the floor. Similar rites are performed later in the evening by the six Shalako‡ and the Koyemshi in the houses where they are to

---

* Without mask, yucca band and red feather in hair, cottons, red garters, buckskin over shoulders (Bunzel 5:1086, Pl. 59a). This godfather to the boy kachina dramatizes the kind of co-operation expected of any godfather who always stands by to help a godchild serving as impersonator, even substituting for him if need be. Compare Bunzel 5:913, 960, 994–95, also Hopi hunt father.

Shulawitsi's "father" is the Badger clansman who "held the blood pudding" or sacred fire at the winter solstice. He appoints the boy kachina from his own family or his sister's family, a child of Badger or a Badger (Bunzel 5:959).

† He prays for the trees, so people may have building timber and firewood (Bunzel 5:967).

‡ Turquoise-colored mask, crest of eagle feathers, and macaw feathers bound to little sticks covered with downy eagle feathers; horns with red-feather pendants; ball eyes and long snout of wooden pieces which open and close by a string and make a great clatter; a unique arrangement which I am guessing is European. The personator pulls the string, but must never look lest he die, so only the Shalako manager knows how it is put together (see Stephen 4: Fig. 230, also p. 269). Long hair, collar of raven feathers and foxskins, dance kilt on shoulders, two embroidered white blankets to which eagle feathers are sewn and which are kept distended by a crinoline. The mask is on a pole carried by the impersonator and supported in his belt, also a European device. The figure towers ten feet.

The impersonator wears under the mask a warrior's buckskin cap decorated around with red ribbon and silver buttons; black cloth shirt trimmed with be entertained.* On coming into town in single-file procession from White Rocks the Shalako have planted prayer-sticks in two places and at Hepatina have performed their running ritual.

The blessing of the house is described by Long Horn in prayer as follows:

> Then my father's rain-filled room
> I rooted at the north,
> I rooted at the west,
> I rooted at the south,
> I rooted at the east,
> I rooted above,
> Then in the middle of my father's roof,
> With two plume wands joined together,
> I consecrated his roof.
> This is well;
> In order that my father's offspring may increase,
> I consecrated the center of his roof.
> And then also, the center of my father's floor,
> With seeds of all kinds,
> I consecrated the center of his floor.
> This is well;
> In order that my father's fourth room
> May be bursting with corn,
> That even in his doorway,
> The shelled corn may be scattered before the door,
> The beans may be scattered before the door,
> That his house may be full of little boys,
> And little girls,
> And people grown to maturity;
> That in his house
> Children may jostle one another in the doorway,
> In order that it may be thus,

---

ribbons; knees painted red, calves yellow; high red moccasins; yarn leglets with little bells. Stone ax in belt, "because he is a warrior." Two impersonators to each of the six masks, Elder brother and Younger brother who take turns (Bunzel 5:969–70).

* They come in with their masks pushed up on their foreheads, exposing their faces. They visit the Shalako and Long Horn houses and standing before the door call the inmates by name in song, twitting them for stinginess, laziness, domestic infelicity, fondness for American ways. In their own house of entertainment "their father," "their speaker," and war chief intone their two-hour chant (Bunzel 5:952).

I have consecrated the rain-filled room
Of my daylight father,
My daylight mother.[103]

Now the kachina are seated ritually and raise their masks. Reed cigarettes are brought, and each kachina smokes with the person seated opposite (in the Long Horn house these are the paramount Rain chiefs) exchanging terms of relationship. Then the host questions the kachina concerning the circumstance of their coming, just as any returned traveler would be questioned. In the recital that follows, like a traveler's report all the events leading up to the present moment are reviewed, and blessings are invoked upon the house, especially the blessing of fecundity.

This litany, chanted in unison by the Long Horn group (Shulawitsi is not required to learn it), takes about six hours. It is chanted in loud tones and very slowly, in monotone except for the last syllable of each line which is higher in pitch, heavily accented and prolonged. The chants of the Shalako, which omit the recital of the twenty-nine springs visited by the kachina on their way to Zuni, and curtail other portions, take about two hours to perform.

All are finished at about 11:00 P.M., when an elaborate feast is served in all the houses to relatives and visitors.* Impersonators take prayer-sticks made by their hosts and bits from all the food bowls to the river for the "old ones," the dead. This night all the dead have returned.† After this all the kachina dance until day in mask or "naked," i.e., without mask in the house of their host, to the songs of the curing society in attendance whose members sit in a circle around their drum to the right of their altar. Each house is visited by the Koyemshi in couples.‡ At sun-

* People will come from different places and they will eat. [Not only this night but throughout their stay.] . . . . It is best to have a lot so that we may not be criticized" (Bunzel 6:11, 14).

† This sounds like a celebration of All Saints or All Souls or both. As in All Souls celebration in Mexico, all the material wealth of the house is displayed, blankets, buckskin, abalone shells; likewise everybody is supposed to have new clothes, everything new. Drinking, trading (Stevenson 2:253–54), probably sexual license are other southern features.

‡ In 1915 a Navaho kachina dance set made the rounds of the ceremonial houses.

PLATE XIV

ZUNI SHALAKO KACHINA (STEVENSON 2: PL. LXI)

rise the heads of all impersonators are washed by the women of the houses where they have been entertained, in token of their permanent association with these houses. Like godchildren, they receive gifts of food, and sometimes of clothing, from their hosts. At the first sign of dawn Long Horn has ascended to the roof of the house, and facing the east, untied the last knot in his tally cord, intoning a prayer and at the end of each line stretching his cord.

Now the several hosts of the kachina lead them to the river-bank where they sprinkle them with meal and leave them, the part of host concluded. Little Firebrand society and Bedbug society flutists and singers escort them across the river (Pl. XIV). In this south field, Shulawitsi is meal-besprinkled by the young men. Then after they bury prayer-sticks in one of the series of holes that have been prepared in this field in advance, Shulawitsi and his "father" leave town for White Rocks. They are followed by the Long Horn party who have also interred prayer-sticks and been meal-besprinkled. At White Rocks Long Horn buries his tally cord and the stick of appointment from the house of his hosts.

The six Shalako masks and the six "younger brothers" have been standing in line in the south field. Now each Shalako runs in turn to a hole for prayer-sticks where stands a Shalako manager. The manager addresses a prayer to the Shalako who buries his prayer-sticks and runs back to the line. The younger brother assumes the mask and runs to the hole to sprinkle meal. As each runner starts, the onlookers breathe from their hands. The running is "to try their strength." If a Shalako fall, it is a sign that the personator has not believed in his prayer, that he has not been *teshkwi*, more particularly continent, some time during the year in connection with his planting. Should one fall, the following day the personator would be whipped by a Blue Horn. Moreover, the Salimobia who have remained out in the middle of the field would forthwith cross the river and in exorcism whip all persons they might encounter.

After the departing Shalako run a number of younger men afoot and ahorse. They intend to overtake and strike the Shalako. The act brings them skill in hunting for the year. Striking a Shalako, a man exclaims "I have killed the deer" and lays it down head to the east, as dead men or dead deer are placed, and sprinkles it with meal, at the same time the personator slips out of the mask.* The personators then plant the prayer-sticks which have been cut for them the day before by all the men of their respective kiva. Returning to the pueblo each personator goes to the house of his father's sister who washes his head.

Early this afternoon, the Koyemshi leave their house and visit the rooftops of the ceremonial houses. They stand in line singing and gesticulating for about fifteen minutes. Then one of them descends and knocks at the house door. He is not asked in, but an exchange of pleasantries and jokes takes place between him and the people within. Then the old woman of the house will come out and throw some liquid over the kachina. Behind her troup the young people, to whom it all seems a great joke. The drenched Koyemshi rejoins his mates on the housetop, and they all proceed to the next Shalako house. They are supposed in this progress not to touch the ground, no matter how high or rickety the places they must climb. Were one to fall, it would be a sign he had been incontinent at some time during the periods of his ceremonial restriction. They are called Mountain Sheep.

During the following four days, as the kivas are presenting group dances, the Koyemshi will come out to play their games in the morning or in the afternoon to valet the kachina. At night they will dance in their ceremonial house, very hard, to the drum and song of the curing society attending them. They dance without masks, the ten masks being set in line near the altar. On the second, fourth, and sixth nights after their house has been visited by all the other kachina groups the Koyemshi will visit the other houses where the kachina are dancing. They are accompanied by their society choir and in each house are the last group to dance. They dance solemnly in a circle, to special

* No white has ever been allowed to see this ritual which is suggestive, to Dr. Bunzel, of killing the god. There is a general belief that a kachina who is killed becomes a deer (Benedict 3:I, 72, 77; Stevenson 2:260). If the Shalako is killed and becomes a deer, that would explain why hunting luck is imparted.

songs; but they may play a guessing game or perform jugglery feats. They carry eagle-wing feathers, and over the right shoulder hangs their characteristic fawnskin pouch.

The final dance night, at midnight in their own house, the Koyemshi will eat a ceremonial meal. Four times Father Koyemshi has to dip his bread into the stew. He may dip fast or slowly as he pleases, but when he has finished, the others must stop eating.* (Their wives or sisters carry away the abundant left-overs.) And from then on to the following midnight they must fast. Were they to eat or drink, gardens and fields would be eaten down by pests. They must also remain awake.

In the morning the Koyemshi are led into the court by their Shalako host and by their society choir. (In 1915 the leader for the choir was a young woman wearing a downy white feather on her head with her bang hanging masklike down to her mouth. She too was a member of the household entertaining the Koyemshi. She was the only woman, by the way, taking any public part in Shalako.) In the court Pekwin joins them and all begin to revolve slowly in sunwise circuit and in their ellipse formation. Presently Pekwin sprinkles ten small meal crosses under the northern wall and on these places seats the Koyemshi, first taking each by the shoulders and turning him in the four directions. Then Pekwin marks each with a line of meal down the forehead. The society members sprinkle the Koyemshi, in farewell, and leave the court. The Koyemshi deposit each the large bundle of eagle feathers from his father's clansmen in the hole prepared for them temporarily in the ground. In conclusion their host sprinkles the Koyemshi and leads them up into the ceremonial house of the Town chieftaincy. There Father Koyemshi tells the paramount Rain chiefs how hard the Koyemshi have worked for the year's crops. All present breathe in. Then the women of the houses where the chiefs' bundles are kept wash the sacred paint off the Koyemshi who stand completely naked before them. The women stand in line and, as each Koyemshi files by, each

---

* Does this ritual meal represent or dramatize the meal of the dead who eat four times only of the offerings made them (Hopi)? Perhaps it is only old-fashioned "table manners." See Index (Manners).

woman gives him a loaf of bread and a roll of wafer-bread
"because she has touched his body." In the court their fathers'
brothers meet them and take them each to the house of his
father's sister where each is sprinkled with water on his mask (a
substitute for washing his head) by his aunt and given a prayer-
stick by all the clansmen for him to pray for their long life and
for rain and crops, and presents of food and other things by all
the clanswomen. (Valuable presents of blankets and clothing
from his real aunts.) All load the presents on head or back, whole
sheep, baskets of bread, trunks, and form a procession into the
court.*

On this last day all the kivas are represented by a kachina
group in the chief dance court, as many as four groups may be
dancing† at the same time in that small court, no group paying
the slightest attention to the others. Dancing in the court on
preceding afternoons or at night indoors in the Shalako houses is
more or less optional, and at the night performances masks are
not generally worn, only three or four dancers may be in mask;
but on the final day each dance set must perform four times in
the morning and once in the afternoon before dispersing at a run
to Red Bank, about half a mile southeast of town, whence after
planting prayer-sticks the kachina are supposed to start for a
visit eastward to Shipapolima. All the men take their masks
to Red Bank.

Before the last dancers have given to the Rain chiefs the corn
which they carry in their left hand (together with prayer-sticks
and wafer-bread for their journey), the Molawia procession arrives in the court, and an entirely separable dramatization is
under way. Meanwhile, after standing a long time by their piles
of goods in the afternoon, the Koyemshi have visited all the
Shalako houses and collected their permanent sticks of appointment; later, in the evening, they collect wafer-bread from all

* Shalako impersonators and impersonators in the Long Horn group have
been paid privately for their work for their hosts (Bunzel).

† The dances are Toichakwena (home or old Chakwena), Chakwena,
Muluktakya (Duck), Hemishikwe, Mahedinasha, Wotempla (all kinds of
Animals or Mixed dance), and each is customarily presented by the same kiva,
i.e., the dance director is from the given kiva and usually a few others, but the
dance director may invite men from any kiva to participate.

the houses, each Koyemshi visiting the houses of his father's clan. Wafer-bread, sticks of appointment, and prayer-sticks temporarily buried in the dance court are all taken to Wide River, all are for the dead. At Wide River, too, Father Koyemshi buries his tally cord.*

Shalako is a ceremony for the dead, but it is also a kachina war ceremony and a hunt ceremony. All the kachina war chiefs are enrolled: Long Horn, the Shalako who carry war clubs hidden in their belt, and whose crooks of office are associated with scalp ritual; the Salimobia, who represent the War Brothers of the Directions; and Shulawitsi, who represents them as little boys; and finally the scouting Koyemshi. Familiar war traits are included: burlesque, sex license (Shalako night) and ritual continence (particularly the prolonged continence of the Koyemshi), signal fire, omen, and ritual killing, finally general participation since all the men are expected to dance. Besides, Shalako is a ceremony for reproduction (see p. 751) and for longevity.†

* Before this they have unmasked, saying, "Now give me long life and a strong body like you used to have when you were a person. Do not draw me back with you." Their Father returns the masks to the house of the woman who takes care of them, praying for the household. On his return to his own house he gives each of the waiting Koyemshi a sip of water. They are sacred until they get this sip. Their Father says, "Even if you have finished your year you must be kind to everyone now so that when our time comes again we may not have a bad name. Our time will come again in four years." Their Father asperses them, and they eat (Bunzel 5:956–57).

† Long Horn reports in prayer:

> Yesterday our daylight fathers,
> Whoever of them wished to grow old,
> Working on plume wands [prayer-sticks] came to evening;
> Working on prayer-feathers they came to evening.
> And furthermore our mothers,
> Whoever of them wished to grow old,
> With aching knees,
> With sweat running down their faces,
> With burned fingers,
> Sitting wearily they came to evening.
> And whoever else wished to grow old,
> Preparing prayer-meal
> They gave it to us (Bunzel 4:757).

They who shorten life can also lengthen it.

Some of the kachina are possessed of features of the hunt: Long Horn who sends the deer; the two kachina in his group who represent trees, perhaps the forest home of deer; little fire god Shulawitsi who kindles fires as Hopi lads once did in the antelope drive (pp. 27–28), comes in with a string of rabbits, and carries a fawn-pelt bag;* Koyemshi who do a mountain-sheep act; and the horned Shalako themselves who in the most esoteric of all the rituals are laid out as if they were dead deer, and give power to deer-hunters. We recall that a meal road is made for dead deer to a place under the Shalako roof shrine (p. 362). Possibly Shalako are deer impersonations, and their running ritual, mimetic behavior. A deer hunt is held before the Shalako ceremony which occurs in the hunting season. Some day a student of Keresan loan terms in Zuni may tell us if *shaiyaik* (*sha'aik*), Keresan for hunter, could become *shalako* in Zuni.

Kachina Rabbit Hunt at Zuni†

The paramount Rain chiefs perform overnight ritual in the room of the War society. At sunrise the War chief who is the warrior of the Hunters society notifies the society that a kachina hunt will be held in four days.

The following day the kachina impersonators make prayer-sticks and at night assemble in their kivas to practice their songs.

The night before the hunt the Hunters society assembles in their room to sing for the kachina who come to dance. The paramount Rain chiefs are assembled in their ceremonial room, where at sunrise they are joined by the Hunters society. Chak-

---

* Upon the association of his "father," blood-pudding holder, with fire (see p. 516) recent information from Santa Ana may throw light. A Santa Ana deer-hunter would fill the deer's stomach with blood (Zuni blood-pudding, sheep's stomach) for people to dip into, the men rubbing a horizontal line under the eyes, and the women, a vertical line. When a Santa Ana man is out hunting, his sister sprinkles prayer-meal on the fire morning and night and prays to Fire Boy (White). Possibly the hunter's sister was once identified with the Mother of Game who among Hopi is the sister of the Fire god.

† From Stevenson 2:89–94. No date is given and the account appears to be from hearsay. The kachina hunt is held, Stevenson states, in connection with the naming and whipping ritual for the children by the Kachina society, likewise in times of drought. Likewise for general exorcism (Bunzel 5:933–34).

wena Woman kachina* enters the court and makes four anti-sunwise circuits, as a rain rite, then ascends the ladder and enters the ceremonial room of the Rain chiefs. Pekwin motions Chak-wena Woman with his hands on her shoulders to the six directions and seats her on a cross of meal sprinkled on a ceremonial blanket. In her scalp lock he fastens a downy red-stained eagle feather. The War chiefs make fire with fire sticks and ignite torches of cedar fiber. These are carried out by two Koyemshi who proceed to set fire to the vegetation on the western road. With them go the Hunters society, Chakwena, the six Salimobia of the Directions, and the kachina Wooden-Ears, Wool-Cap, and Nawisho, owner of deer. At a certain place on the road the yellow Salimobia halts, the other kachina proceed, then the blue Salimobia halts, and thus the kachina string out at different stations on the road. After a Blue Horn kachina deposits a reed cigarette in the river, with the three other Blue Horns and other kachina he goes through town notifying that the hunt is to begin and, as usual, whipping any persons encountered.

All who wish to join in the hunt set forth, on horseback or afoot; girls ride behind their father or brother.† With each Blue Horn is a group afoot. As a group reaches a Salimobia they are chased by him to the Salimobia stationed beyond, the pursuing Salimobia returning to a position on the road in advance of that he left. In this way all the parties pass all the kachina, and the file of kachina moves on. Finally all reach the hunt fire, into which with prayer all throw food. The Hunters pray to the deceased members of the society to help them in the hunt. Chakwena prays that many of her children, the rabbits, be sent to the people. All but the kachina pass their rabbit-sticks through the

* This kachina chief, called also Ku'yapäliᵗsa, parallels the Chakwena mother of Laguna whose personal name is Kisiets'a and who, like one of the Earth Mothers, controls all foodstuffs (Parsons 20:98 n. 4); parallels also Tihküyi of the Hopi, Childbirth-Water Woman and Mother of Game who is not a kachina. On First Mesa the mask of the warrior Chakwena Grandmother is kept in Wikwalobi kiva where is also a shrine of Mother of Game. In Zuni myth Chakwena Woman belongs to the Ky'anakwe who established their claim to own the deer after hiding them away and winning a fight with the kachina (Benedict 3:I, 6–8).

† For many years the women have not gone on the hunt.

fire. A large circle of hunters is formed. Chakwena and the Hunters with their firebrands* drive the rabbits to be killed by the others. When a kachina fails to kill a rabbit which runs between himself and a man, and the man kills it, the man whips the kachina, over each arm and each leg. Should the kachina kill the rabbit, he whips the man. If both fail, they whip each other. A woman snatching at a rabbit and missing it is whipped four times across the back by a kachina.

The first rabbit killed has its nose cut and is handed to Chakwena by a girl. Chakwena rubs the bleeding nose down her legs on the inner sides, a rite to promote puberty in girls and prolific childbearing.†

After the first roundup the women carry the rabbits to the chief and crier of the Hunters society, who stand facing the east, each with a firebrand. They pick off a bit of fur from the tip of the tail of each rabbit and place these bits in the firebrands. The rabbits are laid on their sides on the ground, their heads to the east and facing south; then all draw near, pray, and sprinkle the rabbits with meal.

All the rabbits are carried by the chief of the Hunters society to the room of the paramount Rain chiefs. The rabbits are laid on the floor, heads to the east, an ear of corn is placed between the forepaws of each animal, and meal is sprinkled on it. Meat from the rabbit stew is cast into the fire with prayer: "My fathers, my mothers, my children, eat!"

After the return of the kachina from the hunt they go around town before entering the kiva. At night there is dancing in all the kivas. During the evening Chakwena, led by the chief of the Kachina society, encircles the town, Chakwena depositing food offerings in an excavation to the north, and praying for child-bearing women. The three following evenings Chakwena makes like offerings at the other cardinal points. The other kachina‡

* In a Hopi hunt by kiva there is driving by fire (Beaglehole 2:12).

† A rabbit hunt with girls may be held on Second Mesa after a girl's adolescence ceremony (Beaglehole 2:13).

‡ The circuits of the Salimobia are promissory of seeds; the circuits of Chakwena, of game (Stevenson).

also go around town and dance at night in Chakwena's kiva and in the room of the Hunters society.

In her kiva, after her last offering,* Chakwena is to lounge for four days—a ritual lying-in.† Any woman who has lost children and wishes to perform a propitious rite may remain in the kiva, Chakwena preparing a sand bed for her as in an actual confinement. This woman will bathe and array Chakwena for her domiciliary rounds. On the last of these tours the chief of the Kachina society is in the lead, followed by Chakwena, by the four Blue Horns, by the crier of the Kachina society and the two warriors of the society. Chakwena stands at the threshold of the house visited and extends her prayer-sticks into the room four times; the Blue Horns extend their bows. The woman of the house brings out bread, and the family sprinkle the kachina with meal. On this last tour big-game hunters give prayer-sticks to Chakwena, as do likewise would-be mothers. The prayer-sticks together with some of the food collected in the fawnskin bag are deposited in the riverbank by the managers of Chakwena's kiva.

KACHINA ATTACK AT ACOMA[104]

Formerly the dramatization referred to as "Kachina are going to fight us"‡ was held every five or six years, in spring.§ The Town chief told the War chief to notify kiva chiefs to call for

* I.e., four days after the hunt the confinement ritual takes place; but see p. 526 for this ritual as immediately following the hunt.

† In the Tewa tale of cast-away boy (War gods cycle) the old woman who finds the baby on the ash pile lies in with him four days.

‡ At Zuni the Ky'anakwe were the people who fought with the kachina, taking three prisoners After a famine the Ky'anakwe went to live at Acoma. The Ky'anakwe had with them Chakwena Woman, Mother of Game. Although the War Brothers killed her, she appears today in the kachina rabbit hunt of Zuni. The Zuni Ky'anakwe ceremony is entirely different from Acoma's dramatization, just as the Zuni and Acoma myths are quite distinctive, except that in both myths the War gods kill kachina with the rabbit-sticks given them by Sun, their father.

The Ky'anakwe myth and the myth of the Kachina attack are clear cases of etiological myth, myth to explain existing ceremonial.

On First Mesa Chakwena Grandmother is a war kachina. She arrived with Keres (Mustard clan) who sojourned in Zuni before joining the Hopi.

§ But see p. 541.

volunteers for kachina warriors from their membership. The Town chief's Antelope clan and the War society (O'pi) are to defend the town. To help them the Antelopes call upon the boys and girls they have sponsored at kachina initiation.

Walking through town, the War chief announces the ceremony in eight days. The kachina warrior impersonators begin to practice running, early in the morning and late in the evening. They vomit night and morning. Early the morning of the fifth day each goes out barefoot to the mountains to get wood for prayer-sticks which they make that day. In kiva the mask each is to wear is selected for him and covered with a cloth that can be identified. A man keeps his identity secret, except from brothers or close friends, lest a personal enemy actually kill him during the fight and escape unidentified.* On the sixth day the impersonator kills a sheep and puts the blood from the heart in a gut which he is to wear about his neck during the fight.† On the eighth day, the day of the fight, the Governor sends out eight sentinels, two by two, in different directions, to see that no one approach the town. The sentinels are provided with lunch by the Cooks or Stewards of the War captains. Officers keep watch in town with field glasses!

Early in the morning two red Gomaiowish, impersonated by Flint society men,‡ arrive shouting the war cry and warning the War chiefs against hostile kachina. Several kachina allies walk about town. The War chiefs visit the houses, pressing an arrow-point and a bow against the house walls at each corner to give them strength. Some of the friendly kachina do the same, using staff instead of bow, and others give antiterror herb medicine to the children. Hostile white Gomaiowish arrive from Wenimats[i], saying that the kachina will come bringing presents as usual, but

---

* Murder by Kachina impersonators rings of Hopi Kachina lore; also of the carnival in early Spain and in Mexico.

† Compare the use of this trick by the War gods in their contest with the Eagles.

‡ Compare impersonation of Koyemshi by Zuni societies.

they refuse the cigarettes of the red scouts* and struggle against having their bows taken from them.

Second visit from the white scouts who are still quarrelsome but depart this time for Wenimats[i] with peace offerings of food. West of town a barricade or "town" of poles and hides is put up by men who have to perform this task for life and are succeeded by their sons. For the third time the white scouts approach. The red scouts go out to meet them and overhear threats that all are to be killed or taken captive to Wenimats[i]. In the street red scouts disarm white scouts and take away their moccasins, and the white scouts run away, throwing stones as they run, in the good old way of fighting.

Meanwhile the Antelope men have put a downy eagle feather in their hair and painted their body pink all over and their face red with a streak of black under the eyes. The women have their faces, hands, and arms painted yellow with corn pollen. The O·pi paint their face black above the mouth and white below (like the Hopi Antelope society); they wear a buckskin shirt, red buckskin leggings, with legs painted white from leggings to kilt, a feather down the hair at the back, and eagle down over head and eyebrows.

When the warrior kachina reach the mesa, the Town chief and others go down to meet them and for their big clubs substitute smaller and less dangerous clubs. With their sticks of office the Town chief and the Antelope men hold back the warriors while two friendly kachina chiefs go on to the barricade where they weep, their head down on their arms, and pray. All run up the mesa to the barricade. The warrior kachina, one by one, pray at the "town" and then each strikes it four times. Should any-one strike more often the Town chief would order two warriors to seize and beat him. The barricade is removed to the next station and everything is repeated. At the third station the O·pi[†]

* These red Gomaiowish and white Gomaiowish kachina clowns suggest the clown dichotomy or moiety pattern obscure in the West but marked among Tiwa and Tewa, also among Pima-Papago where the moieties are characterized by white and red.

† The O·pi are representing the War Brothers who in the myth are the ones to kill the kachina (Stirling).

cut the throat (the blood-filled gut) of some of the kachina. To insure having one's throat cut by a friend the impersonator has in advance visited one of the O'pi with a prayer-feather and given him a pass sign. If the kachina has more than one gut of blood, he will have his throat cut again, after being revived by the War chiefs who with arrowpoint and bow touch his head, shoulders, back, and legs.* At the fourth station many throats are cut and again at the fifth and sixth stations.† At the seventh station O'pi seize the white scouts who have been encouraging the warriors, and castrate them;‡ their guts of blood were concealed in their breechcloths. The War chiefs apply their arrowpoint and bow to the white scouts, but they continue to rock back and forth as if in great pain. Now the O'pi and the tenders of the barricade give prayer-sticks to the kachina, placing them in their hands and holding their own hands underneath and praying. The Antelope men give the kachina a ball of cotton with beads inside. The impersonators withdraw to unmask at the foot of the mesa, returning to town after dark.

Continence is prescribed for all participants for eight days before the fight and eight days after; meat and salt are taboo four days before. The townspeople are supposed to be left saddened for days.

THE KACHINA CEREMONY OF THE CORN CLAN OF ACOMA[105]

This ceremony is held every five years, about the last of July. The head man of the Corn clan summons the clan to their

---

* The War Brothers were given this power by Sun when he gave them their weapons (Stirling). As usual, killers are curers.

† While lying "dead" on the ground, the kachina pray that their blood will give new strength to the ground, that it will produce more (Stirling). In the Origin myth the kachina attack was first dramatized in order to kill those who had mocked at the kachina. About ten men carrying prayer-sticks were led unsuspecting in front of the barricade and there actually killed by the kachina impersonators. Possibly such ritual killing was actually performed in early times, but not to check unbelief. That motivation was merely a useful afterthought. Compare the simulated killings at Hopi Powamu (Stephen 4:254) and Zuni stories about killing "mockers" (Bunzel 6:85–88). "To complete your ceremony you must take his head with you," says in ironical despair the grandfather of the mocker.

‡ Recall that Zuni Koyemshi are impotent.

(? maternal) house. They set the date eight days in advance. They inform the War chief, and he notifies the people that Shuracha will visit the pueblo in eight days.

During the first four days there are the usual preparations for a ceremony—making herb brew and vomiting night and morning, getting wood for prayer-sticks, grinding meal. The Corn men and women get help from the boys and girls they have sponsored at initiations into the Kachina organization. (Here is a kind of society organization, see p. 930.) They convene nightly in their house to practice songs and dancing. After four days they begin to make prayer-sticks and prayer-feathers. None of the Corn people may eat meat or salted food from that time on, and all must be continent. On the seventh day they paint their masks and prepare costumes, and some of the Corn men go rabbit-hunting.

At midnight of the seventh day some of the godsons set out for certain mountains or mesas, where they are to build fires by fire drill early the following morning. They go by couple north, west, southwest, and southeast. They may not drink water until they have finished building the fires and have reached the spring and camp of the kachina impersonators.

There are seven kachina—Shuracha represented by a young boy, entirely naked except for his mask; two Shumaashk'ᵘ carrying bow and arrows in lionskin quiver; two K'omutina (transvestites [Stirling]); Kaubata, the blind one, and his mother. Kaubat wears an antelope head, a buckskin shirt, and leggings. His mother who is impersonated by a man carries a bunch of deer scapulas which she rattles to guide her son. Impersonators are chosen by the Corn clan.

At midnight of the seventh day the impersonators have eaten, and from then until after the dance no one may eat or drink except children under about eight years. After their supper the impersonators set out for a spring to the west. With them go the head man of the Corn clan, perhaps some other old men, and some Corn women. About halfway to the spring, they stop and make a camp, where they leave their masks, the women, and the Corn clan's rabbits.

At sunrise the two couriers to the north build a fire on the mountaintop. They go on toward McCarty, westward, building about six fires along the way to the mesa at McCarty. Here the fire is a signal to all the other fire-builders to make their fires and start toward Acoma, building fires along the way. The kachina impersonators at the spring also build a fire when they see the McCarty fire. They pray and deposit their prayer-sticks at the spring. Shuracha fills his pottery canteen and lights his cedar-bark torch. Somewhere he picks up a piece of charred wood.

It is early afternoon when the kachina impersonators reach the camp where the women are waiting with their masks and the rabbits. They put on their masks and set out for Acoma. Shuracha carries the rabbits on his back. Arriving at the foot of the mesa, they dance a bit and then ascend the southwest trail and dance in the rear of the church. Then they go on to the first dancing station, each pair of dancers having their own song. Shuracha does not dance, but lights the pile of wood placed at each station by Corn men. When they have danced in front of the Corn clan house and Shuracha has kindled the fire, some Corn women come out and take canteen, rabbits, and charred wood from Shuracha and carry them into the house. Then all go inside, unmask, bathe, and feast.

The clan head calls the War chief to the Corn house and gives him the jar of water. The War chief takes it to Town chief who orders him to take it to every house in the pueblo, giving each household a few drops. If any water is left, a few drops are poured into the mesa reservoirs. If some is left after that, Town chief sprinkles it to the cardinal points, and any still left he puts in his household jar. The charcoal is distributed by Corn women to each household, a small bit for each fireplace.

NIMA'N KACHINA CEREMONY, WALPI, JULY 15–24, 1893[106]

[Powamu society chief of the Parrot-Kachina clan watches the sun after the summer solstice. He, Crier chief, and Eototo chief smoke together in the maternal house of the Parrot-Kachina clan the night before the announcement, which is made at dawn by Crier chief, eight days before the celebration. In 1893 the announcement was inferably on July 7.]

On July 14 in the evening Shü'himü, the chief of Horn kiva and Wi'nüta, Horn society chief pass around to the houses [of habitués of Horn kiva], saying, "Come to the kiva!" Everyone knows what kiva is meant and for what purpose, so no questions are asked. The men of the house give thanks. It is Horn kiva's turn to present the kachina dance at the conclusion of the ceremony, and as usual they will present Hümis kachina. Horn kiva men are to go to the kiva for preparatory talk and kachina song practice.

FIRST DAY

About sunrise in Chief kiva Intiwa, Powamu society chief and Parrot clan chief, sets up the standard, a blue-green prayer-stick with four feather pendants of eagle-wing and downy yellow bird feathers. Intiwa begins to make "all colors" prayer-sticks, the prayer for flowers and all cultivated vegetation. The two sticks are blue and yellow, male and female. Intiwa makes two sets for each of the four directions, and one set for each of three springs. He also makes prayer-feathers for the kachina shrines near town. Late in the afternoon all are taken out to deposit by Intiwa's son who takes off his trousers, lets his hair hang loose, and puts a prayer-feather on his crown. He runs as fast as he can [in token that the Spirits are to come quickly].

Intiwa also makes a cluster of prayer-feathers for Masauwü and two for Wind. The strings of these for Wind are soaked with saliva and honey. Intiwa had spurted honeyed saliva over all the prayer-sticks and feathers in his tray to supplicate the Winds to stay still, at home. Shortly before sunset Intiwa deposited the Wind prayer-feathers in a rock crevice and Masauwü's feathers with bread and corn-pudding crumbs, tobacco, and a pinch of meal in the shrine below Red cape. Intiwa will sleep in kiva from tonight on, but without fasting.

In the evening, song practice in Horn kiva, as there will be every night until the public performance. Wi'nüta gives notice from house to house.

SECOND DAY

Intiwa makes a prayer-feather for Spider Woman, representing the prayers of the old Hopi women; also four hawk prayer-feathers for the War Brothers, representing prayers of old men and warriors; also more prayer-feathers for the directions to be deposited again by his son in watercourses in the four directions, as supplications to the Clouds to hasten.

THIRD DAY

Intiwa finishes twelve sets of "all colors" prayer-sticks, and his son deposits them before noon, at watercourses in the directions. (Intiwa also makes enough prayer-feathers to give one to each of the Navaho kachina at sunset after their last song. This exhibition is by Singers society, the last kachina dance planned at the winter solstice ceremony to precede Nima'n.) Năka of the Parrot clan is in kiva spinning cotton string for prayer-sticks.

FOURTH DAY

Intiwa makes four long black prayer-sticks and several others. Năka makes prayer-feathers. About noon Intiwa brings from his house his *tiponi*, medicine bowl, corn ears, netted gourds, and Eototo mask; then he brings out the altar slabs and cotton altar cloth from the kiva kachina recess or shrine which he unplastered the first day. Clouds, Tungwup the Whipper kachina, and a dog-head kachina representing the domestic animals are painted on the cloth. After this reredos has been tied up and lightning sticks and their chief sticks placed up against it, Intiwa makes meal lines of the directions and sets his *tiponi* at their intersection. He sets out two wooden corn figurines, "corn mountains," in the same way, also in the same way his crenelated medicine bowl. *Tiponi* and bowl are on opposite sides of the *sipapu* plank from which he removes the plug. On the meal lines of the medicine bowl he places the ears of corn colored according to the directions, the aspergills, and on top of the ears the colored stones or crystals. [This is the altar of the directions made in all Hopi altar ceremonies.] Then he places the crystals in the bowl and a little honey. He sprinkles pollen mixture on aspergills and into the bowl.

Năka fills two pipes for Intiwa and himself. After a prayer by each in turn, they take their gourd rattles and begin the sequence of sixteen songs. At the first dirge-like song Intiwa, pouring water from his gourd, washes off the meal and stones from all the corn ears in circuit into the bowl. At the second lively song, he shakes all the pollen off the aspergills into the bowl, in circuit. Now the water has become medicine water. It will be used in painting prayer-sticks. At the sixth song he sprinkles pollen on everything in circuit and casts toward *tiponi* and vertical altar. At the next three songs he casts meal similarly. At the twelfth song Năka bubbles into the bowl four times with the eagle-bone whistle. A bar or two sung and four calls again. Four repetitions. This to call the Clouds. Năka asperses with whistle after each call and then lays the whistle across the bowl. Thirteenth song, pollen- and meal-casting; fourteenth, Intiwa raps with the plug on the *sipapu* plank, four blows six times, in quick-step measure. He is calling to Müy'ingwa who lives below and to all the other Chiefs of the Directions. At the last two songs Intiwa casts meal, sings a bar or two, again casts meal, and so on, concluding with casts toward altar prayer-stick trays and "mountains" and Eototo mask. Brief prayer. Each smokes the pipe into the bowl. Intiwa takes out the stones, smokes them, and puts them away into their pouch. He bundles up the ears of the directions and hangs them on the wall. This altar ritual has lasted from 2:30 to 3:45.

FIFTH DAY

At yellow dawn four gourds of water are placed on the altar by representatives of Cedarwood, Bear, Horn, and Patki clans who have just fetched the water from springs associated with these clans.

At yellow dawn the directions altar ritual is performed by Intiwa and Năka.

Later Chasra and Suyuku who are the two kachina "fathers" for Walpi and of course members of the Powamu society come down and join Intiwa and Năka in prayer-stick-making. Năka is making small finger-length "all colors" prayer-sticks for the children in the Kachina clan. Intiwa's prayer-sticks are all standard size, from center of palm to tip of middle finger. Besides "all colors" sticks he makes "night" sticks, supplication for rain to fall at night. All the sticks lie on the meal tray. A man comes in to make prayer-sticks for the Deer clan.

In Horn kiva twenty-nine Hümis masks are set along the south end ledge. Each man brought in his mask under his blanket yesterday after dark. Today the old pigments are to be scraped off and deposited in shrine.

In several houses men have begun to carve kachina dolls for distribution.

SIXTH DAY

Directions altar ritual at sunrise by Intiwa and Năka and then they fall to prayer-stick-making. Shortly after sunrise three youths are sent to the kachina mountain Kishyuba for spruce. Intiwa gives the leader two prayer-sticks and meal for the kachina.

Several men come in to make "all colors" prayer-sticks, thirteen including the two chiefs, and 308 sticks have been made. Each man brings his own materials, excepting pigments which are supplied by Intiwa, and places his sticks in his own tray, butts to center in radiating circle.

In Horn kiva the two chiefs are whitening and painting the masks. Some of the younger men proposed to present Zuni Hümis, but the two chiefs objected, "at such a critical drouthy time we should hold to our own kachina."

SEVENTH DAY

Directions altar ritual, and prayer-stick-making by more men.

In Horn kiva mask-decorating, each man decorating his own which accounts for the slight variations in the set.

EIGHTH DAY

Directions altar ritual and prayer-stick-making. Will they never finish!

Between 7:00 and 8:00 A.M. the clan mothers come down, old women or girls. I watch Hümisi of the Deer clan, a girl of fourteen. She goes to Intiwa who has prepared the stems of two sets of "all colors" prayer-sticks for her. He shows her how to tie on their feathers, sprigs, and food packet; she lays the finished sticks in Intiwa's tray. He passes her a pipe of tobacco, saying "my father's sister."* With repugnance she puffs over the prayer-sticks and then scuttles off up the ladder, leaving a chief's prayer-stick for Intiwa to complete with feathers. There are twenty-one or twenty-two chief's sticks, of which eight belong to women. I cannot elicit why all the clans are not represented.† Intiwa makes two prayer-sticks for Masauwü to which all the elders present contribute prayer-feather pendants which Intiwa loops on. These offerings are made because this was Masauwü's country. When the Hopi first came here, they found him living here.

At noon Intiwa makes a sand ridge along the entire front of the vertical altar and in it sets most of the 387 prayer-sticks in the trays. The Directions altar is renewed, and the ritual performed with a third man taking part. Two couriers with prayer-sticks are sent out to springs, to a point in the arroyo washed out by melting snow and to two Masauwü shrines. Food fragments also are to be given Masauwü. Prayers for rain are said before the couriers leave. There have been scattering showers this afternoon. Thunder, it looks as if it might rain tonight.

NINTH DAY

[After all-night practice the kachina dance maskless in the court, before dawn. Then at the kachina shrine at K'owaiwemove the Coyote clan mother whose house cherishes the mask of Eototo, kachina chief, wheels the hair of the impersonators of the kachina women. Powamu chief and the kiva kachina chief sit together watching for sunrise.]‡

* I thought this indicated that Intiwa was a child of her clan; but Intiwa who is probably Hümisi's ceremonial father may be using the kinship term in the same stereotyped way it is used in the smoking ritual of Zuni (Bunzel 4:762, n. 92).

† Probably because this is not the clan ceremony Stephen thinks it is. The women, like the men, are merely members of the Powamu society. It is a kachina society ceremony in which clan associations are merely involved, merely secondary.

‡ Information from Crow-Wing.

At yellow dawn Năka goes down to the kachina shrine and gives each kachina a miniature kick-stick, the small black cylinder that will be tied to the right wrist. Intiwa leads up the Hümis kachina* who carry each a bundle of cornstalks bearing ears. At the three usual dance places they sing and dance, in two columns, the "women" on the right of the men. They stamp with the right foot, and every two bars make a turning movement or right-about-face. After five numbers rabbit rugs and sheepskins are thrown down from the housetops, and the two kachina Fathers spread them on the ground. On these the "women" put down the gourds on which they prop their notched sticks. With their bone scapulas they scrape the stick in quick strokes from the operator, occasionally varying the steady rasp by drawing the scapulas rather slowly over the sticks toward them. They sing in falsetto as the men raise their rattles about breast high, shaking them in front and stamping with the right foot. The song ends in six minutes, and men and "women" stamp without singing as they again face into single files. Intiwa stands at the head of the line throughout with his meal basket and chief's stick.

At Chief court Intiwa sprinkles the kachina, descends into Chief kiva and leads up the society members, men and women who all sprinkle the kachina and at the conclusion of the dance give them each two sets of prayer-sticks and a pinch of meal. Năka puffs smoke on them and they are aspersed from the medicine bowl into which Intiwa had put herbs and refracted by crystal a ray of sun.

Intiwa leads the procession back to the kachina shrine where the prayer-sticks are deposited. Women come with food. At 10:00 A.M. they perform again in Antelope mound or Pillar court and in Chief court and receive more prayer-sticks. They withdraw only to the north edge of town. Here as usual the chiefs gather and sit smoking in a circle, the unmasked impersonators occasionally singing. About noon another performance at Chief court and withdrawal to the north edge to eat the food brought

* In later years their younger brother Avachhoya (Stephen 4:308), the boy Corn-Fire kachina, comes out with them (Parsons 40:99, n. 151).

there by the women. Performances continue the rest of the afternoon.

In Pillar court is planted a small spruce, to which fifteen to twenty prayer-feathers are fastened. At its base are planted two sets of prayer-sticks. Other sticks are planted at the two other dance places.

Hümis kachina wear a helmet mask with a high tablet painted with cloud and rainbow designs and on the back with butterfly and corn designs. Body and limbs blackened with corn smut; the design or glyph of interlocking curves called friendship mark is made by fingernail on breasts and below each shoulder blade. Spruce collar; blue yarn bandoleer; blue leather armlets with spruce twigs thrust in stems down; two eagle-wing or hawk or dyed hen feathers to lower edge of armlet; wrist guard. White kilt, two belts, foxskin at back, ten or twelve spruce boughs tied into belt, stems up. Blue yarn below left knee; tortoise shell rattle below right knee; red moccasins and fringed anklets; gourd rattle in right hand, spruce sprig in left. The "women" wear hair in whorls and yellow leather maskette with a strip of blue black Hopi cloth and painted lines of red or blue at the lower edge to which innumerable bunches of bluebird tail feathers and three to five prayer-feathers are fastened. A red-hair fringe over the face part. Black dress and red-and-blue bordered woolen blanket or embroidered cotton blanket; wrapped moccasins.

The largest distribution of bows and arrows and dolls takes place at the final sunset performance. Intiwa again leads up the men and women of the society, seven women, twelve men, the men in kilt with flowing hair and prayer-feathers on the crown. Intiwa sprinkles meal on the kachina, Nyato of the Tobacco clan puffs smoke on them, Yoyŏwaiya of the Badger clan asperses them from his medicine bowl. The men society members give prayer-sticks to the male kachina, the women society members give them to the "female" kachina. The two kachina Fathers give thanks. As Intiwa leads out, people pluck spruce from the kachina to plant in their fields. Out on the mesa point the kachina impersonators make exorcism, casting meal over the cliff edge and toward San Francisco Mountains.

TENTH DAY

The hatch of Chief kiva is covered with sand, and four clouds and rain are designed in meal on each side.

Intiwa is squatted right over the open *sipapu*, a foot on each side. He and Năka have washed their heads; they wear white kilt and prayer-feather on crown. As they begin to sing their sixteen songs, the kachina arrive and stand in couples on the four sides of the hatchway, Eototo, Malo, and six Hümis.* Hoñi stands with a bowl and a tray of meal and prayer-sticks on the second rung of the ladder. He casts meal toward the northwest. Just as the meal touches Eototo, he passes to Hoñi a circlet (prayer-stick) on the point of a long prayer-stick. This is repeated by Hoñi and all the other kachina. Four Hümis pour water from their gourds into Hoñi's bowl. Hoñi offers a prayer-stick to Eototo and, as Eototo reaches for it, Hoñi withdraws it. Hoñi asperses Eototo and feints again. The fourth time he gives him the prayer-stick. This rite of fourfold feint with aspersing Hoñi repeats with three other kachina. Again Hoñi casts meal, and, as it touches the kachina, they begin to circle around the hatch, and after four circuits Malo casts down the hatchway the branch of box thorn which he carries. This is placed on the altar. Attached to the branch are circlet prayer-sticks and sixteen small gourd disks, painted the colors of the directions and having an owl prayer-feather. [These are implements of a ritual, rain-making game. See p. 981.]

Just as this detailed ritual of casting down the boxthorn began eight young men came in from Wipho springs on a run. Their bodies are whitened; they wear breechclout and silver belt and a bell at the belt. They carry onions, bean plants, chili, cockscomb, squash blossoms, melon vines and in their hair are sunflowers. The little girls despoil them.

* The chiefs or their representatives are impersonating the kachina, whether as members of the Powamu society, as clan representatives, or as society chiefs is not clear.

Now after laying his *tiponi* down on its side, Intiwa leads up the society members and the same rites of smoking and aspersing are performed as were performed yesterday morning. At the conclusion of the circuits lookers-on begin to spit violently. This, that the kachina may carry away all sicknesses. Intiwa leads the kachina down to the shrine where the boxthorn with the colored disks is deposited. The kachina are departing to San Francisco Mountains, their doorway to the Underworld.

Meanwhile, Năka, who has remained in kiva, is exorcising all there with his buzzard feather. When Intiwa returns, he too exorcises.*

Intiwa deposits in his field or the fields of kindred the circlet and other prayer-sticks, also the miniature spruce. The sticks given the kachina or some of them are also deposited in fields close to an arroyo with prayer for rain and a cast of meal on the sticks and toward the Sun.

Same' Invites Kachina from Mishongnovi To Dance on First Mesa, June, 1920[107]

Same' of Walpi wants to invite kachina from Mishongnovi to come over to dance, so he asks men of his clan, Coyote clan, to come to his wife's house in Sichomovi. He asks them because they are going to help him with food and other things. They say it is all right, so the next day Same' goes over to Mishongnovi. When he gets there, he goes to the house of the man he wants to be the chief. He has with him a bag of tobacco and two or three pipes. "Did you come?"—"Yes." They give Same' something to eat. The man (of the house) lays his bag of tobacco down by the fire, he lights his pipe, smokes four times, and gives the pipe to the visitor, saying, "My friend!" Same' smokes out the pipe and, returning it, says, "My friend!"—"I guess you have come for something."—"Yes. I want kachina to come to dance for us."—"What kind of kachina?"—"Ana kachina."—"All right." They say goodbye. The man (visited) goes to his kiva, he makes a fire,

---

* According to Crow-Wing, Intiwa has to sleep four more nights in kiva. And the Badger clan medicine-maker keeps him company, his medicine bowl being still in kiva. The last evening all the society members come in to smoke and pray and be finally exorcised.

he calls out for the members of his kiva to come to the kiva. They come in. Then they will ask why he called out for them. "This morning a man from Walpi came to ask for kachina to go there to dance. I promised him to go."—"All right. What kind of kachina did he want?"—"Ana kachina."

That night they will sing one or two songs. The next morning he (the dance chief) will get some wood to have a fire in the kiva at night, while they practice. He makes a fire every night, he calls out, they come, they smoke, they practice. They do this for several nights. The dance chief says, "Tomorrow I will go to Walpi to tell that man that in five days* we will go to dance, everybody will be glad. You will make moccasins to dance in. Our kachina at Kishyuba will bring clouds, lightning, and rain for everybody so that our crops will grow well."

The next morning the dance chief gets his bag of tobacco and goes to Same"'s house. "Did you come?"—"Yes." First they give him something to eat. "All right, let us go to the kiva," says Same'. They go to Butterfly kiva.† Same' calls out, "Men and boys, come to Butterfly kiva and smoke!" The men go to the kiva to hear what they are called for. They all smoke. Same' smokes his pipe four times and gives it to the visitor who smokes it out and returns it. The visitor refills the pipe, smokes it four times, and passes it around the circle. Same' says, "I guess it smells (for the clouds). What have you come for?" The visitor says, "In four days from today kachina are going to dress themselves at Kishyuba and come and bring clouds, lightning, and rain, corn of different colors, watermelons, everything. (All this is for everybody, for everybody on the earth.) There will be dancing here in four days to give pleasure to the children of the Town chief and to the children of the Town chief woman so that they live to be old." Everybody says, "Thank you for that!"

* Four days, plus the day of announcement; and these days of preparation are given the usual ritual night names, the dance visitors arriving on *totokya* and dancing the next day (see p. 501).

† Ordinarily and at the winter solstice ceremonial, Same' uses the Nashabki kiva of Walpi, but because he invited the kachina to dance at Sichomovi he uses on this occasion one of the two Sichomovi kivas, Butterfly kiva, associated with the Badger clan.

The Mishongnovi men get ready; they make moccasins and what they are to use in the dance. They paint their masks. The next day they put the feathers on the masks. That afternoon the dancers start in a line. The old man who is their Father,* follows them. They carry their things on their back, their mask in their hand. At the foot of the mesa at the trail sits Same' with a bag of tobacco, sitting there until they come. Same' says to them, "Thank you that you come!" They all shake hands with him. He lights his pipe and passes it around four times. Same' leads them, bringing them into Butterfly kiva. "Thank you for coming!" Everybody shakes hands. They hang up their masks for them; all sit by the fireplace; they smoke, many times. Same' says to the boys there, "You boys go around the houses and get food for our friends!" So the boys go out and get food. They have supper. They smoke again. Same' says to the men, "Now you can practice your songs." They practice all night.

At daylight Same' says, "I am glad you have come." Everybody says, "Thank you for coming!" They say, "It is daylight, you better dress yourselves." They get black sunflower seeds and mash them for black paint. Across chest and back and on upper arm they paint with yellow, with two lines down upper arm, down chest and back, and on lower arms. The thighs are painted white. They dress up, go down to K'owaiwemove [the kachina shrine] to wait for sunrise.

At sunrise Same' lays down a prayer-feather "road-marker" for the kachina. Same' stands first in line, the Father† for the [visiting] kachina second. They start for the court in Sichomovi. There Kachina chief stands first in line. He carries an ear of blue corn. The middle dancer [song director] carries white corn, and the last dancer carries yellow corn. Badger woman, the Kachina mother,‡ walks up to the leader and takes from him

* Some member of the Powamu society.

† Chosen by Same'; he happens to be a Tewa Cloud clansman.
Walpi and Sichomovi kachina have a permanent "father" chosen by Powamu chief from members of the Powamu society.

‡ She keeps Shalako and many different kachina in her Sichomovi house.

the ear of blue corn, Same' takes the white corn, the Father for
the kachina takes the yellow corn. Then anybody who wants
to sprinkle meal comes and sprinkles. After they finish dancing,
Same' says he wants them to dance all day to give pleasure to
the children of the Town chief. They go down to K'owaiwemove;
the women carry food down there for them. They eat breakfast;
they come up and dance all morning. They go down again to
K'owaiwemove. The women take them food; they eat dinner;
they come up; they dance all afternoon. In the afternoon the
clowns* come out from Butterfly kiva, four or five. They dance
in a funny way, singing a funny song, saying funny things to the
kachina. Their aunts bring food to the clowns. They eat out
there, eating in a funny way. All the people laugh and are happy
over these clowns (Pl. XV).

Same' steps up to the middle dancer and says he wants them to
dance next day. "So I will take you back into Butterfly kiva."
The clowns follow. They dance there. Then they undress [un-
mask], wash themselves, put on their clothes. Men take them
around to their houses to give them something to eat; make them
their friends. The visitors go back to the kiva; they smoke and
sleep there. Next morning the same men go to the kiva and take
the visitors to their houses for breakfast and to have their head
washed. The visitors return to the kiva. Same' calls out for the
women to bring food to the kiva. They eat again. They go down
to K'owaiwemove. [All the performances of the day before are
repeated.] Different men take them home to eat. Next morning
they do not go down to K'owaiwemove; they go to rest at the
edge of the mesa, and food is taken them inside the house near
by. They eat dinner; they go back to the court to dance. Then
Same' says to the middle dancer, the dance director, "It is time
for you to go home. Your fathers and mothers and sisters are
homesick for you. They are waiting for you. You have been
here a long time. When you go back to Kishyuba, tell your
fathers and mothers and sisters to hurry and bring whatever the
people need."

* Chosen by the Kachina Father for the visitors.

PLATE XV

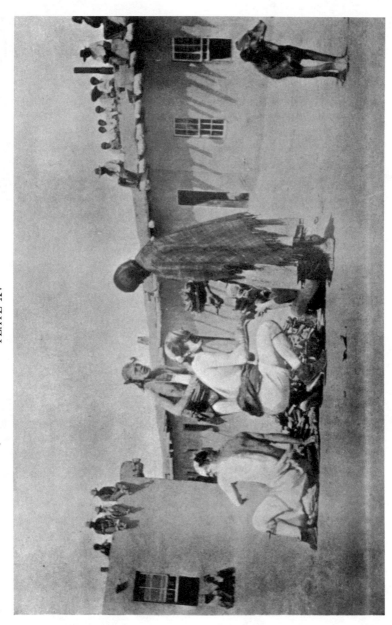

Woman Bringing Food to Clowns, Sichomovi

Same' gives each dancer a prayer-feather.* Their Kachina Father gives each a prayer-feather. Same' leads them to the place at the foot of the mesa where he met them. They smoke; they shake hands; with their things (the presents given them) on their back,† they start in single file. They return to their kiva in Mishongnovi and stay there all night. All the next day they dance at their own village.

This year or the next, kachina from First Mesa will go to dance at Mishongnovi.

CROW-WING HAS THE WATER SERPENT DANCE, HANO, 1920[108]

February 25.‡ This morning I told the men of Chief kiva [Hano] that I was thinking of having a dance for the family. The men said it would be all right. So this evening we will plant corn and beans in kiva. In the afternoon all the men and boys went down to the foot of the mesa to get some sand. I gather up the head men and talk to them. They say it is good for everybody.

March 7. Tonight is my time. I told my kiva partners to tell their folks to cook some meat. We all kill sheep and make nice things to eat. In the evening we all eat meat, and after supper we go to the kiva. I take five boys with me to the house in Sichomovi where they keep Avaiyoe' (the little Water Serpents). The family sets out supper for us. (The food is set down as if for the little Water Serpents, but we eat it.) Then they take the little Water Serpents from the other room, and we take them to the kiva [where we spend the night].

March 8. This morning we all fetch our food for breakfast. This food is without salt, and there is no meat. We do not eat meat or salted food for three days and a half, and we have to stay in kiva; we do not go house-visiting. (I have a man to take care of my sheep.) The corn plants look very well; we have to watch

---

* Same' himself will receive the miniature spruce with its prayer-feathers that has been set in the dance court by the visitors (Stephen 4:375).

† Nowadays hauled by wagon.

‡ The day following the conclusion of Powamu ceremony.

them.* I go to every kiva to tell the men to get ready; in four nights we are going to have our dance.

March 9. The men are now making moccasins for the dance, and some are making belts and other things. Everybody is busy at work. I send a boy to get me spring water. In the morning he starts to the north and goes around the mesa, going to every near-by spring. From the spring he puts water into his little gourd bottle, and puts a prayer-stick into each spring. He comes back in the evening. We are glad he is back. Then we all smoke to have rain.

March 10. All the men and boys are fixing their masks and the other things we are going to use tomorrow night. One of the boys goes to get spruce. He rides a horse and takes another horse to load. He comes back this evening, just at dark. We are all glad for it. We all smoke to pray for rain. After supper the men dress the Muddy Heads (Koyimsi clowns), and then they go around town and to every kiva [to announce the dance. They carry bells and ox-hoof rattles and talk to the kiva chief standing halfway up the ladder. They speak in loud tones so the women and children in the surrounding houses can hear them].

March 11. It is my day. I wash my hair and bathe. While we are making prayer-sticks a Badger clan man from the house they [the images] live in is fixing the dolls which we are going to make dance.† He dresses them. He is the only man who knows how to paint and dress them. I make prayer-sticks half a day, and I finish. But it takes all day to fix the dolls. Until he finishes in the afternoon we do not eat or drink. When we are all finished,

---

* In the performance a miniature cornfield is to be made with this sprouted corn which the children are told has grown under their eyes.

† Or grind. These are two marionettes kept in the Sichomovi Badger house where the Shalako and Wüwüyomo (Sayatasha) masks live. The expert is To'chï who lived a long time at Zuni. This grinding act may be performed also by kachina girl impersonations (Fewkes 12:44, 88). It is to be compared with the spectacular Zuni dramatization, Ololowishkya, the Advent of Kolowisi, the horned Water Serpent represented as a phallic kachina at which two kachina "girls" grind with two He'he'a kachina to wait on them, four kachina flutists and a large kachina circle to dance and sing (Parsons 29:195–99). In 1900 a very similar dramatization was given in Walpi in the court the day after the kiva Water Serpent performance (Fewkes 12:54).

I send different boys out with the prayer-sticks to every direction, east, north, west, south. After the boys come back, we eat our supper. Then we begin to cut the corn we have raised. Some boys bring in some clay and water. They tie corn with yucca blades in little bunches for their roots, and stand them in the mud. Then we put them in baskets, nine basketfuls, one for each kiva. Then the kachina are ready to dress up. Hahai'wuxti or (Tewa) Pokekwiyo (Pour Water Woman) is the mother of the little Water Serpents. Now the men take the little Water Serpents, also two water birds, and two men carry their boards. [The screens or "walls," painted green for the grassy earth, behind which the strings of the marionettes are pulled.] And two He'he'a kachina [Tewa, Mukwęte] carry the grinding-stones for the girls (i.e., dolls). The other kiva men, ten or more, will be kachina of different kinds to sing for them.

We [nine, the eight with the paraphernalia and Crow-Wing] have to go down to the Gap. I am at the head of the men.* When we get down to Coyote spring I have to listen to what I might hear. I hear a water bird singing, and so we are all very glad for it. Just then the rain starts to fall. It is raining when we come up. Everybody is happy.

From the Gap we come up and go to Chief kiva. We have our dance† there first. Then we go to Tewa kiva to dance, then to Sichomovi and Walpi, into each kiva.‡ We go back to Chief kiva. Then they undress those little Water Serpents, and we take them back to the Badger clan house.

March 12. This morning I sent one boy, the best I could pick, with the prayer-feathers down to the spring to pray for rain. He

* He carries a tray of prayer-meal and sprinkles the "road" on which at the edge of the water the serpent images are laid. Prayer-sticks deposited; ritual smoke; prayer; gourd trumpets blown into water; tips of heads of images dipped in water. Trumpeting up the trail (Stephen 4:320-21).

† The Water Serpent images are thrust through holes in the screen; they are suckled by the mother of the kachina, Hahai'wuxti, they struggle with one another or with the kachina clowns; they throw down the "cornfield"; gourd trumpets are blown, Water Serpent's dreadful voice.

‡ Each kiva may present a dance, so there may be in each kiva a program of nine acts. There are outdoor daytime dances also.

has to go down quickly and come back quickly so rain will come quickly. He carries the prayer-feathers each kiva man has had to make for each little Water Serpent, for Hahai'wuxti, for the "wall," and for the kachina figure painted on it. The prayer-feathers of the little Water Serpents were worn around their neck. All these prayer-feathers are taken down by that fast runner.

TURTLE DANCE
SAN JUAN, DECEMBER 24–26, 1925[109]

Christmas day, after the close of Matachina, about sundown, the Turtle dancers are led out from Little kiva by Kossa old man, the clown society chief. He wears his blanket close around him and around his head a *banda* of cornhusk. During the dancing he stands to one side near the head of the line. He does not sprinkle meal on the road, and nobody sprinkles it on the dancers. Before leaving the kiva, the dancers have been aspersed from a medicine bowl by the Town chiefs.

There are thirty-seven dancers, near both ends of the line some boys not over twelve. They dance in line, stomping the familiar kachina dance step and making the usual half-turns in position, like the Good Kachina of Zuni or the Hopi Long-hair kachina. They sing to a large wooden drum. They dance in the two courts in the regular dance places and then in front of Little kiva.

They wear a black kilt with the large white dance belt, the ball fringe pendant at the back; under the right knee the turtle-shell rattle; bells under the left knee; also a belt of bells. In the hair a large downy eagle feather; in right hand a gourd rattle; spruce twigs in left.

Tomorrow the dancers will come out once before dinner and several times in the afternoon, and clowns will be out. Dancers will be wearing a white kilt, the Hopi dance kilt, and skunk fur heel bands. Body painted dark brown, legs above knees and hands whitened. No face paint. Parrot feather between two eagle feathers laid horizontally on one side of the crown, on the other side a tawdry ornament, even magazine pictures; the hair short—in fact, shaved halfway up the head. Silk kerchief around neck and glass beads.

Christmas Eve two groups of Turtle dancers went from house to house to dance and sing and to receive loaves of bread for their sack. From Santa Clara the following Turtle dance song is recorded:

> Long ago in the north
> Lies the road of emergence!
> Yonder our ancestors live,
> Yonder we take our being
> Yet now we come southwards.
> For cloud flowers blossom here
> Here the lightning flashes,
> Rain water here is falling![110]

TAOS, JANUARY 1, 1932[111]

The dancers come out about sunrise from Water kiva and dance in front of the church, then at the three other regular dance places. They come out three times in the morning and three times in the afternoon. The dancers do not eat until they have been out twice. Before their first appearance the church bell rings, and people carry candles to the church. The second appearance of the dancers is at 10:30. First walks the drummer, his huge drum on his back, then the dance leader who is wrapped in a blanket and appears to be carrying something enveloped in spruce twigs. He wears a red-hair belt as a *banda*, the ends pendent on the right side of his head, and from the back an erect eagle feather. On jaws and chin from ear to ear a broken band of white paint, just like the dancers.

The twenty-six dancers wear kilts made of white cotton or of a fringed silk shawl, black or colored: one kilt is of Hopi woolen cloth, white with the scarlet and dark-blue border. Belts vary: there are the red and green belts of the women; there is even an American leather belt with a steel buckle. A few twigs of spruce are stuck erect into the belt, and colored ribbons and silk kerchiefs hang from the belt at the back, instead of foxskin pendent; low moccasins, beaded or buckskin, stained saffron with anklets of brown fur (no skunk fur): bells below each knee (formerly turtle-shell rattle) with colored yarn pendants; necklaces of colored glass beads (no silver or turquoise); I note one necklace of several strands of jet. The hair is parted and done up behind the head, the queue covered by a broad band of cloth or ribbon or by a duckskin, at the top of which are a bunch of brown-and-white hawk (?) feathers and a twig of spruce, and erect from these, two eagle feathers with a parrot or imitation parrot feather or a peacock feather. Nine dancers have a little bunch of small stiff parrot feathers tied to the crown and hanging over the forehead, Zuni fashion. Spruce carried in both hands, a gourd rattle in the right; hands held close together in front of the body, the elbows bent (San Juan position also.).

As usual the middle man is the dance director initiating movements with his rattle. It is the usual kachina stomping step, not very vigorously done, the left foot is hardly lifted. In making the half-turn the right arm sweeps high over the head of the dancer next.* The right-about-face and three songs are repeated in each dance place. During the dancing the leader moves very slowly, inch by inch, in dance measure but barely lifting his feet from the ground, down the line facing or rather shouldering it, his right shoulder toward it. He moves down and then up. He makes two such progresses during the total performance at each dance place.

At the afternoon appearances every dancer in the line wears a silk shawl as kilt, and body pigment is used: yellow over shoulder and chest to a ring of white spots around the body over the stomach and from there to the belt grayish white; yellow to the elbows, white to above the wrists or to a wrist guard when one is worn; the upper leg white to a ring of white spots above the knee, the knee yellow to another ring of white spots below, the rest of the leg white, the same grayish white. In a picture dated 1916 the spotty design is placed like a bandoleer (Pl. XVI).

* Characteristic of the Navaho kachina as danced by Hopi. Possibly this Taos dance *is* Navaho kachina.

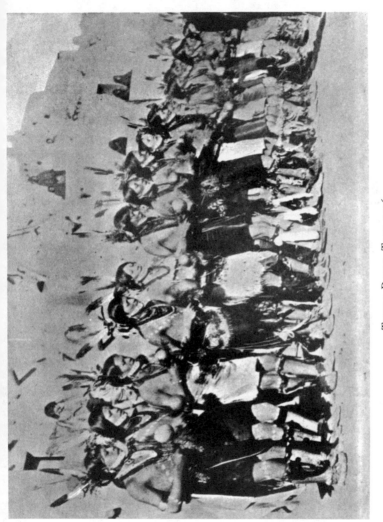

TURTLE DANCE, TAOS, 1916

MASKLESS KACHINA DANCE AT ISLETA* AND RABBIT HUNT†

Thlįwale is called in from "Zuni mountain" or Welima by Chakabede at midnight on September 25. Thlįwale may be heard hollering as he approaches from the west, whence Chakabede leads him into town, sprinkling in front a line of meal. Thlįwale dances in the plaza, first on the east side, then in circuit on the other sides. As it is night, you cannot see how he is dressed or appointed; but he does not wear a mask. Chakabede talks (prays) to him and gives him the prayer-sticks he has made for him, thereby paying him; he sprinkles him with meal, and then Thlįwale "goes back home."

The next day Chakabede bids the War captains call out for the men and youths to come for "four days" to his house to practice their songs, old songs and new. Chakabede has already asked the chief of the Black Eyes for the dance, Chakabede's assistant asking the Shure' chief. During these days it is not necessary to stay continuously indoors, but continence is required.‡ On the third day eight or ten youths are dispatched to gather the spruce which is to be the dress of Thlįwale. They are also to get two spruce trees,§ one for the Black Eyes to stand near in the dance, and one for the Shure'. The leader is given a prayer-stick by Chakabede to put with meal into the spring to ask for the spruce, at sunrise of the fourth day. The stick for the Black Eyes sprucegatherers is of red willow; that for Shure', yellow willow.

On the afternoon of the fourth day the dancers go out to meet the returning spruce-gatherers. The dancers sprinkle meal on the spruce and give thanks. The dancers belong to both moieties—half Black Eyes, led by the Chakabede; half Shure', led by

* From Parsons 52:332-36. Compare the Hopi dance at Jemez and the Hümis kachina on First Mesa, pp. 544, 773.

† Read in connection with the next section on rabbit hunts, but it has seemed better to give this Isletan hunt along with the dance it follows.

‡ In another connection I was told that the dancers would not be released from kiva "even if their father or mother died." Which suggests that the fourday period of dance practice is also a period of strict retreat, also indifference to the usual death taboo.

§ After the dance people like to get these trees to make into house ladders. They ask the moiety chiefs for the trees, with a cigarette.

his assistant—and they divide the spruce to carry to their respective kivas. In each kiva the moiety chief has been waiting in his seat by the fire. The chief stands to receive the spruce, and to place it in the middle of the floor and sprinkle it with pollen. From his medicine bowl each chief takes a little water, drinks some, and from his mouth sprinkles some on the spruce. To each dancer he also gives a drink, the recipient saying, as is usual on receiving a drink of medicine, *aka'a*, (?) father. Before the recipient swallows the drink he sprays some over himself. The moiety chief addresses the dancers. Late that same night from each kiva the dancers come out to dance in the plaza, with their rattles, and shirtless, but without their spruce. As in the afternoon, Chakabede leads the Black Eyes; Chakabede's assistant, the Shure'.

In each kiva six men have been made K'apio, i.e., clowns and dance managers. Also in each kiva is chosen a little boy of six or seven to dance out in front of the line—Aiyayaode. He will be spotted with white and wear on each side of his head a small deer horn. In spite of his horns he represents Wildcat,* who at the Emergence was the leader, with his horns tearing up the earth and making a gap for the people to pass up through.† The Black Eye clowns are striped black and white, the hair whitened, with large "earrings" of cornhusk, i.e., the hair is done up in side bunches. Clout of black cloth; at the back, attached to a bandoleer, little branches of cottonwood. They carry willow sticks, and wear anklets of spruce. Of the Shure' clowns one is painted yellow all over, another red all over, another white all over, and the others red or white. Across the face are stripes of contrasting color. The hair, painted the same color as the body, is plastered down with the pigment and then brought up into a poke on top of the head and tied with yucca fiber.‡ These carry long blades of yucca as whips and wear a bandoleer with cottonwood twigs, and collar, armlets, and anklets of spruce.

The morning of the dance, the clowns come out and two by

* Topirmosan, "coming in without saying anything," cat.

† In the Emergence text and story the K'apio make this gap or gate, see p. 255.

‡ These hair pokes are thought of as horns.

two visit the houses of their aunts, aunts in blood, or if these are few, women of their father's Corn group who have been appointed to act as "aunts" by the group chief. The clowns instruct the women to prepare meal or make bread in the shape of jackrabbits and turtles for their "nephews," to whom they will also give watermelons or chili, silk *banda*, and pottery bowls. While the women are making ready, in the plaza on the ground the clowns draw a "house" into which the head clown takes one of the others and seats him, asking him if he wants to get married. "No."—"Yes, you should get married. You are old enough."—"All right, I will marry."—"You want to get married, but you cannot work. Whom will you marry?" Then the leader names the oldest woman in town and gives his victim a room in the "house," telling him what to do when he lives there with his wife. All this farce is repeated for each clown. Now the "aunts" arrive on the scene, bringing the food into the two "houses." After the clowns eat, they invite visitors from other pueblos to come and eat.

Now the dancers come out to dance on the four sides of the plaza. With them are three men in buckskin mantles to play the notched bone, a deer's leg bone propped against a gourd and scraped with a deer shoulderblade. The Black Eyes come first and start on the east side. When they move on to the north side, the Shure' come in to the east side. The Black Eyes dancers are led in by the Chakabede; the Shure', by his assistant. They dance all day, making anti-sunwise circuits in the plaza. After the last performance they are sprinkled with meal by the Chakabede and by his assistant, and on returning to their respective kivas they are meal-sprinkled by the moiety chief and given medicine water to drink.

The dancers wear a dance kilt with white cotton belt and spruce pendants. Spruce collar and spruce in leg bands and in armlets of leather painted turquoise. Skunk-fur heel bands. Spruce in left hand; in right hand the Black Eyes carry a black gourd rattle, the Shure' a red rattle. Under the right knee is a turtle rattle, a water turtle, for the Black Eyes, a land turtle for the Shure'. The *tablita* or wooden headpiece of the Black Eyes is dark blue and red with black eagle feathers; the *tablita* of the Shure', blue and yellow with white eagle feathers. The visor is plaited yucca; hair flowing.

Before the finish of the last dance the clowns withdraw to their respective kivas, carrying their food surplus. The moiety chiefs give them permission to go to the river to wash off their paint. After sprinkling meal on the water, they wash and dress. They return to the kiva to get permission to carry their food pile to their own houses.

Now Chakabede and his assistant summon the clowns back to kiva and then send them forth to tell people to prepare their lunch for a hunt the day following. The clowns stay overnight in kiva. They decorate themselves and at sunrise sally forth to dance on the roofs on the four sides of the plaza. (In using the kiva ladder the clown has to step on its terraced top, the cloud terrace design.) As soon as the people see them, they get ready to set out on the hunt.*

The head clown has gone to the Hunt chief the night before to ask him to work. So at sunrise a little distance from town the Hunt chief will be making a little fire of which the smoke is to blind the rabbits and keep them from running far. The Hunt chief has got his fire-stick or brand from the house of the Town chief. "When we see the smoke, we start."

The people gather five or six miles to the west. The clowns call out to them not to drive their wagons inside the hunt circle. The clowns also place the hunters and the women who are participating. Now the Hunt chief calls out to everybody to be careful, not to shoot anybody in the circle. Again the Hunt chief calls out; the hunters shout; the rabbits will start up from everywhere, running blindly.

All the rabbits got in the first surround will belong to the Town chief; in the second surround, to the Hunt chief; in the third surround, to the Chakabede, Kumpa, and Black cane War chief. On the following surround the women run up, as usual the woman first to reach the trophy receiving it.

* For the clown societies as managers in the hunt with the girls see Santo Domingo, White 4:147–48; Cochiti, Goldfrank 3:89–91; Jemez, Parsons 41:94.

The clowns are the first to return, in order to go to the river to wash and dress; after the third surround the Hunt chief returns. The day following the women who have received game pay their hunters with a basket of wafer-bread or tortillas and a bowl of stew. The game taken by the clowns is given to their "aunts" in return for the jackrabbit breads given by their "aunts."

The notched-bone dance is a harvest thanksgiving, "for the end of the crops, thanking for them." Also it is to bring frost, to harden the corn and grapes which are to be dried. Therefore all crops such as melons which would be hurt by frost must be gathered before this dance.

MASAUWÜ GOES OUT TO THE FIELDS[112]

After a preliminary retreat for prayer-stick-making and depositing (Mishongnovi) and a rabbit hunt to supply rabbit skin and blood to Masauwü, the impersonator and another society man go to a cave where the impersonator is smeared with rabbit blood and arrayed in a woman's dress,* with different colored ears of corn hanging from his waist, and a mask of bloody rabbit skin with cornhusk circles around eyes and mouth. Under the mask his face is streaked black. Any trespasser near the cave would have to substitute as impersonator.

About the middle of the afternoon Masauwü goes out to the field of the man who has asked for the ceremonial to bless his intertown working party. Masauwü may plant a few holes with mixed seed corn and chase the workers in the planting-party or he may merely ambuscade the party on their return home. When he strikes people with his sack, a small cylinder filled with cotton or anything soft, they fall down as if dead. "All this running about is good for the crops."

While the working party is eating their early supper, Masauwü circles four times around the town. Then Hair kachina (? Anakchina), now called Masauwü kachina, come out to dance, and Masauwü goes off to supper. Comedians (Piptukyamu) appear as cowboys or (?) kachina, one at a time, Masauwü clowns

---

* Tied reversely on left shoulder (Walpi). Formerly Keresan male dress (Bandelier). Compare Koyemshi also.

with each and finally knocks him dead, stripping him and putting the clothes on himself, backward, tying a belt on the left instead of the right or putting moccasins on the wrong feet.

Now somebody lights a cedar-bark flare and advances on Masauwü who falls down dead. They carry him to the mesa edge to roll him over, but he jumps up and chases the men back to the court. The act is repeated but the fourth time Masauwü walks back slowly and stands in the court to receive meal and prayer-feathers and prayers for long life, rain, good crops, and many children. The prayer-feathers Masauwü deposits in a Masau shrine and his costume in a near-by cave.

Masauwü may also come out for an intertown harvesting-party, but no kachina come out, this being out of kachina season. (*Kachina rules do not apply to Masauwü.*)

PLANTING AND HARVESTING FOR THE TOWN CHIEF OF COCHITI, 1922[113]

Before planting the Town chief's corn, the chiefs of the Giant and Shikame societies meet with the Town chief in his house. Here they probably make prayer-sticks, pray, and sprinkle the seeds with medicine. The seeds are carried from house to house by two Koshari when it is their year of service or by two Kurena in their year. At each door a pail of water is thrown over the heads of the clown visitors. At the planting, seeds are dropped by members of the kachina dance society. Women do not go. Only blue corn is planted.

Harvesting for the Town chief was observed the year the Kurena were in charge. After announcement by the War captain, the Kurena went singing through town. Two were masked, wore Hopi blankets, and carried a comb. Two were naked and masked and carried their heavy wands (the Kurena whip) and some black paint with which they streaked the cheeks of all going to gather the corn.* Women were also brushed with the wands; it was called brushing off sickness.

The men and women returned from the field about three

* The Koshari paint people white and are themselves painted black and wear a black mask. They carry a rattle of hooves.

o'clock, led by the War captain, his assistant, and the Governor; and the wagons drove up to the Koshari house. The Kurena stood on one side of the house, singing. The War captain who happened to be a Kurena appeared in full costume on the roof of the Koshari house. Some of his young helpers were with him. The officers made speeches.

A black blanket belonging to the Town chief was spread on the roof. All the perfect ears of corn were placed on the blanket, to be given later to the Town chief to bless and then to be handed over to the Women's society, who will lend them to pregnant or sick women or women desiring the special protection such ears afford.

After all the corn was on the roof, the women and the Kurena approached and received several ears for seed corn. Anyone suffering from lack of corn may ask the Town chief to help out from his store.

HOUSEHOLD CORN RITUALS OF ZUNI[114]

After Pekwin calls out for planting, the man of the household will make a prayer-stick, get out from the fawnskin pouch of seed corn six grains of corn of the colors of the directions and wrap them with the prayer-stick, sling on the pouch, pick up his old planting-stick, and say formally to the women of the household, "We go!" As he steps out, the corn matron hustles after him with a bowl of water with which she lavishly sprinkles him and his pouch, laughingly telling "them" to go.

The planter goes to a well-known spot near the center of the field and digs equally distant from a central point four deep holes in the four directions. By the left side of the northern hole he digs another to represent the zenith and by the right side of the southern hole still another to represent the nadir. In the center he sprinkles a cross of meal, to represent the cardinal points, also the stars that shall watch over his field by night. He plants his prayer-stick at the intersection of the cross and sprinkles more prayer-meal. In each hole he plants seed corn of the proper color-direction, the grain that was wrapped with the prayer-stick and three other grains, chanting a refrain at each hole as he drops the grains. After this song ritual he covers the grains and in lines corresponding to the directions of their four hills plants rows far out in the field.* Now for four days he fasts (? from meat and salt), remains continent, and prays at sunrise by the riverside.

Later the farmer will carefully inspect the ritual corn hills radiating from the prayer-stick. If every kernel in each comes out, the crop will be productive. If, on the contrary, one or two of the grains, for example in the southern hill, have not sprouted forth, part of his crop of red corn will be a failure, not ripening before frost time.

Every night at staving time you will hear women calling in at the doorways as they go the rounds of their husbands' clans, "*She!* Tomorrow we stave." Next morning the men gather and betake themselves to the field and hoe with might and main until about eleven o'clock, then stop to eat luncheon and joke with the girls who brought it down, and who are dressed in their best and have powdered their face with corn meal.

In a field of growing maize, the farmer selects such hills as give promise of speediest maturity. These receive his special care. No sooner have a few ears ripened than he picks the most perfect, as well as a bunch of soot (corn smut) from some neighboring stalk, and tenderly carries them home in his arms. Arrived at the entranceway, he calls to the women within: "We come!"—"Ah? How come ye?"—"Together, happily."—"Then enter ye!" In a basket tray in the center of the room he places the ears of corn, using care that they shall all point eastward, and lays the bunch of soot over them. The women of the house flock to the mantle whereon stands the family bowl of prayer-meal and each takes a pinch of meal, while the "corn matron" hastens away to the granary and carefully lifting the perfect ear (corn father) and the double ear (corn mother) brings them forth.† As she nears the tray she says, "My children, how be ye

* Part of this planting is corn for the kachina, just like the first corn-planting among Hopi.

† In every granary are an ear of yellow corn full to the very tip of perfect kernels, an ear of white corn which has resulted from the intergrowth of two or

these many days?" Then the new corn is supposed to reply through the voices of the other women, gathered near, "Happily, our old ones; happily!" The corn matron puts down the perfect ear and the double ear on the new bunch of soot and all say a prayer, sprinkle their prayer-meal over the tray, and breathe from the hand. This green corn ritual is called the "Meeting of the Children" and is said to refer to the return of the lost Corn Maidens under the guidance of Paiyatuma.

After the general harvest, while the corn is being sorted and corded up around and over the "father and mother" corn ears in the corn room, the finest ears of each kind are selected and laid aside. These and the ears of "new corn," i.e., the corn that was first brought into the house, are laid along the outer edge of the corn pile. Next morning the corn matron slips off her left moccasin and enters the corn room, exclaiming, "My mothers and children, how be ye, and how have ye come unto the morning?" After a moment she herself replies, "Happily!" From the selected ears she takes out eight ears, shells them, and sprinkles them with soot and with a mixture of yellow ocher, a grain of salt (always kept in the corn room, see p. 89), two or three kinds of little yellow flowers, pollen, and water. The seed corn thus medicated is poured into the fawnskin pouch (the kind the Koyemshi clowns carry on their begging rounds) and hung, pouch head downward, on the wall, ready against spring planting.

RITUAL GAMES, CLOWN PLAY, BURLESQUE, RACES AND RABBIT HUNTS

Of all Pueblo games shinny and hidden-ball are particularly played as ritual or with ritual. By Tewa and on First Mesa

more ears within a single husk-fold (flat or double ear), an ear which has been dipped by a Rain chief in Salt Lake, and a bunch of unbroken corn-soot [significant of rain, see p. 397]. Father ear and Mother ear are laid on top of the salted ear and the soot (Cushing 6:167–68).

Father ear and Mother ear, both perfect ears, are bundled separately with white sage stomach medicine and placed one below and one on top of the sweet-corn bake. Medicine bites will be taken from the two ears before feasting by workers and by others at home (Mishongnovi, Beaglehole 3:44).

shinny may be played for fertility; the seed-stuffed ball must be played with until it bursts and the time it takes to burst is an omen of good or bad crops. The ball stuffed with deer hair must be played with until it bursts also at Taos, where also the game is played for crops (and weather); but not by moiety as at Picurís and Isleta. Girls throw water on the players as they pass by a house (Isleta), and the game is played four days after the irrigation ditch is opened. The War Brothers are frequently described as playing shinny; in folk tale, offerings of shinny sticks and balls are made to them. At Zuni miniature game implements are set out on their shrines. The Brothers are called on for support in playing hidden-ball, together with plant spirits, deceased gamesters, or the dead at large. In the hidden-ball game songs of Isleta, Bear and Mountain Lion are asked to help, but the game, like all Isletan games, is primarily for betting.*

The morning of a kachina dance or between performances, the clowns or clowning kachina will play games together, with the kachina or with those they summon from the lookers-on (Zuni, Hopi). At Zuni bean bag and guessing stunts with onlookers are popular Koyemshi diversions. Men and women are called down from the housetop to guess what is under a blanket or what kachina is about to appear in the court. The successful person, more usually a couple, is given the object guessed, generally corn, a melon, food. Hopi Koyemshi will summon people to balance four cones one on top of the other. On First Mesa hidden-ball is played between the clownish Hehe'ya kachina and men impersonating women. At initiations into Zuni curing societies clowning kachina come out.[115]

The games and play of the kachina clowns or of clowning kachina are formal or stereotyped; the play of the clown societies is comparatively free and improvised, although it is directed along the line of caricature or burlesque. With few exceptions, the more sacrosanct the object, the more potent the ritual, the more "valuable" the ceremonialist, the better qualified are all to be

---

* Pueblo games should be studied or restudied, from several overlapping points of view, from that of distribution among the Pueblos and elsewhere in the Southwest, from that of ritual, and from that of education and social psychology.

burlesqued in circumstances of complete publicity, under the eyes of those burlesqued, even under the eyes of White people. White people, all foreigners and their ways, secular and religious, are also subjects for burlesque, Navaho shaman, American schoolteacher, or Catholic priest.

Quite generally burlesques are performed without masks, as in the Piptükyamu play at Walpi, yet there are not only clown masks but the clown societies or clowning groups like the Singers of First Mesa have in their keeping burlesque masks.[116] For the most part these represent foreigners, in a group kachina dance like the Apache or Sioux or so-called Hewahewa dances at Zuni, or as individuals like Rich Man (Rik'ŭs, Sp. *ricos*) or Girl (K'a'mak'as, Sp. *chamaka*) at Santo Domingo. These two and fifteen others are all said to come from the south, from G'o·'wawaima. G'o·'wawaima impersonations are accounted kachina, "but different." They do not appear with the other kachina; they may be seen by White people; impersonators may talk; they do not purge. Some of them function as bogey or sheriff, to scare children away from the ripening fruit or to round up men to cut wheat or perform communal services.[117] These bogey or police functions are performed elsewhere also by clown kachina, by the Koyemshi of Zuni, for example, or by the "grandfathers" of Isleta or of the Tewa, or they may be performed by kachina personages not associated with the clowning societies like Atoshle, the Zuni "grandfather," or the Hopi Natashka or Soyok kachina or in the fields the dreaded Masauwü. The songs of the home-Chakwena of Zuni are of a satirical, personal character.

Hopping or running matches are popular with the kachina clowns,[118] but somewhat more formal races against kachina are also run. These are a kind of handicap race, the kachina whipping the man he overtakes or cutting his hair or pretending to gouge out his eyes or blacking his face.[119] The overtaking pattern appears again in the early morning races run for crops and long life in the Hopi Snake-Antelope, Flute, and Lakon ceremonies, and in the Hopi dance race and Eagle society race at Jemez. The overtaking pattern is suggested in the Tanoan relay race; but what the historical connections may be, if any, is obscure. Possibly the European relay race and the Indian overtaking race were assimilated. Tanoan relay races, we noted, are closely associated with war, as are or were the long-distance races of Taos or of Hopi. Kick races are associated with rainfall.

Zuni and Hopi kick races are highly systematized in a spring-tide series. The Zuni series opens with a race by kiva followed by a race by clan in which clan glyphs are painted on the runners and cut on their kick-sticks.[120] On these kiva or clan races there is no betting. On First Mesa there may be a kiva series of ten races, each of the nine kivas in turn sending around "the announcer" with a bunch of ox hoofs at his belt, and the first kiva repeating,* or an indefinite number of races are run by various groups. In 1921, the year Crow-Wing kept his journal, the series was as follows:

March 13—children's race
March 15—by clan (clan glyph on back, or other clan label in decoration)
March 20—for sister-in-law, i.e., for her crops; racer labeled clan of sister-in-law
March 22—in Hano, Tewa kiva challenges Chief kiva, the War chief messenger saying, "Since in January you beat us in hidden-ball let us now race!"
March 25—by kiva, general
April 5—by women, each for a child of her clan, i.e., a child of her uncle or brother, and each wears a token of the clan the child of her clan belongs to.

In these clan races, at the end, the oldest man of the clan leads the clan members in single file to the houses of their clanswomen where a bowl of drinking water is set out, then to the kiva they started from, to eat the food contributed by their clanswomen. In the women's race the procedure is the same, with change of sex, except that the women do not go to kiva to feast; the men bring them "something."

On the day the "kachina go" at Zuni, the last day of Shalako, a dramatization called Molawia, melons come, is performed. The processional order of the male personators of the Corn girls

---

* Parsons 40:61, n. 100. Inferably the ox hoofs which are "handed" stay permanently in Chief kiva, and Chief kiva always opens and closes the series.

is determined by a race by girls.[121] Inferably there is or was involved here the concept of running to hasten the crops, which is Hopi in character, as is running by girls.

Rabbit drives are held before, during, or after ceremonies. (This has been often noted in the East, but it holds also for the Hopi, particularly in connection with the Wüwüchim ceremony.)[122] The organization of the hunt, the hunt fire, and the assignment of game have ceremonial aspects. Distribution is usually made by the hunters themselves or by the War captains, but in the Hopi Wüwüchim hunt with the novices the rabbits are distributed by men acting as kachina, jesting in high falsetto and carrying a rattle. The "hunt with the girls" is determined upon by the kachina or their dance director (Santo Domingo, Isleta, Jemez, possibly Hopi), and the clown societies are the hunt managers (Santo Domingo, Cochiti, Jemez, Isleta, see p. 788). The hunt with the girls has lapsed in several towns, but at Taos, where there is little or no kachina organization, there never has been a hunt with the girls, although the girls used to go out and count coup on near-by deer hunts. Both girls and kachina go out in the Zuni kachina rabbit hunt.

SHINNY AT SAN JUAN*

Early in March, the day Winter chief gives over the people to Summer chief, "that day they make their plants," i.e., women bring their seeds to Summer chief. From every house a woman brings a basket of seeds to leave in the house of Summer chief for three or four days. Summer chief sprinkles the baskets with medicine. From each basket he takes a few seeds and with the seeds stuffs a buckskin-covered ball. Outside chief, i.e., the War captain, collects the boys and men. Four times in anti-sunwise circuit they play around the town, then they go to the gardens and fields, the men only; "we don't go," said a woman. But as the men go playing around the town, women run out and catch the ball as it passes their house; they take it into the house and then throw it out again, with bread or apples.

* From Parsons 49:230–31. For Taos and Isleta, Parsons 58:27; Parsons 52:239. Shinny is played by Havasupai, Walapai, Mohave, Yuma, and Navaho (Spier 2:339, 345–46), but no ritual is recorded.

HIDDEN-BALL AT ZUNI*

A would-be player calls upon one of the paramount Rain chiefs, exclusive of the chiefs of the North or South. The chief bids him return at night with wafer-bread, beads, and meal. On the ground near the north wall, the chief makes four parallel meal lines, running north and south, as long as from tip of middle finger to tip of thumb. On the most western line, he places a gaming ball, saying to it, "You will remain here through the night." To the gamester the chief gives some wafer-bread, two cigarettes, a sack of powdered *te'na'säli* plant, and a piece of gypsum.

The Governor's crier calls out that the following night a game will be played; the opposite side organizes. There are eight to a side, four players and four watchers to guess the hiding-place. The leader assembles his men in his house. He and his head watcher place each four cornhusks on the floor and in them turquoise, white shell, micaceous hematite, red hematite, corn pollen, and in two of the packages a cigarette. In another cornhusk the leader mixes the *te'na'säli* with water, using the gypsum as dipper and stirrer. Then he dips the medicine into the left ear of each player, across his face under the eyes, and into his right ear. This is to insure seeing and hearing unusual things.† Then the leader sends the head watcher with a package of offerings containing a cigarette to a shrine of the elder brother War god to invite him to come to the court and be with them until the close of the game. A line of meal will be sprinkled from the shrine toward the court. The other three watchers take their offerings out of town to bury them and pray to deceased gamesters. They go a little distance from their excavation, sit down, and listen. Then they move on a little farther, sit and listen

---

* From Stevenson 2:333–41. Compare Zuni, Parsons 53:44–45, Benedict 3:I, 227–28; Hopi, Parsons 28; Taos, Parsons 58:26–27; Isleta, Parsons 52:239–40; Navaho, Matthews 2:1–19. For general distribution in the Southwest, Spier 2:351 ff. In the means of determining the beginner and in the markings of the tubes, Spier notes resemblances between Tewa and Gila River tribes.

† See below. Inferably the spirits of the plant are summoned to show the hidden ball.

again. They do this in all four times. One may not turn around or look back if one hears a step or anything unusual. Omens of success are the Morning Star, lightning, fire or a light, the sound of a summer bird; omens of losing, an owl or coyote. The sound of a mockingbird or snow bird is an omen of trouble between the sides, perhaps a fight.

The leader and his three players go to the house of their Rain chief, removing moccasins and headbands. The Rain chief sings his four songs for rain and crops to the deceased rain-making chiefs. He anoints the ears and under the eyes of the players, who go to the church to deposit in an excavation offerings to deceased gamesters and to listen for omens. If one is touched by the dead, success is assured. From the south side of the cross, the men's side, the leader takes a clothful of earth and leaves it outside the door of the Rain chief. They return to the house of the leader, reporting to the Rain chief there what they have seen. All smoke ceremonially. The players make a visit to the mesa top, presumably to the War god shrine. On their return they make *klo'o*, shell mixture. A man who has been chosen as the "rat" man and sent a cornhusk package carries it as an offering to Wood Rat to ask him, a collector of straws, to aid in winning the straw counters of the game. Rat man then visits the mesa shrine of the War god; he also visits the cactus bed belonging to the Cactus society and gathers a piece, saying, "When I place you in the court, do not let anyone touch you!" He deposits *klo'o* under the "father" plant of the cactus. He collects other plants and takes them all to the house of the leader where with *klo'o* and a quail feather they are wrapped in buckskin. Each of the four watchers binds an arrowpoint to the center of the sole of his foot, the arrow pointing to the toes. All eat heartily, for they are not to eat or drink until the game is concluded. All apply mountain-lion or bear grease under and above each eye, and on top of the grease red hematite. All go to the court.

A man from each side is dispatched for sand. The leader goes to the house of the Rain chief to get the gaming ball which was left on the line of meal. If it has moved from the west line to the east line, it means victory; if it has moved to the second or third line, there is no foretelling the result. The leader breathes from the ball and places it inside his shirt. Returning to the court, he sends a watcher with the black-and-white stone disk to the other side, giving them the choice of black or white for the toss. Standing by the stakes which are piled up in the court, the watcher makes the toss. Each player of the side winning the toss is given a cup.

Sitting by the sand pile, the four players are covered by a blanket. The sand is brushed to one side, and a hole is dug in the center of the place where the sand was; here the plants are buried. Each player makes a small excavation in front of him and in it deposits a cornhusk of *klo'o* and a prayer-feather. The sand is replaced. The leader makes three small holes to deposit a white bead, a bit of turquoise, and a black stone bead. Each player holds his cup to his mouth and prays silently, to Crow that can hide corn and then find it, and to Owl that can carry a ball in its claw undetected. And there are songs to the War gods. The leader rubs the ball of the Rain chief against the ball they are to play with, which he places over the buried plants. He stands a cup over the ball, and places as he likes the other cup, bringing the sand up around them. He then smokes on the cups. The blanket is withdrawn. The leader on the other side proceeds to guess by touching the cups with his hand. If the first cup he touches contains the ball, he loses ten straws; if the second cup contains it, the other side loses six straws; if the fourth cup contains it, he loses four straws; if the third cup contains it, he gets the cups for his side. Between each play the cornhusk offerings are moved a little nearer the plants, over which the ball is always placed. The game continues until one side has won all the straw counters, one hundred and six. It has been known to last five days. All the offerings except the black bead, which is left in place, the leader carries to his house, sprinkles with meal, and then takes to the mesa shrine of the War god. The gaming ball of the Rain chief the leader returns, presenting to the Rain chief a string of beads long enough to encircle the thumb, the left

PLATE XVII

KOYEMSHI, DRUMMER, AND WINNERS IN GUESSING GAME
TS'IA'AWA COURT, ZUNI

thumb, lucky in this game.* The Rain chief adds the beads to those which encircle his fetish.

Koyemshi Guessing, Zuni, September 12, 1918[123]

The morning of the Red Paint kachina dance, the last dance of the summer series at which the Koyemshi clowns are always in attendance, a man and a woman are called down into the court to guess what is inside the hole made in a watermelon. The melon lies on the ground between two rows of baskets of wheat and strings of corn. The man stands next to their Father (Koyemshi), the woman next the man. Man and woman are as usual unrelated. The man is to guess first; he is given four guesses; then if he fail, the woman has her four. But the man guesses right the first time—the tin cover of a pot—and their Father hands him the melon. The man goes to a house on the court, and a girl from inside gives him a handful of prayer-meal. He shares it with the woman, and, saying a prayer in front of their Father, he sprinkles on his head and then on the heads of the other nine clowns. The woman sprinkles but does not pray; no doubt, she does not know the proper prayer. She spreads her blanket and collects into it the grain from one row, the man collecting into a basket the grain from the other row (Pl. XVII).

The clowns leave the court singing and mimicking the dance step of the kachina.

Sometimes couple after couple are called to guess, until the Koyemshi help out. The Koyemshi may not bring back to their house anything taken out to be given away.

Play of Tachükti (Koyemsi) during Powamu
First Mesa, 1893[124]

During night dance in kiva a band come singing and drumming on the kiva hatchway. Our old men inside call repeatedly for them to enter; comic dialogue. They are the Tachükti. The

---

* In the Hopi game the ball must be moved with the left hand. The left, we recall, is associated with the dead. Hidden-ball is played quite generally in the East on All Souls' Night when the dead are in town. Inferably there was some early association of the game with the dead, perhaps as at Zuni, with deceased gamesters.

leader carries a large Havasupai tray in which are four wood
cones. In his hand he has a rod of wood and eagle feather. He
sets the cones up on top of each other near the fireplace about
in the middle of the floor. The others dance around to a roaring
song with much dramatic action. In the tray they heap boiled
corn ears and beans, then seek for a girl, but there is none in the
kiva, so they take a young married woman, bring her to the middle of the floor where she kneels and tries to lift the cones as high
as the staff which the leader holds beside them. They try four
or five women; all fail. They then divide the cones in twos, and
another woman lifts them the required height. All the clowns
fall down and kick their heels up and most of them stand on their
heads for a minute or two. The successful woman is given the
contents of the tray.

These clowns are from Horn kiva. They have the knobbed
mask, their bodies reddened and an old black dress as a skirt,
moccasins, rattle in right hand, and eagle feather in left. Each
carries a pouch of skin or other material slung over his right
shoulder, and in this are corn, beans, and other seeds of which
they give some to the elders and to the women on going out.

During the afternoon dance in the court nine Tachükti clowns
come up from Horn kiva and dance madly around, finally dancing in time with the kachina, the clowns in an irregular group,
barefoot but with blue yarn leggings. The clown rattles are the
globular or pear-shape gourd, some whitened and some pink,
with rings and black crosses. Head, skin, and neck of deer as
pouch.

At 2:20 the kachina go on to Sichomovi, but the clowns stay,
in burlesque of Tewa and other dances, then play ball a few minutes. Their ball-playing does not suggest a game—none tries to
catch it—they merely try to hit each other with it. When struck,
the man falls down and is hauled around by the others until he
gets on his feet.

At 2:25 in comes Cha'vaiyo arrayed in black conical mask
with globular eyes and great teeth and grayish horse or cattle
hair plumes, rabbit rug, bow and arrow in left hand, saw in
right, body pink with white blotches, forearms and legs from

knee down black with white spots, tortoise rattle on right leg, red moccasins. He knocks hell out of the clowns with his hand-saw, chasing them all around. Much broken Zuni is used all through. (A clown with dry sheepskin pretends to be a monster.) Old Cha'vaiyo intones. He demands something from the clowns. They offer him pup's skin fragments, feathers, jerked venison, and wafer-bread. Only venison will he accept. When other things are offered to him, he knocks the offerer with his saw, hard knocks, too. They steal his meat; he recovers it and goes off intoning. He comes back again demanding more.

At 2:50 the kachina return and again face north in line. As they begin to sing, the clowns cease their wildest pranks and dance as before in scattered group around the kachina line.

The clowns are all strong fellows, and they posture finely dur-ing the dance. Old Cha'vaiyo goes off. He returns again hoot-ing. The clowns always pretend to dread him. The old fellow knocks the youngsters who dance in his reach. He has a whip this time and lays it on well. One of the clowns gets a pot of *pigûmi* out of the cooking pit, almost hot enough to burn. They try to eat it, but of course they cannot by reason of their masks. They then plaster it upon the penis and anus of each other, until one of them takes the pot back and gives it to the woman to whom it belongs.

The clowns also go down into Horn kiva and return in their characteristic procession, the drum in front, the other eight in two lines, four in each. They have each a bundle of fine blankets, cotton cloth, yarn, all kinds of textile articles of value, arranged regularly and slung in the loops of a stout cord or rope and car-ried on the back like a low-slung knapsack. One also has the conical cups which they had last night and a Havasupai tray of corn kernels of all colors* and all kinds of cultivated seeds. They lay the tray about in the center of the court and spread a blanket beside it on which they pile all their bundles. One then

---

* These are contributed in the ear by each family of the Kachina clan, and their woman chief shells it. The clowns got it from her house. At the close of the ceremony, Powamu society chief (chief of the Kachina clan) distributed it in small handfuls among all the women spectators to be planted the same night in all the kivas.

sets up the cups atop of each other, and, while he is doing this, the drummer rapidly beats his drum, and the others shake their rattles and sing vigorously. The cups being set up, one seeks out a girl, brings her to them, and tells her if she will take hold of the lowest cone with both hands and bear the four in a pile around Pillar rock and set them back in place without letting any of them fall she will have all the wealth piled upon the blanket, and there is at least $100 worth. But the least jar tumbles the cones down, and they try half-a-dozen or more girls without success. Then they invite the youths to try, and several essay, but none is able to go more than a step, so the prize is left in the original hands, doubtless as designed, although they tell me if any had succeeded they would have given all the things offered. They then bring up a blanketful of cooked ears of corn and place the cones in twos, but none of the girls succeeds—the same person is not allowed a second trial—and finally young Kotka carries them around safely and wins the string of corn ears. He is followed closely around the Pillar by the clowns shaking their rattles and singing and crying, "Don't fall! Don't fall!" (just like the Navaho, this), and, when he lays them safely down in their original place, all the clowns fall down as if dead. Powamu society chief runs and gets a lot of ashes from a cooking pit and lifting the skirt of each clown and pulling aside the breechcloth casts a handful of ashes on his penis.* Then they all get up and dance around in their usual pranks.

Food is brought them, and they make all manner of uncouth attempts to eat it, pushing fragments through the mouth orifice. Some mescal water is brought them, also coffee; some of them pull the handle out of their rattle and, using the gourd as a dipper and holding the head back, pour the liquid through the mask orifice and into their mouths.

BURLESQUE

OF HOPI SOCIETIES, WALPI, JULY 17, 1893[125]

During a Navaho kachina dance a Pip'tükyamu comedian comes into the court from Horn kiva, with a rough imitation of

---

* As a mock exorcism?

the women's Marau society prayer-sticks. The society announcement he slightly burlesques, as he faces the east, squatted, the prayer-stick on the ground in front of his knees. He sits awhile as if watching the sunrise. He rises, and from his basket tray scatters a little meal on the ground about six times, then sings or chants the Marau announcement.

Enter from Horn kiva five comedians singing and stepping sideways. The first wears a Horn society horn helmet. Two carry bows, one a prayer-stick. The last is a Navaho woman with a bundle on her back, her head bent shamefaced, as women hold them in the dance. They move sidling in proper circuit around the Pillar twice, and then retire to Wikwalobi kiva. These are burlesques of the Wüwüchim and Singers when they take out the novices.

An hour later enter from Chief court five Chüküwïmkya clowns as Marau women, each with prayer-stick, and the Thrower. They imitate the Marau dance. The Thrower has a rod in the right hand, and a rod and a sprig of spruce in the left. They circle around in regular circuit. The Thrower imitates playing the flute, leading the circuit. Other Chükü clowns look on and shout admiringly.

The Chükü clowns get foul water from the houses and throw on the Marau burlesques. Women also throw on the Chükü clowns as they collect at the houses. One or two of the clowns imitate copulation with the Marau women.

Enter two burlesquers as Horns, with helmet, horn in hand, and cedar bark. They sprinkle meal over the cliff and march on to Horn kiva. They are whitened and are a very good imitation of Horns, with tortoise rattle on each knee. The two Horn burlesquers return, their torch alight. As they pass by, they scorch the heads and shoulders of the squatted Chükü clowns.

Drums are heard in Chief court. I suppose this is more burlesque of the Wüwüchim processions which the whole of this mummery seems to aim at. It is an imitation of the Wüwüchim sidelong dance in two lines with drum, led by the two Horns. The clowns join with them, and all sing the taunting song. The women drench them with water. The two Horns guard the exit toward Chief kiva court with their lit torches, scorching any of the Wüwüchimtu caricaturists who try to escape. They sing the lecherous taunting song. The women get a lariat and tie up the drummer, and drench, thump, and slap him. Women also grip the clowns, drench and slap them, and roll them on the ground, in pretended anger. The burlesquers get away to kiva at five, just as the kachina come in again.

CARICATURE OF NAVAHO MEDICINE MAN DURING
NAVAHO KACHINA AT HANO, APRIL 26, 1893[126]

The Chüküwïmkya clowns from Walpi come into the village, over the housetops, shouting and romping. There are six of them. As usual, food is brought them from time to time by the women. While the ninth dance is in progress, enter from kiva two characters representing a Navaho medicine or song man and his wife. He wears a grotesque whitened false face and dilapidated overalls and at his back an old pouch, representing the fetish pouch, with a bunch of long eagle-wing feathers projecting from it. The man personating the wife has also a grotesque whitened mask and ragged old skirt. This "Navaho song man" walks with a staff as if an old man, passes down the line of singing kachina, occasionally touching one as if in wonder, and walks down the court as if all were quite strange to him.

He soon spies the clowns who are squatted and eating close to the Court shrine and crosses over to them and tells them he is a song man and has brought his medicine with him. His speech is always in Navaho, and most of the clowns converse with him in Navaho. Two of the clowns say they are ailing, with pains in belly and limbs. The song man says he can drive the pains away with his medicine, but first wants his fee. Some of the clowns run into the neighboring houses and bring out a rifle and a silver bell, and this fee is satisfactory. The song man now tells them to get a blanket for the patients to sit on, the blanket also to be part of his fee. They find one and spread it, and the two patients squat on it, seated side by side facing the east, the song man sitting behind and overlooking them. He takes off his medicine pouch and produces the small chanter's rattle which he elevates, shaking it and beginning his song which is a faithful imitation of the chanter's song. Meanwhile he has instructed one of the clowns to bring a large stone muller and a jar of water, and in the muller the wife places some grass given her by the chanter, pours some water upon it, and begins grinding and rubbing the grass and water into pulp. The chanter ties a bit of string around the head of each patient and in it thrusts several twigs of spruce, also ties similar twigs upon their arms, continuing his song throughout and shaking the rattle and calling on the clowns to help him in imitation of the Navaho chanter. The song ended, he takes one of his long eagle-wing feathers, beats the patients on the back and strokes their bodies with it, then elevates it and blows away the malign influence. Next he produces a short wand, painted blue, with the end of which he presses upon the patient's back and other portions. He takes out of his pouch a small board to which a handle has been fastened and, having rubbed some charcoal on the board, he imprints it on the patient's back. Next he takes out a large cloth ball wrapped with string and, standing back from his patients a little way, he throws it once on the back of each with all his strength, knocking the wind out of them and of course producing a laugh from the spectators, all of whom have followed his proceedings with much interest and amusement. Now he makes his patients lie down flat on their bellies, and stripping off their breechcloth goes to the muller and gets a handful of the grass pulp and slaps it on the anus, and then pretends to insert an eagle feather in the anus, really thrusting the quill between their legs, leaving the feather upright.

The other clowns now ask to be treated, and he causes all of them to lie down side by side on their bellies and treats them with the grass pulp and feather, while all the people shout with laughter. And it is assuredly a most absurd spectacle, especially when one considers that, of the six clowns, five are of the principal men of the Mesa—Sun chief, Snake society chief, Kachina Father, Wikwalobi kiva chief, Horn kiva chief. The chanter then calls to his wife, who has maintained her pulp-grinding, to finish the treatment, and he then withdraws his eagle feathers. She takes a handful of pulp and, beginning with the clown lying on the south side, she turns him over on his back and takes down his breechcloth in front so as to entirely expose the penis, and on it she slaps a handful of the pulp, patting it, and then claps another portion of the pulp in the patient's mouth. She treats all six in this way. The chanter then announces that he has finished, and they get up, sputtering the pulp from their mouths and readjusting their breechcloths. Before the chanter leaves, the clowns all give him a pinch of meal and their thanks.

In an interval while the clowns are squatted and eating, a real Navaho family chances to ride through the court, returning home from Walpi where they were trading. The old man is partly paralyzed, and they invite him to sit down and eat with them. As he leaves, the clowns make free to play some pranks with him, putting his crutches away and pretending to throw him down. Actually they are very careful not to hurt the old man who seems to enjoy the fun as much as they or the spectators.

OF AMERICAN SCHOOL, WALPI, APRIL 26, 1893[127]

Three Pip'tükyamu comedians come in. Two of these and six Chüküwïmkya clowns stand in a row and with the other comedian in American clothes and carrying a cane under his arm and a book in his hand burlesque the school. This is very comic. They imitate schoolboys singing; they have only a few words, but the English accent is very fairly reproduced. The schoolmaster's mask is whitened and has black whiskers. He puts his pupils through sundry facings, and then pulls off the breechcloth from the clowns and the trousers from the comedians, exposing a monstrous false penis in the comedians and of course the natural penis of the clowns. As they stand in line, he has them bend over to touch their toes and while in this position he inserts between the buttocks of each a short twig crosswise and then orders them to stand erect. They pretend great pain and cause much laughter as they waddle around naked and skewered. The comedians retire, but before the "schoolmaster" gets clear of the court the clowns catch him and pull his breeches down, exposing a large bladder penis. They make him stoop over and insert a twig crosswise as he did to them. Then they lead him around the court, waddling with his breeches around his ankles. Finally he waddles off to kiva amid the prolonged shouts and laughter of the crowded housetops.

OF WITCH-HANGING BY NE'WEKWE, ZUNI, JANUARY 12, 1917[128]

Nine Ne'wekwe clowns are out to play during the Mahedinasha kachina dance. In the morning in the court they appear with bows and yucca staffs in mimicry of the War chiefs. Their leader, the Ne'mosi calls down one by one from the housetops nine young men. They drop their blankets, and the clowns tie their hands behind their backs. A rope is thrown over a projecting beam and one end fastened to the leg of the fellow who is the "child" of the society, having been cured by them but not yet initiated. Finally their "child" gets free and after freeing the others they rope the clowns, take away their mock weapons, and haul up the Ne'mosi to hang head foremost from the beam.

In conclusion two clowns withdraw a little way and facing east pray aloud. The young men sprinkle meal on them and on the others standing in line. Then the young men help themselves to the ears of corn piled on two blankets on the ground.

BY KOSSA AT TURTLE DANCE, SAN JUAN, DECEMBER 26, 1925[129]

In the morning someone lets loose a rooster, which runs squawking around the plaza. Immediately, the three clowns rush pell-mell after it, stumbling over themselves and everything in their way. One makes a headlong dive for the rooster, but lands with only a few tail feathers in his hands. Another lunges and captures all that is left of the rooster, which later the clowns will cook and eat. This appears to be a burlesque of a rooster pull, the Mexican *carrera de gallo* common at saint's-day fiesta.[130]

In the afternoon each Kossa dons a red paper cap and a vestment of shabby cloth. A cross in red cloth is sewn on one vestment. The "acolyte," holding himself very erect, brings out from a house a wooden cross which the "priest," the senior Kossa, kisses. Then an American trade journal is produced and held by the other "acolyte" for the "priest" to read from. As he reads, he turns the pages, all in very droll imitation of the ecclesiastical manner. "Priest" and "acolytes" kneel in prayer. A white porcelain bowl is brought out—this is "holy water"—and a broom is used to asperse with. Then they incense from coals on a board. Meanwhile, two visitors, Indians from some other pueblo, have been made to sit in chairs as congregation, and now from this "congregation" a collection is taken up, the "priest" counting from one to five in Spanish for each coin received. A large crowd, mostly Mexican, has gathered and finds this burlesque of a church service hugely amusing. Mexicans and Spaniards love burlesque!

OF FIRE SOCIETY RETREAT, JEMEZ, SEPTEMBER 29, 1921[131]

The maskless kachina dance called Hopi dance is being danced by Squash kiva at the request of the Fire society the day after their retreat. The Tabö'sh clown society is out to play. In the afternoon the clowns conduct a burlesque of ritual that the Fire society has but just been observing in connection with their retreat. The little spruce tree opposite Squash kiva is taken as the altar back. An old man and an old woman are seated there, to represent the society membership. In bringing the woman to her place on the man's left, the clown puts his arm around her neck, gives her a bite from the ear of corn he carries in that hand, bites into the ear himself, gives her another bite, turning her around as if to show her off to the on-lookers, all laughing, including the old girl herself, at her helplessness. An ear of corn set into spruce twigs is set on the ground in front of the old man; this is the "mother." There is a bowl filled with spruce and a liquid, the medicine bowl. From it the clowns will sprinkle water on the dancers and on the Fathers where they sit, in their usual wall seat next the kiva, and on anyone who comes along. The fruits and bread brought in by the dancers are taken by the clowns and set alongside the altar. The rib of a wagon top is brought out and fastened with wire; this is a bow. It is given with an arrow to one who as a war captain stands guard at the altar. Then a man is dispatched at a run with the mock war captain behind him. They return, to run out again in another direction, to imitate the runners sent out at night in the four directions from the society's ceremonial room, runners practicing for their sunrise race.

Women coming up to contribute something to the pile of fruit and bread sprinkle the "altar" with meal. Finally a clown picks up the medicine bowl and carries it to the seat of the Fathers for each in turn to drink from, and then gives drinks to the lookers-on besides taking the bowl into a few houses. He gives me a drink. I am sitting next my dear old host, the assistant chief of the Fire society. The old man is very much amused, and it does not occur to him or to anybody else that some of the secrets he has been withholding from me for weeks are being revealed.

SANDARO* AT SANTO DOMINGO[132]

Late in January or early in February the kiva chief (the two kivas alternate) summons the Principales (former officers) who belong to his kiva to his house. The Principales notify the Town chief, the War captains, and the chief of the medicine society associated with their kiva, the Flint or the Shikame society, and they summon all the men of the kiva to a night meeting in kiva. In the morning the society chief summons the society members and gets impersonators for Santiago and San Gerónimo. All go into retreat for four days, vomiting each morning. They prepare the hobby horses of the saints, also the bull frame that will be managed by the impersonating society member. Feathers will be tied to the horse tails and to the metal crowns of the rider saints who will be blackened under the eyes. Kiva participants at large practice songs in a house apart.

At vespers two Sandaro enter the pueblo, firing shotguns and announcing the dance. All assemble in the house of the kiva chief where the shamans make a meal-painting. Night-practice song and dance. About 3:00 A.M. the War captain assistants drive wagons for participants with their paraphernalia to a hill south of town. Thence in procession, two by two, the horse masks in the lead, to drum and bugle they march into town and to the church, where the sacristan asperses them with holy water. The *mayordomo* appointed by the kiva chief appoints four cooks to

* From Sp. *soldado*, soldier.

make coffee. The Sandaro take food from their suitcases, spread a cloth on the ground, and invite everybody to eat with them. The "Bull" is fed, and the "Horses." To Spanish or English songs the Sandaro dance. Lunch is like breakfast. They dance again; Santiago and San Gerónimo come out, and, sometimes, a burro ridden by San José. People throw coins to the saints. Out comes the Bull; the Sandaro "fight" by throwing their hats, Santiago hits the Bull once with his sword, and the Bull drops to the ground. The Sandaro sing "goodbye"; they are going back to Mexico. The "Horses" are taken to the town corrals, "to bring luck [blessings] to their horses," or increase. At the house of the kiva chief the Sandaro are "excused to go home"; at night the shamans and impersonators bathe in the river, and hobby horses and bull frame are returned each to his custodian. The bugler keeps the white horse, the horse of Santiago.

TEASING SONGS AT DARK KACHINA DANCE, ISLETA[133]

Dark kachina is a maskless kachina dance held in early spring for good weather for the crops. It is conducted and danced by moiety. Comedy or burlesque is supplied by the Grandfathers (three in each moiety) and by the spruce-gatherers, young men sent out by the "man who wants the dance" to White Eagle Mountain where live the Dark kachina.

On the first day the Grandfathers go about town, lowering the house ladders. On the second day the Grandfathers call out to the women to sweep their yards and to the young men each to bring two or three sticks of wood to their respective kivas. On the third day the dancers, led by the moiety chiefs and their assistants, go out to meet the youths returning with spruce, who have to ford the river, using neither bridge nor boat. On the town side, dry clothes are at hand and a fire. The spruce-gatherers dance and sing, teasing songs. Anybody in town may be referred to. The Black Eye boys will tease Shure' people; the Shure', Black Eye people. Gossip of any kind serves. For example, a boy courting a girl had offered her land which she would not accept because only *naera* (some animal smaller than a mouse) lived on it, i.e., it was not arable. The song about this was considered very amusing; "people laughed and laughed." Again there was a song about a boy who was in a girl's house when he saw her parents coming and he ran out through the window. Unable to get an Indian girl for a wife, he began to court a Mexican girl. He asked a certain old man with a beard to help him. Late at night the old go-between carried some beans and two cans of sardines to the house of the Mexican girl. Her father came to the door provoked by so late a call. He grabbed the old man by the beard, and the Isleta boy had to run away. He threw himself on his bed, saying it was no use trying to get married. The next morning he cut off his queue and went out to look for work, because the girls did not want to marry him.

Boys are not only willing to go for spruce in order to be able to sing these teasing songs; they even volunteer. And other boys will tell the spruce-gatherers what to tease about, giving them a cigarette, "paying" them with a cigarette. Whether or not the teasing songs already cited were of actual persons seems somewhat uncertain; but the song about one Francisco Seyo was cited as based upon an actual occurrence, his visit to a woman neighbor who gave him supper. "Where is Francisco Seyo?" ran the song. "And where is María Pinta? Let us go again tonight and eat beans." At this song the wife of old man Francisco got mad and began to shake him. The old man went to the boys and gave them a cigarette to stop their teasing song, the usual way of making them shut up.

The spruce-gatherers come into the plaza to dance and continue their teasing songs on all four sides on the roofs to which the Grandfathers have restored the ladders. (They removed the ladders so there would be nobody on the roofs at this time.) The boys now called Pachu'un dress up as an old Mexican or Indian, carrying a bag or "something funny." Should the padre come out to watch, the Pachu'un would make fun of him, stroke his beard or kneel in front of him, asking for his blessing. They might surround a White or Mexican and not release him until he danced for them. Were a man absent—all should be at hand—the Pachu'un would beat a little drum or can at his house, and, unless he had put a cigarette inside his door, they would take him and throw him into the pond near the town. If the man has made himself safe by putting down the cigarette, the funny men have to take it and merely tell the man to hurry up and go to the kiva. Otherwise, after ducking the man, they run back toward the kiva to which the drenched man has to go directly. There the Pachu'un greet him with *akuwam, poyo!* Hello, friend! as if unaware of what has happened. Following him into the kiva, they shake hands with him, saying: "Where have you been? We did not see you."

By this time it is noon; people go to dinner. Afterward the moiety chiefs, the dancers, and the Pachu'un go to the river to fetch the spruce left there. All the way back to the kivas they sing. Inside kiva the Pachu'un spruce-gatherers have to report on their trip, reporting on everything they did, what they saw, whom they met. Then the moiety chiefs "let them go free," for dinner. When they come out from the kivas, they holler *yayaya-ya!* meaning they are free. Hearing this call, the women and girls come out of their houses to take the Pachu'un back to feed them, a Black Eye woman taking a Shure' boy; a Shure' woman, a Black Eye boy. The boys eat a lot. Left-overs they stow away in bag or blanket. Later, when they meet anyone they have made dance, a poor person or a Mexican, they will give him a tortilla, to pay him for dancing. They set out their food, and visitors from other pueblos are invited to partake. At this time the children are afraid to go out, lest the Pachu'un make them dance or run a race.

Now the Pachu'un go after the Grandfathers to bring them into the plaza. They ask the Grandfathers if they are angry that they do not speak. They will write a make-believe note with a piece of carbon and give to the Grandfathers to deliver to some White man or Mexican in the crowd from Albuquerque. The recipient will of course not understand the note, so the Grandfathers will lead the sender over to explain. The sender will say that the Grandfather is asking for a smoke and "for you to go to the store to buy him something to eat. He comes from a distance and is hungry." When the Grandfather gets his tobacco

or crackers, he takes the giver into the middle of the plaza to hug
or pat him or to make him kneel down and be given the sign of
the cross. Of course, all the people are laughing.

Now the dancers come out, about seven. First come Black
Eyes, then Shure', each set dancing only once, Black Eyes on the
west side of the plaza, Shure' on the east side. The Grandfathers
are out, keeping the lookers-on from crowding up or misbehav-
ing. Pachu'un are out also, to look after any disarray of the
dancers such as loose feathers.

KACHINA RACING, SICHOMOVI, JULY 9, 1893[134]

The group of Pa'shiwawash kachina stand at the southeast
corner of the court and run races not only with the clowns but
with any other person who challenges them. They run against
all comers. They are picked runners and overtake nearly everyone whom they challenge, although as a rule they give the challenger the start of from five to ten feet, and in a little over the
length of the court, say 120 feet, they nearly always overtake the
challengers. These challengers on being overtaken are always
well flogged by the kachina; and, if overtaken by the Hümsomp
kachina, the challenger's hair is sacrificed. It is also considered powerfully invigorating to be whipped by these kachina, and many elderly men and others who do not care
to run go up and ask to be whipped, and the kachina lash
them generously.

A person disposed to run intimates by gesture or otherwise the
kachina whom he wishes to have pursue him. The challenger
then starts off in a swift spurt across the court, from the southeast to the northeast corner or beyond. When the challenger is
overtaken, he is thrashed with yucca, and the kachina returns
to the southeast corner to race some other aspirant. The races
continue for about half an hour, until 4:40 P.M. Most of the running is very speedy. The elders thank the Wawash kachina and
sprinkle them with meal, and the Wawash retire to the kachina
shrine ledge.

LONG-DISTANCE RACE OF SNAKE SOCIETY, WALPI
AUGUST 21, 1891[135]

A Snake member wearing a girdle of antelope hoofs leaves Walpi on a run before dawn. He carries a gourd bottle which he fills with a little mud from each spring he passes on the trail to Antelope Mound, a rocky point about five miles from Walpi. The youthful runners stand in line. The manager motions the gourd to the five directions and then for the nadir, the sixth, he dashes it to the ground, causing the mud and water to flow out, like the great rain that is desired.

In Antelope kiva where the altar is being dismantled Hoñi, the Crier chief who is to be "crook man," has a red feather in his scalp lock and wears a ceremonial kilt. He gathers pinches of sand from the colored clouds of the directions, also from the blue lightning snake, and lays them on the prayer-sticks in his meal tray. From the altar he also takes one of the crook prayer-sticks representing the deceased members of the society. He descends the mesa and on the trail in from Antelope-mound on the site of the "old men's house" he makes with prayer-meal four very large cloud and rain designs with a prayer-feather of eagle and yellow-bird feathers stretched out from the middle cloud. The designs are in line, but each group of three clouds represents one of the cardinal directions. In a near-by shrine at the site of old Walpi, Hoñi sets three prayer-sticks erect in such position that the rising sun will shine directly upon them. He casts meal upon them and then toward the sunrise direction.

About twenty minutes after sunrise the racers approach, about forty, old men and boys. They carry squash blossoms and other flowers. Hoñi shouts, "Race eagerly!" He holds the crook by its end horizontal in his right hand so that the long feather-string hangs down over the first or "northwest" cloud design on the trail. Each racer as he passes touches the curved part and prays: "I desire to be an old man; I wish for long life." Without slowing up, he runs on over the other cloud designs. Hoñi sprinkles each with meal until his meal gives out.

Some young people have met the racers and join them in running past the crook and up the mesa. Above Hoñi stand some girls and boys holding corn plants and vines of melon and squash which the racers touch as they pass.

RACES IN LAKON CEREMONY, WALPI, SEPTEMBER 9–10, 1893[136]

At sunset on the eighth day all the women of the society descend to Sun spring to place prayer-sticks. Three men members, kilted and their arms and legs zigzagged in white, accompany them [and one of these starts the race up the mesa by dropping a basket.—Crow-Wing]. The leading runner carries the standard which she surrenders if overtaken. When the runners gain the edge of the mesa, they distribute bread to the men there. The runners keep on to their kiva. They pass along the meal trail on the north side of the main floor, take a pinch of meal, pray on it, and cast it upon the altar. Then they pass along the meal trail on the south side. About three feet from the trail a man chief holds a crook vertical upon the trail. Each woman in passing stoops down and grasps the crook or presses her palm on it.

At sunrise on the ninth day about twenty men descend the mesa and continue on past Sun spring. About the same time the woman race-winner arrayed in white mantle and with chin, hands, and feet blackened, carries a basket tray down to Sun spring. She is accompanied by two men. When they see the men beyond start to run, one shouts to the maid who then starts up the mesa. She is overtaken and surrenders the tray. The second bearer is also overtaken, but the third one succeeds in being the first to reach the circle of women dancers. He lays down the tray in the gap of their dance circle.

These races are to hasten the ripening of fruits and crops.

KICK-BALL RACE, FIRST MESA, FEBRUARY 12, 1893[137]

In Chief kiva about 7:00 A.M. Kopeli girds himself with a cord to which is fastened a large cluster of oxhoofs and, bare-legged and barefoot, trots to all the kivas on the mesa and tells where to assemble and when. He is called "announcer"; in this spring series each kiva will in turn make the announcement. About two hours later I am in Goat kiva, when Pauwatiwa, kiva chief, brings down five stone nodules from one and one-half to two inches in diameter. Pauwatiwa lays them in a row, across the west end of the fireplace, touching each other, and from his pouch sprinkles them with prayer-meal, casting the remainder of the pinch toward the southeast corner of the main floor. In all the kivas, nodules are similarly placed.

For this race kiva members have prescribed decoration, as follows: Chief kiva, star or cross design in white clay across face, on breast, back and upper arm, front of thighs and calves. Wikwalobi, in yellow pigment, a broad streak across upper chest, leg from ankle to knee and band above knee, all of forearm and three finger marks on upper arm, same finger marks on each side of body, and band around waist. Halfway kiva, blue-green pigment, and, worn by chief only, two eagle-tail feathers. This blue is a double stripe down outside of leg. Blue over the entire body with fingertip intaglio down outside of leg. Horn kiva, white clay annular broad stripes or horizontal broad stripes surrounding body and limbs. Goat kiva, red ocher pigment over the entire body. Sichomovi, valley sand and water over the entire body. Hano kivas, yellow-brown pigment, by all, solid over all, face, limbs, and body. As the racers run through the valley, the women watch them from the housetops and the different decorations permit the women to watch the varying positions of the men of different kivas. When the men are clustered together, kicking the nodules, others, on the outside of the huddle, can watch their legs and thus distinguish the nodules as kicked. But I can get no hint of the reason why the different kivas came to adopt their distinguishing decorations.

At noon lunch is eaten in kiva—corn-meal gruel, wafer-bread, parched corn kernels, and stewed peaches. Runners abstain from flesh food and salt. (Also from sexual intercourse.) Between 1:00 and 2:00 P.M. the kiva members strip and put on their paint. At 1:45 Kopeli, painted and naked save for breechcloth, passes around to all the kivas with final warning of assembly. Directly after this, Chief kiva chiefs go down the northwest trail into the valley, past the Masauwü shrine, each one casting meal on the sagebrush piled there and praying for strength to win.

The chiefs are followed by about eighty runners—from Chief kiva, twenty-five; Horn kiva, fifteen; Halfway kiva, fifteen; Goat, eight; from Sichomovi kivas, three or four; with several stragglers not counted. Each kiva group is led by its kiva chief who carries the stone nodule in his left hand which he has filled with prayer-meal from the tray in the kiva. Each kiva member also has some of this meal in his left hand, which he casts with prayer on the brush cairn of the God of Death.

The kiva chiefs or someone representing them and as many of each kiva as there are nodules belonging to it, arrange themselves in a line facing the main arroyo, about west, each having laid the nodule on the ground, just at his right toe. Kopeli stands on their right flank and a little in front; then, at his signal, all almost simultaneously kick the nodule as far in front of them as possible. They insert the toes under it and give it a good lifting toss. The younger men of each kiva have been gathered around in irregular clusters behind the nodules belonging to their kivas, and, as the nodules are kicked, all rush forward, each striving to keep the nodules of his kiva in the advance, kicking the nodule and running after it, no scuffling. The elder men run around on a somewhat shorter radius, cutting corners, so to speak. The best runners appear to be also the best kickers, lifting the ball with the front of the foot from quite twenty to twenty-five yards. They strive to lift the ball as high as possible. It is quite permissible to move the nodule with the hand to clear it from any obstruction and place it on an open space to kick at. This is no actual race, no keen struggle, each kiva or village group hold pretty well together and the groups are never very far apart.

The kickoff is at 2:20, and the leading group of runners get to Sun spring at 2:57. Thence the Walpi people diverge to the trail leading to Walpi, the Sichomovi people take the trail toward Dawn cape, and the Tewa people hold on toward the Gap. A little way past Sun spring the nodules are picked up, and the men's pace falls to a moderately swift gait. The course is from three and a half to four miles.

The kiva chief who first kicks off the nodule, casts meal upon the nodule and prays before he kicks it. He or another of the group carries a second nodule in case the first one should get lost in the greasewood or roll into a mole or prairie-dog hole. No time is spent looking for a lost ball; the second one is at once brought into play. There is no halt from the first start, and at a little distance, unless one has seen the start, it would be almost impossible to think that they are kicking a nodule along, so evenly do they maintain the pace. The chief prays the nodule to keep away from cactus and yucca, not to lose itself among the sagebrush or greasewood and not to roll into any rat holes, but to keep on the sand and roll smooth and direct. After the runners return, the nodules are laid in the *sipapu*.

The feet of the runners are sore where they have been kicking the nodule. The instep of the foot gets sore and swollen, and small wonder! Warm days are preferred for running, they insure plenty of sweat, plenty of moisture on the body, which is ever a token for rain.

Various explanations of the kick-ball race are given. In Goat kiva they say: "Thus the Hopi did in the long ago, only the race used to occupy a whole day; our young men are lazy and foolish. It has always been well for the Hopi to be able to run swift and far, and in these races the Cloud spirits rejoice to see the Hopi youth run, and he who is fastest wins. His prayers for rain will have special virtue. The Cloud spirits will have seen him run and will be glad to listen to him."

Hahawi of the Horn clan, chief in Horn kiva and in Antelope society, says: "Long ago when the Hopi had no sheep, no horses, no burros, they had to depend for game-capturing on their legs. They then had to cultivate their legs, think much and pray much how could they make them swift. Men strove in earnest to rival each other in fast running, that is why the races were run, and it is well for us to do as the old people did. It is still well for us to learn to run fast and far. We do not take the wide circuits of long ago for we have plenty of horses now, we do not need to be such far runners as the forefathers."

In Chief kiva they say the practical purpose is of course to train men as good long-distance runners, but the deeper significance of the race is that each devout Hopi who engages in it is relieved of all heaviness of heart, all sadness is dispelled, his flesh is made good, his health is renewed. All devout men also pray that the Cloud spirits will look upon the runners kicking the nodule before them, and will send the rain in quantity to fill the watercourses brimming full and rushing as swift as these runners and the water like them strong and swift-running and kicking the nodules before it, the nodules of clay, large and small, which are formed in the watercourses during rain freshets.

KICK-STICK RACE, ZUNI, APRIL 16, 1932[138]

The two races which open the season, the race by kiva and the race by clan, have been held, and today's race is the first of the general series which keeps up until the summer solstice ceremony. This series is more or less in charge of the Sho'wekwe, an informal sort of group whose members know the ritual for the winter gambling games and the spring racing, which is also a form of gambling. Two Sho'wekwe or any two men may assemble the race teams of three, four, or more members. Sometimes the team are all kinsmen, "like Oscar's bunch." Each team meets in the house of its manager the night before the race, with a War chief or a Society man to pray and sing and make food offerings to the War gods and to deceased racers. "They give food to the Earth," and, like Deer Boy when he races against the witches, they ask Sun not to beat down on them as they run. "White fellows rest before a race, but we stay up all night," remarks Jakey, back from boarding-school. During the night, omens are sought from birds or from the dead. Sometimes a spy from the other side listens in; in view of the big bets made on the race advance information is valuable.

About 4:30 P.M. the betting opens in Big plaza. Three or four men representing each side advance in two rows to meet in the middle of the court. Several carry bundles of goods. These are what have been left over after the racers have made their bets in one of their houses of overnight retreat. These plaza stakes may be matched by bettors at large, and now several men carrying what they wish to put up join the central group. Blanket is matched with blanket, and the two tied together, shawl with shawl, silk kerchief with kerchief, belt with belt. All the stakes appear to be wearing apparel*; money is bet, but I think privately, and probably only by the younger men. Jakey has planned to bet privately the shirt off his back, an orange silk shirt his sister has just made him, but luckily for him as it turns out, his taker withdraws, and at the close of the day to the satisfaction of all of us Jakey is still wearing his gay apparel, blue velveteen trousers as well as orange-colored shirt.

The betting crowd is as quiet as Zuni crowds ever are; the matching is done quickly, and without dispute, no voice is raised, it is a smiling, cheerful party. It takes them about an hour, then the piles of goods are left there on the ground, and the crowd, on foot and on horseback, about two hundred men, move across the river by the new bridge to the starting-line on the road to the south.

Here we wait for the runners to appear after they have forded the river by the traditional crossing and have said their last prayers. Each team of four men is led single file by their overnight ceremonialist, in this case a War chief for one team, and an Ant society man for the other. The leader casts a handful of prayer-meal in front of his team before he leaves them at the edge of town. He is "opening the road." The racers continue on, first the Itiwana or Middle team, a few minutes later the Pathltok or east-side team, into a stretch of greasewood where they stoop to pray and sprinkle prayer-meal. The teams scatter, evidently each man is praying on his own. Then in single file the runners come over to the starting-line, the arms of each folded tightly across his bare chest, as if holding in something. As indeed they are doing, the powers of four swiftly flying birds— *anethlauwa* or hawk, *shokyapissa* or red-shoulder hawk, *akwatsu'ta*, and *tse'wia* or McGillivray's warbler—the same birds, at least some of them, Hopi mention in their racing song:

---

* In the tales women's dresses are a favorite stake. (Among the early Aztecs women's dresses were quasi-currency.)

Be racing.
With joyful words
Be racing.
The abdomen, the back.
Hawk (Cooper's hawk), etc.
Be racing.[139]

These powers for "abdomen and back" have been obtained during the ritual of the preceding night.*

The racers wear kilts of nondescript cotton or woolen cloth; torso and legs are bare, and they are barefoot. Itiwan have a white cotton *banda* around the head; Pathltok, a *banda* of blue silk. They all happen to be youngish men, from twenty-five to thirty-five, and their hair is short; but the locks on top are gathered together and tied with a string; inside this bunch of hair is concealed an arrowpoint, ever a protective charm. Protection is needed, for black magic is practiced in these races as in the Isleta relay race or in Navaho and Papago races. Cramps are caused by magic. Ned, a school-bred youth, is afraid to race this year because after remarkable achievements last year he became the victim of magic-induced cramps.

The two teams face each other, and the leader of Itiwan, i.e., the team that was first to arrive, hands the two kick-sticks to the leader of Pathltok to choose his stick. Now the War chief produces some red paint, the ordinary red face-paint, and both sides proceed to paint their stick. The Itiwan leader paints a red band around the middle; the Pathltok leader, a red band around the middle and a narrower band around each end. The sticks are about five inches long, of oak wood, decorticated.

Usually the War chief throws both sticks, but this time the two race leaders throw, and the race is on. Younger fellows in the crowd run ahead, whooping the Zuni war cry—*toha'lala! toha'lala!* A man on a white horse takes the lead and will set the course, first to the south, then east to Corn Mountain and, completing the anti-sunwise circuit, back to the river ford, a run of about an hour and a quarter, seven or eight miles. The road is

* Unfortunately this is not known. Among Papago, Hawk and the Cranes give speed in running. In tale the Cranes give a man kick-ball power, because they pity him (Underhill 3).

soon left, and the country is rough going. The stick may not be touched with the hand, nor may it be held between the toes in extricating from crevices or brush.

After the start the housetops begin to fill up with spectators. This is the time bets are made between the men and the women. Men go out to meet the runners so they return with the same whooping crowd they started with. One of the four in the winning team has dropped out, I notice; he will have been picked up by a horseman. The losing team does not finish; they, too, are picked up by their friends on horses. The stick is kicked high, perhaps twenty feet, well over the heads of the crowd, and covers a short distance, not more than a hundred feet. The final kick is into the river. But the stick is retrieved and will be placed in an arroyo to be carried away by flood waters.

After crossing the river, the runners continue on to Big plaza, run around the pile of bets,* and return to their house of retreat where they are given an emetic. Before the winnings are removed from the court, they are sprinkled with prayer-meal, and again they are sprinkled in whatever house they are carried to.† The people of the house or houses of the winners give a big supper.

Rabbit Hunts at Santo Domingo[140]

Rabbit hunts are held for the Town chief and the War captain Masewi, for the Scalps, for the saint's-day dancers, and, when the kachina impersonators wish, for the girls. Hunt chief, War captains, and Koshairi clowns all participate in one hunt or another.

I

When the Town chief's supply of rabbit meat runs low, Chraik'ats[i] tells War captain Masewi, who calls his little captains to a meeting at his house. The Hunt chief announces the hunt from his housetop the day before.

Hunt chief builds the hunt fire. Nobody is allowed near. If

---

* They pass their hands up the pile, breathing from them and saying, "Just in this way I shall win next time" (Benedict 3:I, 101).

† The woman of the house says, "My clothing, I am glad you have reached us here, and may many of you come to stay with us" (Benedict 3:I, 102).

anyone stepped within the meal circle made by Hunt chief, he would have to join the Hunt society. War captain Masewi talks and prays before the start. They go on foot and ahorse, carrying guns and rabbit-sticks. Guarded by one of the little war captains Hunt chief goes along, and at the end talks "about how they hunted." Each man gives his rabbits to the Chraik'ats[i] at the house of the Town chief where the following morning the little war captains roast them. The girls gather and eat the insides. Then the rabbits are hung bunched on a bar outside the house. Whenever the Town chief wishes to feed his "children," his fetishes, Chraik'ats[i] boils some dried rabbit. Also Chraik'ats[i] gives rabbit meat in the spring to the men who bring wood to the Town chief.

II

War captain Masewi joins the Flint society in vomiting each morning for four mornings before their retreat. On the third day a rabbit hunt is held for "Masewi." It is in charge of War captain Oyoyewi. Masewi and the Hunt chief do not go. Masewi takes some of the rabbits roasted by the little war captains to the Flint society whether to eat the day before the retreat or after it is not clear. The rest of the rabbits Masewi keeps for other societies in retreat. The little war captain doing guard duty for the society will call for the rabbits.

III

Some time before the saint's-day dance* on August 4 a hunt is held for the dancers of both kivas. Hunt chief does not go; no one is in charge. Each man gives his rabbits to the Poker boy of his kiva, and the little war captains come to roast them. The eve of the dance the Poker boys boil the meat for the little war captains to carry to the kivas with bread they have collected from house to house for the dancers' dinner.

IV

A hunt for the Scalps is determined upon in the autumn by Masewi, who is in charge. All the procedure is the same as in the

* Compare Taos, Parsons 58:19.

Town chief's hunt except that the rabbits are taken to the scalp house and given to the keeper, a sometime scalper. His wife boils the meat, roasted by the little war captains for the Scalps.

V

At a kachina dance in the autumn the dancers or the dance director may decide to have a hunt for the girls. Masewi summons the little war captains and Hunt chief to meet with the dancers, and, if they wish, they summon the Koshairi. Hunt chief announces; the Koshairi go around the plaza singing and then go from house to house to summon the men, boys, and girls to the meeting place.* Late-comers are punished by the Koshairi. They make the men stand in line and dance or point in the direction of the hunt with their penis, pulling the foreskin back three or four times. The women have to pull up their dresses and expose themselves. On the hunt, if the Koshairi should find a man and girl copulating, they would make them repeat it in public at the end of the hunt.

As usual the girl who first touches a rabbit keeps it. At lunchtime she pays the hunter with food and the next day she must give him some corn meal.

HOPI HUNT FIRE[141]

The night before the hunt the young men† make eight prayer-feathers for Masauwü and four for his wife, Tihküyi, Childbirth-Water Woman, Mother of Game. The men deposit these under-wing eagle feathers in shrines during the night.

The following morning the man who has wanted the hunt, the hunt leader (there is no Hunt chief) scratches a shallow cavity in any sand mound near where the hunters have assembled. Within this circular depression and below its brim he sprinkles meal in

* Inferably this is the Jemez system for a hunt with the girls. "The kachina want them to go, and the Tabö'sh (Koshairi) make them go" (Parsons 41:94).

† On Second Mesa the hunt organizer makes six prayer-sticks, four for the rabbits, one for Gray Fox, one for Tihküyi, Mother of Game. These sticks he takes in the evening to the house of Badger clan chief. They smoke (? over the sticks) and the Badger man announces the hunt from his housetop (Beaglehole 2:12).

anti-sunwise circuit and with a slight motion toward the cardinal points casts four lines toward the center of the cavity. At the intersection he lays four pellets of rabbit dung* and on each line one of the prayer-feathers he has himself made. With dry grass and twigs he builds a fire in the cavity. He passes his rabbit-sticks through the blaze† as do the other hunters after casting a tuft of grass or a twig on the fire. The fire is covered before they start.‡

ANIMAL DANCES

There are many distinctive kinds of animal dances from the purely mimetic type of the Taos Buffalo dance and the Bear or Lion impersonations of the Keresan curing society through the stylized although in part mimetic Eagle dance (Keres, Tewa) or Hopi winter solstice bird dance to the highly stylized kachina Deer dance of Jemez or maskless but antlered Deer dance of San Juan[142] or Hopi Buffalo dance in which there is little if any imitation of animal behavior.

There is variety also in the objects or functions of the animal dances. The dance in which various game animals, horned animals, are impersonated (Taos, Deer dance; San Felipe, Cochiti, San Ildefonso, Buffalo dance) and at Taos, Nambé, and San Felipe, the Deer Mothers or Mothers of Game, appears to be for the increase of game, "so the Deer Mothers will have many children" (Taos); whereas First Mesa, Tesuque, and possibly Taos Buffalo dances are featured with curing functions, Buffalo is a medicine animal that carries away sickness. He may be associated also with weather, bringing snowfall or moderated cold (Taos, Tesuque).

The Eagle dance of San Juan (? Santa Clara) is a curing society dance. On the third night of the retreat of the Eagle

* Also sand from rabbit tracks (Second Mesa).

† Causing the stick to throw straight (Second Mesa).

‡ "That keeps the rabbits there, that is their home. The fire makes them weak" (Parsons 40:120), because, it is said at Acoma, it scorches their feet and slows them up (Stirling). To this end Acoma hunters cast dung and track dirt in the fire. Each man names the prey animal he desires to help him.

society medicine is given to all who come to the altar, and the chief brushes them with eagle feathers.

The Buffalo dance of Tesuque and the Deer dance of Taos are more (Tesuque) or less (Taos) combined with the familiar saint's-day dance. The clown society comes out only at the Taos Deer dance which they burlesque and police. In the Tewa and Keresan dances the Hunt chief or society takes part (San Juan, Tesuque, Nambé, San Ildefonso, Cochiti, San Felipe). There *is* no Hunt chief or society to take part in the Hopi Buffalo dance, and in the Hopi dance which was introduced into Santa Clara and San Juan the Hunt chief did not figure.

Elk dance is performed on the saint's day at Nambé, October 4, with a preliminary kiva retreat of four days. Goat dance, at Santa Clara, on the patron saint's day.

BUFFALO DANCE, AT SICHOMOVI, ON SATURDAY AND SUNDAY NOVEMBER 20–21, 1920[143]

The day of the week happened to be important because the little children, the school children, were to dance the first day; the second day was for the older girls and boys. I reached the Mesa after the conclusion of the first day's dance. About seven o'clock we heard an announcement called from a house door near by. "That is your father calling to come to the kiva." Sihtaime, of the Patki clan and chief of the winter solstice ceremony, is my "father," his own sister and several clan sisters having washed my head and given me Patki clan names. Sihtaime is the head or chief of the Buffalo dance. At the winter solstice ceremony he makes a prayer-stick for Buffalo.

Presently G'awehtima, Lizard-Snake clansman, the husband of Sihtaime's father's sister's daughter (and chief of the Wüwü-chim society and of the Shalako kachina celebration), and another younger man, together with a troop of the very little boys who danced today, come into our house to invite the fourteen-year-old daughter of the house to join in the dance and the evening's practice. G'awehtima has the function of assembling the girl dancers and collecting their dance paraphernalia. The party of men and boys continue on their rounds, but not until ten o'clock do we all start down the ladder of the kiva, Stove or Meat-eater's kiva, belonging to the Mustard clan. Since Waji, the man who wanted the dance, is a Mustard clansman, his kiva is being used.

"You sit with the girls," I am directed; and as I start to go down the ladder, one of the young men in the choir jokes, "Are you going to join the dance?" There are nine girls sitting on the banquette, and later two Navaho, a girl and an older woman, squat down at the end of the line, next to where the men are crowding in. Navaho females and Hopi alike keep their blankets well up under chin or nose, sometimes covering mouth with hand; but the Navaho woman carries on a lively flirtation of nudges and glances with the Hopi youth next to her, in contrast to the consistently demure behavior of the Hopi girls, who sit for the most part sidewise, their faces averted from the general company. The girls whisper now and then to one another and even giggle, but direct attention to the company of men and boys they withhold. Evidently a very marked etiquette of behavior and posture is to be observed by girl participants in "girl's dances."

For an hour or more the men "practice their songs" around the drummer, a Bear clansman from Hano. But for a brief, high-stepping caper, the Buffalo caper, by four men on their descent into the kiva, there is no dancing. The drummer and a younger man alternate in leading and singing. The young man stands up when he conducts, and his gesticulations are vigorous. There are fifteen or more men in the choir, and from thirty to forty crowd in behind the ladder on the raised floor, most of these men joining now and again in the singing. Even the little boys grouped in the southwest corner join in. In a circle in the middle of the kiva sit some of the elders, smoking. Sihtaime sits here, and G'awehtima, when he is not busy elsewhere.

The circle to the west is kept open, and here on the ground G'awehtima lays down the dance paraphernalia: two gourd rattles painted white with crosses in black, and two lightning sticks, for the two male dancers, and four notched hand sticks for the girls. At the conclusion of each dance, the dancers lay their

things down on the ground; but, in preparing for the dance, while
the young men pick up their things, G'awehtima picks up those
belonging to the girls. G'awehtima is also occupied in matching
dance partners. From each girl couple he learns the names of
the young men they choose as partners,* and then communicates
with these young men in the crowd around the ladder. There is
considerable discussion at times with the girls, of a natural and
unembarrassed kind. Perhaps G'awehtima is making suggestions; but, on the whole, he seems to be merely the girls' messenger.

About half the girls have their hair whorled and are wearing
the native cloth dress; the others wear an American cotton
dress, and a braid down their back. All wear shoes, which are
taken off to dance. The dance is in three parts, just as it is the
following day in the open, and it lasts about fifteen minutes for
each set of four dancers. As there is an odd girl, one of the other
girls repeats with her. In several instances the dancing of the
young men does not please members of the choir, and they step
out and show how it is to be done, with more spirit. At times in
the song shouts or yelps are in order, given by everybody in the
kiva but the girls. At these moments there is a fine pitch of
excitement. In fact throughout the rehearsal there is more personal expression by all concerned than I have ever seen in a
public dance.†

While the last set is still dancing, G'awehtima sends the other
girls up the ladder, and home. It is a careful piece of chaperon-
age. Then the last two girls to dance go up with G'awehtima,
who gathers up the dance paraphernalia; the drummer goes up
and the rest of us, and all disperse, past midnight.

It is eleven the next morning before the first set of dancers
appear. They come out from the maternal house of Waji, on the

---

* Customarily they choose cross-cousins, their mother's brother's sons who
are expected to supply the dance costume, the girls making a food return later
on (Beaglehole 3:79).

† Stephen makes a like observation in connection with a rehearsal of Navaho
kachina. "Several of the youngsters in the ranks occasionally laugh and chaff"
(Stephen 4:297).

court. As they come out of the door, male, female, male, female, one behind the other, Polisi, a son of the house, sprinkles the head of each with corn meal. Polisi represents the family associated with the dance, i.e., the family of Waji,* who had asked for the dance originally, and the day previous had asked for this day's repetition. Polisi then takes a stand to the right of the drummer; to the left stands Sihtaime, and back of them the choir of G'awehtima and five or six other men. The cheeks of G'awehtima and of some of the others are painted red, one man has two horizontal lines in red across the cheekbones. One chorister wears a buckskin kilt and a Navaho silver belt, but the others wear ordinary work clothes. An old man has a crash towel for a *banda* and stuck into it a paper flower. Another has fastened across his back a woman's silk kerchief. Another man carries in his hand two cotton-bound eagle feathers, an imitation warrior badge, "to make his voice sound good."

In contrast to the choir, the dancers are smartly arrayed. They wear the native cloth dress, minus calico underslip, their neck and arms bare, a man's dance kilt draped as a bodice and hung over with heavy necklaces, borrowed as usual from all the family connection. Among the necklaces worn by the daughter of our house are a string of heavy turquoise descended from her mother's maternal grandfather and owned by her mother's sister's son, and a Navaho silver necklace presented to her father by a Zuni friend. While her father fitted the necklaces, her mother fastened the puttees of her moccasins and tied a band of porcupine quill over each heel.

Each dancer wears the big fringed wedding belt, and on the back of each is a sun tablet painted with the face of the sun and encircled with red horsehair and eagle feathers. The hair is left flowing, the bang falling over the face to the tip of the nose, just as Zuni women dancers may wear their hair, a veritable mask.

---

* Why Waji himself did not perform the rite of sprinkling I do not know. Perhaps Waji was sick, and it was his sickness in particular that was being exorcised. If so, it is probable that he was in his mother's house when the dancers visited it. Such would be the case, I know, in a kachina curing ceremonial at Laguna and probably elsewhere.

(As Hopi girls do not bang their hair, like the Zuni or Keres or Tewa, this dance bang is artificial, and of itself indicates a foreign origin for the dance.) On the top of the head is a large bunch of downy eagle feathers, on the right side the conventionalized cotton or wool squash blossoms common to Hopi masks, with a pendant of red yarn, on the left side at right angles some eagle-wing feathers. Slanted across each cheek are two parallel black stripes. The rest of the face and the hands are whitened. Hanks of yarn around the wrists, and silver bracelets.

The feet of the boy dancers, bare but for fringes of buckskin, are whitened, and their legs blotched in white. (Several later dancers wear trousers, the outer seams fringed with buckskin.) They wear as kilt the woman's white woolen blanket bordered with red and blue, and bundled around the waist is the heavily fringed woman's belt. The heavy wig is sheep pelt. Downy eagle feathers are fastened over it, with a feather at the tip of each small horn. From six to eight eagle-wing feathers fan out at the back of the wig. The face is blackened, with white under the chin and across the lips. Across the forehead a band of porcupine quill.

After this first set of dancers withdraw into kiva, they are followed in about half an hour by another set, then there is an interval of an hour or more while dinner is served in kiva from the house of the people who asked for the dance. The day before, Waji's mother and wife baked wafer-bread in his mother's house, with clanswomen to help.

After dinner, at intervals of about an hour, five more sets of dancers come out. The drummer is always the first; he is followed by the choir, then by the boy dancers, who at once begin to caper about, and then by the girl dancers who are given their hand pieces after they leave the ladder, to be relieved of them again at the close before descending. All dance along the short way leading to the court, the choir closing in behind the dancers, singing and now and again yelping and gesticulating. In one dance a gun is shot off several times. While the boys prance around, shaking their rattles, the girls stand side by side moving their feet sidewise, without lifting them from the ground. Their arms are extended at right angles, and at the long-drawn-out notes of the song both are moved either to the right or left, as the dancer has been moving, with a quivering motion which ends, as the long notes end, in shouts, with a gesture of throwing something over the shoulder.

Now the boys spring in front of the girls, and with body bent far forward perform a most spirited dance, stepping high, one hand at the hip, one raised above the forehead, alternately. This whole movement is performed four times, the girls first standing to the south and facing north, then proceeding to the east to face west, and so on to complete the ceremonial circuit. At its conclusion the whole group begins to move back to kiva, dancing the first movement again, a movement in which the boys step backward in front of and facing the girls, to be followed up by them, the girls in turn stepping backward. The gestures of all are from the waist downward, the boy's gesture very sweeping.

Toward the close of the last dance Waji's mother comes out of her house carrying in her hand two prayer-feather bunches and two "road-markers." By someone in the choir the woman is told to wait until the group has danced out.* They have danced about halfway to the kiva when she is summoned to present the "road-markers" to the male dancers. Then, as the dancers move on, the choristers pick up whatever comes to hand in the street to swing around the head, four times, and throw after the Buffalo boys; the girls have withdrawn. The departing Buffalo are to take away with them any "sickness" of the people.

Down the trail on the east side the two Buffalo boys disappear on their way to the kachina shrine. There, like kachina, each will take off his headdress, in lieu of a mask, wave it in the usual anti-sunwise circuit around his head four times, and say to Buffalo, "You may go home." They will lay down their road-markers for the Buffalo, and say a prayer for all the people.

---

* This is one of the very few times I have seen a correction made in any Pueblo performance.

Buffalo (Game Animals) Dance of San Felipe*

"When they want to have this dance, the dance chief gets his men together in the evening," all the men belonging to one of the three kachina dance groups. The dance chief chooses two men for each animal represented, two buffalo, two elk, two deer, two, sometimes four, antelope. The buffalo impersonators choose a woman to be Mother of Game. That night the dance chief notifies the Hunt society.

The next morning participators go to a rented house, where all vomit. The Hunt society has also begun to vomit and fast, for four days. The animal impersonators fetch to their dance-practice house their horns and costumes from the house where together with their kachina masks they are kept. The Hunt chief sets up his altar in the dance-practice house: corn-ear fetish, mountain-lion image, corn meal, etc. The dance chief brings in his paints and grinding-stones, to get ready the dance paraphernalia.

The men who are to be hunters have a house where they practice their songs. For four nights the War captain convoys the animal impersonators to the hunters' house to practice dancing. Sometimes the hunters go to the house of the "animals" and sprinkle them with corn meal.

On the evening of the second day the dance chief appoints two men to go out early the next morning and get spruce, oak, and the grass that deer like. The last night of the retreat the Hunt chief makes a meal road from the door to his altar. The Hunt society starts singing hunting songs, and the Mother of Game starts to dance slowly sidewise from the door to the altar, sprinkling meal from her basket along the road whenever they mention the road in their song. Hunters, "animals," War captains, and all dance to the dance songs of the Hunt society.

Before sunrise the "animals" cross the river, two members of the Hunt society sending them forth in different directions. The War captains round them up and, after being joined by the

---

* White 3:56–60. Compare San Ildefonso, Cochiti (Parsons 49:197–98). Reported from Jemez, December, 1932. The Hopi type of Buffalo dance is also presented at San Felipe (Parsons 49:205).

Mother of Game, drive them to a hill on the north side of the pueblo where the head War captain, Ma·sewi, is standing. All pray. The War captains bring the "animals" down into the pueblo. The hunters come out of their house, beating a drum and singing. They are calling the animals. All go to the court and dance. The "animals" go to the house of the Town chief where society chiefs make a meal road for the "animals" to the ladder. As each "animal" puts his feet on the bottom rung of the ladder, one of the chiefs breaks off a twig of spruce from his collar. They return to the court to dance and then to their house.

Now the hunters go to the house of the "animals" and beat their drum. The "animals" come out led by the Hunt chief who carries spruce in his left hand and a small mountain-lion image in his right. The Hunt chief is followed by the Mother of Game carrying a rattle and a feathered stick in her right hand, and in her left, a small mountain-lion image which she keeps pressed close to her body in the dance. She wears a small black leather cap with two small black horns. She sprinkles a meal road for the "animals," who follow her in single file. In the court the hunters sing for the "animals." The Mother of Game dances between the two "buffalo." Between songs she runs down the line of dancers and shakes her rattle near their heads upon which they duck down and turn around.

After four appearances the war captain calls from the roof of the house of the Town chief to all the women to take food to the house of the dancers. When the women arrive with the food, they are met by two Hunt society members, one takes the food and passes it inside, the other stands with a medicine bowl in one hand and a corn-ear fetish in the other. He gives each woman a sip from the medicine bowl after which she draws a breath from the corn-ear fetish.

The "animals" come out again four or five times in the afternoon. During the last appearances the "animals" begin to break away, a few at first, in the last dance almost all. People help the hunters chase them. When a hunter has caught an "animal," he picks him up and carries him on his back to the Hunters' house where he sprinkles him with corn meal, breaks off a twig of spruce, and gives him a basket of food.

Women of the kachina dance group bring bowls of water to the house of the "animals" and wash their heads. Hunt society members take them to the river to bathe. After they return to their house, the War captain gives them permission to go home. At home the "animal's" head is again washed, by a woman chosen by his mother. This woman gives him corn and sometimes a new name. To this godmother and her family the mother of the "animal" gives corn meal.

BUFFALO DANCE AT TESUQUE, SAN DIEGO DAY
NOVEMBER 12, 1926[144]

At noon the dancers emerge from the Winter people's kiva—the choir down first as usual, ten men to stand in two lines, the drummers in front. The dancers begin to dance as soon as they leave the ladder, taking position in two lines vis-à-vis, eighteen men and women alternating in each line, thirty-six in all. After the short dance in front of the kiva they proceed in dance step to the singing of the choir along the road around the south side of town. In this progress, as in later circuits, they are led by "their father" who during the dancing in place stands off a little distance from the dancers.

Possibly during this processional is sung the following "buffalo magic song making come":

> From faraway frozen Buffalo Country
> Hither now they come with their little ones,
> Rapidly now they walk, rapidly they walk,
> Even now they reach the Red Bird Cap.
> Buffalo Old Man! Buffalo Old Woman!
> Come hither rapidly with your little ones.
> To Y'o pha k'ewe come with your little ones.
> They bring to us long life together
> And even now they reach Tesuque![145]

The men dancers wear rough buckskin kilts except a few who have the tailored buckskin kilt trimmed with metal tags and painted with the horned serpent. Belt and anklets of bells; low moccasins, with skunk heel bands. Horn (cow horn) blackened and projecting from right side of head; on left side, fan of six or more eagle-tail feathers, horn and feathers attached to a beaded headband; hair in belted queue or short. Strips of pelt (? sheepskin) pendent from headdress, armlets, and from below knees. In right hand, rattle of gourd or of cotton-covered can; in left hand, bow and arrows. Upper and lower parts of face black, with a broad red stripe across the bridge of the nose. In one dance line the body is blackened, in the other, reddened;* on backs of all splotches of white paint, and thighs, forearms, and hands whitened. The foremost figure in each line carries the familiar dance standard, an oblong piece of cloth, with pendent eagle feathers, attached to a long pole—red cloth for the black line, purple cloth for the red line.

The women dancers wear silk or velvet dresses with back kerchief. Wrapped moccasins; hair flowing and spotted with bird down; bang to eyes. The hair of four or five of the younger ones is bobbed. A red spot on each cheek; hands whitened, in each, two eagle feathers. One girl has turkey feathers.

Passing into the court, the two lines form at right angles to the spruce-set door of the house of the Winter Town chief. The door opens and out come the Hunt chief who is "their father," then the Fire society chief from a rite of cleansing, then the two Buffalo Old Men with the Buffalo Woman between them. Led by "their father," the Buffalo group dances a serpentine down the middle, the attendant lines executing a special dance movement, the women standing in place, the men stepping out first to one side of the line and then to the other and uttering sharp, shrill hoots or yelps. As soon as the Buffalo group reaches the end of the lines, the movement changes, all the dancers facing now east, now west, and taking a lively stamping step, the men as usual stamping more vigorously than the women, who hold their right arm at right angle to the body, the left arm folded against it. The men make the half-turn to east or west with a quick forward bend of the body. Between these two dance move-

---

* The difference in body pigmentation means nothing. The dancers are mixed, from both Winter and Summer peoples; they are appointed by the War captain, and they do not line up by moiety.

ments, the serpentine figure and the hollow square or turning figure, the standard bearers lead their respective lines around in a circling quadrille-like movement. These three movements are repeated three times.

The whole group passes on to a position in front of the church, with a hopping dance step, the dancers making half-turns to east or west, and the choir following them. Here and again in front of the spruce tree planted within the court and back again in front of Winter Man's house, the three-part dance is repeated. The Buffalo group withdraws into the house, and the two attendant lines return to their kiva. The whole performance lasts three-quarters of an hour. Another appearance before dinner, and two appearances afterward. Dinner is eaten in kiva, women passing their bowls down the hatch.

In the Buffalo group "their father" has his face reddened, his hands whitened, a piece of spruce in his right hand. He wears his ordinary clothes, with a fresh green silk *banda* over his short hair. He looks about forty. Fire society chief is an old man, with a limp. He is dressed in buckskin: buckskin fringed trousers and buckskin mantle over a white cotton shirt; hair in queue, and spotted on top with bird down, and eagle-tail feather in the forelock; face blackened; quiver on back, bow and arrows in left hand; in right, some small feathers and pendent hairs attached to something I cannot make out. Each Buffalo old man and the Buffalo woman carries the same sort of thing in his right hand. In left hand the Buffalo men carry a bow with spruce, the Buffalo women two eagle feathers with spruce. The Buffalo men wear a headdress of two horns with downy feathers at the tips attached to a large piece of pelt (buffalo or sheepskin) falling over head and shoulders; a fan of eagle-tail feathers over the pelt at the back of the head; dance kilt; face and body blackened, with X in white repeated on body, on arms and lower legs, in front and behind. The Buffalo woman wears a white Hopi blanket dress with silk kerchief hanging on the left side, arms bare; forearms and hands whitened; upper part of face red; lower part, black, with white splotches on cheeks; hair flowing, with bang to eyes; wrapped moccasins, with skunk heel bands. The Buffalo woman is a very stout, very sober woman of about forty-five. The impersonator, I am told, should ever be a woman who is not frivolous with men. This impersonator looks the part.

The dancing in the court concludes at a quarter of five, when all the dancers, attendant line dancers and choir, as well as the Buffalo group, withdraw into the ceremonial house for about a quarter of an hour. A matron from another house breaks off the tip of the spruce in the court, together with prayer-feathers. After emerging from the ceremonial house, the attendant lines of dancers dance back as usual to their kiva, in front of which the complete dance is executed. During this final dance the "father" of the Buffalo group stands near by, looking on informally, having donned a pair of overalls and an old *banda*. Inferably the ritual of the Buffalo group has terminated. As on the spruce tip in the middle of the court, so on the tips of the spruces at either side of the door of the ceremonial house, there are prayer-feathers and those, too, are broken off, I note on my return to the court.

During one of the dance appearances I visit the hill range south and southeast of town. In the stone shrine at the highest point are prayer-feather bunches which include a long spear of grass, as do the prayer-feathers attached to the spruces in the court. The feathers, too, are similar—turkey, eagle, yellow bird or warbler, jay. There are also cane joints stoppered with yellow-bird feathers. The feathers carried in the dance will be given to "their father" to offer the following morning in the hills.

A week later I am to meet a San Juan man who attended this Buffalo dance and is communicative. The four men in the Buffalo group were in retreat, observing continence, for four days in the house of the Samaiyo mayo', i.e., "their father" (Buffalo Woman was not in retreat or necessarily continent). During the retreat they put down their "lake" or bowl, i.e., altar, making a circle of meal within which are placed the Buffalo heads (i.e., headdresses). These they feed. The Buffalo heads have to be in a room without fire. (Inferably because the Buffalo are snowbringers.) At this time any sick person may appeal to the Buffalo for help, asking the War captain to ask Samaiyo, with a cigarette. Then Samaiyo will take a buffalo head to the house of the patient upon whose head he will place the buffalo head, and then press it upon the patient's palms and soles. The final dance performance will be in front of the house of the patient. When at the end the whole group withdraw into the house of the Winter Man, they dance there to give him thanks, all but Samaiyo and Fire society chief who withdraw to an inner room, since Samaiyo may not be touched by a woman. Winter Man gives everybody a drink of medicine water.

BUFFALO DANCE, TAOS, KINGS' DAY, JANUARY 6, 1926[146]

About 2 P.M. from all six kivas the dancers come up, as "all the boys" are expected to dance this year. From the three north-side kivas there are seventy-two buffalo dancers and one deer, and from the south-side kivas one deer and sixty-nine buffalo. Four "hunters" from time to time emit a shrill call or bark. A choir of about twenty-five, of whom ten or more beat small pottery drums. The first dance position after assembling is in front of the church, south and north. (I did not see the assembling or whether the Town chief "to whom the dance belongs" led out the whole group.) At the south end stand the choir in double row, then the two "deer" who throughout merely stand facing the dancers, not themselves dancing; then the herd, in rows of four or five. There are some tiny boys in the herd, each alongside an old "buffalo."

The dancer remains in one spot, but now and again turns around. The dance song is repeated four times, with a change of song or movement between, during which the "buffaloes" do not dance, but retain their bent-over position and sway from side to side, giving admirably the impression of a milling herd.

Imitation buffalo heads are worn, made up of bear hair and cow horns. Real heads and hides were once worn, but none is left. To the tips of the horns downy feathers are fastened, and down is stuck over the rest of the headdress. At the back, an eagle-wing feather and hairs from a buffalo beard. Hairs to resemble buffalo beard hang by tendon from the neck in front. Armlets of tendon and of two eagle-wing feathers. Anklets of

PLATE XVIII

BIG EARRING PEOPLE'S KIVA, TAOS

hide, some with hair. Low moccasins, some beaded. Kilt of buckskin or undecorated cotton cloth. Arms, torso, and legs painted dark-red splotched with white. On the face, streaks of blue-black paint, perhaps micaceous hematite. An arrow in the right hand, nothing in the left hand which is held to the waist.

The deer impersonators have the head with its large antlers resting on their head, the hide falling down their back. They lean over, a stick in each hand. Forearms and hands whitened.

The hunters are arrayed in buckskin shirt, mantle, and fringed trousers, a quiver of hide across the back. They stand outside the rows of dancers, and with each stands one of the newly elected secular officers, carrying his cane. The members of the choir who are notably the older men are dressed in their ordinary clothes and blanket. Across the top of their head is a streak of white paint.

After the four repetitions with milling-about intervals, the dance movement changes, and four lines are formed, the inner lines dancing southward, the outer, northward, in a quadrille-like figure. Then all moving in the same direction proceed with dance step to the second dance position, parallel with the front line of the north-side houses. Here everything is repeated, as again in the third dance position, a little farther to the east, and in the fourth position, still a little farther eastward. At the conclusion of the fourth performance the north- and south-side groups separate, the north-side group dancing parallel to the town wall near the north-side kivas; the south-side group crossing the river and forming parallel to the south-side houses near the town wall, with a final position in rather cramped irregular quarters near Feather People's kiva. The north-side "deer" withdraws in advance into Big Earring People's kiva (Pl. XVIII). (I cannot see what the south-side "deer" does.)

During the performance, which lasts less than an hour and a half, the clouds come up, and within half an hour of the close it is snowing—greatly to the satisfaction of one of the townsmen, who remarks that in the morning, clear though it was, he knew it was going to snow later and had therefore put on his heavy boots.

Buffalo dance, in Taos opinion, is a ceremonial for snow—unless my friend was camouflaging in his best manner.

SAINT'S-DAY DANCE AND DEER DANCE, TAOS,
DECEMBER 25, 1931[147]

By 10:30 A.M., if not before, the Black Eyes are out, collecting food from house to house, in shallow Apache baskets: apples and other fruit and small loaves of bread, now and again a bowl of stew. They go mostly singly, sometimes in couples, on a run, and hollering or talking in the high-pitched voice of Pueblo clowns. All collections are taken to Feather kiva. One young man passing by me stops and asks for a gift by gesture and in Tanoan. I put a package of cigarettes into his basket for bread. Later the same man passes by again and gives me an apple from the fruit he is carrying this time. During the morning they may visit the same house for food more than once. In groups of three, four, or five they also go from house to house bidding the dancers prepare or make haste. (If they catch anyone hiding in order not to dance, they will throw him into the river.) I was in several houses when they came in either to get food or to hasten the dancer. There was nothing of a ritual character; no meal-sprinkling, no prayer. In one house a Black Eye asked a man to give him his blanket, a joke parried by the man asking the Black Eye to give in exchange his sheath knife. "They wouldn't trade their knife today for anything. This is the day they need it"—for cutting meat, our host might have added.

During this house-to-house visiting there are intervals of play. A Black Eye comes out with an antlered deer head on his head, the pelt down his back, as the Deer dancer is arrayed; the others stalk him, then throw a lump of snow at him, and he falls down "dead," is "skinned," and deer head and skin are carried away on another fellow's shoulder. Again near the river three or four do a dance, a capering step, to the singing of one who sits down beating a drum. One gets down into the hole cut through the ice and splashes the water up on the others. A food-collector finds a buffalo head in a second-story house; he puts it on and does a few dance steps on the terrace.

The hair of the Black Eyes is tied up on either side of the

head, as adolescent girls once wore their hair, and into each bunch
is fastened a large bunch of cornhusks, the tips pointing backward. The hair on top is painted white. One Black Eye has a few
husks on the top of the head. Another wears a wreath of dried
yellow flowers, wild sunflowers gathered when they went to the
Lake. Another has two hawk wings as part of his headdress, and
he carries a wing in his hand. The shoulders and a space above
the waist are whitened, the upper body is blackened; the arms
are banded black and white. The face-painting varies, although
all are painted a solid black around the eyes. On some there is a
white triangle on the forehead, the rest of which is black; the
cheeks may be white with black diagonals; one had circular
bands of alternating black and white over his entire face. Old
trouser leggings are worn held up by a string attached to a cord
around the waist, with two shabby pieces of blanket doubled
over the back and front, in the style of the old breechclout. On
the feet, old moccasins or the heel-less shoes which pass muster.

Saint's-Day Dance

About three o'clock the choir and the dancers assemble outside the churchyard. The choir of about ten men, middle-aged
and old, from Big Earring kiva, stand bunched together and
rotate slowly in anti-sunwise circuit, the drummer in the middle.
First the men dancers join them, five, circling on the outside;
then from their house come the women, to circle outside the
men. A short song, then two lines of dancers face each other,
east and west, the choir sitting down in an oval, between the
dancers and the wall. The singers clap to the drumbeat. The
men dancers stand in the middle of the lines, three on one side,
two on the other. Their step is stomping from foot to foot, not
at all vigorously. The women's step is still quieter; they move
their bent arms up and down alternately in the familiar woman's
dance motion. After dancing in line two or three minutes, the
lines break up into groups of four or five who move around in an
anti-sunwise circle and then renew the line. This is the only
distinctive figure; it is repeated three or four times.

Meanwhile the Black Eyes, five or six, burst through the

eastern line and, shouting to their own drum, begin to burlesque the dancers.

The women dancers wear their silk or cotton dress in the old style, left shoulder and arms bare; but not a single dark woolen dress is to be seen. There are a few red and green woven belts. Ribbons of all colors hang from the back of the neck and from the belt. They wear their boots, not the wrapped or puttee moccasins. Their hair is flowing, with a small stiff feather in the forelock, and white paint on top; necklaces, earrings. Red spots on each cheek. In each hand a twig of spruce. Black Eyes give each woman some of their wild sunflowers to hold with the spruce.

The men dancers wear a kilt of colored silk or cotton, a foxskin pendent from the back of the belt. Their body is nude, unpainted; their hair flowing, an eagle-wing feather tied in horizontally at the back. Gourd rattle. After dancing at the two regular dance places in front of the houses on the north side, the men dancers withdraw into Knife kiva, and the women, into Big Earring, the choir sitting down on the wall around this kiva. Food is brought to the kiva by two women from the south side, two heaped-up baskets covered with white cloth.

Deer Dance

The three repetitions of the saint's-day dance took less than an hour. About 4:30 we see the Deer dancers emerging from the hatches of Old Ax and Water kivas. Five or six elders who have been sitting at the wall at the northeast gap together with as many more from the wall around the hatch of Big Earring kiva at once proceed as choir toward the Middle where on the river side a fire or rather smoke has been made—the hunt fire—and around it they sing. The choir is furnished by Big Earring kiva.

Meanwhile I can see the dancers forming in two single files, outside the wall and I can also see one antlered figure leave the line to stand alone, facing the east, as if in prayer. Then the files follow the trail outside the wall and enter through the northeast gap. They are led by two of the deer watchmen; the other two watchmen are rear guard. The watchmen wear fringed buckskin shirts and leggings, and on their backs carry a large quiver with arrows. One of the rear watchmen is an acquaintance, and he smiles at me as he passes. Behind the watchmen in the lead come the two Deer chiefs. They are whitened all over, antlers and body, and wear a white kilt and the kind of net leggings used by Hopi dancers. Then come other deer, antelopes, four buffaloes, a little coyote, two wildcats, two mountain lions. All wear kilts and moccasins; their body nude and unpainted. The head of the animal is over the dancer's head, the pelt hanging down his back. A bit of spruce is in the mouth of the deer. Downy feathers are fastened to the tips of the buffalo horns. All carry in each hand a short stick to lean over on, the better to imitate animal posture. The older men come first, then the boys according to size, some very little ones at the end.

The dancers proceed to the dance place in front of the church-yard wall, where the choir and the Deer Mothers join them, also the saint's-day dancers who merely form an outer ring, not dancing. Each Deer Mother heads a file of "animals" to form spirals, circles, diagonals—it is difficult for the eye to follow the two files as they twine in and out, packed very close together. Their progressions are definite figures, however, not merely the milling around as seen in the Buffalo dance. The Deer Mothers take very short dance steps, moving forward steadily but very slowly. They hold their arms forward, rather high, but flexed as usual at the elbow. Now and again they shake the gourd rattle held in the right hand; in the left hand are held two eagle-tail feathers and some spruce. At the back of their head are some erect parrot feathers and an eagle-wing feather, and below hangs a wild-duck skin (covering the hair and the butts of the feathers which were described as held together in a hollow corncob). On the top of the head is a bunch of small parrot feathers, on the cheeks are shiny black spots (micaceous hematite), and around jaws and chin a black streak of "sacred paint." The dress is like that of the saint's-day dancers, belted and with pendent ribbons, but the material is of white cotton, to look like the ceremonial Hopi blanket dress which was once worn. Had they wrapped moccasins, they would wear them, but as it is they wear their buckskin boots.

After the weaving in and out figures, at a signal from the Deer Mothers made with their gourd rattles, all the animals crouch down on their heels, and the Deer Mothers dance down the middle of the oval and back, very slowly, very impressively, in fact all the movements of the Deer Mothers are impressive, conveying a sense of drama.

Meanwhile the Black Eyes are performing their hunting burlesque. All carry roughly made bows and arrows about a foot and a half long. As soon as one of the boy wildcats or mountain lions puts his hand on a deer—the wildcats and lions stand outside the dance lines to act as hunters—the nearest Black Eye shoots an arrow into the head or pelt of the "deer," then seizes and flings him, quite unresisting, over his shoulder. If the "deer" is big, the Black Eye merely runs down to one end of the dance oval with him and drops him; but a little "deer" he will try and run away with across the river and into Feather kiva. All the bystanders, including women, will come to the rescue, and if anyone gets any sort of a hold on the captive the Black Eye has to drop him. There is no struggle. A lot of chasing and fun—for all except the little "deer." They do not look as if they enjoyed it. As many as twenty must have been successfully carried away.

Their *pas seul* concluded, the Deer Mothers signal to the animals to get up; then the Mothers withdraw, their two male attendants wrapping black shawls around them and escorting them away from the crowd and behind the houses to the next dance place. (The Deer Mothers should not be touched, they are sacred impersonations. The men looking after them are the Big Hail society men who have supplied their headdress, handpieces, and black face paint.) The animal dancers straggle back to the northeast gap, where they re-form to come in again as at the beginning, and to be joined by the choir and the Deer Mothers to repeat the dance.

Meanwhile the saint's-day dancers have repeated their dance before the wall of the churchyard. After it, again they form a circle or rather half-circle around the Deer dancers, the choir sitting at the west end to sing and clap to their drum.

At the close of the second and last performance the Black Eyes go about among the saint's-day dancers giving them bits of raw deer meat. Perhaps they are picking out those who re-captured the little deer.*

Early in the evening there is to be in kiva a brief ritual of feeding the deer, i.e., the deer heads, giving them pollen and feathers and rubbing meal on the head, before each man takes home his own deer head.

SAINT'S-DAY DANCE[148]

The patron saint's day is celebrated by Mass, procession, and dance. After the morning service in the church the saint is car-ried in procession to an embowered altar erected in the court. Near by sit the church officers, the secular officers, or the Prin-cipales. The dance groups come out once in the morning at a late hour and then, after dinner, several times until sundown. In many houses out-of-town visitors, Mexican or American, are en-tertained at dinner. It is the sole occasion non-Indian guests are traditionally welcome. In Mexico a market is generally part of a fiesta, among the Pueblos there is some house-to-house trading and in some towns a few Mexican vendors will set up booths, but there is no market. Besides the dance there may be races or a rooster pull, and the houses of the saint's godchildren may be visited for largess. But these activities are more usually con-fined to fiestas other than the day of the patron saint when attention is concentrated on dances and on clowns.

The dance performance is usually by kiva; there are two dance groups and two choirs of drummers, singers, and standard-bearer. The groups alternate, one coming into the court as the other leaves it, until the final joint dance. In several towns the dance group is led in by a member of the Koshare society, and Koshare clowns are out to play. There are a number of quad-

* At San Felipe and San Juan the "animals" run away at the close of the dance. At San Juan the women pursue, and a captor is given meat by the house-hold of the captive (White 3:59; Parsons 49:195).

rille-like figures. Men and women dance, the women often wearing the high head tablets which give the dance one of its names, Tablita or Tablet dance. By Mexicans and Indians it may also be called Pascua or Bashk'ᵒ, and by other New Mexicans, Corn dance.

FIESTA OF PORCINGULA, JEMEZ, AUGUST 1–2, 1922[149]

The evening of July 29 a War captain is heard announcing dance practice in the kivas. The clown society (Ts'un'ta tabö'sh) will go from house to house, gathering up the dancers. The clowns carry a rattle of olivella shells wrapped around a corncob.

July 31 there is a rabbit hunt "for Porcingula."

Toward sunset, August 1,* several women are sweeping in front of their doors. An hour later, "the Pecos bull is out," I am told, and hasten to the Middle. There the bull mask is out playing, with a following of about a dozen males, four or five quite little boys. They are caricaturing Whites, their face and hands whitened; one wears a false mustache, another a beard of blond hair. "U.S.A." is chalked on the back of their coat or a cross within a circle. They wear felt hats, several garlanded with yellow flowers. They shout and cry out, "What's the matter with you, boy?" or more constantly *Muchacho! Muchacho!* They carry a staff to prod the bull as they chase him or get in his way, tumbling over and sprawling on the ground as he makes a rush. Again, they will quiet down and go with the "bull" to a house door, to receive bread from the inmates which two or three boys will carry into the house of the Pecos Eagle-watchers society. Of that society these bull-baiters are members, the small boys merely designated members.†

The bull mask consists of a large frame covered by several patched pieces of dark blue or black cloth, spotted all over with white rings. The long and not at all realistic head is covered with sheepskin; from it flaps a red tongue. Back of the head within

---

* In Mexico this would be the day of vespers, *las visperas.*

† A case is on record of an eagle-hunter of fifteen losing his eagle because he was afraid to hold it, and the case is cited as justifying unwillingness to initiate mere boys.

the frame is fastened a bunch of flicker feathers. Still further back but almost hidden from sight appears the head of the man who is carrying the frame. He wears a dance kilt and belt, knitted stockings gartered under the knees and dance moccasins with skunk heel bands; he is dressed as would be any kachina impersonator.

While the "bull" rests from his careerings about the plaza, at the foot of the kiva ladder, from the house of the clowns come out six men, older men, dressed in white cotton shirts and trousers, with woven belts, *banda*, and moccasins, each carrying a corncob shell-wrapped rattle. They stand in a row facing east, to sing a short song, then singing and walking abreast they make an anti-sunwise circuit of the town, followed by a War captain. Paying no attention to the singers, another War captain has been shouting a summons to the dance practice for the evening.

The bull antics are renewed, this time with attempts of his baiters to lasso. Finally they succeed in dragging him in front of their house, where he breaks away again, to be caught again and dragged into the house. From the house a bugler steps out and plays "Wedding Bells" and ragtime tunes for the bull-baiters to dance to in couples, "modern dances," ending up in a tumble. Two by two, in their brown habit and sandaled feet, four of the Franciscan Fathers pass by. It grows dark, the bugler sounds "taps," and this burlesque, reaching from the Conquistadores to the Great War, is over for the night.

August 2, after Mass, about 10:00 A.M., Porcingula is carried in procession from the church to the bower built for her in the plaza. On either side is planted a small spruce. On the ground in front of the saint's table or altar stand a crucifix and two high candles. Within the bower sit some of the Fathers, among them the chief of the Arrowhead society and the chief of the Clown society who walked alongside the Franciscan Father in the procession. In the morning Antonio Toya, the chief of the Pecos Eagle-watchers society, does not appear, but in the afternoon he sits in the bower, prominently forward on the left-hand side, the corresponding position on the right-hand side being occupied by the Town chief. Toya is the outstanding ceremonialist among the descendants of the Pecos immigrants, and in his house lives Porcingula, the Pecos saint.

The bull mask is out,* with the pursuing gang. After some antics the bull is tied to the foot of a house ladder where now and then somebody on leaving the plaza will approach, touch the mask, pray to it, and sprinkle meal. Now a table is brought out and covered with bowls of meat and baskets of bread. One woman takes her food offering first to the bull mask, and prays, giving the bull a bit from the bowl before she places it on the table. The older men among the bull-baiters enter the saint's bower, shaking hands demonstratively with those sitting there, and, speaking to them in Spanish, noisily invite them to table. Included among the guests is the sacristan who has been standing alongside the bower. These table guests eat rather perfunctorily, and for only two or three minutes, and then withdraw to the bower. Then the bull-baiters themselves sit down to the table, and fall to, voraciously. The table-talk burlesque is a string of profanity and obscenity, mostly in English. Twice into the midst of this noisy party the bull plunges, upsetting the table and spilling the food.

About noon the Clown society chiefs make another singing circuit of town. The dancers are out about 3:00 P.M. They are to dance in two sets, alternating from the two kivas. The first set out is from Turquoise kiva. In each set there are about forty-four dancers, half male, half female; and in each choir around the drum from fifteen to twenty men. Seven clowns. The hair of the clowns is parted on the crown, painted yellow on one side, blue on the other, and wrapped into two pokes, in one, downy eagle feathers, in the other a bunch of sparrow-hawk feathers. Face, body, and limbs are also parti-colored, blue with white stripes, or yellow or white with black stripes, the striping horizontal. A piece of Hopi embroidered cloth serves as a loincloth; around neck and body are twined wreaths of clematis. In the right hand, a short hoof rattle stick, in the left a spruce twig.

The men dancers wear the Hopi dance kilt and belt and

* In 1933, Santiago hobby horses of the Santo Domingo Sandaro type came out to play with the Bull (King, B. M. Personal communication).

pendent foxskin, moccasins with skunk fur heel bands, yarn in various colors with bells under both knees, and armlets painted turquoise with spruce twigs above and below. The body of the Turquoise dancer is painted blue; the color of the Squash dancer is hardly distinguishable. In the hair a bunch of parrot feathers, tied into the hair if flowing or onto a band of yucca if the hair is cropped. Under the eyes a streak of red paint. Gourd rattle and spruce.

The women wear their dark blanket dress over calico slip. Several little girls in calico slip dance at the end of the line. All are barefoot. In both hands spruce twigs. The hair flowing, and tied on by thongs under the chin is a high *tablita* headdress, painted turquoise with a cloud design at the top of alternating red and white scallops and two turkey feathers at the corners.

The dance is in two parts, lasting about forty minutes. In the first or entrance part there are two lines, facing the saint's bower, men and women alternating, and at the head of each line a clown. Here, as in kachina dances, they are the roadmakers. To one side dances the choir. The two lines dance down to the bower where they turn and dance back, during which dance progress the clowns have been dancing within and without the lines. Their step is quick and high, and they gesticulate a lot, with outstretched arms or, scout fashion, the hand shading the eyes. In the second part the lines break up into sets of four or six dancers who circle anti-sunwise and return to position in line.

In the set from Squash kiva are several children. One woman has her little boy, not more than four years old, dancing next her, like a mare with a foal.

At the close of the first appearance of each set, each dancer kneels within the bower and prays to the saint. Then a single line is formed and at a walk is led out by one of the clowns. As one set goes out, the other set comes in. Late in the afternoon the Town chief and the others leave the bower to go to his house for supper. Afterward they return to the bower.

In conclusion, after sundown, the set which has been dancing, instead of withdrawing, remains dancing while the other set

dances in. Both sets form two continuous lines and dance together. At the end the seven clowns walk slowly abreast down
the lines, and back, praying the while. Twelve times they walk
the length of the dance lines, before their prayer comes to an
end. It is a very impressive finale, although the dancers are
standing at rest, whispering together a little, even laughing, here
a man relieving a woman of her headdress, there another gathering up from some of the men dancers their foxskins, those no
doubt which have been borrowed for the occasion, and still
another going the rounds of the women to collect their *tablita* and
carry the handsome turquoise-colored bunch into Squash kiva.

The dancers scatter homeward, leaving the solemn clowns
standing in line facing the west. The Town chief steps out from
the bower and up to the clowns, sprinkles each with meal, praying the while, and walks on up the "middle" to his house. As the
clowns take up their position in front of their own house, other
men come up to sprinkle them and to pray. Now the little saint
is picked up by a woman and carried under a canopy supported
by four men toward the church, into it for two or three minutes,
and out again up the west side of town, to her own house, the
house of Antonio Toya of the Pecos people. From the church
children have carried candles, and now before the door of the
saint's house they light the candles and carry them into the
house.

Matachina, San Juan, December 24–25, 1927*

Early in the afternoon the ten dancers form in two rows, the
two Mexican players of violin and guitar being seated at one end,
a San Juan drummer standing alongside, and next him the little

* From Parsons 49:218–33. Danced at Santo Domingo, San Felipe, Cochiti,
Jemez, and Taos. It is a variant of the sword dance Morismas or Los Moros
introduced by the Spaniards into Mexico. See p. 1069. Matachina proper is
danced by Tarahumara (Bennett and Zingg, 297–303), Huicholes, and Mayo-
Yaqui.

As Los Moros is danced today in Mexico (also Philippines), clown-devils or
old men, usually two, come out with the Moors and Christians or Santiagos.

In 1598, on completing the church at San Gabriel, across the river from the
present San Juan, Los Moros was danced by Oñate's followers (Hammond, 320–
21).

PLATE XIX

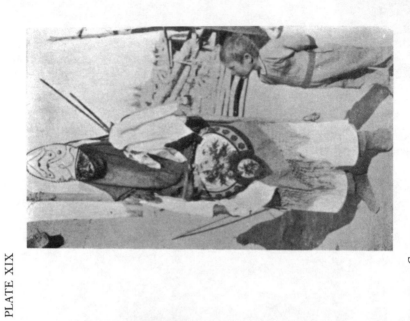

MATACHINA AT COCHITI

boy "bull" whose back is covered with a complete hide, including horns and tail. The boy carries two sticks to bend over on, like animal impersonators in the game-animal dances. Monanka (Monarco) stands between the dance rows, with the Malinche, the little girl dancer, behind him. She is about ten, with short brown hair and a light skin, heavily powdered. Yellow cotton dress, with wide sash, a handkerchief pinned in front; wreath of white artificial flowers, white woolen gloves, wrapped moccasins. Sometimes Malinche dances arms akimbo, but mostly with arms crossed in front, taking small Indian-like steps, dancing very soberly, surely, and unperturbedly.

In the first figure, each Matachin revolves where he stands, to right or to left, taking European gliding steps and moving his three-prong stick, *matachina ma* or hand, languidly, fanwise, in front of himself. Stick in left hand, kerchief-covered rattle in right hand. The headdress of the Matachin looks like a bishop's cap, with small gilt or silver crosses pinned in front, and on each side an eagle feather. The eagle-wing or tail feathers are tipped with downy feathers except in two cases where tiny American flags are substituted—cross, eagle feather, flag, symbols to us of the threefold culture of the Pueblo! The face is hidden by a fringe of jet to the nose and by a silk kerchief raised cowboy fashion from the neck to the mouth. Beaded cloth trousers, beaded moccasins, beaded armbands, and belt of bells.

In the second figure, Matachina kneel on both knees (one knee, Cochiti, Pl. XIX), each vis-à-vis couple in turn. Monanka sits in a chair at one end. He gives his stick and his kerchief-covered rattle to Malinche, who proceeds to dance alone, weaving in and out of the kneeling figures. She returns the stick and rattle to Monanka, making passes which may be the sign of the cross. In the third and final figure there is a variety of quadrille-like changes of position by the Matachina, Monanka weaving in and out with Malinche dancing close to his heels. Music and dance figures are much the same as in the Mexican performance at Alcalde; but the steps are executed with much greater spirit and precision or rhythm. In fact, the rhythm is so much more marked that the steps seem almost more Indian than European.

Moreover, the feet are placed on the ground, in a way I can only call indefinitely Indian fashion, more deliberately and circumspectly, with more staccato than in the slipshod, gliding Mexican motions.

Meanwhile the two Abuelos, the Grandfathers, have been valeting the dancers, straightening out displaced streamers, or picking up pebbles from where the dancers are to kneel. The Grandfathers wear ordinary store clothes and shoes, and each a large mask of hide, with nose and ear flaps, the back and top showing a fringed seam. On the side of one mask are painted a horse and five-pointed star. "Merry Christmas" and other words are scrawled on each mask. Each Grandfather carries a thong whip, and calls out in falsetto.

At the close of the third figure the "bull" makes a dash at one of the Grandfathers, who falls as if gored. A gun is shot off by somebody behind the musicians, and the bull drops dead. Then the other Grandfather goes through the motions of quartering the bull with his whip. Throughout the performance a War captain has checked the crowd of lookers-on, and two or three old men have stood on the outskirts of the dance group. Now one of the old men speaks to the musicians, bidding them accompany the dancers for dinner to the house which is labeled in large letters "Governor of San Juan."

About five in the afternoon there is a church service, and after it three saints are carried out. Each is carried by four townswomen, the little image set on a trestle. Over all is a canopy, a square cotton cloth fastened at each corner to a pole held by a townsman. Behind the saints walk the choir of Indians and Mexicans, singing in Latin. In front of all a cross is carried by a short-haired townsman in riding boots. As the procession leaves the churchyard, it is met by the Matachina, dancing toward it from the court. Monanka takes very lively steps in front of the saints and of little Malinche, who now walks just ahead of the saints. To one side march the bull impersonator and the impersonators of the Grandfathers, without bull horns or masks. As the procession starts eastward, the little bonfires or *luminarios* of crisscross pine sticks set in the churchyard and on either side of the route are all aflame, vesper lights for "our blessed Mother."

The procession halts several times for more lively dancing by the Matachina. One halting-place is at the usual dance place in front of Little kiva. Finally the dance processional wends westward to the churchyard where in Mexican fashion a final figure is performed before the saints are carried into the church.

NOTE

The afternoon of December 28, 1925, the Mexican performers of Matachina dance in the court of the ranch house in Alcalde, the Mexican town three miles north of San Juan. There are ten boy Matachina; Monarca; a little girl of six, Malinche; a little boy of four, the bull; Grandfather, who wears an unpainted leather mask or hood covering the entire head, with slits for eyeholes, an ordinary coat and trousers and carries a wagon whip; and Grandmother, also a man, who on this occasion wears no mask and is in overalls. Grandmother is generally in charge, leading the "bull" by a rope fastened to the sheep horns of his cap, or seeing to it that Malinche keeps up her dance behind. The little girl is dressed in a white satin frock with a wreath of white flowers in her hair.

The ten Matachina and Monarca dance quadrille-like figures, forming for the most part in two opposite lines, and gliding to the music of violin, guitar, or drum. Ordinary clothes overlaid with silk kerchiefs, around waist and over shoulder, with ribbons. Headdress of artificial flowers on a metal frame, from which falls a bang of jet beads over the eyes; silk neckerchief up to the mouth; same dance stick and rattle as at San Juan.

In one episode Grandfather touches his whip to the outstretched foot of the seated Monarca. The meaning of this is unknown to Tranquilino, who calls Malinche the sister of Monarca. Another time Malinche waves a kerchief at the "bull" who begins to gore Grandfather. Grandfather falls over, then the "bull" stretches out as if dead, and Grandfather jumps up and quarters him with his whip. At other times Grandfather would fasten the "bull" to a tree or to the leg of a chair. Tranquilino thinks of the performance as a whole as a mock bull fight.

A little more farce than in the Indian presentation, steps more gliding, headdress, mask, and costume less elaborate, less "finished." The Indian dance has style that the Mexican lacks, an impression that will be extended for any visitor in Mexico familiar with Pueblo dances.

ALL SOULS

As among Spanish Indians everywhere* All Souls, *día de los muertos*, the day of the dead, is celebrated in all the pueblos, excepting the Hopi. At Zuni on the night of Grandmothers' Day, *ahoppa awan tewa*, also at Acoma and Laguna, boys go singing from house to house, and are given food. They make the sign of the cross and in garbled Spanish say the familiar prayer. The cry *tsalémo* (Zuni) or *sarémo* (Acoma, Laguna) is from *salvemos*, we save.[150]

At Jemez and Taos, loose turkey feathers are put down outside the town, toward the north, at night or twilight. At Taos, food and water are taken to the graves in the churchyard, and candles are burned on the graves. At night hidden-ball is played in the old sacristy, and all night the church bell is rung. The day is called "Corn deposit day" from carrying corn to the church for the priest who asperses it.

The game of hidden-ball is or was played on All Souls' Night also by Tewa and at Sia. The Sia Fiscal tells the men to throw their winnings to the Grandfathers.[151] The game is not played on Grandmothers' Day at Zuni; but it is associated with the dead (see pp. 800–801).

At Santo Domingo the Grandfathers, who are assumed to come from the west since the day is called "Coming from the

---

* In Mexico All Saints (November 1) and All Souls (November 2) are generally combined as a single celebration for the dead, lasting two nights, the first night for the child dead, the second night for the adult dead. This distinction is not observed by the Pueblos; and only at Isleta is All Saints celebrated. Compare Santo Domingo (see below).

west,"* are "fed" at noon. Everybody digs a hole, anywhere outside town, and buries a bundle of food and of prayer-feathers, saying: "Here eat, Grandfathers, Grandmothers! After you eat, bring us crops!"

The day before there has been a rabbit hunt for the dead or a kachina dance, usually Tsaiyadyuwitsa, the most sacred of the mask dances.† The Governor sends his captains and the Fiscales to collect wood from house to house for an all-night bonfire in the churchyard. Men gather around the fire and sing. The church bells ring until sunrise. Women bring food to the church, and in the morning people bring corn and wheat which the Fiscal sends to the priest.

The night of the initiation into the Hopi Wüwüchim societies both witches and the dead are said to be in town (Oraibi), and Horns and Agaves patrol. People stay indoors, not even looking out, on pain of rheumatism (a sickness from the dead). At Oraibi food is set out for the dead in the houses of half the town. These houses are deserted, people taking refuge in the half of town the dead are not to visit.[152] I surmise an acculturation of All Souls. Papago set food on the floor and then abandon their houses the night of All Souls (Underhill).

COCHITI[153]

At this time every family offers to their dead and deposits in the church wheat, corn, beans, peas, watermelons, *tortillas*, wafer-bread, the sweet made of the roots of germinating wheat, and boiled meat. There are sometimes in a church as many as twenty wagonloads of these provisions. The provisions are supposed to be given to the priest, but in larger part they are stolen by the very persons who offered them.‡

* Compare Cochiti: "Their Grandfathers arrive from the west" (Goldfrank 3:74).

† From mask and from notched-stick-playing it may be equated with Hemi-shikwe (Zuni). Note that this dance falls actually on Todos Santos, All Saints.

‡ Today in Acoma, where there is no resident priest, boys and old people come for the wafer-bread and stew put down on a platform in front of the church. A Fiscal gets for the priest the candle that has been lighted and left with the food.

During the night of the dead, masses of candles are placed in the church and in houses. It is believed that persons remiss in carrying out this practice will have the tips of their fingers burned by the dead. Ears of corn on the stalk are also deposited in the church. They are the canes the dead use to go to Shipapu.

In a corner of the room, food is placed in bowls for the ghosts to eat. People believe, too, that the food deposited in the church is eaten by the dead. All the people fast to help the dead support their woes. The preceding day or night everyone is expected to stay indoors—the men in kiva, the women in their houses. The house doors are left open so that the dead may enter and visit their kin.* In the houses the blankets, the shawls, all the wealth of the house is hung on the walls, and the animals are shut up in the corrals. The dead, they say, are pleased to see their kindred prosperous.

The church bell is rung twice in succession at distinct intervals during one night and one day.

The society members, nude with their corn fetish in front of them, are in a place apart from the others. Members of Turquoise kiva, of Squash kiva, and of the Kachina society, all likewise assemble separately. All sing the entire night. Kachina society members go from house to house to dance a few moments to entertain the dead. In each assemblage of men everybody contributes some offering to the dead, pumpkins, melons, or bread. These things are cut in small pieces and thrown outside for the dead to eat. Bundles of turkey feathers are also buried on this day in different places in the pueblo that the pueblo may come under the protection of the Mother Uretsete. The dead are supposed to carry away the food and in their dance decorate their heads with the feathers. (The Shiwanna wear them.)

* Long ago when their grandfathers came back, they came back alive, but so many people cried that the grandfathers wanted to stay. At that time, too, the women tried to go back with them. Therefore, the grandfathers do not return nowadays alive (Goldfrank 3:74). This is the Zuni explanation about the kachina. Was Koko awia (Shalako), The Kachina Arrive, originally associated with All Souls' Night? There is the same display of wealth; kachina go dancing from house to house; the Rain chiefs (high priests) chant; there is a midnight feast. In Mexico *los viejos*, the old ones, go masked, from house to house.

NAMBÉ[154]

An old man in the family arranges the food offering for the dead. He sits in the middle of the floor, barefoot. The older members of the family—the young, unmarried ones do not participate—hand him the food with their left hand, on his left side. He crumples it all up into a big pile from which he puts some crumbs in a cloth for each participator. Taking with him the straw broom or the poker, the old man goes out first. The others follow in single file, the last taking that one of the two implements the leader has not taken. They go to a field to the north,* paying no attention to sounds heard behind them, sounds made by the dead. The line turns, facing the east. Everybody prays and from his left hand throws his food bundle backward, i.e., to the west, as far as he can. Then with a little stick in the left hand everybody makes four parallels on the ground "so the dead will not come back and follow them." Again in single file they return to their house, the last to come being the first to go, or the leader of the line. Reaching the door of the house he leads the line around the house, antisunwise, four times, after the fourth circuit entering the house.

Before leaving the house each had taken a piece of charcoal and outside had marked on his left sole and on his left palm the crosslike track of the chaparral cock, so that the dead would not make him sick or do him any harm. The chaparral cock has power (*piñan*). Each had also put a bit of charcoal under his tongue, which on the return to the house, he chews and spits out, spitting several times. The leader goes to the windows and doors and spits, then waves what he carries, broom or poker, in four antisunwise circuits. Similarly, the last in the line goes to the fireplace, spits, and waves in circuit what he has been carrying. What is spat out is called "dead medicine." As everyone came into the house, he gave the familiar ritual greeting, "May you live long!"

* There is no church at Nambé. At Acoma before they had a church they took the offerings to a field to the north (White 7).

ZUNI[155]

The Saint's crier or sacristan (*sakisti*) announces Grand-mothers' Day,* after the crops are harvested. He calls from the housetop, four days in advance. Large quantities of food are prepared from the year's products, to be offered by the women in the fire, before supper, or later by the men at the river. Men say this prayer:

> This day my children
> For their fathers
> Their ancestors
> For you who have attained the far-off place of waters
> Have prepared food for your rite. . . . .
> From where you stay quietly
> Your little wind-blown clouds,
> Your fine wisps of cloud,
> Your massed clouds you will send forth to sit
>   down with us;
> With your fine rain caressing the earth,
> With all your waters
> You will pass to us on our roads. . . . .
> Your waters
> Your seeds
> Your long life
> Your old age
> You will grant to us.
> Therefore I have added to your hearts
> To the end, my fathers,
> My children:
> You will protect us. . . . .
> You will bless us with life.

* 1915, October 30; 1916, October 17; 1918, October 17; 1927, November 9.

CEREMONIES

	Zuni	Hopi	Keres
Winter solstice ceremonial	*itiwana* (middle): synchronous meetings of societies and chieftaincies. Participation by certain clans in new fire ritual and in impersonations (kachina). Ceremonial appointments for year. Participation by all in prayer-stick offering and in taboos on fire outdoors, taking out refuse. War god ceremony	*soyala* (go in). All males make prayer-sticks or feathers (grouped by clan). Sun prayer-stick-making. (They turn the Sun back to summer.) Dance plans made for year (*soyala* is preceded by fire-making ritual of *wüwüchim*, and by *soyal* kachina) War chief weather and curing ceremony and phallic ritual	Synchronous society meetings. All males make prayer-sticks (Acoma, Laguna). Clan chiefs make prayer-sticks (Laguna formerly). Fetishes and masks repainted (Cochiti). *K'obishlaiya* (kachina) impersonations (Acoma). Shpi'nyinyi or a kachina dance (Santo Domingo, San Felipe). Mock combat or war dance by kiva (San Felipe, Santo Domingo). *Kashina* society altar set (Acoma)
Kachina ceremonies or dances	*koyapchonawe*, winter dance series by kiva *koko awia*, the kachina come, or *shalako* (Nov.–Dec.). Summer dance series by kiva, beginning at summer solstice, including *ololowishkya* drama *ky'anakwe* (sporadic, Nov.).	Sporadic by kiva, initiative by individual *powamu* ceremony (Feb.). Spring dance series by kiva Zuni Shalako (First Mesa, sporadic, July) *rima'n*, Home-going ceremony (July)	Sporadic or after society retreats or during Catholic celebrations, by kachina dance societies; Turtle dance (San Felipe) Summer rain dance (Acoma) Fight with the Kachina, sporadic (Acoma) *shuracha* (Acoma), *shuruka* (Laguna) drama by Corn clan (sporadic, July) *kohashtoch'e* drama
Snow-making or wind control ceremony	By Wood society, Big Firebrand society (stick-swallowers), War society Retreats by War society, February, April	War society and Stick-swallowing society ceremony Snow-making ritual by Town chief, after harvest Wind control ritual, *powamu*	Laguna: *kapina* society ceremony to control winds, or wind control ritual in kachina cult Cochiti: By *toahe* (*tabahi*) society, for snow
Curing ceremonies	Sporadic and private, by medicine order of society for the sickness associated with the society; general at winter solstice ceremonial	Sporadic and private, by doctors not organized into a society By society chief for the sickness associated with the society	Sporadic and private by societies; general at solstice ceremonials or at ceremonial spring purification
Initiation ceremonies	Sporadic, autumn–winter, into curing societies, War society Into Kachina society, before first dancing kachina Whipping of boys	In connection with regular ceremony, *wüwüchim* (Men's societies), *powamu*, Flute, etc. Whipping of the children, at *powamu*	Sporadic, into societies; before first dancing kachina Of annual War chiefs (Acoma) Whipping of the children
Races	Spring kick-stick races by clan, kiva, and general *molawia* ceremony race	Spring kick-ball races by kivas Spring kachina races by kivas Ri:e in ceremonies and in salt expedition	Spring kick-stick races by kiva

Ceremonial			
Summer solstice ceremonial	Pilgrimage to lake or spring. Participation by all in prayer-stick-making and taboo on trade	Sun prayer-stick-making. (They turn the Sun back to winter.)	Laguna: one night ceremony, by *kashare* society and by *shiwanna cheani* Kachina dance (Acoma, San Felipe)
Rain retreats	*klétsishemaü'pe* (in to call rain) by Rain chiefs in successive sets, beginning at summer solstice / Throughout year, at new moon, by high Rain chiefs		By all societies, successively in agricultural season
Irrigation, growth or harvest ceremonial	*thlé'hewe* corn ceremony, quadrennial or sporadic, in August / *molawia* (melons come), ceremony of *ne'wekwe* society, at close of *koko awia*	Women's ceremonies: Marau, Lakon, Oaqöl, in autumn	Ditch-opening ritual / *owe'*, night circle dance, spring (Acoma, Cochiti, Santa Ana, Santo Domingo) / Laguna: *yakohana*, Corn people, kachina dance / Cochiti: In harvesting for Town chief
Hunt ceremonial	Rabbit hunt with kachina, sporadic, May / Ritual during *koko awia*	Rabbit drives	Rabbit drives / Animal dance, Hunt society altar (San Felipe, Cochiti)
War ceremonial	Scalp dance (initiation into War society and Coyote clan ritual) / *owinahaiye* (installation dance)	Scalper ritual (Coyote clan) / *hoinatwe* / *masauwü* ritual in wild-plant-gathering, at corn-planting or harvest	San Felipe, Santo Domingo: Scalp dance / Cochiti: *a'hena* after bear kill; scalp dance (*ats'ät'anyi*); formerly Tanoan war dance (*sikarapo*) / Installation of officers: war dance
Women's dances	Buffalo / *thla'hewe* ceremony (Tablet or Corn dance)	Buffalo / Butterfly dance (*politit*)	Santo Domingo: Buffalo / Cochiti: Buffalo; *aiyashdyukurtsa* (Tablet or Corn dance) / Acoma: Butterfly dance / Laguna: *talawaiye*
Catholic ceremonial	Saint's childbed, January (Christmas) / Saint's dance, September / All Souls' Day (Grandmothers' day), October, house-to-house singing		Christmas: Scalp dance, *a'hena*, animal dance / Saint's Day: Tablet or Corn dance or borrowed dance / Holy Week: kachina dancing, Tablet dance (Cochiti) / All Souls' Day, tithes to the Church; house-to-house singing

TABLE 3 (cont.)

	Jemez	Tewa (Western)	Tewa (Eastern)
Winter solstice ceremonial	*pesa* (sun-work): Sun observed by Town chief; synchronous society meetings, 8 days Prayer-stick-making by societies and by laymen Retreat by Snake society	*i'an'aii*: all males make prayer-sticks or feathers, grouped by clans War ceremony, including snake ritual and growth ritual	*i'at'aire*, "Sun lives now." About Jan. 7, San Juan, during 4 days Sun goes to report to the Mother births of year: "people, animals, plants, everything." No smoking outdoors, no refuse out. Each Town chieftaincy observes retreat 2 days. San Ildefonso: Winter chief in retreat 4 days, fasting from meat. Conclusive kachina dance in kiva
Kachina ceremonies or dances	Sporadic or after society retreats, by kachina dance societies	Sporadic, by kiva, initiative by individual Child-whipping ritual	Santa Clara: after harvests, New Year's night, Kings' Day night San Ildefonso: after solstice ceremonies and rain retreats San Juan: one night early in December; *oku share*, Turtle dance, maskless, Dec. 25–26
Snow-making or wind control ceremony	By *totwahe'sh* society; and (?) by *ts'an'la-tabö'sh* By Morning Star and Cactus societies for thaw, March	*kabena* society (extinct)	Kings' Day, Buffalo or Deer dance
Curing ceremonies	Sporadic and private, by Arrowhead and Fire societies; general at winter solstice ceremony	Sporadic and private, by doctors not organized into a society By *shumaikoli* society	Sporadic and private, by *pufona* societies; general in epidemic (Nambé, probably elsewhere)
Initiation ceremonies	Into War society Into 2 Men's societies, at annual ceremonies Into dance society before first dancing kachina Whipping of boys	Into *shumaikoli* society in connection with ceremony	Into women's *tse'oke* society (Santa Clara), sporadic, at *puvere* ceremony
Races	Spring kick-stick races Rite at dances	Spring kick-ball races by kivas Spring kachina races by kivas	Relay races, by moiety, *pufona* exorcising, on Saint's Day

Summer solstice ceremonial	*peta*: Sun observed by Town chief; synchronous society meetings Prayer-stick-making by societies and by laymen	*i'ibit'ani'olo* (they work for the Sun)	Summer Town chieftaincy in retreat (one night, San Juan; four nights, San Ildefonso, with fasting from meat)
Rain retreats	By 6 societies after summer solstice, and again in September, with Water Serpent ritual	*tanpen* (*shumaikoli* society)	San Juan: By 6 chieftaincies or societies, August San Ildefonso: By 5 chieftaincies or societies with repetition, Aug.–Oct.
Irrigation, growth or harvest ceremonial	*siawe'e*, night circle dance, with irrigation and kick-stick races Flute dance by Women's societies, Sept. In harvesting for Town chief; prayer-stick ritual by Women's societies		*t'embishare*, San Juan, San Ildefonso
Hunt ceremonial	By Eagle hunt societies, Dec. Rabbit drives	Rabbit drives	Kings' Day, Deer dance, Buffalo dance ? Eagle dance Rabbit drives
War ceremonial	Scalp dance Ceremony after bear kill		Santa Clara and San Ildefonso: *puwere*, sporadic *p'angshare*, Captive dance, sporadic
Women's dances	Buffalo	*kwatihih* (line-up dance)	Buffalo, Butterfly, Basket *powinshare owe* (San Ildefonso) *tidi*, shield dance (San Ildefonso)
Catholic ceremonial	Saint's Day: San Diego, Nov. 12; Porcingula, Aug. 2 Christmas and New Year dances Kings' Day: Buffalo, Matachina Holy Week: Kachina dancing All Souls' Day (Grandmothers' night), feathers to the Dead		Saint's Day: San Juan, June 21, *fraeshare*; Santa Clara, Aug. 12, *yandewa*, Goat dance; San Ildefonso, Jan. 23, *wilara*. Christmas: San Juan, Turtle dance, Matachina; Santa Clara, *yandewa*, Ute dance Kings' Day, Buffalo, kachina (Santa Clara) All Souls' Day: tithes to the Church; Mass for growth

	Isleta	Taos
Winter solstice ceremonial	*napé'i*: by Corn groups, Dec. 1–20, White Corn one day ahead, and by medicine societies Dec. 15, ceremony of Snake war society	Sun observed by Cacique Kiva societies assemble (*natoiyemu*), Dec. 1–Jan. 10, with initial ceremony in charge of Big Hail society and conclusive ceremony in charge of Town chief; people "stay still" these 40 days except during Bear People's (?) war ceremony
Kachina ceremonies or dances	*kompŏr* or Pinitu or Spruce dance, maskless, in charge of Chakabede, Sept. 25–Oct. 5 *thliwahlichapŏr*, kachina basket dance Turtle dance by moiety Dark *thliwana* Jan.–Feb., June 20, kachina dances by Laguna colonists	*ahataana* or Turtle dance (maskless) by Water People, Kings' Day ? Feb.–March kiva dances Pilgrimage to Blue Lake (Aug. 24–27)
Snow-making or wind control ceremony	By *shichu* corn group, for snow (Feb.) By medicine societies, to quiet wind (March)	Big Hail ceremony (see above) Kings' Day. Buffalo or Deer dance (Big Hail society in charge of Deer Mothers; Black Eyes out), night ceremonial Spring ceremony against high winds by Old Ax kiva chief and another chief
Curing ceremonies	Sporadic and private by Town Fathers and Laguna fathers General purification (*shunad*), early spring	Sporadic and private by doctors not organized into a society, probably also by societies
Initiation ceremonies	Into medicine societies (Feb.)	Initiation into kiva or kiva society through training over 18 months, the 6 kivas rotating and overlapping
Races	Relay races for Sun (? and Moon), March–April. Sunday races by children and others in spring	Relay races by kiva, for Sun and Moon, Cross Day (May 3), San Gerónimo Day (Sept. 30) (pole-climbing by Black Eyes) Long-distance races (?) January or spring Sunday races in spring by children and others

		Sun observed by Cacique
Summer solstice ceremonial	By Corn groups, June 1–20	
Rain retreats	*thlcchide*, retreat 12 days, July, by Town chief and other chiefs; repeated in drought	By 6 kiva societies, beginning middle July
Irrigation, growth or harvest ceremonial	Ditch-opening ritual and circle dance	Ditch-opening ritual: preceding circle dances, in kiva by night, and outdoors by day (see below) One-day springtime ceremony with ground altar, outdoors, by kiva groups
Hunt ceremonial	Ceremony by Hunt chief, late October Rabbit drives	Deer or Buffalo dance, Christmas or Kings' Day ? Eagle dance Rabbit drives
War ceremonial	Scalp ceremony sporadic, in connection with races	Arrow assemblage (January)
Women's dances		*yunataana*, "Navaho" circle dances, Feather kiva sings, after Feb.–March night kiva dancing *tanapotaana*, men and women in line, throw-away, Feb.–March Round dance, on any occasion
Catholic ceremonial	June 25, 29: San Juan's Day, San Pedro's Day Aug. 28: San Agostin's Day Sept. 4: San Agostinito Day Dec. 12: Guadalupe Day Christmas: *hawinaa'ye* and various dances Kings' Day dance (by Laguna colonists) All Saints' Day	*konthli*, Christmas, Kings' Day, Cross Day, Santa Ana's Day, Santiago's Day Christmas Vespers: Children's dance, dance-procession with saints Christmas, Kings' Day: Deer dance, Buffalo dance, Matachina, house-to-house dancing by children (Kings' Day) All Souls' Day: tithes to the Church; feathers to the Dead

CHAPTER VII
REVIEW, TOWN BY TOWN

By this time in the multiplicity of detail we stand to lose the general picture. By way of review, therefore, I propose to give in this chapter, before going on to our final discussion of social processes, summaries of the ceremonial life, town by town, selecting in each tribe the towns about which we are best informed—Walpi, Zuni, Acoma, Laguna, Santo Domingo, San Felipe, Cochiti, Sia, Jemez, San Juan, Hano, Isleta, and Taos.

WALPI

Hopi town sites, including the sites of ruined towns in Antelope or Jeddito Valley, are conspicuous instances of clash between the need of security against enemies and the need of water. The only permanent water supply is from springs along the southern edges and spurs of Black Mesa, an extensive catchment area north of the Little Colorado River; and from this plateau the valleys are flooded and rendered fertile for farming. By tree-ring chronology mesa-set Oraibi was settled eight hundred years ago, but it was not until after the Great Rebellion of 1680 that from their valley fields and springs fear drove the Hopi of First and Second Mesas to the mesa tops.

Coronado's captain sacked Kawaika in Antelope Valley, and the town was partly abandoned. Forty-three years later, in 1583, Espejo and his Zuni escort found Sikyatki across the wash below First Mesa abandoned. Missions were established in 1629 at all three mesas and at Awatobi in Antelope Valley, where four years later the missionary was poisoned. The missions at Shumopovi and Oraibi (Mishongnovi and Walpi had been reduced to *visitas*) were destroyed at the Rebellion. Then there were punitive expeditions by Spaniards and, it is said, by Hopi themselves. In 1700 an Oraibi chief, called Espeleta, visited Santa Fé to seek assurance of peace without conversion from the

Governor.[1] He failed to get it, and soon after Awatobi, containing a pro-Catholic party or at any rate acquiescent to a baptizing
friar,* was attacked by Oraibi and other Hopi, sacked, and
abandoned (1700),† and First and Second Mesa people began to
move up to their present mesa sites,‡ undoubtedly from fear of
raiders, whether Utes or Spaniards. Refugees from the East
were being harbored, and pursuit by Spaniards and reprisal were
dreaded by both the refugees and their hosts. Governor Martinez' visit in 1716 was not reassuring (see p. 914), and Hopi and
Tano (Thano; Tewa of Hano) must have been well satisfied to
be on top of their Rock.

Missionaries came to preach,§ but none was allowed to live
in Hopiland until late in the following century when sometime
after 1870 a Moravian mission was founded at Oraibi and in 1875
a missionary school at Keam's Canyon. Thanks to their own
"stubborn" spirit and to Navaho buffers who terrorized travel
for a century or more, Hopi were exempt from that long period
of direct Hispanization the other Pueblos experienced through
the Church or through Mexican colonists. Mexican or Spanish
influence may have been felt, but only indirectly, through other

* Summoned from Zuni by Espeleta before he went to Santa Fé; but, after
the friar finished baptizing at Awatobi, he was not allowed to proceed to Oraibi.
Inferably there were two parties at Oraibi, a pro-Spanish or at least a conciliatory
one, headed by Espeleta, and a stiff-necked one, and in characteristic Pueblo
fashion policy vacillated.

† The massacre is described as general, yet only one kiva assemblage is specifically accounted for as shot to death or suffocated by throwing down burning
brush and red peppers. In the Snake chieftaincy of Walpi tradition held that
near Mishongnovi prisoners were slaughtered and *tortured*, a very unusual procedure, but women with ceremonial knowledge were spared (see p. 1133, n. ‡),
also two men who knew about growing peaches and sweet corn (Bloom, quoting
Fewkes, 206, n. 41). Chili, peaches, and sweet corn—Eastern or perhaps direct
friar influence here.

‡ Walpi made more than one shift. I find to my surprise that Sichomovi was
settled before a part of Walpi. After his eight-day survey in 1775, Father Escalante reports: Within a stone's throw of Janos (Hano) is a settlement which
has only fifteen families "because of the new settlement which the Moqui are
making at Gualpi," within gunshot and accommodating 200 families (Thomas,
151).

§ In 1707, 1716, 1723, 1730, 1741, 1744, 1745, 1775, 1780.

Pueblos or through Hopi returned from sojourn in the East.*
Spanish secular government was not imposed, the Church calendar did not confuse the solar or lunar calendar, nor did Spanish
witchcraft notions come in, until comparatively late. Clowning
and burlesque flourished as they have never flourished in the
eastern pueblos under the eyes of the Church. Spanish ideas
about property, sheep excepted, did not affect the descent of
property, in the female line, through lineage or clan.

Clanship is the paramount principle of Hopi social organization, since clanship affects not only marriage choices and all
forms of hereditary property but chieftaincy and ceremonial details of all kinds. The chief of a ceremony or society is the clan
chief. Theoretically he is the oldest son of the oldest sister in
the lineage in charge. The chief keeps his fetishes or bundle in
his maternal house, and his mother or some woman of this house
is considered the clan mother. Walpi Sun-watcher and Wüwüchim society chief has each the usufruct of a field attaching to
his office, a system more general on the other mesas. At Shumopovi ten large plots were owned by the societies or assigned to
their chiefs.[2] Walpi chiefs, women chiefs excepted, compose a

* Among the 441 "converts" convoyed by the friars in 1741 from Hopiland
to the east (? Tiwa settlers at Payupki) there were probably some Hopi. In
1777–79 there was a great drought in Hopiland. Thirty-three Hopi went to
Zuni and thence, led by the Spanish alcalde at Zuni, to Sandía (supporting the
idea that among the Payupki-Sandía people there were Hopi). In March, 1780,
seventy-seven Hopi were brought to Santa Fé by Father García and placed by
Governor Anza in various pueblos. Later this number was increased to two
hundred, "coaxed out in small parties." The Governor had sent word to the
Hopi that he would give them a site on the lower Rio Grande, "free from working fields, giving service or any other labor for their missionaries or for any other
person," but this plan was not carried out. Had a Hopi pueblo been founded in
the east, in view of the perpetual Ute and Navaho menace other Hopi might
have migrated and latter-day Hopi history been quite different. As it was,
although the tribe was reduced from 7,494 (1775) to 798 (1780) by death and
migrations to Havasupai and Navaho as well as to the east, none of the "indomitable rebellious nation" followed the conciliatory Governor back to New
Mexico, no lasting migrating route was set up, and some of the Hopi scattered in
the eastern towns probably did return to the homeland, although they were distributed in the more remote pueblos so they would be unable to return. Others
came to be settled in that mixed Genizaro population of Abiquiu (Thomas,
26, 29, 146, 166, 223, 224, 237, 243, 244).

council which chooses the Town chief,* apparently from any clan, although a properly qualified kinsman of the lineage of the deceased chief will be preferred. The present Town chief is of the Horn clan. He and his precedessor have been chiefs of the Flute ceremony.

The other nine clans of Walpi including Sichomovi are Bear, Snake-Lizard-Sand, Kokop (Cedarwood-Fire-Masauwü), Rabbit-Tobacco, Patki (Water-Corn, etc.), Reed-Sun-Eagle, Kachina-Parrot, Mustard-Chakwena, Butterfly-Badger. Next to the Town chief is the Bear clan chief, the "Bear man," who is in charge of the Place of Emergence, and who was probably once, as in other Hopi towns, the Town chief. Two other chiefs, Crier chief of the Snake clan and Eototo chief of the Kokop clan (in charge of the mask of the father of the kachina), figure importantly in ceremonial but are not chiefs of ceremonies. The other Walpi chiefs are chiefs of Powamu or Kachina society, of the sometime war societies of Snakes and Antelopes, of Sun and winter solstice Soyal societies, of the War society, of the four Men's societies (Singers, Wüwüchim, Horn, and Agave), and of the women's Marau, Lakon, and Oaqöl societies. The clan mothers have roles in the kachina ceremonies, but women chiefs do not attend council. Nor does the Badger clan chief who is in charge of Zuni Shalako, a sporadic early summer kachina celebration. At Oraibi the Badger clan has control of the kachina cult jointly with the Kachina (Parrot) clan. Both clans are said to come from Ki'shiwuu (First Mesa, Kishyuba), sixty miles to the northeast, whence spruce for the kachina is fetched by all the Hopi towns.[3]

There are many kachina dances but only two kachina ceremonies: Nima'n, the Home-going July ceremony, and Powamu, the February ceremony for exorcising cold and wind, for initiating into the Powamu society,† for cleansing the fields, for getting

---

* Not always easily (see p. 1041) or without starting a feud (Stephen 2:67; and see pp. 1134–35).

† At Oraibi children aged from five to ten are initiated, at an evening kiva ceremony at which Chowilawu, a very secret kachina who never appears outside, dances on a sand-painting. There is no whipping, nor are these children whipped

crop omens for the year, for curing rheumatism, for whipping (which probably means exorcising) the young children and providing them with godparents not only for kachina initiation but for initiation into all the societies the godparents belong to.

Both Powamu and Home-going ceremonies are in charge of Powamu society chief; the seven kivas of Walpi and Sichomovi take turns year by year in supplying the kachina dance set for Nima'n* and the bogey kachina for Powamu. Each kiva has a dance membership composed of men who frequent the kiva, generally because they live near it. After the one-day or one-night winter retreats of most of the societies there may be a kachina dance; there is a more or less fixed series of kachina dances in spring and early summer; and kachina dance visits are exchanged sporadically between all the towns.

Besides serving as a sort of dance club, a kiva is a race club—the kick-ball race series is run off by kiva—and an assembly room for most ceremonies. (Sun, War, and Flute ceremonials are observed in the maternal house.) Originally the chief of the ceremony may have been the proprietor or trustee of the kiva but such connection today is obscure in Walpi. Today the kiva proprietor is merely one who has built or rebuilt the kiva, or his descendant, although the only time the kiva is associated with the proprietor as such or with his lineage or clan is at the winter solstice ceremony. Chief kiva is properly so named, for it is used for important societies or ceremonies, for Singers society which conducts the Wüwüchim ceremony, for the Water-Corn clan chiefs who conduct the winter solstice ceremony, for the main Powamu and Home-going ceremonials, and by the Antelopes in the Snake-Antelope ceremony. The chiefs meet in council in Chief kiva, indicating its particular communal use.

---

at the regular kachina whipping of the children. Powamu society members make the "road" for the kachina, besprinkle them with meal, give them prayer-feathers, and pray, all as "Kachina fathers." At Oraibi the girl initiates will later put up the hair whorls of the Powamu kachina maids, sprinkle corn meal, and act in Powamu ceremonials whenever women are needed (Voth 2:93–94).

* After observing Nima'n three years, Stephen remained baffled by the inter-relations of society, clan, hierarchy, and kiva. There are no records at all for Second and Third Mesa. The ceremony should be studied.

Kivas are borrowed by the four Wüwüchim or Men's societies, always the same kivas, so there is a fixed association between kiva and society. Initiation into one of the Men's societies is necessary for adult status, to dance kachina or to take part in the winter solstice ceremony. All four societies have war traits: Singers and Wüwüchim* supply clowns; Horns and Agaves are watchmen or scouts. The Agaves are associated with fire, fertility, and with the underworld; they sang for the people as they emerged from that world; the butts of their prayer-sticks are always black to represent the black of the Nadir; at Oraibi they have a unique kind of corn fetish and they represent the Nadir not by the southwest but by the northwest; at Walpi their chief is or was a member of the small cult group or society of Masauwü, god of Death.

The organization of this Masauwü society, Maswïmpkya, is obscure at Walpi, probably because in Stephen's day it consisted only of three men and was lapsing;† but at Mishongnovi the society was organized like any other Hopi society. The chieftaincy was in the Eagle clan.‡ Men cured of swellings on the head or of headaches joined the society, as well as those caught by the Masauwü impersonation as he ran his night circuits to deposit prayer-sticks in the Masauwü shrines and burial places. When asked for by a planting or harvesting party and arranged for at the winter solstice, the Masauwü impersonator and presumably the society went into retreat for four nights, the impersonator sleeping by day and fasting from salt and meat. His

* This society paints yellow like the War society of Oraibi, and the circle dance of the Wüwüchim is like the Oraibi warriors' dance (Titiev 3). Initiates into the Men's societies are seated with knees drawn up to chin, as are war initiates.

† After the harvest ceremonial of 1891 Masauwü did not come out again until 1924, for a wild plant harvest in May (Stephen 4:994–95). But see Forde 3: 396-97, quoting Freire-Marreco on an appearance in 1912 at an intertown planting-party for Snake clanspeople of Walpi. Two impersonations were out, planting seeds, distributing leftover seeds to the girls, and chasing people.

‡ I was told that the Walpi ceremony was in the Coyote clan, where Masauwü belongs; but on Second Mesa no Coyote clansman could be a member of the Masauwü society, he would be too powerful: if he hit anyone with Masauwü's sack, the person would really die.

night circuits diminished as the Clouds drew nearer. On the third day there was a rabbit hunt with a member of the society as hunt chief, every hunter contributing his first rabbit to the society for Masauwü's bloody arrayment. Masauwü's behavior in field and dance court (see pp. 789–90) is highly suggestive of human sacrifice.

The War society proper [Momchit, Oraibi; Kaletakwïmkya, Walpi] is associated with the War Brothers. A stick-swallowing group (Nasosotan, Walpi; Nakyawimi, Oraibi) was affiliated with the War society.* On First Mesa there is no tradition about any organization of scalpers (scalps were cast away in fissures of the mesa), but on Second and Third Mesas there was a distinctive group of scalp-takers who at Oraibi are referred to as the real warriors. The Kokop (Coyote-Cedarwood-Masauwü) clan was in charge,† arraying the scalper and taking him to certain shrines for exorcism. "If he is not lucky, he will see his son (victim) coming after him as a real Masauwü"(Titiev). Only one or two scalps were ever taken in a fight (Second Mesa), and these might be given away‡ to would-be initiates into the group of scalp-takers.

The Snake-Antelope ceremony is popularly referred to as for

* Stephen 4:94; Titiev 3.

† Just as the Tewa were given land on the mesa top after they defended Walpi against a Ute raid, so the Kokop people were admitted to Oraibi after they defeated the big-foot Chimwava (? Chemhuevi) for whom, in spite against being kept out, they had secretly sent.

Masauwü is the *wuya*, the ancient, of the Kokop, and the Kokop would send out two impersonations against the enemy. The Kokop introduced the real Warrior society, also images of the War Brothers. Anyone who, like Kokop, bragged of war exploit had to join the real warriors, so if any one asked "Who killed this enemy?" the warrior would answer, "My *wuya* killed this one" (Titiev 3).

‡ The scalper might throw the scalp on anyone who would then be initiated as a war chief, sitting on a bearskin within a circle of meal for three days, the fourth morning washing his head in kiva and having it washed again by his "aunt" before dancing with the scalp on a pole in the court, accompanied by his aunt (Shipaulovi, Voth 5:57–58, 60–61). The circle of meal, the "house" of the initiate, was drawn close to toes and buttocks for those who did not belong to the Momchit war society; for members, there was a little space for extending the feet (Oraibi, Titiev 3).

rain, the prayers recorded by Voth at Oraibi and Mishongnovi are definitely for rain, and the Antelope society chiefs impersonate the Chiefs of the Directions, rain chiefs. However, the societies are war or sometime war societies. Formerly the Snakes were warriors, and, when they went out on the war trail, the Antelopes who were old men stayed at home to make war medicine. In the current ceremonial the Antelopes pray in kiva to keep peaceable the snakes that are being hunted.

The snake-bitten may be initiated into the Snake society, but the whole story of curing by the society is not known.* Infants are taken into one of the society assemblages,[4] I surmise, for treatment for swollen navel. (An infant's sore navel is blown upon by one who has been snake-bitten at Zuni and Laguna.)†There is initiation by trespass, i.e., through encounter with the snake-hunters.[5]

Ritual may be performed by the Hopi society chief for anyone sick of the disease associated with the society.‡ At Walpi rheumatism is associated with the Powamu society, swellings with the Snake society, wounds (?) and lightning shock with the Flute society, "twisting sickness" (?), paralysis, with the Wüwüchim and Marau societies, and venereal disease with Marau and Lakon societies. At Oraibi deafness is associated with Marau but sore ears with the Winter solstice society; with the Horn society twisting and twitching (? palsy) of face and neck are associated; with Oaqöl, a hornlike swelling on top of the head; with Lakon, eczema in upper part of body;§ with Powamu

* At Mishongnovi men join the society who have been cured by the society chief of snakebite or of a swelling of the stomach (Lowie 4:340), snake sickness.

† Parsons 22:103. At Isleta, by one who has experienced either snakebite or attack by the Navaho who use venom-poisoned arrows.

‡ He will sing the discharming song of the society (Voth 2:148–49; 4:45). Neither Voth nor Stephen describes in detail any treatment of this kind; probably neither ever saw one. In 1896 Voth saw the Snake society chief put roots from his bags into a bowl and take it out of kiva, presumably to one affected by snake sickness. Snake society members will be brought into kiva to be treated. Infants also are brought in to be rubbed and *sucked* (Voth 3:330, n. 1, Pl. CLXXVII B).

§ Can this be smallpox? The devastating epidemics experienced by Hopi must have been associated with some society.

society, swelling of kneepan and contraction of the tendons about the knee; and with the War society, bronchial affections.[6]

Other ailments or afflictions were treated by the Poboshtü and the Yayatü societies which were lapsing at the close of the century. The Yayatü practiced jugglery and cured for burns; the Poboshtü sucked out witch-sent disease, witch "arrows," objects that looked like a headless centipede, said to be used also by the curing societies of Zuni. Very little about witches was recorded by the early Hopi observers,* but Stephen remarks in a letter to Washington Matthews that the Poboshtü, "eye-seekers," were so closely connected with the Powa'ka, the sorcerers, that he believes originally they were the same.[7]

Women's ceremonies, Lakon, Marau,† and Oaqöl, are very similar, in the Spirits addressed, in altar ritual, and in public performance.‡ For the Lakon ceremony the three *tiponi* (all belonging to the Water-Corn clan) are laid down in Goat kiva where the standard is erected and where the five women chiefs will eat and sleep. The five chiefs make prayer-sticks, smoke over them and have them distributed by two young women who have been anointed with honey and given a hair prayer-feather. This ritual is repeated for eight days. The fourth day there is a new standard, and the altar is completed, with painted slabs, corn meal "mountains," figurines of Müy'ingwa, Lakon Maid, "their mother," and "their uncle" Sho'tokününgwa and with a sandpainting of the first two. Night ceremonial of songs and prayers, and of initiation through head-washing,§ other women and several men (seven) also participating. An altar of the Directions is made; the walls are marked with meal, also the left cheek

---

* Recent observers report all the witchcraft beliefs and practices that occur in the East.

† Mamau is Shoshonean (Southern Paiute) for woman.

‡ Tradition supports the hypothesis that they are variants of the same ceremony, developed in different towns. Both Marau and Oaqöl are reputed to be derived from that treasure town of ceremonies, Awatobi; Lakon is identified with Walpi.

§ Novices have been grinding corn in the houses of the women chiefs. The rite of passing novices through the yucca ring is observed only in Marau and Oaqöl.

of each attendant, by the woman of the Town chieftaincy, using her left hand. The sand-painting is gathered up. At dawn a procession of the women to sprinkle meal along the cliff edge and deposit the prayer-feathers of the novices in a shrine. On the eighth day, the final prayer-stick-making, the offerings to be carried in procession in the afternoon to Sun spring and the following dawn after the night ceremonial to the Water-Corn clan *sipapu* in the court. On this day the *tiponi* may be renovated. In the late afternoon a race by the society women up the mesa into kiva, where they touch the crook of longevity held by a Water-Corn clan chief and society member and song leader. The next morning, a men's race. The standard or a basket tray is carried and passed on to the overtaking runner. Both races are to hasten the ripening of the crops.

When the men runners come up, the society women are dancing their circle basket dance in the court. This is danced again in the afternoon, two women and a man performing a trail ritual from kiva to dancers. The man closes the trail with meal, and the women throw corncob darts onto the meal lines. The two women carry baskets, basins, and food balls which, after joining the dance circle, they throw to the lookers-on. The two women are replaced several times during the afternoon performance.

Besides the circle dances of the women's ceremonies and their warlike traits of throw-away and burlesque, there are so-called girls' dances: Buffalo, danced by successive couples, and Butterfly, a *tablita*, line dance. Maiden and youth impersonate in several ceremonies—Snake, Antelope, Flute, winter solstice ceremony; women clan representatives figure importantly in the two kachina ceremonies, and women race and play hidden-ball.

Not only in the women's ceremonies but in almost all Hopi ceremonies there runs a definite pattern: prayer-stick-making or prayer-feather-making or smoke or chiefs' talk the morning or night before the housetop announcement; eight days later the standard set by the chief at sunrise, at hatch or ladder; on the first day the altar is begun, to be finished on the fourth day, the first day or first four days a meal altar of the Directions being used for medicine-bowl ritual, afterward the main altar for a

PLATE XX

Hopi Girl

nightly ceremonial of song and prayer, with smoking, aspersing, rattling, whizzing, whistling, or flute-playing. During the first four days prayer-sticks or feathers are addressed to the Chiefs of the Directions and deposited in an ever narrowing circuit. Offerings are made in springs whence water is fetched in gourds for the altar to be poured later on the fields of the chiefs. Prayer-sticks or feathers are made for various Spirits, throughout the retreat. Adoptions or initiations are made generally on the fourth day, after the completion of the altar. Adoption consists only of giving a handful of meal to a godparent and of head-washing and naming ritual; in initiation the novice undergoes abstinence taboos or a girl (Pl. XX) will grind for her godmother; youths go ahunting or wood-gathering; youths are painted; daily prayer-feathers are deposited; and, finally, the novice is shown an impersonation of the patron of the society. On the ninth day the public dramatization or dance will be performed, and there is general feasting, the ceremonialists not eating, however, until the close of the day. They have already been exorcised or separated from supernatural power at the close of the eighth-night ceremonial, when the altar is usually dismantled. The important days or nights are the first, fifth, and eighth. The eight-day cere monial may be thought of as a reduplication of the four-day ceremonial.

Ceremonies are timed by lunations, by chief notifying chief that it is now his turn, or by the position of the sun at the horizon during the solstices.

At Walpi winter solstice celebration varies in several particulars from the Oraibi ceremony (pp. 556 ff.).* The Water-Corn (Patki) clan is in charge, forming what has been called a Sun chieftaincy, and the clan kachina come out. Dramatization of the sun's progress differs; all the dramatizations differ. The novices of the Men's societies are more conspicuous at Walpi, as is the Soyal Maid at Oraibi.

* Stephen 4:3–4. The ceremony should be studied comparatively in all the Hopi towns.

Zuni has not always been called Itiwana, middle place;* an older and still current name is Halona, Ant place. At the time of the Conquest Halona was one of the reported Seven Cities of Cibola of which nation Hawikuh, the walled town seventeen miles to the southwest, and Matsakya, three miles to the east below Corn Mountain, were the largest. Matsakya, "the best, largest, and finest" town, was reported in 1540 to have houses seven stories high, the highest in the country, the top stories having embrasures and loopholes for defending the lower roofs. The houses of Hawikuh were from two to five stories. Three towns, probably Matsakya, Hawikuh, and Halona, had two hundred houses, "the others somewhere between sixty and fifty and thirty houses,"† the total population being from 3,000 to 3,500.[8]

Hawikuh was discovered in 1539 by a dark-skinned, bearded native of northern Africa, Estevan, Stephen, who is referred to as the slave of one of the Spanish captains but who figures as a brother-in-arms. Scouting for Fray Marcos, the Franciscan of Nice, and other seekers after gold and souls, Estevan crossed the *uninhabited* mountain country between the Gila River and Cibola with an escort of three hundred Pima, Opata, or other Mexican Indians, and, heedless of warnings (see pp. 363, 385), given no doubt by the War chief of Hawikuh, entered the pueblo and was killed, probably as an unwelcome sorcerer, a witch. Estevan's "bones" were kept.[9] Had we but a record of that head or scalp ceremony!

The following year Coronado and the advance guard of his Spanish and Indian followers from Jalisco, over a hundred horsemen and foot soldiers, captured Hawikuh, after Coronado was wounded by the rocks hurled down‡ upon him from the house-

* Zuni is a Keresan term meaning "middle place" (Boas).

† Six, not seven, towns are indicated. The next news from Cibola, in 1581, gives only six towns, and it has been suggested that the Spanish use of seven in this case approximates the Pueblo use of four as a favored numeral (Spier 1:271; Hodge 3:56–57).

‡ Rock-throwing was a fighting technique of Acoma and other pueblos, and of Northern Paiute (Steward). It was (and is) widespread throughout Middle

tops. The women and children had already fled to the other towns, and that night the men abandoned the town to the hungry Spaniards, who made themselves at home in the houses, finding enough corn, beans, and squashes to last through the winter. The Ashiwi sought refuge atop Corn Mountain. Coronado's party went on to the Rio Grande, but on their return to Mexico by way of Cibola they left several of their Indian allies there, and, just as after the retreat of Estevan's followers, stragglers were picked up and detained.

Three of these Indians were found living among the Ashiwi, perhaps at Matsakya, in 1583 by Espejo and Fray Bernardino: three "Christian Indians," Andrés of Coyocán, Gaspar of Mexico City, and Anton of Guadalajara, culture-carriers for over forty years, and the two sons of Gaspar were found by Oñate in 1598. The son named Alonso "spoke a few Mexican words, but understood none."[10]

Fray Bernardino remained at Hawikuh for only a few weeks. The first mission was established in 1629 and possession taken by "hoisting the triumphal standard of the Cross." The people began at once to serve the missionaries* by bringing them "water, wood, and what was necessary," being "knowing people and of good discourse,"[11] yet three years later two of the four missionaries then in Cibola were killed, and the people fled to Corn Mountain to stay there three years. About 1643 the Mission was re-established at Hawikuh and later at Halona,† and

---

America. Possibly it was a factor in building multiple house stories. Upper stories were also well-protected storerooms.

* Fray Roque de Figueredo had preached many years in Aztec and in the language spoken in the valley of Toluca. What dances may Fray Roque have introduced during the three years he was resisted by the "sorcerers"? No dances are recorded, only a well-staged spectacular public baptism of *principales* and infants, "since with the water of baptism a soul is *born again* to a new life of grace." The principal cacique, given the name Don Augustín, made a great exhortation to the people.

† At Hawikuh, La Virgen de la Purísima was patron saint, her day being December 8, the feast of the Immaculate Conception; at Halona, Our Lady of Candelaria (February 2) was patron. For several years the only missionary lived at Halona.

now at last the Church exerted continuous influence until 1670, when the Hawikuh missionary was killed by Apache, or until 1680, when the Halona townsmen themselves killed their missionary. The people were found back again on their mesa of refuge in 1692 by Vargas. This time three hundred children were baptized. Nevertheless, a year later some Ashiwi aided in the Jemez revolt.

But the Ashiwi came down from Corn Mountain and rebuilt Halona across the river, or perhaps better said a new town was built by all the refugees, from Halona and from Hawikuh. In 1699 a new mission was established, and Our Lady of Guadalupe became patroness. But the maintenance of the Mission appears broken and troubled until 1744 when there were two priests at Halona.[12] In 1821, Fray Antonio Cacho abandoned Zuni (Pl. XXI) on account of danger from Navaho* and the Mission was not re-established until 1920,† when, despite town opposition but encouraged by the Federal Agent, a zealous Catholic, the Franciscans built outside the town a new church, a monastery, and a school. The friars are said to be taking the long view and paying attention only to the children.

Native Zuni history, "from-the-beginning talk," concludes with the arrival of the Conquistadores and a flight to Corn Mountain, ever the mountain of refuge.‡ Characteristically, there is no mention of abandoning towns;§ unless the story of

* Twitchell II, 640. Possibly he was also discouraged by the "small attendance of the inhabitants at church" as reported by the deputy alcalde in 1813 (*ibid.*, p. 574).

† During this century the town was probably visited from time to time by Catholic priests. I heard of such visits before 1920. The priest stayed in the house of the wife of Jesús, the Yaqui.

‡ But this may have been the first time it was resorted to. No sherds indicating pre-Spanish occupation have been found (Spier 1:276).

§ This had begun by 1604. Escobar, the chronicler of Oñate's expedition to California, writes that four of the six pueblos are "almost destroyed although all are inhabited" (Hodge 3:76). What happened between Oñate's two visits, 1598–1604, to cause this destruction or rather withdrawal? Kechipawa, small and inferably from its refuse heap briefly occupied, about three miles from Hawikuh, contains the ruin of an unfinished church, indicating that it was inhabited after 1629; but it was to be abandoned probably soon after 1680 (Spier 1:276,

PLATE XXI

ZUNI, 1916

Wall of graveyard in front of church ruin. Corn Mountain

the Ky'anakwe rain society is a version not of intertribal but of interpueblo war. But the concentration of the tribe into one town had inferably the same important consequences as concentration had elsewhere, reduplication or elaboration of ceremonials. This is indicated not only by the myth of the Ky'-anakwe rain society with its black corn bundle, its quadrennial ceremony, and its identification with clan and kiva; in the myth of separation and reunion of the Wood society* and the combination of its ceremony with War society ceremonial; in the duplication of war functions by the Cactus society (said to come from Hopi;† compare Agave society); in the association of Pa'utiwa, the Kachina chief, with different clans; in the association of the Shalako with Hawikuh and the amazing elaboration of the whole ceremony, and finally in the way Pekwin's functions overlap those of Town chief. In myth Pekwin is a later functionary; he does not "come up" with the people; his use of the shrine at Matsakya, important among the early towns, may

---

277; Hodge, 101). Kyakima (K'ia'kima), likewise briefly occupied, was still inhabited in 1680, but not resettled after the descent from Corn Mountain. Nor was Matsakya, which inferring from its deep and extensive ash heaps had been inhabited a long time. Identification of the other towns is uncertain. At Pinawa, on the river a mile and a half west of Zuni, Spier uncovered the deepest refuse heap in the valley. Wares from the upper levels are the same as those from the lower levels of Matsakya, but Pinawa was probably abandoned even before the Discovery.

* See pp. 223, 234. When a Pueblo is faced with the introduction of something foreign, say a kachina from another town, his standard explanation is that the kachina is merely a variant of an earlier home kachina. Analogously, a foreign society, like the Wood society, is merely a home society that separated and then returned. For the most recent version of the trek of the Wood society, given by Ts'awele, see Roberts 1:8–9.

The "return" of the Wood society may have been kept alive in tradition by the ruin of the "Village of the Great Kivas," as Dr. Roberts has called it, near Nutria. A small band of immigrants from the north built this village containing several small kivas and two immense round kivas and occupied it for about twenty years, together with a group from the south who built a separate block of houses.

† Stevenson 2:413. No Cactus man may join the War society ("priests of the bow") until he has taken four scalps (Stevenson 2:570). There is some sort of grading, obscurely indicated, among Zuni, Hopi, and Jemez people in relation to War society or chieftaincy and Cactus society.

have some historical significance.* Similarly, there may be significance in associating the Pathltok Rain chieftaincy of the East with Katikia (see p. 234). With its six major Rain chieftaincies and its six kivas Zuni gives the impression of being a planned town. In fact, not to go farther back, it is tempting to see several of the towns of ancient Cibola represented today in the major or minor Rain chieftaincies. One of the minor Rain chieftaincies did come in tradition from Hawikuh, the Water Serpent chieftaincy; another, the extinct Black Corn chieftaincy, came from Heshatoyala near Hawikuh (Water Serpent was painted on the wall of its ceremonial room);¹³ Shalako kachina come from Ojo Caliente, the vapory spring south of Hawikuh, and Shumaikoli and Mahedinasha kachina are associated with that town. In bulk the kachina live at the junction of Zuni River and the Little Colorado, but organizing the cult is associated in the Emergence myth with Matsakya (possibly explaining Pekwin's close association with the cult). A close study of the springs and shrines visited by all the ceremonial groups, particularly by the Rain chieftaincies, might reveal historical connections.

Coming up at the Emergence were the Rain society chiefs, the Ashiwanni, carrying with them their water and seed fetishes or the bundles from which their power derives. The paramount Rain chiefs are associated with the directions, the chieftaincy of the North being the Town chieftaincy, which consists of the Town chief and two assistants. (The office of "woman chief" has lapsed.) These four high chieftaincies descend each within the maternal lineage of the house where their fetishes are kept, but not strictly,† so that more than one clan may be represented

---

* See p. 998 for trait of speakership among Papago. One of the curing societies, the Shuma'kwe, "the last to come up," Pekwin is credited with having introduced into Zuni (Stevenson 2:530). In origin tradition (Parsons 53:2–5) Shuma'kwe come from the east, from Chipiakwi, Sandía Mountains, where there was a fight with other Pueblos; but Stevenson opines, to be sure on casual hearsay, that the society songs are in Pima. Moreover, piercing the septum for a feather, as is done by this society, is a southern trait (Beals, 175), a Piman, Yuman, and Southern California trait, and see below for Shumaikoli kachina.

† Kroeber 2:165–66. Sons as well as brothers or maternal nephews will be included in a Rain chieftaincy. No close analysis of the trend to patrilineal suc-

in each chieftaincy of several men and one woman. The chief of
the Zenith, Pekwin, Crier to the Sun, and the chief of the Nadir,
Elder Brother Bow chief, War chief, chief of the scalp-takers
society, are associated with the three Town chiefs and the head
chiefs of the three other major Rain chieftaincies to form the
Council. Pekwin may be referred to as "chief of them all, the one
who holds in his keeping the whole town,"* and he is certainly a
more distinguished personage than the Town chief proper. The
War chief serves as executive messenger of the Council, even to
performing the duty of striking a chief who "has no sense" on
the chest, "even though he is a chief."[14] The War chief is or
should be a stern and much feared man. Only a member of the
Hunters society would think of thwarting him or refuse to be
"caught" for initiation into the War society.[15]

These high Rain chiefs and societies are called "daylight people" in distinction to the minor Rain chiefs or societies, the
"night people," of whom there are eight sets including the group
in charge of Water Serpent. These groups also descend in maternal lineages; each has a ceremonial room, fetishes or bundles
and altar, and they observe retreats, one-night retreats in winter and a summer series following the series of the paramount
Rain chiefs. All the Rain chiefs may be referred to as Corn
fathers; "they make the corn ripen";[16] but those "darkness
chiefs" with one exception control no ceremonial matters other
than their own.

The exception is the Ky'anakwe Rain chieftaincy whose chief
is chief of a nine-day ceremony. He is of the Corn clan; Corn
clansmen and members of Chupawa kiva, the Corn clan kiva,
impersonate the ancient Ky'anakwe enemies. Corn clanswomen
wash the heads of impersonators and receive seed corn. There
are songs for grinding pigment to be used on dance moccasins.
The Ky'anakwe kachina may whip against bad dreams; they
bring handsome gifts of venison and feathers to the high Rain

---

cession or of the composition in general of the Rain chieftaincies has been attempted. It could be done only through genealogies.

* Bunzel 6:54. Note that a meal altar such as is made by Pekwin represents
the town (in Isletan opinion).

chiefs and throw gifts to the populace.[17] For the public dance
the Koyemshi are out. Warriors are impersonated and the three
kachina captives. It is a kachina war dramatization and seems
to be an attempt at historical record.*

The Council appoints performers in war and corn dances, the
impersonators of kachina chiefs, and the secular officers, the
Town chief giving the officers their canes, and Pekwin giving
the kachina chiefs their sticks of office. The mask of Pa'utiwa
is in the house of the Town chief who, inferably, remakes the
mask, since his prototype made the first Pa'utiwa mask;[18] the
Koyemshi clown masks, made traditionally by the Ne'wekwe,
are in the house of the Rain chiefs of the West; all the Rain chiefs
are prominent in asking for the repetition of kachina dances:
otherwise, kachina organization is separate from the Rain chieftaincies.

The office of chief of the Kachina society descends in a lineage
of the Antelope (Deer) clan; the office of "speaker" descends in
a lineage of the Badger clan; the two warriors are from the War
society. Every boy must be initiated into the Kachina society,
joining one of its six constituent kiva memberships. The boy
goes into the kiva of his ceremonial father, the godfather to
whom he was given at birth.

The kivas are used almost exclusively for kachina ceremonial.
Each kiva has a dance director, also managers for particular
kachina chiefs such as Shalako and Salimobia. Other kachina
chiefs, Pa'utiwa, Long Horn, Kiaklo, are in the hands of small
cult groups that fill their own vacancies and, as instructors, pass
down the ritual—dramatic behavior, prayer, or chant—required
of the impersonation. The kivas conduct kachina dance series,
summer and winter series. Theoretically, the kiva that dances

* The Ashiwi in exile who talked to Fray Marcos told him that "toward the
southeast there was a kingdom called Marata in which there used to be many and
large settlements . . . . houses of stone and many-storied, and that this kingdom
was and still is at war with the lord of the Seven Cities, through which warfare
the Kingdom of Marata has declined greatly, although it still holds its own, and
is at war with the others." Another report mentions a village "one day from
Cibola," and at war. The Marata have not been identified (Spier 1:267, 268).
The Ky'anakwe are spoken of as a southerly people.

first in the summer series will dance first in winter, and the six kivas rotate sexennially,* like the Hopi kivas in presenting Home-going kachina. He'iwa may be considered chief Kiva.

Some of the curing societies present kachina at initiations, their own society impersonations, and clownlike kachina, He'he'a and Nawisho, are pictured at an initiation into the Fire order of the Uhuhukwe;[19] the Ne'wekwe present burlesque kachina dances and supply clowns for kachina dances and an important personage to deposit prayer-sticks throughout the year; Little Firebrand society supplies kachina musicians at the kachina Water Serpent dance (Ololowishkya) and as escort to the Sha-lako; Big Firebrand society, whose own Black kachina and White kachina come from Sandía Mountains,† makes the sand-paint-ings of the kachina at the whipping of the children; and all the curing societies may furnish a choir for kachina dances. Other-wise the curing societies are separate from the kachina cult, also from the rain or weather cult except for their rain rituals at the winter solstice, and excepting the Shi'wanakwe rain society and the snow-making Wood society. The curing societies function through the animals whom they impersonate violently‡ and from whom they get medicine or power. Prays the medicine-water chief of Little Firebrand society:

> Lion of the North, give me power to see disease.
> Bear of the West, give me power to see disease.
> Badger of the South, give me power to see disease.
> White Wolf of the East, give me power to see disease.
> Eagle of the Zenith, give me power to see disease.
> Shrew of the Earth, give me power to see disease.
> Thou, my Sun Father, give me power to see disease.
> Thou, my Moon Mother, give me power to see disease.
> All ye ancient ones, give me power.[20]

* Stevenson 2:64. Actually this order is not followed. See p. 520. Cf. Bunzel 5:886.

† Compare the Dark kachina of Isleta and Sandía Mountains; also Black kachina and White kachina of Apache.

‡ Stevenson 2:525, 556–57, 562, 563. The curing society is the part of Zuni ceremonialism least known to recent observers who therefore underestimate, I think, the "orgiastic" potentiality of Zuni character, also the hold of witch-craft belief.

Only the medicine order of the society conducts cures and with certain exceptions only medicine members are possessed of the corn fetish.* There are Fire, Jugglery, Stick-swallowing, and still other orders in several societies. All these are associated with weather control, except perhaps the Fire order in Hunters society (at a hunt, coals were cast in the six directions to attract game). Only in Little Firebrand and its derivative Bedbug society is there a Paiyatemu or Flute order. Little Firebrand is traditionally derived from Hopi, its flute ritual being got from a supernatural,[21] we may note incidentally, in characteristic Plains or Apache mode.

Wood society, a sometime war society, conducts a ceremony jointly with the War society during each of the two winter moons "given" to the Wood society in which to call snow or rain; the Ant society functions with the War society at Scalp dance and the Owinahaiye harvest dance; the Big Firebrand society functions in the new-fire ritual of the winter solstice ceremony; and the rabbit-hunt fire is built by the warrior of the Hunt society:[22] with these exceptions the societies conduct public ceremonial only the year they hold an initiation. Shamanistic feats are performed at initiations, and society members dance. Initiations are held only in November or after the winter solstice ceremony; never in the agricultural seasons, which belong to the kachina organization or to the Rain chieftaincies.

The paramount Rain chiefs initiate or, as would be said at Isleta, give permission to hold the Thla'hewe (Rabbit-skin blanket) ceremony which is the women's quadrennial growth or corn ceremony, and also Owinahaiye, the annual war celebration. For Thla'hewe Pekwin makes his stepped meal-painting and appoints the dancers, from the family connections of the Rain chiefs with the Dogwood and Corn clans figuring. The War society and its understudy, the Ant society, manage Owinahaiye with the

---

* Wood society has no medicine order, but it has a single corn fetish or bundle of corn ear and reeds; also it cures for sore throat. Shuma'kwe has no medicine order, curing through Shumaikoli kachina for convulsions or cramps, with a spiral shell as "mother"; but each officer whose nose is pierced for the feather has a corn fetish. Hunters society has no medicine order, but each member has a corn fetish (Stevenson 2:411, 416, 417, 530).

co-operation of the kiva groups, of whom two furnish choirs for the dances by warriors and girls. After a long interval Thla'hewe was performed in 1920 and then again not until 1932; the last performance of Owinahaiye, as far as I know, was in 1910. Also omitted for a long interval, about thirty years, from the autumn calendar was a kachina visitation to First Mesa; then a dance visit was made in 1931.[23] Ceremonial that has lapsed at Zuni is never quite as dead as it may seem.

ACOMA[24]

From Hawikuh, Coronado sent on a detachment to explore Acuco, about seventy-five miles distant. The Spaniards were met below the mesa, with presents of many turkeys, piñon nuts, corn, flour, much bread, and tanned deerskins. The trail up with handholds and footholds and rocks at the top to roll down on invaders was described by Captain Alvarado, who inferably led his men up across the formally closed trail. There was no fighting at this time, but in 1599 after Oñate's field officer, *maestre de campo*, was killed within the pueblo a punitive party captured the pueblo and burned and slaughtered.* Only one of the seventy Spaniards was killed.

About 1629 one of the indomitable Franciscan friars, Fray Juan Ramirez, went to Acoma and ingratiated himself by acting like a medicine man and reviving a child, casting on it the holy water of baptism. Fray Juan succeeded in getting his church built and, as he lived in Acoma many years, in well indoctrinating the townspeople. However, Acoma joined in the Great Rebellion, killing its missionaries, and in 1696 the town made a final gesture of resistance by keeping Vargas, the reconqueror, off the mesa. The best Vargas could do was to shoot four captives and ravage the cornfields.

Most of Acoma's fields lie twelve miles to the northwest in the valley of Acomita and during the last few decades, when life in

---

* The population was reported reduced from 3,000 to 600 (Twitchell II, 462), incredible figures. Alvarado set the population at 200. In 1680 the population was 1,500.

the valley has been secure,* an almost complete exodus from the mesa top to the valley takes place during the agricultural season. This dispersal must have had considerable effect upon the calendar, but there is no definite information about it.† The Town chief and probably other ceremonialists remain continuously at Acoma (Pl. XXII).

Acoma's Town chief is chosen within the Antelope clan and, as far as information goes, within one lineage, by the Antelope clansmen. He has an assistant who succeeds to office. When the new Antelope man is installed, perhaps a year after the death of his predecessor, the assistant is chosen. For the installation there are a rabbit hunt, a kachina dance, and for all a drink of the Town chief's medicine. The Town chief sets dates by solar observation for the solstice ceremonies as well as for other ceremonies, even permission to hold society initiations must be obtained from him, and he decides on the ceremony of exorcism by the societies; he decides on what kiva groups are to dance in the summer kachina dance; he appoints kiva chiefs who have charge of the masks, and he instructs the children in kachina lore; he is the Father of the kachina; he instructs the War chiefs about the prayer-sticks they have to make; he appoints all the annual officers, and he fills vacancies among the ten lifelong *principales*, Antelope clansmen, who are advisers with the Governor and with all the chiefs; he allots lands, theoretically all the land belongs to him. He does his own field work, but he may draw on the communal store of corn. The Town chief has no altar, but at the solstices and the kachina initiation uses that which the Kaвina society chief sets for him, with buckskin and feather fetishes

* But even at Acomita houses built high up in the girdling mesas are still used, and people climb laboriously up and down the mesa with burdens of water and provisions when they could live on the level below if they wished. "Their conservatism seems to be organic," exclaims Dr. White, "below the level of thought entirely," rational thought, as are many of the things we do "to feel safer."

†Along this line of effect upon calendrical integrity as well as along several other lines both of disintegration and of reconstruction, ancient Pueblo processes, Pueblo colonies should be studied. We know nothing about Moenkopi, about Zuni's farming colonies, about beautiful Paguate, or the other permanent colonies of "old Laguna."

PLATE XXII

Acoma
From the air

called Tsamai'ye and Tsamahi'a, and a large stone lion in the middle. These fetishes are male and female and have become very large from the prayer-feathers contributed by everyone who addresses himself to the altar asking for man-power or manliness.* Kaʙina was a war, not a curing, society. Another Antelope clan or Town chief altar is depicted with a set of large upright befeathered crooks and in front animal figurines (White) or several masks (Stirling).

The Outside or War chiefs, head chief and two adjutants, are annual officers; but they have so many more important ceremonial functions than annual War captains usually have that they had better be called War chiefs. Two "cooks" supply the War chiefs with deer meat and corn meal for offerings, with corn and cattail pollen, and with the lunch needed on ritual trips; as executive aids there are ten "little captains." "Broken prayerstick" is handed on by the War chiefs as well as other paraphernalia, and chiefs and cooks live together in a special closely guarded room. At their installation in Chief kiva, a four-day ceremonial, the War chiefs are whipped by the Kaʙina society, they as well as the outgoing chiefs and any townsmen who wish thereby to gain strength and luck in hunting, racing, or gambling. The two adjutant War chiefs, who are called Shu·ti (Canyon Wren) and Mockingbird and represent the War gods, fetch wood for prayer-sticks from the mountains for Town chief and societies as well as for themselves. Throughout the year the War chiefs and cooks must observe continence and at intervals of eight days the chiefs take turns in making the circuit of four springs and depositing prayer-sticks.† In their first circuit they bring back water to pour into the town reservoirs that they may always be full. Every day the War chiefs are expected to make kiva rounds to see that all is in order (Stirling). In filling the secular offices and in all ceremonials, the War chiefs act as executive messengers. The head War chief starts and judges the

* Stirling. The altar was given not by Iyatiku but by Tiamuni, her husband. Elsewhere among Keres the Town chief is called Tiamuni, but only at Acoma is he given a male patron, or the Corn Mother a husband.

† Compare the water-fetching trip of the Oraibi War chief, p. 558.

kick-stick races; he makes the kick-sticks, and, finally, deposits them as an offering. He also makes the arroyo offering of miniature kick-stick and annulet.

The War chiefs have charge of the communal cornfields, directing the planting, tilling, and harvesting. The crop is stored in the War chiefs' house to be used by them, also to feed kachina dancers or townspeople whose crops have failed. Wafer-bread is made for the War chiefs, and wood is hauled for them. Foreign spouses are met ceremoniously by the War chief. He conducts the newcomer up the mesa trail, making a road of corn meal. Near the top he asks Town chief's permission for the stranger to enter, asking four times, and then he convoys the couple to the groom's house, where their heads will be washed.

The War chiefs build the hunt fire and conduct the rabbit hunt, having taken over some of the functions of the Hunt society which is extinct,* just as their two cooks or stewards seem to have taken over some of the functions of the Chraik'ats[i] (? pollen-collecting), in charge of game and wild food plants whose offices became extinct about fifty years ago.† (However, it is the "little war captains" who are referred to as Chraik'ats[i].)‡

* In tradition the oldest man of the Eagle clan (compare Zuni) was made Hunt society chief (Sha'ak) by Iyatiku, given songs, prayers, and altar, and taught how to make prayer-sticks and prey-animal fetishes. On a big hunt fetishes were borrowed from the Hunt chief (Stirling), as at Zuni.

† In tradition, on the other hand, Outside chief, appointed from the Sky clan by Mother Iyatik to relieve the Antelope Man (Town chief) and to outrank all the chiefs, has lost some of his original functions to the Town chief. Outside chief kept the solar horizon calendar and announced solstice, planting, and kachina initiation dates. Through his permanent prayer-stick he drew all the people together and had power over them: they were "tucked under his arms and their minds were tucked in his temples," i.e., he had to think for them and speak for them (Stirling). This prayer-stick is "the centre pole, four earths down and four skies up" which holds sky and earth together. It is called prayer-stick broken or bent as if it were a crook, but it is depicted as a figurine (of Iyatiku) girt with beads and downy eagle feathers. The image is repainted yearly by the Kaʙina society chief and the beads renewed by the new War chief. (Keresan terms for prayer-stick broken and prayer-stick holding are very close, and I surmise some confusion.)

‡ For the cooks, the *cusineros*, compare the *prioste*, cook or steward of the Spanish *cofradía*, or the woman *birioste* of the Tarahumara (Bennett and Zingg, 304). Or compare the kettle-bearer assistants to the war leader of Plains tribes (Smith, 440).

The society of scalp-takers is also extinct, and it seems probable that the War chiefs have taken over some of their ritual functions.

A scalp-taker and his "brother," the man he flung the scalp to, were exposed on a red-ant hill. Newly taken scalps brought in on a pole were baptized by the sacristan. The warriors were met by women, and girls carried in scalp hairs fastened to branches of cedar. The Scalp ceremony was in charge of two groups of K'ashale in different kivas and was the occasion for K'ashale initiation (Stirling). (K'ashale gave their own sons to the society, which established a relationship between K'ashale and kivas.) The K'ashale assembled the women dancers and instructed them in kiva practice, and they got together the costumes of the women and of the Opi. The K'ashale had an altar. They used stuffed birds, canyon wren (*shu'tᶦ*)* and mockingbird, with a grain of corn for their heart,† placing them on the altar and hanging them around the neck, and in the Scalp ceremony one K'ashale was called Canyon Wren Youth and another, Mockingbird Youth (the others, Sun Youth)‡. As the society diminished in numbers, men were *made* K'ashale for the ceremony. At its conclusion women of their father's clan fetched the K'ashale and washed their heads. The dance has come to be used as an installation dance for the War chiefs, a two-day dance in which two kivas alternate, four women and their Opi manager dancing in and out among the singers, and two women dancing like the Shake girls in the Zuni Scalp dance.[25]

There are four societies, Fire,§ Kaʙina, Flint, and Shiwanna; Snake doctors practice on their own. There is no Ant society, but medicine men in the societies know how to make the Ant

* Compare the mud hen used by First Mesa clowns, their "sister" (Stephen 4: 489, Fig. 281).

† Just as Zuni Ne'wekwe give heart to their baton or stick of office (Stevenson 2:437).

‡ These bird K'ashale were to chatter (or mock) like the mockingbird, and, like the canyon wren, they go in anywhere, into any house or kiva, into any ceremony. This is why the the War chiefs also are called Canyon Wren and Mockingbird, besides, birdlike, they carry messages (White 2:99; Stirling).

§ With its own chamber which is referred to as kiva.

altar including a sand-painting of Horned Toad (devourer of ants), and know the prayers and the brushing technique.* Shiwanna or Thunder Cloud treat for lightning-shock† and broken bones. The other societies cure as usual for witch-sent disease, by sucking or by "whipping away" with eagle feathers, i.e., by "brushing," and as usual the patient either pays down or joins the society. A crystal is used for diagnosis. The object sucked out is spat into a bowl. Herb medicine is given to the patient and his household. During the four-day cure the doctors remain continent, fast from salt and meat, and may not bathe. There is recruiting by trapping, through encountering a shaman engaged in ritual, through asking for a cigarette, or, by the Fire society, by lines of ashes;‡ and, if anyone builds a fire outdoors or carries out live coals for a set time after an initiation, he, too, must join the Fire society. The society throw an initiate into a fire pit and have a stick-swallowing dance. Certain kachina masks may be worn by shamans, but the societies do not own masks or use them at initiations. A shaman conducts the child-naming ritual, presenting the infant to the Sun,§ and a shaman paints the face of the deceased and performs ritual four days after the death.

Chiefs of five of the six kivas have charge of kachina masks and dance groups, and impersonate the Gomaiowish messenger kachina who announce the coming of the kachina. Boys join the kiva of their father. Boys and girls are given a kachina initiation. Their ceremonial father is a friend, usually a clansman, of their father. The initiation is held in Chief kiva, the kiva associated with the Town chief; initiates are whipped by the

---

* Stirling. In other words, the Ant cure is a detachable ceremony like a Nahavo chant.

† In the tradition sickness from Lightning or Clouds is treated by the Flint society. There is or was a Shiwanna society at Laguna. The Acoma Flint society chief performs ritual for kick-stick racers. The society uses Chief kiva.

‡ Made, also, between kachina dancers and spectators by K'ashale to trap recruits.

§ Naming ritual may be performed also by the father's kinswomen.

horned kachina Tsitsünits, "Big Teeth," who is impersonated by the Kaʙina shaman. Four Gomaiowish are along. Initiates are referred to as G'uirana chaiani* or society member. There is no G'uirana or Quirena society as in other Keresan pueblos; but on occasion men acted like Quirena, i.e., were "made" Quirena, any men who were associated with the K'oʙishtaiya, the winter kachina.[26]

As many as ninety distinctive kachina appear as individuals and in groups, at the winter and summer solstices, in the two kachina dramatizations given "every five years," at the summer rain dance, and at the autumn harvest dance. As the societies of Acoma do not conduct a series of retreats as elsewhere among Keres, the pattern of kachina dancing after an esoteric retreat does not occur. Special kachina are associated with special kivas. Summer kachina come from the west; winter kachina who are called not kachina but K'oʙishtaiya come from the east. Among them are Sun and the four mountain chiefs of the directions who also are seasonal chiefs, Chiefs of Winter, Spring, Summer, and Autumn. Possibly the K'oʙishtaiya were once impersonations without mask, like the cosmic impersonations who appear at the winter solstice ceremony in its long form at Walpi. K'oʙishtaiya cure and impart vigor. They look "ugly" or "ferocious" (Stirling).† Temporary K'ashale clowns come out with the kachina, at the bidding of the War chief.

As at Laguna, the Corn clan is associated with the fire kachina dramatization, and formerly the Parrot clan (and the Squash clan) conducted the salt trips. In tradition the first chief of the Hunter society was selected as an Eagle clansman, and the first chief of the Fire society as an Oak clansman (oak is strong fire wood), and the first War chief as a Sky clansman. Formerly the War or Outside chief was always from the Sky clan because he had "to rule on the outside" (Stirling).

---

* Hopi initiates are regularly called sparrow-hawk. Sparrow-hawk is the Quirena society feather. Instead of calling his kachina novice sparrow-hawk, the Acoman calls him G'uirana.

† Compare the angry kachina classification of Oraibi (Voth 2:118).

LAGUNA

San José de la Laguna or San José Coquicamé (Kawaika) is said to have been founded* by Kerest from Santo Domingo, Cochiti, and La Cienquilla, the rebel stronghold near Cochiti that Vargas captured in 1694.[27] Possibly about this time Keresan rebels also went to Hopiland, returning later to settle at Laguna; or, in the famine-stricken years of 1777–79, Hopi (and Zuni) may have sojourned at Laguna; 116 Indian "settlers" are mentioned. In the repatriation of refugees to Hopiland in 1716 ten persons returned to Laguna.[28] There is at least one Hopi lineage in the Sun clan of Laguna. There are also Zuni and Acoma and Navaho lineages or intermarriages at Laguna.

Given this history, it is not surprising that Laguna was the first of the pueblos to Americanize, through intermarriage. In the late sixties or early seventies, George H. Pradt, a surveyor, and the two Marmon brothers, one a trader, the other a surveyor, married Laguna townswomen and began to beget and rear large families. Walter G. Marmon, appointed government teacher in 1871, married the daughter of Kwime',‡ chief of the Kurena-Shikani medicine men and father of Giwire, who was to take his father's position. This group led the Americanization faction§ and was opposed by most of the hierarchy, by the other clown society, the Kashare, by the Town chief and the War chief or head of the Scalp-takers, by the Flint, Fire, and Shahaiye societies or their chiefs. According to José or Tsiwema,[29] who was a Shahaiye shaman, the withdrawing ceremonialists first took their altars and sacrosanct properties up a mountain to secrete and protect them, and later brought them down to

---

* This river site was occupied about 1582 by westward-moving Apache called Querechos (Hodge 3:111). Pueblos using pottery of little Colorado type were hereabout still earlier (Mera).

† In 1707 the population was 330; in 1765, 600 (Thomas, 102–3).

‡ Kwime' or Luis Sarracino was educated by Catholic priests in Durango, Mexico, but became an apostate to Protestantism. See p. 1079, n. ‡.

§ Marmon made the old Spanish stocks into seats for his schoolroom which everyone probably approved, but when he insisted on burial grounds away from the churchyard, one for Protestants and one for Catholics (Gunn, 96–97), that must have caused acute dissension.

Mesita, three miles east of Laguna. Meanwhile the two kivas of Laguna were torn down by the progressives, while Robert G. Marmon was Governor, and there was a meeting at which the old women in charge of what was left of sacrosanct things brought them out and gave them up. At Mesita the Kashare and the Town chief continued to live; but about 1880 the Flint, Fire, and Shahaiye chiefs moved on to Isleta, to become affiliated there with the two medicine societies known today as the Town Fathers and the Laguna Fathers.

The Town chief of Laguna has long since died,[30] and he has had no successor; but the Kashare society continued itself, for in 1920 three Kashare from Mesita visited Laguna and conducted winter solstice ceremonial in a Water clan house where war fetishes had been kept before the Great Split. In another house, merely a loan house, for many years Giwire* and Tsiwema had also conducted winter solstice ceremonial. Tsiwema, the Shahaiye shaman, had gone to Isleta and returned to Laguna. In 1919, Giwire died, and Tsiwema, who was generally known as a Shiwanna shaman, was assisted by Martín, who had been initiated as a Fire shaman at Isleta where he grew up. At these winter solstice ceremonials uninitiated substitutes or "raw medicine men,"[31] also assisted, men never reborn or, what may be the figure, cooked on the hot sands of childbed.

After the Great Split and the laying of the railroad through or on the edge of town, there were no kachina dances at Laguna for some time; then in some obscure way a demand arose for their revival. The chief or "father" of the Chakwena, K'ausiro, was from Zuni. K'ausiro's Zuni wife was of the Badger clan. Now at Zuni, we recall, the "fathers" to the kachina are Antelope and Badger clansmen. K'ausiro's son, We'dyumă, was to become at Laguna "father" of the kachina, and the Badger kinswomen were to do the housework of the kachina impersonators. In the absence of the Kashare a new clown group was needed; the

* Giwire lived in the Encinal colony. His maternal house stood a ruin. Probably it was one of the two storied houses admired by Morfi in 1782. "The houses are all of stone, all of two stories along the upper part (of town), and well constructed. They are very clean and neat within and without, painted and whitened" (Thomas, 102).

Koyemshi of Zuni, corresponding to the Kashare, were introduced, and We·dyumă became custodian of the ten masks
(Gumeyoish)* and led in the kachina. (In earlier days Giwire,
the Kurena chief, led the kachina.)† The Zuni Koyemshi myth
began to circulate in Laguna. The Zuni kachina prayer-stick
showing the reversed duck feather was introduced into Laguna
prayer-stick ritual.

We·dyumă became blind and decrepit, and in 1920 Ts'iwairo
of the Antelope clan took his place as head of the three kachina
dance groups. Ts'iwairo went to Acoma to be installed by his
clansman, "the Antelope Man," Town chief. Another kind of
kachina prayer-stick was made; perhaps other cult changes. It
would have been an easy step at this time to have adopted the
whole Acoma pattern and made Ts'iwairo Town chief, but Laguna had got on for so long without a Town chief that there was
probably no demand for one, the annual secular officers plus the
secularized council were too firmly established as adequate government. With this secular rule, two or three shamans for sickness and solstice ceremonials, clan heads with a few ritual functions, and three kachina dance groups Laguna seemed quite satisfied.

When the town was first studied, twenty years ago, its ceremonial disintegration was so marked that it presented an obscure
picture of Keresan culture. But, with recently acquired knowledge of that culture in mind, today Laguna and her nine colonies
offer unrivaled opportunities to study American acculturation
and the important role played by miscegenation.

* Parsons 33:219–24. In the kachina dances at Isleta, Gumeyoish appear,
but without masks; because, I take it, no one in the Laguna colony had the right
to make Gumeyoish masks which are made at old Laguna in the Parrot clan.

† At the kachina initiation the Kurena sang songs of birth; the hair prayer-
feather of the initiate was given to the Kurena chief to deposit in the river
(Parsons 33:265). See p. 887 for a Kurena-kachina association at Acoma. Playing a flute and forbidden to speak, the Laguna Kurena chief led out the Scalp-
takers (Boas 2:208). In the scalp dance he led one line and the Kashare chief
led the other. For this dance twelve men called Sho·t'ʸⁱ (Canyon Wren) went
from house to house in two parties to get out the people (Boas 2:289; Parsons
33:257, n. 4). Compare Acoma, p. 885, and compare the bird Fiscales of Cochiti
(Dumarest, 202) and the function of getting out dancers assigned the Red Paint
People in the Taos Scalp dance.

SANTO DOMINGO[32]

The town was visited by the early Conquistadores, but the first visit of moment was paid in 1598 by Oñate, who held a council of the chiefs in kiva and talked about Phillip of Spain, protection from enemies, and baptism. The speech was interpreted, so by this time some townsman must have learned to speak Spanish. The chiefs *kneeled and kissed the hands* of the Governor and of Fray Juan de Escalona. A Franciscan mission was established, and Fray Juan got a church built between 1600 and 1605. In 1607 the friar died and was buried in the church which was shortly to be destroyed by flood.* The town was rebuilt and again destroyed by flood, and again in 1886 flood carried away the two churches and many houses. Of all the Pueblos, surely the people of Kiwa or Santo Domingo, as Oñate named the town, have cause to believe in Water Serpent!†

In the Rebellion of 1680, Santo Domingo killed some Spanish administrators and three priests, leaving their bodies before the altar. Before Otermín's punitive expedition the small population of a hundred and fifty fled to Potrero Viejo above the Cañada, where they found refugees from San Felipe and Cochiti, from the Tano pueblo of San Marcos, from Taos and Picurís. Otermín burned eight pueblos, among them Isleta and Sandía, and sacked Cochiti, San Felipe, and Santo Domingo, burning the kivas.‡ (Masks were found in Santo Domingo.) The Indians are said to have returned to their towns by 1683, but in 1692, De Vargas found the houses of Santo Domingo in ruin.§ Santo Domingo people joined Jemez people and built a town north of Jemez. In the Jemez rebellion of 1696 a chief of Santo Domingo, a leading spirit, was captured and shot, and Santo Domingo rebels joined in founding Laguna. But they could not have been more than a handful, since, by 1707, the population of Santo

* My guess is that about this time some families migrated to First Mesa, and that some migration kept up during the following hundred years.

† Actually they believe that flood is caused by a foreign shaman (Densmore).

‡ The wooden image of Dawn woman of First Mesa, a Keresan goddess, has had her head badly scorched (Stephen 4:966).

§ Here was another probable period of migration to First Mesa.

Domingo had increased to 204. At the close of the century Santo Domingo is said to have received immigrants from the Comanche-beset town of Galisteo, a Tano town.

Santo Domingo is a conspicuously conservative town, conservative alike of Indian and of early Spanish custom (much as are the remoter villages in Yucatan[33] or other parts of Mexico). The so-called Mexican kachina, whether Spanish or Indian, refer to the early Spanish occupation, as does the dramatization of Sandaro. The presence of drummer and bugler at Sandaro, saint's-day celebration, and rooster pull is early Spanish practice. The practice of wrapping the priest's stole around bride and groom was retained at the request of the townspeople after it was discarded in other New Mexican churches.[34] Weddings are celebrated on the saint's day, a widespread Spanish-Indian custom. Bourke saw old women approach the Saint on their knees and kiss the hem of her gold brocade. Not for nothing was Santa Domingo the Catholic ecclesiastical capital.*

The Spanish division of the town into *barrios*,† for herding horses, and the Spanish-Indian plan of secular government and communal service is probably to be seen at Santo Domingo in its original form. There are three lines of service or office: (1) the Governor, Lieutenant-Governor, and six Capitani; (2) the two War captains and their ten helpers;‡ and (3) the six Fiscales or church servants. Service is graded, men work up to the top in each of the three lines§ of mutually exclusive services. The Town

---

* From 1610 on, the capital for the Province, the Tano and the Rio Grande Tiwa (Scholes 1:29).

† My belief about this districting being Spanish is corroborated by a recently edited letter of Bandelier: "I have come across the trace of the former *barrios* (at Santo Domingo) here (at Cochiti) called *cuarteles*" (White), as they were probably also called at Santo Domingo. "This comely village (beautiful like all those of the kingdom if they be the possession of the Indians)," writes Morfi with rare discernment in 1782, "is divided into four uniform quarters leaving in the center a regular and adequate square" (Thomas, 98).

‡ They also have each a stick of office, as have the *topiles* in Mexico. The Tarahumara *dopi'le* has charge of all the canes (Bennett and Zingg, 202). *Cabo de vara*, corporal of the cane, was a current Spanish term. These horse-herders might have been called *cabo de cavalleria* (Twitchell, II, 2).

§ The triple line is indicated also in Cochiti.

chief, the Cacique, who is the Flint society chief, selects the War captains, one from one kiva, one from the other, and their helpers; the Shikame society chief selects the other officers.

The Town chief initiates or approves all ceremonies. He fasts and prays for the people. In his ceremonial house he keeps a basketful of small clay images representing the townspeople. The people farm for him; they hunt to supply rabbit meat to his fetishes. This meat is cooked by the Town chief's helper, "Bow." Bow or Chraik'ats[i]* looks after the ceremonial house; he announces the time for harvesting or when it is expedient to hold a general exorcising ceremony or a rabbit hunt for the Town chief. It is not known how Bow comes into office. The Town chief is appointed by the War captains from among the Flint society members. The War captains supervise kachina dances and initiations and guard assemblages of the societies. The War captains may punish drastically, confining an offender in a "circle," to the point of exhaustion.[†] Men who have served four terms as War captain are called "Mother."

Flint, Shikame, Boyakya,[‡] and Giant are the four major societies curing for witchcraft. Minor specialized societies or shamans are Kapina, who treat sore eyes;[§] Toad, Ant, and Snake, who treat ailments associated with these creatures or who keep the creatures out of town. There are four Toad shamans, shamans peculiar to Santo Domingo (see p. 993, n. §). The Ant shaman was a Zuni married into town. He died in 1932. The Snake society cures and initiates for snake bite. Snakes are kept in the room of the patient-initiate, so they will not bite him thereafter, and then they are taken back where they were found. Snake-bitten women are initiated into the society, but have only economic functions.‖ There is a Hunt society. The

* In other Keresan towns officials by this name are associated with the hunt.

† Compare Cochiti, Dumarest, 201. The initiate into the War society of Oraibi remained sitting in a corn-meal circle for an exhausting period (Titiev 3).

‡ Songs are in "Tewa"; possibly it is a Tano society. Reported in Cochiti as of Pecos (Benedict 2:16).

§ Extinct in 1927.

‖ Note the elements of the Hopi Snake society.

War society of scalp-takers is extinct, but the scalps are still housed. Their custodian is a Flint society man who succeeded his own father as scalp custodian. He is called Bear. The scalps are fed daily and washed on three saint's days, San Juan, San Pedro, and Santiago; the water is given to young men to drink. The War captain will visit the scalp house. Formerly in their dance the faces of the scalpers were painted black; like the Hopi Snake-Antelope men they wore a buckskin kilt painted in black with the Horned Water Serpent and trimmed with jinglers. All Flint society members are Koshairi, but not all Quirana are Shikame. The Koshairi are associated with Turquoise kiva, the Quirana with Squash kiva. Wik'ore is the Quirana patron; Pai-yatyama [? Sun Youth], the Koshairi patron. They appear in mask at the society initiations. Initiates are self-dedicated in sickness or dedicated by father or father's father in childhood. A person would join the society associated with his kiva; he belongs to his father's kiva. Through the Flint-Koshare-Turquoise kiva alignment and the Shikame-Quirana-Squash kiva alignment, the principle of moiety is quite well expressed. Matrilineal clanship controls marriage choices but figures in no way in the ceremonial life.

Foreign marriage is carefully scrutinized or not allowed. It is forbidden with Americans and Mexicans and with Navaho it would be condemned. A Domingo woman marrying a Pueblo from another town would probably go to his town. There are at present no foreign husbands in the town. There are a few foreign Pueblo wives. A Taos woman would not be received, because at Taos "there aren't any Shiwanna (kachina)." There was the same marriage taboo on Isleta until "they got Shiwanna from Laguna."

The Kachina cult is organized by kiva, each kiva having a chief and various groups which are recruited by self-dedication or by paternal dedication, just like the Clown societies.* In these kiva groups of assistants to kiva chief and of Poker or fire boys, succession to chieftaincy is based on seniority, not on age

---

* Other dance parts are assumed in the same way, also the part of kiva drummer.

but in order of initiation. Women are included as helpers to the kiva chief, they outnumber the men; but their functions are merely domestic; they are not even told that the kachina are impersonated by men. (Possibly here are factors, too, of the town conservatism: large groups of interested but ignorant, i.e., mystified women.) The Shikame society once had general charge of the kachinas; now they share the charge with the Flint society. The kiva chief organizes dancers and is custodian and painter of the masks. The Koshairi and Quirana have charge of the Gowawaima* masks of their respective kivas. These impersonations are burlesque, bogey, and police-like, "Shiwanna but different."

The Winter solstice ceremony, Haniko, is observed by the four major societies who "work for the sun to go north." Each society has its own ceremonial house, and here the members vomit for four mornings. Then the meal-painting is laid and prayer-stick-making follows. Outsiders who have joined in the rite of emesis make prayer-images of what they want. The bundle of images and offerings called Sun is placed on the meal road to the altar. The slat altar is raised, and a night song and dance ceremony is held. The men dance with bows and arrows. Women members are curtained away from the altars, but one by one the girls are given the Sun bundle to dance with.† The clown members present make fun of the bundle.

There is also a general layman's solstice ceremony, managed by the War captain, who appoints men to act as shamans and war captains. Men and women meet at night in one of the kivas, the Turquoise people sitting on one side, the Squash people on the other. First they are visited by the real shamans and the real War captains, all wearing the costume of the Opi; but with bear-leg skins on their forearms. They come in a procession of two single files and make noises like a bear and dance. The shamans slash about with their eagle-wing feathers. After they

* Compare the Hopi kachina shrine called K'owáwaimü. At Sia, a song word, *kowaiyätu*, is translated "door of Shipap" (Stevenson 1:126).

† Compare the girls' dance at the winter solstice night ceremonial of Walpi (Stephen 4:18).

go out, male dancers* wearing a *tablita* with eagle and turkey feathers and a "butterfly" back tablet, and representing, one set Turquoise kiva, and one set Squash kiva, perform alternately until sunrise. At midnight the *made* shamans and captains come in and act just as the real ones did. They use mock materials in their get-up, otherwise there is nothing of a burlesque character. Shpi'nyinyi is danced by kiva. The Town chief, the Shikame society chief, and the War captain talk in turn about what they have been doing. Everyone washes hands and face in the river and goes home to eat. It is about noon.

Christmas Eve after the midnight Mass there is a dance in the church, Buffalo, Navaho, or the Ahyana war dance. Dances follow for four days. At this time, and this time only, White or Mexican visitors may spend the night in town. On New Year's Day there is a war dance for the new officers.

Early in February is presented a kiva dramatization of the arrival of the Spaniards, Sandaro, in which Santiago and San Gerónimo are impersonated, and sometimes San José on a burro. The Saints appear, and there is a burlesque bull fight as at the Jemez *fiesta*, but the performance as a whole is for show; it is not a saint's-day celebration. It is organized much like a kachina celebration. There is a Santiago caballo shrine (Densmore), a horse shrine!

Later this month Matachina is danced, and the Koshairi have their dance.

Late in March the War captain starts the work on the ditch. He and the Ditch official (if not Chraik'ats^i) bury prayer-sticks made by the Town chief, in the middle of the ditch. For about two weeks under the Governor and the Fiscales all work on the ditch, excepting the chiefs of the four major societies. On the last day the Gowawaima kachina may appear, at the option of the war captain, coming out with the girls who bring lunch to the workers. The kachina act as sheriffs against shirkers. Through the Governor, the prayer-feathers of the Town chief are placed in the ditch before the water is run in.

---

* These dancers are recruited just as are other kiva functionaries, by dedication for life.

Follow the Comanche dance and Aiyahenats, a war dance, for rain. In April in the court there is a general anti-sunwise circle dance for the crops. Everyone dances, carrying an ear of corn in each hand, men and women alternating; choir and drummer in the center. In each kiva there is a man in charge of this dance, serving for life. He invites the Gowawaima kachina of one kiva or the other, ten or twelve coming out and dancing anywhere near choir or circle as would the clowns at a saint's-day dance or kachina side dancers at a kachina dance. At Eastertide, the saint's-day dance.

Now begin the spring and summer series of rain retreats by the four major societies, four days of morning emesis and of sleeping overnight in the respective ceremonial house, and four days of fetching water from a sacred spring, of altar ritual, prayer-stick-making, and fasting. The first night of this period and later on, too, the shamans and women members "dance like Shiwanna." During these days a War captain sits on the roof, also a woman appointed by the society chief. They watch for clouds or rain. In the evenings the shamans visit the house where the kachina impersonators are in retreat practicing their songs. The third evening the shamans sprinkle from their medicine bowl the masks that have that day been painted. The fourth evening the shamans throw the meal from their meal-painting into the river and bathe. The women of their families bring them food, shaking their hands in greeting, for "they have just come back from Shipap." The society chief arrives with the kachina chiefs, Heruta and Nyenyeka. The women are frightened, the society chief enters, the kachina move on. That night the society chief brings prayer-sticks and feathers for each kachina impersonator and lays his meal altar in the house of the kachina impersonators where he will stay during the following day, the day of the outside dances.

The kiva dancers have been vomiting in their special house for four days. The masks have been taken out of their plastered-up kiva shrine which is called Wenima, each man carrying his own, placed in a row on the floor, and at meal time offered food. The masks are to be repainted; only the kiva chief can apply the turquoise paint. Boys are sent to the mountains for spruce. The shamans have provided the prayer-feathers.

Early in the morning Heruta and Nyenyeka, one shaman, and the War captain visit the Town chief to ask if he wants the kachina to dance. The Ma·sewi War captain followed by a shaman leads the kachina in single file into the court. The other shamans and War captains are impersonating kachina with the kiva members. They dance six times in the morning, six times in the afternoon, dancing finally in their house. The kiva chief removes their masks and sprinkles the impersonators with medicine water.

The Quirana dance or initiate in September. Together with the Koshairi they come out at saint's-day or other Catholic dances. "Raw" or temporary clowns come out with them. The Town chief appoints a man from each kiva who with the presentation of a ritual cigarette has to gather the other clown impersonators.

SAN FELIPE

In 1540, Katishtya (San Felipe) was located at the foot of Black Mesa. After the Great Rebellion in which San Felipe took part because, they said, their kivas had been burned, the town was sacked, and those "houses of idolatry" were burned again. The town was rebuilt in a less accessible place, on top of Black Mesa, at the very edge; yet it was attacked by Jemez and other pueblos because of its pro-Spanish stand. At one time it gave refuge to a missionary fleeing from Cochiti. Within a decade or two this mesa town was abandoned, and the people came down to the Rio Grande to settle on the western and less accessible side. Eventually a bridge was built, but the town can be easily closed and is closed, for kachina dances, by blocking the bridge.

The Town chief is the center of control and influence. He is the Father of the kachina and their host when they come to dance. He is the chief of the Flint society and of the Koshare. All his farm work is done for him by the townsmen, and rabbits are supplied to him from the ritual hunt. Weekly he feeds the scalps and stone fetishes in his ceremonial house which is also the house of the Flint and Koshare societies. After advising with the chiefs of the Giant and Shi·'k'ame societies, he appoints all the annual officers and he instals them. In addition to this small consultant group, there is a council consisting of Town chief and society chiefs and of the secular officers and *principales*, former officers.

The Town chief holds office for life after appointment by the War captain. This War captain and his lieutenant are representatives of the War gods. They are chosen annually by the Town chief, Ma·sewi from Turquoise kiva and Oyo·''ye·wi from Squash one year, the next year, Oyo·''ye·wi from Turquoise and Ma·sewi from Squash. These officers are responsible for the enforcement of the *costumbres;* they supervise work in the fields of the Town chief and direct the communal rabbit hunts. They guard the curing societies during their ceremonies against witchcraft. They act as heralds in the winter solstice ceremony and as custodians of the scalps in the Scalp dance, and they appoint the permanent custodians of the scalps, a man and a woman. They might properly be called war chiefs and their eight assistants, war captains.

The war society of scalp-takers, the O·pi, is extinct; but they are represented in the war dance called Ahe·''na, sometimes danced at Christmas, and in the Scalp dance every five years. In both dances a buckskin kilt painted with a horned water serpent in black is worn. The scalps are carried on poles in the Scalp dance which is danced by kiva. A girl dances with the O·pi, a different girl in each appearance, and she and the clanspeople of the O·pi throw gifts of food to the choir. The head O·pi is called Mountain Lion.

Kiva chiefs, the *na'wai* and his assistant, are appointed to serve for life by the War chief. The kiva chief is also the kachina dance chief; he keeps the masks, he paints them and he animates new masks and the kachina dolls. The masks of Turquoise kiva are kept in the house of the Giant society. Youths join their father's kiva or kachina dance group. There is a third kachina dance group, "All kinds of beads," the Mixed Dancers, unattached to kiva. There is no kachina initiation nor whipping ritual. A few women (Pl. XXIII) are attached to the kachina dance groups.

There are four curing societies, Giant, Flint, Shi⋅'k'ame, and Snake. The Snake society consists of men who have been cured of snake bite. Curing for snake bite is the only function of the society. The society meets in the house of its chief. The other societies have each its own ceremonial house. All these societies cure for witch-caused disease, by sucking or by retrieving the stolen heart. A single shaman may visit the patient and be paid in corn meal or the whole society may come and conduct their ceremony. In this case the convalescent joins the society. There is initiation by trapping.[35] The initiate is whipped.

The clown groups, Koshare and Quirena, are associated, respectively, with Flint and Shi⋅'k'ame societies. Every Flint shaman must be a Koshare, every Shi⋅'k'ame, a Quirena. Koshare and Quirena do not doctor; nor do the women society members who, although they assist at cures, are referred to as Koshare or Quirena. Women members of the Giant society are called Shiwanna. Women members and clown societies join in the summer rain retreats which begin toward the end of May in the following order: Giant, Flint-Koshare, Shi⋅'k'ame-Quirena. These four-night retreats may be repeated. Retreats are followed by kachina dances. During the retreat the shamans are supposed to visit I'atik'ᵘ to ask her to send the kachina.

There are kachina dances also before the harvest, and sometimes in September the Spruce or Turtle dance or maskless kachina dance. At the winter solstice ceremony late in November or early in December the curing societies assemble, setting up their painted slab altars. In Squash kiva there is night war ritual and a ritual combat between Squash and Turquoise. At the summer solstice, a kachina dance with Koshare. At the winter solstice both Koshare and Quirena may come out. The War chief determines the appearances of these groups which have no kiva affiliations. In late winter or early spring there is a communal night cure by the societies.

PLATE XXIII

SAN FELIPE GIRLS

COCHITI

Santo Domingo, San Felipe, and Cochiti speak the same Keresan dialect and are supposed to have been an undivided tribe living in the Rito de los Frijoles and on neighboring *potreros*, whence because of Tewa hostility groups migrated southward. The Cochiti group was found at its present site by Oñate in 1598. The mission of San Buenaventura was established. In the Rebellion of 1680 the population of three hundred withdrew to found with their allies the fortified town of La Cieneguilla on Potrero Viejo, where they remained until routed by Vargas in 1693.

Cochiti, as described by Esther S. Goldfrank in 1922, has a Town chief, who is chief of the Flint society, and, theoretically, two assistant Town chiefs, the chiefs of the Giant society and of the Shikame society. Practically these chiefs do not appear to function together. Nor is there any hierarchic council. Besides the three curing societies—Flint, Giant, and Shikame, which is also the hunt society—there were in 1893–1900 as described by Father Dumarest, Ipani, Fire, and Snake societies. In 1922 the Town chief is accounted a member of the Fire and Snake societies, but as there are no other members of these societies the membership appears to be but a nominal matter. Related to the Flint and Shikame societies are the clown groups, Koshari and Kurena, who in alternate years are in charge of the rabbit hunts for the Town chief, of planting and harvesting for him, and of the kick-stick race. The Town chief has to be a Koshari. The senior member of the Flint society who is a Koshari qualifies as Town chief. Similarly the chief of the Shikame has to be a Kurena. Between the Giant society and the Kachina dance society there is also an association, the Giants make prayer-sticks for the Kachina society who keep their masks in the house of the Giants, and both societies visit the same shrine. The women's societies, Thundercloud and Women's society, are associated, the first with the Giant society, the second with the Shikame. Because of these intergroup relations, Goldfrank inclines to see a tendency to a tripartite pattern of organization at Cochiti.*

Recruiting in all the societies, except the Kachina society or dance group, is by trespass or by vow in sickness or dedication in childhood. It is felt that strength adheres to a group whether or not it is a regular curing agency. Instead of a society, a clan may be joined; it is cheaper. To the Kachina society all the males belong. They are partly initiated by whipping in childhood; when old enough to dance, about eighteen, they are instructed at home about the kachina.

The two-kiva system prevails, and, as usual, the Koshari and Kurena are associated with the kivas—the Koshari with Turquoise, the Kurena with Squash, the chief of each kiva being appointed from the clown group associated with the kiva, appointed by the chief of the clown group. With the kivas the secular government is linked to the extent that the offices are divided between the kivas, i.e., if the Governor is Turquoise his assistant must be Squash and vice versa. And so with the War captain and his lieutenant, and with the Fiscal and his lieutenant. Besides, Governor and War captain must be members of different kivas, and the helpers of Fiscal and War captain, six to each, must be equally distributed between the kivas, three of each group belonging to one, and three to the other. The Giants appoint the Governor and his lieutenant; the Town chief appoints the War captain and his lieutenant; the Shikami appoint the Fiscal and his lieutenant.

In Father Dumarest's time there was a war society of scalptakers and a War chief, the Nahia, who installed the Town chief, directed dances, and safeguarded the *costumbres*. Nahia might or might not be chief of the War society. Nahia's position was important enough to give the hierarchy a double-headed character. Today the war society is extinct, and some of the functions of the War chief are undertaken by the War captains. They arrange for dances, act as guards for ceremonies, and announce certain ceremonial events, and the head War captain instals the

* This were an anomaly in the usual Keresan system. I incline to think that the tendency toward this schematism has been exaggerated by the observer.

Town chief.* War captain and lieutenant are named for the war gods, Ma'sewi and Oyoyewi.

The ceremonial calendar of Cochiti consists of solstice ceremonials, with rain retreats by the societies after the summer solstice; Hunt society ceremonial followed by burlesques and animal dances on Kings' Day (January 6); kachina dances in winter and at Easter, by night in kiva, and in summer after each society retreat, in kiva or outside; a general midwinter curing ceremonial; kick-stick races run by kiva at Easter and *tablita* dancing which is also performed on various saint's days; Plains and other dances at Christmas; ritual planting and harvesting for the Town chief, and ritual rabbit-hunting; ritual before irrigation; All Souls' Day ceremonial.

SIA[36]

When the Espejo expedition stopped at Sia in 1582, they found a prosperous, orderly town of more than a thousand houses three or four stories high, built around five courts. The Spaniards were given turkeys and so many tortillas that they had to return them. After the Rebellion of 1680 the Spaniards destroyed the town and slaughtered most of the people. Today the one-story houses inclose two courts, and the population is 177, a great shrinkage from the last Spanish figure of 508, in 1765,[37] but an increase over earlier American figures which were in 1850, 124, and in 1889, 113.

The Conquistador chronicler mentions three chiefs, probably they were the Town chief, Chraik'ats[i] and the War chief. Today the War chieftaincy has lapsed. The Town chief has neither clan nor society affiliation; a vacancy once filled by the War chief is now filled by the annual War captains. After consulting with the society chiefs, the Town chief appoints the two War captains, their four assistants, and the other secular officers— Governor, his lieutenant and four "captains," and two Fiscales. The Town chief also appoints the three stewards called Chraik'ats[i] to collect and cook the rabbits from the communal rabbit

---

* He installed even the Nahia (see p. 595), to which puzzling arrangement, if it really existed, the historical key is missing; but see p. 1145, n. ‡.

hunts as food for the fetishes. These men are consulted by the Town chief on his appointments to secular offices. The Town chief watches the sunrise, sprinkling prayer-meal. He tells the War captains when to prepare for the solstice ceremonies. The Town chief should not leave town and should spend much time fasting and praying. The land of the Town chief is worked for him by the townsmen, and he is supplied with firewood.

The societies are Flint, Giant, Kapina, Fire, Snake, Ant, Shikame, and Hunt (Shaiyak). The Flint society was formerly affiliated with the War society, now extinct. The Koshairi and Quirena hold no relations to the other groups. The societies perform individual cures, and in February at the bidding of the Town chief they perform a ceremony to drive all sickness from the town. They hold summer rain retreats which are followed by a kachina dance. Seven group kachina dances are reported, and twenty-two side dancers or individual impersonations.

In Stevenson's day the Quirena had charge of the kachina dance. Today White finds four other societies in charge—Giant, Flint, Ant, and Koshairi. In their ceremonial houses all these societies have custody of various masks which they prepare for dance use. Each society assembles men at large to dance kachina. When the particular society goes into retreat, the dancers begin to observe continence, to vomit in the morning, and to practice dancing at night. On the third day they fetch spruce for dance costumes. The night before the dance a ceremony of prayer-stick-making and altar ritual is held by the society. The masks are laid out on the meal altar, and the impersonators sleep in the society house. The War captain and some shamans lead the kachina into the dance court, where at the close they are thanked in formal speech by the Town chief and the War captain. At night the impersonators bathe in the river, throwing into the water their spruce trimmings. The impersonator of the Kachina chief, Heruta, breaks his two-day fast. There is neither kachina society nor kachina dance group at Sia. Formerly there was a whipping ritual of kachina initiation conducted by the Quirena. Inferably both Quirena society and kachina organization have lapsed at Sia because of diminution of population. For

PLATE XXIV

SANTA ANA CHURCH. SANTA ANA KIVA. SIA KIVA

a long time but one kiva (Pl. XXIV) was in use. Unfortunately, we do not know how it was used or how the two present-day kivas are integrated into the town life.

The winter solstice ceremony is said to be determined by the Town chief on a horizon calendar; but as elsewhere in the East the ceremony is performed the end of November or beginning of December. The societies go into retreat for four days. The fourth night the ceremony is open to all. The shamans sing at their altar of painted slats, sand-painting, and fetishes. People dance; there is a midnight supper. At sunrise the shamans deposit their prayer-sticks. The summer solstice ceremony is similar, but curtailed and less well attended; people are at work in their fields.

In early spring, "after the witches have been busy all winter and have got too thick," the Town chief may decide upon a communal curing ceremony. This is conducted like a private cure, but by all the societies. Town chief represents the patient, but all the townspeople may attend and be cured.

Various saints' days are observed—San Juan (June 24), Santiago (July 25), San Pedro (July 20), San Lorenzo (August 11)—by rooster pull, horse races, or by throwing gifts from the housetops by the saint's godchildren; and on August 15 is celebrated the fiesta of the patroness, Nuestra Señora de la Asuncion.

JEMEZ[38]

In the Jemez River Valley as many as eleven towns were reported by the early Spanish chroniclers, but by 1622 because of famine or Navaho raids most of the towns were depopulated. In 1627 their Franciscan friar persuaded the people to concentrate in the two towns where there were chapels, one dedicated to San José, one to San Diego.

During the second half of the seventeenth century the Jemez fought on and off against the Spaniards acting in league with Navaho and with other Pueblos. In 1692, Jemez and Santo Domingo refugees were living together in a mesa-built town whence within two years they descended to raid the pro-Spanish towns, Sia and Santa Ana; in turn they were attacked and badly beaten by the Spaniards, with eighty-four persons killed and three hundred and sixty-one made prisoners and sent to Santa Fé. The mesa town was abandoned, but two years later Jemez in the valley killed their friar, and again took to the mesa where they were helped in a fight against the Spaniards by warriors from Acoma and Zuni. After this fight Jemez people went to live among Navaho or Hopi, being among the first of those refugees to the West that were to be such a thorn in the spirit to Spanish administrators. (Of all Pueblos, the Jemez and the Keres of Santo Domingo, independently or together, put up the most determined opposition to the Conquistadores, and to this day they have resisted penetration by White people.)

Most of the Jemez returned east within ten years, building near or at the site of their present town where they were enumerated in 1704 as a population of 500.[39] But sixteen families stayed behind at Walpi and remained there until 1716, whence they were escorted home, a party of 113, by two War chiefs and twenty young men.[40] Quite a number of Hopi ways were acquired during this sojourn of twenty years at First Mesa (see p. 985, n. †). Besides, as all the Jemez sojourners did not return, contacts were probably maintained for some time.

The people of Jemez speak a highly differentiated dialect of Tanoan, similar to that spoken at Pecos, eighty miles distant. When Pecos people had been almost exterminated by the Comanche, in 1840 the twenty survivors migrated to Jemez, escorted by Jemez townsmen, and were given houses and lands. To the ceremonial life of Jemez the Pecos contributed their Saint Porcingula, i.e., her image and her birthday celebration including a sacrosanct bull impersonation, and the Eagle-watchers* or Flute society, including three Mothers or fetishes and, I was told, the society mask.†

---

* This somewhat distinctive Pecos-Jemez society should be considered in connection with the important eagle-kills of Papago. See p. 999.

† Slim evidence for the use of masks at Pecos. No mask material was found there, although there is a masklike design on a bowl of sixteenth-century ware, possibly pre-Conquest.
The latest tree-ring date for Pecos is 1612. Probably growth either in population or in ceremonialism occurred but little after this date.

The Keresan Flint (Arrowhead) and Fire societies are represented at Jemez; as among the Tewa, they are the only curing societies; and these societies together with the war or Underchiefs society, the two clown societies, and the Eagle-watchers or Flute society conduct two series of rain retreats, in summer and in autumn. At the solstices, again in Keresan style, all these societies conduct synchronous ceremonies at which kachina appear and game animals, in Isletan style, are drawn in.* Prayersticks or feathers are deposited on Mount Redondo (summer solstice). Following the retreats there are races and dances: a maskless kachina dance, Flute dance of the Women's societies, the kachina Deer dance, or the kachina dances Sürni (Zuni) and Dawiye (Jemez) which have kiva associations, Sürni dance with Turquoise kiva and Dawiye with Squash kiva. The kiva dance managers are appointed by the Council of chiefs.

Boys and girls belong to the kiva of their father, the girl at marriage transferring if need be to her husband's kiva. Boys of eight and upward are initiated into one of the men's mutually exclusive societies, Eagle or Arrow society; initiates are whipped by a kachina. These societies control wind or snowstorm; the War chief's fetish is placed on their altars, and they have still other war god associations.

Boys are whipped by the kachina, at Easter, and probably boys are whipped again before dancing kachina (the statements are contradictory).† Women may dance kachina, but, unlike men, they are not given a kachina name. A kachina Father or chief appointed by the Town chief is trustee of a Mother and is in charge of initiatory whipping ritual.

The clown societies are associated with the kivas, the Tabö'sh with Turquoise, the Ts'un'tatabö'sh, also called Ice society, with Squash. Almost all the men belong to one or the other. There are also women members. The Ts'un'tatabö'sh come out for the

---

* Bunzel 6:61. Also, in this account by a Zuni visitor, the padre. "Wherever he passed by, there was wheat lying on the floor."

† Compare, too, statement made by an Isletan visitor that all the boys who are not returning to school are whipped, with cactus. Before this they know nothing, afterward they may know everything (Parsons 52:287, n. 84; Parsons 41:66, n. 3).

Porcingula fiesta, talk backward, and do not eat outdoors; the Tabö'sh come out for the San Diego fiesta and the autumn dance series, eat outdoors, and wear Jerusalem cherry necklaces. In summer dances the chief of the Tabö'sh is leader or road-maker; in winter dances, the chief of the Ts'un'tatabö'sh. The Tabö'sh chief "makes" his dancers race, in the Hopi or maskless kachina dance, late in the afternoon, between dance performances; and the Tabö'sh race with the men's Eagle society after they come out from their January retreat. This may be a relay or quasi-relay race; the track runs east and west and, like the Taos track, is marked by a small boulder shrine. Black-paint-all-over starts behind; when he overtakes a runner he checks him by holding out his arm and then smears him with black paint,* for good luck (power) in hunting. The Hopi dancers also run a sunrise race, the leader having been appointed or invited by the society in retreat. The leader carries a buckskin and an ear of corn which he relinquishes when overtaken, in the Hopi style. He has practiced running four nights preceding, each night in one of the directions. The same kind of race may be run by women the afternoon of the Hopi dance.† In the early spring a series of kick-stick races is run off by kiva, the last race being on the day the irrigation ditch is opened. (It is not surprising that in this sometime belligerent town Pueblo racing standards are kept up.)

The War society or Under-chiefs probably once consisted of slayers of men or prey animals; their chief is called *opi* as were Keresan slayers, and he is in charge of a Navaho scalp. He corresponds to the Nahia (Under) of Keres, whose office is now extinct. The War chief is installed at a scalp dance; he is appointed by the Town chief and the Council, from the Badger clan. With the Town chief he may call meetings of the Council. He has one assistant, and altogether there are six Under-chiefs, who are supposed to know everything, to be admitted to all ceremonies, to supervise and conserve the customs. The two annual War captains called Ma·sewi are their executives or representa-

---

* Compare the Cochiti masked Kurena who marks people on the cheek with black for good luck (Dumarest, 183; Goldfrank 3:93).

† Reported on October 2, 1932.

tives. The War captains are in charge of racers, they are on guard duty during society meetings, and together with the Town chief they ask for the appearance of kachina groups or chiefs. They have six youthful aids.

The Town chief is chosen by the Council. He has a right-hand man and a left-hand man (as has the chief of most of the twenty ceremonial groups), but these assistants do not necessarily succeed to office. Town chief and assistants are appointed from the Young Corn clan or the Sun clan. The Town chief watches the sun for the solstice ceremonies. His assistants summon the society chiefs to a preliminary meeting in his house, to what the Hopi would call a smoke talk. The Town chief may summon the Council; with the Council he appoints chief and members of the Under-chiefs society and the chiefs of the clown societies. The land of the Town chief is worked for him by men appointed by the War captains. Rabbit and deer are provided for the Town chief by the Mountain Lion society, which probably conducts certain hunts, the hunts opening the season, for the Town chief.

Neither this hunt society nor the Under-chiefs have any functions after a bear or mountain-lion kill. The bear-slayer is expected on his return to stop about a mile out of town and to shout, as in war. All the men go out to meet him, each receiving a piece of bear meat which he wraps around the barrel of his rifle. Women come out and strike at the bear with fire pokers. The relatives of the slayer take prayer-feathers and prayer-meal to the chiefs of the Arrowhead and Flint societies, asking them to wash the bear. On the fifth day the altar is laid. Men made Opi' for the occasion, dressed as Ma'sewi, attend and contribute food for the feast. The bear legs are given to one of the altar-making shamans who becomes the "younger brother" of the slayer. The head of a mountain lion is also washed, but the slayer returns to town unnoticed, and "he needs no brother." The animal heads are placed in a shrine with red-painted miniature weapons.

Town chief, War chief, every society chief, has a Mother, a befeathered corn ear which belongs to the society; at initiation society members are also given a cotton and feather-wrapped Mother. One of the three Mothers of the Eagle-watchers or

Flute society is a flute. At the installation of a new society chief the Mother may have to be moved to his house, carefully guarded by the War chief. Even if they move the Mother, "they like to keep the Mother in the same clan."

The Mothers of the Directions are referred to, the Mothers, instead of the Chiefs. Cloud or Rain people (*dyasa*), kachina (*k'ats'ana*, also *dyasa*), and the Dead are all confusedly identifiable, as among Keres. The kachina and the Dead live underground, toward the north, whence the people emerged.

The ceremonial system of Jemez is in general Keresan*—we recall that the town lies only four or five miles north of Sia, and that it was grouped with Sia and other Keresan towns in the Spanish jurisdiction. The Jemez Snake society is probably modeled on the Sia Snake society; like the Sia society, it holds four snake hunts and conducts its ceremony in a house or cave distant from the town, after its summer solstice retreat. Yet Jemez is a meeting-ground for the different Pueblo forms of social organization: the curing society or collectivistic shamanism, the matrilineal clan, and the moiety. The society is the outstanding form, but a few chieftaincies are associated with clans, and moiety is expressed through the two kivas, the two Men's societies, the two kachina dance groups, and the two clown societies which are especially inclusive and influential. A feeling for duality may have expressed itself also in having two Women's societies, two eagle-hunt societies, and celebrations for two patron saints, for Saint James on November 12 and for Porcingula† of Pecos on August 2.

SAN JUAN[41]

After Oñate established his capital of San Gabriel in 1598 in the Tewa pueblo at the junction of the Chama and Rio Grande

---

* There is a notable exception in the ritual of infant-naming. The infant is not presented to the Sun, Keres fashion. Instead, the ear of corn that has been laced alongside the cradleboard is taken out, pointed in the four directions (south, north, east, west), passed alongside the baby's nose, and then breathed on as the name is given (Harper). Compare the Isletan reference to the corn name.

† The mission name of Pecos was Nuestra Señora de los Angelos de Porciuncula.

PLATE XXV

SAN JUAN AND THE RIO GRANDE

rivers, the Indians abandoned their houses and finally resettled on the east bank of the Rio Grande, and their town of Ohke was called San Juan de los Caballeros, gentlemen as they were to give away their land and houses, said the Spaniards.* Today only a few ruined houses and a hillside shrine mark the site where Los Moros w s first danced in New Mexico, but the resettled population h⹁ more than held its own. To be sure in both blood and culture it has been Mexicanizing (Pl. XXV).

Although Pope' was a native of San Juan, his agitation was not welcome, and he had to go to Taos to plan the Rebellion. At the Reconquest the population aided much, writes Father Morfi, by their "fidelity and valor." When San Juan's seventy families (1744) were reduced to fifty in 1765, there was a total of 316 Indians against 175 neighborhood Whites.[42] More houses are owned by Mexicans,† and there appears to be more intermarriage in San Juan than in any pueblo except Nambé. I never saw elsewhere as many Mexicans at a saint's-day fiesta.

In San Juan, as in all Tewa towns, the moiety is the outstanding social classification. There are Summer people and Winter people. Membership is patrilineal. Marriage choice is not affected; but, if a woman is of the opposite moiety, frequently she undergoes the ceremony of adoption into her husband's moiety which is called "giving water."‡ The two moiety chiefs are the Town chiefs, the Winter Man in charge of all the people from autumn to spring, the Summer Man in charge, from spring to autumn. Each moiety has its kiva. Races, games, and dances may be carried on by moiety.

* So runs legend; but Father Morfi remarks in 1782 that Los Caballeros refers to Oñate's own knights (Thomas, 95).

† Out of 119 houses, 11 are listed with Mexican affiliations (Parsons 49:40 ff.).

‡ This is probably the moiety naming ritual noted at Isleta and in 1632 at San Juan. One day in January, while men were playing a game with beans (*patoles*) and reeds in kiva, a woman came in with an infant. One of the players, a Fiscal, took the infant in his arms, while they brought a bowl of water into which they put the beans, washed them, and took them out. Then they threw them up in the air as if playing, and some fell down on the infant. Taking some water in the mouth, each man spat it into the infant's mouth. Then they all rubbed the infant's head, hands, and feet. They said that this was to give a name in their language to the infant (Scholes 2:240–41).

Each moiety Town chief has a right-hand assistant and a left-hand assistant, the left hand succeeding to the right hand, the right hand to the chieftaincy, subject to the approval of Pikę, Mountain Lion, i.e., the Hunt chief, and of Apienu, Red Bow Youth, a woman war chief. Hunt chief installs the Town chiefs, after a year.

The office of Hunt chief is filled by the chiefs, from the paternal family of the deceased chief. Hunt chief is in charge of rabbit hunts and of the Deer dance. Hunt chief keeps the scalps. Presumably he took over this function from the War chief as well as the function of installing the Town chiefs.

The woman war chief was formerly appointed by the War chief. She has assistants who may be called Blue Corn Girls. These offices may be filled through self-dedication or "trapping." This woman's society is important because together with the Hunt chief the women control, at least theoretically, appointments to all the chieftaincies.

There are two outstanding curing societies, Flint and Fire. They are recruited through self-dedication or vow in sickness. Their patrons are Bear and four kachina of whom one whips at the initiations. These are the cleansing or exorcising groups; they "clean" the people, the houses, the fields, the race track.

Another curing group, the Eagle people, presents the Eagle dance, and on the third night of its retreat welcomes anybody sick of anything (?) who wants a drink from the medicine bowl on the altar. The chief is also a Flint shaman.

Of the clown groups the Kwirana are or were recruited by dedication in infancy; sick infants, male or female, are given to them. The Kwirana come out to play at the request of the War captain, but the group is lapsing. The Kossa are recruited through trespass, anyone straying into their ash house, a semi-circle of ashes on the ground, is caught and in due time initiated. Payachiamu, an anthropomorphic image, is their patron; they also pray to Fire Boy for a good day when they are to come out to play and to the Horned Water Serpent for water.

The old men or chiefs form a council. They appoint the secular officers who are installed by the Town chiefs.

In November the Summer Man gives the people to the Winter Man. Sometime later the Winter kachina come to dance. (Masks are kept by the Town chiefs; there is no separate kachina organization.) Similarly, after the seasonal transfer of spring, there is a rain dance by the Summer kachina. Turtle dance (maskless kachina) and Matachina at Christmas; Buffalo dance on Kings' Day; ritual ditch-opening; Women's society ceremonial; general exorcising; spring rain dances and pilgrimage up the sacred mountain which may be repeated later by the societies in case of drought; Buffalo or Deer dance at Easter; saint's-day dances with relay racing; society rain retreats; harvest dance; All Souls' Day; and throughout the year, as they come due, the initiations into the various groups or the installations into office.

HANO*

According to tradition, New Mexican Tewa were invited by Walpi chiefs, Bear clan chief and Snake clan chief, to come to their aid against the Ute, early in the eighteenth century.[43] They came, defeated the marauders, and ever since have considered themselves warrior protectors.† "We Tewa men are the watchers for the Snake clan. They came after us when we lived at Chwęage,‡ so we are their children."[44] At first the newcomers

* Parsons 44. The tribal name of the Tano (said to be a southern Tewa branch) was T'hanuge, from which derived Taha'no and Tano (Thano) (Handbook) and, probably, Hano. T'anuge'ịntowa abbreviated to T'anutowa, live-down-country people, refers to habitat and was applied to Pecos and to Keresan as well as to Tewa-speaking Indians who inhabited the great plain called T'anuge south of the Tewa country (Harrington, 576).

† An attitude and a tradition they may have found helpful in preserving self-esteem. The second night of the Hano winter solstice ceremony the Town chief "tells his men and boys about his way and how his (Bear) clanspeople came to this place, and where he comes from. Also why the Tewa people came here. (Note the suggestion of a different origin for the Bear clan or some of the people in Chief kiva.) He tells us that we must remember the story of how those Walpi chiefs sent for us. *Whenever any Walpi person says anything bad to us remembering the story we must not mind what is said to us*" (Parsons 40:122).

‡ Tsawarii, above the present town of Santa Cruz (see Handbook, Hano). Tano from San Lazaro and San Cristobal (between Galisteo and Pecos) moved into this neighborhood after the Rebellion, appropriating the lands of ousted Spaniards. At the reconquest, in 1695, Vargas made San Lazaro consolidate with San Cristobal and then after the harvest he made them all vacate houses

were assigned land below the mesa, but later they moved to the
mesa top, where their houses are within a stone's throw of
Sichomovi, the suburb of Walpi.

In the first Spanish picture we get of these immigrant Easterners they are on the mesa top, determined not to be removed (for
a third time within thirty-five years) by the Spaniards. In 1716
Governor Phelix Martinez assembled a company of 109 Spaniards and 317 Pueblos* and marched to Awatobi to recover by
persuasion or by force all the refugee "apostates" from the East,
Tano, Tewa, Tiwa, and some lingering Jemez. At Awatobi the
sixteen Indian peace emissaries Martinez had sent on ahead of
him from Zuni reported that on the "impregnable rock" where
the Tano had established their pueblo all the Hopi and Tiwa†

---

and fields and withdraw to a tract at Chimayo (Twitchell I:241 ff.). There is a
tradition at Santa Clara that the Hano people went west from Chimayo. Tano
did go to the Hopi (Handbook, San Cristobal). In 1707, Tano were in asylum at
Tesuque, 150 Tano, whence they went to Galisteo where their resettlement survived nearly one hundred years (Thomas, 92; Nelson, 30). (Possibly these visitors introduced the distinctive features of the Buffalo dance of Tesuque.) A
Tano of Galisteo asks permission in 1718 to visit the Tano at Moqui (Twitchell
II, 187). In 1775 Father Escalante of Zuni reports on the "Janos (there they
say Teguas)" (Thomas, 151). It seems fairly certain that Hano was settled by
southern Tewa or Tano who first moved north and then withdrew to First Mesa.

Espeleta, the Oraibi chief who visited Santa Fé in 1700, may have got into
touch with the unsettled Tano and suggested migration, not because of Utes, of
course, but because of Spaniards who only six years earlier had driven the Tano
out of Santa Fé, where they had settled after the Rebellion, and shot seventy
warriors, and enslaved four hundred women and children (Bancroft, 205).

Eastern Tewa may also have migrated to First Mesa. Stephen was told that
the migration was in two groups, from Abiquiu which is in the northwest corner
of Tewa territory and from which we know the Tewa were crowded out by
Spaniards and Genizaros, as Indian converts detached from their tribe were
called, as well as from near Peña Blanca, now a Mexican town near Cochiti
(Stephen 4:1085).

* Quotas and numbers mustered out of this all-Pueblo army who were to be
together for two months are of considerable interest: Taos, quota 15, mustered
19; Picurís, q. 10, m. 12; San Juan, q. and m. 10; Santa Clara, q. 6, m. ?; San
Ildefonso, q. 10, m.?; Pojoaque, q. 6, m. 5; Nambé, q. and m.5; Tezuque, q. 10,
m. 8; Pecos, q. and m., 30; Galisteo, q. 4, m. 5; Cochiti, q. and m. 20; Santo
Domingo, q. and m. 10; San Felipe, q. and m. 20; Santa Ana, q. and m. 12; Sia,
q. 25, m. 20; Jemez, q. 20, m. 30; Isleta, q. and m. 5; Laguna, q. 10, m. 12; Acoma,
q. and m. 25; Zuni (Alona), q. 30, m. 25.

† Tiwa were living two leagues distant from First Mesa.

chiefs accepted the peace and friendship of the Spaniards, only the Tano *"remained silent without saying a word."* * Even when the Governor camped below the mesa, sending up more Indian emissaries and the padre who was with him, and the chiefs came down, El Pinjui, the well-known Tano chief, refused to come down, being "very weary and sick." Finally after a fight with Hopi and Tano, in which eight Indians were killed and many wounded, and after destroying the standing crops in the fields below the mesa, Martinez proposed to the Walpi chiefs to allow him to ascend the entrenched mesa and make the Tano prisoners. Thereupon a great confusion of counsel must have ensued on the mesa top, for from "the middle approach" came out a Hopi saying that the Tano were malevolent, had led them astray, and were responsible for the killing of their people and that the Spaniards could ascend the mesa and would not be annoyed. Juan Barthólo, the Tiwa negotiator, was sent for. Descending the mesa to a great rock, he told the Governor to approach and then a Spaniard for once heard in good Castillian what Indians, even one who "knew the eternity of Heaven and Hell," thought of Spaniards. Peace in no form was wanted by Barthólo or any Indian, "they got along very well without the irreligious† Spaniards." The rest Martinez does not record. It was a dramatic defiance. And costly. The army was turned loose in the fields and "before their very eyes" crops were destroyed.‡ For six days with a rest of one day the Spaniards continued to save the Indians from the Devil by ambushing and seizing people, cattle, or flocks, destroying fields, and "doing all the damage possible to the Apostates" of First and Second Mesas and of the Tiwa settlement. Oraibi was too far away. By night horses and mules

* Just as two centuries later when Christian Indians and Protestant missionaries invaded the mesa, I saw Crow-Wing silent without saying a word except to counsel all to stay within their doors. "Not one of them (Tano) has come to see me," complained Martinez, who was probably more forgetful of the Santa Fé slaughter than some of the refugee Tano.

† For one thing, the man who had sent them a Cross was devastating Cross-guarded fields.

‡ As was done by American cavalry in their campaign against Navaho in 1862 (Gunn, 95).

and cattle were pastured in the fields, making "great ruin and destruction." Bean and squash patches were not overlooked. After very few fields remained to be destroyed and these "very insignificant," Governor Martinez felt that "the enemies of our Holy Faith" had been properly punished and concluded his very remarkable visit of twenty days, marching back to Zuni.[45] With him went, of course, the Christian Pueblos who had been ordered out also to "pull everything up by the roots," a most unusual experience for maize ritualists and one that must have been well broadcasted throughout the pueblos, as bearing upon the disposition of Spaniards.

After seeing the first good crops they had had in four years thus destroyed, it is perhaps not surprising that the people of Hano remained there and, although they forgot the unforgetable conduct of the Spanish Governor* (at least no recent historian has heard it referred to), came to consider themselves "watchers" for their Hopi hosts. And soon they began to intermarry, i.e., Hano men married into Walpi or Walpi men married into Hano. By 1893 out of 62 children in the population of 163,† only

---

* Largely, I believe, because they substituted fancy for fact through the tales of why they moved westward and why Awatobi was destroyed. Why the Spaniards have been so thoroughly ignored in Pueblo folklore is very intriguing. Perhaps their own quarrels have greater and more sustained interest for them. In a Shipaulovi account of what appears to be Martinez' campaign, the emphasis is on the treachery of the chief of Shongopovi (Shumopovi), who was a witch and had flown to Santa Fé overnight to summon the Spaniards (Voth 5:62–63).

Comparatively recent behavior of Spaniards or Mexicans is referred to merely by the stereotype "Mexicans are mean." No illustrative anecdotes are told such as was recorded in 1807 by Lieutenant Pike (Appen. to Part III, p. 13): "Before we arrived at Santa Fé, one night, we were near one of the villages where resided the families of two of our Indian horsemen. They took the liberty to pay them a visit in the night. Next morning the whole of the Indian horsemen were called up, and because they refused to testify against their imprudent companions, several were knocked down from their horses by the Spanish dragoons with the butt of their lances; yet, with the blood streaming down their visages, and arms in their hands, they stood cool and tranquil: not a frown, not a word of discontent or palliation escaped their lips."

† Estimated by Escalante at 110 families in 1775. Eight families of Tano had been "brought down," i.e., convoyed to the East thirty years or so earlier by missionaries inspired by the successful bringing-down of the Tiwa of Payupki (Thomas, 160).

6 were pure Tewa.[46] Hano families became bilingual; but Hopi do not learn to speak Tewa. Tewa women retain their bangs and queue.* The Tewa kinship nomenclature is retained but whatever was the clan system of the immigrants, if any, today the Hano system is completely Hopi. Sacrosanct paraphernalia and chieftaincies are handed down in the maternal lineage or clan, Hopi way, as is property in houses, lands, or springs, and in kivas. There are only two kivas in Hano, although whether or not this is a moiety survival is not certain.† Otherwise, except in traces of a double Town chieftaincy, the moiety system of the eastern Tewa has disappeared.

Every Tewa belongs to one of the two kivas, Chief kiva or Corner (or Tewa) kiva, but at the winter solstice ceremony at least two clans, Cloud and Cottonwood, split between the two kivas. In 1893 the eight clans were Cloud, Bear, Corn, Tobacco, Pine, Sun, Earth (Sand), and Kachina. In 1920 the Kachina clan was being called Cottonwood (Crow); Pine was accounted a lineage of Bear; Sun was extinct.[47] In 1920, Satele of the Bear clan was Town chief, Poętoyo (in New Mexico, Summer Man, chief of the Summer moiety)‡ and winter solstice chief in Chief kiva where in 1898 he was functioning as assistant chief; in Corner kiva a Sand clansman was chief of kiva and his brother, kiva chief at the winter solstice ceremony. It is indicated that the Corner kiva winter solstice chief would be called in New Mexico the Winter moiety chief.[48]

* An intensive comparison of the domestic life of Walpi-Sichomovi and Hano would be of great interest. Everybody is impressed by the bold or enterprising character of the Hano Tewa compared with Hopi, and there are comparisons of ceremonial, but no comprehensive cultural comparisons have been made.

† The paucity of the circular partly subterranean kivas in Tano ruins (Nelson, 111) suggests that organization was by moiety rather than by clan.

‡ Stephen makes no direct reference to Poętoyo, but already in 1893, Satele (Sateli) was a chief and the maternal house of the Bear clan was important since it was possessed of a *tiponi* corn fetish and was a place of chiefly assemblage (Stephen 4:392).

This house of Pobi and her brother Sateli became closely intermarried with the house of the Town chieftaincy of Walpi, as did the Bear maternal house of Walpi. The sister of Kotka, Bear Man of Walpi, married Tü'ïnoa, Town chief of Walpi; and Sateli, Town chief of Hano, married the sister of Tü'ïnoa.

The date for the winter solstice ceremony (*t'ant'aii*) is taken from Walpi, but the Town chief goes into Chief kiva, not in the early morning, but late in the afternoon, together with Tobacco clan chief and Corn clan chief and the Bear man who exorcises.* The Corn man has to make the road of meal, after the altar is put up, from altar to door.† (A Corn man also goes in to Corner kiva for this function.) The following day all members of each kiva go into their respective kiva to stay three days, during which members of Chief kiva fast from food and drink until the close of the day.

The first evening initiates chose their sponsor or father with a handful of meal. These "new boys" fast from salted food; with their "fathers" they bathe early in the springs; and they are sent out to gather prayer-stick willow.⁴⁹ Inferably all this is a substitute for Wüwüchim initiation or for not belonging to kiva or winter solstice ceremony through birth into one moiety or the other.

The morning of the fourth day all have their heads washed and proceed to make prayer-sticks or prayer-feathers, for wife, offspring, and livestock, for clanspeople and paternal relatives. Early in the afternoon women from every household bring food to the kivas, and there is a feast, the food brought first by the

* Almost certainly he is the custodian of the Bear mask which is depicted with a pine (spruce) tree and which gave the custodial lineage the name of Pine. The tree was Bear Old Man's ladder when he led the people up from the lake of the Emergence.

The Bear mask is identical with the mask of the Fire society of Jemez, and I believe it is the Fire *pufona* or shaman mask of the Tewa. Did it reach Jemez via Hano or vice versa during the Jemez sojourn at First Mesa? Or did it reach both Jemez and Hano from the Keres?

The obsolete Hano term for doctor is *kieh*, bear, the New Mexico Tewa term, and formerly there was a Bear doctor society in Hano; the songs were known to the custodian of the Bear mask.

† Meal-road-making for any general ceremony is a function belonging to the Corn clan. This clan feels bound to feed people in times of scarcity, to entertain strangers and interpret for them (Robbins, Harrington, Freire-Marreco, 98). Also the Corn clan owns Chief kiva, calling it "Corn-silk heap house" (Freire-Marreco). Note that all these are functions of the Town chieftaincy of eastern Tewa. My guess is that the Corn clan was originally associated in Hano with the Town chieftaincy before the Hopi association between Bear clan and Town chieftaincy was adopted.

Bear woman, the Tobacco woman and the Corn woman being first eaten, "to become strong old men." (Formerly girls from these clans used to join the kiva assemblage, "because they got their winter solstice ceremony from Cactus Flower girl.") After sundown the men distribute their clan prayer-feathers. They go in single file, grouped by clan, with the senior clansman in the lead.

Returning to kiva,* they undress and take places to form a spiral, "like a snake," near the altar on which stand two corn-ear fetishes (Stephen), prayer-sticks or feathers to represent deceased chiefs or common people, and a clay image of Water Serpent, in Corner kiva, three feet long, stuck with twelve upright eagle feathers (Stephen, Fewkes) and with horn, teeth, and eyes of corn kernels (Parsons, Fewkes).† On the north side stand images of the War gods (Awęlę)‡ and Spider Grandmother.[50] Half the night they sing war songs, "to make the Tewa men brave" and the hearts of their enemies weak; the young men go out and shoot. There are twelve songs: two Rattlesnake, two Big Snake, two Sun, two War god, two Bear, and two Wildcat; "fine anthem tunes," writes Stephen, "very impressive, the Bear song sounds like a peal of victory." Then into the early morning

* Chief kiva to which Crow-Wing belonged. But there is also ceremonial in Corner or Tewa kiva.
Why is Tewa kiva so called? Was Chief kiva that of the Tano proper?

† The cloud-rain design recalls that on the Oraibi Soyala altar. We might infer that the idea of having Water Serpent on the altar was borrowed from the Walpi altar in Chief kiva except for the prominence of Water Serpent in the San Juan Kossa altar (Parsons 49: Pl. XVII). To be sure, Water Serpent is patron of Kossa, but in this eastern Tewa altar, despite the erratic composition by the draftsman, we find other parallels to the Hano altars: cloud and lightning meal design; befeathered "road"; crenellate medicine bowl; and large jar representative of a cosmic spirit.
Among the pictographs of the Tano ruins is a horned serpent over twenty-five feet long (Nelson, 93; n. 3).

‡ Compare the altar found in a small blocked-up chamber in Pueblo Largo, one of the Tano ruined towns. On the raised earthen base stands the stone image of the god, presumably the war god, face painted red and body, green, all glistening with what was perhaps powdered mica. Miniature jars and canteens, arrow-points, petrified wood, a small boulder of iron ore, pebbles with polished facets and a thin circular disk of shale were in the cache, over which was found a stone slab fireplace filled with ashes (Nelson, 91–93, Fig. 12).

they sing solstice songs, among them in Chief kiva the song of running water (*poẹka*), the song of the early *sipapu* in the far east where the water is always in motion. Poẹtoyo, the Town chief, is the chief of running water.[51]

At midnight the seed corn that has been brought into kiva and placed upright on the altar is laid lengthwise as if mature and ready for harvest. Peaches of flour and clay images of the domestic animals lie also on the altar.

Tewa do not join the Hopi Powamu society, nor do they have their own Powamu or Kachina society; yet they have "kachina fathers" and whipper kachina, and Tewa children are whipped in Hano during the Powamu celebration. There is no kachina Home-going celebration in Hano and no seasonal restriction on kachina dancing. Otherwise kachina dances are Hopi model. Tewa claim to have brought with them from the east four kachina: Po'haha, the girl warrior (Cottonwood clan, War chieftaincy), Yeenu (Bear clan, Town chieftaincy), Bear Old Man (Bear [Pine] clan) and the starry Whipper kachina (Tobacco clan) (also the Shumaikoli shields or masks). These are all kachina chiefs, but there are many group kachina, any of which will go to Sichomovi or Walpi to dance; and Hano frequently supplies the clowns for kachina celebration in Sichomovi or Walpi. These Kossa or Koyala or Paiyakyamu (Paiyetemu, Keresan for youth) were formerly an organized group with chief* and altar paraphernalia: painted cotton cloth, medicine and medicine-water jar, and crook prayer-stick.[52] They initiated through sickness or trespass. In appearance and clowning behavior these Hano Kossa are similar to the Kossa of eastern Tewa.

Besides its clown society Hano has a Shumaikoli (Somaikoli) society which cures for sore eyes, is possessed of masks (shields, Stephen) similar to those of the Shuma'kwe society of Zuni, and holds an annual summer ceremony called "they work *tangpeng*,"

---

* The chieftaincy was in the Cottonwood (Kachina) clan (Stephen 4:146, n. 1, 182, 371, 392; Parsons 40:68, n. 112), but in 1920 I believe that Alạ, the Corn clan chief, and chief of Chief kiva was Koyala chief (Parsons 40:113; Stephen 4:1032, n. 2). Alạ was in charge of harvesting for the Walpi Town chief (Parsons 40:114).

from a sort of rattle with wooden links carried in the ceremony. About the time of the summer Snake or Flute ceremony of Walpi, Shumaikoli chief announces the ceremony in four days. Members go to the chief's house* for a half-day to make prayer-sticks (for the shields which are set out in a row), and in the afternoon women members and wives of male members contribute food. That is all there is to the ceremony unless the chief decides to have the Shumaikoli kachina come out; then there is a public dance, Zuni Yaya (Mothers) dance.† The chief appoints a man to assemble in kiva the girl dancers. In the afternoon four or five men go into kiva to sing for the girls. They all come out, the girls forming a circle alternating with young men similarly gathered up. Out come some of the women society members carrying meal in baskets, and followed by men members, singing and escorting Shumaikoli. One after the other the six Shumaikoli are brought out from kiva by different sets of men and women. In conclusion the six Shumaikoli, with a man and woman to each and with the society chief in the lead, come out into the court which they circle four times and then go "home," i.e., to the Gap, where they undress.

Four other ceremonies are to be noted: Tiyogeo' ("they act as summer"), the summer solstice ceremony ("they work for the Sun"), the following month prayer-stick-making for rain by all the chiefs with mountain pilgrimage,[53] and a lapsed war ceremony called Kahbena. Tiyogeo' which is observed during the March moon‡ appears to be a survival of a moiety transfer ceremony. The chiefs go into Chief kiva to make prayer-sticks: Town chief, Sand clan chief (winter moiety chief), Corn clan

* In 1892–93 Kalashai of the Sun clan was chief. Nineteen members, all but three being Tewa men. Kalashai died in 1895, the clan became extinct, and K'elang of the Cloud clan became chief (see Stephen 4:818 ff.; Parsons 40:104, Fig. 41).

† Compare Stephen 4:343. The Zuni Yayatüh and Sumaikoli come out from Walpi in the Water Serpent celebration. Sumaikoli and their leaders called Wiki are known at Laguna (Parsons 20:116). Wikoli is a term for a Keresan society official, and the whole complex appears like that of a Keresan society.

‡ Observed in 1893 on May 28 in the Bear maternal house of the Town chieftaincy (Stephen 4:392).

chief, who is chief of Chief kiva, and Sun-watcher of the Cloud clan who is also keeper of the War god images and chief of the Shumaikoli society. They stay in overnight only, all but Town chief who is chief of the ceremony and who stays in four more nights. They sing the solstice song of running water.

For the summer solstice ceremony Town chief watches the sun, and the ceremony is observed from four to six days after the Hopi summer solstice ceremony. Town chief, Corn clan chief, Tobacco clan chief, Cloud clan chief, and two men of the Pine lineage that keeps the Bear mask go to the maternal house of the Town chief to make prayer-sticks, sending out depositors, and to sing. The chiefs are not in retreat, but for four nights they must remain continent.

Kahbena* was a war ceremony celebrated one night during the January moon in Corner kiva. The chiefs were the Corn clan chief who was in charge, Town chief and Bear (Pine) clansman. Early in the morning a woman (? Red Bow Youth of the eastern Tewa) would call down Corner kiva that they were to bundle up their wood and put it on the kiva roof to dry, for four nights. "That way they knew they would have Kahbena." Later the woman announced at the kiva, "Sweat in our hands!" referring to the ritual posture of folded arms and closed hands which sweat. "That way everybody knew about it." Inferably this meant a four-day retreat. On the last night all members of the winter solstice ceremony of Chief kiva had to assemble with the Corner kiva members. The War chief who was the last man down sat by the ladder. Men sat in a spiral to represent the Big Snake. All, including the women present, sang men songs, songs to be brave. In conclusion the Kossa clowns arrived from Chief kiva and performed their act of striking ashes off a feather, peering through the ash cloud, and in a lively colloquy pretending to see the approaching kachina.† Then kachina with fruit and seed came down to dance and "make people happy." But,

---

* Note resemblance to Kaʙina or Kapina, the Keresan warlike society.

† This contrary exorcism was performed at Powamu, 1893, by Hopi clowns from Wikwalobi kiva (Stephen 4:205). Compare eastern Tewa, Parsons 49: 166–67.

however happy they were over the distribution of the kachina gifts by the Kossa, they might not laugh; anybody who laughed during the evening had to join the Kossa society. After the clowns and the kachina withdrew, the songs were resumed until sunrise, when a Corn clan girl passed around a drink of parched corn meal in water, exchanging terms of relationship, "my father, my daughter."

Being a war ceremony, this ceremony was kept very secret from the Hopi. The ceremony was associated in some way with the 'Yu"yuki (? Cactus) society who whipped one another so men would be brave and hardy and so the ground would freeze. We recall that the Acoma Kaвina society place the altar for the installation of War chiefs who are whipped.

Scalps were kept at Hano, possibly in the house of the War chief. The War chieftaincy is in the Cottonwood clan. The War chief (Potali) is watchman against witches who cause sickness or epidemic. The War chief keeps the mask of Po'haha, the warrior girl. Another hint of the associations of women with war characteristic of eastern Tewa is afforded by the Man dance, the victory dance by two men and two girls, the girls who went out to welcome the returning war party, perhaps the Blue Corn Girls.[54]

In the ceremonial organization of Hano there is still much that is obscure, but tentatively I conclude that the Hopi system of chiefly succession by inheritance within the maternal family has been taken over, although in the conduct of ceremonies most of the chiefs participate and society members are recruited in the familiar Eastern way, through sickness or trespass.

ISLETA[55]

The early history of the Tanoan-speaking tribes is very obscure; Tiwa, Tewa, Tano, Towa (Jemez-Pecos), and Piro. Much of the cultural history of these tribes will never be known, but it is to be hoped that at least the direction of their migrations will be learned together with the dating of their ruins. The Proto-Tanoan language may have been like that of Taos, although there is no reason why Tiwa morphology may not have grown up later, with Tewa and Towa (Jemez) developing along parallel but not identical lines.[56] At any rate, of the Tiwa dialects, Taos is the most archaic.

Isleta probably stands on or near the site that was occupied in 1540, the year of the Spanish discovery, when twelve Tiwa pueblos were reported along the Rio Grande by Castañeda, the historian of Coronado's discoveries and ruthless conduct. In one Tiwa (Tiguex) town the Spaniards burned two hundred men at the stake or shot them down as they tried to escape. Most of the river Tiwa towns were abandoned, the people concentrating in two towns which ultimately were besieged by the Spaniards and captured. Many townsmen were killed, in one town two hundred, and in each town one hundred women and children were captured. It was not an agreeable introduction to Spanish culture, and it is not surprising that the two friars in the next Spanish party to visit one of these Tiwa towns, in 1581, were killed after their small military escort departed. The Mexican Indians in the party remained, nineteen, but what became of them is not recorded. The historian of the expedition describes the town we take to be Isleta as having 123 houses of two or three stories.

Spanish captains and friars persisted, and by 1629 there was a Franciscan mission in San Antonio de la Isleta. There were at this time eight Tiwa river towns, with a population of six thousand. In 1674 and later Isleta received accession from three of the Tiwa mountain towns abandoned because of Apache depredations.* By this time all southern Tiwa were concentrated into four towns: Alameda, Puaray, Sandía, and Isleta.

Isleta did not join in the Rebellion of 1680, although some of the townspeople fled when 1,500 Provincials from the ranches of the lower river took refuge in Isleta before retreating into Chihuahua. The next year, when Governor Otermín returned, all the Tiwa towns were abandoned except Isleta. Otermín burned the towns and stormed Isleta, taking 519 of its captives to the southwest, of whom 115 escaped and others settled about

---

* What became of the other eight towns reported in 1581 on the eastern slope of the Manzano Mountains is obscure.

fourteen miles below what is now El Paso at Isleta del Sur.* The rest of the Isletan population of 2,000 abandoned the town for a sojourn in Hopiland lasting until 1716† or 1718. Some of the Oraibi who accompanied the returning Payupki-Sandía "converts" in 1742 settled at Isleta, as the near-by suburb called "Oraibi" bears witness. But they and probably those at Sandía "deserted little by little."[57]

In this same Oraibi suburb about 1879 a group of from thirty to forty immigrants from Laguna, forty miles west, were allowed to settle. These Keres began to intermarry and to become bilingual. They joined the matrilineal Corn groups, equating their clans with these groups‡ and giving up their exogamous custom. The shamans among them were received into the Laguna Fathers if they did not start that organization. The immigrants kept their own office of Town chief and their kachina mask cult of which the Town chief is Father, presenting their dances in the

---

* In 1744 the population was 498 Indians and 54 Spaniards; in 1765, 429 Indians and 131 Spaniards (Thomas, 110). By 1901 only 25 persons were speaking Tanoan. The Cacique and his assistant, the "lieutenant cacique," were the source of all authority. The Cacique called the meeting to elect the officers: Governor, *Alguacil, Capitán major,* and four other *capitánes.* Officers and all the sons of the pueblo were subject to the Cacique and had to maintain him and his family. He handed on the canes of office, and he himself had a short black cane, "our mother." Permission to hold dances was got from the Governor, and the War captains directed dances and hunts (hunt fire, surround, and girls went out and ran for the game), but all this after consultation with the Cacique. There were several dances: saint's day in atrium of church and then before the house of the *mayordomo;* as at Taos, a Christmas dance by children; a women's throw-away "red pigment" dance or Hawina war dance; scalp dance (obsolete) with a woman holding the scalp pole; a quadrille-like, kachina-like (maskless) dance, and a dance by two clowning, bogey Grandfathers (one male impersonation, one female) in buffalo-hide masks, called Turtle dance, from the turtle-shell rattle (Fewkes 10).

The latter-day history of this town might yield interesting acculturation information, as might also the more Mexicanized town of Senecú, about six miles from Juarez, Chihuahua, a Piro settlement made also after the Great Rebellion, with a scattering of Tano, Tewa, and Jemez "progressives."

† In this year five Isletans returned East (Bloom, 170). Inferably these scouts made a favorable report, and the others followed.

‡ For example, the Lizard clan joined the Yellow Corn or Earth people, Earth or Sand being another name for Lizard clan at old Laguna. Sun clan people joined the White Corn or Day people.

town proper, and assisted in policing by the Isletan Grand-fathers, the moiety masked clowns. The kachina come after the field-cleansing ceremony of the shamans and after the summer solstice ceremony. Dance practice is in the house of the Laguna Fathers.

The Laguna colony contributes a Kings' Day dance to the Isletan calendar. Their Town chief gets permission to present the dance from the Isleta Town chief. The Isleta War chief or captain appoints twelve K'apio clowns, six from each moiety. Besides, a few Isletans have been invited to dance by the Laguna people. Two groups of men and women alternate. The men dancers wear back tablets representing Sun or Moon. Sun, Moon, and Stars and other Spirits were painted on the walls of the chamber[58] of the Laguna Fathers by Juan Rey, the Fire society stick-swallower of Laguna.

The Town chief has two assistants or executives or guards, Kabew'iride* or Bow chief who succeeds, and Kumpawithlawe or Pą'ide, Pouch War chief or permanent war chief, who is Scalp chief and Snake society chief as well. In recent years Pą'ide has been acting Town chief.†

The land of the Town chief is planted and harvested for him; he may not cut wood or do any but ritual work. He keeps the supply of ritual tobacco and of ritual game food and he maintains flint-made fire. His corn-ear fetish is the paramount fetish, and the Town chief himself is the source of all the ceremonial life. To hold ceremonies or dances or to get power, his permission must be asked; he may initiate or ask for the ceremony of general exorcism or other ceremonies; he oversees food offerings

---

* Compare the Town chief helper called Bow, also Chraik'ats^i, at Santo Domingo. The Keresan Chraik'ats^i were formerly chiefs in charge of game and wild plants. Possibly Kabew'iride corresponds to the Chraik'ats^i. It is not known how Kabew'iride is selected.

† According to one poorly substantiated theory, the lifelong office of Town chief is filled from the Corn groups in rotation. The annual office of head War captain is filled this way. Twice in recent years he who was Pą'ide has become acting Town chief. In 1885 and in 1896 the office of Town chief became vacant by death and the council of elders was unable to agree on anybody (Parsons 25:158–59). The installation is elaborate, and it is felt today that nobody knows how to direct it, so the situation of not having a *real* Town chief continues.

to Wȩide and the dead; final report of a ceremony is made to him. During the solstice ceremonies he remains in his house to receive reports, but he does not conduct ceremony. The long summer rain ceremony, which may be repeated, is conducted in his ceremonial house; he makes the meal road in the irrigation ceremony; with the curing societies he conducts a ceremony to bring in Salt Woman. He "clothes the sun" and helps him in his course; inferably he represents or is closely associated with the Sun. The spring races are called Town chief races.

In these relay races the first two runners are started by the Pą'ide war chief who with the Town chief and Shichu chief has performed a ceremony the night before. Pą'ide paints half the runners with red, Shichu paints the other half with white.* Pą'ide stands behind the runners and gives them a push with his bow. In the race in connection with the Scalp ceremonial Pą'ide moves the scalps in the directions and hits each scalp-taker thrice with the scalp. Pą'ide leads out the runners of one side, the Town chief those of the other side.

Pą'ide is an executive for the Town chief, but he gets his "power" from the serpent Ikaina† for whom he conducts a ceremony. He has a bundle of scales from the Serpent which he keeps in his pouch, together with a powder (? pollen) to rub on the eyes to give clairvoyance and make him act like a snake, turning and twisting and hissing. On Pą'ide's moccasins lightnings are painted. Pą'ide uses special words, talking backward and for the cardinal directions cornerwise. He is dreaded by witches whom he paralyzes with fear. Formerly he shot witches with his bow and arrow, and he and his helpers or society still guard ceremonial assemblages against them. These Kumpawithlawen are recruited by vow. "If a man gets sick, he can promise to become Kumpawithlawe." If he recovers, there is an initia-

---

* These colors are associated with Sun and Moon by the Jicarilla Apache, who have borrowed the relay race from Taos, if not from Picurís. Inferably Kumpa is painting for the Sun, and Shichu for the Moon.

† Ikaina is almost certainly Rattlesnake, not the Horned Serpent as I formerly stated. Ikaina is never associated with water, but with war, lightning, and the Sun. Quite generally in California Sun is the patron of the Rattlesnake shaman.

tory dance; if he dies, the society is in attendance.[59] In 1920 there were several members,* including two women. We have here a war Snake society.†

The two women Kumpawithlawen (also called Mafornin) do the work in the Town chief's ceremonial house and once a week in kiva feed the scalps. At the victory dance they carried the scalps, and in the presence of Pą'ide they chewed the scalps, and mixed what they spewed out with mud to make cornhusk-enveloped mud cakes as a medicine against anxiety. Although the Town chief may not kill, "not even an insect,"‡ he has general charge of the Scalps,§ can interpret the meaning of their "noises," and keeps the anti-worry medicine from the water used in scalp-washing, after he has decided to give fresh air to the scalps, i.e., to hold a scalp ceremony which is held irrespective of scalp-taking.‖

The scalp-takers, three old survivors of a sometime larger group, take part in the Scalp dance or ceremony and for a month take care of the scalps. There is no rain association with the scalps. They cure for toothache¶ and for worry. You strew corn meal before their kiva niche, feeding them, and your toothache goes; or, sick from worry or longing (? caused by the dead), you medicate with the water the scalps have been washed in.

* In 1937, four.

† And several Navaho (Apache too?) traits are indicated: Navaho warrior carried a bundle containing among other things pollen off the big snake that "lives in a den and never comes out"; moccasins painted with lightnings, etc.; "war talk" (for animals or other booty); two women in a war party (Hill, 10, 11, 12).

‡ And yet in a recently acquired picture he is represented holding a bow and arrow. He wears antelope horns, and his face is black with white spots. His headdress and buckskin suit are Plains-like. I think the war and peace functions of the Town chief have become confused, possibly by a Keresan peace overlay on a Tiwan war character or merely because Pą'ide, the war chief, has been for so long acting Town chief, peace chief.

§ In tale a scalp was brought to the Town chief; the scalp-taker was made Kumpa (withlawe) or second to the Town chief and succeeded to the Town chieftaincy (Lummis 3:169 ff.)

‖ Compare Maricopa, Spier 3:186.

¶ Compare p. 625, n. ‡.

The annually elected head war captain is called War chief of the Cane, and his cane of office, "Black Cane Old Man." He and the assistant war captains he has appointed—all together they are twelve, six from each moiety*—have the usual functions of executive messengers, of assisting in rabbit hunts, and of guarding against witches and intruders. "Cane war chief" has no ceremony but he may ask the curing societies to perform a ceremony of witch-finding against epidemic.

The Hunt chief and two assistants supply prayer-feathers and other offerings to individual hunters, and conduct a ceremony in which rabbits and, some say, a deer are "drawn in" to the chamber, for the Town chief. There are taboos on killing bears, eagles, and snakes.

The moiety organization, Black Eyes (winter) and Shure' (Gopher) (summer), are all-inclusive. A child belongs to the moiety of his parents if they belong to the same moiety, otherwise the eldest child is given to his father's moiety, subsequent children are given alternately in order of birth to both moieties. If a child is given to any other ceremonial group, he will also be given to the moiety his ceremonial father belongs to. Anyone may get a child for his moiety by spitting† into the child's mouth and sponsoring it at the moiety initiation or name-giving held after the Opening of the Ditch. A meal altar is used by the moiety chiefs, but they are without corn-ear fetishes which are possessed only by the Town chief and the curing societies. Each moiety chief is in charge of two kivas, a rectangular chamber and a "round house." The round kiva of Black Eyes is called Fog kiva; that of Gophers, Protecting Wall kiva. Moiety chiefs as well as the Town chief receive a visit of deference from the Town chief of the Laguna neighbors. Black Eyes use a dark drum, a turtle-shell rattle, and sparrowhawk feathers; Gophers, a red drum, a gourd rattle, and turkey feathers. (In the Spruce dance the rattle of the Black Eyes is water turtle, that of the Gophers, land turtle. The Black Eye prayer-stick is red willow; the Gopher stick, yellow willow.) Black Eyes talk backward. They are

---

* They too have canes, with colored strings, red beads, and turquoise.

† Spraying water? As at San Juan, see p. 911, n. ‡.

"elder brothers" to the Gophers who wear their hair in a poke on top because their prototypes butted a way up at the Emergence. In each moiety there are four masks worn by the grandfathers or watchmen, i.e., scouts, when they come out in the otherwise maskless kachina dances. The masks are of buckskin, painted a solid white, yellow, or red.* The masks are kept by the moiety chiefs in their kivas and used in the winter kachina dance. In one maskless kachina dance the spruce-gatherers on their return sing satirical songs and do burlesques. A maskless kachina impersonation and a maskless kachina dance are in charge of Chakabede. Various dances, kachina and others, are performed by moiety. The moiety chiefs, being kiva chiefs, are virtually dance chiefs. One rabbit hunt is in charge of moiety clowns.

The seven Corn groups are also all-inclusive, and, like the moieties, they have nothing to do with marriage choice. A person belongs to his mother's group, but, as in the case of the moiety, he or she has to be adopted ritually into the group,† at its solstice ceremony. The groups have special names, but they are named and associated conceptually and ritually with the corn of the five color-directions: Day People, white corn, east; Poplars and Shrikes‡, black corn, north; Earth People, yellow corn, west; Water-bubbling People and Cane-blowing People, blue corn, south; Corn People, Eagle People, Goose People, Shichu, speckled corn, up, down, and middle. These groups conduct retreats and ceremonies at the solstices, the Day People taking precedence by going in one day earlier than the others. The chief of Shichu takes part as noted in racing ceremonial; he presents a maskless kachina dance in which his godchildren dance;§ he co-operates in planting ritual and in the ceremony of

* According to a later picture, these Grandfather masks are white with short horizontal lines in red from the corners of the mouth and eyes. Nose and ears projecting, back of head showing—a European false face. See p. 1005, n. †.

† A child may be taken also by his father's sister to get a name from her Corn group. This aunt would have to give presents at dances.

‡ Not Magpies as stated in Parsons 52.

§ Compare Acoma and Hopi pattern, pp. 765, 865.

bringing down the moon. From Bat* he gets his power; inferably he represents or is closely associated with the Moon. The solstice ceremony of the group is the last day by one day, and, when ritual is performed in rotation by the chiefs, Shichu chief is the last in order.

There are two curing or medicine societies, Town Fathers and Laguna Fathers, who are recruited by convalescents and otherwise. They include a childbirth doctor, an Ant doctor, a Snake doctor who has power from Lightning, a veterinary,† a newhouse doctor, a hunt shaman, a detective or thief-catcher. The supernatural patron of the Town Fathers is Elder Sister Corn or Earth Mother, of the Laguna Fathers, Younger Sister Corn or Earth Mother. Besides cures, private and communal, ceremonies to quiet wind and to call rain, and initiation ceremonies, the Fathers perform solstice ceremonies, going in two days after the White Corn group.

Solstice ceremonies are conducted by the Corn groups and the curing societies according to the Julian calendar. And at this season Kumpa holds his Serpent ceremony to clean up the town, at which all the ceremonialists assist. Four maskless kachina dances are held, in winter for snow, in early spring for rain and crops, in summer for rain (a long ceremony), in autumn for frost; and, as noted, Laguna neighbors hold masked dances. There is an irrigation-ditch ceremony including a ritual of forced crops, also there is ritual shinny, both conducted by moiety organization, and the moiety chiefs conduct seasonal transfer ceremonies, in March and November. Ritual races in the spring, sporadically a scalp ceremony, and in the autumn a hunt ceremony. Animal dances are notably lacking. Catholic fiestas are fully observed— Guadalupe Day, Christmas, and, by Laguna people, Kings' Day; also the days of San Escapula, San Juan, San Pedro, San Agostín, San Agostinito, and All Souls. Like Santo Domingo, Is-

---

* Bat figures prominently in Navaho, but not in Pueblo, ceremonialism.

† Compare horse doctor of Western Apache (Goodwin, personal communication). Navaho believe that being thrown from a horse or being kicked by one means being pursued by a supernatural (Franciscan Fathers, 379). Compare Zuni Koyemshi power.

leta is tenacious of early Spanish custom. A bride is "asked for," church weddings are usual, a man is buried in the black cowl and knotted girdle of a friar. Candles are offered in the hills, and Dios competes in display of power with Węide, a high god of a sort, if not a kachina chief. Then there are the mountain-dwelling *thliwa* (kachina) and the Chiefs of the Directions, the prototypes of the moiety clowns, Sun, Moon, Stars, the Earth Mothers, the Water People, Wind, the animals—Bear, Mountain Lion, and Badger, Eagle and Rattlesnake—and the Dead.

TAOS[60]

In 1540 and 1541, Coronado's captains visited Taos and estimated the population at 15,000, "the most populous village of all that country." (Probably here as in other cases they overestimated, since in 1680 the population was 2,000.) People dressed in deer and buffalo skins; turkeys were not bred. (One family breeds turkeys today.) Early in the next century the mission of San Gerónimo was established.[61] Curiously enough, there is no tradition about the Rebellion of 1680, although Pope' planned or directed it from Taos and all but two of the seventy Spaniards near Taos were massacred. During the troublous period of "pacification" the townspeople twice abandoned the town for a fortified canyon. By 1707 the population was reduced to 700, and by 1765 to 505. In the eighteenth century the fighting was with Apache, Ute, and Comanche, and Mexicans were abandoning the region.* They returned, however, and, by 1815, 190 Mexican families were living on Taos lands,[62] basing their claims in part on support given against Comanche. By 1896, Mexicans were occupying half the Taos grant of twenty-seven and a half square miles. After the Treaty of Guadalupe, Mexican insurrectionists involved Taos in a fight with the newly instituted American authority. Some Taos men visited the American sheriff to ask for the release of two prisoners. On being refused, they killed the sheriff and prefect, and then went to the

---

* Thirty-six families were listed in 1765, but only two ranches were occupied in 1782, Las Trampas and San Fernando, and "these even promise a short existence, being on the Comanche line" (Thomas, 96).

PLATE XXVI

TAOS NORTH SIDE HOUSES, AND TAOS PEAK

house of Governor Bent and killed and scalped him and two other men.[63] When troops arrived, the population of Taos was considerably reduced, 150 being killed in escaping from town and 15 prisoners being executed.

The population of 674 is housed on either side of the little stream which flows into the Rio Grande from Blue Lake, twenty-seven miles to the northeast. The terraced houses pinnacle into four or five stories, but the upper, lightly built stories are used merely as storerooms, no longer as a retreat from enemies. Nor is the town wall a barrier against anything but foreign customs or ways of living. All townspeople are expected to live within the walls during the winter kiva ceremonies (Plate XXVI).

There are seven kivas, including one which is used merely as a shrine. The kivas of Big Earring People, Day or Sun People, Knife or Dripping Water People, are on the north side of the river; and the kivas of Feather People, Water People and Old Ax People are on the south side. The Big Earring Man is chief of the north side kivas. He is also "chief of the houses" or Town chief, the presiding officer of the Council. Big Earring Man and for the south side kivas Water Man and the Cacique who is head of the Catholic religion,* make nominations for the annual secular offices (Governor, Lieutenant-Governor, two War captains, ten junior War captains or executive messengers, and Fiscal). These nominees are voted on by the Council, a group of about thirty men "who sing and do not dance" and consist of the chiefs of the kiva memberships or societies, of the head secular officers, and of former Governors and Lieutenant-Governors. The Lieutenant-Governor acts as sheriff, whipping or fining offenders. Fines go to the officers. Sanctions at Taos are comparatively secular and strong-armed.

Each kiva has two chiefs. Every infant, male or female, is given to a kiva by its parents but not necessarily to the kiva either parent belongs to. Boys go through an eighteen-month period of observing certain taboos and of training for kiva mem-

---

* Spaniards or Mexicans appear to have picked their own chief (but see p. 1105), just as Americans did among many tribes, including Hopi. Among other Pueblos the secular officers were available.

bership; girls are not trained, nor do they attend kiva ceremonies, apparently they are called upon merely sporadically as
plasterers or to grind prayer-meal. For dance practice a girl goes
to the kiva of her father; a married woman, to the kiva of her
husband. The kiva groups take turns training or initiating, two
groups overlapping each year. Until they are trained, boys may
not take part in the February-March kiva dances or go on the
pilgrimage to Blue Lake. There is some adolescent ritual for
girls. The girl grinds for four days, protected from the sun, lest
after marriage she bear twins. She grinds corn and fasts from
Mexican food and from salt. Her dress and headdress are
changed, and she puts on the Kaiowa-like women's boots. Not
until after this ritual may a girl go into the springtide circle
dances or on the pilgrimage to the Lake.

Associated with each kiva are one or more small societies
whose members may be "trained" or untrained, i.e., they may
or may not belong to the large kiva membership. They sing
and need not dance. These societies are: Big Hail in Big Earring
and Water kivas; White Mountain in Day kiva; Black Eyes in
Knife kiva, mostly; Corn Mother in Knife, Feather, and Old Ax
kivas; Papta in Feather kiva; and Bear in Water kiva.

The Big Hail society is in charge of the period of forty days
which begins the end of November, and they are referred to as
winter people. (Spring, summer, and autumn groups are referred to, but the applications are obscure.) Big Hail society
performs a four-day ceremony for snow, and they array the Deer
Mothers and are in charge of them in the Deer dance.

The retreat of Big Hail society initiates the period of "staying
still" when all townspeople should move within the walls, and
nothing may be moved about, including wagons or automobiles,
no digging in town being allowed, or wood-chopping, or plaster-
ing. Singing and dancing are taboo; also body-painting and hair-
cutting. All the kiva societies are functioning (? for power or
medicine, *natoiyemu*). In conclusion, after Kings' Day, the Town
chief "takes his four days alone," and he and all the townspeople
bathe ritually in the river.

White Mountain People hold an exorcising ceremony after an

eclipse. The solar eclipse ceremony is attended by all the men; the lunar eclipse ceremony, by men, women, and children. This society is possessed of an anthropomorphic stone fetish called White Mountain. White Mountain was the place of the Emergence. The membership list of the White Mountain society and of the Day or Sun People kiva are almost identical. Sun and Moon are associated with hunting; the chief of the Day People is the Hunt chief.

Black Eyes are striped black and white, like Kossa or Koshare clowns; but their hair is bunched on either side of the head. Their clowning and disciplinary functions are typical. They may say "anything mean or funny"; they might throw any person intruding on them into the river or splash him with urine; they burlesque dance or deer hunt; they fetch absentees, at the Deer dance, or if anything is lost at this dance—the only one they come out for—they will look for it; they make food-collecting trips at the Deer dance and doctor sick boy infants who may be "given" to them; two or more cave-kept masks were once worn or associated with them;* they climb the pole on the Saint's Day. Their chief must belong to the Dripping Water People.

Little is known about the Corn Mother society and still less about the Papta society which in ceremony is identified with the Feather People. Since one of the functions of the Corn Mother society is gathering plant medicines and their name seems to refer to the fetishes of Keresan and Isletan curing societies, the society may be a curing society. Curing for ant sickness or for loss of consciousness is performed, but by whom is not known. Only well-paid doctors who cure on their own are mentioned, but it is almost certain that "medicine men" are associated with the groups who sing and do not dance. The Bear People have a ceremony in December for curing bear or snake bite (more probably bear-sent or snake-sent sickness).

* Possibly these masks were kachina and not clown masks. Jicarilla Apache have two kachina masks. The Taos masks were in charge of the Water People, who dance the maskless kachina dance (see below).

Bear society chief is the permanent War chief;* in war the society "worked" for the absent warriors, praying to Bear and Rattlesnake, and they "worked" during the Scalp dance. Trophies other than scalps were given the War chief for his bundle. Scalps are kept in the kiva the Bear society assembles in, Water kiva. On January 1 the Water People perform outdoors the maskless kachina dance, known at Isleta and at San Juan as Turtle dance. The Bear People chief who is also the War chief sings for the south-side racers in the relay races of Cross Day (May 3) and the Saint's Day (September 30), and the Knife People (Black Eyes) sing for the north-side racers. A Bear man and a Black Eye "brush" the runners. The races are for Sun and Moon.

It is not known if there is any distinctive society associated with Old Ax kiva People, but the kiva group functions distinctively in a ceremony against snow-drying winds, in the Earth Mother (or Sun-Moon) ceremonies of spring, and in initiating the summer-rain retreats by all the kiva groups. Old Ax People are called the Grandfathers "because they are the beginners."† They are possessed of an anthropomorphous stone image called Summer Eagle-tail. Old Ax People and Day People are or were associated with the Buffalo dance or with buffalo hunting.

Permission to dance Buffalo or Deer or saint's-day dance must be formally obtained from the Town chief. Town chief and Water Man conduct in alternate years the August pilgrimage to Blue Lake, where live the Thlatsina (kachina) and some of the dead. The summer rain retreats are going on at this time, and, according to one account, the kiva chief who is engaged in one has to take charge of the pilgrimage, completing his own ceremony on his return.

The seventh, disused kiva belonged to the Red Painted People, who had warlike functions, getting out scalp-pole dancers and ducking shirkers.‡ They were painted red and offered

---

* Just as at Isleta the chief of the Snake society is the permanent war chief.

† Future inquirers should keep in mind the age-class society of the Plains.

‡ Compulsion of skulking dancers, by whipping, is noted among southern Utes (Spier 2:270).

red pigment together with pollen and feathers to the Night People: Stars and inferably Moon. Probably this extinct group may be equated with the Shuré of Isleta who duck shirkers in the irrigation round dance, with the Kwirana (Kurena) of Keres and Tewa, if not with the Tsanati of Jicarilla Apache, a Pueblo-like dance group figuring in their Bear ceremony.

Into this group or into the Taos Bear society, scalp-takers apparently were not initiated; consistently with Plains practice, they and other warriors formed a merely temporary group. In the scalp dance the scalper was the "first man"; other warriors ranked in the order they came up to the dead enemy, or touched the scalper on his return, an expression of counting coup. War regalia taken from the dead enemy were given to the War chief for his bundle.

The Taos pantheon consists of "our fathers" or Sun, Moon, and Stars, of Earth Mother, the Stone Men, Red Bear, Rattlesnake and Big Water Man (or Bear), described as a monstrous frog with functions of the Horned Water Serpent; Spider, Gopher, and Coyote; Echo Boy, Dirt Boy, the Winds, Red Boy, and the Cloud Boys (Thlatsina) including Lightning or Thunder (Thlatsi). In Taos tales as in Tewa tale Sun as he travels places his twin sons on either hand. He gives them a hunter's medicine bundle. Sun is addressed by hunters. Moon is asked to mature the crops. (In the Jicarilla story about the relay race which they have borrowed from Taos, the two sides represent Sun and Moon. If Sun wins, it will be a good season for game; if Moon wins, the crops will prosper.) Earth, "our mother for corn," is addressed also by hunters. She was also prayed to in war, as were Sun and Stars. Once Morning Star killed seven Redheads* so that the Corn Girls could bring in the heads on a pole. The "Stone Men," the Hayunu' (? little Kaye', Tewa for spirit stones), are presumably the War gods. The Stone Men images in their mountain shrine are prayed to for strength and life. Formerly they were addressed in war. Bear and Snake are also associated with war. Big Water Man causes landslide and flood. Spider and

* Aztecs represented enemies with red hair. Redhead enemies figure in several Taos tales. The Coyote-Firewood Hopi clan are called Redheads.

Gopher are helpful old women; Coyote appears in his usual role of trickster and nuisance; but he is also helpful, bringing the buffalo to Taos* and by his calls foretelling weather and coming events. Echo Boy is asked for clothing; Filth Boy lives in the small refuse pit at the house threshold and is addressed by hunters or their wives and given food. Wind Old Woman causes rheumatism; but Refuse Wind is the terrible "sickness man" who brings smallpox and other epidemics. He is exorcised by aspersing outdoors. Red Boy or Spotted Corn Boy may be the war god kachina of the West. (Red Boy is an outstanding *hash-chin* [? kachina] of the Jicarilla.) The *thlatsina* (kachina) live under lake or on the mountains. They bestow blessings. They are not the dead; but men dying on the mountains and devout men (? chiefs) may become *thlatsina*. Suicides too. The *thlatsina* "came up with all the others."

Only fragments of the Taos Emergence myth have been recorded. Red Person (? Red Boy) led the people up from the Lake at White Mountain after Black Eyes scouted ahead to see if Earth Mother was soft or hard. The people scattered by kiva groups. The Feather People settled above Ranchos; from the south the Water People swam as fish up the rivers,† becoming people after they were switched with bean vines.

---

* Coyote liberates the buffalo in Lipan Apache myth. Formerly Lipan Apache lived near Jicarilla Apache (Opler).

† This associates them with the kachina cult they are in charge of. Compare the Zuni myth of the origin of kachina as river creatures (p. 222), and the curious Tewa reference to ceremonialists as "Fish people."

CHAPTER VIII

VARIATION AND BORROWING

Some of the interpueblo variation now familiar to us may be put down to differences between observers or historians as well as to unequal opportunities for observation. Observation differs within a single pueblo, take Zuni. Cushing, the poet and craftsman, did not see the same facts at Zuni as the museum collectors who were there at the same time. Thirty years later Kroeber visited Zuni and devoted himself to those aspects of culture which in the interval had become more significant to the trained observer of Indian life, to language and social organization. Cushing, Stevenson, and Kroeber—to these three would any culture look alike! Familiar with the medicine-bundle complex of Plains Indians, Kroeber could see homologues in the cane or corn-ear fetishes of Zuni and appreciate the significance of their role in the ceremonial life. But the actual use of these fetishistic bundles or of other ritual objects, Kroeber unfortunately had no opportunity to see, as had Stevenson or, among Hopi, Voth and Stephen. These scrupulous observers of Hopi ritual were allowed to be present at kiva altar ritual; Stephen was initiated into three societies and was himself the subject of curing ritual, as he gallantly records before he dies. Is Zuni ritual less intricate than Hopi, or is it merely that part of its complexity has not been recorded? Matilda Stevenson, who usually failed to distinguish between what she saw and what she heard about,* was far from being an accurate recorder, nor did she have any facility for interpretation or evaluation. As described by her, the ritual of Zuni societies appears to vary considerably from Hopi

* Nor does she distinguish between her own records and those of her deceased husband, James Stevenson, who made two field trips to Zuni in 1879 and 1881, of six months each. At this time no townsman spoke English; two spoke Spanish fluently, two spoke it a little (Stevenson 2:20, n. b). According to Bourke, all the older men spoke a little Spanish (Bourke 2:201).

ritual—actually does it vary so much, at least the ritual of the Rain chieftaincies, including the kachina cult? The ritual of the Zuni curing society, we now know, is more like that of the Keresan society than Stevenson led us to suppose, good as were her opportunities to compare Sia and Zuni ritual. Search for the witch-stolen heart—in fact, the whole witchcraft complex—is characteristic of the Zuni curing society as well as of the Keresan society. But enough crying over Stevenson! Fortunately, more comparable reports may be expected of recent students who have had more or less the same training, who go over one another's work, and who are learning the tribal languages. Bunzel's Zuni texts bring out many parallels heretofore unknown between Zuni and other pueblos.

However, all students, old and new, have been faced with the baffling inequality of conditions for inquiry that exists in the eastern and northern pueblos compared with the western. In the East the very existence of societies, let alone their ritual, is hard to come by—Keres and Tanoan peoples are so much more secretive than Zuni or Hopi. When the Tanoans borrowed the Keresan society as at Isleta and Jemez and in Tewan towns, we infer that they took over the ritual complex or most of it, and the same is true of the kachina cult; we infer—as yet we do not know. During years of inquiry by several investigators no medicine man has been of aid, not a single thoroughly informed, frank, and reliable informant has been found. Not a single inside ceremony has been witnessed by any ethnologist, excepting at Sia, nor even an outside kachina dance. At Zuni I was invited into the dressing-room of kachina* impersonators as they made up; whereas at Jemez a piece of sacking was hung across the high little window of my temporary prison lest I see the feet of the Deer kachina as they came down the hillside trail. On First Mesa, Stephen not only saw the women's burlesque war dance but was allowed into their kiva and initiated into their society. How different my approach to the women's burlesques among Tewa! References by timid and unwilling informants were so meager that I could not even learn whether or not a Women's society exists at San Ildefonso corresponding to that at Santa

* Accurately speaking, near-kachina, the Navaho dancers.

Clara. Only on my third visit to the Tewa, from a chance word to a visitor from Hano who repeated it, did I get any assurance that mask dances actually occur at San Juan.

Of greater intrinsic interest than the handicap or attitude of outside observers is the attitude of Pueblos themselves toward variation, and their own capacity for observation. In general, I have found them quite blind to the religious differences between pueblos; only a few spectacular distinctions are noticed. "We have no Bear medicine like that to the south," I have been told in Taos. That the "Snake dance" is peculiar to Hopi and "Shalako" to Zuni (the Hopi borrowing is overlooked) is generally known, also that Western Pueblos allow Whites to see kachina dances, thereby falling away from their *costumbres*, the Eastern Pueblo will add resentfully, appreciating that some of his own secrets are being betrayed. But the eastern, say the Isletan, visitor to Zuni, is unaware that the functions of the Town chieftaincy are far more decentralized at Zuni than at Isleta or that the Zuni clan is not the same as the Zuni society. Even the Isletan visitor to Taos will tell you that they have Corn groups there as at Isleta, overlooking the fact that the Taos kiva-society groups have no female membership, Bear society excepted, and are not based on maternal descent. When Crow-Wing and I set out from First Mesa to visit the other Hopi pueblos, he told me that I would find just the same ceremonies and the same clans in all the pueblos. "They *have* to be the same," said this witness to Gestalt psychology, and it was not until he interpreted for me on Second Mesa that he admitted they were not the same. Similarly, Stephen was told by Sikya-piki, the Snake chief of Shipaulovi, *who was also a member of the Walpi Snake society*, that the Snake rituals of Shipaulovi and Walpi were the same.* This characteristic assumption of homogeneity or lack of any conception of heterogeneity† is, I presume,

---

* "They are not," Stephen curtly remarks, after pointing out in his day-by-day record many differentiations.

† One of Dr. White's Acoma informants once told of the shock of surprise he got when, after talks with White, he became conscious all of a sudden of Pueblo variability. Certain variations he had known, but the concept of variability was utterly strange.

as it is frequently among White Americans, an expression of tribalism or nationalism, arising from the feeling that all being, let us say, Hopi, all are alike, all *have* to be alike. And as the townspeople are disinclined to discuss ceremonial affairs with outsiders, the assumption of likeness is never tested. The attitude within the group, town or tribal, converges with the attitude of Bandelier, who held that from peublo to pueblo the variations were but slight and negligible, or with the attitude of many Southwestern archeologists who, indifferent as they are to knowledge of language, social organization, or religion, transmit the impression that but for difference in pottery or building Pueblo culture has been uniform throughout the centuries.

The equalizing attitude of the White man together with certain terms he uses to describe the Pueblos has had an effect in this connection on Pueblo conceptions. Take the Spanish term "cacique." Ask any Keres about the Tewa cacique, and you will find that he knows nothing about the dual chieftaincy of Tewa not only because he assumes that the Keresan principle of single headship is general but because, if ever he happen to ask a Tewa about chieftaincy, he would use in speaking to him the term "cacique," which implies the single, not the dual, headship. The use of the term "clan" in the northern pueblos is another verbal source of confusion. At Taos, where there are no clans, and even among Tewa, where the clan is negligible, this English term is supposed both by Indians and by Whites to refer to societies, so that even anthropologists have been misled at Taos into listing societies as clans. Any English-speaking citizen of Taos would likewise assure a Pueblo visitor, say from Laguna, that there were clans at Taos, "but we do not speak about them," he might add, as Lucinda of Isleta remarked about the Corn groups of her pueblo so significantly that I am requoting her: "At Laguna they always ask us right away about our clams [the usual pronunciation for clans], but we don't tell them." Thus from characteristic secretiveness* complicated by verbal con-

---

* Variation in secretiveness from tribe to tribe corresponds somewhat to variation of intensity of belief in witchcraft, and I surmise a causal relationship. Ritual may be invalidated through witchcraft. Fear of practical interference

fusion, Isleta and Laguna remain unaware of the differences in their social classification.

Often secretiveness conspires with erring evaluation to render faulty the observation of the townsman. From some minor similarity or dissimilarity he will infer general homogeneity or heterogeneity. Zuni Shalako and Hopi Nima'n are entirely different kachina ceremonies, but a Hopi will describe Shalako as the Zuni Nima'n or Home-going ceremony because in both ceremonies the kachina leave town en masse. (But see too p. 972, n.†.) An Isletan visitor to Taos reported on the existence of the same Corn groups at Taos as at Isleta because he found retreats being observed at Taos at the same season as at Isleta: the ceremonial groups were "going in" the first week in December, so, of course, thought he, they were the same groups. I am reminded of the attitude of a Taos man in regard to a visitor from China. Long ago, opined the Pueblo, his people and the Chinese must have spoken the same language because today they have the same word for "queue." The occurrence of a like song or even a few words in a song will lead to the inference that the ceremony as a whole is the same. Similarly, the import of a minor differentiation may be greatly exaggerated. When Lusteti of Zuni and I were met at the head of the Acoma trail by our host, as we walked along I overheard Lusteti inquire of the Acoman about the direction of their Kothluwala, their lake of the kachina and the dead. The muttered answer I did not hear, but later Lusteti told me with derision that their sacred lake was only a little pool somewhere below the mesa. That it was not a large lake to which pilgrimage was made gave him a sense of differing from

---

combines, of course, with fear of magical interference. In the East, Franciscans and Mexican neighbors have aroused both fears. "Americans" are rarely thought of as witches, but they have frequently interfered with ceremonial, and so they, too, fall under the ban of secretiveness as a protection against "bad people," i.e., witches.

Idle curiosity may be just a bore. When Pedro Baca was guiding me over the range from Jemez to Santa Clara he pointed out an outcrop of fantastically eroded rocks as "where they were turned into stone" (the inhospitable townspeople by the war gods), and then to my question he shut up as tight as you or I might do on being asked to explain fully a reference to Sodom and Gomorrah.

the Acoma out of all proportion to the fact which arrested his attention, a familiar tourist attitude. And I doubt if he ever learned at all about the more important difference, i.e., that the dead of Acoma go not under water to a kachina dance hall but back to their great Mother underground.

I have been giving scattering illustrations of the ignorance of one pueblo about the other. We should know much more about this as a factor in interpueblo variation and borrowing. People do not borrow what they are unaware of. Esoteric kiva ritual lends itself far less to imitation than does the public exhibition, say a kachina dance. The openness of the kachina performances has been, of course, a factor in the spread of the cult* and a reason for its comparative uniformity. In war or medicine societies there is undoubtedly a greater degree of differentiation; such groups are comparatively secret, although a Hopi society is as hospitable as a Hopi clan, although Zuni and Keresan societies entertain foreign medicine men at initiations,[1] even intra-society visitors† being invited, and although doctors treat patients from another pueblo or go abroad to practice, sometimes to live.

In such ways single rites or methods may be learned and perhaps copied, as in fact we find Hopi and Taos doctors making use of Keresan curing methods; but group organization and ceremonial are not always imparted.‡ Not even the group name is learned. Taos people sometimes go to Santa Clara for Bear medicine, but they do not know if the doctor they visit is Fire

---

* Only in Santo Domingo and Sandía, as far as I know, has there ever been any exclusion of other Pueblos; here visitors from Isleta and Taos, who are without kachina masks, have been excluded from masked dances.

† At the initiation of the Big Firebrand society in November, 1891, Shuma'-kwe and Little Firebrand society members were present (Stevenson 2:498).

‡ An interesting instance is that of the Ant doctor of Zuni living at Santo Domingo and extending his practice to San Felipe and other towns (White 3:40, n. 48; White 4:67–68). He was visited by his Zuni society, and, when he refused to return to Zuni, they confiscated his paraphernalia. He refused to initiate anyone and thereby institute a permanent society in Santo Domingo. Juan Rey, the Laguna stick-swallower who went to Isleta at the time of the Great Split, did impart his ritual; when he planned to desert Isleta for Sandía, his paraphernalia were also confiscated (Parsons 47:611–12).

or Flint. When Hunke of Zuni, a Ne'wekwe doctor, visits Laguna with his Laguna wife, I doubt if they compare Ne'wekwe with Laguna Koshare organization. In 1921 the chief of the Jemez clown Tabö'sh visited Taos for the San Gerónimo fiesta. He saw pole-climbing by the Black Eyes (some day it may be introduced into Jemez) but I bet he learned nothing about the Black Eyes organization. In accordance with Pueblo manners or habit, probably he asked no questions. Pueblo friends well aware that I "know something" about other pueblos never ask me questions about organization and only the most trivial questions, if any, about ceremonial. Pueblos, like other Indians,* do not learn by question and answer.† And, of course, questioning in itself, any Pueblo would think, tends to reveal too much.

Where there is no curing and no public dance or ceremony, as in the rituals of the Rain chieftaincies of Zuni or in the inside altar rituals of Hopi societies, differentiation is probably greatest. But for the fact that the genius of Taos does not tend to ceremonialism and so may be content with marginal scraps, not developing anything on its own, we should expect to find Taos ceremonies the most distinctive of all, for they are the most exclusive, no visitors being admitted, not even kindred from Isleta, nor are Taos ceremonies held in dwellings, as often happens elsewhere, with members of the household coming and going and looking on, if so minded.

Between West and East the conspicuous and consequential differentiation in the ceremonial organization, as in the entire social organization, is the clan or kin in the West as a conceptual and functional unit as against in the East the society or the moiety-kiva group. However, at Zuni society and kiva groups are co-ordinate in general importance with clan or kinship groups. Paramount social control is vested in the kin groups constituting the major Rain chieftaincies, and clanship or lineage has figured in curing society organization, more formerly, perhaps,

* Note that among Papago, for a junior to ask questions of a senior is considered forward and discourteous (Underhill 3).

† And here is the simple reason why riddles do not take among Indians; they are resisted like any other form of questioning.

than today.* Among Hopi, clanship is to the fore, but even
here it is primarily the maternal family within the clan rather
than the clan as a whole that counts. Among western Keres the
clan begins to disappear from cult; among eastern Keres and
the other Rio Grande pueblos it practically does not figure, and,
as among western Keres also, the principle of paternal descent
comes forward in determining kiva or moiety membership. At
Isleta bilateral descent figures in moiety membership with the
paternal line preferred. In the other ceremonial groups, the
Corn groups, into one of which every Isletan child is taken,
matrilineal descent rules; but, as these groups do not affect
marriage choice, they are not clans in the general Pueblo sense.

At clanless Taos the office of one of the major chiefs, the
Cacique, is hereditary, from father to son, and there is a tendency in practice if not in theory for a son to succeed his father in
the two major chieftaincies of north- and south-side kivas. Kiva
membership which is partially identified with society membership is determined by dedication in childhood, as is kiva membership at Zuni. Parental dedication figures elsewhere in the East,
but cure or convalescence is the basic principle of admission into
the curing societies of the East and Zuni. Hopi join the societies
their kachina or Wüwüchim godparent belongs to. Trespass
and, except at Zuni, mere volunteering are other recruiting devices. Cases of volunteering seem to be for the most part, if not
always, cases of vow or promise to join, given convalescence or
other benefit. Societies not specifically for curing, but with
curing functions like the War society of Isleta, may be recruited
similarly. Among Tewa and at Cochiti even the other moiety or
another clan may be joined in hope of benefit. There are traces
of this point of view in connection with dedication to the kiva-
kachina society of Zuni and to the Hopi tribal or Wüwüchim
societies; but, on the whole, joining a group through vow is distinctly an Eastern trait.

---

* For example, the Frog clan owned and was responsible for the upkeep of a
spring near Black Rock, from which a clansman would fetch water for ritual
purposes (Stevenson 2:59, 60)—all quite in the Hopi mode. The spring was
destroyed when the Black Rock dam was built.

The extent to which women are involved or share in the ceremonial life varies greatly from one cluster of pueblos to another. Where clanship, matrilineal clanship, prevails and figures in religion as among Hopi and to a lesser extent at Zuni and among western Keres, women have a larger part and interest in ceremonial. Fetishes are kept or "handed" within the maternal family and looked after by the women, and throughout the ceremonial life women have more functions to perform, both ritualistic and housewifely. Among eastern Keres, where clanship is merely a principle of exogamy, although there may be more female than male society members, as in Santo Domingo, the females are referred to as "outside" and have purely economic functions. At Jemez and among Tewa, where clanship is even weaker, women have a place theoretically in the societies, actually there are few women members; women attend the ceremonies of the pseudo-clan Corn groups of Isleta and have some functions, in the rest of the ceremonial organization women take little or no part; in clanless Taos women have no part even in theory in the kiva society system on which the ceremonial life of the town is based. However, in all the Tanoan pueblos, Jemez excepted, a few women are assigned important war or scalp functions, and the Tewa women called Red Bow Youth control appointments to ceremonial office.

At Taos more men than women own houses; in the other Eastern towns you find house proprietorship about equally divided between the sexes with a preponderance of female proprietors as you move west; in the West with recent exceptions no men own houses. A Hopi chief keeps his paramount fetish in the house of his mother or sister, the clan mother; or, let us say, the son, brother, or uncle of the woman in whose house the fetish is kept is chief of the ceremony. Between chieftaincy, fetish custody, houseownership by women, matrilineal clanship, and participation in the ceremonial life by women there are close functional relations and, I suggest, genetic relations as well.[2] Exclusion of women from ceremonial, houseownership by men, patrilineal moiety, and tendency to inheritance of chieftaincy in the male line is the opposite complex as held by northern Pueblos.

Tribal initiation affects the size of the ceremonial groups. Where every boy has to be initiated into some group, as into one of the four constituent societies of the Hopi Wüwüchim, or at Zuni, Acoma, or Taos into one of the six kiva groups, group memberships are necessarily large. The Corn groups and moieties of Isleta are large for analogous reason, likewise of course the moiety kiva groups of Keres and Tewa. Jemez clown society memberships are large, inferably as an effect of the moiety principle; and yet the clown groups of Isleta and of Tewa and Keres, in which the moiety principle is also expressed, are small. Why there are not more "Grandfathers" at Isleta, I do not know, possibly because the "Grandfathers," likewise the temporary K'apio, are borrowed groups. Tewa and Keresan clown groups are small because they are controlled by the curing society rather than by moiety organization. The membership of curing or shamanistic society is small everywhere except at Zuni. Here the principle of paying as you go, i.e., of paying the doctor outright has vogue only in minor ailments; he who has been "saved" is initiated into the society. Consequently, the society that effects many cures will have a large membership, including women. In the Eastern curing societies, on the other hand, where the doctor is more usually paid down and recruiting depends on vow or on trapping, there are few members.

The organization of the society varies in its headship. Among Hopi there is the single head or chief as in the Wüwüchim societies or a plural chieftaincy as in the Antelope society or Lakon society; at Zuni, excepting the rain and war societies, there are the chief, his "speaker," and two guards or warriors loaned from the War society, a pattern of four; among Keres, the chief has usually one assistant; among Tewa and at Jemez the chief has two assistants, his right-hand man and his left-hand man.

In war organization, headship varies; it may be single, dual, or plural. The War Brothers have been prototypes for the Zuni war society, giving it as heads, Elder brother Bow chief and Younger brother, and the myth also finds expression in the temporary impersonations of the Hopi war ceremony, although there is but a single head to the Hopi war society or societies. In the East the Outside chiefs or War captains vary in number, but in several Keresan towns there are two who are called by the names of the War Brothers, Masewi and Oyoyewi. Women scalp ritualists are most prominent among the Tanoans, possibly because among them female effects on warriors were most deleterious. Hence both abuse of the scalp by women and use of it in making medicine.* Tanoans were closest to the Plains tribes among whom women figured in the conventions of war.

There is a single-headed Town chieftaincy everywhere except at Zuni, where three men form the chieftaincy, and among Tewa, where the principle of moiety classification is expressed in a dual chieftaincy. The Zuni-Hopi office of Crier or Speaker chief is lacking in the East. At Zuni the office is most important, combining with the office of Sun-watcher.

This Sun chieftaincy at Zuni is a clan office not in the usual way through a maternal family but through appointment by the high Rain chiefs from the Dogwood clan at large. As to succession in the Town chieftaincy, we find matrilineal succession in the West and at Taos a tendency toward patrilineal succession. Among Keres, as usual, the system is mixed, the Town chief is drawn from a particular clan (Acoma), or the office shows clan affiliation of some kind, or, most commonly, it shows society affiliation, or it is independent of either society or clan. Tewa Town chieftaincies are quite independent of group affiliations, being recruited by vow or dedication. In the West and at Taos the Town chief appears as a member of a council of chiefs rather than as an outstanding figure. The Town chief of Taos who is chief of the three kivas of the north side shares authority with the chief of the three kivas of the south side and with the cacique or exponent of Spanish or southern Pueblo influence. Town chief supremacy is a Keresan (and Isletan) trait.

The authority of the Town chieftaincy varies, and in general the form of chieftaincy or headship varies, but throughout the

---

* But this must remain highly speculative until more information is secured about the Bear society of Taos and the Tewan society of Red Bow Youth.

pueblos the relations of the society members to the chiefs appear much the same: the chiefs are responsible for the proper performance of ceremonial, the other members of the society are their errand men or helpers. Chiefs go into retreat as a rule before other members, and upon them ritual restrictions bear most heavily. Theirs the responsibility and theirs the control. Custodians of the fetishes or what the people live by, with knowledge of ritual technique, of song and of prayer, orators or experts in "hard words," the chiefs are "valuable men" (West), "powerful men" (East). As office is lifelong, the chiefs are generally found among the older men; among hereditary-minded Hopi there are regency practices. Gerontocracy is not diminished whatever the differences in the prevailing unit of social organization, whether clan or lineage, as in the West, moiety as in the North, or as in the middle area, shamanistic society.

How do these three units or organizing principles lend themselves in general to the social organization and temper as we compare the more socialized West with the more individualized East? Of the three—clanship, moiety, and shamanism—shamanism favors individualism; it is of personal benefit to patient and doctor, the patient being cured or otherwise benefited, the doctor, paid with goods or prestige from "knowing something" or having power. At Zuni, shamanism has been accepted but is greatly socialized by giving the patient to the curing society, by large membership lists, and by being related functionally to noncuring groups; among Hopi, shamanism is of even less consequence, although a curing function attaches to the weather-control societies. Among Keres, Jemez, and Tewa the shamanistic society occupies a kind of middle ground, showing an individualistic trend in curing, and in weather ritual a communal trend which Keres consider the more important (White). The importance of the Keresan Town chief, the supreme weather or seasons man, who is not necessarily a member of any society, also indicates this attitude. At Taos, curing is individualistic, but there is an eclipse ceremony for the purification of all; Bear People and Black Eyes have cures; and it is quite possible that other kiva-societies have special curing functions in the mode of the Hopi society. The cosmic control that prevails at Taos, control of sun and moon, weather and flood, is community service, through kiva-moiety organization.

Outside of Taos there is no organization by kiva among Pueblos; kivas are associated with prevailing social units, more particularly with moiety and clan. The society in the West, especially the Hopi society, may borrow a kiva for its ceremony but the eastern society of Keresan type does not. Scalps are kept in kiva only by Tiwa. Dance groups, especially kachina groups, make use of kivas so habitually that between a given kiva and a given dance group a fixed association may develop. This has occurred most notably at Zuni. The Zuni kiva chief is the dance director. Zuni kivas are little but dance clubs within the Kachina society.

The Kachina cult varies a great deal according to how it fits into the prevailing social organization, by clan, by moiety, or by society. In the West masks are cared for by lineages within the clan, by kiva dance chiefs, or by individual owners; in the East they are cared for by societies, by the Town chief who may or may not be connected with a society or who is a moiety chief, or, in the case of clown masks, by clown societies or by moiety chiefs. Since kiva chiefs in Keresan towns are practically moiety chiefs, kiva-kept masks are also moiety-kept. Kachina dramatization including recital is particularly elaborate at Zuni and is perpetuated, perhaps developed, through self-filling cult societies or permanent kiva directors. And only at Zuni is there any thoroughgoing individual ownership of masks, the mask being secured through ritual and being buried at death, inferably for use at Kachina town. This identifies a large group of the dead, but not all, with kachina. "Poor" people, i.e., nonceremonialists, may get value through acquiring a mask (if they are not economically too poor). The Kachina cult is set off quite generally as the "poor" man's cult.

The lack of curing societies of Keresan-Zuni type among Hopi results in several differentiations in its Kachina cult. Hopi kachina are "brought in" not by society members but by permanent deputies of the Kachina society chief, by Powamu "kachina fathers." There are no society altars or choirs; all kachina groups must sing for themselves. Solitary dancers have none to sing for them; they can only "go around." The presentation of Zuni Shalako on First Mesa is necessarily much altered by the lack of societies. All the masks are kept in a Badger clan house. The woman of this house is known as Kachina mother, which would be strange to a Zuni but is consistent with the Hopi maternal-house complex. Shalako is obviously an overlay on First Mesa; so, less obviously, is most of the kachina cult, and not only on First Mesa.

Given numerous ceremonial groups and comparatively large memberships, the ceremonial calendar will naturally be fuller than where a few groups of small membership await their turn to perform their ceremony. The prevalence of the principle of sequence or succession in celebration (Western) or of the principle of contemporaneous celebration (Eastern) is another factor in calendrical determination. Whether the ceremonial is predominantly for weather control and crops or for curing also affects the character of the calendar, curing ceremonial occurring more sporadically than seasonal ceremonial. For these reasons the calendars of the western pueblos, Hopi and Zuni, seem alike fuller and more set than those of the eastern pueblos, where the shamanistic society prevails with its comparatively small membership, its principle of contemporaneous celebration, and its self-determined dates for initiation, for exorcising or purification, or for other ceremonial. In so far as the shamanistic society functions for weather control as, for example, at Jemez, or everywhere at the solstices, its calendar is more rigidly determined by the general calendrical sequence.

Differing degrees of solstitial observance make for variation in the calendar. In the West the solstices are carefully observed on a horizon calendar, and they determine ceremonial incidence: the winter solstice ceremony itself; at Zuni, the summer pilgrimage to the Lake, the initial rain retreats, and the initial summer-rain dances; among Hopi, the completion of planting and the ceremony of the departure of the kachina. To the east and north, solstice observation has less significance. There are references to the Sun's house and to his "turning," but use of a horizon calendar has either lapsed or was never developed. The important winter ceremonial occurs at the beginning of December, not at the close. The pilgrimage to the Lake at Taos is the end of August, not the end of June, and, unlike the Zuni pilgrimage, it probably has nothing to do with solar observation. Throughout the East very little attention is paid to the summer solstice. Solstitial observation and ceremonial are Western and particularly Zuni traits.

There is considerable variation in the calendar as affected by the Kachina cult. The Hopi kachina season is from the winter solstice to the summer solstice; the Zuni kachina season is unrestricted in theory except for very brief ritual periods, but in practice there are no kachina performances during about two autumn months and two late spring or early summer months. Acoma confines kachina performances to three periods, summer and winter solstices and an autumn period, or, like Zuni, presents a dramatic ceremony at long intervals; again, as at Zuni, the summer kachina are more sacred than the winter kachina, who are called, not kachina, but K'oᴃishtaiya, and come to cure or strengthen rather than to bring rain by dancing. In the East there are no distinctive kachina ceremonials, rather the kachina come out as a conclusion to other ceremonials, since the societies while in retreat for rain are supposed to fetch the kachina from underground Shipap. Some of the kachina performances of Keres and Tewa correspond with the Catholic calendar of Christmas or Eastertide. The saint's-day dances observed in the East give an aspect to the calendar it does not have in the West. As these dances or festivals combine with trading and with the tradition of hospitality, they are very favorable to interpueblo communication and borrowing, and celebrations are quite uniform.

By and large in the East the ceremonials are short and simple compared with the long, elaborate, and dramatic ceremonials of the West. And yet this distinction is easily exaggerated, for the esoteric term of ceremonial in the East is less well known than the corresponding term in the Western ceremonial, and the sixteen- or eight-day term of the Western ceremonial contains many nonritualistic days. Besides there is more ceremonial disintegration in the East and extinct ceremonies are cut down in description, an important point for students of variation to hold in mind.

However, dramatization in the East, if it occurs at all, appears to be of a type different from the performance of the West. Possibly Eastern rites and paraphernalia have in themselves a higher dramatic content, with a closer and more arousing mythical reference, in the manner of the Navaho chant or, let us say, as the cross carried in procession or kissed on the altar would differ from a dramatization of the Crucifixion.

One outstanding difference in ritual goes with, perhaps necessitates, the comparatively longer Western ceremony or retreat—the greater use of prayer-stick and prayer-feather. A large part of the time in retreat is spent in making these prayer offerings which are much more elaborate and much more numerous in Western than in Eastern ritual. In the Northeast, in fact, the prayer-stick figures little if at all; only feather bunches or loose feathers are offered. In the middle area, among Keres and at Jemez, only the chiefs make prayer-sticks or tie feathers. The Jemez word for shaman is feather-tier. The prayer-stick is more developed at Zuni than elsewhere. A far greater number of prayer-sticks is offered, and more craftsmanship is displayed. Keresan and even Hopi technique is inferior to the technique of Zuni. The sticks are less carefully cut, the feathers less beautifully mounted, and fewer feathers are used. Sticks are not made for the dead by or for each member of the household, as at Zuni, nor at the solstice ceremonials are sticks made as abundantly as at Zuni by "poor persons," persons unattached to ceremonial groups. There are no yearlong impersonators to make monthly offerings as at Zuni; only at Zuni are monthly offerings made by curing members. Yet the prayer-stick painted with designs as elaborate as corn ear or clouds with falling rain is peculiar to Hopi. So is the solstice prayer-stick for deceased kindred.

The use of the duck feather reversed in the kachina stick is confined to Zuni and Laguna. At Zuni, except in the Ne'wekwe society, feathers are never bound at the butt end of the stick, a characteristic feature elsewhere. Usually this butt-bound feather is turkey and such features are probably always thought of as the blanket or clothes of the stick. The spacing of feather pendants down the length of the stick occurs among Hopi, also at Isleta and Jemez, probably one of the many things brought home by the eighteenth-century refugees. The use of prayer-feathers,* particularly trail prayer-feathers or road-markers, is characteristic of Hopi.

The use of pine needles in prayer-feathers is confined, as far as I know, to Hopi, and among them the use of plants on prayer-sticks is conspicuous, but at Jemez and Zuni grasses are now and again bound in. The bead offering† seen on a Zuni prayer-stick is not found elsewhere, except rarely at Isleta or Laguna.

Everywhere meal is sprinkled on prayer-sticks, but peculiar to Hopi is the tying of a package of meal and honey to the stick. Spurting honey over sticks or holding it in mouth while smoking is notable among Hopi, but honey and meal are placed on the cotton wrapping distinctive of Jemez sticks.

The outstanding feature of depositing prayer-sticks, in the West, more particularly at Zuni, is the "planting" of the offering so that part of stick and feathers is buried. Even in stone shrines, sticks are usually "planted," not merely thrown in. In a disused Laguna shrine I found such a planted stick; but Laguna sticks today are placed in rock crevices or in a crater pit, under a cedar or in a little hollow weighed down with stones. Similarly the only Sia sticks I have found were lying unplanted, in shrine or on hillside. Jemez sticks are not planted, except those, it is said, for cornfields. Jemez sticks are placed in very roughly made shrines or under cedars; kachina sticks are cast into the river. Commonly Hopi stick-makers do not deposit their own sticks.

* An ancient usage in Hopiland. Note the downy feather bunches in the medicine kit from Medicine Cave, an early Pueblo site in the San Francisco Mountains (Bartlett 1:Fig. 30.)

† Bead offerings in springs or caves are found in southeastern Arizona and southwestern New Mexico, notably in the hot springs of the San Francisco River drainage (Hough 1:19, 41, 70).

A conspicuous Hopi detail is depositing sticks nearer on successive days, for the approaching Spirits.

There are many other details of variation in placing or making prayer-sticks, for at every point the technique is related to variations in ceremonial organization and in pantheon; besides, every town has developed its own patterns,* quite as distinctive as its other art patterns.

Sticks of office are found everywhere, generally as canes or staffs, but among Hopi they are horizontally carried bars. The bundled-seed-filled cane fetish is peculiar to Zuni, although its prototype may be the single cane, the "husband" that accompanies the corn fetish among Hopi. In the arrangement of the corn fetish there are several differences, the basket base of the Zuni *mi'li* not appearing in the Hopi *tiponi* or Keresan *iyatiku*. The bundled-stick *tiponi* of the Hopi Women's societies is unique. So is the Hopi stick or cane of longevity, or rather the rite of touching it.

Annual manufacture of War god images is a peculiar Zuni feature, and the carving of both wood and stone fetishes is more elaborate at Zuni than elsewhere. To this generalization the kachina dolls of the Hopi are an exception. They are quite as elaborate as Zuni "dolls," if not more so. Hopi "dolls" are more secularized, given or sold to visitors openly, nor are they quite as carefully preserved as at Zuni or Jemez. In elaboration of carving and of apparel both Hopi and Zuni "dolls" are distinguished from Keresan and Jemez "dolls" which are comparatively shapeless boards or cylinders. Peculiar to Hopi are their marionette-like images of grinding-girls and of Horned Water Serpents. Prayer-images are made in all the Western towns, but their use is marked at Acoma and is conceptually related to the way the Mother creates, by making the images in her basket come alive.

Altar equipment is more elaborate in the West, whether as sand-painting, which is used but meagerly to the northeast, or as carved and painted frame or uprights which are not used

* A prayer-stick monograph is in preparation. The subject is even more esoteric than masks and hardly less so than prayers and songs, and so one is slow to publish what is inevitably inadequate.

there at all and are seen in their most elaborate forms at Zuni. Here again Keres show mixed forms, the same society having for different occasions the wooden frame altar and the altar with meal or sand design. Keres definitely associate meal designs with rain-making and sand designs with curing. Clown societies who do not cure have only meal altars. The Pekwin of Zuni makes only a meal altar, likewise the Rain societies or chieftaincies. Hopi do not observe consistently this distinction between meal and sand altars, nor that between slab altar and ground-painting altar, using both types at the same time. The trail design in meal, the cloud glyph, is peculiar to Hopi. Elaboration of altar screen or reredos is also peculiar to them; in the Oraibi Oaqöl reredos there are eighty-three slabs. The altar of the Northeast is little but the elementary juxtaposition of sacrosanct objects on the ground.

Altar rites such as "road-making," meal-sprinkling, and aspersing are probably general, but they are certainly more ubiquitous in the West. Aspersing kachina passing by a kiva is peculiar to Hopi. The direction-color schematism which contributes not a little to altar elaboration in the West appears to be slight or nonexistent in the Northeast, although in Tewa and Taos conceptualism about Corn Maidens and Cloud People or kachina it is a feature. The color circuit itself varies—one for Hopi, Zuni, and Keres, except for variation for zenith and nadir, and others for Tewa and Tiwa, approximating the Athapascan direction-colors. Picurís, Isleta, and Navaho direction-colors are the same. For Isleta and Taos the circuit starts in the east, not as elsewhere, in the north, and there are five directions instead of six. Three and five* are the favored numerals at Isleta instead of as elsewhere four and six. Taos uses five, but also four and six. Notice at Jemez, just as we might expect, both the four-pointed and the five-pointed star![3]

Head-washing with naming ritual occurs throughout, but, as a preliminary to ceremonial, head-washing is observed only in

---

* The use of five seems anomalous, but there are other instances in the Southwest (Paiute, Lowie, in some cases Navaho) and Mexico (Tepecano, Mason; in some cases Aztec).

the West, possibly among eastern Keres. A ritual river bath at the conclusion of ceremonial, often to wash off sacred paint, is a trait of eastern and northeastern Pueblos. But bathing within doors does occur in the West and is very noticeable in Hopi infant-naming ritual, as each "aunt" has to give the infant a complete bath. Ritual emesis, a trait common to the tribes of the Southern Plains and the Southeast,[4] is most characteristic of Keres, although it is common enough on First Mesa or at Zuni. Only at Isleta is it an altar rite. Ritual continence is marked at Zuni and Acoma; of Pekwin (Zuni) and Outside or War chiefs (Acoma) it is required during office, and it was required of the Zuni scalp-taker for one year; it is required of kachina impersonators at Zuni for longer periods than elsewhere. Masks are more numerous and more elaborate in the West, where there is a distinction between permanent or chiefly masks and more personal dance masks. At Zuni copies of chiefly masks are used when use of the originals is not prescriptive. The art of maskmaking is highly developed, like most of the arts, at Zuni. Tiwa, Sandía excepted, do not use masks excepting clown masks of simple European type. Kachina dolls are associated of course with kachina masks and Tiwa do not make these dolls, nor do even mask-making Tewa. Impersonation without mask is also an outstanding Western, particularly Hopi, trait, and, as noted, dramatization is developed far more elaborately in the West than in the East. Maskless kachina dancing is more common in the East, not only among Tiwa who have no kachina masks but among Tewa and Keres. Kachina music is notable at Zuni, since the kachina not only sing for themselves but are sung for indoors by society choirs that have distinctive kachina songs.* The relay race on a permanent race course is characteristic of Tiwa, the kick-stick or ball, over a wild course, of the other Pueblos.

To sum up the variations in ritual: offerings, altar and altar service, kachina equipment in images and masks, also, we may add, in personal pigmentation and costuming, and dramatic im-

---

* Similarly at Santo Domingo a society may sing for kachina impersonators in their ceremonial house, not outdoors (White 4:94). As noted, Hopi kachina have no choirs.

personation, by and large all these traits are more substantial and elaborate in the West than in the East, with the middle Keresan area showing as usual mixed forms, but on the whole tending to the simpler abbreviated ones of the Northeast. My impression is that both dance and song are more highly developed in the West, and Herzog reports this is so of music in general (see p. 413). It may be said that the ritual arts reach their highest development in the West, perhaps at Zuni, where style is a very notable trait throughout ritual. From the pictorial, plastic, musical, and dramatic arts of Zuni which flower in ritual to artless and nonritualistic Taos is a long, long step.*

Shamanistic practices which are on the whole literal or realistic center in the East, among Keres and at Isleta. The Isletan ritual of "bringing down" Sun, Moon, and Lightning appears distinctive,† although it may turn out to be equivalent to the Hopi practice of flashing the sun into kiva by crystal or a sun-hole device as in the Zuni Rain chief's roof. Crystal-gazing is a prominent practice at Isleta, where every shaman wears a crystal pendent from his necklace of bear claws; and peering into the medicine bowl for second sight, particularly for witch-finding, is characteristic of Isleta and of Keres, among whom disease is notoriously witch-sent. Keres and other Pueblos follow both widespread methods of removing disease-causing objects, by sucking

---

* An illustration from war ritual is particularly apt. The Scalp dance of Zuni is or was on the verge of dramatization. In 1921 it was still thought necessary to have a scalp, but nobody bothered about how it was obtained beyond saying, consistently with myth, that it was the scalp of a Navaho girl (at an even earlier date, old scalps were used; Cushing got the scalp he needed from Washington), and I surmise that if the dance is ever given again in Zuni there will be a completely ritualistic substitute such as that of the winter solstice ceremony when a twig is kicked for a scalp or such as that used in Hopi Women's ceremonies. The Zuni scalp performance rehearses the return of the victorious war party; dramatizes it. Now Taos could have done the same thing, the war practices and traditions were there and even example from Comanche Sun dance; but the dramatizing impulse was lacking. And so Taos does not try to get around its rule that after losing a scalp there can be no celebration until a scalp is taken. (This, by the way, is Navaho-like. Enemy way or War dance is suspended at once at a death until a new scalp is secured [Haile]).

† Compare the performance of "making the Sun travel" at Cochiti (Dumarest, 198).

out or by brushing (stroking) out, but the "brushing way," as Dumarest calls it, is conspicuous in the East. Stick-swallowing and fire-handling or jugglery are particularly characteristic of war societies and of societies Keresan in type, yet curiously enough the practices are not found at Santo Domingo or San Felipe. Stirring boiling food or water is peculiar to Acoma and to Tewa. Shamanism in the East, ritual art in the West.

Shamanistic ideology centers around "power" and witchcraft; the ideology of the cult groups of the West centers about the state of mind or behavior proper for religious efficacy which we might call righteousness. The shaman will impute drought to a witch, probably in a neighboring town; Rain society people will impute it to a lack of harmony which repels Cloud, discord at home, or, more usually, in another town. These two very different concepts should blossom in different ways. Do they? How do the "valuable men" of the West compare with the men "with power" in the East? Are they less self-assertive, more devoted, holier? Or in psychological terms is the tension from socialization relieved by fighting witchcraft just as much as by developing ritualism. Are Hopi and Zuni or some of them more equable and peaceable peoples than they of the Rio Grande, less given to envy, suspicion, or, as the Pueblo uses the word, meanness? Here is enterprise for the social psychologist who believes with Dr. Cora Du Bois that in any social group it is "important to know whether the apparent character formations, deduced from institutions, are actually present, and to what extent?"

As a ceremony is a complex of rites, what has been said of ritual variation will apply to variations in ceremonies; but the distribution of certain type ceremonies may also be noted. There are war ceremonies in the West which do not occur in the East: the Scalp ceremony and early spring ceremony of the War society of Zuni, the Scalp ceremony of Acoma, the winter War god ceremony of Hopi. The irrigation or ditch-opening ceremonies of the East in charge of clown groups or Town chiefs are not paralleled in the less irrigated or more recently irrigated Western region, nor is the ceremony of general exorcism by the societies cleansing fields, town, and people altogether paralleled. Flute

and Snake-Antelope ceremonies are peculiar to Hopi, if we except the Snake ceremony of Sia and the Hopi report (1893) that
the Snake-Antelope ceremony was used in Acoma.[5] Hopi Wom-
en's ceremonies are also distinctive.* The distribution of kachina and saint's-day celebrations we have already mentioned,
noting how in the West there are distinctive kachina ceremonies
like the Shalako, also the Ky'anakwe, of Zuni, the Powamu and
Nima'n of Hopi, and we may add the Corn clan ceremony of
Acoma which is a fragment of Shalako, and the Kachina Fight,
and how in the East kachina exhibitions tend to be merely ap-
panage to the retreat or esoteric ceremonies of other groups. One
of the Hopi Girl's dances, the Butterfly dance, and the saint's
dance of Zuni are the only equivalents of the numerous saint's-
day celebrations in the eastern pueblos. The Buffalo and Deer
dances of Taos at first sight appear unique, but in the Buffalo
dances of Tesuque and San Felipe a number of fundamental
traits are recognized; the impersonation of various game animals
with the use of a stick or sticks to lean over on, and in particular
the female impersonation of Mother of Game to whom a peculiarly sacred character is given; also the functioning of war
captains as herders or watchmen; and the capture of the animals,
by the hunters at San Felipe, by the clowns at Taos. In spite of
these common traits the animal dances are very distinctive at
Taos, the presentation is so much less formalized than to the
south, and the dancing much more naturalistic or mimetic. At
San Juan the Deer dancers are led in from the hills by the Hunt
chief, but pelts are not worn, the antler headdress has a conventionalized ornament, and the dance movement too is stylized.
At the close women run after the escaping "animals," and a
captor is given meat by the household of the impersonator.
There is no female impersonation. The performance approximates the kachina Deer dance of Jemez or of Zuni. (The Zuni-
Hopi Buffalo dance is quite different, a performance by successive groups of men and girls, two men and two girls, or, as introduced into San Felipe, four men and four girls.) Distinctive at

* From town to town all Hopi ceremonies vary considerably and within the
same town a ceremony may vary in details from year to year (Voth 3:291).

Taos is the prolonged initiation of the boys into the kiva groups which is more in the nature of training, such as the warpath training of Apache, than of ceremonial. The Taos pilgrimage to the sacred lake, religious camping party for all but uninitiated boys and preadolescent girls, differs considerably from other pilgrimages which are made by "valuable men" to lake or mountain to deposit offerings and pray for rain or bring back the kachina.

The kick-stick or kick-ball race of the West is associated with the Kachina cult, the relay race of Tiwa with the cult of Sun and Moon. Zuni and Acoma bet on most of their kick-stick races, but Hopi do not bet on any of their kick-ball races which are so little competitive as to be hardly races at all, merely expressions of mimetic magic. Long-distance racing was particularly characteristic of Tiwa and Hopi. Hopi youths run from mesa top to valley spring for a ritual bath, couriers from other towns attend a kachina dance, a race is fitted in to most of the big ceremonies, and Hopi women run ceremonial races, the only Pueblo women* who race.

Isletan relay racing is closely connected with their Scalp ceremony. There is no running ritual in the Zuni Scalp ceremony. Outside of dramatizing the return of the war party and of dancing around the pole, Zuni and Isletan victory dances vary as much as do the ceremonial organizations from which they flower. No initiation ritual for scalp or scalper occurs at Isleta, where the War society is recruited through a vow in sickness and the Scalp is not a rain and seed being but a diviner, a curer, and a bestower of the strong spirit needed by runners who are not only exposed to black magic but inferably are representing Sun and Moon.

Moon, likewise the Stars, the Night People or Fathers of Taos, have more distinction in the pantheon of the Northeast than in that of the West. Moon changes sex, and Moon Old Man (Taos, Isleta, Jemez, Tewa) is more of a personage than Moon in the

---

* Excepting Jemez women imitating Hopi women, and excepting Santo Domingo women at a saint's-day celebration (White 4:156); possibly another Hopi imitation, if not a very recent innovation.

role of Sun's younger sister (Zuni). (Yet in Zuni prayer Moon our Mother is often referred to.)[6] The stars or particular constellations (Pleiades and Orion) have more supernatural significance or weight for the Tanoans than for the other tribes, and Morning Star is definitely associated with war.

Sun is everywhere of paramount importance. This is not true of his sons, the war spirits, the little war gods, the War Brothers or Twins, as they are variously referred to by the ethnographer, in native circles they are called by name or, by Tewa, the Little People. As the Stone Men they are referred to at Taos where there are tales of Speckled Corn Boy or Echo Boy, war god beings elsewhere but not at Taos. Nor are the Ash Boys, Fire Boys, Poker Boys, or Corncob Boys, of Tewa and Cochiti lore distinctly identified with the Twins of the West; they are beings of folk tales rather than of myth.* Little Bleary-Eyes or Tousle-Head or Bushy-Head of Taos or Isleta are disliked as were the War Brothers and like them triumph over enemies, but they become chiefs rather than gods. Mythology about the War Brothers is richest at Zuni where, as among Hopi, Navaho, and Apache, one boy is the son of Sun and the other the son of Waterfall, of Dripping Water; in the East both boys are begot by Sun. At Zuni, too, the War Brothers are considered to be the source of customs and institutions; they are founders and inventors, culture heroes, and they are mentioned continually in all sorts of ways.

Keres are less feminist in many ways than Western Pueblos yet their pantheon is dominated not by the War Brothers but by the Mother or Mothers of the Underworld, beings of vegetation and of all creation. Analogously, the outstanding spirit of vegetation or germination of Hopi is male, Müy'ingwa, as much of a maize spirit as Iyatiku of the Keres. In Hopi lore some of the creative function of Iyatiku at or before the Emergence is as-

---

* Poker Boy is introduced into the Emergence myth recently recorded from Mishongnovi (Nequatewa, 18). Poker Boy advises the chiefs to have Chipmunk in to run up and down the pine tree and with his song make the tree grow to the upper world. This is Keresan-Tewa tale incident, possibly derived from Hano. (Note that formerly at Cochiti's Santiago Day celebration a pine tree and a squirrel were brought into the court (Goldfrank 3:46]).

cribed to Hürü'ingwühti, Woman of Hard Substances; but I incline to identify Tihküyi wühti, Child-Medicine Woman, with Iyatiku. Child-Medicine Woman, also called Sand Altar Woman, is thought of as the sister of Müy'ingwa and the wife, sometimes the sister, of Masauwü. In Walpi she has a shrine in the kiva that has various Keresan associations, Wikwalobi. Dawn Woman is another underworld Hopi-Keresan Mother, and in all the Hopi Women's ceremonies Müy'ingwa is given a female companion. Although in Taos folk tales there are Corn Maidens (Yellow and Blue, but in one tale White Corn Girl is mentioned), corn fetishes are unfamiliar and the Earth Mother is a somewhat different personage from the Earth Mothers elsewhere. She is associated with the hunt (so is Child-Medicine Woman); and she was prayed to in war.

The Hopi pantheon is perhaps the most distinctive of all—given Müy'ingwa and Woman of Hard Substances who is not unknown, however, at Zuni, and Masauwü who is Skeleton, Death, Fire, the First Denizen of the mesa tops, a being not found in any non-Hopi pueblo.* Badger is the Hopi doctor, not Bear, the doctor of the Keres. Bear among Hopi (also at Jemez and Taos) is associated with war. Zuni is eclectic in medicine animals. Bear of the Keres and Badger of the Hopi both figure. Bear and Mountain Lion are the most conspicuous ritual animals.† Achiyelatopa, Knife-Wing, the prominent personage represented on or rather above Zuni curing society altars, may be identified with Kwatoko of the Hopi; but in the East their equivalent has not been noted. The mythical water creature of Taos, "big water man," is a monstrous frog, not the Horned Water Serpent that causes landslide or flood in the other pueblos. Yet both are fearsome and punitive, particularly Water Serpent in the river towns of the East, where "the last day" is to come through flood.

---

* Except Laguna, where the name occurs but where the conceptualism is obscurely identified with that of the War Brothers.

† Animals, Zuni themselves call them; and this term is preferable to beast gods (Stevenson, Bunzel), a grandiloquent and misleading term for the Indian spirit animal.

Poshaiyanki, who is associated with Zuni curing societies as a benevolent human curer, was probably known to Hopi in connection with the Pobösh curing society which is now extinct. In the East he is identifiable with Poseyemu, who is something of a culture hero and, in speaking to Mexicans, has been identified with Montezuma. Poseyemu-Poshaiyanki was associated with jugglery, and the traditions of western Keres indicate that his cult was once opposed. In up-to-date Acoma mythology, if he can be identified as Pishuni, he is First Witch and the Snake in the Garden. T'aiowa of the Hopi, Bitsitsi of Zuni, and the supernatural patrons of Koshare, Kossa, and Kyapiunin (Keres, Tewa, Isleta) all vary in details, but may be taken by and large as homologous supernaturals.

The supernatural groups referred to as Chiefs of the Directions, Cloud chiefs, kachina (some of them), and the dead, i.e., the old ones, the ancestors, overlap in conceptualism and present many difficulties to classification. At Zuni the dead are closer than elsewhere to Cloud spirits and kachina, both in conceptualism or myth and in ritual. Among Hopi there are ancestral-like kachina, but the dead as a class do not appear to be kachina, although they have been referred to as kachina, also as Cloud spirits. Distinctive food, cooked food, is given the dead, as at Zuni, and distinctive prayer-feathers.* Zuni and Hopi Cloud spirits or chiefs may also be distinguished from the kachina. At Acoma, Isleta, and Taos, among Hopi too, the Chiefs of Directions are mountain or lake and spring spirits, rain or weather spirits, having little or no association with the dead.† At Isleta there is a cult of the dead including ritual for the Stillborn. The ritual of the Catholic day of the dead, All Souls, is observed in all but Hopi towns, although possibly the food offerings made to

* In the Home-going kachina ceremony of Walpi offerings are made to the dead, to "old Hopi women" and to the children dead. Offerings to the dead are made by Marau women at Oraibi, and at the winter solstice ceremony a great many prayer-feathers are offered to the dead.

† The idea of special personages joining the underlake great house or kiva-dwellers occurs in Taos tales. Also a man who dies in the mountains may become an underlake spirit (Parsons 58:70).

the dead at Oraibi during the Wüwüchim ceremony is an All Souls observance.

The Pueblo cult of the saints is much less elaborated than among most Spanish Indians. At Isleta and elsewhere San Escapula stands out as a miraculous saint or curer and medicine clay is fetched from his sanctuary, Santiago or St. James is recognized as the horse saint (Acoma, Santo Domingo, Cochiti) and Saint Christopher as the protector of travelers (Santa Ana), but between a town's patron saint and the other saints whose fiestas are celebrated probably little distinction is made. At Zuni there is but one saint.

The origin myth of every town is an emergence myth, but in the Northeast (Tewa, Taos) the Emergence is from under water, elsewhere from under earth. The concept of the underworld as stratified is confined to the West. In Zuni-Acoma myth the sun existed before the Emergence; in Hopi-Laguna myth the sun had to be placed in the sky. Sun is not mentioned at all in the origin myth recorded from Tewa. The intent of the rather fragmentary Eastern origin myths is to account for the hierarchy, its functions and organization. The Zuni myth rather accounts for certain ceremonies. As might be expected, Acoma myth accounts both for ceremonies and for hierarchy. Indeed it is the most frankly etiological of all Pueblo origin myths, in Navaho style bestowing a warrant for the whole range of ceremonialism. Mother Iyatiku ordained all of it, although, as was to be expected, she conflicts in tales with those potent culture-carriers of Zuni, the War Brothers,* and, as Benavides would say (see p.

---

* Iyatik and the brothers Ma'sewi and Oyoyewi lived together at White House, and every night the Brothers would dance before the Mother's altar so that clouds would arise from the altar bowl and spread over the world. Now Iyatik became indifferent to the nightly ceremonial, so the Brothers deserted, carrying with them corn they collected from all the houses. They buried the corn in a deep hole, with Horned Toad as watchman, and Iyatik saw the water in her bowl and in the town's spring dry up. Despite Iyatik's appeals to the Rain chiefs of the Directions and to the kachina who came and danced, drought and famine ensued, and the people began to perish. Not until Iyatik's bird emissaries found the Brothers and she sent them something they really liked to eat, would they send back seed corn or return from their underground abode at Flower

156, n.†), the shamans lose out to the warriors. Hopi myth accounts for the sun, moon, and stars and, like the Zuni myth, for death; otherwise it is little but a stringing together of tale incidents. The clan origin or migration myths of Hopi have a few fragmentary parallels at Zuni and among western Keres, but none in the East.

In the West the great volume of tales is about the War Brothers and the kachina. The comparative absence of these personages in the East gives a different character to the folk tales. There are fewer novelistic tales, more episodic animal tales, more witch tales. War god or kachina exploits are made into nursery stories about the little Poker or Ashes Boys or about Magpie-Tail Boy, who lives at Cottonwood place.

On the whole, religious variation between the towns follows variation in language, i.e., the tribal divisions based on language show religious divisions. The cluster of towns speaking the same language are more alike in religion than any one town is like another town speaking a different language. But there are some notable exceptions, particularly where dialectical differentiation is marked. Jemez in ceremonial organization is more Keresan than Tewan, although its language is a dialect of Tanoan, as is Tewa. (For communication, to be sure, Jemez and Tewa are virtually separate languages.) Similarly, Tewan religion is more Keresan than Tanoan. Isleta has borrowed so many Keresan traits that it approximates Laguna or Santo Domingo rather than Taos. Hano retains Tewan speech but is more Hopi than Tewa in religion. Hano shows convincingly that borrowing in religion goes on across language barriers and that, given intermarriage and close neighborhood, religious changes may proceed rapidly, far more rapidly than linguistic changes.

Mound. After one night on the altar, the seed corn multiplied; it rained four days and four nights; the Brothers visited the fields (a Walpi reminiscence, p. 789), and the crops matured at once. Then the people realized that the Brothers possessed great power, and after the harvest they set aside a day to visit them. A charming myth of cultural clash! Do we see in the Keresan Corn Mother cult that of the early maize growers, and in the war and clown cult that of invaders?

In the foregoing survey of differences between the towns several factors that make for variation have been suggested. In the Hopi country there is no permanent stream, no true irrigation, which may be a reason why rain-making appears so much more important in the ceremonies than curing or any other function or why these flood farmers hold a distinctive ceremony for Water Serpent, the god of terrestrial waters, or why the kachina "go away" in midsummer when torrents threaten the fields. River-set Isleta gives distinction to its river beings, the Water People.*
More important or less hypothetical than differences in environment, however, are differences in the general social organization, from matrilineal clan to patrilineal moiety, inevitably affecting the ceremonial organization; differences in the ceremonial unit itself, in its size or predominant function, affecting, among other particulars, that combination of rites which is ceremony, and also the character of the calendar; differences in mythology which account for differences in impersonation or dramatization,† and in quasi-ritualistic narrative; differences whatever they are which focus attention and interest either on witchcraft or on ritualism; finally, differences in the degree of secretiveness or esotericism that prevails, conditions which either favor or preclude imitation or borrowing.

Borrowing from other groups, it is well known, is a foremost factor in cultural variation. Among Pueblos interpueblo loans must be considered as well as loans from other Indian cultures, and from the intrusive Whites.

There are several ways in which town borrows from town, through visits, temporary or prolonged, personal or by cere-

---

* Given more information, these Water People may prove to be homologous with the Uwanami or Cloud People of Zuni who live in all moisture (Bunzel) or with the Water Old Men of Tewa or Western Apache (Goodwin 2:26).

† Whatever the original relationship between myth and ceremony, once made, the myth supports the ceremony or ceremonial office and may suggest ritual increments.

monial groups, through marrying in* or immigration by family, through formal purchase of ceremonial or exchange.

Buying a ceremony is not a usual Pueblo procedure, but there are a few accounts which indicate that it is not unfamiliar. In 1883 eleven Zuni chiefs went to First Mesa to beg the Hopi to initiate them into the Snake-Antelope societies, offering two large oxen, ten or more sheep, much wheat, rawhide, moccasins, and other wealth.[7] The offer was refused "lest the medicine lose its virtue." The Elk dance of Nambé is said to have been bought from Taos, for ten turquoises, five red beads, twelve dance blankets, and twelve deerskins,[8] the Hunt chief of Nambé promising the Hunt chief of Taos that the ceremony would always be properly or strictly performed. When Buffalo songs were acquired from the Sioux living in Gallup,[9] they were undoubtedly paid for. Kachina dance songs are probably exchanged quite informally between Pueblos,[10] but masks, it has been reported, may be bartered. Sia passed on their disused Shumaikoli masks to the chief of the Zuni Shuma'kwe, trustee of Zuni Shumaikoli masks, when he was visiting Sia, and in return a Sia youth was initiated into the Zuni Kachina society (1891) in order that he could impersonate Koyemshi in Sia. The chief of the Shuma'kwe was his godfather.[11]

The ways in which loans are made will affect their character. Loans through immigrants will be fuller and more exact than loans made through observation by visitors. The Zuni immigrant family who introduced the Koyemshi masks into Laguna also introduced the Zuni kachina prayer-stick with its reversed duck feather, a very characteristic detail but one that a mere dance observer would miss. Immigrant family groups like Zuni

* In recent years a few persons from other pueblos have married into every pueblo: into Zuni, two or three Hopi (noted in 1893 and earlier), one Laguna woman, one Acoma woman, and one Isletan woman; onto First Mesa, some Zuni (Stephen 4:310, 1001 n. 1); into Acoma, one Hopi man, one Zuni man, one Jemez woman (White 2:35); into Jemez, two women from Sia, two from Cochiti, two from San Ildefonso, one from San Felipe, one from Tesuque, and one from Santa Clara (1925). The father of the Jemez Town chief was Zuni; the wife of his "right-hand man" was Hopi; the mothers of three Fire society members were from San Felipe and to one of these women the chief was once married.

famine sojourners among Hopi, at Acoma,* at Jemez or else-where in the East† or permanent groups like the Laguna at Isleta or the Pecos at Jemez, the Tano or Tewa on First Mesa, perhaps the Tano at Santo Domingo, can introduce ceremonial more fully than individuals marrying in. Laguna people introduced medi-cine society rituals, the back-shield dance, and in a way masked dancing; Pecos people introduced a saint, Porcingula, and at least one society, the Sun society; First Mesa Tewa introduced clowns, the Shumaikoli curing society, ritual shinny, and pos-sibly the Butterfly dance; Tano from Galisteo may have intro-duced into Santo Domingo the Boyakya society. Several Hopi societies are said to have been introduced by survivors from Awatobi. From Palatkwabi, the Red Land of the South, several ceremonial traits may have been introduced: the office of Sun-watcher or rather the Sun chieftaincy, the Lakon society, and myth, perhaps ritual, relating to Horned Water Serpent and the human sacrifice to check flood.‡ On the other hand, the Tusa-

* See Benedict 3:II, 199–201, for a charming account of how an improvement in making wafer-bread was introduced by Zuni visitors, likewise a masked dance and the custom of taking food in bowls to the dancers.

† In the great drought of 1777–79, which scattered the Hopi, a large number of starving Zuni also went East to "our interior pueblos," writes Governor Anza (Thomas, 230). Movements from East to West during the refugee period, 1680–1716, then from West to East.

‡ All these traits are associated with the Patki or Water-Corn clan. Am I reviving the discredited migration-by-clan theory? Yes, in a measure, but with different emphasis. My emphasis is on the fetishes or ceremony, in Hopi term, the *wimi*, not on the actual trustee group, the clan. Tradition of provenience accompanies the *wimi* and is more reliable than tradition of clan provenience or origin.

There is a general Hopi tradition that the Water-Corn people represent a late migration from the south (Stephen 4:943–44) with a migratory association with Zuni. Their flood and child sacrifice myth is told at Zuni, and, as we shall see, derives from Pima-Papago. The flood presupposes a great river. In the last recorded version, Palatkwabi is described as having had "an irrigating sys-tem from the river which flows through that country" (Nequatewa, 85). This describes Hawikuh; it also describes the Gila River Valley, which had an impres-sive system of irrigation.

These Water-Corn people state definitely that they stopped at Homolobi, near Winslow, on the Little Colorado (and then before joining Walpi, at Pakat-chomo, four miles south of First Mesa [Fewkes 8:252]). The pottery of the Little Colorado ruins is related to Zuni wares (Spier 1:305), and in archeological and yan men who married into Santa Clara and San Juan and taught the Hopi Buffalo dance did not pass on the curing aspect of the performance (I am fairly certain), merely the dance form. A visiting or even an immigrant shaman would be likely to keep his secrets to himself, as did the Zuni Ant doctor married into Santo Domingo; his esoteric or professional knowledge helps to establish his position, besides being a source of income.

However, the patients a foreign doctor cures learn a good deal about his treatment. At Acoma a medicine man or woman marrying into town is expected to join the local society. This rule probably applies elsewhere, and it must give considerable opportunity for borrowing. At installation it is customary among Keres to invite representatives of the same society in other towns. In 1891 two Fire shamans from Sia participated in the initiation ceremony of the Big Firebrand society of Zuni, and Stevenson opines that they showed more facility in playing with fire than their hosts.[12] Visiting delegations, visiting doctors, members transferred through intermarriage—it is easy to see how the Keresan society spread almost everywhere, not to speak speculatively of early connections of Keres with Antelope and Zuni Valleys or with other places.

The Hopi who first learned kachina dancing from Zuni* did

native opinion Zuni-speaking people came into the Zuni Valley from the west, from the Little Colorado. Possibly the Water-Corn people were a trickle of Zuni-speaking people so thin that the language was lost. See pp. 1026–27.

In a prayer by a Water-Corn man of Oraibi I notice a Zuni-like use of the term light for life: "Then will these corn-stalks be growing up by that rain; when they mature, we shall here in the light (archaic for in this life), being nurtured, be happy" (Voth 3:320).

* By way of Awatobi? Tradition goes that there were Zuni immigrants at Awatobi, Badger clanspeople, who after the destruction of the town went to Walpi (Stephen 4:944) and to Second Mesa, to Mishongnovi. (Some of these may have constituted the group of thirty Zuni sojourners among the Hopi who in 1716 were persuaded to return to Zuni [Bloom, 170].) By two or more Mishongnovi Badger families the fields or gardens of Awatobi are still cultivated (Forde 1:369; Brew). Designs of kachina masks have been found on Awatobi kiva walls (Brew). (Mishongnovi physical data are distinctive [Hrdlička]).

Note that when Zuni visited Hopi in 1892 to dance kachina they went by way of Awatobi and after stopping at Sichomovi they went on to dance at Mishongnovi (Stephen 4:944). To'chii, Moccasin, a Badger of Sichomovi married in later not learn that the impersonator carries in his belt the seeds which give the dance its efficacy;[13] but they learned a great many other things about the Kachina cult. The Zuni association of the Badger clan with the kachina was passed on to Third Mesa, where the Badgers control the kachina for half the year; also to First Mesa, where the Badger clan chief is chief of the Shalako celebration. The Shalako celebration was lifted bodily from Zuni to First Mesa.* Zuni has closer relations with First Mesa than with the other Mesas, and Shalako is celebrated only on First Mesa, where it is actually called Sio Shalako.† Sio Shalako is

---

life into Zuni, was with this Zuni party and inferably arranged it. My guess is that Moccasin was an Awatobi descendant. At any rate, he was an important ceremonial middleman between Zuni and First Mesa (Stephen 4:1131).

* To Sichomovi. In 1853–54 and again in 1866–67 Hopi suffered smallpox and drought, and people went visiting to other towns, to Zuni, to Jemez, and elsewhere; Sichomovi was almost abandoned; Hano was decimated. (In 1843 it had also suffered from smallpox.) Zuni pottery designs were brought back to First Mesa (Bartlett 2:36; Stephen 4:1022, 1148) and at this time, too, Sio Shalako was introduced. Hopi pottery shows a still earlier Zuni connection (Bunzel 1:80).

In turn may not Molawia have been introduced into Zuni? It has the ear-marks of Hopi ceremonial: racing for crops, racing by females, a Ne'wekwe with headdress and face painting like a Singer, and clan affiliations. The clans are Tobacco (on First Mesa trustee of chieftaincy of Singers society) and Mus-tard, a clan said to have reached Zuni from the East and then to have moved on in part to First Mesa.

It is fairly certain that Ololowishkya was introduced from First Mesa, possibly through Moccasin, expert on painting or dressing the puppets of the kiva exhibition on which the outdoor performance was based (Stephen 4:1131).

In the drought of 1777–79 (followed by smallpox epidemic of five months in 1781) Hopi also went to Zuni but did not stay, as Zuni too was suffering from drought.

† To distinguish these kachina from native Hopi kachina, a brother and sister, instead of four (Zuni, six or twelve) brothers. Possibly the Shalako couple were introduced earlier into the pantheon and so seem native, possibly Hopi Shalako (which in Zuni terms would be called home-Shalako) is merely a social fiction. See pp. 529, n. †, 875, n. *, 1163.

Later. Hopi Shalako is not a fiction. The couple were presented on the last day of the Home-going kachina ceremony at Shumopovi in 1937. The ten-foot figures standing at opposite ends between two lines of singing dancers, bobbed up and down or ran from one end to the other. They were attended by Eototo and Hahai, Kachina Father and Mother. Theirs was the last dance appearance; they danced in three places, and they, instead of the usual Hemis group, were given prayer-sticks and were smoked on. They wore the eagle-feather skirt and performed sporadically, not annually as at Zuni, and only the more public parts of the matrix ceremony are given. It is a superficial performance from which much ritual, notably prayer-stick plantings and chants, is omitted.* These traits, sporadic or optional celebration, omission of the esoteric, together with lack of integration into the rest of the ceremonial system—all these are the earmarks of a borrowed ceremony. It is because kachina celebrations among Hopi, even including their Powamu and Nima'n ceremonies, have this character when compared with Zuni celebrations that I infer Zuni provenience for the kachina dance cult.† Hopi kachina chiefs or clan ancients may have had a quite independent history.

Clowns or clowning behavior is ever part of the kachina complex. One of the four or five clown types of the Hopi, the Tachükti or Koyimsi, appear in the Shalako and Horned Water Serpent celebrations and at Powamu and are plainly of Zuni provenience. Like the Koyemshi of Zuni, the Koyimsi wear a knobbed mask‡ and carry a fawnskin bag. The black cloth of

---

a blanket over the shoulders. The mask was without horns or snout. Paraphernalia were kept in a Sun clan house. When given at all on Second Mesa—only three old men were familiar with the performance—this home-Shalako is always associated with the Home-going ceremony (Kennard). This may explain why Hopi have called Shalako at Zuni a Home-going ceremony (Stephen 4:945). For Papago associations see pp. 999–1000.

* See p. 509, n. *. Compare Stephen 4:352. But more Zuni ritual, readily observed ritual, has probably been added at each Hopi performance, since Hopi continually visit Zuni during Shalako. At the January performance in 1900 appeared Zuni kachina not appearing in 1893, the first performance in thirty or forty years, perhaps since the introduction. Also in 1900 the kachina danced at the shrines (like the Zuni Long Horn group [Stephen 4:416 ff.; Fewkes 12: 26–29]). In 1912 and 1914 walls were marked with meal and switched (Stephen 4:441 n. 1).

Night dancing in the houses entertaining the Shalako is necessarily omitted, since Hopi societies do not furnish choirs to the kachina, Zuni way.

† The miniature kick-stick is a Zuni-Keres-Jemez type of prayer-stick in the kachina cult. This prayer-stick offering figures in Hopi kachina offerings, although, as the Hopi use a kick-ball, a miniature ball might have been expected. The miniature kick-stick is used in the Home-going ceremony as well as in the Snake-Antelope and Flute ceremonies.

‡ Tachükti means "ball-on-head" as does the proper Zuni term for the impersonation, Molanhaktu.

the women is worn as kilt or dress; mask and body are painted with pinkish clay. They sing Zuni songs, pretend to talk Zuni, and even make Zuni prayer-sticks. Their origin myth is the Koyemshi brother-sister incest story; their play, phallic or obscene; and their games, those of the Koyemshi. They are sprinkled with meal as sacred figures, and rain-making is an attribute of their eponymous supernatural. Like the Koyemshi they have no altar paraphernalia and no fixed organization of chieftaincy or membership. Incidentally, I would point out again that in borrowing much has been lost. Zuni Koyemshi have a yearlong function of prayer-stick-making and depositing. There are ten personages and each has his own name and individuality. Of Hopi Koyimsi there are an indefinite number; there is no individualization, and impersonation is for the occasion merely. Nor are the kachina clowns by any means the important and "dangerous" personages at Walpi that they are at Zuni.

Hopi Wüwüchim and Singers societies have the clowning traits of jesting with women society members or singing at them, in obscene terms, and Singers or Wüwüchimtü volunteer to clown for the kachina. These clowns wear red-stained tufts of rabbit fur at the ears, and their faces are striped red, like Singers, or they paint yellow, like Wüwüchimtü. Some copy the black-ring face-painting of the Kossa or Paiyakyamu clowns of their Tewa neighbors. Some of their clowning may be copied, too, from Tewa: ash house for temporary initiation, contrary exorcism, coming in on the housetops, valeting the kachina or burlesquing them. Are the mummers, in mask or maskless, who carry out elaborate farces, sometimes with the clowns or kachina, derived from the East? Probably not. At any rate, these mummers were borrowed by Santo Domingo and at one time imitated at Zuni (see pp. 646, 648).*

The ritual shinny that is played on First Mesa was introduced, I believe, by Tewa; it is played by eastern Tewa, and it is not

---

* As was once an Eastern Koshare. At the Ne'wekwe initiation of October, 1884, with the thirty men and five boys who came out painted gray as usual with the mud from their sacred spring was one who was banded black and white (Stevenson 2:436).

played on Second Mesa or at Zuni. The Hopi Butterfly dance is the saint's-day dance of the East, and it appears to have been introduced by Tewa.[14] The Hopi Buffalo dance came, of course, from the East, through some relay from the Plains,* but Hopi tradition that it came by way of Zuni is probably sound, for the bang to the nose of the girl dancer is a Zuni trait. Recently the Hopi variant has been introduced into eastern pueblos. For Santa Clara and San Juan the very dates are known and the introducers: danced on January 6, 1926, as taught by Philip, a Hano man married into Santa Clara; danced on January 19, 1926, as taught by the Shipaulovi man married into San Juan.[15]

Hopi borrowings from Keres are less clear than those from Zuni or Tewa. The now extinct Poboshwĭmkya[16] was undoubtedly of the contemporary Keresan curing society type, but it may have reached Hopi through Tewa, through Zuni, or even through Hopi themselves back from their trip to the East after the killing drought of 1777–79.† The fire pit of the extinct Yayatü, the Mothers, is reminiscent of the initiatory fire pit of the Fire shamans of Acoma (and of the Little Firebrand society of Zuni). In general character the Snake-Antelope ceremony appears Keresan; the songs are in Keresan and contain references to the *chamahia* stone fetishes or people of the Keres,[17] and to their monstrous mythical snake, the yellow Horned Water Serpent of the North;‡ another animal, possibly mythic, is called by the same term (*shuhuna*) by Keres and Hopi; the impersonation of the Direction chiefs (by the Antelope chiefs) and the Bear and Lion impersonations at initiation are characteristically Keresan, and so is the dedication of infants to the societies. Acoma once

* The Hopi Buffalo is a medicine animal as among Navaho and Plains tribes. In 1851 a mimetic Buffalo dance was performed among Omaha by ten couples in mask around a wounded man who was aspersed with water (Kurz, 66).

† Returned Hopi may have brought back both the curing society and the smallpox scourge of 1781.

‡ Ka'toya of Tokonabi, the junction of the San Juan and Colorado rivers, whence Snake people of First Mesa and Acomans are said to have come (Stephen 4:716 n. 4). See p. 184.

had a public snake performance;* Sia still has one in which almost all the Hopi features appear: a four-day snake hunt in the
directions, with the uninitiated warned away, Lion sand-painting, exposure of novice to the snakes, snake bower, dance, and
snake release. The only notable difference is the absence of the
Antelope society or what would correspond to it. Now at the
rain ceremony of the Sia Snake society the Kapina (Spider)
society is present. Spider Woman is the Mother of the Antelope
society, and at Oraibi the society belonged to the Spider
(woman) clan.† I surmise that the Hopi Antelope society is to
be identified with the Keresan Kapina (Spider) society.‡ If the
Antelope society reached Hopi by way of Acoma,§ it may have
got its name because of the close relationship at Acoma between
the Kapina society and the Antelope clan. Antelope Valley,
twelve miles southeast of First Mesa, may have been the seat of
an early Keresan population.‖

* In 1582, described by Espejo as "juggling feats, some of them very clever,
with live snakes." (Note, incidentally, that jugglery with rattlesnakes is reported
from the Yukuts of British Columbia.)

† I surmise that the lineage in charge of the ceremony was called Spider.
The Spider group is generally associated with the Bear clan.

‡ Chamahia implements are on the Kaʙina society altar at Acoma. S'amahi-
ya was the initiating kachina of the Kapina society of Laguna (Parsons 20:116
n. 5). Compare the obsolete, warlike Kahbena society of Hano (Parsons 44:216–
18). Kahbena-Kapina societies have been noted only among these Tano or
southern Tewa and among the western Keres.

§ There is a Hopi tradition that people living at the spring Amüba, on the
east side of First Mesa, migrated to Acoma (Stephen 4:679, 713–14); but there is
also a Hopi tradition that the Snake ceremony was known at Acoma before it
came to Hopiland (Stephen 2:44).

‖ Here the mesa-top ruin next to Awatobi is called Kawaika, Laguna. Hopi
also apply the term generally to Keres. Awatobi was occupied from late Basket
Makers on throughout Pueblo history. Pueblo III pottery affiliations are indicated with the Kayenta area of the San Juan and with the Little Colorado
(Brew, 134). (Compare cephalic index for Acoma and Mishongnovi.)

With Santo Domingo I surmise early First Mesa connections, made possibly
through Santo Domingo immigrants after that town was burned by Otermín
after 1680 (see Parsons 59; note on p. 410 the same name for Santo Domingo
masks belonging to clown societies and for First Mesa kachina shrine) or possibly
later via Laguna. Among the "apostates" who were released from "the captivity
of the Devil" in 1715 and terminated their sojourn among Hopi were ten
Laguna people (Bloom, 170).

Hopi Flute society songs are also in Keresan. The reception of the Horn clan in the Flute ceremony of First Mesa is very much like the ritualized reception accorded a foreign spouse at Acoma.[18] On First Mesa the Flute society is closely associated with lightning and arrowpoints shot by lightning, a conceptual relationship with the Keresan Flint society. The Flute ceremony, like the Snake-Antelope ceremony, is a curing as well as a rain ceremony, to treat wounds and to keep Masauwü, Death, away,[19] dramatizing the encounter with Masauwü at the Emergence. The extinct Drab Flute society was in charge of the Squash or Sorrow-making clan who were probably of Keresan descent. As there was a relationship in warlike traits between the Keresan Flint (Lightning) society and the O'pi, so on First Mesa there was some relationship between the Snake-Antelope societies, sometime war societies, and the Flute (Lightning) societies which may have been named Drab* and Blue from their supernatural patron, Locust, "the humped-back flute player," also a brave fellow unaffected by lightning and so medicine for wounds. The twofold organization is a Keresan trait.

Songs of the Singers and Wüwüchim societies are said to be in Keresan, and the reference to the long-form initiation ceremony is in Keresan, they say: *naashnaiya* from Keresan for father (and) mother. Wüwüchim's affiliated Women's society sings in an unknown language. The underworld language before the Emergence was Keresan. Indeed, according to Walpi tradition, the bulk of the ceremonial organization is either Keresan or from Awatobi: Snakes, Antelopes, Flutes, Singers, Wüwüchimtü, Mamsrautü, Oaqöltü.† If we compare Keresan societies, specialized as they are at Cochiti,[20] with Hopi societies each treating a special ailment, dissimilarity of function is less than is usually assumed.

The Snake-Medicine society of Zuni is a late local develop-

* The Drab Flute of Oraibi said to derive from the East (Voth) were named from the immature or *gray* locust (Eggan). Again, bows are called drab or blue (Apache bows) (Beaglehole 1:19), and the Flute carry bows.

† How Oaqöl was carried from Awatobi to Mishongnovi and thence to Oraibi is told very circumstantially, i.e., with the names of successive chiefs (Voth 4:3).

ment, but in type it is Keresan, as are all Zuni curing societies, a fact well appreciated in Zuni tradition. Zuni curing animals live at Shipap; society kachina visit Shipap; in fact all the group kachina from Kachina town pay a courtesy visit to the East, to Shipap, at the close of Shalako. The Ky'anakwe, the old enemy of Zuni kachina, live at Acoma and inferably Chakwena giantess lives there, too, since she was with the Ky'anakwe. A Chakwena dance group is from Laguna, their songs in Keresan.[21] Then there is the office of Pekwin; in all his functions and in several attributes he is homologue of the Keresan Town chief. Like him he makes solar observations and like him he appoints to office and instals and is ever solicitous about *all* his children. But for the Rain chief of the North who is called explicitly "chief of the houses" we would have to call Pekwin the Town chief. The office of Pekwin appears to be derivative or unauthentic since it is without supreme fetish or bundle and takes its rules from the Town chieftaincy or from the Pathltok rain chieftaincy of the East. Pekwin did not "come up" with the people, although that may be because conceptually there was no reason for his existence in the *sunless* lower worlds.

Speculation about the office of Pekwin is brash;* about curing societies, less so. How was this complex, which bulks so large today and in organization is Zuni stereotype, carried there?

* There is another confused line to hold in mind: a parellel with the Outside or War chief of Acoma who has or had functions of crier and sun-watcher, announcing solstices and first planting, who appointed to office and installed, who had a crook of office (Pekwin's characteristic prayer-stick), and upon whom continence taboos were peculiarly strict. No war functions attach to Pekwin (except that he gives their first cigarette to youths in token of warrior status [p. 623]); in Keresan terms he is Nahia but not War chief (Dumarest, 199). His altar design, the Acoma "field" design, associates him with fertility, as does his own growth ceremony, the Thla'hewe, and perhaps Ololowishkya. He is said to have introduced one of the Keresan-like societies, Shuma'kwe, into Zuni. Only a history of early Keres-Ashiwi contacts can explain the office of Pekwin.

Out of these contacts too, *probably in pueblos long since extinct*, came forth part of Zuni Shalako, a remarkable agglomeration of ceremonials, too recent as such at least to be accounted for by myth, either separately or in the Emergence myth, and too recent to have spread anywhere except to First Mesa. As a yearlong ceremony with periodic visits to springs it suggests the Acoma War chief's functions. Then the Shulawitsi-Shuracha Zuni-Acoma kachina groups are similar.

Probably through Acoma if not through closer Keresan settlements now extinct, or indeed if not through settlements of Keres encountered by the Ashiwi when, abandoning the Little Colorado, they came into the Zuni River Valley. At any rate, the ceremonial connections between Zuni and Acoma have been close, judging from the mark of Zuni upon the ceremonial system of Acoma. Acoma borrowed the Kachina cult or parts from Zuni, and at Acoma the cult was fitted into the ceremonial system more integrally than in Hopiland. The Kachina cult at Zuni is associated with the Town chieftaincy and the other paramount Rain chieftaincies, and with the Antelope-Deer clan (and the Badger clan). At Acoma, Antelope clansmen sing at the kachina initiation at which the Town chief is present. Here we have another hypothesis for the association at Acoma between the Town chieftaincy and the Antelope clan. This Keresan anomaly may have come through the Kachina cult as borrowed from Zuni. Instead of developing such an independent kachina organization as the Zuni, the Acomans clustered kachina traits or functions about the Town chief; and because the chief of the Zuni kachina-kiva organization was an Antelope clansman, the Acoma Town chief had also to be an Antelope. The Acoma origin tale of how Antelope and Badger recovered or rescued the kachina[22] was, of course, a posteriori myth. Kachina dramatization at Acoma is borrowed from Zuni. The signal-fire dramatization of the Corn clan is virtually the advent of Shulawitsi and the Long Horn party in Shalako. The Gomaiowish (Koyemshi) clowns of Acoma* are carried on the back in announcing kachina performances; they use a knotted tally string; and the kachina count is in more than one instance decimal—all Zuni traits.† Acoma

* These masks are found at Laguna, Santa Ana, Sia, and Jemez; not at Cochiti, Santo Domingo, or San Felipe (White 7).

† At Zuni it is the Koyemshi who carry another kachina on the back, Kiaklo. Kiaklo, by the way, has a mask like that of the warring Ky'anakwe (Bunzel 5:981, n. 77). Ky'anakwe are reported to sing in Keresan (Stevenson 2:218). In tradition the Ky'anakwe came out of a great cave southeast of the kachina lake; they are not *really* kachina (Bunzel 5:1009-10). Note transvestite impersonation in Acoma-Laguna dramatizations and in Ky'anakwe; also their Corn clan affiliations. Ky'anakwe (Laguna, Shturuka)-Kiaklo-Chakwena appear to be a borrowed Keresan group.

kachina carry a seed pouch, Zuni-like. The Fight with the Kachina has a Zuni flavor, although Hopi also put on dramatizations to check unbelief. Spacing elaborate dramas over considerable intervals is Zuni-like.

Exposure to ants is a trait peculiar to Acoma and Zuni which spread probably from Zuni to Acoma since it is not reported from other Keres.

The Acoma Town chief is virtually over-chief of the Acoma kivas, a Keresan, not a Zuni, trait; nevertheless, the Acoma kiva system has been affected by the Zuni system; it is not the two-kiva system of the other Keresan towns but the six-kiva Zuni system, and, as at Zuni, the kivas are peculiarly related to the Kachina cult. Kiva chiefs are dance chiefs, and each kiva presents its own kachina group, as at Zuni, for the summer-rain dance. As happens frequently in borrowing, this Acoma celebration is less elaborate than the Zuni summer kachina dances. At Zuni each of the six kivas presents in turn its dance for one or two days at intervals of several days or weeks; at Acoma there is but a single celebration, with two kivas presenting their groups each for two successive days. (Possibly the Keresan two-kiva pattern of dance presentation may have had an influence, although in the Keresan pattern proper the two kivas alternate each day.) The kick-stick race, which is associated with kachina ideology, probably passed from Zuni to Acoma and other Keres. At any rate Acoma and Zuni kick races are alike in several particulars; in betting, the wagers being stacked in the court; in painting the sticks, and in supervision by War chief.

The association noted at Acoma* between ceremonial functions and clanship is a Zuni trait, but it is still more a Hopi trait. The legend of how the Acoma Corn clan got into their clan Shuracha, the virgin fire god, is typically Hopi. The clan head meets Shuracha making his bonfires to heat the Earth Mother into fecundity. "I am glad to receive you and welcome you," says the clan head, "I want you to be our head." So the kachina

* Not only of clanship to Town chieftaincy but in tradition to other chieftaincies; see p. 246.

stayed with the Corn clan.[23] That Acoma in developing its clan system was in close relation to Hopi is proved by the fact that the paternal aunt gives her godchild one of her clan's stock of personal names, a naming complex peculiar to Hopi.

Acoma shows other Hopi traits. Its two-part kachina initiation, first the whipping of the children, boys and girls,* and later the indoctrination of the boys, appears to be very much like Hopi ceremonial. In both the Acoma kachina dramatizations the clanspeople in charge are helped by those they sponsored at the kachina initiation, just as Hopi young people join the societies of their kachina sponsors. There is an intriguing similarity between the appearances of Whipper kachina and the K'oвishtaiya and of the Hopi Whipper and Cloud chief, Hail chief (in mask), Ice chief, and T'aiowa, also mountain seasonal chiefs, at the winter solstice. Acoma has an altar for the kachina, Hopi way; nowhere else is there a kachina altar. For little children of First Mesa and Acoma, kachina and crows are identified in reference: "Watch for the crows flying by in blue moccasins; kachina stockings [? netted stockings] are crow stockings; the crow bring presents."[24] Acoma's summer-rain dancing does not follow upon rain retreats, as among eastern Keres and at Zuni (in part), but is concentrated into one long performance, as in Nima'n, the Hopi summer kachina ceremony. In Nima'n there figure a broad paddle-like prayer stick, gourd disks painted in the colors of the directions, a miniature yucca ring, and pencil-shaped prayer-sticks: all implements in a ritual game called *toki^amoti* at Acoma: the balls are rolled to make thunder and lightning between goal posts (pencil prayer-sticks).† The kachina masks of Acoma are kept, as on First Mesa, in a side room or recess of the kiva. The built-in drum or slab resonator which is danced on over the *sipapu* is another common Acoma-Hopi kiva trait. Ma'sewi k'am, the house of Ma'sewi, under a boulder, sounds like Maski, the house of Masauwu, a cairn. The returned scalper

* Eastern Keres do not whip at the initiation, and Zuni do not whip girls.

† Stirling; Stephen 4: 529, 570, 573, Figs. 320–22. Compare Zuni Rain chiefs' thunder balls, p. 378. A stone disk is used in a different game of quoits, *k'oti'*, stone-shooting, played at Hano.

may throw the scalp at another man, at Acoma to get a "brother," on Second Mesa to get a substitute. Other ritual parallels are: scrotum rattle; stuffed birds used by clowns; honey in smoking; deer skulls painted; prayer-feathers fastened to images by altar visitants; the War god image of Walpi[25] or the image of Dawn Woman of the Horn society compared with that of Iyatiku (Stirling); the frame and meal altar of Horn society and the Acoma altar type; use of the Galaxy as wall- or sand-painting design; a red war prayer-stick pointed at both ends; marked use of prayer-images. Mating the corn goddess is an Acoma–First Mesa parallel: Iyatiku and Tiamuni, Tihküyi and Müy'ingwa, both underground couples; and the "husbands" of the corn are represented on Hopi altars. At Acoma and Walpi the Chiefs of the Directions are more outstanding than elsewhere. In both Acoma and Hopi Emergence myth Badger and Locust are the first to be sent up to find an opening. The Acoma corn fetish is called by the Hopi term for badger,* probably because Badger and not Bear is or was, as among Hopi, the outstanding curer animal (see p. 190). Finally, we may note in passing that the peculiar traditional functions of the Acoma War chief—solar observation, water and corn ritual—are those of the Patki clan of First Mesa as well as of the Pekwin of Zuni.

Western influence is less marked at Laguna; Laguna retained the typical two-kiva system of Keres, also the affiliation of its Town chieftaincy was with society rather than with clanship. However, one Laguna lineage (in Sun clan) is recognized as Hopi, and clanship is associated with ceremonialism in the Western mode. Kick-stick races were run by clan. Salt-gathering, as at Acoma, was connected ritually with the Parrot clan. There are clan grinding-songs. Clan heads addressed prayer-sticks, Hopi fashion, to the eponymous creatures of the clan. Clan heads may have functioned at the solstice ceremonials, and it is possible that the corn-ear fetishes, the "mothers," were originally kept, again Hopi fashion, in the maternal houses of the clans and loaned, as they are loaned today,† to the shamans.

* Compare Hopi and Acoma terms for full ear.

† Parsons 33:214 ff., 254–55, 277; Parsons 20:96. Of course, lapse of society organization as well as loss of kivas may have given lineages new functions.

The Kachina cult shows Hopi-Zuni influence. Certain masks are kept or used by certain lineages or clans. The head of the cult at one time was of Zuni descent, old man Surni of the Badger clan, custodian of the Gumeyoish (Koyemshi) masks. Many Laguna kachina have Zuni names; I heard of a Laguna man living at Zuni who was initiated into the Kachina society and danced kachina at Zuni. Laguna are the only people against whom the Big Shell may not be blown in war or the Shomatowe war songs be sung.[26]

Between western Keres and Sia there are several parallels in the Kachina cult which suggest borrowing;* a close relation of the Kurena society to the Kachina cult (at Sia the Kurena chief was custodian of masks and directed dances; at Laguna the chief led in the kachina; at Acoma the kachina initiate is said "to be made Guiraina chaiany"); Sia girls as well as boys are or were initiated into the Kachina cult as at Acoma and Laguna but excepting Santa Ana this is not the case in other Keresan pueblos, and there is a whipping rite in the initiation; as stated, there are Sia Gumeyoish (Koyemshi) kachina and a Sia Snake ceremony. Sia like Acoma has preserved the ancient chieftaincy in charge of the wild food supply, although at Acoma the three Chraik'ats[i] or "stewards" are associated with the War chiefs and at Sia, with the Town chief.

After Laguna ceremonialism was shattered to its foundations in the seventies, and conservatives departed to Isleta, their society rituals were welcomed and incorporated into the Isletan system. The Laguna Fathers were co-ordinated with the Isleta Fathers in ceremonial and in myth, the home society representing the Older Sister of the Corn Mothers, and the Laguna society, Younger Sister. Stick-swallowing and fire-handling rituals were introduced by the immigrant shamans. The immigrant women who introduced decorated pottery and paint brushes of yucca fiber also taught how to ask Clay Old Woman for clay.[27] The Bear medicine complex with witch-finding and witch-fight-

* Possibly union. See White 5. But it must be remembered that resemblances in language and even in pottery are a better argument for sometime union than resemblances in ceremonial traits which are more readily borrowed and are besides less ancient.

ing was borrowed probably much earlier, from Keresan neighbors.

Other traits were also borrowed from Keres. Between Isleta
and Acoma there are striking parallels. In both towns the Town
chief is supreme, and relations between Town chief, War chief,
and curing societies are virtually identical. Each town has a
single summer rain ceremony. The four Rivers addressed by
Acoma societies may be compared with the Water People of
Isleta. Acoma and Isletan societies paint their walls with pictures of Bear, Eagle, Mountain Lion, Snake, with Koshare and
Kachina.* The Isletan association of the father's sister with
dance presents and naming indicates Acoma, if not Laguna (or
Hopi), influence. The way infants get names at ceremonies is
Hopilike.

A few features at Isleta may indicate Santo Domingo influence: the Pinitu dance and the rabbit hunt with the girls, temporary clowns and the office of Kabew'iride or Bow chief who
may parallel the Bow chief or Chraik'atsi of Keres, keeper of
game and wild food.[28] In turn, periodic washing of the Scalps
together with the use of Scalp wash medicine at Santo Domingo
may have been borrowed from Isleta, since it has not been
recorded in any other Keresan town.

Comparing Isleta with Taos for hints on what Isleta (or other
southern Tiwa) may have borrowed from Domingo, Acoma, or
other Keresan neighbors, we note in Isleta the importance of the
Town chieftaincy, the guards and warlike helpers of the Town
chief (Kumpa and Bow chief), curing societies, several maskless
kachina performances, temporary clowns, cave-dwelling mythical serpent and the ceremony of bringing him into the "round
house" kiva,† finally the principle of associating descent with
ceremonial groups. Between the heads of these groups, the
chiefs who are called Corn Mothers, and the paramount Rain
chiefs of Zuni, who in ritual phrase are called Corn chiefs, there

* But wall-paintings are made elsewhere also (see p. 356, Pl. IV).

† The report in 1714 that there were no kivas or subterranean chambers in
the abandoned town of Isleta (Twitchell II, 328), proves that the Keresan-like
"round houses" were built after the return from Hopiland (1718), if not indeed
much later.

may have been some historical connection. Yet Isletan Corn groups, the heart of Isletan ceremonial organization, are enigmatic and probably will remain so, for lack of information about those extinct Tiwan towns to the southeast or east, some of which (eastern Piro) were abandoned even before the arrival of the Spaniards.

Between Isletans and Hopi visiting relations are a matter of record (see p. 925), and, as suggested, the ritual importance of "aunt" or "made" aunt at Isleta and naming infants at a ceremony may be from Hopi, also a principle of matrilineal descent and in particular the tradition of how Eagle people got their name from an eagle feather dropped on a crybaby (pp. 257–58).

Eastern Tewa as well as Isletans borrowed the Keresan society, specifically Flint and Fire societies, and so did Jemez whose ceremonial organization in general is Keresan.* Jemez and Tewa, also Isleta and Taos, borrowed the Kachina dance cult from Keres; Jemez quite fully, Tewa, particularly San Juan people, less fully. At San Juan there is said to be but one masked dance during the year, at night, in kiva. But there are other kachina dances without mask. Turtle dance, which is a variant of the Good Kachina dance of Zuni, is performed without mask at San Juan and at Taos. "Jemez dance," the notched-stick dance, performed in the West in mask, is performed at Jemez ("Hopi dance")† and at Isleta, without mask. It is significant

---

* Only recently (1922–33) the Santiago hobby horse was introduced from Santo Domingo into the Porcingula fiesta. "Horses accompany the Santo Domingo Bull, why not the Jemez (Pecos) Bull?" may have thought some Jemez visitor to Santo Domingo [if not to Cochiti when on Santiago's Day, July 25, the stick horse which is kept and fed by the Town chief is ridden by him or by a Koshari clown (Goldfrank 3:46).]

Recently, by the way, the Santa Clara Eagle dance has been introduced into Jemez, songs and all.

† In time of famine Jemez was resorted to from First Mesa and from Zuni (Stephen 4:1022, 1046; Bunzel 6:59–61). "Hopi dance" and "Zuni dance" may well have been introduced by these visitors. Surni of Zuni, who tells us of his boyhood, yearlong visit at Jemez, says that the Zuni visitors were asked to dance. We may note various Hopi influences or parallels at Jemez: The Women's societies in relation to the Clowns, and the women's Flute dance (Basket dance); the powerful society of Under chiefs and the affiliated Cactus society (compare Hopi Agave society and the extinct 'Yu"yuki society of Hano); an identical

that throughout the East these basic kachina dances are performed as maskless dances.

What reached Keres from Tewa? Probably the two-kiva system with its patrilineal membership. Also the moiety principle as applied to the clown organization. This is very marked at Cochiti, where Koshare and Kurena alternate annually as managing societies.* Elsewhere among Keres (also at Zuni) the two clown groups are associated, respectively, with winter or with summer dances. The moiety or dual principle spread to the medicine societies at Santo Domingo and affects the kachina cult and the appointment of the secular officers, the alignment being: Turquoise kiva and kachina dance group, Flint society (Town chief), Koshairi, War chiefs and staff and Squash kiva and kachina dance group, Shikame society, Quiraina, Governor and staff.[29]

As moieties are less marked at Picurís and still less marked at Taos than among Tewa, the principle appears to have spread northward. It spread through kiva and racing organization, rather than as a principle of descent. The racing alignment actually or conceptually is North- and South-side peoples, Sun and Moon, game and fruits.†

---

kachina mask (Bear mask of Hano and Bear mask of Jemez Fire society); the race in which the overtaken one is painted black; "Hopi dance" including meal-sprinkling by the Fathers (compare Nima'n kachina); sunrise racing; racing by men or by *women* overtaking the bearer of sacrosanct things; Water Serpent ritual, i.e., bringing an image in from the spring and probably other unrecorded serpent ritual; wrangling; the Navaho-like, feather-stoppered reed war offering; crook and miniature kick-stick among prayer-sticks; a long string prayer-feather; petrified wood in shrines (the Jemez pieces were probably brought from Hopiland). The hair cut of the little girl, Jemez and Hopi, is the same, shaved on top and a fringe around (Stephen 4:Fig. 104; Harper). Jemez children play with stuffed squirrels (Harper). Did not some Jemez visitor to First Mesa, child or adult, get this idea from the clown play with stuffed animals? We recall that twenty-year visit of the Jemez "apostates" to Walpi.

* In turn the Kurena spread to Tewa. At Santa Clara besides two sets of Kossa there is a Kwirana (Kurena) group. The chief of the Nambé Kwirana lives at Cochiti, "where the Kwirana belong" (Parsons 49:132).

† Expressed in Isleta and in Tewa myth (Parsons 42:15) and in Jicarilla myth (Opler).

Spanish writers of the Conquest refer to tribal neighbors of the Pueblos, but little about direct cultural influences can be inferred. Study of the distribution of parallel traits is more fruitful, although conclusions are still very uncertain. The affiliations of two of the Pueblo languages, Zuni and Keresan, are still obscure. Hopi belongs definitely in the Uto-Aztekan stock, a Shoshonean language, the dialect closely related to that of the Shoshoneans of southern California (J. P. Harrington). Tanoan and Kiowa are more or less related, and they are classified by Sapir under one of his six major linguistic groups, Aztec-Tanoan. Zuni is placed here as a guess. Keresan is placed in the major Hokan-Siouan group.[30] Boas, who is the authority on Keresan, finds no affiliations. Keresan is one of the most complex of Indian languages; it has the earmarks of a very ancient one. Bearing upon Sapir's classification is the fact that between Pawnee (Caddoan-Siouan) culture and Pueblo culture there are some marked similarities.* To be sure, the Caddoan Wichita, neighbors of the Pueblos on the southeast, were closer to the Tanoan-speaking Tiwa or Piro than to Keres. Tano-Kiowan and Shoshonean show resemblances with Southeastern languages (Swanton; Harrington). The linguistic picture is still highly problematic. Furthermore, affiliations in language do not necessarily determine other cultural affiliations which may arise, everyone knows, quite apart from language.

Students of California peoples opine that Pueblo traits, notably secret society and initiation, impersonation of Spirits, curing by Spirit impersonator people made sick by the Spirit, ground altar and altar sand-painting,† fetish bundle, and the whizzer,‡ spread anciently into California from the Southwest.[31]

---

* Parsons 51; see pp. 1034–37.

† Dr. Boas has just reported, by the way, a "sand-painting" altar among Dakota, a circle in red ocher.

‡ Pole-climbing is also mentioned; but pole-climbing occurs only at Taos and may not be aboriginal. Note foot-drum where Kuksu spirit cult is found. Note the rabbit boomerang stick in southern California.

In turn, Pueblo moiety and clan in their ceremonial aspects have western traits. Distinctive animals or plants or paints are associated with the Summer and Winter moieties of Tewa and with the Black Eye and Red Eye moieties of Isleta, as among various California peoples.[32] Clan and lineage organization of Shoshonean Luiseño, Cahuilla, Cupeño, and Serrano of southern California parallels that of Shoshonean Hopi, except that descent is patrilineal instead of matrilineal; there is the same complex of clan chief (priest), clan bundle, and clan house. The lineage subdivides and takes on a new name but avoids marriage with the parent group; clans as they begin to lapse merge with larger groups, forming, as among Hopi, pseudo-phratries. The bundle, *maswut*, is covered with reed matting[33] and reminds us somewhat of the wicker-covered bundle of canes of the Hopi Marau society or of the Zuni Rain society. In the Cupeño bundle are crystal-bearing wands, eagle feathers, eagle-feather skirts, eagle-down headdresses, feather wands (? prayer-sticks), and shell money. Women of the household feed the bundle, and presents are made to it. The chief or priest obtains his power from the bundle which he talks to in bundle, i.e., esoteric, language. The bundle and the house it is kept in are very sacred. The bundle is the "heart of the house" (Cahuilla). Contents of bundles vary according to clan or tribe. The main fetish in the Serrano bundle is a long feathered string. The clan priest goes into retreat in the big house or dance house three days prior to the ceremony, when the bundle is brought out and smoked.[34]

Other parallels with Pueblos are the clown-messenger who is feared for his "charms," i.e., black magic; transformation of shamans into bears by putting on bear skin; curing by sucking out disease object and by brushing;* sickness from soul loss (heart, Pueblo); black magic by evil shamans and by non-shamans; stinging-ant ordeal (Zuni, Acoma); piercing of septum of initiates (Cahuilla) (Zuni, Shuma'kwe officers); salt, meat, and grease taboos at critical periods, also cold-water taboo and

---

* Here, as in the case of many traits I shall be citing, the distribution is quite general in the Southwest or beyond. In some correlation or another, inclusion may be of value and is preferable to drastic exclusion.

baking at childbirth (Zuni, cooked at birth); semicouvade for father; self-scratcher (Hopi); girl in adolescence ritual kept covered (in shaded room, Hopi) and fasting from salt and meat; knowledge of datura (the use is dissimilar); bead string measured on hand of chief as payment; ritual smoking; the rite of exhalation (to blow a spirit to its destination); purification by bathing and by emesis; six repeated month names;[35] clan ownership of eagles and ritual killing of eagles and burial with offerings; eagle dance (?); "enemy songs" or songs of ridicule (of other clans) during ceremony.[36]

But in southern California it was among the coastal peoples that Pueblo-like traits occurred in greatest numbers: most of the above-mentioned traits besides rain prayers, meal-sprinkling, smoking on fetishes, aspersing with spring water; and the distribution of all these traits in California has been from west to east. To account for this, the opposite of what might be expected in considering Pueblo sources, Strong has suggested that early connections were severed by the intrusion of the Yuman peoples of the Colorado River,[37] followed later by the southerly movements of the Shoshonean Paiutes and of the Athapascans, who are without ceremonially organized clan or moiety.

YUMAN PEOPLES

Before reviewing parallels with other groups in the great Shoshonean populations hemming in the Pueblos, with the southern Paiutes and southern Utes, or with the Uto-Aztekan peoples of southern Arizona and Mexico, let us pause among the Yuman peoples of the Colorado and lower Gila: Havasupai, Walapai, Mohave, Yuma, Cocopa, and Maricopa. With these Yuman tribes Pueblos have war traits in common, notably the fetishistic character of scalps and dancing around the scalp pole.[38] With Maricopa in particular, close neighbors to Pima, there are Pueblo parallels: purificatory retreat including vomiting by scalper (sixteen days), scalp-washing in order to adopt scalp, verbal attempts to make scalpers laugh (compare Pueblo rules against laughing, p. 467, n.*), bringing old scalps out in ceremonial (Isleta), guarding scalps in jar in communal chamber by scalper custodian, belief that scalps are noisy, dreaming in connection with scalps (Isleta).[39]

The striking Maricopa-Hopi parallel in naming has been noted (p. 60, n.†) and see p. 1055, n.†† for self-scratcher. Other Pueblo parallels are: six month names repeated; counting the duration of a ceremony by nights; four-day fast from salt, meat, or grease; fire jugglery; smoking for rain, for curing, or as a generalized prayer act; curing by brushing, spraying spittle, blowing, and sucking; sickness from animal (deer) and curing through power from animals or birds; search for lost soul by shaman; bewitching by shaman; paying dance visits and receiving presents (throw-away); talking backward by clown, in cotton mask or with face painted black and red; backward or contrary behavior imputed to the dead; plural deaths and transformations (Hopi); ordeals (ant hill, Acoma, Zuni; whipping) for youths or little boys; races (relay and kick-ball) at which runners are exposed to black magic (Isleta, Zuni).[40]

Special Zuni parallels are: semicouvade (general among Pueblos but specially marked at Zuni); hot bed* for delivery or confinement; twins referred to as elder brother and younger brother (compare War god twins); formalized friend (M., *kiyi'*; Z., *kihe'*); datura diagnosis;[41] piercing the septum.[42]

Yuma at the confluence of Gila and Colorado rivers also pierce the septum, fast from meat and salt, and have a kick-ball race, at which black magic may be practiced. For war training boys sling at each other hard mud balls from the tip of a willow stick (compare Hopi mud-flinging kachina). Corn (unground) is scattered on ceremonial persons or objects or into excavations for a ceremonial house. The doctor both causes and cures bewitchment; but anybody may suddenly get the power to bewitch. The doctor looks into a bowl of water (or today into a mirror!) to learn the circumstances of bewitchment. The soul may be taken by deceased relatives (compare Havasupai, Zuni). Cloud spirits bring rain, and they may be thought of as dancing. (One of the songs brings rain because it makes the Cloud spirits

---

* Noted among other Yuman peoples: Yavapai, Walapai, Havasupai. A Yuman source for this Zuni-Acoma-Sia trait is indicated. But see p. 46, n.*.

dance.) The rain-maker, who not only brought rain for the crops but a thunderstorm to confuse the enemy *while he remained at home*, looks after the Scalps, taking them out and brushing the hair (Isleta). When the Scalps cry, their guardian knows a projected raid against their people will be successful. The scalp is kicked, four times, and thrown into the air, to the rising growls of the warriors (Zuni). Women dance in a circle around the scalper, who bathes and fasts for four days. According to one early account, the hearts of certain enemies were taken out (compare Hopi) and eaten or burned. Father Font reported in 1775 that the Yumans believed fierce animals lived underground; Pima had told them so. The Jesuit also reported that Yuman shamans practiced blowing, a far-flung Indian rite that seemed everywhere to annoy the friars. Yuma timed their planting period by the rising of the Pleiades or Orion (compare observation of these constellations by Tewa).[43]

Yuma got their Hopi cotton blankets or black cloth through the Mohave-Havasupai trade route,[44] but Mohave themselves were not itinerant traders, and between them and other Southwestern peoples there appears to be a gap in religious practices and in ideology (Kroeber), although the dream design which is central in their culture is not altogether unparalleled.* Another northern Yuman people, the Havasupai, are visiting neighbors with Hopi, and cultural borrowers. The most conspicuous loans are of kachina and of clown;[45] other common Havasupai-Pueblo traits we have already mentioned.[46]

PIMA-PAPAGO

Pima and Papago are the Uto-Aztekan peoples who are today the nearest tribes to Zuni on the southwest and with whom trade or travel connections have existed for centuries.† Although the

---

* The cultural function of dreaming throughout the Southwest and peripheral regions should be studied.

† Fray Marcos heard a great deal about Cibola from the Sobaipuri (Soba Jipuris) tribe on the San Pedro tributary to the Gila, and even talked with an old man from Cibola, probably from Hawikuh, since he said that was the largest town (Hodge 3:18). The old man had fled from home because of some troubles

general ceremonial system of Pimería differs from Pueblo systems, shamans or chiefs perform a number of Pueblo-like rites or ritual complexes in curing or in controlling weather. Scalps taken from Apache were kept by the Pima war chief in a jar in a cave or special house to be used, Zuni way, in calling wind or rain.* The Scalps of Pimería caused and presumably cured paralysis. We recall the twisting sickness caused and cured by the sometime war society of Hopi, the Wüwüchim, and by its affiliated women's Marau society, and that Isletan Scalps cure certain ailments. Like Tiwa Scalps, Pima Scalps might be noisy.

Pima curers, like Zuni curers, are differentiated from shamans for weather and crops and war. Unlike Pueblo shamans, Pima shamans have dream experience,† are visited by their super-

---

(a witch in exile!). A "red house" lived in by people from Cibola was noted by Coronado, probably in Sobaipuri country (Hough 1:37).

Piman Indians who had lived fifteen and twenty years in Cibola talked with another Spanish explorer in 1540 (Hodge 3:47, 49). Much polychrome pottery, also cremation, both Middle Gila River traits, were found at Hawikuh (Hodge 3:15). See p. 1027, n.* for further discussion. Poisoning arrows was another common trait (Velarde, 128).

Sobaipuri also traded with Hopi, "holding fairs" (here was a source of macaw feathers [Pima bred macaws] and of cotton), until there was a fight, sometime before 1716, and "Pimas killed many Moquinos." Then Apache occupied the pass of the Gila River and cut off communication, although the road between Sobaipuri and Hopi was only three days (!) (Velarde, 129, 139). Eventually, the Apache-harassed Sobaipuri merged with Papago.

* In 1716 there was weather control for war, "to make snow fall when they are going to fight the Apaches or other enemies, or to make the wind blow hard against the faces of their adversaries so as to make their own arrows go more directly to the mark, or to raise fogs on the hills in order not to be seen by their enemies, or to make the rain fall and take away clouds" (Velarde, 135-36). Navaho warriors also prayed for wind and snow (Hill, 12), and Navaho and Apache were believed by Pueblos and Papago to be able to control the kind of weather they wanted in raiding, mist or rain (Parsons 42:166; Underhill 3). The Papago shaman himself blew smoke toward the enemy to cause mist or fog, and there was a fog-making song (Underhill 4). Here are conceptual clues to why or how weather control at Zuni or elsewhere came to be associated with the Scalps.

† This trait and many others Pima share with their Yuman neighbors, the Maricopa, but to what extent Pima have been influenced by Yuman culture opinion is divided or suspended.

Between Maricopa and western Pueblos there is a specific "bad dream" resemblance, sickness being caused by dreaming (Spier 4:6–7) and, among Pima and western Pueblos, treated by whipping by masked personages.

natural patron, and may pass on power by throwing a sharpened stick (arrow) at the heart of an apprentice—a curious echo from the far north. Held responsible for misfortunes or all unexplained ills, as bad shamans, not as witches, they may be killed. Yet probably among Pima, as among Papago and Pueblos, fear of witchcraft (and of gossip) regulates conduct.[47]

In general, Papago shamans resemble the Piman. One type of Papago shaman divines causes of disease, the position of the enemy, the direction from which rain will come, and which is to be the winning side (Isleta). Through dreams he secures an animal helper. The curing shaman is also a dreamer, singing his dream.* His animal helper or guardian spirit gives him power (over one kind of sickness). His songs are rendered unintelligibly in order to keep his power to himself (Hopi).[48] There is a specialist sucking curer.

In Pima-Papago theory several animals and birds cause disease: among Pima, badger, bear, deer, coyote, dog, gopher, jackrabbit, mouse, horned toad (rheumatism), rattlesnake (stomach trouble in children), turtle (crippled legs),† eagle, hawk, owl‡ and buzzard; among Papago, badger (swelling, neck boils); butterfly (diarrhea and sleeping spells in children); coyote (itch); deer (cough, tuberculosis); frog (body sores); Gila monster and horned toad (sore feet, from stepping on them; as among Pueblos, something red should be tied around the creature's neck);§ owl (sleepy and dizzy "heart-shaking"); quail (sore eyes); chapparal cock (stomach pains); snake (abdominal pains); turtle (foot sores); gopher (menstrual cramps from sitting on a gopher hill). Sickness also comes from winds, including Whirlwind, and from plants (Papago). Sickness in children may be caused by what occurs in pregnancy; sores from Buzzard, if

* In a song dreamed after killing an eagle, a little (Zuni) Kolowisi serpent is named.

† To cure, a rattle is shaken. (Any Pueblo conceptualism between turtle rattle worn under the knee and cramps?)

‡ In Papago opinion the dead appear as owls (Underhill 3). Compare the Zuni story of the ghost woman changing into owl (Parsons 1:250).

§ Isletans ask it for a belt or dress (Parsons 52:211 and comparative note). Compare Toad doctors at Santo Domingo.

a buzzard eats some of a hunting husband's kill; fever from Cow if the husband torments a cow; convulsions from Rabbit, if the husband kills a rabbit (Papago). Compare Zuni pregnancy taboos. The fundamental concept in curing is the same among Papago and Zuni: using some part of the disease-causing creature or, as among Papago and Hopi, an effigy. Possibly the use of animal effigies on altar among all the Pueblos was once similarly motivated.

Pima have or had a kachina-like cult. Their Vipinyim live below a spring or pool at the foot of a mountain; they are impersonated in gourd masks; they do not dance, but sing to notch stick and basket on which their loud-calling masked leader (Kâksh'pakam; compare Zuni term Kok'okshi, Good Kachina) sprinkles corn meal. Standing in front of a patient, they make passes with a long, painted stick. They caused the sickness which they cure, perhaps a lingering sickness like tuberculosis. Navichu is in charge of their masks. He himself wears a mask of cotton cloth.* He is the doctor whom the family of the patient has invited with a bag of meal. He makes domiciliary visits to collect food, also pigment for his ritual stick. If anyone following him fell down, he would whip or stroke him, against rheumatism. He carries exorcising eagle feathers. He assembles ritual paraphernalia (? altar). His supernatural patron lives on a mountaintop.†

The spring in which Vipinyim live was once about to flood the world.‡ A boy and girl were arrayed and sent into the spring.

* Pima in the north painted their cotton clothes red and yellow (Velarde, 132). Compare not only the Koyemshi cotton mask but Hopi Snake kilts, also painted altar cloths.

† On Santa Catalinas, north of Tucson (Russell 2:266, n. a.). This spirit causes swollen knees and inflamed eyes. Navichu shamans are also rain-makers. Russell misidentifies as Navichu the Yaqui Pascola mask which he figures (Fig. 26).

‡ Piman myths of flood are mentioned in 1716: "the Deluge of which they also have their tales" (Velarde, 139).

A Papago version of the flood was that it was caused by the tears of an infant after the Emergence (Underhill), a curious hint of the Aztec belief that the little children to be sacrificed should cry on their way to death to make it rain. Note below too the crying of the sacrificial Papago children.

If the year is to be dry, the children are heard to cry,* and food, beads, and money are cast into the spring, which is a shrine in Papago country. We recognize the Zuni-Hopi myth, the myth of the Water-Corn clan.

Other myth incidents common to Pima, Papago, and Pueblos are: placing sun, moon, and stars; creation from epidermis; Emergence from underground† (by clan and search for the Middle, Pima; Papago emerge in the east, search for the Middle, and travel west, overcoming inhabitants who *live in adobe houses in walled towns*, scattering them north and south); people led by Elder Brother (I'itoi) who has quarreled with Earthmaker (quasi Younger Brother) over their creations after the flood when a new population was made from clay (Papago, compare Acoma, even to term Iyatik‡ for Elder Sister); Elder Brother plants prayer-sticks to indicate where to settle; Coyote as trouble-maker at the Emergence, and Gopher as scout (Papago, Isleta, ? Pima); Elder Brother kills off monsters: man-eating eagle and one who sucked people into his spring (Papago); efficient brother and marplot brother (Papago, Zuni); after ceremonies are instituted Elder Brother returns underground (Papago, Keres, Zuni); mark of flood on a bird's tail (Pima); magical impregnation; twins with powers (Pima), which in actual life, among Papago as at Oraibi, do not persist beyond childhood.

Pueblo-like rites or ritualistic concepts besides those mentioned for Pima are: prayer-feathers and prayer-sticks which are bundled in a set of four or more, like Zuni sticks, and deposited in springs, in field,§ under house posts, at ruins,‖ in shaman's

* Compare the Santo Domingo kachina heard hollering in their spring (White 4:91).

† They "have a fear of the depths of the earth (compare Zuni), although in the same silly way as that which they show in speaking of the Deluge" (Velarde, 136–37).

‡ Compare also Papago term for sacred things: *iyakta* (Underhill).

§ Shamans for crops, weather, or war will bury a stick three or four inches long in the middle of a field, a *wheat* field (Russell 2:258). Compare the three-inch splints stood upright facing east in the fields of the Totonac of southern Mexico (Starr, 188).

‖ "Feathers and arrows for the ancients" (Velarde, 131).

grave, or pressed on the body of a patient, or used in warfare, or kept permanently; smoking for rain, smoking the sick, smoking over sacrosanct objects; exchanging kinship terms in ritual smoking; cornhusk or cane cigarette as offering; anti-sunwise circuit; color-directions (east-white, north-yellow, west-black, south-blue); four the favored numeral; repetition by four in songs,* with a change only of color-direction term or special word (Herzog); arrowpoints from lightning, particularly white ones; diagnosis by crystal; sucking out disease or ailment; blowing on patient; spitting to cleanse; salt abstinence; fetching salt with ritual;† taking fire into mouth;‡ jugglery for magical growth of crops.[49]

Several of these rites have been noted among Papago:[50] eagle or turkey down on sticks which are pointed at butt to be planted (eagle down is independently an offering, compare Tewa downy offerings); diagnosis and discovery of witchcraft§ by crystal; town exorcised of witches (Isleta, Keres); brushing with shaman's eagle feathers; sacred object passed down body or special parts touched; sucking out disease; blowing on patient; use of animal fetish by singing shaman; jugglery (shaman causes drops of water to fall from eagle feathers or crystal), also fire-eating and sword-swallowing; passing cane cigarette and exchanging kinship terms (as preliminary to all important procedure); anti-sunwise circuit; fumigating; and salt (grease, meat) taboo.

Other Papago-Pueblo rites or practices are: offerings of ar-

* See p. 1027, n. †, for Pima-Pueblo similarities in corn-grinding music. Pima rain songs and creation myth songs have some general resemblances to Pueblo music (Herzog, 309).

† They walked with eyes fixed on the trail, i.e., soberly and concentratedly, like Zuni gatherers leaving the salt lake, and they made ceremonial circuits. Like Pueblo warriors, they were segregated on their return, observing continence (?) (Russell 2:94).

‡ This trait as well as others may have been acquired by Pima from Western Apache with whom, as we shall see, Pueblos have several traits in common.

§ An evil shaman would cause epidemic by burying something "out of his heart" placed inside the quill of an eagle feather. The crystal-gazer goes with his helpers to pull up the feather which has sprouted, while in the council house men sing to give him power. When the feather is burned, the evil shaman dies. Isleta all over!

rows, beads, tobacco; tobacco-filled cane cigarettes puffed four times in the directions and then offered; bird down to represent clouds; down worn on head; strewing corn meal (ground from double ears) or putting it in hand preliminary to any request; taboo on naming the dead (Zuni); use of datura, but use generally disapproved; shells associated with war; deer for ceremony strangled (Zuni); notch-stick-playing (for growth songs), gourd rattle (for rain); standard outside council house; use of caves as shrines or depositaries of sacrosanct objects, a widespread and probably early Middle American trait (Bunzel); breathing in from sacred object; also breathing out on it (mask); elaborate effigies carried in ceremonies: birds, deer, clouds, mountains, rainbow (Zuni, Hopi); prayer-images. Ironwood sticks will be buried near a shrine, to represent squash and thus increase the crop, prayer being said to the Spirits of the Directions, who bring the crops. Assemblages were also once held "to sing up the crops" at which were set out effigies of the crops—corn ears carved from giant cactus rib; squash made of ocatello stems covered with buckskin dyed yellow; beans represented by small, spotted pebbles; giant cactus and cholla fruits made of clay and painted wood. Myths of corn or squash were told, and songs sung to notch-stick-playing. The next day the prayer-images were placed in fields or hills by the shamans.

Keeping the scalp in the house of the scalper as "his child" is a conspicuous parallel between Papago and Oraibi. The Papago "child" will work for the family like any relative. The hair has been made into an image of an Apache man, dressed with buckskin shirt, with moccasins, and with a feather on its head. (Compare kachina doll!) The "scalp" may consist of only a lock of hair, even four hairs are enough, two from each temple (compare Zuni Shuma'kwe scalp hairs). Papago Scalps bring rain like Zuni Scalps and whistle or are noisy like Pima and Tiwa Scalps; and scalp-takers cure sickness from Scalps. Love sickness or malaise is caused by Scalps. Scalp-takers, likewise wounded warriors (? Hopi), are segregated. For their sixteen days purification (Pima also) they have ceremonial fathers or godfathers, old men who have themselves been enemy slayers. During these nights men and women holding hands, with fingers interlacing, dance anti-sunwise around the scalp or trophy pole which has been brought in by an old woman. The girls went out first to meet the returning warriors and seize their weapons; then the girls danced and sang and had to be paid before giving back the weapons. Papago belief that the enemy's death lets loose power which you must tame lest it kill you is a widespread belief held inferably by Pueblos.

The major Papago fetish in every village is kept by the Village chief or cacique. It is for rain, a bundle or basket containing stones, arrowpoints, carved stone figures, sometimes a stone frog, and prayer-sticks. This basket is kept in the chief's house, the "big house," a round house. He is a man of peace, and the people used to work his land. He chooses his successor within his patrilineal family (compare Taos). He knows the wise speeches (the prayers). He also has a speaker. The emphasis on speakers for all groups (speeches approximating what elsewhere are called prayers) is very marked (compare Zuni).

The Village chief presides at the rain ceremony preliminary to planting. From the different villages Chiefs of the Directions are impersonated and are the first to be served the ritual liquor. In the Emergence myth shamans are placed on mountains, mountain-dwelling chiefs. The rain shaman called *sivanyi* (compare Zuni *shiwanni*) performs feats of jugglery at the rain ceremony and predicts rainfall. A *sivanyi* leads the salt pilgrims. The handholding, counter-sunwise circle dance of men and women at the rain ceremony "to pull down the rain" may be compared with the Keresan-Jemez-Isleta circle dance before opening the ditch.

The red and white moieties of Papago call to mind moiety-like odds and ends among Pueblos: the red and white Gumeyoish scouts of Acoma;* the red and white sides in the Tiwa relay race run at Isleta and Picurís by moiety. Like Tiwa, the Papago run relay races, on a permanent race track. (For parallels in kick-ball racing see p. 823.) Races are not ritualistic but the

* Compare with Papago race challengers who are chased back to challenger group.

winner brings luck to his locality, i.e., rain. Intervillage visits to race or play gambling games or dance may be compared with Zuni-Hopi intertown dance visits, races, or games (First Mesa). The elaborate naming songs and ritual of visitors whereby those named and therefore blessed have to contribute presents may be compared loosely with the simple song-tying practices of Hopi and Isletans. Possibly song-tying was borrowed from the south by Pueblos and its significance lost.

The Papago salt trip, like Pima and Zuni trips, was a ceremonial enterprise. The volunteer had to go to the Gulf four times (compare certain Pueblo undertakings, pp. 632, 633) else he fell sick. If many volunteered, the date was set eight days ahead; if few, four days. During this period continence was observed and running was practiced. As on the war path, a special vocabulary was used. The men spoke slowly, in low tones, or not at all. They went single file. Prayer-sticks were planted at the Gulf or thrown into it, and corn meal was cast. Omens were observed which were near-visions. Anyone in danger of drowning would not be rescued. The drowned man would turn into fish or bird or after a long time return as a powerful shaman (compare Zuni kachina origin myth). On the return journey nobody might look back. At the close of the journey there was a race (compare Hopi salt trip race, p. 1084). After ceremonial of purification, salt pilgrim, like warrior and deer hunter, remained secluded for four days (compare kiva retreat by Hopi chief after ceremony). The salt was breathed from, for power. The experienced salt-collector, like warrior or eagle-killer, could cure any sickness resulting from taboos broken in the adventure. Indeed any participant in a ceremony was qualified to cure sickness similarly caused. (We may compare the curing ideology of Hopi society, but here the comparison ends, for achieving individual supernatural power, through getting sea shells, eagle feathers, or scalps, is not in Pueblo character.)

Eagle-hunting is very important ceremonially to Papago as to Hopi, Jemez, and in less degree to other Pueblos. Account of the prolonged Papago ceremony of purification after killing an eagle recalls certain Pueblo associations: the prolonged purifications of Zuni Shalako, the use of effigies (taking the Shalako rig as an effigy), and the killing of Shalako to get power in hunting (in Papago ideology the eagle gives hunting power; in Hopi belief Hawk was the great hunter). We recall that the Hopi eagle-be-feathered Shalako appears at Nima'n and that eagle sacrifice concludes Nima'n.

Papago reckon nocturnal time by the Pleiades, also season (compare Tewa). At the winter solstice Papago hold with Hopi that the sun stands still for four days, and at this time the origin myth is told. The Town chief (Keeper of the Smoke, compare Isleta), is requested to tell the myth, requested in familiar Pueblo fashion by putting some corn meal into his hand. He has to fast from meat, grease, and salt, and listeners may not fall asleep.

Other Papago practices or attitudes to be compared with Pueblo are: license during certain ceremonies; intervillage messengers called Mockingbird speakers (compare Acoma Mockingbird war captain); impersonation (as noted in the rain ceremony he who represents each participant village figures as one of the rain gods of the directions, and Sun and Moon and the children sacrificed in the flood are impersonated in procession or dance); mask transformation, with mask on "we are not ourselves"; messengers or errand men required to run (Hopi); racing by women; black-face summoner to dance (compare kachina or clown sheriff); formal, enigmatical language as, for example, in the rabbit hunt for the rain ceremony calling the three fire stones the three shamans or in the salt pilgrimage calling the salt, corn; bowed head and folded arms in religious posture; Clay Mother; no wastefulness of natural resources and, as among Pima,* reproduction encouraged. Toward the close of the November cleansing ceremony (sickness from killed deer), deer meat was cut into small pieces and everybody rubbed a piece downward over face and body, saying, "Make we well!" (Compare Taos.) Food, crops, are the center of ceremonial concern for Papago as for

---

* Fish bones are thrown into the river to become fish. Is such the reason why no fish bones have been found in the refuse heaps of Pecos?

Pueblo, and this is insured by compulsive magic by a group in behalf of all.

Papago like Pima have the Pueblo-like or specifically Shalako-like Vi'pinyim cult and the Vigita or Wiikita* so-called harvest ceremony is celebrated every four years, during ten days in December, by the northern villages in concert.† There are a director-in-chief and for each village a director. Each village camps separately. The contingent is led by the clowns carrying toy bows and arrows (see below). Announcement is made eighteen days in advance. All officials are continent for ten days. The speech-prayers must be kept secret, on pain of dying automatically. There are hereditary song-composers, but the young men who carry the large effigies‡ in dance-song circuits volunteer for four years. They wear a cotton kilt with bells or shell rattles at the belt, and a gourd mask painted with horizontal stripes of black, white, and red. (This mask may be made by anyone. It descends from father to son, and the wearer is probably the owner.) According to one account, the dancer's body is spotted white to represent grains of corn. In each group (theoretically eight bearers or dancers from each town) is an impersonation of yellow corn, Koshpakam, a young boy, wearing, according to one account, a parti-colored blue and yellow gourd mask,§ with the gourd stem forming a snout. In a high piping voice Koshpakam sings the first and last words of each song, or at the close of a song shouts *kuh*.‖

There are Nawichu clown-curers, about ten from each village, wearing a cotton, befeathered mask with hornlike turkey feathers and with cloud designs. They carry a pole (for gather-

---

* *Viik*, bird down, *ta*, suffix meaning made, i.e., prayer-stick-making (Underhill 4).

† At one village the celebration is annual, for one day in August (Underhill 4).

‡ On a trestle, just as images of the saints are carried.

§ Compare the Grandfather masks of Isleta del Sur.

‖ Koshpakam may be compared with Shulawitsi of Zuni and Avachhoya of Hopi (Fewkes 12:83, Pl. XXI; Parsons 40:99, n. 151) who comes out with Hemish kachina at Nima'n. See, too, Acoma, White 2:79; Laguna, Parsons 20:101, n. 1.

ing cactus), also machete, grotesque bow and arrow, and a tobacco pouch, and they wear a shell bandoleer. Legs and arms
are whitened with dabs or spirals. They shoot at deer impersonations, perform burlesques, collect firewood, and visit houses or
camps to collect food for the singers. All objects are passed close
to the ground, including the cigarette that is smoked (Hopi).
They speak in a squeaky voice, since they are supposed to come
from the north and to speak an unknown language. They visit
the fields to cleanse them, mimicking farmers. They are themselves farmers; they brought the squash (compare Zuni Molawia), and some say the corn. They police the ceremonial inclosure. They are feared, for they have much power. If a sick
man is breathed on by Nawichu, he recovers, at the Vigita ceremony or at any time at home when Nawichu is summoned and
the Vigita ceremony is sung to cure sickness resulting from having broken some Vigita rule. Nawichu also brushes his cactus
pole over the sick present at the ceremony or those wanting good
fortune. Nawichu keeps his mask in a jar in the hills; it is too
strong and dangerous to keep near by. The office of Nawichu
descends in the family through the father. (Compare the patrilineal connection of Zuni Koyemshi and of Acoma Koshare.
Other Koyemshi or Pueblo clown parallels are obvious.)* Hereditary functionaries (Chui'wa'tam) sprinkle corn meal for Nawichu and on people against sickness and for longevity. They
stand at the door of the brush inclosure and sprinkle on any who
enter and toward dawn sprinkle everybody present. Their faces
are painted with black specular iron. Sun and Moon are impersonated,† Moon by mask, Sun by a man carrying a tablet-
standard; and the children sacrificed in the flood‡ are impersonated by two boys and two girls who dance to song and notch

* For kachina name see Zuni, Bunzel 5:991–93; Laguna, Parsons 20:101, n. 1,
Fig. 11; Acoma, White 2:76, Pl. II*e*; Santo Domingo, White 4:112, Fig. 24;
San Felipe, White 3:31, Fig. 6. See too Nahalisho, Crazy Grandchild boy im-
personation, Zuni, Bunzel 5:1065–66; Parsons 29:173, 174–75.

† Compare Aztec impersonations (Sahagún, 149).

‡ There was a gaping hole from which poured water that could not be checked
until two boys and two girls were put down into the hole.

stick and basket rasp, and are meal-besprinkled by the Chui'wa'-tam. The boys are painted red with white spots to represent corn, and the girls carry an ear of corn in each hand. For four days afterward the head men fast and observe continence.[51]

Papago of Sonora hold a Vigita mask ceremony which varies in particulars of considerable comparative interest. The ceremony is held yearly, early in August, for rain, good crops, health, and longevity. The fetish is the "heart" of Water Serpent, a green stone. After a great flood when people fled to the mountains, a large pool or lake was left, and here lived Water Serpent with power to draw people to him and to swallow them alive. Montezuma let himself be swallowed and then cut out the heart of Water Serpent, making it into two shapes, male and female, and giving rules about caring for these and holding a ceremony. Each "heart" was laid upon downy eagle feathers in a deer-skin bag placed in a medicine basket which was placed in a jar. Both jars were hidden in a cave whence long ago the male fetish was stolen. But the female fetish is brought out at the full moon and cared for by the old woman who is sister of its trustee, one who appoints his successor. The "heart" is turned in its bundle and the feathers renewed, but nobody looks at the "heart," which in its basket is placed on a platform behind the old woman. *Eto'ne* and Rain chieftaincy of the Water Serpent of Zuni, and Sia Water Serpent myth!

Other special parallels are: road-making with meal by the three men who come out with the two masked dancers from each circular bower, walking with them in single file; meal dropped to mark dance position (compare Oraibi Antelope dance); meal ground from perfect ears (Navaho more than Pueblo); fasting from food and water by the meal-sprinkler, and from food by a choir of four notch-stick players and the woman guardian of the bundle at the altar; buckskin masks and feathered staffs; singing by masked couple stomping opposite each other; dancer relays by all the males, each relay dancing four times, four being the numeral of completion, and on the eve of the final performance making four sand piles in front of the *capitán*'s house; sprinkling the sand piles with meal, in one placing a bunch of medicine feathers and into the other shooting a small arrow.* In the afternoon of the dance two masked clowns put on a mock hunt and a cooking and eating act. The night is given over to drinking *tizwin*, first ceremonially and then drunkenly with induced vomiting.[52]

Papago at Kavorik near the Mexican border have clowns of another type referred to as Devils (Sp., *diablo;* P., *djidjiaur*) or Fariseos (Pharisees) or Nanawichu who come out during Holy Week. The horned masks are made of leather: calfskin, peccary, or buckskin. The Fariseo is licensed to appropriate anything outside the yard, but if pursued with a crucifix (Spanish) or offered a cigarette (Indian) he has to drop his stolen goods. On Holy Saturday a pile is made and whatever is not redeemed with a cigarette is burned, together with the masks. Fariseos run after people, touching them with their staff of cactus rib and they scare the children. On Holy Saturday flowers are thrown on the Fariseos (flower-throwing is a Papago-Catholic prayer for rain) and then each Fariseo is whipped with cactus by a man selected by the "old man" in whose house or under whose direction the masks were made. The impersonators have taken a four-year vow in order to get blessings.[53] The Fariseo clown has spread to Papago, as we are about to see, from northern Mexico.

The Uto-Aztekan peoples best known in northern Mexico are in the northern mountains, the Tarahumara with a population of about forty thousand; in the southern mountains the Cora and Huichol; and toward the Pacific Coast the Cahita-speaking Mayo and Yaqui. All these peoples have traits in common with Pueblos.

---

* These sand piles in the Arizona celebration mark the corners of the sand "fields" made by the five participant villages. Turkey feather prayer-sticks from the fetish basket are placed in the piles. Sand-painting with mountains!

Near the center of the ceremonial scene is placed a tuft of turkey feathers significant of the founding of the village, a very striking Jemez-Tewa-Keres parallel. The dancers will make a circuit around these feathers (Underhill 4).

MAYO-YAQUI: TARAHUMARA

The most spectacular resemblances of Mayo-Yaqui* and Tarahumara[54] with Pueblos are in the behavior of ceremonial clowns and of the masked dancer called Pascola and in dancing Matachina. Chapaiyeka (Yaqui) or Chapeónes (Tarahumara), called Fareseos also, wear crudely painted leather or wooden masks. The Chapaiyeka mask is a helmet type with horns or behaired as a grandfather; the Chapeón has white hair and beard, a face mask which may be shifted to the back of the head.† The clowns carry a painted wooden lance or sword and sometimes wooden dolls or stuffed animals; in their mouths they keep a small crucifix as an amulet, and their rosary protects against sky-dwelling spirits causing body swellings (Mayo). During the Lenten season, the Mayo-Yaqui clowns accompany the image of Christ whenever it is taken from church, and the clowns visit the *rancherías*, as beggars for their organization. They receive an offering in the left hand, turning away from the donor. In general, they act backward. They burlesque, they pretend to consume voidings, they perform chores, and they police, enforcing all regulations and punishing in particular sexual offenses. They themselves are under restrictions of continence, and, if they break them, the mask will stick to the face;

* For a speculative war dance parallel see p. 635, n. †. There are incidentally other parallels, but unfortunately Dr. Beals has not yet published his Mayo-Yaqui information.

† It is like the Mayo-Yaqui Pascola mask. The Mayo-Yaqui leather Chapaiyeka mask is not found among Tarahumara. The grandfather mask of Isleta and the Chapio of Laguna and Acoma is of the Chapeón face type of Tarahumara or Mayo-Yaqui Pascolero.

The Mayo-Yaqui leather helmet is comparable with the Tsabiyo (Grandfather) mask of San Juan (and Alcalde), of Cochiti, Santa Ana, (?)Jemez (Pecos).

It is possible that the Mayo-Yaqui wooden Pascolero (Pascua dancer) face mask spread to Tarahumara (Chapeó), to Isleta (K'apio), Acoma and Laguna (Chapio) (Pascolero dancers from the Yaqui colony near Tucson or from Mexico are invited to Holy Week celebrations by Papago, a few of whom know the dance [Underhill 4]) and that the Mayo-Yaqui leather Chapaiyeka mask spread to Papago (Fariseo), and to San Juan (Tsabiyo), Cochiti (Chapio), etc. Or these masks may have been introduced in all these places by the Spaniards. The two traits, masked clown and Matachina dance, may be associated (Pueblo) or may not be (Mayo-Yaqui).

The derivation of the common clown term is puzzling. Is it *diablo?*

women may not approach them. They bury anyone dying during Lent; one of their own at death is laid out wearing a mask which is burned at the burial (Yaqui). The clowns have godparents and are baptized after their paraphernalia (two masks excepted) are burned on Holy Saturday. Recruiting is by vow, for one to three years (Mayo) or for life (Yaqui), by trapping, or by infant dedication.

It is not clear how Tarahumara ·Chapeónes are recruited. The head Chapeón who alone goes masked has a position of some distinction: he sits in with the officers at trials. Mayo-Yaqui Chapaiyeka appear at the same celebrations as Matachina dancers, but they have no special connection with them as have Tarahumara Chapeónes, who are in charge of the dancers, valeting them, getting them out to dance, or filling vacancies. Standing to one side during the dance, Chapeónes will mark time or call out in falsetto. They may perform the ritual of dedicating liquor.

In all three tribes Matachina is danced for a vow. Among Mayo-Yaqui there is a permanent head man. Music, dance step or figures, dance stick and array are comparable with the Pueblo, but there are no little girl Malinche and bull burlesque as at San Juan. Matachina is danced not only at Church fiestas (*not* during Holy Week among Tarahumara),* but at wake or memorial service, particularly if the deceased belonged to the dance group.

The Pascol or Pascolero dancer appears in the Tarahumara Holy Week celebration, leading processions and dancing his rapid jig to violin and guitar. He is painted but not masked. Among Mayo-Yaqui, Pascola wears a wooden mask (compare Tarahumara Chapeón mask) and dances to flute and drum. With his mask on the back of his head he makes stereotype

* When special groups called Judas and Fariseo perform a dance which is a form of Los Moros sword dance.

Among Mayo the Chapaiyeka are called Fariseos. Possibly Chapeónes do not appear during the Tarahumara Holy Week because at the time they were introduced to Tarahumara the Judas and Fariseos were already established. Also Matachina is not danced during the Tarahumara Holy Week, and with Matachina the Chapeónes are closely associated.

satirical comments comparable with those of certain Pueblo kachina.

The kick-ball race of Tarahumara has many traits in common with the Pueblo kick-race: preparatory ceremonial retreat; "medicine" carried in belt; bewitching the course (Isleta); betting and tying the stakes together (Zuni, also Papago); painting legs white (Taos); crossing the arms (Zuni-Hopi); and affiliation of some kind between runners and warriors. Tarahumara races are held on religious occasions, but they are reported as having no religious significance such as rain-making. Papago runners get power through dreams.[55] Zuni racers may dream prognostications the night before the race; Tarahumara shamans dream diagnosis.

Other Tarahumara parallels with Pueblos are: curing or exorcising fields, animals, or persons; rites of aspersing, fumigating, and breathing;* sucking out noxious things including maggots which squirm; burning hair in exorcism; ashes in exorcism or curing; slashing the air with a knife in exorcism; observance of the ritual directions; five, four, and three as favored numerals (recall that five and three are favored at Isleta, three being a Pueblo anomaly); conclusive, exclamatory thanks; notched-stick-playing (associated by Tarahumara with witchcraft); belief that hunters have bad luck or that a traveler's animal falls sick because of misbehavior of wife; plant animism and the practice of carrying roots in belt; whistling as the language of birds; belief in Water People who are identified with dangerous rattlesnakes (?)† and live in whirlpools,‡ and in dangerous, sickening Whirlwind People; belief that sickness may be caused by the envious or by persons aggrieved in matters of food or drink;

* By breathing on the sick, the curer strengthens the soul sick from fright.

† They sicken children. Recall the Pueblo relation between the snake-bitten and in infants swollen navel; also the mythological sacrifices of the young to Water Serpent. Tarahumara formerly sacrificed children in the court (but as a blood offering).

‡ We are reminded of the Water People of Isleta; the offering of prayer-feathers in whirlpools; the connections between the Tewa Kossa and Water Serpent; and the springs from which emerged the patrons of Kossa and Koshare whose circular face marks represent a whirlpool.

belief that the soul of the doctor travels after the lost soul of the patient, retrieving it; belief that the soul is the breath and is in the heart; great fear of the dead; offerings of food to the dead, especially to deceased group members; belief that everything connected with the dead goes by contraries, the land of the dead being a place of opposites, and the left hand being used in handling food or drink for the dead (a very marked Isletan and Zuni trait).* The dead function at night. The seasons are reversed for the dead, as in Hopi ideology they are reversed for the kachina. Tarahumara observe a sunset horizon calendar for planting at the summer solstice; Orion is observed for bean-planting, and the Pleiades figure at corn-planting. The early world was soft (the sun came too near) and had to be hardened by dancing.

CORA-HUICHOLES

Of all extant Uto-Aztekan peoples, Cora-Huichol tribes[56] of the Nayarit Sierra in Jalisco are the closest in culture to Pueblos. Like Pima-Papago and Tarahumara they are *ranchería* people, yet living in towns under the same early Spanish system of government that prevails among Pueblos, Tarahumara, and generally in remote regions in Mexico. The appointment of the Huichol annual secular offices is in charge of several elders (Kawitero) who dream appointees,† a very striking piece of Indian-Spanish acculturation. The self-appointive Kawiteros instal the officers with their canes. Before the houses of the officers they sing the Jesucristo myth at the nine-day carnival, and they impersonate Jesucristo, who was the first Kawitero. The women of the house regale or smoke the singing Kawitero with incense. Their dream technique apart, the lifelong Kawiteros may be compared with both the Rain chieftaincies and the kachina cult groups of Zuni: they appoint to annual office, they are keepers of

* Marked among the Maricopa of southwestern Arizona as are almost all the foregoing traits. See pp. 989 ff.

† Keepers of the votive bowls and *mayordomos* of the saints as well as secular officers. The bowl-keepers serve for five years. They have to fetch spring water before a ceremony (Zingg). They are subject to fasts.

song or chant myth, they impersonate a supernatural who is the patron of their society.

Huichol shamans are distinguished as curers and as singers, the singers singing the "myths"* throughout a ceremonial night somewhat as do Rain chiefs or kachina impersonators on Shalako night at Zuni. A Huichol singer has two assistants.[57] Curers are unorganized; they qualify through peyote pilgrimage and fasting five days in a sacred cave where they are visited by the Spirits and instructed; they dream diagnosis. All shamans get power from peyote as sorcerers do from datura, Jamestown weed.†

Jesucristo is the teacher or culture hero for all Mexican ways of life. He was killed in Mexico City, as was his dim counterpart in Pueblo lore, Poshaiyanki or Poseyemu or Montezuma. The Huichol earth goddess, our Grandmother Growth, may be compared with Oraibi's goddess of seeds or with Iyatiku, the great underground Mother of Keres, certainly a growth goddess; and the other Huichol wet-season or corn goddesses who are also clouds‡ or water serpents living in the western ocean§ may be compared with Keresan or Isletan Corn Mothers or with Zuni Corn Maidens who hide in the ocean from Sun Youth.‖ The importance of the rain goddesses in Huichol religion and their affiliation with Water Serpent seem to derive from the same

---

* These texts have not been recorded. Zingg has recorded myths as narratives. Presumably song myths are quite differentiated, as at Zuni. The songs of the Tarahúmara chanter are wordless.

† Jamestown Weed Man was a sorcerer, singing a false myth. He had a stone for a heart. Kauyma'li, the hero-trickster, killed him (Zingg). Kauyma'li is the counterpart of Coyote, the Pueblo trickster and sorcerer.

Among Tarahumara datura is greatly feared; it is not used or even touched except by a shaman who can uproot it (Bennett and Zingg 138, 347).

‡ When the clouds loom up and a Zuni woman exclaims to a child, "Your Grandmothers are coming!" the reference may not be to the dead but to rain beings like the Huichol Grandmother or Mothers, to long since forgotten Cloud beings.

§ In Zuni tale these serpents, like all water serpents, are male; but note the female Water Serpent in Hopi ceremonial, their mother (Stephen 4:300, Fig. 171).

‖ Possibly an echo of the conflict between Sun and the wet season or rain or Corn goddesses conspicuous in Huichol mythology.

ideological source from which derived the title of Serpent Mother for one of the two paramount chiefs of the Aztecs, and the titles of Corn Mother or "our Mother" for the Corn group chiefs of Isleta and the Town chiefs of Keres and Tewa. Huichol supernatural water serpents like Pueblo serpents live in water holes, and Wind, which is evil, causing sickness, lives Hopi-like in rocky fissures. Other Huichol spirits live in springs or water holes, like kachina. For first curer, Grandfather Fire, for Masauwü, for Acoma's first Fire shaman, there may be a common prototype. Between the ancestral stone beings of Huicholes and Pueblos the parallel is close. Besides, to both Huichol and Pueblo (and Papago) stone or crystal is fetish, and gods have hearts of precious stones. Huichol gods have animals attached to them, "pets," Hopi would say.

There are many ritual parallels: prayer-sticks and prayer-feathers; prayer-meal which is sprinkled on the canes of office and on the altar, cast on the saints (Huichol),[58] rubbed on the face of ceremonialists, and given as pay; honey with meal offering, done up in cornhusk and very suggestive of the little package on Hopi prayer-sticks; food offering into fire; blood from game animals smeared on fetishes or images or impersonations; miniature prayer-images; staff or cane of office; standard carried behind singers (as for the Pueblo saint's-day choir); masking or impersonation without mask; heads of enemies brought to the ceremonial chamber (Cora); ground altar and sand-painting (Cora); circuit (anti-sunwise) and processional, with five as a favored numeral (compare Tiwa); pilgrimage; smoking in the directions;* bonfires for rain clouds;[59] aspersing to the four directions and zenith with feathers (or flowers); aspersing persons or anything sacrosanct; back shield; drum, notched rasp, and gourd rattle; arm gesture of drawing something in; reciprocal hand kiss; breathing on patient or into one's own hands; spray-

* The Cora who did it for me did not observe the usual Cora anti-sunwise circuit; he puffed east, west, north, south, down, up, and then, just as they do at Zuni, he circled his head with the cigarette.

ing medicine; omen from ease with which new fire* is kindled; stomping as a means of communicating with the Spirits, as in Zuni, Hopi, and Acoma ceremonials and possibly in kachina dancing; also the bowl (votive or medicine) as a means of spirit communication; fasting from salt or meat or sexual indulgence, i.e., from adultery, by ceremonial celebrants;† vigil; automatic sanctions;‡ vow taken in sickness and other circumstance to impersonate or to hold office; purificatory ashes; purificatory bath in river; brushing with grass or feathers in purification or exorcism; blowing on patient; sucking out witch-sent (or god-sent) objects (corn kernels, lizards, stones); whipping which is punitive and apparently of Spanish provenience.

We found no association between disease and animals or insects which is so marked among Pueblos (and Papago); but it is reported that a Huichol witch will put down a prayer-stick against his victim, and the prayer-stick§ will turn into a snake, a lion, or other creature and attack the victim (Kleinberg), or that, after an "arrow" is put down near the victim's house, a wolf appears and kills him. The shaman kills the wolf (Zingg). A suggestion here of nagualism.‖

The function and form of prayer-sticks or arrows is extraordinarily Pueblolike. They carry messages, i.e., prayers, requests.

* The Huichol new fire is that of Holy Saturday. If the flint and steel work easily, it is a good omen; if not, someone may die. The keeper of the canes (*vartero*) kindles the fire (Zingg). Women light their candles from the fire as in village Spain.

† Cora singers, *mayordomos*, and dancers will observe a five-day retreat, eating only one meal a day (Parsons).

‡ If a woman servant of the church (*tenanche*, Spanish-Indian term) is incontinent, i.e., adulterous, her censor will break; the cane of an adulterous officer will break; deer do not fall into the traps set for them because of the adultery of the hunter or his wife (a close parallel to Pueblo belief); sickness or death befalls the person who falls asleep during a chant (Huichol, Zingg).

§ Possibly it is the witch, not the prayer-stick that transforms, in accordance with widespread Pueblo and Mexico beliefs.

‖ There is a similarly obscure suggestion in the small cross called *nawili'ki* set alongside the three large crosses in the Tarahumara yard. This *nawili'ki* is associated with sickness, and food is offered to it whenever food is placed on the altar (Bennett and Zingg, 275).

They talk to the personage they are sent or shot to; and they are placed in the hair to indicate sacred business. The Huichol "shaman's plume" is the regular Zuni prayer-stick with pendent feathers; the Cora-Huichol wheel prayer-stick may be compared with the netted shield prayer-stick of the Zuni War gods, to which miniature bows, arrows, and clubs are attached just as miniature objects are attached to Cora-Huichol prayer-sticks.* Cora use the netted wheel prayer-stick,† Zuni-like, in connection with war; it is addressed to the head taken in war, after five days (inferably there is a ceremony for the head of an enemy), and in time of drought, because the dead enemy is a rain-maker. The Nayarit peoples, like the Pueblos, associate sticks dressed with different kinds of feathers‡ with different Spirits; the prayer-stick made by the Cora War chief is addressed to Morning Star; another type of stick is addressed to Earth Mother (for corn), another to Sun, another to Moon. For the dead and for the spirits of the mountains both Cora and Huicholes make prayer-sticks. Huicholes deposit prayer offerings in rock crevices and in springs and lagoons (Lumholtz). Cora dancers deposit prayer-sticks early in the morning following the dance. Huichol hunters deposit prayer-feathers bunched, a feather from each hunter, in mountain deer shrines (Zingg). Cora and Huicholes capture and cage eagles to supply feathers for prayer-sticks.

The Huichol *sipapu* in court or god house is strikingly Pueblo-like. It is under the fireplace; the Hopi *sipapu* is near the kiva fireplace, a Hopi mother will strike on her fireplace when she is summoning a bugaboo kachina, and the Suyuku bogeys are sup-

* Some of these, like the shaman's chair, may be prayer-images. Many of the animal prayer-images found at Hawikuh are perforated as if to hang (Parsons 19:Fig. 38). Perforated prayer-images have been found in Jalisco (Parsons 63: 470).

† Huicholes associate the netted wheel ("god's eye") with male infants; it represents a male squash blossom (Zingg), as it does on kachina masks. Compare the squash effigies in Hopi squash patches.

‡ According to Lumholtz, the feathers are from the birds associated with the particular Spirit addressed. This is a clue to the use of prayer-feathers among Pueblos, to the association of particular feathers with particular societies, and to the placing of bird skins on Hopi altars.

posed to come up from under a fire in the valley.[60] Huichol spirits also emerge from the *sipapu* in which offerings of food and drink are made, Pueblo-like, also candles instead of prayer-sticks, and which is covered by a disc.

Cora dance masks are sacrosanct; Huichol masks are not.* Huichol masks are new each year, but Cora masks are old; they are kept in a ceremonial chamber and, like enemy heads, fed corn meal. One is called Lightning and comes out on the summer pilgrimage to a sacred mount† for rain. Cora have a snake ceremony preceded by snake hunts.[61]

The behavior of the mask-wearing clown of Huicholes is typically Pueblo clown behavior. He polices or keeps people awake during the ceremony; he leads the wood-gatherers for the ceremony and gets drink for them; he mimics or burlesques the shaman; he may urinate or defecate into drink or food. He carries a rattle (inflated bull bladder in Mayo-Yaqui Chapaiyeka or Tarahumara Chapeón fashion) or a cane. At the carnival celebration there are burlesques of Spanish soldiery or hobby-horse-riding and of bull-baiting comparable with the performance of Sandaro (Soldier) at Santo Domingo and of the Pecos Bull at Jemez. The two Huichol Bull impersonators have abstained from salt, meat, and sexual intercourse. The horns lie on the altar; candles are placed on the tips (instead of feathers, Pueblo style). The burlesque of a Mexican treasure hunt, in which all

---

* Kleinberg reports only one mask at San Sebastian, which is worn by the clown leader of the six dancers at the installation of the Governor on St. Francis Day, October 17. At Tuxpan, Zingg reports only one mask, of Mexican make, worn by the clown in the rain ceremony. However, Lumholtz figures a bark mask of one of the Corn-Serpent Mothers which was kept in a cave, belying statements to Preuss, Beals, and Parsons that there are no sacrosanct masks.

† San Blas, said by Preuss and Lumholtz to be visited also by Huicholes. Kleinberg reports that during an August drought the singer shaman sent offerings to the nearest mountain summits: prayer-sticks, gourds containing miniature tortillas, and clay effigies of animals, of cow, horse, dog, and deer. The effigies were to protect the animals so that the Mountains would allow them to roam anywhere and not harm them by lightning. The other offerings were given to the Mountains so they would send, not winds, but rain. Offerings to Mountains or Mountain spirits are indeed a far-flung trait, Pueblo and Mexican or Middle American.

the officials are roped for hanging, might be staged by any Pueblos.

Huichol treatment of the Spanish canes of office expresses a fetishistic attitude even more than does the Pueblo treatment. Huichol canes are incensed, given candles and flowers, honey and corn meal, the blood of a sacrificed bull, and before them, placed erect in the ground, people kneel, making the sign of the cross and saying in Spanish the usual prayer. At the installation the retiring officers do this, followed by the incoming officers and the Kawiteros, who then give the canes to the officers. After this the canes are placed on the altar of the *casa real* before they are restored to their permanent place in the box of Jesucristo. The Kawiteros themselves carry a staff—a staff of old age like that of Grandmother Growth.

The account we got of the ground altar in the ceremonial chamber of the Cora is curiously like that of a Pueblo altar: prayer-sticks in a row and a row of corn ears, hollowed out and filled with seeds, as are Pueblo corn fetishes or "mothers." They are also the "mothers" of the Cora who, like Pueblos, sprinkle the "mothers" with corn meal and medicine water. There are altar sand-paintings.

In Huichol mythology there is a marked dichotomy of the wet-season supernaturals (Grandmother Growth and the other corn-rain or serpent goddesses) and the dry-season supernaturals, Sun and Fire, with whom rattlesnake, deer, and peyote are associated.* The dichotomy which is expressed of course in the calendar has a possible bearing on the Hopi calendar which so deliberately or artificially restricts kachina or rain-god celebrations to one-half the year. Dichotomy shows also in the ceremonial calendar of Zuni: shamanistic or curing celebrations in winter, and the most sacred or authentic rain ceremonials in summer. Cora-Huichol (and Tarahumara and Papago) distinction between singers or chanters and curers is suggested by the

---

* Note in Isletan myth (pp. 260 ff.) the opposition between Sun, with whom Rattlesnake is associated, and the pursuing Corn Maidens, or, differently expressed, the opposition mentioned before between the Zuni Corn Maidens and Payetemu, the Sun Youth.

Zuni distinction between Rain chieftaincies (and dancers) and curing societies.

Shalako, Zuni's great enigma, is characterized by several traits that occur in the Huichol celebration of carnival or that are in general Huichol-like and in some cases not Zuni-like. The welcome to visitors and their lavish entertainment is unusual; so is or was the heavy drinking that went on Shalako night and the very great distribution of food, including mutton. To count the days for the peyote pilgrims, the Huichol use two tally cords, untying the knots, Shalako style. In one Shalako ritual Koyemshi clowns come in wearing their masks on top of the head, a unique and very surprising arrangement for any Pueblo mask, but occurring for the Huichol clown mask (also for the Mayo-Yaqui mask). The Bull impersonators at the Huichol carnival in certain details recall the horned Shalako impersonators: the Huichol Bull has an understudy; the two impersonators have to fast from salt, meat, and sexual indulgence before the celebration; if any mishap befalls, like a sprained ankle, it is imputed to broken taboo; the impersonation has a characteristic roar or cry. The Bull horns lie on the altar like kachina masks during the eight days of preparation. Altars in houses, new houses, offerings in pit within house or in ground outdoors, and most particularly singing the myths or myth references in these houses are all Huichol· as well as Pueblo features. Another Huichol feature of Shalako is the preliminary deer hunt (from which must have derived the slaughter of sheep or cattle characteristic of Shalako and of Huichol and Tarahumara celebrations). Zuni Shulawitsi is a hunter, also a sun or fire god, quite in character with Huichol mythology, and in Huichol character too he is a virgin. Huicholes stress virginity in connection with fire. Fire may be "tamed" only by a little boy (or girl) too young to have had sexual intercourse. The virginity of the Shulawitsi impersonation is unique in Pueblo circles, and no explanation is available in Zuni myth. This Fire-Corn little boy of Zuni, Hopi, Acoma, Laguna, and of Pima and Papago is surely a southerner.

AZTEC

Of some of Zuni's forebears at Hawikuh, Luxán wrote: "Men and women are pure Mexicans (Aztec) in walking, in crying, and even in their dwellings, but neater than the Mexicans."[62] Between early Aztec and Pueblos there are many ceremonial parallels, in rain and curing cults, in rites of all kinds, and in the pantheon. The mountain rain gods or chiefs, associated with the color-directions, and Lightning, god of fertility and war, are common to both Aztec or Nahuan and Pueblo religion. So are Sun god and Earth goddess and the War Brothers. Pueblo and Aztec or Middle American gods at one time retreated or withdrew underground, sometimes staying under temple or kiva. Pueblo, particularly Hopi gods, have each several traits and names, like Nahuan gods who vary from town to town as do gods of the Pueblos. Aztec and Pueblo gods* are impersonated by their priests or by designated persons. The impersonation may be for a year, and during that year the impersonator is called by the name of the god.[63] Rain gods and their representatives alike wear masks, actual or cloud masks. Animals are the companions or pets of the gods as is the snake or lizard of War and Lightning god,† or like Mountain Lion of the Hopi War gods or Dog of the Whipper kachina. Horned Water Serpent is anthropomorphized on a great scale in Mexico as Quetzalcoatl, on a lesser scale as the lover of maidens who descend into his spring, among western Pueblos. Aztecs also had water serpents that sucked men into their waters, and also a water animal (*ahuitzotl*) that was an agent of the rain gods and drowned anyone *whose company they desired.*[64] Besides, there are horned or double-headed or mul-

---

* Mayan gods also. "In the Temple of Chac Mool found in the substructure of the Temple of the Warriors at Chichen Itza there is a fresco representing five men wearing the mask and the headdress of God B, the Maya rain-god. . . . . These are called God Impersonators, and it is believed that they impersonated the *five* Maya rain-gods who, like the *five* Mexican Tlaloque, were set at the four cardinal points and at the center of the heavens" (Book of Chilam Balam of Chumayel, 67, n. 5).

† Compare his fire snake stick with the snake chief stick of the Hopi. Horned Toad, who is a lizard, sends thunder (lightning) knives (stone points) (Isleta, Lummis 3:76).

tiple-headed serpents that suck men into their caves, among Aztec[65] and Pueblo. In Aztec-Pueblo opinion movements of such great snakes cause flood or earthquake.

Sacrifice of a boy and girl is associated with Water Serpent by Pueblos who, like Aztec, conceive of ritual killing by drowning* as well as by cutting out the heart or cutting off the head.† Sacrificed humans are dispatched to and join the Spirits in Pueblo opinion,‡ and this concept surely entered into the Aztec immolation complex. Just as the Cochiti Bears took out a man's heart so he would live with them forever, so the Aztec god impersonator whose heart was cut out above the temple stairs may have been attached permanently to the god. Another trait in the Aztec sacrificial complex is suggested dimly, in Pueblo ritual and tale, by game or race allowed the victim as, in our terms, a sporting chance. In tale, losers in races lose their heads (as did certain losers in the Mayan ball game). The Hopi kachina cuts off the hair or in tale the head of the man he overtakes, but he does not always overtake a man. The Aztec practice of putting on the skin of the flayed victim in ceremonial is suggested by

---

* Taos, Parsons 64; Isleta, Parsons 52:366-68, 400-402; Tewa, Parsons 49: 302-3; Zuni, Parsons 35:161; Benedict 3:I, 206; II, 117-21; Hopi, Parsons 49: 183:85; Cochiti, Dumarest, 209, n. 2. Consider, too, that in Zuni myth the most important kachina are the children drowned in crossing a river. Possibly ritual drowning was the source of the belief that the weather supernaturals and their cult representatives dying normally live below water. Ritual drowning appears to be related conceptually to the ritual smothering of animals which is to enable the animal spirit to live again at home.

After Blue Corn Girl of Taos enters the kiva under the lake, an ear of blue corn comes up and drifts ashore as sustenance for the people. The ritually drowned girl of Isleta returns as their Mother. Is it possible that once the corn fetishes had to be invested with a spirit obtained through sacrifice just as witches have to get power by sacrificing a relative?

† Boy and girl die from being merely touched by the two witches who bring corn to Zuni and in order to get rain for it must kill two children (Stevenson 2:30), an out-and-out Aztec sacrifice.

‡ Excepting the boy who is offered every year to Lightning, in Tewa tale (Parsons 42:86); this sacrifice is to *feed* Lightning. But compare Parsons 49:302-3 and Benedict 3:I, 10-11; II, 117-21, for the youth who dying *becomes Water Serpent* and for the witch youth who becomes a supernatural in life and has, of course, *to be sent to Kachina town under the lake*. Dispatching anybody or acquiescent departure to Kachina town seems to connote ritual killing.

Masauwü's rabbit-skin mask or by wearing a piece of the enemy's skin in the Laguna war dance.[66] Masauwü wears also a more permanent kind of mask (see p. 237) that scares people away, and he wears it against the enemy. Possibly this was the aim for the near-mask worn by Aztec warriors, the Eagle Knights,[*] so very much like the Eagle headdress worn in the Tewa Eagle dance.[†] In a general way the jaguar pelt worn by the Tiger Knights may be compared with the bear pelt worn by Isleta shamans. (Recall identification of *shuhuna* as jaguar.)

Pueblo suicides are rare or indirect, but in the only folk tale of a direct suicide that I know, the Taos tale just mentioned, Blue Corn girl drowns herself to join the Fathers and Mothers,[‡] the rain beings, just as Aztec suicides went to Tlalocan, the home of the rain gods. Those mountain rain gods, like the kachina, caused certain diseases, and persons dying of those diseases joined the gods. Among Pueblos persons cured of disease join the society of those who cause disease and cure it, and after death Pueblos join the deceased members of their group or society, whether rain-makers or curers. Aztec killed by lightning went to Tlalocan. Compare the treatment of the lightning-shocked at Zuni. They are fed corn meal, like supernaturals, and treatment is conducted by the Rain society of the West. During the ceremonial of this society "there is always lightning, *and someone is always killed by lightning.*"[§] The Hopi who because of sickness in the family presents a kachina or Water Serpent dance may be compared with the Aztec who sick from a mountain-sent disease vowed to make offerings to the Mountain and hold a feast.[67]

---

[*] Compare the bird masks of the Early Chimu culture of northern coastal Peru (Means, Fig. 12). The same type of helmet-like half-mask appears in Mayan bas-reliefs (Chichen ball court temples).

[†] Curiously enough this does not give the impression of being a very ancient or deep-rooted dance. Possibly a colonizing Tlaxcalan taught a Tewa how to make the headdress. See p. 1069, n. §. Did one of Coronado's Indians (see p. 873) introduce Shalako as an Eagle Knight?

[‡] In the Laguna variant, Yellow Woman goes to the drowning place in the lake leading to the lower world (Boas 2:178, 220).

[§] Benedict 3:II, 109. Compare the Isletan "father" whose patron was Lightning and who was killed by lightning (Parsons 52:455–56).

The picture of the masked Aztec priest impersonating his mask-wearing rain-god Tlaloc in procession is strikingly kachina-like, even to the flowing hair (a wig) and the black "smear" on the face under the mask.[68] It was a mask of Tlaloc together with a mosaic turquoise mask of Quetzalcoatl ornamented with a serpent that Montezuma sent to Cortez on his fateful landing,[69] the sort of gift no Pueblo chief would make to *any* visitor, the only analogy, a very remote one, being the presentation of kachina "dolls." Aztec hung small bejeweled masks on the images of the gods;* they were not processional or dance masks such as were worn by the priests.† Between the two types of masks there may have been some such distinction as exists among Pueblos between the masks of kachina chiefs (the gods) and dance masks, some of which are constantly redecorated and even used now for one kachina, now for another.

In the Aztec rain ceremony of every eight years all the gods were believed to appear and, in the semihelmet mask character-istic of the Eagle Knight dancers, impersonated birds, butterflies, bees, and various animals.[70] There were also impersonations of poor people, wood-carriers and peddlers, and of sick persons. This sounds like maskless kachina dancing and comedy like that of the Hopi Piptükyamü. Still more the following: "A hunch-back mask provoked great mirth"; there was obscene dancing.‡ Sometimes in a dance "certain men start to imitate the men of other nations, wearing their clothes and burlesquing their speech. They indulge in other kinds of buffoonery, pretending they are drunk or crazy, or imitating old women. These turns cause great amusement and laughter amongst the dancers and on-lookers."[71]

Aztec chiefs had court jesters. The Sun has his jesters among

---

* According to Peter Martyr, the mask was placed upon the face of the god whenever the sovereign was ill, not to be removed until he either recovered or died (Saville, 19). Compare the Zuni practice of putting the mask on the patient.

† Worn by all the priests in the ceremony of the seventeenth month (Sahagún [a], 95).

‡ Thompson, 241, citing Torquemada.

Pueblos, and so have the kachina.[72] "We have nobody to amuse us," lamented the Keresan Mothers, and created the Koshare; and did not the old ones, the Tewa chiefs, return to the Lake of Emergence and bring up the Kossa to make their sad people laugh and grow cheerful again?

A dance performed in honor of Montezuma *and in his patio* suggests (with variation in details) the familiar Pueblo dance formation and dance array. "They dance in two long lines with linked arms one behind the other. Two well trained dancers head the lines, the others follow them in their movements. When the two leaders sing, the rest reply, or if the arrangement calls for it, only a few. All together they raise or lower their arms and heads, achieving a graceful unison as they move together as though they were all one single dancer." Dancers carry flowers or feather "fans"; they wear feather headdresses or masks in the form of heads of eagles, crocodiles, jaguars, or other wild beasts.[73]

Even the Pueblo saint's-day arrangement would seem to have an Aztec parallel. For the goddess of flowers and dancing, a bower was erected and in this the image of Xochiquetzal was seated. Close by, imitation trees decorated with sweet-smelling flowers (instead of prayer-feathers) were set up.[74]

Kachina processional and dance, saint's dance and bower, burlesque and comedy—all are paralleled in Aztec celebration, ceremonial or honorific. Compare the winding in-and-out movement of two women and a man or of two men and a woman of Aztec and Pueblo war dances; compare also in Aztec and Pueblo rain dances feats of snake or stick-swallowing.[75] In an Aztec war god ceremony a live snake was carried in procession.[76] In the fourteenth month of the Aztec calendar, in November, preliminary to festival in honor of the Otomi war god, a ceremonial hunt, a surround, was held[77] which may be compared with Pueblo ritual hunts. The last five days of the Aztec year were called "idle days"; they did not work during these "unlucky" days, and they refrained from quarreling.[78] Refraining from quarreling at set ceremonial times has a decidedly Pueblo ring, and in Pueblo terms those idle days would be called "staying still," taboo periods found at Taos, Isleta, and, at what might be called the end of the year, at Zuni. The danger which Hopi attach to the December moon might correspond to some Aztec concept the Spaniard would call unlucky. The Aztec procession of virgins carrying seed corn that has been sprinkled with "oil" to the temple of the Corn god and the goddess of sustenance or food plants[79] may be compared with the Powamu procession of Hopi maids and youths who carry to the kivas spruce-enveloped ears of seed corn, women's corn which will yield very abundantly.

At this Aztec maize ceremony as at other ceremonies men and boys make domiciliary calls and are given food. We recall the house-to-house calls by the Hopi meal-gatherers, by the Natashka and other kachina, and by the clowns. The practice is widely distributed among Indians. So is the Aztec-Pueblo practice of taking left-overs home.

Ducking in water for ritual negligence was an Aztec practice,[80] as it is today at Taos, Isleta, and Laguna, perhaps elsewhere.

New fire, drill-made, is carried out from the temple of the Aztec Fire god[81] as it is carried out from the Hopi kiva where ritual has been performed for Masauwü, god of Fire. Like the Aztec "old men," Hopi chiefs throw their offerings into the fire. In both cultures this ritual is performed at a ceremony which features tribal initiation and was one of those annual ceremonies which among both Hopi and Aztec were performed more elaborately every four years. At the Aztec and Hopi ceremony, initiates are carried on the backs of their "godfathers," and there is a special dance by the "lords" or "old men." Aztec infants are presented to the Sun in ritual referred to as rebirth. Water is applied to the tongue, the breast, and the head of the infant, and the body is then washed.[82]

Aztec traders, traveling men, carried walking-sticks or canes, solid, light, black canes, which they would tie in a bundle and venerate with food, flowers, and incense.[83] On returning from the extraordinary trips they made, the cane was placed in the calpulli or "district church" and later in the house shrine, where before eating the merchant offered it food. "Black Cane Old Man" is the name for the cane of Isleta's annual war chief. Zuni have always asserted that their war chief canes "came up with them," i.e., anteceded the Lincoln or Spanish canes or *varas* of office; Sahagún's account of Aztec canes, not only the canes of the merchants but the war chief stick,[84] works in with this tradition, as does also the attitude of the Tarahumara toward their sacrosanct canes. Pueblo canes of office, we recall, are sprinkled with meal or with "holy water" and have a distinctly fetishistic character. They are placed on the altar. The Hopi chief's stick, a horizontally carried stick often carved with the Water Serpent, certainly antedates the Spanish *vara*. To be considered also are the crook sticks placed on Hopi altars to represent deceased members of the society, the crooks of longevity, sticks touched at the end of a race or at other times, and the crooks in prayer-stick bundles, including the crooks offered at Acoma as a prayer for strength by men about to take a journey.*

Aztec seem to have used "gum paper" very much as Pueblos use prayer-feathers. Gum paper was tied to canes and placed around the images of the gods, as feathers tied to canes, i.e., prayer-sticks, are bundled at Zuni around War god images; and Aztec hung gum paper around the neck of an image, just as Hopi and Acomans hang prayer-feathers. Miniature arrows and "torches," i.e., sticks of candlewood were placed by Aztec on graves. As death ritual Aztec also made a feather-stick or cane, tying together the white feathers of the heron, two by two, and fastening these little feather bundles to a cornstalk cane; then these Pueblo-like "prayer-sticks" were carried to a stone pile where they were burned.[85] We recall the prayer-feathers burned to the god of Death and Fire by Hopi. Aztec attached feathers to the tips of feathers[86] as do Pueblos and other Indians, and in both cultures feather down is used in ritual. The crook stick of Quetzalcoatl[87] and the befeathered stick of the impersonator of the Salt goddess[88] remind us of the ritual crook or staff of the kachina (and of the Growth goddess of Huicholes); and the ritual shields of the Aztec remind us of the shields used by Hopi imper-

* Compare the crooks held by pack-carriers (? traders) depicted on Hohokam pottery of a period corresponding to Pueblo I (Gladwin, Haury, Sayles, Gladwin, Pl. CLXVIII).

sonators of the gods in the winter solstice ceremony. Back shield or tablet and fending stick (see p. 1028, n.*) are common traits, also the use of ritual footgear, sandals* or moccasins.

Pueblo use of clan designs on boundary stones, on kick-stick or on the back of stick racer, petroglyphs of the Spirits and certain conventional designs on altar ground-paintings, screens, tiles, and slabs, on masks and prayer-sticks, for corn, rain, clouds, and lightning are not very far removed from Aztec picture-writing. To explain what my newly acquired Hopi name meant, my "father" drew me the cumulus cloud and falling rain "glyph" familiar to all Pueblos.† Had Hopi wanted to make historical records of persons or periods or tribute, they would have produced something closer in style to Aztec glyphs than, let us say, to the skin-painted records of Apache or of Plains tribes.‡ As it was, they were developing an interest in place records.[89] We recall their title deeds on stone and that the "friendship mark" (interlocking crescents) on the rock near the Gap, First Mesa, which is used as a place-name reference records the numbers of Apache slain or taken captive.[90]

Fasting and continence are both Aztec and Pueblo traits,§ and such abstinence is observed for four ritual days, a "retreat"

* We recall the artistic elaboration of the Basket Maker sandal which was possibly a ritualistic elaboration. (Sandals were worn by Pueblos up to the Conquest.)

† This is a Maya glyph, a Maya day sign (notes Seler on seeing it at San Juan in 1887 [Seler V, 7]). Like Pueblo stick racers, Maya chiefs or leaders had glyphs written on their body (Chilam Balam, 68).

The step or house terrace cloud design is found in early Chimu and in Toltec art. Once in the Teotihuacan museum a Pueblo friend and I were looking at the fragments of Toltec sculpture, separately. We met in front of a stone "cloud," looked at each other and grinned. Here was a "glyph" we both understood without a word. This simple design is used on tiles and walls of the Alhambra and elsewhere in southern Spain, but no Spaniard would have reacted as did my Pueblo friend.

‡ To be sure, the object that the kachina Chowilawu dances with in the Oraibi Powamu initiation seems to be a book of illustrations merely (Voth 2:Pl. LI). Compare Laguna gossip about clan books (Gunn, 102).

§ They are widespread Indian traits, practiced, for example, in a culture of early coastal Peru, in time of famine, and in a much later culture of highland Peru where the fast was from meat, salt, and pepper (Means, 62, 256).

which concludes with the dance on the fifth day.[91] Fasting may consist of one meal a day, or certain ordinary food elements may be omitted, like lime in cooking corn (Aztec) or chili (Aztec) or salt (Zuni, Hopi). Variations are played upon ritual abstinence among both Aztec and Pueblo.[92] The periods of taboo may vary; they may precede or follow the ceremonial. Comestibles may be served or dressed in special ways or eaten formally, e.g., by four mouthfuls. When the continence taboo is broken, venereal disease results or the mask will stick to the face.[93] In both cultures, exorcism* or purification is expressed by spitting[94] and throwing from the hands,[95] by the use of ashes or arrowpoints,[96] and by bathing to wash off ritual paint,[97] etc.; offerings are made of bread "fashioned into diverse figures"; food offering is thrown into the fire before eating;[98] food is offered to fetishes[99] and blood is smeared on their mouths;† corn meal is strewn;‡ popcorn is used ritualistically;[100] miniature offerings are in vogue;§ there is an offering of incense or of tobacco-filled cane or cigarette;[101] images and impersonators (or their masks) are smoked;[102] smoke is swallowed,[103] a practice referred to in Pueblo tales as a test of power, or enforced as punishment (Taos); insects are used in medicine;[104] snake- (and frog-) swallowing is performed in the rain ceremony of every eight years;[105] an anti-sunwise ceremonial circuit is observed;[106] there are rites of running,[107] as-

* It is quite apparent that Sahagún had no conception of exorcism, of ritual to overcome supernatural danger, or the bad effects of broken taboo. All such rites he calls penance or punishment. It seems probable that ritual blood-letting was, like flagellation, a rite of exorcism (or a blood offering) rather than a penitential rite (note Sahagún [a], 131).

† Sahagún (a), 151, 159. At Zuni, we recall, the blood of a deer is smeared on the mouth of the mountain-lion fetish.

‡ Sahagún (a), 114. In the early Chimu culture of northern coastal Peru white corn meal (and red ocher) is strewn (for the sea) (Means, 61. Compare Bourke 1:510). The Mixe, a large mountain tribe of Oaxaca, strew corn meal in shrines (Beals) and, at Tepustepec, on the cane and head of the alcalde (Starr).

§ We recall that among eastern Pueblos miniature costumes are offered to the Sun, and very small, if not miniature, water jars are used in the rain cult.
I find no suggestion of the inexhaustible motif or of "much from little" in Sahagún, but in Zapotec folk tales it occurs in just the same mode as in Pueblo folk tales. The miniature prayer-image of what is wanted is another parallel between Zapoteca and Pueblos.

persing,[108] including spraying by mouth, and of divination by peering into a bowl of water;* birds are observed as omens.[109] The time it takes to kindle new fire is another common omen. In both cultures there are images of the gods, permanent or temporary,† including effigies of sacred mountains.[110] The Aztec "tabernacle of painted boards for the god's image" may be compared with the painted slab altar of the Pueblos, or even with the painted roof shrine, however Catholic it may look, in the Zuni Shalako house.

Road-guarding by snakes is a conception that finds expression in both cultures (and elsewhere in Middle America). Figurines of snakes are on the Hopi War chief's altar and the stone coils in Hopi trail-side shrines probably represent snakes. Snakes, also clashing mountains,‡ have to be braved by the hero in Pueblo folk tales, and by the Aztec who dies and journeys to another world. For this journey the deceased Aztec is given credentials of paper,[111] the deceased Pueblo, credentials of feather.

EARLY MOVEMENTS IN THE SOUTHWEST

Between the plateau of Mexico, the mountains of Nayarit, northern Mexico, the coast of California, and the valleys and mesas of New Mexico and Arizona there are vast distances. How account for linguistic and other cultural parallels among Aztec, Cora-Huicholes, Mayo-Yaqui, Papago-Pima, Tarahumara, and Pueblos? Possibly these peoples were peaks in a cultural distribution§ which was broken into long before the Spanish Con-

---

* Sahagún (a), 27. Witches are seen (Pueblo) or see themselves (also a stone knife, Aztec) in a bowl of water.

† Compare the corn kernel-incrusted clay image of Horned Water Serpent on the winter solstice altar of Hano with the dough image of the Aztec god which is given teeth of pumpkin seeds and eyes of black beans (Sahagún [a], 46); and compare the tradition of eastern Tewa that originally the image of the Kossa god was of dough. We recall that the prototypes of Zuni Ne'wekwe and Keresan Koshare were of human cuticle or of the Corn Mother's cuticle, i.e., of corn meal.

‡ Pima pointed out to the friars an actual hill of this kind. It was divided in two, and anyone passing between was never seen again, thanks to Montezuma, the magician (Velarde, 131).

§ This is also Strong's final hypothesis for the parallelism between Pueblo and coastal Californian cultures: "a spread of basic ideas presumably from the south" (Strong 1:54–56).

quest by peoples of a quite different character, nonagricultural and nomadic peoples long since extinct.[112] Intrusive in some such way were the Shoshonean groups from the north who isolated Californian Shoshoneans from Hopi Shoshoneans, or the southeastern Apache who evacuated the populations of southern pueblos, Piro and Tompiro, before and after the arrival of the Spaniards. Chililí, a Tiwa town about thirty-four miles southeast of Isleta, was abandoned between 1669 and 1676 because of Apache raids, the population joining the Tiwa on the Rio Grande or the Mansos at El Paso.[113] These "very comely, well featured and robust" people who lived below the Piro on the Rio Grande, may also have been harried to death by Apache to the north, if not by those nomadic tribes to the south so "barbarian" that they would "not even let themselves be talked with."[114] The Sobaipuri, a Piman group that was a link between Pima and Pueblos, were eliminated not so long ago by Western Apache.

Whether or not harried by hostile neighbors just as Pueblos have been harried in recent centuries, Uto-Aztekan peoples in northern Mexico began to migrate sometime at least before the twelfth century. Nahua tribes moved south, the Aztec reaching the Mexican Plateau in the fourteenth century. Was there a Nahuan trickle to the north, complicating Hopi culture? By pottery dating, Oraibi was settled about A.D. 1150; a kiva beam dates 1370.

Tree records show that from 1276 to 1299 there was a severe drought in the Southwest which contributed to the abandonment of the great pueblos in the north and a movement southward,[115] including the memorable visit of Pueblos to the Salt River and Gila valleys where they lived one hundred and fifty years, from 1300* to 1450, and built great structures: Casa Grande, Casa Blanca, Los Muertos, and others. When these sojourning Pueblos "withdrew" where did they go? Southward to the San Pedro, to the Mimbres? Northward to Cibola or Zuniland, to the Little Colorado whence they started out, to Hopiland? Does the story

---

* Between Pueblos of the Salado culture in Tonto Basin and the Hohokam of the Gila there had been infiltration for a century or more before (Gladwin, Haury, Sayles, Gladwin, 266).

of the Water-Corn People of Homolobi, Pakatchomo, and Palatkwabi, the red land of the south, throw back this far?* At hand here is explanation for the occurrence of the Zuni myth of the sacrificed children, for the Maricopa myth of the Twins, perhaps for the Pima-Papago mask cult, and for other ritual Pima-Pueblo similarities, always assuming that the other occupants of the valleys, the so-called Hohokam, were ancestors of the Pima or at least passed on some of their culture.†

Pueblo history prior to concentration into large towns and great buildings, periods of small villages or hamlets or single houses when the roundhead, head-deforming, bow- and arrow-using‡ newcomers of the eighth century were assimilating with

* These people are the most plurally named of all Hopi clans (Water, Cloud, Rain, Snow, Frog, Corn, Corn-in-Ear (Wilted Corn), Corn-on-Stalk, Sage (rabbit bush) and their main name, Patki, cannot be etymologized, although it is translated Water House, deriving from the small water vessel said at Oraibi to be their *tiponi* fetish (Voth 5:48 n. 2). Plural naming and non-etymologizable names are both Yuman clan traits.

The Gila River ware found at Hawikuh (see p. 991, n. †) is more than trade pieces could account for. Found at Hawikuh in late deposits were two bowls decorated with a Shalako-like mask, and the mask design of Shalako Maiden is common in Hopi ware (1700–1850) (Bunzel 1:80). Between Zuni Shalako and the Papago-Pima Prayer-stick-making ceremony we noted many parallels.

From Papago come further suggestions. The Papago ceremonial house is called *vahki*, water house, and this is the name they give the Casa Grande ruin. In Papago creation myth plant lice produced the gum from which, flattened out, Earth-maker made the earth (Underhill 4). Plant lice are associated as patron insects with the woman's Lakon society which on First Mesa is "handed" in the Patki clan.

† Circumstantial evidence that this happened lies in parallels between Pima-Papago and Pueblos along lines perhaps even more persistent than ritual— along domestic lines. The music of the corn-grinding songs of western Keres is notably Pima in character (Herzog), suggesting that grinding songs traveled north with maize. Food is currency among Papago as among Pueblos, and gift exchange is conspicuous. Notice the common ways of lip-pointing and of saying "I am going" for goodbye; of sensitiveness to scolding, of personal unobtrusiveness and of peaceableness. Resemblance in burial practices between Papago and Hopi are striking: seated position and roofed-over grave made with great care. Like Zuni, Papago do not mention the dead by name; they believe that the dead can call the living, in dream, or fly back as an owl (compare kachina flying as duck) (Underhill).

‡ The earliest arrowpoints found in the Southwest are reported from Snake-town Hohokam from a pre-Pueblo I period (Gladwin, Haury, Sayles, Gladwin, 252).

the longhead, *atlatl* and grooved "boomerang"-using Basket
Makers, archeologists are reconstructing along economic lines,
but there is little or nothing available for a history of social
organization or, apart from what may be inferred from burials, of
religion. No doubt many fundamental habits of mind date back
to these early periods; for example, we surmise from the Basket
Maker throwing-stick, grooved with four lines, and possibly from
their use of the cross (see p. 38), that four, not five, was their
favored number;* but the social or religious traits which are distinctively Pueblo must have taken form very largely during the
period of living in sizable groups, after the single-house *ranchería* economies that have been called Basket Maker and early
or developmental Pueblo, after this near-nomadic culture became a town-dwelling, highly socialized type of culture. But
even of this latter period, when the great kivas must have been
used by large groups, we do not know how these groups were
organized, or indeed who used the small kivas so often placed
in front of or near the houses. Households, with membership
through the father, Keres-like? Lineages, Hopi-like? Mere
neighborhood club fellows, again Hopi-like? Of ceremonial, if
any, conducted in kiva, there is still less to be said; the assumption that the kiva was ever for ritual seems to be unwarranted.

During the fourteenth century towns were abandoned and

* Aligning them, by the way, with Keres, Zuni, or Hopi, but, and this is more
significant, not with Tanoans. What was the language of the Basket Makers?
Languages are highly persistent among cultural traits. It is unlikely that the
language of the people whose distinctive economic traits persisted to the end of
the eighth century (in the San Juan region) has not survived.

Let archeologists play a little with ideas about the language or languages
spoken by some of the peoples of the widespread Basket Maker culture or by
early Pueblos, not forgetting that changes in food supply through new weapons
or greater use of maize might affect head measurements within a short period.
Actually change in head form may have been quite gradual. Long heads as well
as broad heads were found in the Pueblo I remains of Kiatuthlanna (Roberts
1:171). No head measurements are available for the cremating Hohokam excepting two brachycephalic skulls found at Snaketown; Pima are dolichocephalic.
Hawikuh heads are longer than Zuni heads (Hrdlička).

The throwing-stick, by the way, is unfamiliar at Taos, where in ceremonial
rabbit drives use of bow and arrow is required. A grooved stick like the Basket
Maker stick was also Mayan, perhaps a fending stick against atlatl spear
(Amsden).

populations vanished somewhere, raising serious problems in the reconstruction of Pueblo history—problems which can be solved not merely by pottery records. As Dr. Steward has well said, ceramic history is not culture history; pottery technique spreads beyond its source. Labeling a period of four hundred years (1300–1700) Pueblo IV by its pottery sequences and letting it go at that, with perhaps slight references to exposure to nomadic tribes or infiltration of Spanish influences, has not been helpful in bridging the intolerable hiatus between Pueblo ethnology and Pueblo archeology due to ignorance of the culture history through archeological records of the fourteenth and fifteenth centuries. The influence of Mesa Verde, dated last of the great settlements of Pueblo III in the San Juan drainage appears in the Rio Grande Valley in the fourteenth century. Does this mean an actual migration and were the migrants the forebears of the eastern Keres? Are the forebears of Acoma, perhaps of Santa Ana and Sia, to be related to the populations of Antelope Valley and of Kayenta towns? Such determinations are material to reconstructing the history of both earlier and later periods.

PLAINS TRIBES

In the historic period the tribes in contact with Pueblos have been Paiute and Ute, Navaho and Apache, Comanche, Kaiowa, and, more recently, other representatives of the tribes settled in Oklahoma. Oklahoma "dances" have been coming into vogue in the eastern pueblos,* and within the last thirty or forty years the Peyote cult† has been introduced from Oklahoma into Taos, where it has led to considerable conflict. Its spread to San Juan has been resisted.[116] Although the cult emphasizes individual experience and does not fit readily into the Pueblo system of societies or, except as plant animism, into Pueblo ideology, who

* One of the Tewa saint's-day dances is called Comanche; Comanche is danced by Hopi, and at Zuni there is a kachina Comanche dance, also a very animated pleasure dance by two men and two girls called Comanche. Cheyenne was danced at Taos and a tepee put up (Parsons 58:Pl. 13D). Tourists and fairs are regularly treated to Plains dances by Pueblo entertainers gorgeous in war bonnets or in Kaiowa feather dance disks.

† The plant was known as long ago as 1631 (see p. 1095, n.*).

knows but peyote will spread, perhaps as an order of a medicine society and be described, say at Zuni, as brought up at the Emergence!

But even before the interchange of visits between Oklahoma and Taos there were contacts between southern Plains tribes and Pueblos. Hunting and trading parties from Taos encountered Plains parties with whom they fought or traded. Plains parties came in to the summer fair held annually at Taos under Spanish direction.[117] Comanche would visit Taos (or Pecos) one year to trade, the next year to raid.[118] In 1751, after trading at Taos, a band of three hundred, they attacked Galisteo; Picurís and Nambé as well as Taos were raided in 1774, and throughout this century and into the next Comanche (and Kaiowa) continued to raid on Pueblo territory. Warriors from Taos and other pueblos were associated with Comanche in Spanish punitive parties against Apache.* Plains war fashions spread. Taos warriors counted coup. General Kearney and his dragoons were greeted at Santo Domingo with a sham battle in regular Plains style: warriors and horses were painted and arrayed with feathers, tails, claws, and buffalo horns; the warriors war-whooped and shot under the bellies of the horses. Hopi warriors, like Plains warriors, wore necklaces of claws—the claws of bear, porcupine, and badger;[119] Hopi and Navaho carried shields. To be sure claw necklaces and shields are widespread and ancient Indian war fashions, as are scalping and decapitation, common to Pueblo and Plains tribes.

Like Plains war societies, Pueblo clown groups scout or police or function in war ceremonials, and part of their clowning behavior or convention is characteristic of the Plains societies— initiation by trespass, showing mock fear, inspiring real fear, backward speech,† perverse or foolhardy or gluttonous‡ behavior. Keresan Kurena and Isletan Shure' clowns use leafy wil-

---

* In 1810, in a Spanish-Comanche-Pueblo campaign, San Juan warriors brought back some Apache scalps (Twitchell II, 555).

† Northwest Coast (Kwakiutl, Tlingit) also (Boas, Lowie 1:607).

‡ Kurz, 166. Inferably the glutton feasts are war society celebrations. And what of the habit of jeering Kurz mentions (p. 143) as characteristic? Is not Isleta-Hopi song-tying an equivalent?

low whips like the clowns in the Comanche Sun dance.[120]
Kachina warriors in one instance play the clown, talking and
behaving backward, and begging food.[121] Clown masks have
been used by Plains tribes,* and masks were worn in the Buffalo
medicine dance (see p. 975, n.*). Plains warriors returning from
counting coup blackened their faces. (Compare black-face Taos
war dancers, Zuni war society initiates, black-face Chakwena
kachina, Buffalo youths, and Snake-Antelope dancers.) Special
or ritual importance attaches to the first camp (Taos) or to the
last camp (Zuni, Isleta)[122] as part of the warpath, this "road"
being something of the ritualistic conception which the road of
life is to a Pueblo. War, like life, was a journey. Supernatural
power was imparted to the Plains war party by those who usually remained at home (compare Hopi Antelopes and Taos Bear
society). In a few cases mist or dust was brought to the assist-
ance of an attacking or pursued party.[123] Although the treatment of the scalp as a fetish for curing or rain-making with adoption into the tribe is Yuman (or Pima-Papago) rather than
Plains,† there are in Pueblo scalp ceremonials Plains features:
counting coup (Taos), abusive or obscene behavior toward the
Scalp by women (Zuni, Taos), possibility of scalp-taking by a
woman (Tewa-Taos tradition),[124] custody of Scalps by women
(Tewa, Isleta), importance of women in war dances, procession,
outlay made by victors or their families,[125] calling out personal
names,‡ and conventional bragging (Taos). The Taos scalper
had to compose a song about his feat and sing it night and morn-

* Comanche: in Sun dance, large false noses of mud and conical willow twig
helmets to shoulders (Linton, 422); Arikara: the captain and one member of the
Buffalo society wear masks, and the mask of "Crazy Buffalo" is bearded (Lowie
2:661). See p. 730, n.*. Clowning is widespread not only on the Plains and in
the Southwest but among Iroquois, Western Ojibwa, and Yukon River Athapascans, in California and on the Northwest Coast (Lowie 1:607).

† However, Kaiowa Scalps were associated with curing (Parsons 50:110).

‡ An Oraibi who kills a coyote in January, the month for girl's dances, may
call for a dance, taking his favorite "aunt" as partner. The dance song will nar-
rate how the coyote was killed. [Navaho were commonly called coyote.] In the
war dance, scalp-takers were mentioned by name (Titiev 3), as at Zuni and
among Navaho (Haile, 26, 55)—for all these peoples a unique use of personal
name in ceremonial.

ing through town for four days,[126] behavior strongly belying Pueblo attitudes. Returning Hopi warriors were not allowed to say that they had killed anyone; they attributed success to Kwatoko, the monstrous eagle, or to supernaturals associated with their clans. If anyone did say he had made a killing, he had to be initiated as a scalp-taker, and this few desired.*

Among Plains tribes elder warriors remained in the home camp; but it is along the line of the mediator or purveyor of supernatural power for the war party that Plains parallels with the Pueblo home-staying and praying war group is to be looked for.

Crying out the orders of the day which is particularly marked at Taos is a Plains trait, although it also occurs among Athapascans and other Southwestern peoples.[127]

Two types of Hopi prayer-sticks, the crook with string across and the stick with feather pendants spaced lengthwise, are miniatures of Plains lances. The Keresan-Hopi rattle-stick and the Hopi chief's stick, the stick horizontally carried, are similar to sticks of Plains war societies. In turn, ritual sticks suggesting prayer-sticks were not unknown in the Plains, among Pawnee (see below) and Assiniboin. In the Assiniboin "great place of sacrifice dedicated to the sun and moon a bepainted buffalo skull set on the summit of a small mound is encircled by other skulls of buffaloes and of enemies. In front of every skull a bit of white down is placed on a small stave"[128]—this more Papago than Pueblo!

In the Pueblo Buffalo dances, in both western and eastern types, there are enough elements to suggest some borrowing from the Plains Sun dance which might well be called Sun-Buffalo dance. The relation between Sun and Buffalo comes out in the Hopi dance where the women dancers carry on their back the sun tablet or shield. Dance steps in this western type of Buffalo dance, the Zuni-Hopi type, is reminiscent of the Comanche dance

---

* Titiev 3. On Second mesa a scalp-taker even had the privilege of giving away the scalp to anyone who wished to be initiated (Beaglehole 1:23). Joining the Bow chiefs was not desired at Zuni, either. Men had to be "caught" (Bunzel 6:37).

step. Possibly the Buffalo dance reached western Pueblos through Comanche.* (Ceremonial Buffalo headdresses have been found at Pecos.) But it is in the eastern type of the animal dance, in the ideology and ceremonial of the Mother of Game, Buffalo Woman or Deer Mother, that Pueblo and Plains parallels are closest. Possibly the motif of the animals led by their Mother reached Taos from the Kaiowa.[129] Why the female impersonation became associated at Taos with the Deer dance rather than with the Buffalo dance is of course puzzling,† particularly as in the southern pueblos the female impersonation is a Buffalo Woman. Another hypothesis is tenable, that the impersonation idea, the whole complex of animal impersonation, spread from Pueblos to Plains tribes. Whatever the direction, there has been some historical connection between Pueblos and Plains tribes in the dramatization of the Mother of Game bringing in the animals. The Taos summer pilgrimage to the Lake is suggestive of the summer hunt of the Plains tribes, overlaid with kachina conceptualism and ritual.

Besides those mentioned, ritual parallels between Plains tribes and Pueblos are: sacred bundle, including for Pueblos the warrior's hair piece and bandoleer which are as close to war honors as Pueblos ever came; jugglery or the so-called *iruska* complex of rites including spear- or arrow-swallowing, fire-walking or fire-handling, stirring boiling water, with ritual continence before

* Since writing the above, I note that Hopi told Bourke that once a large group of Comanche traders remained two years in Walpi (Bourke 1:529).
  Other Comanche (Sun dance)-Pueblo parallels are: ritual bathing before and after the dance; backward-speaking War whip-bearers who get out the dancers and who have dreadful magic power; dramatized battle or victory (compare Zuni-Isleta scalp dance); performance of knife-swallowing and other tricks by shamans who are the dance directors. The dancing and whistling were mimetic of young eagle not yet able to fly. (Compare Tewa Eagle dance, and possibly the Hawk dance in Hopi winter solstice ceremonial [Linton, 424 ff.].) It must be remembered that any Pueblo-Comanche borrowing would date only from the eighteenth century as Comanche did not reach Pueblo territory until after 1700. Comanche themselves as they moved down from the north were borrowing the Sun dance from Plains tribes.

† Note the Taos folk tale of Deer woman who visits the hunter's camp (Parsons 64), and compare with Papago belief that the deer who appears to hunters in their dreams and makes a tryst is a doe (Underhill 4).

all such shamanistic feats to display power, not to speak of shamanistic organization and animal mentors; general purificatory rites of continence, fasting, and bathing; fear of menstrous women before fighting or (?) after being wounded (Taos); food offering (corn) into fire; burying food offerings in the four directions; cleansing by fumigation; blowing smoke to the corn fetish or other fetish; offering smoke in the six directions, to the gods or to deceased medicine men; smoking in sign of agreement, smoking to the Spirits (in the directions)[130] and pipe offering as a form of initiation (compare Acoma initiation on accepting cigarette); spraying medicine; whistling to Eagle to get his power; calling a line (used in decoration) the road of life; use of arrowpoint in curing or cleansing; and dancing before the homes of leading men who make the dancers presents.[131]

Of all Plains tribes, Caddoan-speaking Pawnee are closest in ritual to Pueblos. In the seventeenth century Pawnee raided Pueblos for horses, and there were Pawnee, Panana, visitors in Rio Grande pueblos in later times, but ritual similarities point either to very early Pueblo associations when Pawnee were agricultural village dwellers, or to sources from which both Pawnee and Pueblo ceremonialism was derived.

As at Zuni, there is a marked distinction among Pawnee between medicine or curing societies and societies possessed of a rain bundle which is referred to as "rain-storm wrapped up" and consists of two decorated ears of corn, known, in Pueblo fashion, as the mother of the people. These are white ears with glumes or tasseled tips, perfectly kerneled, with the first section of the stem left on. In each bundle society there are four leaders or chiefs whose position is hereditary; through the paternal line they are descendants of the first keepers of the bundle which as in Pueblo vernacular is "handed down." The chiefs of the society choose the members, within limitations, from kindred of deceased members, a method of selection not unknown to Hopi and Jemez. The chief of the society is the keeper of the ritual and the bundle, although actually the keeper is the wife, often the sister, of the chief, again a marked Hopi and Zuni feature. The corn bundles are said to have been carried from the southwest whence the people came,* i.e., the origin myth is in Pueblo style a migration myth.

There is a Pueblo-like hierarchic council, consisting of the chiefs of the four main bundles, and these chiefs rotate in the office of supreme chief, each chief holding office for a half-year, reminding us of the terms of office of the Winter Man and the Summer Man of Tewa. Each of the four paramount Pawnee chiefs has a crier or speaker, and each selects a warrior who in turn selects three police, men with clubs. These positions of warrior and police are lifelong. Again we are reminded of certain relations between the secular and ceremonial officers of the Pueblos.

There are two Pawnee medicine lodges, West and East. In each bundle society there are north and south moieties, the north side leading in winter ceremonies, the south side, in summer, a seasonal division bringing to mind that of the Tewa and of Taos.

Pawnee bundle rituals form an annual series, beginning with the planting and ending with the harvest, i.e., there is a ceremonial calendar which may be compared, if only loosely, with the Pueblo calendar, although the outstanding Pawnee ceremony is typically Plains, for it occurs at the first thunder in the spring when the lance paraphernalia are renewed. (But recall the Zuni spring war ceremony after which corn-planting is proper, p. 525, n.*). Fertility or phallic practices attach to both Pueblo and Pawnee war groups. Specifically, the Pawnee spring

---

* Bands of Caddoan Wichita were southeastern neighbors of Piro. With these Wichita it has been proposed to identify the Jumanos, often mentioned by the chroniclers but never satisfactorily localized. Grinnell reports that in Pawnee tradition they used to live in stone houses in the far southwest whence they traveled northward together with the Wichita. Archeologically, Pawnee show relations to the Southeast and not to Pueblos (Strong). However, between the Mogollon culture and the Southeast, relations have been indicated recently (Haury), also it must be recalled that we know comparatively little about the southernmost Piro or Tiwa populations in whose neighborhood southern Caddoans might have lived. Most Pawnee-Pueblo parallels are paralleled by Papago. Pawnee maize is related to Southwest maize (Longley).

When an early American Q complex by way of the Gulf is worked out ethnologically as well as archeologically, Caddoan peoples may fit into it (Sapir, Mason, Strong), and even Pueblo peoples. Hrdlička finds the dolichoid Pueblo crania (Taos mesocephalic, Hawikuh, Salt River) resembling the Algonkin, and the high vaulted brachycranic Hopi (also Puyé) identical with the Gulf type.

to autumn bundle rituals may be compared with the summer-rain retreats of Zuni or Jemez. The Corn bundles themselves and their priests remind us of the Isleta Corn groups.

Pueblo-like offerings of eagle feathers and of beads are made by Pawnee, and offerings may be thrown into water, into the river, or into a certain pool in a crater cone; downy red feathers are worn in the hair, and there are several references to what I take to be prayer-sticks or prayer-feathers. In war, ritual offerings of tobacco, blue beads, etc., are fastened to willow sticks, measured from the tip of the middle finger to the shoulder, pointed at the butt, decorated and stained red. These sticks are "planted" in the different directions, with prayer. Other parallels are a water monster (serpent) image; tying the penis in ritual (Zuni Koyemshi practice); painting the face of the warrior with vertical parallels, two on each cheek; breathing on the sacrosanct; tree-conservation ritual; the occurrence of a ceremonial lodge under water; foot-racing with the one overtaking snatching at the fetish carried in the lead; giving the newsbringer a smoke before hearing his news; new fire ritual.[132]

Among Arikara, another Caddoan-speaking people associated with Pawnee as late perhaps as the eighteenth century, eagle feathers are fastened to the tips of ceremonial trees (Strong) and are placed on the ground altar for Mother Corn. One of the twelve tail feathers of the eagle is to be worn on any serious undertaking. Eagles are pit-snared, and a man goes into his eagle-pit on an empty stomach, for fifteen successive days.[133] Compare the importance of eagle pit-snaring among Papago.

Members of one of the Arikara Women's societies danced, carrying an ear of seed corn set in sage in each hand, and at corn harvest bundle owners were invited to bless the fields. An old man went from corner to corner, sang his songs, and made an offering of smoke. He "fed" the corn by passing meat over some ears and then depositing the meat in the field.[134] In one ceremony a calico-wrapped ear of corn, Mother Corn, is cast into the river (Strong). (Compare the casting of prayer-sticks to the Water People at Isleta.)

Membership in the Women's societies was through matrilineal

descent. (Compare Jemez, Hopi.) Between Women's societies and Men's societies there was fraternal relationship, the women's River Snake society being very generous to the Men's societies. The women's Goose society danced in a circle, side-stepping like warriors. In the war dance women put on warrior toggery *not as burlesque* but as a form of conjugal bragging.

As traits in the Men's societies we note painting of novices (compare Hopi), dance-procession, night-time appearance without "full dress," breechclout with fancy-work border (see p. 400), hide bundle drum, hoof rattle, and notched bone rasp. Noted elsewhere is the use of boiling water and of a Buffalo mask. For ruthlessness we may compare Black Mouths, the village guards or police, with Black Eyes or Koshare. The Foolish People society, corresponding to the Pawnee Children of the Iruska and the Skidi Children-of-the-Sun society, acted and talked backward. When they were around, people had to look out for their children.[135]

PAIUTE AND UTE

Plains influence may have been indirect, through the Southern Athapascans as they moved down from the north, or through Shoshonean tribes other than Comanche, who from an early period surrounded the Pueblos. We recall that Hopi is a Shoshonean language. What implications of early contacts there may be here, we can but guess. But at least one word stands out for us with a peculiar significance, the word for witch, or shaman, *powaka* in Hopi, *puhāga, pu'hāgant, puaxa'ntⁱ* in Shoshonean.* To Hopi the Paiute or Ute shaman would certainly appear to be a witch, just like Apache or Yuman or Havasupai shaman, each practicing on his own and through a familiar spirit. (The Bear doctor of Northern Paiute with his transformation into Bear would seem quite familiar to Keres or Tewa.) Most sickness is caused by shamanistic sorcery, i.e., putting something noxious

---

* *Pocahanti* is a current term for magic among Pueblos and Whites of the upper Rio Grande. Its derivation was enigmatic until Dr. Lowie drew my attention to the Shoshonean term.

Another interesting word is that for people, persons: Paiute, *nümü*, Hopi clan people, *nyümü*.

into the victim or using contagious magic. Several traits noted for Yuman shamanism in common with Pueblo (p. 990) may be mentioned for Shoshonean shamanism: sucking and blowing (compare Havasupai), search for lost soul, fasting from salt and grease (before hunt). (The Northern Paiute hunter prays to the Sun at dawn.) A few scattering distinctive Pueblo parallels may be cited: association between wind and war, wind shamans acting as war scouts (Chemehuevi);[136] wind-making for spite; use of datura for finding lost objects (Zuni, Chemehuevi, Northern Paiute); chasing with firebrands (Chemehuevi, compare Zuni); exacting confession from witch (shaman) (Chemehuevi); love magic somewhat suggestive of Zuni love magic; shaman's fetishistic cat's-claw crook staff (compare Hopi Flute society rattle staff); holding a smoke before ceremonial, Hopi fashion, and smoking in the directions. Chemehuevi and Southern Paiute shamans in general are specialized as Rattlesnake, Rock (for falls), Arrow (for wounds), Rain or Wind, and Horse.

Southern Paiute* were raiding Hopi towns at the beginning of the seventeenth century (p. 367, n.†) and probably long before. In 1892–98 a Paiute boy "sold by his father" into Oraibi was living at Hano.[137] A Paiute burlesque was presented on First Mesa during Powamu in 1893 with Paiute dance steps and songs to a bundle drum. The year before, on March 12, a Ute dance was performed, two couples, male and female, between two lines of men.

---

* Unfortunately, Dr. Kelly has not yet published most of her information about the Southern Paiute, the Paiute we look directly to for Southwest parallels. But even among Northern Paiute there are striking parallels: Summer months unnamed, five the favored numeral (Tiwa), racing so wild crops would grow well, running to shorten the season, telling time at night by Pleiades and Orion, eagle domestication, meat and salt taboo, sprinkling pine nuts or seed or wheat meal on ground for ghost who is urged not to return in dreams, or on ghost representations in the dance, round dance by men and women interlocking fingers, giant cannibal bogey, and ceremonial buffoonery (Lowie, Steward, Kelly). When we recall other Northern Paiute parallels in adolescence, marriage, and death practices, in hunting, in the practice of communal irrigation (for wild seeds which are ground on stones to song), and in female ownership of the houses built by the men, we incline to agree with Lowie that Pueblo culture has resulted largely from the superimposition of the agricultural-ceremonial complex of the south upon "a primeval ultramontane layer."

Utes were visiting Taos and San Juan in the eighteenth century, trading,* perhaps raiding. (Centuries earlier they may have troubled Pueblos of the San Juan drainage.) Ute dances are or were given at Taos, and Ute doctors are esteemed. Patients go to them or they are invited to Taos, and Taos doctors are said to use Ute methods in curing.† Possibly Tanoan practices or traditions about women scalpers or scalp custodians were also derived from Utes, who became militarized along Plains lines when they took over the horse complex. Women camp followers scalped and stripped the enemy, and such women participated in war dances or parades. As the Ute hunter was expected to distribute his meat, so the warrior distributed his loot to those who came out to meet him, in the Scalp dance, and to poor persons who might come in a group to his tepee to dance in his honor (Marvin Opler)—the throw-away of Plains and Pueblos.

Temporary hunt leaders (compare Hopi) is a trait of Shoshoneans, Northern and Southern (Lowie, Marvin Opler). As is girl's adolescence ritual (Lowie), a marked trait also among Southern Athapascan, Yuman, and Pima-Papago tribes. The indifference to first menstruation practices among Pueblos, excepting Hopi, is outstanding enough to be thought of as a case of resistance.

NAVAHO AND APACHE

Warfare with Apache and Navaho was the most important if not the first fighting engaged in by the early Pueblos, so it is not surprising to find many parallels between Pueblo and Athapascan warfare. This warfare probably dates from the time these southern Athapascans came into the Pueblo area, an undetermined period. One hypothesis is that the fateful thirteenth-century drought caused them, too, to migrate and as they moved southward led them to harry the pueblos of the San Juan drainage. At any rate, Apache and Navaho were raiders over a large territory before the arrival of the Spaniards, although it

---

* Hides and meat, for meal. Utes state that to their southern winter camps Taos and San Juan sent pack trains of trade goods (Marvin Opler).

† But a bad doctor or witch would *not* be killed at Taos, in the Ute way (Lowie, Parsons 58:60).

appears that the Western Apache did not camp between the Gila River and Cibola when the first Spanish expeditions traveled that rough country.[138]

Spanish administration probably stimulated raids in early years by its policy of capturing and enslaving women or children, but in the eighteenth century it held the nomad raiders somewhat in check through punitive expeditions. After Mexican independence in 1823 until Kit Carson's campaigns, raids went on unrestricted by American authority, both Apache and Navaho raids. In 1862, Carson was ordered to kill all Mescalero Apache men encountered and, the following year, all Navaho who failed to surrender before a fixed date. Utes and White civilians also went Navaho hunting for several months until they were called off by gubernatorial proclamation. It is not surprising that except by Hopi, who never took scalps from Navaho,* all scalps are referred to nowadays as Navaho scalps.

Navaho and Pueblos raided each other, but they also traded together, raced, and probably played games† together, rendered each other services and hospitality (if sometimes murderous), attended the celebrations each of the other,‡ and intermarried. In the western pueblos, particularly Hopi, broken Navaho has been spoken. Some time in the eighties an old Tewa of First

* This was not reciprocated. In the Navaho "gesture" or victory dance, even though the victory was over another people, there had to be a Hopi scalp (Hill, 18).

† First Mesa Hopi sang their game songs of hidden ball in Navaho (Stephen 4:257).

‡ One hundred Navaho were present at the Powamu ceremony on First Mesa in 1893, also at the Shalako celebration (Stephen 4:235, 242, 254, 437). I have been at Shalako at Zuni when there were just as many Navaho. Stephen describes a Navaho family on its way through Walpi that was teased by the clowns at a kachina dance, and of how Navaho were admitted into kiva during prayer-stick-making (Stephen 4:384, 471, 524). In 1934 I heard of a Navaho in Walpi taking the Wüwüchim cure for "twisting sickness." I saw two Navaho women sitting with the girls during the kiva dance practice of the Buffalo dance in November, 1922, and to the Yeibichai(kachina) dance on the last night of the Night chant which I attended with Hopi and Tewa friends the First Mesa people had been invited to send a dance group (Parsons 26). On this occasion they had not accepted the invitation, but not uncommonly they do contribute dancers to the Yeibichai.

Mesa reported that in his boyhood Navaho lived all around the Hopi mesas and came to the pueblos,* lots of them every day.† They carried in wood or water. In time of famine they might sell a child or just abandon it in a Hopi household.[139] That is how, I infer, two Navaho came to be initiated at Oraibi into Wüwüchim societies,‡ which are pretty exclusive groups. Simo, Town chief of Walpi, was three-quarters Navaho. His mother's mother was stolen as a child by Navaho§ and married a Navaho, as did her daughter, Simo's mother.[140] When the family was fetched back to First Mesa, Simo's brother remained Navaho, but he visited First Mesa a good deal and had the run of the kivas. Once in Goat kiva he gave Stephen a Navaho interpretation of certain prayer-sticks on the Nima'n kachina altar. After Simo's death, in 1893, this Navaho brother claimed Simo's property, his secular property, not his fetish bundle and not, of course, his office. These went back to the senior family of the Horn clan that had been sojourning in the Rio Grande pueblos|| and could not be found when Simo was given chiefly office.

* Particularly, I infer, to the pueblos of First Mesa. Nowadays Hopi of Second Mesa refer contemptuously to the people of First Mesa as Navaho (John Otis Brew, after Mishongnovi acquaintances met at Awatobi). But First Mesa people themselves are as quick as other Hopi to burlesque or disparage the Navaho. Crow-Wing writes characteristically: "We heard that the Navaho were coming to call for us to go and dance (in the Yeibichai of the Night chant), but they were afraid to come and call us because we are sure to beat them at dancing" (Parsons 40:22). Pueblo conceit, although well-founded!

† In 1863, after Carson's campaign against the Navaho, many were removed to New Mexico, but many remained north and west of the Hopi. Until the seventies the Navaho were a check on American visitors or Agents (Bartlett 2:34–35), just as in the eighteenth century they checked Hopi from moving eastward, dissuading or bullying or in at least one case killing migratory bands, all of which Governor Anza attributed to "Infernal seduction" (Thomas, 146).

‡ Voth 5:265. Subsequently these two men joined in a Navaho-Walpi raid against Oraibi.

§ Possibly she was in the Walpi party of forty families who in the famine year 1780 while waiting to be convoyed to the east by Governor Anza went on to the Navaho "persuaded that they would give them shelter as friends, as they had done at other times." The men in the party, excepting two who escaped, were killed and the women and children kept as prisoners (Thomas, 232).

|| From which region, in their tradition, they originally came (Stephen 2: 67 ff.).

Simo's office was primarily not the Town chieftaincy, but the chieftaincy of the Flute society.* The Flute ceremony has several Navaho features or parallels. Larkspur petals are used. Bird and mountain effigies figure on the altar, as on Navaho altars; also on a stone slab Locust is depicted playing the flute. Now in the Emergence myth, Hopi and Navaho, Locust goes forth playing the flute, is shot with lightning by the Chiefs of the Directions, and revives. Locust is described in Navaho myth as pierced by two crossed arrows.[141] Locust, I surmise, is the pet or guardian or war medicine† of the Flute ceremony, just as Beetle is of the Snake-Antelope ceremony (or Cornbug Girl with Pollen Boy of the Navaho Shooting chant). The Flute ceremony is a dramatization of the Emergence,‡ and I venture to predict that some of the same Emergence features will be found in one of the many Navaho chants still to be studied. The Emergence myth of First Mesa and of Navaho near Keam's Canyon have a good deal in common: the reed used to ascend on; ascent by Badger as well as by Locust; presence of Spider Woman; creation of Sun and Moon through blankets and two youths;[142] quarrel and separation of men and women; creation of gods or monsters through masturbation by men or women;[143] flood caused by Water Serpent.§ Horned Water Serpent is referred to by Navaho as Water Ox that draws Holy Man down into the water.‖ There is a chant for people hurt by water or dreaming of Water

* In the seventies or before, one of the Walpi Flute societies lapsed with the extinction of the trustee clan. I surmise that it was fear lest the whole ceremony lapse that prompted the search for Simo's maternal family.

† Compare Cushing 7:167–68. Locust is medicine for mortal wounds. In petroglyphs (see p. 359) he is seen shooting mountain sheep.

‡ Besides Locust, the bird scouts, and the four mountains, there are rattles, the so-called water rattles on which four disks represent the four underworlds, and shells sound the commotion at the *sipapu* exit (Stephen 4:772). Masauwü, who in myth stands at the *sipapu*, is impersonated. The standard is made up of some of the same things the sun was created from.

§ Stephen 3. For other Navaho parallels: Coyote scattering the stars and establishing death, see Goddard 5:138.

‖ Navaho also refer to the "Big Serpent that never ends" that seems to be identified with Lightning but has the punitive function of Horned Water Serpent among the Pueblos. Big Serpent can slay in a moment, punishing any "sin" (theft, lieing, sexual offense) or any ritual offense such as singing or praying when

People. Enemy Slayer (Elder Brother War god) and other Holy People find people *under the lake*. Enemy Slayer visits the Mountains and is given altar sand-paintings,[144] just as the War Brothers visit Shipap and are instructed about the societies. Enemy Slayer, Slayer-of-Alien-Gods, wears flint clothes, but it is the Thunders[145] in Navaho sand-paintings who are to be compared with Flint or Knife Wing above Zuni altars. In Zuni myth Flint Wing was worsted by the War Brothers. The widespread myth of all the early monsters destroyed by the War Brothers is most developed among Navaho, but it is prominent also among Hopi and Zuni; in the East it peters out into nursery tales.

Alternating with the Flute ceremony is the Snake-Antelope ceremony which has traits in common with the Shooting chant, a ceremony to cure afflictions from zigzag moving things, lightning, snakes, or arrows, also to cause rain; the Antelope sand-painting is practically a Shooting chant sand-painting,* the same zigzag snake design representing Snake Youth and Snake Maiden† and the very same pictorial style. The Antelopes are said to sing in kiva to make tractable the snakes hunted‡ by the

---

a man should not or divulging secrets and thereby giving them away from the tribe (Parsons).

* Nevertheless, Hopi doctoring for snake bite seems to have been preferred at times by Navaho to a performance of the Shooting chant. On August 17, 1889, the very day of the Snake dance, a Navaho boy was bitten by a rattlesnake. The boy's father rode to Walpi, and the next day the Snake society chief and two members arrived at the hogan, used their medicine on the boy, and cured him (Stephen 4:XXVIII, n. 3). See p. 1040, n. ‡.

† Note that the pair is a common Navaho and Pueblo trait (everything in nature is dual, say Hopi); also that Snake Youth is given the ceremony or instructed in it in the same mythological way that a Navaho chant is imparted. In general, between myth and ceremonial there is a closer conceptual relationship in Navaho chant than in any Pueblo ceremony. "Navaho organize religion, Pueblos organize themselves" (Reichard).

‡ My guess is that the snakes were originally hunted for their venom for arrows. A snake pen was excavated at Hawikuh. Oraibi described the Navaho method of collecting venom as follows: They would suspend a rattlesnake and place a vessel under it, into which the putrid matter from the decaying rattlesnake dropped. They would mix with this matter poison that they had extracted from the fangs of the rattlesnakes, and with this stuff they would poison their arrows (Voth 5:266, n. 1). For the distribution of the use of poisoned weapons among Apache and other peoples see Beals, 195; Spier 2:258–59.

Snake society; but whether or not there is any curative aspect of initiation into the Antelope society is obscure. A Bear impersonation performs before the Snake society initiate[146] as before the patient of the Shooting chant. Navaho warriors painted on their bodies snakes (compare snake on Hopi Snake man's kilt), bear tracks (compare Isletan Fathers), or human hands in red ocher, white clay, blue paint, or charcoal. The snakes gave a man power and made him feared as the snake was feared; bear tracks made him fierce and brave like a bear. Snakes were also painted on the soles of moccasins (compare Isletan war chief's moccasins),[147] and sand or soil is put into moccasins to give strength (compare chaparral cock feather in Zuni moccasin, p. 624 or cotton into Isletan's shoe, p. 6, n.*).[148] Navaho war sickness was inferably respiratory (compare Hopi War society) since today a girl inhaling the steam of the water in which she washes a White man's clothes gets war-sick.[149]

Both Snake-Antelope and Flute ceremonies, as noted, indicate Keresan influence. There is a tradition on First Mesa that early Keresan immigrants made a sojourn among Navaho long enough to drop Keresan and learn Navaho.* On returning to First Mesa they learned to speak Hopi. However this may be, it seems probable that Navaho contacts on First Mesa were largely through its Keresan (or Tewan)[150] immigrants.

After the Great Rebellion Jemez people also sojourned among Navaho, although most of them moved on to Hopiland. Navaho say they got their clowning Black Ears from Jemez (Reichard) (see p. 31 for possible early contacts). In the West Black Ears or Black dancers may have been influenced by Zuni Ne'wekwe or vice versa. Ne'wekwe and Black dancers† are painted with mud

* In a Navaho grave found by Dr. Kidder in Canyon de Chelly the woman wore the wrapped moccasins of the Pueblos. The burial has been dated as of about 1810. Navaho say the Canyon Navaho women were so beautiful and desirable *because they were of Pueblo descent* that the Mountain Navaho would steal them (Hill, 3). For other Hopi sojourners among Navaho see Nequatewa, 108.

† Black dancers represent the Hard Flint boys, the Pleiades, "little winds" or the small whirlwinds of summer (Haile, 35). The mud vagina associated with the Black dancers (Haile, 54) reminds of the vagina stick carried by the Hopi Singers.

from springs. Their warlike, starry patrons settle at springs or water holes; they travel by rainbow or Milky Way.

The Naakhai ("Yeibichai") dance during the last night of the Night chant is the Kok'okshi of Zuni or the Hopi Anakchina, with "their grandfather" behaving very much like Heruta (Keres). The clown in Night chant or Mountain chant acts like Pueblo clowns, particularly the Koyemshi. Navaho "begging gods" carry the same kind of fawn sack carried by Koyemshi, and the Walpi term for this sack is a hybrid Hopi-Navaho word.[151] The appearance of Navaho masked gods singly during a curing ceremonial and at its conclusion collectively are Keresan features. Just as in Keresan mythology ceremonial was developed at White House, so in Navaho mythology the masked gods gave their ceremony to Navaho at White House (Canyon de Chelly). The Naakhai mask dance has been copied at Zuni and on First Mesa, but that the mask cult spread from Zuni or Hopi to Navaho and to Apache there is to my mind no question, the mask dance is so restricted among both Apache and Navaho, and the rest of the kachina complex, including the whipping of the children during the Night chant,[152] is so much simpler than among Pueblos.* The kachina of the southern Apache represent merely the chiefs of the color-directions who are mountain spirits. The Jicarilla Bear and Snake ceremony including its masked personages† appears to be a deliberate replica of Pueblo ceremonial groups—kachina, shamans, and clowns (Opler).

Navaho account the "inner forms of mountains and cardinal points" among their holy people,[153] reminding us of the Pueblo Chiefs of the Directions. Sun makes his diurnal journey to the house of White Shell Woman, and, as at Isleta, he pauses at noontide (Reichard). White Shell Woman or Changing Woman

---

* The motivation appears similar. The Navaho "Grandfather" whips to preclude the children (boys and girls) from ever being sickened or made blind by the Ye'i (Matthews 4:119). Adults who feel under the influence of malicious beings may also be whipped at this time or during other Ye'i ritual (Parsons).

† This ceremony warded off epidemic. Vaccination was opposed as irreligious and it was decreed that no vaccinated person could impersonate, a striking case of suicidal resistance, for as more and more boys were compelled to be vaccinated nobody was left to dance kachina (Hashchin) (Opler 6:11).

(the same woman or sisters), mother of the War Brothers and the most powerful and revered of Navaho gods, who creates from her own epidermis or from ears of corn and who is never impersonated (Matthews), may be compared if not identified with Iyatiku of the Keres. The War Brothers cycle of adventure is southern Athapascan mythology. As in Laguna myth, Sun is a secondary creation, made as in sand-painting or mask, a horned blue disk with black eye and mouth marks and a yellow band across, made by First Man; and Sun has to make four attempts before he moves at the right distance not to burn the earth. Coyote does not come into this, but Coyote does scatter the stars and by stealing Water Serpent's boy and girl causes Water Serpent to send a great flood which subsides only when Coyote returns the girl: the boy he keeps; with the boy's white fabric, says Coyote, he will cause male and female rains and make the black clouds; he will cause flowers to grow on the mountaintop and vegetation to spring up[154]—a new twist to the Papago-Pima-Zuni-Hopi myth of the sacrifice of the children. Coyote also establishes death after the first woman to die is seen below the hole of the Emergence as she sits combing her hair. She is seen by the two pall-bearers who *put on masks before visiting the place.** Between Coyote as a Pueblo witch animal and Wolf in Navaho witchcraft there is some conceptual relationship. In Navaho as in Pueblo tale Bear fights for the camp or guards it, and Mountain Lion hunts for it.[155]

Navaho war paraphernalia or ritual in war or ceremony may have spread not only, as suggested, to the War chief of Isleta (p. 928, n.†) but to other Pueblos. Navaho carried shields painted with designs of bear paws, with Big Snake, Lion, Sun, Moon, Lightning, Rainbow, and Monster Slayer; Hopi shields were painted with identical or comparable designs.[156] Curiously enough, the only masks of Isleta or Taos, the clown masks, suggest the wildcat or other animal-skin caps of Navaho warriors, caps that were made to fit (Hill) like masks. The Wildcat dance impersonation of Isleta wears another Navaho-like headdress.[157]

* Just as do the two couriers carrying dance invitations among the Athapascan Ten'a of the Yukon River (Parsons 27:63).

We recall that the Hunt (War) chief of San Juan is called White Wildcat Man. (To be sure, Tewa Kossa and Hopi and Zuni warriors all wear a cap headdress.) Navaho-Pueblo war practices were retaliatory attacks (Zuni); listening for omens (Zuni); knots untied in cord to count time (compare Shalako time cord); no levity on the warpath (compare Hopi Snake society rule); women in war party, two only (compare Tewa warrior women); closing trail against pursuing enemy by drawing across it with an arrowpoint straight lines or zigzag representing lightning, sun ray, or rainbow (compare Pueblo, also Jicarilla Apache, trail-closing at death); prayer to Sun and to Wind (compare Hopi); scalp-chewing by scalper[158] (Acoma or, by young males, Hopi);[159] scalps cast into rock crevices (Hopi); smoking by youths indicative of warrior status (Zuni); gift exchange in throwing gifts; emesis in training for war (or warlike racing, Pueblo); obscene gesturing in war dances of men and women (compare the Hopi Singers' "gesture dance"). The Zuni Shomatowe song ritual at the close of the Scalp ceremony has parallels not only in the Yaqui Coyote war dance but in the Navaho War dance: pottery drum and loop drumstick addressed as fetishes in prayer; Coyote associations; the idea that hostile Spirits are to be forced underground and kept fast there,[160] and a myth about the scalping of two girls at the river.* Houses are serenaded, and food representing war booty is thrown or given in both the Zuni ceremony and the Navaho (also in actual Navaho warfare); personal names of "warriors" are mentioned, the only time such naming occurs in either tribe; and continence is observed four days *after* the ceremony. Between the Zuni Scalp ceremony proper and the Navaho ceremony there are further similarities. Scalper (Zuni) or invalid (Navaho) is identified with the war god (Ahaiyuta or Monster slayer, Slayer-of-Alien-Gods) and blackened to look like him, and scalper and invalid have to be saved from the malignity of the Scalp or alien ghost. In general, identification with the Spirit or impersonation is a marked trait among Pueb-

* Taos girls attacked by Navaho (Haile, 147 ff.); or girls scalped by Zuni Ne'wekwe or Kushaile (Koshare, Black Eyes) during the early Zuni migrations (Parsons 36:33).

los and Navaho. Navaho gods are impersonated in mask in
Night chant and Mountain chant, and in the Mountain chant
Bear may be impersonated, also in the varied entertainments of
that ceremony occur burlesque or obscene impersonations quite
in First Mesa style.[161] Navaho chanter impersonates the War
god; Pueblo doctor impersonates Bear. The Navaho patient impersonates through being painted; the Pueblo patient who is
initiated also impersonates. The Navaho patient gets power
from those he or she impersonates (Reichard). This may be the
meaning of impersonation of kachina or Bear by the Pueblo
patient.

Holding a dance or initiation ceremony for the sick or menaced
"to save him," which is an outstanding concept or practice not
only in the Zuni Scalp ceremony but in the Kachina cult and in
the Zuni or Hopi Buffalo dance, may be derived from Navaho
whose ceremonies are almost entirely for curing or salvation.
(Note in particular First Mesa or Plains parallels.) The essential
belief of the Navaho chanter is that the patient has suffered some
improper and discordant contact with the supernatural, disease
results from discord; if the supernatural ones can be induced to
come and be treated in the proper way, they will bring the
accord which means health.[162] No succinct and explicit ideology
of this kind has been expressed among Pueblos (except the belief
that causers of disease are also its curers, Navaho belief also,
in the case of animals); nevertheless, it throws light upon Pueblo
rituals which insure the presence of the Spirits or properly speed
their departure and upon Pueblo belief that emotional accord is
necessary to efficacy. Common to Pueblos and Navaho are holding a ceremony in long or short form and ideas that for efficacy a
person must go into a ceremony four times* and that a person
cannot perform a ceremony until he has had it performed over
him, a widespread idea held even in modernistic psychiatry.

There is little question that the sand- or ground-painting

* Note Shake girls in Zuni Scalp dance and men members of Walpi Women's
societies. For kachina initiation Zuni require only two whippings against four
whippings required by Navaho.

reached Hopi through Navaho, in its later development.* Probably it was taken over as a single element, introduced into the Snake-Antelope ceremony or into the Powamu ceremony where the initiate stands on the sand-painting, Navaho style.† The sand-painting situation is reversed for prayer-stick ritual, which is more complex among western Pueblos than among Navaho, indicating that Navaho were the borrowers. In a minor detail we may note an exception: the comparatively recent change at Laguna from depositing prayer-sticks in stone shrines to placing them under cedar brush seems due to Navaho influence. Navaho use crook prayer-sticks (Zuni, Hopi, Jemez), wands with downy feathers (Zuni Wood society, Walpi), and annulets for Wind; facets on sticks represent the female;[163] and with prayer-sticks they notify, invite, or summon the Spirits (Hopi), prayer-sticks conveying messages. Prayer-sticks are made to a song series (Isleta), and the set made during the day and placed directionally in a basket‡ are carried off in a cloth to be deposited, on a run (Hopi). In connection with long ceremonials there is a four-day period of prayer-stick-making (during which morning emesis is practiced).[164] Prayer-sticks are stood on or stepped on in protection (Reichard); they are given as sticks of office to messengers, they are set up around the sand-painting and represent deceased mythical persons,[165] and they are kept permanently in ritual bundles.[166] Prayer-feathers are used, including the Hopi-Laguna type of "road-marker." Shell mixture, or, to use the Navaho-Zuni term, hard substance, is sprinkled on prayer-sticks;

* The meal design on trail or altar, the meal circle (for snakes, Hopi; for ants, Keres) or, indeed, the "road" of meal or pollen may have been a basis for the sand-painting and of independent development among Pueblos. We noted the ground-painting in southern California as an early Pueblo-derived trait.
Neither the painted sandstone slab of Hopi altar nor the painted buckskin "bundle" of Apache (Bourke 1:591 ff.) should be overlooked.

† Whether or not the initiate gets power or strength from the painting, as would the Navaho patient, has not been noted directly; but the Big Firebrand initiate of Zuni is rubbed with the sand (Stevenson 2:564).

‡ The position of prayer-sticks in the basket and elsewhere, tips out, is observed by Pueblos, but it appears more important among Navaho, part of what Matthews calls the rule of butts and tips.
Butts of Navaho prayer-sticks are pointed (Matthews 4:93).

turquoise, white shell, redstone, abalone, and jet (cannel coal), and shell or stone beads, sometimes attached to prayer-sticks,[167] are offered; also pollen (from cattail and corn) and powdered blue flowers (Goddard; Matthews). Turkey beard hairs and a bit of yarn are used in offerings (Reichard, Matthews). A crystal is used to deflect a sun ray (onto prayer-sticks, Navaho; onto altar, Hopi). Crystal or other precious stone may be kept in pollen. Ashes in cleansing* or laicizing, and arrowpoints as amulets are common to Navaho and Pueblos, but only Navaho explain the practices by myth;[168] both practices have a widespread distribution. Navaho (and Apache) use a turquoise bead as an amulet; the turquoise beads of Zuni strung around ceremonial pots or fetishes *may* have the same meaning. I have seen turquoise set into a Navaho cradle board and heard a turquoise cradle board sung about in a Laguna lullaby. The olivella shell is also an amulet (compare its use in Pueblo wrist guard or bandoleer).[169] Calling upon *virgins* to grind medicine (Zuni) or prayer-meal (First Mesa) is a common Pueblo-Navaho trait. Others are: meal or pollen strewed on trail (blessing it, rather than opening it), on altar, on masks, on fire (Matthews, Bourke), and on tree or plant left behind, the part taken having been asked to give itself (Parsons); meal "road"; meal or pollen smeared on house beams, face, etc.; meal rubbed on after ritual wash (Hopi); waving four times around the head (pollen, after being applied to patient) (Parsons); offering of cane cigarette stoppered with feathers; painted cigarette;[170] smoking in the six directions with a final circular puff (Zuni); aspersing medicine water, and cotton-bound turkey-feather aspergill; fetish reed container bundles; perfectly kerneled ears, sacrosanct;† beating

---

* Strewing ashes on scalp, Navaho call "killing with ashes" (Haile, 32). Compare sprinkling "powder" on scalps by Taos War chief in order to "kill the noise" (crying of Scalp).

The Navaho chanter places ashes on a crow-feather brush and strews on patient (Parsons).

† Matthews 4:63; Goddard 5:127, 146–47, 160. First Man comes into being with a white ear, and First Woman with a yellow ear; Matthews 3:69, 217; Matthews 4:43. Such ears are used for grinding sacred meal. Curiously enough, the corn-ear fetish is not found.

time with fetishes; pressing fetishes or sacrosanct things against the body, from feet to head or vice versa; passing patient through a hoop or circle prayer-stick; longevity crooks represented in a series; smoking set-out masks; putting mask on patient, yucca fiber mask for woman (Navaho masks belong to the shaman chanter); various forms of fumigation; meal altar as well as sand altar; representation of home or house of supernaturals in altar design (but at center rather than as periphery); placing altar properties such as prayer-sticks[171] or fur pieces outside the ceremonial chamber to signify closure; closing the road with a mark;[172] pouring water from the directions into the altar bowl-basket; sacred water from spring, pool, or stream; color circuit (identical with Isleta and Picurís);* medicine sips from shell; corn cake baked in earth pit as a ritual dish (compare Hopi *pigumi*), and tasting four times only;[173] salt abstinence;[174] eaglebone whistle (see p. 380); whizzer;† lightning frame; back tablet representing Sun or Moon;[175] yucca suds-making (Navaho, for bath anticipatory of a visit from the gods); downy or soft hair feather for patient or initiate or courier (to make light-footed);[176]

* This is particularly significant, for it indicates that in the earliest days when the intrusive Athapascans were integrating Pueblo-derived traits their contacts were with Tiwa (possibly Tano and Piro had the Tiwa color-directions), *not* with Keres, Zuni, or Hopi. Their own merely directional circuit, their sunwise circuit, they did not alter except perhaps in one particular, nor their favored numerals: 4, 12, 32. But 5 occurs among Navaho as among Tiwa (Newcomb and Reichard, 80).

I find no use of 32 by Pueblos, but 12 is common enough, particularly in matters of war, and possibly it points to Athapascan influence. Consider, for example, that the mourning period for a chief at Nambé is 12 days and that persons of Navaho descent live in Nambé, including a man in the summer moiety chieftaincy.

The alteration referred to in circuit is in coiling baskets: the Navaho marriage basket must be coiled countersunwise. Today, Paiute and Ute make these baskets for Navaho, and they have had to change their own sunwise circuit (Weltfish) to conform to Navaho rule (O. C. Stewart), a neat little illustration of how pattern may alter to meet trade requirements.

† Of lightning-riven wood, with turquoise inlay for eyes and mouth (Matthews 1:436). Thunder is dreaded by malignant beings. It is a protector (Parsons). This idea would explain the use of the whizzer by war chiefs or scouts at the close of Pueblo processions, but I have not heard this protective idea expressed by Pueblos.

blackened chin, also blackened arms and legs to represent black rain clouds (Hopi, Agaves);[177] painting songs;[178] "bright sand" on face (compare Jemez); use of double triangle or "queue" design which among Navaho and Pueblos is a sort of glyph for the War Brothers or any war personages; ritual continence* (for four days or until paint is washed off on pain of blindness unless Night chant is performed);[179] breathing in from the Sun (patient in curing War ceremony),[180] from the directions† with a drawing-in gesture made by both hands (cf. p. 392), from any ritual object or from "anything you have wanted and just got,"‡ any valuable thing; breathing out or blowing;[181] spraying medicine;[182] the motif of much from little;§ concern expressed in one way or another that the Spirits recognize or identify the ritualist (compare Keres);[183] fourfold feint (very marked among Navaho); feeling that power or efficacy accumulates from repetition in song, prayer, or any ritual performance, the fourth day being the efficacious day when pollen, meal, the whizzer, the wand, or the chanter's bundle all achieve their greatest potentiality to "restore," or, if not used properly, to harm. In the house-to-house visits of the Ye'i beggars, the first day only two Ye'i go forth, the second day, four go, etc. (Parsons). The Navaho concept that performance in reverse is specially potent[184] may be related to contrary behavior among Pueblos.

Oratory as a chiefly function is marked not only among Pueblos and Uto-Aztekan peoples but it was a trait of the Navaho until their political organization lapsed: their twelve Peace chiefs were orators.[185] Orations are made at ceremonial gatherings today. After a fourth inquiry or request information or

* Compare Navaho phrase, "to keep things holy," and Zuni-English for *teshkwi*, "to keep sacred."

† From the four directions with a fifth inhalation and circle gesture for all the directions, just as smoke is puffed out.

‡ Parsons. I incline to think this is Pueblo practice also, at least in the East, where I have seen instances.

§ Offerings—white shell, turquoise, coral, abalone, jet, specular iron ore, blue pollen, cattail pollen, of each a tiny bit or a single bead—become a great heap (Goddard 5:162). This motif is very widespread (Apache, Opler; Pawnee, Weltfish; Zapoteca, Parsons).

compliance should be given or made.[186]   The Black dancers (clowns) use riddle language, calling earth, wood, stone, water, or horses by special words. "Even if a horse has kicked or thrown a person it may simply be called 'a live one's plume.' "[187]

Navaho or Apache influence is plain among Pueblos in divination and feats of jugglery.[188] Divination is a far more important element among Navaho than among Pueblos, and the very conception of individual shamanistic power which underlies divination, also feats of jugglery, is Apache or Navaho rather than Pueblo. Navaho used to send meal-sprinkling messengers to other peoples to invite them to attend their Mountain chant at which stick-swallowing, fire-handling, yucca-growing, and feather levitation were all exhibited, and to contribute their own magical performances.* This would be a sort of competition and may be related conceptually to the rain-making competition with outsiders that figures in Pueblo myths.

In several instances where divinatory and juggling feats are described among Pueblos it is explicitly stated that they have been learned from Navaho or Apache, and all Pueblos testify to the divinatory and other magical powers of Navaho,[189] particularly in finding stray animals. To divine for lost objects Tsatitselu of Zuni practiced the Navaho method of motion-in-hand.[190] In his youth this old Ne'wekwe doctor was married to a Navaho and lived with the tribe. The granddaughter of a former Town chief at Isleta told me that her grandfather had great power, he had learned from a Mexican captive among Navaho "how to make wheat grow under your eyes."† This plant-growing trick was familiar to the Towahish (Tubahesh) society‡ of Jemez,[191] which is to be identified with the Tubahi of Cochiti, who were associated with Apache jugglers.[192] And with

* Franciscan Fathers, 377; Matthews 1. The visitors at Zuni from another pueblo noted on p. 971 were probably invited in some such way. Compare the Hopi couriers to kachina dances (p. 735). Compare Ten'a practice, p. 1046, n.*.

† The sprouting of corn under one's eyes is a Hopi trick to impress children, whereas the forced growing of corn (or beans) is for the elders a rite of mimetic magic or omen. (See below.) An alien would be treated as a child.

‡ There was some doubt at Jemez as to whether this group was a veritable society, just as we might expect if its Navaho affiliations were suspect.

these Eastern societies must have been connected the tricky Yayatü of Hopi, a society extinct in Stephen's day, although a few members survived.

My guess is that shamanistic feats were formalized or ritualized in Pueblo circles into the bean- and corn-growing rites of Powamu and the *tawinide* or display of the coming crops of Isleta; in the Isletan rite of bringing down the Sun and Moon;* in practices of producing live animals, deer or rabbits, in kiva, "drawing them in" by shamanistic power (Isleta, Jemez, Keres); in widespread rituals of bringing the Horned Serpent or Rattlesnake into town;† and in the initiation and other rites of stick-swallowing (including swallowing of piñon saplings) and fire-handling by societies (Keres, Jemez, Zuni, Hopi).

To be sure, all this jugglery complex of Navaho-Apache and Pueblos is shared, as we noted, by Plains tribes, and we must bear in mind the possibility of direct transmission to Pueblos as well as transmission through the Athapascans, who had early Plains contacts. The boiling-water feat practiced at the installation of a Tewa Town chief, the Winter Man,[193] is peculiarly Plains-like.

The concept of getting power from animals or other things in nature is so widespread and probably so ancient that I would not look for any comparatively recent diffusion among the Pueblos. It is only when the power is not wholly integrated‡ or socialized in Pueblo style that the problem arises whether the trait is very old, "pre-Pueblo," or a late borrowing from Plains culture or from southern Athapascans or others. Imparting the powers of

---

* Compare the mirror and radiating scarlet feather effigy of the Sun made to move up and down against a plank in the Mountain chant (Matthews 1:438–39).

† Possibly the snakes of the Snake-Antelope ceremony were once supposed to be "drawn in," appearing for the first time in public at the bower of the Snake dance, this being the reason outsiders were kept away so carefully from the snake hunt.

Rattlesnake is "drawn in" by Kumpa, the War or Snake society chief of Isleta.

‡ As integrated as Spider, one of those ear prompters or monitors pointed out by Goddard (Fly or Wind, among Athapascans) as a kind of guardian spirit.

strong flying birds to runners* is an instance; the resemblance (a Pueblo version for power) between Mockingbird† and Shuti, Canyon Wren, the prying bird, and the Acoma clowns or War chief is another instance; the power imputed to twins at Oraibi,‡ power derived from twin-born antelopes, still another.§ Isletan statements that Kumpa gets his power from Rattlesnake and that Shichu chief gets his from Bat sound Athapascan, as do Pueblo attentions to Horned Toad, the Navaho patron of diviners, or to Buzzard, the curer.‖

At one time adolescence ritual for girls was performed on First Mesa, with segregation, the use of a head-scratcher, corn-grinding, new headdress. Grinding and a change in hairdressing are observed at Taos, but with one exception¶ the head-scratcher is not used in other Pueblo circles. The self-scratcher is a conspicuous Athapascan trait, and one might surmise Navaho** or Apache influence.†† I surmise Apache influence in

* Parsons 56:53. Under the stones on the Jicarilla Apache race track are placed feathers of four fast-flying birds: ? sand-hill crane, cliff swallow, prairie falcon, hummingbird (Opler).

† Hopi societies get their songs (and so, power) from Mockingbird (also from Shrike, and from Snake [Stephen 4:XXIX, 137–38]).

‡ Note that twins have special power among Shoshonean peoples of southern California (Drucker).

§ Eggan. (Zuni also associate twins with deer [Parsons 10:381]). Oraibi twins can cure urinary or digestive complaints, but only while the twins are young. At Laguna unless twins are medicated "they will know all and become witches" (Goldfrank 1:387), i.e., persons with improper power. Inferably what they will know is something about urinary disease, for they have been medicated with their mother's urine by which they were caused, when a witch rolled two balls of earth wet by their mother in the direction she took after urinating. I surmise both borrowing and resistance to what has been borrowed.

‖ On the other hand, Navaho near Ramah who use stinking beetle or tumble beetle as snake-bite medicine (H. Tschopok, personal communication) may have heard of the Hopi Snake society beetle medicine or of Zuni lightning-shock medicine.

¶ Girl novices in the Oaqöl ceremony of Oraibi use the self-scratcher (Voth 4:10–11).

** However, Navaho near First Mesa do *not* use the self-scratcher, which is some evidence for aboriginal Hopi or Shoshonean usage.

†† But not to be overlooked is the use of head-scratcher in girl's adolescence ceremonial by southern Californians (Drucker), by other Shoshoneans, and by

the Taos attitude of avoidance of women in war. Continence taboos appear elsewhere in the war complex,* but only at Taos are they observed deliberately as necessary because of the weakening effect of menstruants.

Although fear of the dead is probably among the oldest emotional attitudes held by Pueblos, it may have been intensified by Apache or Navaho influence. The idea at Zuni that rheumatism is caused by handling the corpse suggests the Navaho or Apache† attitude, as does the Tewa opinion that digging up bones results in depopulation,[194] or at Oraibi the temporary desertion of houses where food is set out for the dead on what appears to be All Souls' Night, or at Walpi staying indoors when the dead are abroad during Wüwüchim. On First Mesa scalps were not kept in town but in a fissure of the cliffs as among Navaho or Apache.‡

If a pregnant Navaho woman or her husband touch or even look at a corpse, the war ceremony (against alien ghosts) may have to be performed sometime for the child. This requirement seems to be based on the belief that, if a warrior whose wife is pregnant look upon a corpse, the unborn child will resemble the dead person, just as whitish hands in a child are believed to be caused by his father using white clay on his hands in dancing kachina before the birth of the child. All this is typical of Pueblo belief and practice, particularly at Zuni (cf. pp. 90–92). A pregnant Jicarilla Apache woman may not attend the Bear

---

Maricopa (Spier 3:325), nor, in view of the common Maricopa-Hopi naming practices, the fact that among Hopi the husband of the "aunt" makes the self-scratcher. For self-scratcher among Paiute and southern Californians see pp. 58, n.*, 989. The self-scratcher is a widespread and inferably very ancient Indian trait (Lowie 6:314–15).

* In scalp ceremonies, also in the belief of the Snake society that the smell of a woman is offensive to the rattlesnake, making him bite the man who has been in contact with a woman (Stephen 4:659).

† Among Jicarilla Apache the young are thought to be particularly susceptible to the disorders contracted from ghosts and so, as at Zuni, have nothing to do with a corpse (Opler 2:223; Parsons 18). Out of some such general idea among Pueblos may have developed the kachina whipping or cleansing of the children.

‡ Western Apache (Goodwin); Navaho, Hill, 17. "The idea of taking a scalp into the hogan was thought to be ridiculously funny."

dance on the last night when the painted dancers are out (Opler).*

Of the many groups of Apache, the Jicarilla of New Mexico have been closest to Pueblos, to the eastern Pueblos, and, among them, to the people of Taos and Picurís. There has been some intermarriage; and probably considerable trade† and visiting of public ceremonies. The character of the "long life" ceremonies of Jicarilla appears to be influenced by Pueblos. The creation of animals and birds by Black Hashchin from his clay images reminds us of Iyatik's acts of creation. (Creation from epidermis is a common Athapascan-Pueblo myth feature.) Jicarilla offer turkey feathers in their cornfields. I note in the folk tales that their ritual meal consists of four mouthfuls; undoubtedly many other practices will be seen to parallel Pueblo practices or rites in Dr. Opler's forthcoming Apache ethnography. The Taos relay race has been borrowed, and probably the Black Eye clowns;‡ and from Tewa the Jicarilla may have borrowed the Hashchin or Kachina ceremony which they held in spring or fall for the crops, for rainfall or harvest, also in case of much sickness or epidemic. The ceremony has lapsed.§ In turn the animistic conceptualism of Taos seems to have been affected by Jicarilla, also personages in the pantheon: the character of Earth Mother is Apache-like; the Apache Water Man, Frog, takes the place of the Pueblo Horned Serpent, and White Mountain and Red Person are Apache-like personages. Weide of Isleta may be compared with

* Nor may a menstruant, probably for other reasons. Cf. p. 1120, n. *.

† Trading co-operation and probably intermarriage occurred in the eighteenth century at Quartelejo, a trading post in western Kansas settled or visited by Spaniards, Pueblos of Taos and Picurís, and Jicarilla Apache (Twitchell II, 189, 236). This may be the source of Taos tradition about its lost colony.

‡ Opler 2:215–16. The horned cap is Tewan. The association between clowns and warriors noted among Pueblos was expressed by Jicarilla when the clown gave his characteristic cry into the mouth of the departing warrior so that his war cry would terrify the enemy (Opler 2:211).

§ Opler 6:140 ff. Possibly a like ceremony has lapsed at Taos and possibly the masks of the Water People were as noted (p. 935, n. *) kachina masks.

White Hashchin* of the Jicarilla; among other Pueblos this god would be the kachina chief.

Among Jicarilla there were four old men to whom the new scalps were handed to be sung over and cleansed. They scraped the fat off, mixed it with red pigment, and painted their faces.† They had complete charge of the scalp dance.[195] Probably these elders are to be identified with the Bear society of Taos and the extinct Red Paint People. Jicarilla (also Mescalero and Chiricahua) do not eat bear, believing that sickness can be contracted from Bear. A similar attitude is implicit in Pueblo Bear "medicine," and I recall in particular that Lucinda of Isleta never stepped on my bearskin rug without muttering an "apology" to him who was "once somebody just like us."

Western Apache, if not Chiricahua, raided Hawikuh in 1670, killing the friar, and throughout the eighteenth century and into the nineteenth they threatened or perpetrated attacks‡ on Zuni. Then trade took the place of war. Up to about sixty years ago the nearest group of Western Apache, the White Mountain, had trading relations with Zuni, mescal cakes were bartered for wafer-bread, and Apache attended Shalako.[196] In the pantheon and ritual of the two peoples there are several parallels which are of course not confined to them but which have some little measure of particular resemblance: Sun as a near high god or paramount holder of the roads of men; Dawn Boy and Dawn Girl who are prayed to at daybreak (note the spirit pair as Apache as well as Navaho-Pueblo pattern). Turquoise Boy and White Shell Girl§ and among kachina and clowns Black god (compare Zuni Big Firebrand society kachina or perhaps Chak-

---

* Black Hashchin is another kachina-like personage.

† Compare the use of rattlesnake grease by Zuni War society, pp. 415–16, and the red paint used by Hopi snake-hunters.

‡ As, for example, in 1715, when the officers of the Spanish detachment in Zuni report to Santa Fé that the townspeople are in a state of alarm (Twitchell II, 180). In 1772 fifty Apache attacked Zuni, killing six persons. In 1785, ninety-two Pueblos campaigned with Navaho and Spaniards against Western Apache (Thomas, 7, 46–47).

§ The mask colors of Zuni Good Kachina, male and female, by the way.

wena) and the clowning Gray One (compare Zuni Ne'wekwe).
There are Water People (White Mountain, compare Isleta) who
send rain but are differentiated from Cloud People and the potent
Lightning People, who in autumn go home to the other side of
the sky. Lightning is associated with a great underworld
snake.[197] The War god myth cycle is familiar. Hummingbird, as
in Acoma myth, finds the roving kachina (*ga'n*). While dancing,
the *ga'n* begin to levitate and disappear into the air, just as does
Sun's son and mistress in Tewa tale. Compare the incident of
submerging on top of a spruce tree (Isleta), also, as a widespread
Pueblo incident, the inexhaustible water cup given to the man in
the eagle's nest.[198] Eagle-feather prayer-sticks are deposited in
cornfields (San Carlos).[199] Note the seductive power imputed to
Butterfly. Although circuit and associations vary from those of
Pueblos, note the extreme emphasis on color-directions. Note
that persons killed by water, lightning, or certain animals go not
to the land of the other dead but to the abode of their slayer.
Apache ghosts,* like Zuni (and Havasupai) ghosts, cause bad
dreams and carry away their relatives.[200] The Zuni rule that the
scalp-taker must have intercourse with a woman other than his
wife before he resumes conjugal relations is inferably borrowed
from Apache; this scapegoat rule applies to a remarrying
widower among Jicarilla Apache,[201] but it has not been reported
from Western Apache.

Hopi also were raided or traded with by Western Apache. In
their clanship system, which appears to be Pueblo-derived and in
some details derived from Hopi more than from Zuni, there are a
few ceremonial traits[202] which do not occur in other Athapascan
groups. Clans are named from places like Navaho clans, but
among White Mountain Apache animals or plants are associated
as relatives with the clans or phratries and conceptual relations
occur in Hopi fashion: the clan related to deer had special luck
in hunting deer; clansmen related to eagle were asked to pluck
eagles; an old man attributed his great endurance to the *ga'n*

---

* Note a curious resemblance between Athapascan (Jicarilla) for ghost
gok'o'sh (Opler 2:222) and Zuni for Good Kachina, *kok'okshi* (*koko*, kachina,
k'okshi, good). Keresan for ghost is *gu'upo, gu'uko*.

(kachina), his clan relatives.* Clanship figures in the Pueblo-derived *ga'n* curing ceremony for *ga'n*-sent sickness, a twisting of the body. Masks and body-painting belonged to certain clans, and the position of dancers in line might be clan determined (not Pueblo). Clan designs were painted on the body in the Scalp dance (excepting White Mountain Apaches). A local group might have a hereditary chief, a member of its dominant nuclear clan (White Mountain). Compare the Town chieftaincies of Hopi and Acoma and the Pekwinship of Zuni.

White Mountain Apache tell the Hopi Snake clan myth, relating it to the Lightning songs[203] in their Snake ceremony, in which a snake is prayed to with pollen and released. In the new 1920 cult which started as a cult against witchcraft there was a snake hunt in the cardinal directions followed by a snake-carrying dance. In their Lightning ceremony four youths and four girls impersonate Lightning.[204] During kachina dancing sleep is taboo, theoretically. A messenger wears a downy feather in his hair as safe-conduct. In the girl's adolescence ceremonial she has to run to and around a crook (Sun's cane, and chief's cane, compare Hopi longevity crook), and throw-away of blankets and seed corn occurs in this ceremony.[205] Sacred objects are pressed against the body to draw away disease; as among Navaho the patient is passed through a befeathered hoop (compare Hopi Marau rite, Acoma discharming rite, and the familiar witch rite which also occurs in Apache tale as a technique of transformation); the body is brushed (but not sucked) or breathed on to blow off disease; smoke is puffed toward the being addressed; supernatural power both kills and cures.[206] From sand-paintings, as from Navaho and Hopi paintings, sand is applied to the patient or taken home as medicine. Anything that is painted with ceremonial design (*ge'eschin*) has power and may be prayed to,[207] a general Indian concept† that crops out frequently in Hopi

---

* It is interesting to find borrowing along the easy familiar line of analogy. Hopi-Zuni clan fetishes have not been borrowed, being more esoteric and involved with extensive complexes.

† Compare the power (for evil, for sickness or death) attributed by Plains tribes to White artists (Kurz, *passim*). There were some unfortunate coincidences between the presence of these visitors and devastating epidemics, but

ideology, in connection with masks, "dolls," and altar tiles or slabs.

Apache neighbors to the south are the Mescalero east of the Rio Grande who were buffalo-hunters* and were orientated toward the culture of the Southern Plains, and the Chiricahua, comparatively unaffected by the Plains Indians and ranging west of the Rio Grande and north toward Acoma and Laguna. In the seventeenth and eighteenth centuries these southern Apache destroyed several pueblos of the most southerly portion of the Tanoan stock, Piro and Tiwa,[208] and Apache raids kept up on Isleta until recent times. Although described as White Mountain, it was probably a Chiricahua outfit that raided Isleta and was overtaken on the Puerco River and yielded at least one scalp to Juan Domingo Lucero of Isleta (see p. 31). It was not the first raid by this band for among them was an Isletan whom they had captured in childhood. Later when this captive returned to Isleta he said he had got used to his captors and called them his brothers.

Isletans show contacts with Apache in ceremonial costume, wearing fringed buckskin coat and trousers, and buckskin leggings, and in hunting practices, making a hunt corral,† orientating the head of the quarry, and leaving the guts for the animals.[209] Among Apache (noted among Jicarilla) grandfathers are the jokers and disciplinarians (Opler); the professional jokers and disciplinarians of the Pueblos, the kachina clowns or bogeys are frequently called grandfathers, and for this group of masks at Isleta I know no other name. Isletan Grandfathers wear fringed buckskin garments. The masked clowns of the Mescalero-Chiricahua are associated as scouts, mimics, or

---

of course behind this were preconceptions of the power of pictures. Rottentail, a Crow chief, ascribed success in taking scalps to a piece of painted cloth given him by the trader, the same piece which had caused influenza within the tribe (Kurz, 213).

* In the Buffalo dance on First Mesa in 1893 an Apache song was sung, "perhaps the best song of the day" (Stephen 4:128).

† This is general Apache (Gifford); among Pueblos it has been noted only at Isleta (Parsons 52:433) and Cochiti (Goldfrank 3:87).

bogeys with the other masked spirits living in caves of the mountains.[210] We are reminded of the Isletan K'apio, temporary clowns who fetch spruce from the mountains and, Apache-like, satirize in song, of the mountain-dwelling Thlịwale, and of Chakabede, who may correspond to the Apache shaman who summons the kachina-like mountain spirits. The curing functions of their Gahe and clowns have parallels among Pueblos, but still closer ones among Pima-Papago.

Lipan Apache, who in recent times have joined the Mescalero but at a very early period were neighbors of the Jicarilla (Opler), believe that fog or fire harasses the wicked after death, with snakes or lizards as their only food (Jicarilla, Cochiti). As among Western Apache, dead relatives fetch the living. The mask spirits appear as deer; and in one tale, in Tiwa mode, a man walks into the lake whence voices are heard (Opler). In another tale a Lipan puffs smoke on a magic stick and asks for what he wants. Marking a shaman with pollen is to pledge faith in his ceremony and to ask its benefits. (Have we here a possible interpretation for Pueblo meal- or pollen-sprinkling or, more rarely, marking?) In asking a man to tell a tale or to cure, you give him tobacco (Opler).

The Mescalero-Chiricahua shaman has personal power. Isletan shamans are grouped together, but each is more of an individual practitioner with greater power than is typically Pueblo, also ordinary persons are possessed of power quite atypically. Possibly all this is due to Apache influence; any Apache may be the recipient of power. Power not properly handled is dangerous. Songs, prayers, and rules may be taught to another, but, if he misuses them and angers the power, his teacher will suffer from the power (Lipan). Compare the general Pueblo attitude of danger from sacred things and specifically at Isleta the return of love magic or power to the shaman. Compare the horse doctor (for sickness from Horse) of Isletans and Apache (Western, Lipan). The Isletan Pouch War chief or Scalp chief got his eye "powder" or pollen for clairvoyance from Apache if not from

Navaho.* Isleta-Laguna crystal-gazing may have been affected by Apache practice. The Isletan reference to having to confess in sickness is Apache-like,[211] also the practice of menstruants not attending ceremonies (or church), also an Isletan account of being frightened by a bear and of being cured in a ceremony in which bear pelts are used.† The high god of the Apache, Giver-of-Life (Mescalero-Chiricahua and White Mountain), suggests Weide,‡ also the Acoma creator.

There are several other Mescalero-Chiricahua and Pueblo parallels: casting pollen in the directions, smoking in the directions, smoking the patient, sucking the patient, ritual pigments consisting of red ocher, specular iron ore, and white clay, arrowpoints as lightning arrows,§ hide beaten as drum, continence as

---

* However, Walpi War chief and Taos War chief use "powder" (see p. 1050 and Parsons 58:22). Incidentally, note that in Lipan migration myth White Cane is guard (compare Black Cane Old Man of Isleta).

† Parsons 52:445 ff.; Opler 1:67; Bourke 1:505. To be sure, Juan's bear is described not as a power but as a witch. In both Pueblo and Apache belief relatives are done to death. Is this from Spanish witchcraft or from an Indian concept of investing the living with power? Among Jicarilla it is payment to a man's power (Opler 2:214). To the Pueblo the whole Apache complex of individual relationships to powers would seem to be witchcraft, if grasped at all. See Parsons 42:166 for a picture of a San Juan man ignoring the meaning of an Apache vision.

‡ Giver-of-Life also suggests Dios of whom knowledge may have spread in very early days through Apache slaves. Distribution of traits through Indian captives of whom there were many in the Rio Grande Valley should not be overlooked. In 1733 certain Indians of different tribes, including Jumano (that mystery tribe south of the Tiwa, possibly Wichita), Apache, Ute, Kaiowa, and Pawnee who had abandoned their tribal relations and embraced the Catholic religion, and who were living at various towns and pueblos in New Mexico, petitioned to be allowed to settle in the abandoned pueblo of Sandía. The petition was denied, but the petitioners were to be allowed to settle at established pueblos (Twitchell I, 353). Some years later Abiquiu in abandoned Tewa territory was settled by Mexicans and by Genizaro half-breed or foreign Indians, among them Hopi, ransomed captives or refugees (Twitchell I, 25-27).

§ A Chiricahua medicine woman Bourke knew wore from her neck an arrowpoint amulet found at the foot of a lightning-blasted tree, and Bourke notes the use of arrowpoints among the women of Laguna and other pueblos (Bourke 1: 468-69).

Bourke notes as general Apache traits: shamanistic power to visit the "house of spirits" (compare Keresan shaman visiting Shipap), crystal-gazing, imparting

a technique for success (in roasting mescal). The Apache afterworld is underground, a hunter's paradise like Wenima.[212]

Recent study of Apache culture indicates that it is much more
elaborate than has been supposed, yet its ritualism compared
with Navaho is simple. Is this not only because of the warring
character of the Apache but because all the Apache groups,
excepting Western Apache in a late period, have been neighbors
to Tanoan pueblos, whereas Navaho have been neighbors to the
more ceremonially developed Hopi and Keres?

WHITE PEOPLE

The first Spaniards, Coronado's troop, introduced domestic
animals and metal implements, and they got well rooted the still
vigorous belief that "Mexicans are mean." The Mexican Indians
who stayed on may have introduced other things about which
we will speculate later. But there was probably little Hispanization before the permanent Missions and the Spanish soldier-
colonists* of the seventeenth century. Then, if not before, from
friars, ranchers, and administrators spread wheat, chili, watermelons, peaches, and the vine; knowledge of herding and breed-
ing;† plow and cart, ox or mule drawn; a new technique in rope-

---

power to bundle through lightning-riven twigs, use of rhombus made from
lightning-riven wood (among western San Carlos for rainstorm-making in time
of drought, with Wind spirit depicted), the rite of exhalation (a northern Athapascan trait), and a use of tule or cattail pollen as ubiquitous as the Pueblo use
of corn meal. A pollen pouch is carried at the belt of every warrior. The war
shaman would sprinkle pollen ahead of a wounded man *to make his road easier.*
Every Apache *blows* pollen to the Dawn, and on going out to fight or hunt or
plant he casts pollen to the Sun. A little bag of pollen is fastened to the neck of
an infant or to his cradle (San Carlos). At all critical times pollen is put on the
tongue or rubbed on the person. It is cast on dancers. It is ritual food for Snake
or Bear. Pigment is cast to the Sun (Bourke 1:461, 465, 477–78, 501, 505, 513,
548.

* These soldiers were paid by the *encomienda* system: a soldier *encomendero*
was appointed receiver of the tribute, mostly maize and cloth (*manta*) exacted
from the Indians of a specified district. This system would of itself involve close
contacts. Also the soldiers seized Pueblo "orphans" as house servants (Scholes
1:83, 103), involving both interpueblo and White contacts.

† The friars owned great flocks and herds, and these were herded by
Pueblos. Pueblos served as muleteers on the caravan trips to Mexico (a line of
communication we should not overlook).

making (*trabil*), a new type of oven, chimneys* and doors, novel political and religious systems, new folk lore, notably about bewitchment, and new diseases: smallpox,† syphilis, trachoma, tuberculosis, measles, whooping cough, malaria, typhoid, all possibly witch-caused, in Pueblo opinion.

Witch trials with hangings‡ were held by the Spaniards in New Mexico in the seventeenth and eighteenth centuries.[213] Pueblo medicine men or chiefs like native priests everywhere else were called witches (sorcerers) by the Spaniards. In 1675 forty-seven medicine men were rounded up for trial§ as sorcerers.

* As late as 1883 at Oraibi hearths without flue or chimney were to be seen, only an oblique smoke hole in the wall (Cushing, Fewkes, Parsons, 255).

† Smallpox epidemics are dated more closely than the other scourges. In the epidemic of 1780–81 more than five thousand Indians died, a large number being Hopi (Twitchell II, 287). Smallpox occurred again in 1788–89, 1800. See p. 972, n.*.

‡ Gibbet (and whipping-post) stood in the center of the Spanish plaza.

§ As practically all the Spanish archives before 1680 were burned by the Indians, there is no detailed record of this notable trial. Records are available (Twitchell II, 142 ff.) for a much humbler yet very illuminating witchcraft trial in 1708 in which two middle-aged or elderly Indian women of San Juan are defendants, and Leonor Dominguez, a Spanish girl of twenty, is plaintiff. Leonor swears that her husband has boasted of having an Indian mistress in San Juan and another in Taos, and so, "being extremely ill with various troubles and maladies which seemed to be caused by witchcraft" and knowing that many women have suffered from witchcraft (she names four), Leonor testifies that on Holy Thursday in the church at Santa Cruz (near San Juan) she overheard an Indian woman tell another who she, Leonor, was and then say, "Now!" the other woman answering, "Not yet." Whereupon Leonor, "full of terror," left the place where she was kneeling and fell on her knees farther off, but not too far to overhear, "It would be better now." The Indian woman then came close to her and put her hand on her back beside her heart, and at once Leonor's entire body began to itch and since then she has not lifted her head. The rest of the jealous wife's story is so thoroughly discredited by her husband and other Spaniards that the charge of witchcraft is dismissed, but throughout no skepticism about the nature of the charge is expressed by anybody save one of the Indian defendants who affirms that *Spanish women say that whatever sickness they have it is bewitchment.* (You are told today in Taos that it is prudent to avoid Mexicans, for if they fall sick they charge you with bewitching them.)

Several other trials of Indians for witchcraft are on record. There were cases against Indians of San Ildefonso, in 1725, against Indians of Santa Ana, in 1732, and against the "Cacique" of Isleta, together with a man and woman, in 1733. In 1730 Felipe of Isleta died in prison under a charge of witchcraft. The San Ildefonso man convicted of bewitching Fray Antonio Barreras in 1799 com-

Three were hung.[214] Pope' of San Juan, the leader of the Great Rebellion, was one of the forty-seven and when he and the others were released, thanks to pressure from a delegation of Tewa warriors, he began his anti-Spanish agitation forthwith; so that this trial of *chiefs* for witchcraft was the immediate cause of the Rebellion.

Spanish witch trials were conducted by the Alcalde who was both judicial and military officer. It seems probable that witch-baiting among the Pueblos, if not guarding against witches, developed as a function of the Pueblo alcalde or war captain to whom policing against bad people came to mean little else but detecting and persecuting witches. The witch complex is associated primarily with the Keresan society or with that type of society at Isleta and Zuni and among Tewa. Among Hopi, where there are no out-and-out curing societies and no war captains, there is comparatively little witchcraft lore.* Witchcraft lore occurs at Taos, where relations with Mexicans are close, but I think it came in here later than in the pueblos to the south and was not associated with the political administration; until very recently witch-baiting has not been a function of the war captains.† The lack of the Keresan type of society in Taos is another reason for the failure to persecute witches and for the absence of

---

mitted suicide. As a result of this "false trial," the Spanish Alcalde was suspended and the removal of the friar was recommended. The following year another friar petitions to leave the Province on account of illness and fear of witchcraft (Twitchell II, 194, 197, 200, 202, 397, 399, 409).

But witchcraft cases in connection with Spaniards or Hispanized Indians date back to the establishment of the Inquisition in the Province, to 1626, or before (Scholes 2:218 ff.). They involve love potions for erring husbands, bewitchment through food, tossing an invalid about like a ball, evil eye, also sticking thorns into images and burying them—all familiar Spanish practices (though unfamiliar as such to the historian who calls them Indian superstitions!).

* However, the Oraibi War chief appears in one folk tale as a rescuer from witches (Voth 5:127).
Early observers report very little about witchcraft among Hopi; but recent observers report a lot, at Second and Third Mesas.

† It is reported that charge of witchcraft is now being made against the rebellious "Peyote boys," one more instance of the witchcraft complex serving for standardization or control.

black magic at Taos compared with the southern pueblos or Zuni.

Current Pueblo belief that anyone may be a witch looks Spanish (or southern Athapascan). Among Tarahumara aged shamans might become witches; Pima and Papago and Yuman tribes killed shamans who failed to cure; black magic was in the hands of the shamans; the good shamans overcame the bad shamans; there were no witches at large. I incline to think this was the early pre-Spanish, if not pre-Athapascan, attitude of the Pueblos, although all shamans were better protected in Pueblo circles because better organized. To be sure, the nobody who boasted of power, like Nick when he was drunk, may have always been castigated as a witch, an attitude which converges with that of the Church toward any independent claimant to supernatural power or authoriy.

Witch doll, ball of fire, evil eye, transformation into domestic animal, and blood trail are all Spanish witch traits. Power to transform into animal form, into coyote,* rattlesnake, butterfly, or bear, is Indian. Also the power to transform one's self into animal or bird without malevolence as does shaman or kachina who becomes a duck or as do the Eagle or Hawk People who live above the sky.[215] I incline to believe that the bulk of belief and behavior about witchcraft is Indian, but that it was greatly stimulated by Spanish witchcraft belief and behavior so that matters not originally conceived of in witchcraft terms came to be so thought of. For example, the Hopi fast runner who is called a Wolf boy, in the East would be called a Witch boy, or sickness imputed once to ghosts is now imputed to witches. During the unusually long confinement period of the Hopi women, twenty days, a fire or embers should be kept burning. If the fire goes out, it is at once renewed, and the day is not counted. The child will be a fire-meddler. If anything is baked or roasted in the fire, he will also be given to playing with fire.[216] Now in the East there is also a confinement fire, and on it an

---

* Jicarilla Apache believe that a ghost (that part of the body which does not accompany the "breath" to the lower world) turns into a coyote (Opler 2:222). Most Pueblo witch transformations are into Coyote.

herb powder is sprinkled that the smoke may keep away the witches.²¹⁷ This is Mexican custom* also. I incline to think that the early Pueblo fire-making custom has lost its aboriginal meaning and been read into the witch complex.†

Elements of European folk belief other than witchcraft and many Catholic rites are found today in Pueblo religion, and whether they are also aboriginal has been an open question. Notable are ritual continence, ritual fasting or abstinence from particular comestibles, head-washing with naming and sponsorship, incensing or smoking sacrosanct objects, aspersing and the use of holy water as medicine, anointing with water or oil, touching the sacrosanct or kissing it, which is equivalent to breathing upon or from it, ritual of the cross, ritual flagellation (through the discipline administered by the Fiscales or possibly through the example of the Penitentes),‡ use of carved wooden images, dressing images or offering clothes, shrines and altar pieces,§ the cross, the standard, the altar candle (of course not originating but possibly affecting the use of the prayer-stick),‖

---

* In a conspicuous Spanish witchcraft case of 1631 involving two Ladina or half-breed women from Mexico, mother and daughter, both wives of Spaniards, the infant held in her arms by Juana the daughter was cured by being smoked with a burnt bit of Juana's clothing (Scholes 2:222, 238). Evil eye cured by sympathetic magic—Spanish or Indian?

These witches had power to travel rapidly like the nun María de Jesús, who about 1620 made flights from Spain to New Mexico (Parsons 52:265, n. 87). Juana the Ladina traveled in an egg.

† To be sure, the Aztecs believed that newborn infants were subject to evil influences.

‡ Benavides reports in 1634 that the Pueblos entered the procession three days a week during Lent, when they all performed penances in the church, and during the processions of Holy Week they flagellated themselves (Hodge 3:125). See p. 1102, n.†.

§ In the Zuni church there were six angel caryatides around the altar of which two remained in 1881 (Bourke 2:115). Everywhere the friars taught carpentry (Benavides, 33, 67).

The frame altar of the Zuni society appears to be comparatively late. The Wood society did not adopt one until 1902 (Stevenson 2:454).

‖ At Acoma a prayer-stick in the shape of a cross or with a cross painted on the tip is offered to Dios. It is always accompanied by a stick for the Corn Mother (White 2:128–29).

the prayer-image,* use of trees and greens in fiesta, use of bells, carnival burlesque, dancing and collecting food from house to house as in Las Posadas or on Kings' Day, vow, religious dancing in general, and masking.

All these ritual elements are conspicuous in the Kachina cult, and a case has been made for the borrowing of that cult itself from Catholicism, from the cult of the saints, as it was presented to the Pueblos by the friars† and their followers, White‡ and Indian,§ from Mexico. We recall that today at Alcalde, the Mexican town near San Juan, Matachina is danced as it is danced in San Juan itself and in other eastern pueblos with only slight variations of Pueblo-like nature. In the so-called Tablita or saint's-day dance of the pueblos these variations are more marked, dance step and song are Pueblo, and the Pueblo clown societies supply the Grandfathers, but the dance figures are still quadrille-like. The saint is carried in processional to an altar in

* Of this it must be pointed out not that it is Indian, this is indubitable, but that it is also a European practice. At a Mallorca sanctuary I saw twig crosses offered by harvesters as a prayer against injury by scythe. In a chapel at Schwarzensee, Austria, iron figurines of domestic animals are placed not as *ex voto* but as a wish (*American Anthropologist*, I [1899], 795).

† Published records of the Church in New Mexico are very meager, but as yet no references occur to teaching dance or music to the Indians as was done on the grand scale in Mexico. And yet most if not all of the missionaries had experience of Mexican methods. Spanish musical instruments were probably scarce. Boys were taught singing (Benavides, 67).

‡ Too little is known about the influence of Colonials of the eighteenth century, a very restless period for the Indians when town groups were removing or being removed (see p. 913, n.‡) and "Mexicans" were pouring in to Indian neighborhoods. I surmise that Mexican settlers did more to Hispanize the Pueblos than the Church ever did directly.

§ See pp. 872–73. Note, here, that in 1680 Tlaxcala Indians were occupying a ward (*barrio*) called Analco in Santa Fé (Twitchell II, 271). In the Espejo expedition of 1583 there were one thousand Mexican Indians. Mexican Indians and Pueblos were attached to the caravans as muleteers. Spanish or Mexican muleteers are ever story-tellers, so here Pueblos had special opportunities for learning Spanish folk tales.
Indian slave traffic through the caravans—in the eighteenth century there was a great annual caravan to the January fair in Chihuahua (Bancroft, 277)—was a means of contact for New Mexican Indians with Mexican Whites and Indians.

the plaza, and the dance is in honor of the saint. In the parade of the saints at San Juan and at Taos, the dancers, Matachina or children dancers, take dance steps or pause to perform a figure, which is a marked feature of the early Spanish procession.²¹⁸ The maskless kachina dance is much like the Tablita dance.*

The ideology of saint and kachina is identical; both are beings who once lived as men, who now are associated with mountain-tops or springs or the sky, whence they send blessings of rain with fertility in crops, also in offspring. Also they cure sickness. They are represented in images and by impersonation with mask. The impersonation or kachina dance follows upon the ceremony of a society much as the saint's dance follows the Mass. Kachina, like saints, are for "poor people." Possibly the Tablita dance† was developed into the Good Kachina dance, presumably in the seventeenth century,‡ and that from Zuni it spread to Hopi and Keres, becoming more and more efflorescent and less and less recognizably European. This hypothesis which is based on the dance alignment common to both kachina and saint's-day dancing§ and on intrinsic similarities between saint and kachina ideology, finds support negatively in the fact that no masks or mask materials have been found in excavations of pre-Spanish period‖ and that, excepting Luxán, the earliest chroniclers make

* The chief difference is that the kachina sing; the saint's dancers have a choir.

† Pekwin's precious Thla'hewe ceremony is a Tablita dance (cf. Stevenson 2: Pls. XXXVIII, XXXIX), a Corn dance or dramatization.

‡ During Otermín's retaliatory campaign in 1681 many masks were captured and burned (southern Tiwa, Keres) since, as Dr. White points out (*American Anthropologist*, XXXVI, 626–28), Spaniards as well as Indians associated masks with the indigenous cult.

§ Similar alignment, let us not forget, occurs in the Aztec dance in honor of Montezuma (see p. 1020).

‖ We have already mentioned the archeological evidence for pre-Spanish use of the mask recently come to light through Dr. E. W. Haury, who has studied in the Peabody Museum of Cambridge the approximately fourteenth-century collection made in 1887 or 1888 by F. H. Cushing from a ritual cave near Phoenix, Arizona. A ritual stick, perhaps a prayer-stick, perhaps a kachina "doll" or "baby," has painted on it an indubitable kachina mask, parti-colored, with the characteristic kachina doll ears. A bandoleer is painted on the nude body. The stick suggests the encradled "baby" used by Keres and at Jemez and associated no mention of masked dancing. In his account of the Espejo expedition in 1583 Luxán writes: "Throughout this nation (Tiwa) they have many masks which they use in their dances and ceremonies";[219] but it is improbable that the Spaniards actually witnessed any "dances or ceremonies." The Tiwa, having recently killed the friars of the Gallegos expedition, fled before the Espejo party. Granted that there was masked dancing at this early period, possibly it was introduced by those Mexican Indians* left behind by Coronado. The three "Mexicans" Espejo found among the Ashiwi were undoubtedly familiar with both Aztec and Spanish masks, two men being from the Valley of Mexico and one from Guadalajara,[220] where Spanish masks were also introduced at a very early date.

Whether or not masking to impersonate a god or to burlesque foreigners or other funny people was a pre-Conquest trait among Pueblos as among Aztecs, Peruvians, and other Indian peoples,† the Spanish mask was taken over, as may be seen in some of the Chapio or Grandfather clown masks of the East and in some of the Gowawaima masks of Santo Domingo. All these masks are referred to as coming from the south. Chapio appears in Mexican dances or celebrations, with the Matachina or at fiestas. Montezuma, the Monarca, brought the Grandfathers from the

---

with cave shrines (Dumarest, 141–42, Fig. 3). Infant spirits, we recall, are the first Kachina in Zuni myth. See Kidder 2:Fig. 78*b* for masklike design in a biscuit ware bowl of Pecos which is probably pre-Spanish. Mask designs on pottery which may be pre-Spanish are reported from Awatobi (Brew, 126).

* Did not these Indians introduce the Aztec or Mexican-Spanish term for Catholic priest, *totache* (Nahuatl, *totatzin*, our reverend father > *tatli*, father, *tatsintli*, reverential)? Compare Zuni, *tutatsi*, Hopi, *tota'ichi*, Santo Domingo, *doɒach*, Laguna, *t'rra·ch*[shu]? And what of the term for governor? P. 147, n.*.
Nequatewa of Mishongnovi says the priest term means "a grouchy person that will not do anything himself, like a child"(!).

† Masking and clowning occur among the Iroquois, on the Northwest Coast, and among Eskimo and Athapascan Tinneh of the Yukon. Among the Tinneh there are grotesque masks of foreigners and clown masks called "have-fun-in-it" who may dance behind masked impersonations, burlesqueing their movements (De Laguna, 575, 582).

mountains.[221] The Gowawaima masks are not sacred, since they may be seen by white people, and before wearing them emesis is not necessary. Among these pseudo-kachina, Mexican personages are represented: Rik'us, Rico or Rich Man, and K'amak'-as, Chamaka or Girl, and all the Gowawaima kachina talk, using any language including Spanish or English.[222] Gowawaima kachina act as police in communal enterprises, like ditch work or cutting wheat (Mexican activities, we note). If masking in the kachina cult was of Spanish provenience, the Gowawaima masks show an early stage of the development. On the other hand, Gowawaima is a Hopi word, the word for the most important kachina shrine, and Gowawaima may have been used at Santo Domingo to label borrowed masks, first from the Hopi,* then from any group, including Mexicans.

To what extent the Spanish devil-clown, with or without mask, was adopted by the Pueblos is uncertain. Throughout Spanish America, the devil-clown-old man (grandfather) appears at Catholic celebrations. In Mexico the clowning couple attend on or valet or burlesque saint's-day dancers very much as do the Pueblo clowns at kachina or saint's-day dance.† Among Mayo-Yaqui and Tarahumara, clowns associated with Holy Week or saint's day also have the same satirizing, policing or punitive functions that characterize Pueblo clowns. Clown and dancer are associated among Navaho, Apache, Havasupai, Pima, and Papago. Probably all these people took over the clown when they took over the Kachina cult, and that may not be so very long ago. The Havasupai call the clown by the same term they

* Possibly via Sandia. See p. 1092, n.*. Inquiry into the Kachina cult at Sandia is important.

† In Acoma tradition Koshare arranges all the details of this pleasure dance, going from house to house to summon the people, appropriating the shaman's drum and rattle, pushing the singers together but in no order, and so calling it "singing grapes" (no doubt it was Iyatik, too, and not the friars who introduced the vine), rehearsing the dancers by showing the men how to lift both feet and the women how to move their arms in rhythm. (Possibly the clowns in the dances are not mimicking the dancers, but rehearsing them!) (Stirling.)

called their masked figure,* *gĭdjĭna,* a term undoubtedly derived from the Hopi word "kachina."†

The evidence remains baffling, but I am tentatively concluding that the clown and kachina mask, the Kachina cult, is of independent Indian origin combining with Catholic contribution. Also I believe that the history of all the other ritual elements mentioned as jointly Catholic and Pueblo has been that of the mask, the end product is a convergence rather than an out-and-out borrowing well acculturated. Aboriginal usage or rite has been fed or stimulated by the Catholic rite.

The use of bells is an exception; the European bell was obviously borrowed and fitted into rattle usage. The cross is certainly both Indian and Catholic, and only the way it is used at times indicates provenience. As a sign of the directions, of star or of sky, it appears to be Indian (and very ancient);‡ as a charm against sickness§ or evil it appears to be Catholic.‖ Used in a

---

* His function is to frighten nonparticipants into dancing, at the annual dance around a pole. He beckons them to enter with the switches he carries; if they fail to heed, he drags or scourges them into the circle. He uses switches on children and dogs, going through a pantomime of shooting them with a gun and pretending fear of them, all in a clownish manner. His trunk is painted with black and white horizontal stripes; he wears short black trousers with torn, flapping legs, and a white cloth mask, a bag drawn in about the neck with short sticks to which down is attached fixed like horns (compare Stephen 4:412) in the upper corners (Spier 2:262).

† Curiously enough from the point of view of this distribution the Hano-Hopi clowns do not use masks.

‡ The inclosed cross was a common design on Basket Maker sandals, and on post–Basket Maker (and Hohokam) pottery (Morris, 197). It is also an early and widespread petroglyph design. In 1716, Pima were calling a people to the north (not Hopi) Cruciferos because that was their sacred sign (Velarde, 117). Navaho? They make their cross from west to east, from south to north.

§ One of the first missionaries to the Hopi was challenged at Awatobi to cure a boy of twelve or thirteen of congenital blindness, and he did, by laying a cross, a miraculous one bestowed by the flying nun María de Jesús, on the boy's eyes

[Footnote (§) continued on next page]

‖ Actually analysis is not simple. On the forehead or body of the newborn Laguna infant is smeared a cross of ashes, and on the fontanelle of the medicine man a cross is painted in red, to keep away witches. Witch belief being both

[Footnote (‖) continued on next page]

secular officer's prayer-stick tied with wool (Laguna) it is certainly Catholic,* but as a message stick, a passport, a token of
good will it was used alike by Spaniards and Pueblos.† The use
of the kiva standard in procession or dance may be derived from
the unfailing use of cross (or flags) in conducting ritual or procession, but the standard as a seal against intrusion looks Indian.
Breathing *on the thumbs*, which is peculiar to Zuni, was derived, I
think, from the Catholic rite of kissing the thumb held over the
index finger as a cross, performed at the close of making the sign
of the cross, but ritual breathing was an ancient widespread
practice.‡ Similarly, continence and fasting are too deeply in-

---

(Benavides, 29). As Benavides passed in 1626 through the still unconverted
Indian *rancherías* south of the Piro pueblos on the Rio Grande, he would set up
a cross, telling those peaceful "Mansos" that should they touch it with faith
they would be cured of sickness. "It was a sight to see those that came quickly
to the holy Cross on their knees, to touch it and kiss it, as they had seen me do.
. . . . I saw come an Indian with toothache; and with great trouble she opened
her mouth with her hands and brought her molars close to the holy Cross. And
another, in the pains of childbirth, came with the same faith and laid her belly
to the holy Cross" (Memorial, 15, also 61). Like Pueblos as well as Catholics,
the Mansos believed in contagion by contact.

Indian and Spanish, as is also the ritual use of ashes, is this infant or doctor cross
Indian or Spanish? Again how construe the large cross placed by Pueblos as by
other Spanish Indians in the middle of a cornfield (Awatobi, 1717 [Bloom, 197]).
I have seen one near Zuni. But making the sign of the cross in self-protection
was definitely *resisted* by Pueblos. I have never seen one crossing himself.

* Not so certainly! In 1540, Castañeda reported finding at a spring near
Acoma "a cross two palms high and as thick as a finger, made of wood with a
square twig for its crosspiece, and many little sticks decorated with feathers
around it, and numerous withered flowers, which were offerings" (Winship, 544).
Here, in our first account of prayer-sticks (White), is the Laguna type of cross
prayer-stick!
When Espejo marched into Walpi in 1583, he found in the court "a cross newly
erected and whitewashed, with an inscription after Spanish custom, with many
feathers and much *pinole* (corn meal) scattered over the sign and ground"
(Luxán, 100).

† By one of his Pueblo ambassadors, a Sia man, Governor Martinez sent a
paper cross to the Hopi who, apostates though they were, sent Martinez a
cross of painted green wood, the size of a Jemez Indian (Bloom, 192, 199).
(Compare the green-painted crosses of Middle America.)

‡ From Alaska to Middle America (Parsons 27:65–66; Parsons 62:313).

grained practices in far-flung Indian cultures as well as among the Pueblos to question their aboriginal character. Fasting from salt is peculiarly Indian, not Catholic at all.* Besides the friars did not seek to impress fasting and ritual continence upon converts; in Spain itself, as compared with other Catholic countries, fasting has been little observed; not every friar even by personal example would have drawn attention to fasting† or continence as condition of holiness; properly or improperly in Pueblo tradition the early friars are accounted incontinent. Ritual continence is most marked at Zuni and except for the impersonations of the Shalako ceremony it follows sacred performance instead of preceding it, Catholic fashion. Incensing, aspersing, breathing (kissing), head-washing with naming and sponsorship, the vow, are all widespread Indian rites; but they are peculiarly emphasized among the Pueblos and other Hispanized peoples. After planting the Cross, baptism was next in order, and it was the one sacrament that always took, if the missionary was suffered at all. As medicine or exorcism it probably appealed in general to the Indian, although each culture where it was readily accepted might present special conditions. I think the Pueblos already had similar practices, spraying or rubbing on medicine, washing as purifying and renaming, possibly as purification or exorcism also, the new name being given to save from vengeful or pursuing spirit,‡ the whole initiation or salvation being a rebirth to this end, washing and renaming being first a war practice and then spreading to curing societies§ and to the Kachina

* Yet Father Kino in the Pimería "ever took less food without salt" (Velarde, 153).

† Benavides opines that the fasts of the friars never fail, even to the more severe fasts of the Lent of the Blessed (Memorial, 67).

‡ This was South American Tupinamba practice (Métraux, 163–64).

§ The Hopi wounded in a fight is taken to the house of the man who rescues him, his "father," and given treatment for four days (Nequatewa, 58–59). See p. 55 for Zuni practice. When Tsashji of Laguna was struck by lightning, he was taken to an empty house and treated four days by a Shikani doctor (Parsons 33:275). Possibly any accident or grave sickness appears or once appeared to the Pueblo as supernaturally caused and to be saved the afflicted has to be ceremonially treated, reconciled with the god through a sponsor.

cult. Sponsorship was familiar in Pueblo organization as a curing or educational arrangement before the Catholic godfather of the candle or of baptism was heard of, so that the *compadre* system took hold easily among the Pueblos, not in the early days of wholesale baptism of course, but after Spanish godparents were available. Mexicans still serve as godparents in Catholic baptism, a linkage between Pueblos and Mexicans which is socially valuable. The vow to hold office or perform a role, often for a given number of times, is also both Spanish and Indian. It enters into the technique of Spanish *cofradía* organization which carried on the cult of the saints, including custody of the image, responsibility for candles and for fiesta celebration. A *cofradía* and its *mayordomo* or head are mentioned in a law suit of 1774 in Santa Fé,[223] but lacking fuller information about the *cofradía* or *mayordomía** in New Mexico we cannot press parallels with Pueblo organization. Nor can we more than speculate about service† and subsistence as rendered friars and *encomenderos* or as rendered Town chief, or about other Town chief and friar parallels. When Government complained that friars had plenty of horses while some soldiers had none and that each friar had from a thousand to two thousand sheep, the friars retorted that in famine they fed both Spaniards and Indians,[224] just as we have seen the Town chief providing for his "children."

The Pueblo calendar has incorporated a good deal from the Catholic calendar, all the pueblos but Zuni and the Hopi having a fixed patron-saint's day and observing other saints' days, Holy Week, Christmas or Noche Buena, and All Souls. Even Zuni has a saint's dance, which is movable and not held every year, and observes "Grandmothers' day." Throughout Mexico house-to-house visiting occurs during *las posadas*, the nine guest nights before Christmas Eve, and again on Kings' Day, when masks visit and dance. The people of the house regale their visitors, especially the children or young people the nine nights. Possibly the house-to-house visiting by boys and little children that

---

* See p. 925, n.* for *mayordomos* at Isleta del Sur.

† The field of the padre of Taos is still worked for him, by the bachelors, to offset wedding fees. The sacristan has a field for his services.

occurs the evening of Kings' Day at Taos together with "pleasure dances," i.e., dances borrowed from other tribes (Navaho, Cheyenne, Ute, Apache, Sioux, Pawnee, Comanche), and the regaling of dancers[225] is a shift of Las Posadas to King's Day, in honor of the new secular officers whose houses are visited. At Acoma I saw the same kind of domiciliary performance by the young people, on January 27,[226] a still later shift due to fitting in the ceremony of installing the War captains.

Granted that the Kachina cult has been prompted, or at any rate, stimulated by the cult of the Saints (and of the Souls, *las animas*), that would mean a still further enrichment of the Pueblo calendar, a momentous elaboration. That the Kachina dances tended even to overcrowd the calendar and had somehow to be regulated may be inferred, I think, from the "Kachina come" and "Kachina go" periods of Western calendars. The Homegoing Nima'n kachina of the Hopi and the less drastic farewell at the close of the Zuni Shalako seem to be dramatic devices or rationalizations, whether post-Catholic or pre-Catholic (see p. 1001) to keep kachina ceremonial in its place.

Such deliberate adjustments of calendar have been known in the case of saints' days. For example, San José had his birthday shifted at Laguna from March 19 to September 19 because there is more food in this month of harvest. The kachina initiation of Acoma has been shifted from winter to summer in order that the children may be home from boarding schools.[227] If the Zuni Shalako* was originally a carnival or a Christmastide celebration, as has been suggested, that too exemplified calendrical adjustment, by a month,† that it might not interfere with the win-

---

* The wicker framework of the impersonation and the movable snout or jaw are features of the European mask, the giant masks still familiar in Belgium, in Mallorca, Spain, and in Mexico (Parsons 48:602; Parsons 62:244). The Flemish Giants go around as family groups, like the Soyok or Natashka kachina of Walpi. On the other hand, movable mask jaw and marionette-like figures (there is a Shalako maid marionette on First Mesa) are Northwest Coast traits (Nass River).

† Little or no adjustment was called for if Shalako was the celebration of the patron-saint's day, December 8. It might have been the original celebration, the sporadic saint's-day celebration coming in later, from the East.

ter solstice ceremony.* In the East the Christmastide held its own and possibly the solstice date had to shift, to an advance date excepting at San Juan when the solstice ceremonial is twelve days after Christmas, January 7, the day after Kings' Day.

To the Pueblo pantheon, the saints and possibly certain kachina are the foremost Spanish contributions; God the Father, Dios, remains the "Mexican God," exciting little interest and receiving little attention, although the conception of a supreme or high god has probably affected the character of Węide of Isleta or even of the Hopi sky god Sho'tokününgwa. What became of the Virgin and her Son is even more problematical. As Catholic divinities they are rarely, if ever, mentioned. I surmise that Mary was assimilated with Mother Iyatiku, by Keres. At Laguna I found Iyatiku referred to in very much the same loving spirit as is Mary among Catholics. Iyatiku is the Child Medicine Woman or Sand Altar Woman of First Mesa, and possibly the image of Sand Altar Woman carried in Wüwüchim procession was a sometime Virgin introduced through immigrant Keres, if not one of the *santos* "buried" at the Great Rebellion. As for Jesus, to us he seems identifiable with the Zuni-Hopi kachina, Shulawitsi-Avachhoya, virginal fire or corn spirit, or again with Payatemu-Poseyemu, Sun Youth, but there is no direct evidence of identification by Pueblos, whereas kachina similarity with Huichol fire virgins is close. Nor is there direct identification between the Catholic story of the Virgin birth and the widely spread Indian story of magical impregnation. But Jesus has been identified with Montezuma;† both performed miracles, both

* It has been customary at Zuni for the children in the boarding-school at Black Rock to return home, not at Christmas, but at Shalako. A Catholic Agent wanted to change this arrangement. The townspeople were much upset. The Agent came to our house, and the Governor's wife and I talked him out of his plan. Had we failed of persuasion, it is possible that Shalako would have been shifted into the Christmas vacation and the winter solstice ceremony placed in the beginning of December, Eastern style.

† "Montezuma is like Christ. He and Christ are the same thing" (San Juan). Like Poseyemu, Montezuma has been magically conceived through a piñon nut given Salt Girl by Our Lady of Lourdes! (Espinosa, A. M., 98). Cf. Bandelier 3.

were persecuted or killed by their own people,* both promised to return, restoring the past† or bringing a happier day.‡

The promise is for this life, for Pueblos, like many Indians, remain indifferent for the most part to Catholic dogmas about life after death. To the Pueblos life goes on as usual yet the idea of future punishment, by transformation into insect or snake or by fire, does occur, particularly among Hopi. At Zuni, too, I have been told of punishment after death,§ by fire. At Cochiti two guards examine the prayer-feathers the deceased has carried to the Mother at Shipap and then the deceased goes on either to Wenima or, if he is a witch, to hell, which is the fourth under-

---

* Montezuma was said to have been stoned, and this is the Mexican story of his death, not a derivation from the story of Jesus.

† Conservatives among Papago call themselves the party of Montezuma. Undoubtedly the Pueblos heard a good deal about Montezuma from their early Mexican Indian visitors and later they found Montezuma a "god" that might be mentioned conveniently to White people. Compare Espinosa, A. M., 97 ff.

‡ See p. 202. One literary source is indicated. In 1864 there was in circulation among the Indians a "highly esteemed" document said to be derived from Mexico City, stating that Montezuma was born at Tognayo, an ancient New Mexican pueblo, in 1538; that he was a prophet, foretelling events, and a wonderworker. He was expected to come again (*Report of the Commissioner of Indian Affairs*, 1864). Possibly this was the "book" buried with Kwime' of Laguna (Parsons 20:97-98).

But there is the older widespread tradition of the return of the god, the white god or chief, with which no doubt these stories were assimilated. The first Catholic sermons the Ashiwi heard, in 1629, gave them "to understand the coming of the Son of God to the world" (Hodge 3:83). The most recent version of the second coming is from Second Mesa, where as at Jemez and elsewhere prayer-meal was offered to the rising sun to hasten the advent of the Bahana (Americans) who would be able to identify witches at sight and bring peace (Nequatewa, 50-51). Compare the tale told in Walpi in 1883 of the chief long since departed who returned one day at sunrise to restore harmony and the ancient days (Stephen 2:67).

§ The early Pueblos buried the dead, but cremation was observed in Cibola by Coronado's party. Pima cremated those killed on the war path; Navaho sometimes burn the body with the lodge (Spier 2:293 ff.); and cremation occurred among the Yuman peoples and in southern California, until it was ended by Mission pressure.

Inferably the friars opposed cremation by the Pueblos. No evidence of cremation after the Conquest has been found in Zuniland. (The Church also made a change, of course, in the place of burial, from refuse heap to churchyard.) Was there any ideological clash or agreement over cremation or hell fire?

world. He goes into a round house of flames where he has to stand upright forever. Other sinners have to stand in a circle of shell drawn by Masewa, the War chief of Shipap, and eat only the fleas or worms that come into the circle.[228] In Tewa tale witches are burned alive. Possibly all these references to punishment by fire are reminiscent of the teachings of the friars. To be sure, Masauwü is the Hopi god of fire as well as of death, and the Tokonaka or Agave who guards the death trail is his servant; so there may be some aboriginal basis for the hell fires of the Hopi. The Keresan circle of confinement is based on the punishment inflicted on the living.

What of Wenima, the terrestrial paradise in the west, a place ever green and watered, rich in crops and well stocked with game, the home of kachina who are both farmers and hunters? Was Wenima suggested by the Catholic heaven in distinction to the underground or underlake abodes of the Dead—Shipapu, Kothluwela? More probably it was derived from Apache or Plains notions of the afterworld. In Mescalero-Chiricahua belief this hunter's paradise is underground. Nor is it to any Indian, Apache or Pueblo, a place of reward. Reward after death has even less place than punishment in Indian ideology.[229]

When Nick was rescued from the church beam where for two days he had been kept hanging (? Spanish fashion) as a witch, cut down by the American soldiers from Fort Wingate, witch-baiting at Zuni had to take a new turn. Suspects were nagged rather than tortured* into confession† and loss of power. Otherwise I doubt if belief in witchcraft has been directly affected in any pueblo by the century of contacts with Americans who "because they do not believe in witchcraft are not troubled by witches." To be harmed, just as to be helped, you must believe.

* As late as 1891, Lummis reports from Isleta a case of torturing a witch by having him sit with legs crossed and weighed down by neck-stocks (Lummis 3:145).

† However, nagging was probably nothing new, for it approximates examination and re-examination of witnesses or defendants in Spanish days and getting statements sworn to "in the name of Our Lord God and under the sign of the Holy Cross," by the First or Second Alcalde.

Once at Zuni during an epidemic of measles when the American doctor tried to point out that the children were dying in town under native treatment and not one child had died at the Black Rock school under his care he was told that it was because there were no witches at Black Rock, so many Americans lived there.

Although Pueblos have been not wards but American citizens, since the Treaty of Guadalupe, they do not vote or pay taxes; in conflict with outsiders they depend on Federal Agent or Commissioner and few besides Nick have applied to American authorities in internal disputes.* American influence has been for the most part along economic lines. Aside from the fight at Taos which was an aftermath of the Mexican war, the Treaty of Guadalupe in 1848 opened the way for peaceful penetration and American trade. Unfortunately, we have no record of the early barter, but at the turn of the century in almost every pueblo or in its neighborhood the oldest living American resident was a trader. Changes in house-building and furnishings and in dress have been made; windows enlarged and window glass used; entrance by ground door instead of by ladder and roof; rooms enlarged; wooden instead of dirt floors; planked and plastered ceilings; stoves, tables, chairs (for block stools), and bedsteads have altered ways of cooking, eating, sitting, or sleeping; men have given up white cottons, their Spanish garments, for cloth suits, and women have replaced their native cloth dress with cotton dress or slip or added a long sleeved underslip to their armless cloth dress. Headdress and footgear have changed less, but in most towns the younger men wear hats (over short hair), and American shoes and stockings are replacing moccasins and

---

* An old Cochiti man told Father Dumarest that he was once charged with unbelief (refusing to dance or showing contempt for any ceremonial, in this case I suspect the charge was witchcraft) and stood upright in the circle, until he fainted and then "confessed." He was delivered, and the next day he fled to Santa Fé and applied for American citizenship (?). "*This audacious and unprecedented move brought him the contempt of everybody even of his children.*" Even today and even in Taos, that town of fighters, a man is very reluctant to appeal to an American court. Recently a youth was about to be disciplined by his kiva chief by being made to smoke strong tobacco (perhaps he had to swallow it also); his champion took the matter to the American judge, but, when he found he would have to reveal *costumbres*, he withdrew the case.

leggings for men and women. Wagons, buggies, and automobiles have come into use; horses have taken the place of oxen, mules, or burros, and agricultural implements have been introduced;* because of a ready American market for wool, and the disappearance of game animals, the interest of sheep-raising has encroached upon that of agriculture and through trade has been a means of introducing American goods of all kinds. From San Ildefonso comes a report that agriculture is losing out to the tourist trade in pottery; men are helping women in their quasimass production. How some of these new goods or new economic ways have effected changes in religion we shall consider in a later discussion on disintegration, also the effects of the wage system, of the Protestant missionary and of schools.

Many of these changes were resisted by the hierarchies, the chiefs. The Taos Council has opposed innovations in hair or dress, in food containers or furnishings, and to this day has kept window glass out of the walled town. The Zuni schoolhouse was once mobbed because hair was being cut short, a shortcut into unpopularity much favored by schoolteachers.† During the Great Rebellion some of the leaders proposed to burn up the seeds of all plants introduced by the Spaniards.[230] Certain agricultural implements have been now and again forbidden. Santo Domingo decided that well water was not to be substituted for water from the ditch, and destroyed their newly installed hydrants. Wheat threshers offered by the Indian Bureau were rejected (Zuni, Acoma, Jemez, Taos [machine burned], and probably elsewhere). Just how modern water supply and farming machinery clashed with Indian preconceptions has not yet been

---

* As late as 1807 there were no horse-drawn vehicles, and hoe (*coa*) culture prevailed (Pike, Appen. to Pt. III, 9). In 1855 and 1857 congress made grants of $5,000 and $10,000 for farm implements; a farmer was assigned to every Pueblo in 1899.

† In early Spanish days the friars cut hair to punish "for errors and light faults," a practice forbidden by royal decree in 1621 because it so deeply affronted the Indians that it drove some of them to live in the unconverted pueblo of Acoma, "returning to idolatry" (Scholes 1:155). Long hair is associated with cloud spirits by Pueblos and by Jicarilla Apache (Opler 6:XI).

explained.* In 1892, when there was talk of a railroad through Zuni country, it was objected that it would make the earth tremble (always a fearful thing) and so much disturb the perfect quiet of the bundle fetishes that they would withhold rain or snow.[231]

Ceremonialists will often resist novel things or methods merely in connection with ritual so that the old-fashioned thing or method takes on a ritual character, for example, like tearing and not cutting cornhusk for cigarette (Acoma) or getting a light for smoking from burning husk or wood, or getting fire from a drill, to the preclusion of the sulphur match as in the Zuni hunt with the kachina or at any time in the ceremonial house of the Town chieftaincy.[232] Digging-stick and even Mexican hoe (*coa*)† are used in the Snake hunt in preference to American implements. Native-grown cotton will be used in prayer-sticks after it has gone out for clothing. Old-fashioned dress or ornament, headgear‡ or footgear becomes conventional dance array or array for images; old-fashioned foods become prescriptive ritual dishes, and food innovations are taboo; eating light or fasting during ceremonial gains distinction from being contrasted to three meals a day, today's routine, rather than to the earlier routine of two meals. The kiva has to be ascended or descended by ladder§ as

* A hint from Santa Ana. Shovel work on the ditch *would hurt the Spirits living there*, so at the request of the ditch boss the Koshairi remove the Spirits (*maiyanyi*) temporarily and then restore them just as the water is about to be turned in, when the ditch boss prays to Water Serpent and to the other Spirits (White).

† Introduced by Spaniards and much sought after by Pueblos (Bloom, 167).

‡ Removing hat or even *banda* at a ceremony is another case in point. Acomans resisted the hat in general by holding that the hair parting should not be covered because it represented the Galaxy—a rationalizing invention?

§ After the Rebellion, Pueblos occupied Santa Fé and converted the chapel in the round tower of the palace into a kiva, at least Vargas and the padres thought so. The Indians walled up the door, made a hole in the roof, and descended by ladder.

(Vargas had the Indians open the door, whitewash the interior, and build a foundation for an altar. The Fathers *resisted* taking over as a chapel a place that had been desecrated by "diabolical meetings and dances" until Vargas reminded them that the principal cathedrals of Spain had been previously mosques of the Moors!) (Wuthenau, 177–79).

in the day when every house was entered by hatch; the kiva itself, the subterranean kiva, appears to be the early pit house surviving as a ceremonial chamber. Old-fashioned games become ritual games, such as Koyemshi play, or like the game of throwing dough balls which is no longer played except by the Zuni kachina Hetsululu, who throws clay balls, or by Mishongnovi salt-gatherers at their Sparrow-hawk race.[233] The early practice of head-taking instead of the later practice of scalp-taking, is imitated in dramatizing a ritual execution.

CHAPTER IX
OTHER PROCESSES OF CHANGE

RESISTANCE

Cultural contact does not necessarily mean borrowing, and the question of selective borrowing—why one trait is borrowed and not another—is very baffling. The hypothesis generally entertained is that resistance to taking over an alien trait or indifference to it is greatest when there is nothing resembling it in the culture of the potential borrower or when the new trait clashes with an existing trait or is incompatible with the spirit of the culture. Suggest to the most intelligent Pueblo you know that he give you information about his religion or *costumbres* so that his grandchildren may know their tribal history, and you will get an immediate illustration of this theory of resistance. In Pueblo history, as we attempt to reconstruct it, there are many illustrations, certain or probable.

The Western clanship principle spread to the East until among Tewa it encountered the moiety as a unit of organization. The Tewa moiety is patrilineal. Here was a real clash of concepts for Keres and Tewa who might intermarry.* The outcome was that the matrilineal clan got little recognition from the patrilineally set Tewa; clanship furnished nothing but a few group names, and these sometimes to paternal as well as to maternal groups. The clan did not come to control marriage choices because that idea was too foreign; it was not part of the moiety plan, the Tewa moiety not being exogamous. The leaning of the Tewa clan, such as it is, to patrilineal descent is, I think, a good case of adapting the borrowed trait, matrilineal clan, to an existing trait, patrilineal moiety.†

* Note that theoretically Tewa men would be marrying Keresan women. The men would be carrying with them the patrilineal moiety principle, but there would be no women to carry to Tewa the principle of matrilineal clanship.

† Reinforced, possibly, at a later date by Spanish patriliny, particularly at Santa Clara (see p. 1137, n.*; also Parsons 49:91 ff.).

Clanship has been too unobtrusive or slight a matter among Tewa to spread through intermarriage to Taos. It is probable that under Americanization it will disappear from Tewa culture and never reach Taos at all. Even with a strong development among Tewa, the matrilineal clan would be resisted at Taos, first, because its bilateral system tends toward paternal descent; second, because there is no expression at Taos of reckoning descent in large groups: descent does not figure, at least overtly, in Taos expressions of moiety which are ceremonial. An inconspicuous model and internal contrariety—why clanship, matrilineal or patrilineal, did not spread at Taos is clear enough. It is an excellent illustration of one way in which a trait, a complex of traits, or a culture area may receive a boundary.

The case for the matrilineal clan was a little different at Isleta, and the result has been curiously different. Isleta has been in contact for a long time with western Keres—she has today a Keresan colony in her midst—and clanship is comparatively well established among these Keres. Isletans in mass visited the matrilineal Hopi for a term of years. I take it that matrilineal clanship was forced on their attention; possibly the concept of descent was associated with their moieties at an even earlier period. The Tewa case indicates that it was an early Tanoan idea. At any rate, some of the Isletan ceremonial groups, the Corn groups, became, we may assume, matrilineal groups. True clans they never became because the idea of a group outside of bilateral lineages affecting marriage choice was never established. In fact, all that was borrowed was the idea of regulating membership in a ceremonial group through matrilineal descent. Only an element of clanship was borrowed, not the whole clan complex.* If the early Isletan moiety *was* patrilineal, it too has been invaded by the idea of matrilineal descent, since the children of a family are divided between the moieties of their parents if their parents happen to belong to different

* See p. 1035, n.*, for the possibility that the Corn groups and, I would add, their matrilineal character were derived from non-Pueblo cultures to the southeast. Survivors of the Mansos below the Piro on the Rio Grande and intermarried with Piro are said to have Corn "clans" (Blue, White, Yellow, Red) and Water "clans" (Handbook).

moieties. Yet it may well be that this distribution of offspring is nothing more than an expression of bilateral principle characteristic of northern Tiwa. Again, proveniences may be foreign.

In the West clanship is associated with ceremonial; in fact, the *wimi* (fetish and ceremony) are the heart of the clan.[1] Why did this association wear thin among western Keres to disappear among eastern Keres, not reaching Tewa at all? Because the body of fetish and ceremony was comparatively slight, and because of clash with the group around which ceremonial was already concentrated and in which fetishes were personal property, the shamanistic society. The shamanistic Keresan society, organized otherwise than through kinship, operated to prevent the Keresan clan from taking on ritual functions. The matrilineal clan was borrowed but shorn of ceremonial functions. Acoma was a battlefield for this clash between clan and society. Here the Town chieftaincy was associated with a clan, the Antelope clan, but formerly the Kaʙina society and now the Flint society erects the altar of the Town chief, and the societies retain a veto on his nominations to office. The Town chief is chief of the Kachina cult. The Western association between Kachina cult and clanship is further expressed at Acoma in the Shuracha kachina dramatization by the Corn clan; when this was borrowed from the Zuni Shalako, the clan relationship probably slipped in with it. But why salt-gathering and its ritual came to be associated with Parrot and Pumpkin clans, with clanship at all, we cannot even guess.* No such association is recorded among Zuni or Hopi.†

To return from a speculative detail to the major matter of resistance to the spread of the clan system, let us note how negligible was the resistance among Tewa immigrants to First Mesa, because of contiguity to an impressive clan system and intermarriage which could not fail to bring the system to im-

---

* Still, after learning more about the great importance of Pima-Papago salt-gathering, I am making a guess. Parrot feathers were acquired by Pueblos in Pimería. Acoma (possibly Hopi) traders may have introduced a salt-parrot association.

† A Pumpkin or Squash clan became extinct on First Mesa sometime, let us say, in the eighties (Stephen 4: 1086).

mediate attention, and perhaps because of previous experience with clanship.* At any rate, among these immigrant Tewa, moiety and shamanistic society were in no position to oppose the introduction or strengthening of the clan; as we shall see later, they could not hold their own. And so, in a remarkably short period, clanship blossomed at Hano just as in what was probably an even shorter period it broke down in the Laguna colony at Isleta, in both cases mostly by way of intermarriage and, let me add, because of a change in the system of owning houses.

It has been pointed out that houseownership by women and clanship go hand in hand.[2] I believe that the clan principle developed locally, among Hopi, as a by-product of their Shoshonean housing complex (see p. 988). Hypothetically, a house cluster of Hopi women relatives, owning several contiguous rooms or "houses," was given a name, probably by outsiders, much as we might call a settlement of related families named Smith "Smithtown." The name stuck to the men and women who "came out" of those houses, the men to marry into another house cluster and the women to remove from the original house cluster, because of lack of space, and to start another cluster. This second cluster might or might not take on a secondary name, thus contributing a name in the first case to the original group name.[3] The idea of exogamy followed the group name, an exogamous rule having prevailed in the original house cluster. When the younger women removed, they would not take with them the family fetishes, which remained in what we have called the maternal house of the clan. That house belongs theoretically to the oldest sister whose oldest brother or son is chief of the ceremony associated with the fetish. Minor ceremonial duties would be delegated to the scattered kindred or, as a ceremony developed, new duties or functions might be assigned these junior branches. Through ceremonial the group would be held together long after memory of common blood was forgotten. On failure of the leading lineage, other lineages would become responsible for

---

* Tano were closer to the more weightily beclanned Keres than were northern Tewa.

ceremonial or would be entitled to houses or lands. This reconstruction is supported by contemporary Hopi data.

What happens or happened at Zuni? Houses belong to the women, and maternal lineages are recognized, with ceremonial functions, but, except through the Rain chieftaincies, without distinctive names. If Zuni borrowed the clanship idea from Hopi, they dropped out the feature of secondary clan names,* of naming lineages (but see pp. 219, 223). However Zuni clans "got their names," the curing societies of Keresan type held clan domination in check, and involution in clanship did not progress at Zuni as it did in Hopiland.

To sum up, clanship among Pueblos may spread through intermarriage or be checked, and it may spread as part of a cult system or be checked by a cult or unit of social organization contrary or indifferent to its principle of kinship. Do these processes hold on a large scale in the distribution of clanship among Indian peoples in general?

As the principle of clanship centered in the West and spread eastward, so the principle of moiety centered in the Tanoans and spread south and west, a little. Keres are not divided into Summer people and Winter people, but they do express patrilineal moiety in their kiva membership: children belong to the kiva of their father which is also the kiva of their mother, as *at marriage a girl automatically* joins her husband's kiva.† This modification in the moiety idea indicates that it is thought of among Keres as a ceremonial expression rather than as a principle of kinship. At Acoma kiva membership based on moiety has all but disappeared, leaving only the tendency to initiate children into their father's kiva or, if he were a Koshare, into that society. I take it that the patrilineal moiety did not "take"

---

* Some of these in Hopiland are due to affiliations between clans in separate towns—affiliations which might well have been made in Zuni Valley before the seventeenth-century concentration of population at Itiwana or modern Zuni.
Are clans differentiating in contemporary Zuni colonies?

† Passage at marriage from one moiety to another is not unfamiliar among Tewa, but it is performed with an elaborate adoption ceremony. Possibly a breakdown of moiety.

further among Keres as a principle of descent because of the existence of the matrilineal clan.

But moiety as a ceremonial trait had a better chance. It trailed along with summer-winter kachina and clown distinctions. Witness at Acoma the winter K'oβishtaiya, at Zuni the importance of summer dances and the seasonal functions of Ne'wekwe and Koyemshi, and among Keres the general association of Koshare with summer and Kwirana with winter (excepting the curious modification at Cochiti from seasonal to annual alternation). In group organization, however, the Clowns cease to express moiety. The moiety, like the clan, lost out to the Keresan society. From being moiety war groups the Clowns became shamanistic societies.

But not without opposition. Inferably there was resistance to the jugglery complex that characterized the Clowns, at least in Keresan towns. On the traditional migration southward Cochiti society chiefs, jealous of the Clowns, criticized them for performing "miracles" and doing "whatever came into their heads." So the two Koshare returned to Shipap to get authority from the Mother who had given them power; but Iyatiku supported the medicine men and told the Koshare that they should not perform miracles; they were only to amuse the people, dance, and bring in the kachina.[4] P'ashaya·'nᵞ'i (Bacheani), who was the son of Giantess or who made himself out of an arrowpoint, introduced jugglery to Laguna people. From his toe he brought out two burros, fully bridled. He took pebbles and bits of cloth from his mouth, or piñon nuts or corn kernels from his chest. The Koshare liked this, and do it themselves to this day, for they still believe in P'ashaya·'nᵞ'i. But P'ashaya·'nᵞ'i deceived the people,* and in the end the Mother had to send Masewi to drown him in the ocean.[5] At Acoma, Pishuni was the arch-

---

* It is tempting to see in this adumbration of ancient feud by a partisan of the Kurena and the Whites a reference to the turmoil of the Reconquest and to Pope' (Pos Pec), the medicine man who led the Great Rebellion. But the feud is probably more ancient, referring to the conflict in myth between the Underground Mother and the War gods (p. 247) or, among Papago, between Elder Brother and Earth-maker. Giantess came from the south.

witch and has even been identified with Satan, the serpent-tempter.

Resistance to the spread of the Keresan clown appears to have occurred at Isleta. At the time of the migration from Laguna to Isleta, the Kurena (Kwirana) society chief remained at Laguna, where he was the leader of the Progressives, but the Kashale (Koshare) men moved away, and one of them at least went on to Isleta. *"He did not like it there* and returned to Mesita." Possibly he was not made much of at Isleta, as he did not fit into their moiety clown organization. Isletan moiety clowns are borrowed today by the Laguna colonists for their kachina performances, just as Hano clowns are borrowed for Hopi kachina.

Zuni has been the center of the Kachina cult. From Zuni the cult spread successfully to Keres,* but there is fragmentary evidence of some early resistance, again by the medicine societies. Possibly the Acoma ceremonial of the Fight with the Kachina, the Zuni Ky'anakwe ceremonial, and the Laguna tradition of the punishment of the kachina by Iyatiku are obscure echoes of such opposition. In the Ky'anakwe tradition, Chakwena Woman is killed by the War gods. Her heart is in her gourd rattle; in other words, she is a witch. The sister of the oldest shaman of Laguna, the Kurena chief, told me that, when the Chakwena came to Laguna about a hundred years ago,† they were called witches and spat upon by the people. Less speculative is the idea that the medicine societies, the customary depositaries of ceremonial paraphernalia, took over the custody and even the use of the masks, in some cases a monopolistic use, i.e., only a shaman may impersonate a certain kachina. And only the shamans may bring the kachina into town, through the good offices of the Mother whom they visit at Shipap during their rain retreats. Clan kachina of the West are changed into society kachina in the East. Here, too, Acoma reveals the early issue. The Town chief,

---

* I am not closing the question whether in still earlier days use of masks may have spread from East to West.

† Three Laguna men went to Zuni to ask for the Chakwena. The masks were refused, so they stole them. There is an independent Chakwena dance group today in Laguna (Parsons 33: 223–24).

Antelope clansman, appoints the chiefs of kiva who have charge of the masks, but the appointments have to be passed on by the shamans. The Town chief's kachina altar is put up by the Kaвina society chief. Kick-stick (kachina) racers are medicated by the Flint shaman. Kachina initiates are whipped only by the Flint shaman who impersonates the whipper kachina, and initiates are actually called Kurena people. Formerly the Kurena chief of Laguna controlled the Kachina cult of Laguna. Laguna masks were made by one of the societies. In the East Town chief and societies achieved complete control of the cult.

But it is fair to say that this Keresan history shows acculturation rather than resistance. Actually the cult was accepted and then fitted into the prevailing social pattern. It is only when we reach Tewa and Tiwa that resistance or indifference is unmistakable; mask cult or usage is slight among Tewa, and among Tiwa, excepting Sandía,* nonexistent. This is all the more strik-

---

* Isletans and other Indians have asserted that there are masked dances at Sandía, but there is no description of them. Isletans are not admitted to them.

Sandía (Napeya), where many Provincials were killed in the Great Rebellion, was burned at the Reconquest (1682), and refugees from the population of three thousand went to Hopiland, founding Payupki near Second Mesa. In 1742 they were led back to the East by two friars, and, after living about in Jemez and other pueblos, in 1748 they obtained the right to resettle in Sandía as "Moqui converts" (Stephen 4:1163; Twitchell, I, 400; II, 221). They may well have acquired the mask cult during their Hopi sojourn.

Except for the fact that the present population of Sandía speaks Tanoan and not Hopi, the resettlers would have to be described as Hopi, as the friars and the Santa Fé authorities consistently refer to them as Hopi without any reference whatsoever to an earlier Sandía history, as in the following petition of Friar Juan Miguel Menchero: "For six years I have been engaged in the work of converting the gentiles, and, notwithstanding innumerable trials, I have succeeded in planting the seed of the Christian Faith among the residents of the pueblos of Acoma, Laguna, and Zia, for all of which I hold instructions from the Most Excellent Viceroy of New Spain, to construct temples, convents, and pueblos, with sufficient lands for each, water, watering places, timber and pastures, which I have obtained for all of those whom I have been able to convert; and having converted and gained over three hundred and fifty souls from here to the Rio Puerco, which I have brought from the pueblos of Moqui, bringing with me the *cacique* of these Moqui pueblos, for the purpose of establishing their pueblo at the place called Sandía . . . . which I have already examined and found unoccupied, so as to prevent my converts returning to apostasy, as by locating them at any other point they may escape to their former homes, being the most remote" (Twitchell, II, 221).

The puzzle of why the Payupki Tiwa were so persistently called Moqui

ing because underlying kachina ideology is developed—belief in
cloud beings, benevolent bringers of rain and bestowers of crops,
dwellers in spring or lake, on mountaintops. But beyond the
Tewa the mask itself and much of its ritual have not spread.
The idea of masking is familiar, as is shown by the clown masks.
Isleta has looked on for perhaps half a century at kachina
masked dances performed in her very streets by Laguna immigrants, and annually a maskless kachina impersonation visits
Isleta from Zuni Mountain. Although described as an afterthought in the ceremonial life,[6] maskless kachina dances* are
performed at Isleta (and at Taos).† No criticism of the use of
masks in the other pueblos has been recorded from Isleta or
Taos. The ground appears to be fully prepared for mask usage
and the more elaborate part of the kachina cult, yet there is a
very notable resistance. Our theories of clash or of lack of cultural springboard break down, although not entirely. Whatever
their early history, modern Tiwa are without the techniques of
design essential to mask-making and to the prayer-stick-making
which is part of the kachina ritual complex. As we have elsewhere noted, Tiwa are inferior craftsmen; they weave little if at
all, their pottery is undecorated or crude,‡ they are not wood-
carvers or painters. I know from observation that in drawing
ritual objects they show no sense of conventional design. I infer
that Tiwa do not use masks and prayer-sticks *because they do*

(Hopi) is solved by the report of Father Escalante, dated Zuni, 1776, that "God
in order to save these souls [Oraibi families] allowed a grave discord over the
election of a chief in Oraibi. On this account the pueblo was divided into two
parties, who took arms against one another. The least powerful . . . . took
refuge on the little mesa [Payupki] on which the Tiguas were already" (Thomas,
159), which accounts for Menchero's reference to the Moqui cacique, for the use
of masks at Sandía, and, by the way, for the presence of good pottery at Payupki.

* The maskless kachina dance occurs in all the towns. Why impersonators in
such masking centers as Zuni, the Hopi towns, or Santo Domingo go without
masks is not clear.

† Hopi visitors in 1742 may have danced kachina, and, if so, without masks,
for they would not have carried masks with them on this friar-conducted
journey to the East. Note that the fifth Corn group of Isleta conducts a maskless
kachina dance, and that this group is a sort of omnibus, afterthought group.

‡ Early Pecos pottery was comparatively poor; were all the Tanoan-speaking
peoples inferior craftsmen?

know how to make them. Recently at Taos I heard Antonio
Mirabal say that he wanted his sons to be taught painting and
carving, in school. The Mirabal family were in charge of the
clown masks, and Antonio's father is chief of the kiva that presents the one maskless kachina dance of Taos. My guess is that
Antonio wants his sons to become craftsmen in order to make
dance masks.

The Mirabals are the center of the opposition at Taos to the
introduction of the Peyote cult. The Mirabals face toward the
south and the Kachina cult;* the "Peyote boys" face toward
Oklahoma. Their new cult is fundamentally contrary not only to
the Kachina cult† but to the general temper of Pueblo ceremonialism. It emphasizes individual emotional experience as
against communal, ritualistic performance. At Taos, after it
spread a little within family groups, peyote became associated
with a group of Americanized individuals inclined to rebellion
against the hierarchy. One of the Peyote leaders is a Carlisle
graduate, a traveler, and a very independent thinker. As a
younger man he enjoyed circumventing group control; after he
and two others were expelled from the hierarchy for Peyote
activity, he became bitter, hostile, and more ardent in supporting the foreign cult. Excepting Nick of Zuni, I cannot compare
Lorenzo of Taos with any other Pueblo of my acquaintance, although no doubt there have been others, notably among leaders
of feuds big enough to cause migration which is always undertaken, by the way, as far as the record goes, by the conservative
faction.‡

* Features of this cult may have been once opposed at Taos. At any rate, the
Mirabals have been a center of feud for a long time, ever since they entertained
Miller in 1896 (see p. 1154, n.*), and probably long before. The reason for feud or
for opposition to any group may be a posteriori, among Pueblos as among
American political parties, or just as myth is to ritual.

† Among Mescalero and Lipan Apache there is some evidence that the
masked dancer cult and the Peyote cult were antagonistic. Songs of the masked
dancers should not be mentioned in the Peyote meeting nor should a masked
dancer come in there (Opler).

‡ Why is this? Possibly because conservatives feel that harmony is essential
to the efficacy of the ceremony they still believe in, and so they seek a place to
live in peace.

When peyote was first* used at Taos, there was no opposition, only after its development as a cult did the hierarchy oppose. "It was good for medicine† but not good for god."‡ However, some opposition at least was due to the shaman in the Mirabal family who practiced Keresan medicine, peyote interfered with his individual practice, *for peyote cures bewitchment.* Probably when the "Peyote boys" began to show indifference to Taos religion in general—for one thing they have infringed upon the rules of "staying still" during the ceremonial winter period—Porfirio Mirabal found it easy to organize opposition. "Peyote is not the work given to us," the chiefs began to say. "It will stop the rain. Something will happen." Peyote boys retorted that peyote brought rain. As an instance of cultural clash the future of the Peyote cult at Taos will be well worth following up.

The year the Taos controversy over peyote was at its height—a Peyote meeting was raided and shawls and blankets confiscated, and all the secular officers resigned—two Taos men happened to be traveling south. They were refused hospitality at San Juan; the War captains went from house to house ordering people not to become their hosts. And so they spent the night at a White man's ranch near by and told us the story.

* I refer to recent years. Peyote was known much earlier and *proscribed by the Spanish administration.* In 1719 a Taos Indian was tried for having drunk a beverage made from the "herb peyote" (Twitchell, II, 188). Probably peyote was thought of by the administration as a drug of black magic, for as such it appears in declarations about witchcraft made to the Provincial Inquisition in 1631–32. It gave a vision of the witch to the bewitched person (Isletan fashion!); also it gave a vision of persons in the New Spain–New Mexico caravan. A mulatto deposed that in New Spain, after he had been robbed, he took a big dose of peyote and an old woman appeared to him and told him where to find his stolen goods (Scholes 2:219–20)—a most surprising Navaho-Zuni parallel! See p. 1098.

Possibly *tenatsali*, the Zuni plant for finding lost things (see p. 414 and Stevenson 2:569, n. a) is to be identified with the unidentified Papago plant *chi·nashat*, a narcotic with in-dwelling anthropomorphic spirits, used privately as a love charm (Underhill). On one occasion (see p. 75) *tenatsali* was used in a love affair at Zuni.

† Inferably, peyote was used as medicine, as a society medicine, after 1719. I get this impression from certain general remarks dropped at Taos.

‡ The history of the cult among the Winnebago is similar. In the beginning not much religion was connected with eating peyote. Then the leaders became indifferent to the tribal religion and then hostile (Radin, 4, 9, 17).

These men were not "Peyote boys," but word had come to San Juan of the dissension at Taos, and all Taos people were considered "dangerous"; they were nonconformists, individualists, a threat to town harmony. With this unfavorable feud-making reputation it is probable that the Peyote cult will be resisted successfully in other pueblos. At Zuni, it would certainly be resisted, for peyote hallucinations would be classified with the "bad dreams" the kachina are called upon to flagellate away.

(Dreaming is considered so dangerous at Zuni, by the way, that one wonders whether dreaming was not at some early period definitely resisted as too individualistic for the highly socialized Ashiwi. Dreaming or dream shamanism belongs to the cultural core of the peoples of southern Arizona, to Pima-Papago and Yuman tribes. Contacts with these peoples might well have set up dream resistance. Indeed, considering the religious role of dreams among all neighboring tribes, and considering that dreaming as a means of getting omens was familiar to Pueblos, the fact that dream functions did not spread into the religious life or organization argues a definite resistance.)

Among Mescalero Apache the problem of introducing peyote as a cult was reconciling it with individualistically minded shamans, and this was done for a while.[7] Among Pueblos the problem is just the opposite; in order to "take," peyote would have to be socialized. This might have been done, at least at Taos, poor as it is in doctors. Peyote addicts might have organized a curing society within their kiva societies, taking over not the whole peyote complex but a part of it. Plant animism is a perfectly familiar concept, and, as noted, peyote has actually been familiar at Taos as medicine for centuries.* "Peyote boys" had but to say "we have always had Peyote, only a little different." It is believed that peyote, like other sacred things, is dangerous if not properly used. Peyote ritual lends itself well enough to Pueblo ritual.† Despite these favorable circumstances

* Did proprietary users of this medicine resent encroachment and lead the fight against the new cult?

† In the Taos cult several practices familiar to Pueblos are observed: cigarettes are offered Peyote chief, the "button" which lies near the "moon" of yel-

when the Oklahoma borrowers insisted upon introducing the whole complex, with meetings independent of the kiva-society organization, and when they betrayed indifference or antagonism to ceremonial routine, they got in bad with the hierarchy.

We may conclude from the history of peyote at Taos, as well as from the eastern spread of the Kachina cult and the western spread of clown traits, that there may be less resistance to the adoption of one or two traits of a complex than to the adoption of a complex as a whole. A few traits can be fitted into existing schemes,* but a complex requiring new organization, say Catholicism if not Peyote, runs the risk of arousing the hostility of the vested interests, unless the "interests" themselves choose to initiate the affair, as did those Zuni chiefs who went to First Mesa to buy the Snake-Antelope ceremony.

Here was a case of resistance not within the borrowing group but within the group asked to lend. No doubt this type of resistance has occurred more than once among Pueblos and has checked the spread of a ceremony altogether or as a complex. Probably something of the kind happened in connection with the spread of Shalako from Zuni to Sichomovi. The superficial aspects of that elaborate ceremony have been reproduced on First Mesa; certain matters that would have to be taught, like the night chants or the cord tally, have not been reproduced. The retreats of the various ceremonial groups and their yearlong ritual have been dropped out altogether—in fact, most of the ceremonial organization has been omitted. Badger clan has charge of masks and of some ritual, otherwise Shalako on First Mesa is little but a performance by temporary impersonations. The complex as a whole was not acquired. (Another case of partial complex provoking no opposition; the Powamu society

---

low sand, and Peyote is asked for a good living in characteristic utilitarian terms. Sage is rubbed between the hands, which are passed over the body. The ritual meal consists of four mouthfuls from each of four dishes.

* As, for example, a neat little one, when Lucinda of Isleta was learning new styles in pottery from her Laguna neighbor and they went together to get clay and the neighbor taught Lucinda how to ask the Clay Mother for her substance. One more Mother, that was not hard for corn-mothered Lucinda!

in this case was not antagonized. Besides, it may have been known at Walpi that the Badgers at Oraibi shared control of the Kachina cult with the Powamu society.)

Let me give a few instances of introduced or rumored matters which did not "take," inferably because of resistance or of indifference which is a form of passive resistance. My Zuni friend Tsatiselu, who learned the Navaho method of divining by motion-in-the-hand, failed to learn or to borrow two features: addressing the lizard (Gila monster) as patron spirit* and getting the technique as a direct personal experience.[8] Tsatiselu planned to teach his son; direct personal experience is inconsistent with Pueblo attitude. In the usual Zuni methods of divining, the little spirit couple of the plant medicine appear to the diviner as guides.† Plant medicine, the narcotic datura or Jamestown weed, is also used in Zuni-Navaho motion-in-the-hand; the spirit couple control the hand;[9] that is why, I think, in borrowing the technique of motion-in-the-hand the lizard "medicine" was not borrowed. Familiar medicine and familiar patrons were substituted.

During the winter solstice ceremonial of Zuni in 1891 a Hopi resident was observed by Stevenson to make prayer-feathers of two downy eagle feathers and two pine needles for all those present in the house, including Stevenson.[10] Here the Hopi winter solstice prayer-feather, and notably the use of pine needles, was being introduced into Zuni. But we never hear of it again; it did not take.

At this time or earlier the Hopi type of burlesque or comedy by improvised players was also introduced, probably by Hopi residents in Zuni (see pp. 646, 971, n.*). This form of comedy did not take, perhaps because the celebration into which it was introduced was doomed, the Owinahaiye or annual ceremony of the

---

* He is patron because his foot trembles when he lifts it.

† In looking for the lost or hidden Corn Maidens, the Rain chiefs first summon the spirit couple of their *tenatsali* plant; then they summon the Jamestown weed couple, who give their leaves to the little son of the Town chief to eat and thereby fall into trance (Benedict 3:I, 34–38).

War society, a lapsing group, perhaps because it conflicted with the established functioning of the Ne'wekwe clown society.

The Hopi practice of wrangling has not even been introduced, as far as I know, into Zuni, although it is probably known about and in a Zuni tale about a Hopi sojourn is even described, inaccurately: "The Hopi boys and girls taught the Itiwana (Zuni) young people for three nights how to play"; the boys tried to pull the girls out of the windows, and the girls snatched at the boys' blankets; if a girl got a blanket, the boy had to redeem it with food.* I surmise that wrangling is incompatible with the conventional behavior in public of Zuni girls.

Incompatible with the general Pueblo attitude against individual distinctions were the Plains war traits of counting coup and of bragging songs. Adopted at Taos in a way, these practices, as far as we know, did not spread. Pueblo killers or scalpers remained conventionally adverse to joining their war society; any rash Hopi braggart felt penalized by having to become a war professional (see p. 867, n.†). Nor did the Plains vision on the eve of war ever displace the Pueblo omen. The function of each was the same, but for Plainsman (and Apache) the individualized vision or dream and for Pueblo the socialized omen!

Not that the vision and power through it were unknown to Pueblos. We recall the San Juan man who learned about an Apache vision (p. 1063, n.|). In Pueblo folk tales a vision is not uncommon, or even power from vision. For example, a young hunter from Hawikuh is addressed by the Mahedinasha Antelope or Deer kachina. He is frightened and loses consciousness. Coming to, he sprinkles meal on the head of Mahedinasha, who tells him that because of this he shall always succeed in killing deer.[11] Another Ashiwi (Zuni) hunter gets power through meeting Coyote (p. 194). We may properly infer that individual power through vision was resisted as incompatible with the ceremonial organization. Along this line a plausible case might be made out for wish fulfilment through folk tale.

Consideration of Hopi attitudes toward the dead yields re-

* Benedict 3:I, 33–34. The fourth night, the night before the departure of the Zuni, was for "laughter"; they slept together, everybody was happy.

sistance data. Hopi remained indifferent to the Ghost dance cult. In 1890 four Hopi went to the Havasupai to trade. During their visit, a Havasupai chief who had been traveling to the westward reported that people there were saying that the game animals were to return to their haunts. Just how, the Hopi men did not very well understand. A Navaho visitor to First Mesa also reported that Paiute were telling the Navaho that Mountain Lion and Bear were to lead back those who had been done to death by the witch these animals had worked for. Pole-climbing to get a vision of the dead was performed by Havasupai during the above-mentioned Hopi visit. To all these rumors of the spreading Ghost dance cult little credence was given on First Mesa, comments Stephen, and no importance attached to them,[12] because, I take it, no Hopi would want to believe in the return of the dead.

Contemplation of the dead enters less into Hopi religion than into Pueblo religion in general. At Zuni the Clouds and kachina are more or less identified with the dead. By Hopi this identification is far less clear. The Hopi clan ancient or mask is in a very limited way a clan ancestor, a supernatural the clanspeople met in their original migration, not a deceased clansman; whereas most Zuni kachina started as the children lost off maternal backs in fording a river. This myth is not told, as far as I recall, by Hopi. Again, at Zuni a man's mask is buried when he is buried, for use after death. Not so among Hopi, who have no individual masks. Among Hopi one hears comparatively little of the idea that the dead return to make rain. Nor is prayer-stick-making for the dead nearly so common as at Zuni. Prayer-sticks and prayer-feathers are given the deceased Hopi, and at the winter solstice, at Oraibi as at Zuni, everybody offers prayer-sticks to the dead.* The idea of offerings to the dead is certainly familiar and might have spread in

* Stephen makes no mention of winter solstice offerings to the dead. The only Walpi offerings to the dead noted by Stephen are made at a kachina dance to the children dead (Stephen 4:487). At Oraibi, of all the winter solstice offerings, prayer-sticks for the dead are by far the largest (Dorsey and Voth 1:57 n.). Prayer-feathers and balls of cooked food for the dead are thrown in four places around the town by Marau society women (Voth 8:30).

Hopi ritual as in Zuni ritual had it not met with resistance of some kind. I surmise that the resistance was a strain of Athapascan fear of the dead. Not that Pueblos have no fear of the dead, but it is far less marked than among Navaho[13] to whom, for example, cherishing scalps in a dwelling has seemed an outrageously silly idea. Hopi have enough of the Navaho attitude to object to the ubiquitous presence of the dead in ritual and ideology. This would account for the facts we have been citing; it may also account for the disposal of scalps in the rocks, on First Mesa, the mesa which has had the closest contacts with Navaho. It may account also for not taking over any of the All Souls ritual* which has been very "taking" not only among Pueblos† but among other Catholicized Indian peoples.

There are several important features in Catholicism or Christianity which have been resisted not merely by Hopi but by all Pueblos: the conception of a high god, the Jesus story and more particularly the story of the Crucifixion with the dogma of redemption, and concepts of hell and heaven. In the Pueblo pantheon some spirits are more important than others, but they are not grouped into a pinnacle, all are departmental, so to speak, a conception not hospitable to the conception of a su-

---

* Titiev reports ritual in connection with the Wüwüchim initiation at Oraibi that appears very much like All Souls ritual. In the houses in one half of town feasts are set out for the dead, and house doors are left open. These houses are deserted by their owners, who take refuge in houses in the other half of town which is taboo to the visiting dead. This initiatory night none may venture forth excepting Horns and Agaves who patrol against "witches." A Horn would beat up an intruder; an Agave has the right to kill him. This is the culminating night of initiation, and Titiev suggests that the dead have been summoned to the ceremonial. It is probable that the idea is entertained on First Mesa also because anyone who even looks out this night will get rheumatism, a disease from the dead (and the kachina); but on First Mesa the practice of setting out food for the visitants has not been observed. (Note that Horns and Agaves are guarding against witches during an initiation just as War captains do in the East.)

† But even when All Souls is observed, there is little or no recognition of deceased relatives who rarely if ever at any time are prayed to or asked for anything. It is a dangerous or witchlike practice. In Zuni tale a Corn clansman who asked for help from the uncle killed by a Navaho died as soon as the ghost touched him (Benedict 3:I, 10). A witch might bury a prayer-stick for the deceased kinsman of somebody the witch wishes dead, asking the deceased to draw to himself his living relative.

preme being. It is significant that even when Dios is as much acculturated as he is at Acoma where he is given prayer-sticks, the offering is always accompanied by an offering to Iyatiku, the underground Mother.[14] At Zuni, Dios may have been associated with the Sun and may have strengthened Sun's position in the pantheon, but even at Zuni, where the Sun cult is more developed than elsewhere, Sun is not a supreme being. Once I thought I had found a Pueblo high god in Wẹide of Isleta; the references of my chief informant were certainly expressed in such terms, but other Isletans led me later to believe that the Chiefs of the Directions, if not the kachina, were being collectively referred to, not a single, paramount spirit. Even if Wẹide is held by some Isletans to be a single being, he is to be identified not with Dios against whom in folk tale he competes but with Giver-of-Life of Apache mythology, if not with White Hashchin (kachina).

That the story of the Crucifixion did not take at all among Pueblos* is because the concept of redemption is quite alien to them and the concept of sin is almost so. Ritualistic failure or broken taboo or quarrelsomeness which keeps away the game animals or the clouds are the nearest approaches, and in connection with such offenses there is no way to entertain the idea of personal salvation by grace of God or the idea of redeeming the world by sacrifice.

Since misbehavior to the Pueblo has social rather than individual consequences, being crime, not sin, the conception of penance did not take; neither penance† nor confession is prac-

---

* Here, as among many Spanish Indians, is a striking illustration of a ritual practice, use of the cross, being acculturated without its myth.

† An interesting instance of resistance to flagellation as penance is reported by Benavides from the "great pueblo" of the Xumanes (Jumanos), neighbors to the Piro or Tompiro. Angered by the wave of conversion, a "wizard" shouted: "You Spaniards and Christians, how crazy you are! And you live like crazy folks! You want to teach us to be crazy also!" "I asked him," continues Benavides, "wherein we were crazy? And he must have seen some procession of penance [Penitentes] during Holy Week in some pueblo of Christians, and so he said "You Christians are so crazy that you go all together, flogging yourselves like crazy people in the streets, shedding [your] blood. And thus you must wish that this pueblo be also crazy!' And with this, greatly angered and yelling,

ticed,* as far as I know, through the Church. Outside the Church there are a few instances of confession to preclude or remedy disaster and many instances of extorting confession from witches; practices Spanish enough in form but wholly Indian in motivation.† And this is true also of the rite of fasting. Fasting as a penance was certainly resisted by Pueblos (Bandelier to the contrary) not only because of the lack of ideology about sin but because of pre-existent theory of the function of fasting as a means of compelling results or getting power. (Fasting as purification may not have been resisted.)‡

The Pueblo idea of life after death as merely a continuation of this life is incompatible with dogmas of hell and heaven. In this life the Spirits do not reward or punish; why should they after death? Besides, proper or improper conduct, ritualistic conduct, has immediate consequences. The few departures from this ideology noted at Cochiti or among Hopi, punishment by detention, by carrying burdens, by transmigrating into an insect, or by cremation and plural deaths on that journey after death which is policed by Agaves, these exceptions§ may be influenced by Catholic dogma heeded long ago and thoroughly reset. The

---

he went forth from the pueblo, saying that he did not wish to be crazy" (Memorial, 21). This left the Spaniards laughing and Benavides convinced that the Demon was in flight: counterresistance.

* Dr. White writes that one of his Santa Ana acquaintances, after declaring the town was Catholic, opined that going to confession was ridiculous—"of course we don't go." (But see p. 83, n.*, for possible exception.)
It follows that church-going Pueblos do not take Communion. At San Juan, Indians group on one side of the church and Mexicans on the other side, and I recall seeing the entire Indian group withdrawing before Communion.

† Except in one case. Girls in the Hopi Butterfly dance, the Eastern type of saint's-day dance, had to name their lovers.

‡ In order to take Communion, the Catholic must be "in a state of grace," that is, having fasted and having remained continent from the preceding midnight, and having gone to confession. The early Church in Mexico held that the Indians were not capable of receiving the sacrament of communion, and this may have been the attitude of the friars in the Province. In this case we have resistance to spreading a trait rather than resistance to accepting it.

§ Another theory of provenience is that these are dim echoes of Yuman traits (see Spier 3:298–99).

widespread Pueblo notion of transmigrating into a domestic animal because of racial incest is partly, if not wholly, European.

ACCULTURATION

We have discussed the borrowing of single traits rather than complexes and the greater ease with which such traits may be fitted into the existing system. Such fitting-in was plainly what happened when parts of the Zuni Shalako were introduced into First Mesa. Clans or lineages undertook the organization of the quasi-ceremony. There is general prayer-stick-making by most of the clans, and four lineages see to the special prayer-stick ritual of the Shalako houses in one of which the principal masks are kept permanently.[15] This house and the Shalako chieftaincy belong to a lineage of one of the clans associated with the Kachina cult at Zuni, the Badger clan. It is probable that nothing ceremonial, not even a medicine society,* gets itself firmly acculturated in Hopiland unless its ritual is well established within a given lineage.

The same acculturative process of fitting a borrowed element into existing organization occurred at Isleta, but in opposite terms, when one element of clanship was borrowed, matrilineal descent, and fitted into existing ceremonial groups, the Corn groups. (Always assuming that the Corn groups and their matriliny were not of southeastern derivation.) Here a clan element was grafted on to a ceremonial group, whereas at First Mesa ceremonial was taken over by clanship.

Isleta and Taos both seem to have borrowed the office of caciqueship from Keres, adding this type of Town chieftaincy to their own moiety Town chiefs. The Isletan Cacique is plainly an afterthought in the mythology, just as Pekwin was at Zuni, but he presides over the other groups, whereas the Taos Cacique is merely co-ordinated with the moiety Town chiefs, or the same man is both Cacique and chief of the south-side kivas. The Taos Cacique is thought of as a Spanish officer; he hands the canes, i.e., instals the annual secular officers; he is in charge

---

* There is no indication that the lapsed shamanistic societies, Yayatü and Poboshwïmkya, were ever associated with clan or lineage.

of the Catholic religion. The office is hereditary in the male line; there is even a tradition that it was established in a certain family by documentary title. Inferably the office was introduced into Taos by persons, whether White or Indian, who were familiar with Keres and Spaniards,* a case of that chief-making by outsiders which occurred among many Indian tribes.

At Isleta and Taos the favored numeral is five, not four or six, as elsewhere, where four or six gain in significance through association with the cardinal directions. Taos makes this association of number and direction through beginning and ending its ritual circuit in the east, a count of five; Isleta makes the same count by starting also in the east but by adding the composite direction up, down, and middle, to the other four directions,† a curiously ingenious acculturation with Keresan and other Pueblo pattern.

Let us analyze another equally ingenious but more elaborate acculturation of single traits in the Kachina cult. Hilili, we recall, is a scalp-taking Keresan kachina, first borrowed by Hopi and then by Zuni, probably through Hopi. Hopi could or would not tell Zuni about the significance of the "stone knife" on top of the mask, so the Zuni eliminated it and substituted other significant things: a duck's head and sun, moon, and star designs. (Nor would or could Hopi explain the songs, so songs were made up of meaningless syllables with some Zuni words.)‡

---

* Hereditary chieftaincy, from father to son, caciqueship, Spanish administrators always impressed upon Indians or took for granted among them. In 1716, when Don Juan Nicolás, "cacique" of Zuni, was sent by Governor Martinez to the Hopi with a cross, some bundles of tobacco, knives, beads, sashes, and hoes, he was told in Oraibi that their principal cacique who had been in Mexico said to his son, before he died, "Take this blessed Christ [crucifix] and this silver [headed] cane, so that when the Spaniards enter they will with it give thee peace." The son had become cacique and governor of the province, Governor Martinez reports Don Juan of Zuni as reporting (Bloom, 169–70). Don Juan Nicolás was presumably the Governor of Zuni or possibly the War chief, and the "principal cacique" of Oraibi inferably caused the dissension which prompted some Oraibi to join the Tiwa at Payupki (see p. 1092, n.*).

† Compare the Huichol reconciliation of five with the cardinal directions: the four directions and the center.

‡ The words of one Zuni Hilili song are Keresan (Herzog, 324).

But Zuni knew they had a *dangerous* kachina, and they planned to make him more so by giving the leader a snake which is associated with war and with Hopi. We recall that only a year or two earlier Zuni had sent a delegation to Walpi to buy the Snake ceremony and had been refused it. The ceremony could not be fitted into the society system, but something could be done about it in the kachina catch-all system. So a stuffed snake (a live snake, people say now) was added to the recently borrowed Hopi mask. This was so frightening and so novel that it was more than some could stand. "The people were all afraid because they were carrying snakes. They were not rattlesnakes but they were real snakes and the people had no medicine to cure the bite of these other snakes."[16] The Rain chiefs were appealed to, and they in turn appealed to a visiting Hopi, who argued that since Zuni societies gave prayer-feathers to the snakes there was no reason to be afraid of them. Then word was sent to He'iwa kiva to go on with the dance.

But this was not the end of the opposition, and so stuffed snakes were substituted for live ones (if they really did have live snakes in the beginning), and later two Hopi Eagle kachina were added and the plea adduced that snakes (Hilili) are good climbers; they can climb the high mountains, and so they can get the eagles; they will bring the eagles. Now the Eagle kachina represent not only Hopi kachina, but the abundance of eagle feathers enjoyed by Hopi and craved by Zuni, so every evening after the Hilili performance the two Eagle kachina visit Corn Mountain or another mountain, put down wafer-bread for the eagles, unmask, and say to their masks: "Now, our father has told you to stay here and to call the eagles to build their nests in this place." All this sounds more Hopi than Zuni, at least it is a bit of innovation in kachina performance by Zuni. Borrowing, recombination, resistance and innovation—the Zuni Hilili-Eagle dance is stirring to the foreign theorist as well as to the practical townsman who may be pleased to think that nowadays Zuni are getting as many eagle feathers as Hopi, if not more.

Its Corn clan kachina ceremony Acoma borrowed from Zuni, but this is quite forgotten, and the ceremony is well fitted into the general origin myth by imputing its introduction to the War Brothers while they were still living with Acoma people. Returning from one of their many journeys, the Brothers reported that they had met a group of kachina belonging to the Corn clan. They carried oaken crooks, and one of them, Shuracha, a little one, always had fire with him and a miniature canteen of water. "They belong to us, then," said the Corn clan of Acoma and their "first man" went to a shaman to ask him how to summon these kachina and how to make an altar. He wanted Shuracha to bring water for the Town chief's bowl, so the people would never be out of water, and to kindle a fire in the Middle from which people could light their hearths and always be provided with fire.[17]

Now what of borrowed traits that cannot be fitted in, through ingenious myth, to existing patterns? Even in communities that feel as strong an urge to integration as do Pueblos this type of loan must occur. It has occurred in fact among Pueblos in the case of several dances borrowed from other tribes. They are considered mere pleasure dances, these Comanche and other Plains dances and even the saint's-day dance (Acoma),*without ritual or ceremonial import even if the regular ceremonial dance groups are the performers. A Zuni way of fitting in outside dances is to give them kachina masks but to put them into the class of burlesques by giving them a Ne'wekwe leader.† Then there is the case of the Mexican rooster pull which is a part of

* To be sure, this was instituted by Iyatiku and Outside or War chief and Kashale, but it is not a sacred dance, says an Acoma commentator, since men make up their own songs, and all dance who want to. The Pascua step is with two feet and the kachina step, with one foot; there is no patterning upon kachina dancing since Iyatiku had instructed that the sacred kachinas were not to be imitated in any way. Perhaps an uneasy recognition here of the actual resemblance between kachina dance and saint's-day dance! I recall that the Acoma commentator is an unusually good Catholic. He used to entertain the padre at the saint's-day dance at Sant' Ana (his later home), and I recall vividly the time after the fiesta he drove the padre and me across the Rio Grande in his buggy and knew as little then about Pueblo ways as he knew about Catholic ways when he was narrating the Emergence myth to an anthropologist.

† However, I am not sure that all such Hewahewa masked dances should not be considered merely native burlesques, although of course they include loan traits. Here as elsewhere burlesque is a form of borrowing.

the saint's-day celebration in several towns, Acoma alone attempting any ceremonial assimilation. (A Flint shaman and a Fire shaman make medicine at the house of the War chief and give the medicine to the rooster with prayer, "rooster blood is good for rain."* The same medicine is put into the white clay the prayers paint on their hands. The two men *appointed* to seize the rooster from the cross bar before the general chase begins are given each a reed cigarette and some prayer-feathers by the War chief.† From an individualistic struggle the sport has been converted into a communal ritual, or nearly so. But how did the sport come to be taken over at all, it is so alien to Pueblo life? Here, as often, you do not find the resistance you expected.)

Getting supernatural power in the way of neighboring peoples, as individual revelation or proprietorship, has been a difficult trait to take over and yet difficult also to ignore or perhaps suppress. What happened? The power was restricted to chiefs or societies, or, as in making fetishes, imparted through them, perhaps temporarily (Isleta). Or, the power was held to be anti-social witchcraft. Moreover, the power concept was itself changed; no direct transmission was made at all, but in resembling the Power, *in acting like it or being called by its name you acquired it*, like causing like. Thus Isletan War chief got power from Rattlesnake, Acoma War chief and Kashale putatively from birds, and the doctor from Bear or Badger.

Analysis of witchcraft among Pueblos yields abundant phenomena of Spanish-Indian acculturation, as well as of resistance, processes ever difficult to keep not theoretically distinct

---

* This is curiously like the chicken or turkey sacrifice still found in various tribes of Mexico, although the "sacrifices" are an expression not of historic connection but of convergence. Among the Chorti of eastern Guatemala the rooster pull of San Juan's day is associated conceptually with the beheading of the saint (Wisdom).

† White 1:106. At Santo Domingo, too, the rooster pull is in charge of the War captain who at the close of the day makes a long address to the horsemen. *Principales* sit together and all day are given smoke by the Fiscales (White 4: 155-58, including comparative note). The rooster pull occurs also among Papago (Underhill).

but factually separate. That the shaman can kill as well as cure is widespread Indian belief, part of the general attitude toward Spirits and toward "medicines"; shaman, Spirit, or medicine has power, for ill as for good. To this characteristic attitude was added among Pueblos, I believe, the European belief about the ill-disposed neighbor, that any malevolent person might be a witch. In other words, the power to do harm magically became generalized; anyone might become possessed of it. This European conception that anyone may be a witch is current today among Pueblos, although the earlier attitude of restricting black magic to persons with "power" often expresses itself today in directing suspicion particularly against the ceremonialist. Witches in European belief are organized as a society. Belief in the witch society is current among Pueblos, and I incline to think that it has been borrowed, fitting very readily into the societal pattern. An individualist may be accounted a witch; but even a witch must be regularized by being put into a society. The hypothetical witch society is organized like a curing society, with supernatural patron and myth, with chief and assistants, with initiation. The idea of sacrificing a member of your family to the witches is both European and Pueblo. The European concept of a witch transforming into an animal is held by Pueblos. It is close to the Indian concept of curers getting power from animals through wearing their claws or paws, through the practice of impersonating animals. The Bear doctor becomes a bear; the witch puts on the pelt of a wolf and becomes a wolf. In Pueblo folk tale, as very commonly in Northwest Coast tales, the animals take off their pelts and become human.

One of the most characteristic European ideas about bewitching is found among Mexicans in the Southwest, bewitching through food, but it is not current among Pueblos, and here I think is a case of resistance. The prevailing Indian mode of bewitching is through sending noxious objects directly into the body.* This satisfying concept precluded interest in the related

---

* Pueblo technique or supposititious technique for doing this is not known. Compare the Navaho way of shooting the victim with something. In their cave, witches make a ground picture of the victim in colored *ashes* at which the witch

idea of bewitching food. The cure of sucking out the witch-sent object could not be applied easily to bewitchment through food. The purificatory rite of emesis might have been so applied, however, had the idea of bewitching food been entertained. Possibly the practice of hospitality, of offering food to strangers, worked against that idea.

Bewitching through evil eye, *mal ojo*, is familiar to eastern Pueblos, but as it is still associated with Mexicans,* i.e., it is not practiced by Indians, it cannot be said to have been taken over.

Another European mode of bewitchment *has* been taken over, using an image of the victim to stick noxious things into. This is obviously quite close to the mode of sending noxious things directly into the body. Father Dumarest's account of the early use of the witch image or doll shows just how the European practice may have come in, if you exchange the roles of Mexican and Indian as assigned by tradition. "A century ago there lived at Cochiti a Franciscan who had as herders an Indian and a Mexican. One day he punished these boys for some mischief. After some time the Indian boy made a coarse image of the priest with earth and his urine, saying to the Mexican, 'You will see how sick the priest will be when we come in this evening.' He then stuck cactus needles into the ears and stomach of the image. On returning from the fields, the Mexican was greatly surprised to see the missionary in agony. The little Indian drew the thorns out of the image, which he kept hidden in his *serape*, and relief followed. The Mexican thought he should disclose the thing to his master, so the next day he said to his companion, 'Go ahead of me and I will overtake you; I must go to the field and look for something I forgot.' He took the image, which was hidden in a cave, and gave it to the priest. The priest called the

---

chief with a small bow shoots a turquoise. Where the stone strikes, the person is affected (Valkenburgh, 52). Compare p. 225. Apache blow something into the body.

* Goldfrank 3:100; Parsons 58:14. To be sure, at Zuni something much like the evil eye was once reported. Whenever any witch suspect came into a house where there was an infant, its face was covered (Stevenson 2:392).

Indian, showed him the image, and said, 'Show me what you did to make me sick.' "* A like practice still occurs at Laguna. The spittle or hair of the victim may be rolled up in rags into which cactus thorns are stuck, producing pains, for example, tuberculosis, in the victim.

Now let us note a related practice at Nambé. Here a witch might make a doll to represent the victim and fill its stomach with noxious things such as chili seeds or a bit of cloth from the dress of the victim.[18] This idea, that a person or spirit is sick or evil because his heart (or stomach) is filled with material evil, is, I take it, an Indian idea. The heart of a witch at Cochiti is described as full of thorns.[19] We recall that Arrowpoint Boy, the Corn Mothers, even the Sun, all have had their heart cleansed or replaced.[20]

Evidently if the heart can be replaced, it might be stolen. In Keresan opinion it *is* stolen, to produce illness. It is stolen and, as a kernel of corn, placed in the witch doll which has to be retrieved from the witches by the doctors and returned to the patient.[21]

The witch doll has been invested with the life of the victim. It fights with the pursuing shaman; it talks. The War captain shoots it. This fetishistic concept of a vivified image appears to be both Spanish and Indian† and in view of the early Spanish trials and executions of witches in New Mexico the concept of killing the witch may also be Spanish, although the concept was at hand in the practice of killing unsuccessful doctors among Pima-Papago and Yuman peoples.‡ At Zuni and in Hopi towns,

* Dumarest, 165; from a Mexican woman of Santa Cruz, one hundred years old, the same story has just been recorded (Espinosa, J. M., 172), and the narrative concluded: "If you wear the medal of San Benito, witches can do nothing to you."

† Compare the Papago scalp doll that works for the family, the Plains medicine doll, the kachina doll, the saint's image or the doll for *el Niño*.

‡ But among them all the killing was done by relatives. Also, it is doubtful that any Zuni chief or society doctor however much suspected of witchcraft would ever have been killed by the War or Bow chiefs. Bow chief offerings of miniature bow, arrow, and club suggest some such ritual execution as practiced by the Navaho witch. See p. 305.

all towns farthest removed from the Spanish witchcraft complex,* the witch doll is not found. My guess is that the witch-doll agent shot by the War captain is derived from the witch-doll victim "shot" by the witch. Indian ideas about the thorn-filled heart combine with Spanish ideas about sending thorns into the heart or body; the doll victim becomes the doll witch.†

Besides the ritual loans already discussed, there are many scattering illustrations of acculturation with Catholicism. Take the various ways in which All Souls is observed. Throughout Spanish Mexico All Saints' Day and All Souls' Day are both observed as days of the dead; first return the children dead, then the adult dead, food and candles being set out for them in the house or carried to the graveyard. Pueblos make the food offering, but in their own way, burying it or casting it into the river. Candles are used, but also prayer-feathers, and prayer-sticks may be made by shamans who assemble as for an indigenous ceremony (Cochiti). Rites or practices usually associated with the dead in native ceremonial may be observed, using the left hand, not looking backward, and most of all, exorcism by closing the trail with four marks, by spitting, or by motioning with ashes. Also association of the dead with the game of hidden-ball, a winter night game, played on All Souls, is pre-Spanish. (Zuni players made offerings to the dead and seek omens from them; and, if one is touched by a ghost, success is assured.) Except at Taos, where people appear to be less apprehensive about the dead than elsewhere, visiting the graves on All Souls is not customary; that Catholic practice did not take; perhaps it was considered too dangerous. More Pueblo elements characterize All Souls at Nambé than elsewhere in the East, and yet the ceremonial life is so disintegrated in this Mexicanized town that its kiva is not kept in repair or even closed against strangers.

---

* Also the towns farthest from Plains influence. See p. 318, n. †, for Plains medicine doll.

† In the Sia tale, "The Medicine Men Cure an Evil Spirit," the disease-maker caught at the communal ceremony is not a witch but the red Horned Water Serpent. After he is shot, the shamans cut out his heart, clean it of cactus spines, and replace it. Water Serpent comes to life, and, as he departs by river, he assures the people that he is not going to be bad any more.

But there is no church at Nambé, and so the Catholic celebration is completely in the hands of the townspeople. (Here is an instance of a general principle in acculturation: If the model-setting group withdraws or even partially withdraws, there is a much greater degree of acculturation, a more thorough binding-together of old elements and new, than if the group continues to direct or dominate.* The foreign origin is more easily forgotten, a point for later discussion.)

The provenience of the cross has been discussed (p. 1073). It is hardly questionable that it "took" so thoroughly because it was identified with the Chiefs of the Directions, with the Sky, or with the Stars. Oñate writes (1598) of the "province of Zuni": "In all these pueblos we found crosses which the Indians reverence and to which they are accustomed to make the same offerings as to their idols, which consist of flour, small sticks painted with different colors, and turkey feathers"[22]—prayer-meal and prayer-sticks! Fifteen years earlier, Fray Bernardino had erected a cross next the "devil's prayer-house" at Hawikuh,[23] giving the same kind of push to the acculturation of the cross that was given everywhere by the friars throughout Spanish America.[24]

Why is the cross prayer-stick, the "Laguna prayer-stick," associated at Walpi with sheep? And why is the Star fetish of the Walpi War chief the fetish of all the domestic animals? One conceptual tissue at least we can appreciate, the one that was woven around the cross as a star sign and so a war sign. From the Spaniards came the domestic animals, also a great insistence on using the cross design. When people have no common language and attempt to convey more or less abstract concepts, signs for them may get curiously interpreted. And so, we may

---

* The Pecos cult of Porcingula at Jemez together with the Bull come to mind. At the time of the immigration from Pecos the Church was not represented at Jemez, the cult got firmly established in Indian hands, and later the Church had to join in honoring an unknown saint and an animal "idol." The cult of the Saint at Zuni, where Catholic control was much interrupted, is a still better illustration. The *santu* who is a *shiwanni*, a Rain chief, "sits down in her sacred place," and the Fiscales who look after her are organized like a Rain chief taincy (Parsons 12:259 ff.; Parsons 6:171).

suppose, the War chief who represents warrior stars became the spiritual keeper of domestic animals when they were to be acculturated into the general religious scheme.

What "idols," by the way, did Oñate see? Stone or wooden images of the War gods (or were wooden images made only after the saint's wooden image became known?), or stone images of the animals such as were found in the Village of the Great Kivas? In Catholic as in Pueblo lore, it is quite possible for stone once to have been alive, but turning people into stone *in punishment*, like the adulterous Mexican queen and the son of the Isletan cacique or like the Isletan war captain who was incontinent before his antelope hunt,[25] seems to be a Spanish notion[26] that was resisted by Pueblos, except in one case, the War Brothers turn inhospitable folk into stone.

Naming ritual such as presenting the infant to the Sun (Papago, Aztec) was aboriginal, but in what degree head-washing at naming, the baptismal rite, was aboriginal, and in what degree Spanish, we can but guess.* At any rate, Spanish baptism was readily accepted and as part of it the godparent complex, which also had aboriginal antecedents. As a rule, Indian and Mexican godparents are kept separate, but at Cochiti the Sun godparents are the same persons as the Church godparents. Many of the Church practices in regard to godparents are paralleled by Pueblo godparents: preclusion of marriage; different sets of godparents for different occasions—birth name, confirmation (initiation or whipping of children), and sickness (*padrinos de vela*, godparents of the candle);† present-giving or other close relations between godparents and their children on

---

* Ritual headwash in Zuni is *awatenakya;* Catholic baptism is *tutatsi wukoshokya,* priest wash (*wokoshona,* the ordinary word for wash).
[When the Koyemshi are head-washed by their "aunts," the term in use is *chakoshoi* (*chale,* child, *wokoshona,* wash.)]

† For this early Catholic practice see Parsons 62:69. The candle godparent takes the goldchild to the altar, lights a candle, and hangs ribbon and medal around his neck. Compare the Pueblo godfather who has his godchild look upon the altar or visit a shrine and who makes him prayer-feathers or sticks; and compare the ritual of Pima godparents for a child sick with dysentery (Russell, 266–67).

ceremonial occasions;* broadening the circle of persons to depend on in the emergencies or crises of life.†

The political circles established for Pueblos developed features
of acculturation as well as of resistance. If Santo Domingo presents a picture of the form of self-government as it was planned
for the Indians after 1621 or before, the other pueblos appear to
have resisted this scheme at various points. Santo Domingo is
districted into five parts according to the cardinal directions, the
fifth part being the middle. Little War captains are appointed
from these sections, two from each. The little War captains,
two by two, herd the horses, and weekly, turn by turn, the sections contribute men and boys to help their herder representatives. The sections have no other functions.[27] As the same system is found in parts of Mexico,‡ it seems plain that the town
sectioning of Santo Domingo was a Spanish plan, more or less
associated with the ward or *barrio* scheme. In Mexico the *barrio*
became in many places a unit of religious organization, each
barrio having its own chapel; in Santo Domingo and in other
towns grouping by *barrio* remained limited to the matter of
herding; it did not spread at all.

Three classes of officers are provided for in Santo Domingo—
the Governor and his staff, judicial officers or alcaldes (War
captains) and their constabulary, and church officers. Service in
one group precludes in the lower ranks service in the others. A
year of service is expected of every adult male from time to time,
with progress upward from rank to rank. Former Governors and

---

* Marriage godparents are not paralleled; there is no place for them in
Pueblo marriage custom, Hopi custom excepted, and here kinship controls.

† In the Zuni whipping of the children, Kyäklo kachina says the ceremony is
held "in order that people may have someone whom they call their second father
(or mother)" (Bunzel 4:691).

‡ Parsons 62:158 ff. The errand men or executives are called *topiles* (Aztec).
They have short sticks of office, as have the little War captains of Santo Domingo. At Mitla, Oaxaca, the church *topiles* herd the Saint's bulls. In building
the square bull fence, men work on the side they live.
    Among Tarahumara the term *topile* is applied to the keeper of the canes; the
errand men are called *capitanes*, as among Pueblos (Bennett and Zingg, 202,
206 ff.).

alcaldes form a group of elderly respected citizens referred to as *principales*. (All this is typically early Spanish, in Mexico).*
Now at Zuni there are no *principales;* the idea of annual office was familiar, but not well established;† the tenure of the secular, Spanish officers followed the principle of tenure during good behavior, the prevailing principle for chieftaincies, combined with a principle common in filling minor ceremonial offices or impersonations, rotation in office by several sets of incumbents. There are different sets of secular officers at Zuni just as there are different sets of clown or kachina impersonators: Koyemshi, Long Horn, or Shalako impersonators.

"Alcalde" is a term never heard among Pueblos, although it was used regularly in Spanish administration. The Spanish official in charge of several pueblos was called "Alcalde mayor," and there was an alcalde at each pueblo, but whether he was always a White man is not quite clear. At any rate, the judicial and punitive functions of alcalde probably clashed from the beginning with the functions of the Pueblo War chief. The War chief was identified with the alcalde but never so called;‡ he remained a lifelong chief—for a time; and the constabulary officers became subordinate to the War chief as war captains. Hints of the original idea of the alcalde may be seen today in the Sipaloa *shiwanni*, Mexican chief, of Zuni, who is co-ordinated with the Governor and his staff, in the "lieutenant-governor" of Taos who is the punitive officer, and in the War chief of the Cane of Isleta who heads the annual War captains, and is called Cane War chief in distinction to the War chief of the Pouch or "War chief from the beginning," permanent War chief. Isleta, Taos, Jemez, Zuni, and Hopi preserve their War chief or chiefs, but elsewhere the lifelong ceremonial war chieftaincy has lapsed.

* In Santa Fé the *cabildo* (*ayuntamiento*) consisted of Governor, four *regidores* (councilmen), and two *alcaldes* (Scholes 1:94).

† Compare Tarahumara, where the Governor and with him *all* the officials hold office indefinitely, as long as the people back him or he is willing (Bennett and Zingg, 205). Papago Governors also came to hold office for life (Underhill 3). The office even went down from father to son.

‡ Alcalde (Alcante, Alcaide) and *capitán* are interchangeable terms among Tarahumara (Bennett and Zingg, 202).

As it lapsed,* the secular annual constabulary, the *maestres de campo* or Outside chiefs, took up its ceremonial functions, representing the War gods and in a measure, particularly at Acoma, conducting their cult. The annual war captains of Acoma are so markedly ceremonial officers rather than secular officers that we have referred to them as War chiefs.

Spanish canes of office were readily adopted, assimilated to ritual sticks of one kind or another—Zuni Rain chief's staff, Keresan War chief's crook, or Hopi bar of society or kachina office. The Spanish *vara* or the Lincoln cane is aspersed by *cura* or by Town chief, and is passed on and breathed from† in just the same way as are fetishes or other society insignia, one more thing with power to bring good life. The cane of the Cane War chief of Isleta is called Black Cane Old Man. The cane of the Cacique of Isleta del Sur, a stick of black wood, the length of the forearm, with a silver head and a cross inlaid,[28] was called "our mother."

One of the important tasks of officers of the cane is superintending irrigation. Irrigation by ditch was not unknown to Pueblos before the Conquest, being practiced at Hawikuh and Acoma and probably elsewhere, but contemporary methods are of Spanish introduction, and so work on the ditch—cleaning and repair—is naturally in charge of the secular officers, or, at Santo Domingo, on the last day, in charge of the Mexican kachina; but when it comes to opening the ditch, prayer-sticks or feathers are deposited or made by Town chief or shamans, since Water

* Stevenson and Dumarest report two War chiefs (priests) at Sia and Cochiti, the chiefs of the Opi or Scalpers society. Thirty years later White and Goldfrank find only the annual War captains.

† That is, kissed, just as canes and candles and official hands are kissed everywhere in conservative Mexican Indian circles. The hand kiss "took" among the Pueblos (see p. 1074), but not the foot kiss, although that, too, was introduced. "And to give that people [of Hawikuh] to understand the veneration due to the priests, all the times that they arrived where these were [1629], the Governor and soldiers kissed their feet, falling upon their knees, cautioning the Indians that they should do the same, as they did; for as much as this the example of superiors can do" (Hodge 3:81). Foot-kissing was also practiced at Santa Clara (1629) (Benavides, 49, 50).

Of course, foot-kissing may have continued and lapsed only after it lapsed for Whites, but I doubt if it ever "took" at all.

People or Horned Water Serpent control the water's flow, just as they control the water of the Rio Grande.

Comparable with carrying over ritual from river to irrigation ditch is carrying over ritual from wild life or aboriginal crops to introduced or domesticated fauna or flora; for example, from deer to sheep, or from corn to wheat, like a Tewa singing of Wheat Maidens in the same breath he sings of Corn Maidens (see p. 412). To instances of this simplest of all kinds of acculturation given elsewhere[29] we may add: leaving turquoise or shell and prayer-stick next a steel trap just as these offerings were left near a deadfall (Mishongnovi),[30] the use of metal-tipped arrows in ritual,[31] the use of bells instead of bone rattles, or embroidering dance kilts or blankets with wool. The association of all the domestic animals with the Stars (Tewa) must have been, as suggested, more complicated, as was also the use of horsehair dyed red as a "beard," as rays, for the Sun, or in very early style as string skirts for fetishes or kachina impersonators.[32]

INNOVATION OR INVENTION

Even in our society, in matters that cannot be patented or written up, innovation often goes unrecorded and anonymous; in an unlettered people it is as hard to "catch" the birth of innovation through an individual as to note exactly the moment a leaf falls from its twig. And yet individuals, even standardized Pueblos, undoubtedly do innovate in all sorts of ways. Nampeyo, the wife of a Hano workman employed in excavating Sikyatki, studied the sherds and in the course of years produced designs inspired by the old pottery and yet distinctive, and this famous potter has been copied by all her neighbors. After Julián Martinez and his wife María Montoya of San Ildefonso were exposed to pottery and to enthusiasts in the Museum of New Mexico at Santa Fé (Julián was janitor), they began to invent new pottery styles.* I have just heard of the death of

* From such instances Dr. Bunzel concludes that sudden changes in decorative style are the result of general cultural instability working upon the mind of a sensitive individual: an analysis that may well hold for changes in other cultural particulars.

Lusteti of Zuni, married for twenty years to Margaret Lewis from Oklahoma. Although he remarried ten years ago, before he died he asked to be buried with their four deceased children in Margaret's field, "the first Zuni not to be buried in the church-yard." (Margaret's historical knowledge is as poor as any Pueblo's.) This was the last but not the first time Lusteti, the song-maker, innovated. Once in Gallup he heard an organ-grinder play "Marching through Georgia," and forthwith he set the melody to Zuni rhythm, quite appropriately for Comanche dancers. In old Lina Zuni's account of the indiscreet little Zuni boy about to be killed by the kachina, his grandfather gave tongue to bitter irony, and the boy's father raised his gun to his shoulder—unheard of rebellion that may have started something (by ending something), just as something was started at a later date by Nick's rebellion against being strung up as a witch. In the sand-painting of the Walpi Snake society a mountain lion is figured, a single lion; but until about 1850 there were two lions in the design. (Just as in the escutcheon of the State of Jalisco, and I would not be surprised if the Snake society got its original design off a banner from Guadalajara.)* It was Nachiwa, the great-uncle of Kopeli, the Snake chief Stephen knew, who changed the design from two lions to one.[33] Perhaps it was Nachiwa again who changed the race marks of Middle kiva (the Snake clan kiva) from a white band across the body and over the right shoulder to blue-green pigment over the entire body.[34] Ordinarily in making sand-paintings the sand is poured from the fingers without preliminary outlines, but in 1901 the Mishong-novi Antelopes worked with outlines.[35] The changes in altar-painting must have been done deliberately—you could not over-look a lion or start to make an outline from carelessness—but minor altar arrangements are often varied from mere inaccuracy, Voth observes, especially when the chief or even an assistant is

* Various objects from White culture have been seen on Hopi altars, and a picture of a Sia altar (in the Bureau of American Ethnology) shows two Chinese porcelain dogs in company with images of Mountain Lion and the other Beast Gods (White).

a new man or even when material gives out.* When I first heard of ceremonial friendship at Zuni, I was told that Dick, that garrulous, vain, and atypical friend of many Americans, had invented the custom, and Dick himself supported the claim. But the Zuni term *kihe'* is like the Maricopa term (*kiye'*) for this relationship which before Dick's day was known to Cushing and which is a familiar Plains (also Kaiowa-Apache) war trait. It seems probable that ceremonial friendship was a war trait at Zuni, as elsewhere, that it was lapsing, and that Dick, if not long ago another Zuni, had the bright idea of reviving it in kachina guise.

It appears that elements, "inspiration," may be gotten from various sources and be developed into a fresh complex, which is what happened, I think, with the kachina cult as a whole, say at Zuni. Where individual leadership or invention occurs, it is easy to picture a new development; but where there is little opportunity for invention by the individual, as in Pueblo ceremonialism, and historical data are lacking, imaginative reconstruction is difficult and perhaps, as Dr. White holds, as unauthentic as any folk tale. I am not going to attempt reconstruction beyond suggesting that the kiva groups were originally war groups, devoted not only to fighting but to war dances; that upon their initiation of the youth as warrior† was based kachina initiation, a singularly brutal performance by people tender-hearted for children; that sex restrictions imposed upon kachina impersonators derived in part‡ from sex taboo in war,§ and secretive-

---

* When Wishkwaya, the male chief of the Oraibi Marau society, changed the colors of the cloud designs in repainting the images, he said it was because the proper pigments gave out. However, Wishkwaya did not seem to feel quite easy about this innovation and, adds Voth, "did not seem to like it that I had noticed it" (Voth 8:45).

† Compare the flagellation of War chiefs of Acoma.

‡ Continence is required, by the way, in contemporary Mayan rain cults; it is probably a far-flung ritual trait in America.

§ Continence on the eve of war or on returning from war is to preclude weakness in the warrior or danger from the scalp, the enemy dead. Continence before dancing kachina or after offering prayer-sticks cannot be interpreted in these ways. It is difficult to interpret at all. Possibly it is merely a transferred rite with the meaning lost. (Zuni *teshkwi*—continence and fasting—certainly sugness about kachina derived in part from the secretiveness of the warrior, a widespread characteristic; that the ideology of the kachina was basically that of the Chiefs of the Directions or Cloud spirits with a flavor of Catholic hagiology; and that kachina dancing grew out of saint's-day dance, war dance for the dead, and hunt or animal dance. Impersonation of the Spirits with dramatization was a very old practice which lent itself to impersonation through the mask; the god or priest-chief mask was also an old trait, but the dance mask or general mask usage may have been encouraged or developed comparatively late through head- and face-painting at death for chiefs or animals (recall the masklike eyes put into a deer skull, and the Hopi-Zuni cotton death mask), through animal or other head-dresses, or through the pelt coverings* of curing, hunt, or war†groups, including war scout or clown police groups.

War or hunt‡ burlesque in which the sexes exchanged roles or particularly men impersonated women, and in which the enemy or any foreigner as potential enemy was ridiculed, was probably the basis of clowning and burlesque in connection with kachina dances. Clowns burlesqued war dancers. The old woman's obscenity toward the scalp may have been a source of clown

gests the Catholic "state of grace," as does specifically "dancing before break-fast" by certain Zuni kachina or by First Mesa Wüwüchimtü.) The rule that menstruating women should stay away from kachina dances (Zuni) or from church (Isleta) may be similar transferences.

* Note how the Zuni Bear kachina may come out either in mask or wearing pelt and head (Bunzel 5:1031, 1055). On First Mesa, Buffalo may be danced with or without mask.

† Note the making of a stone mask, a helmet, by the Zuni War Brothers in conflict with the cliff ogre (Parsons 29:7). Note the way the Hopi god Masauwü uses his mask to scare off persons who might catch him or to terrify raiders; and note the black paint across the nose of the kachina impersonator, a warlike mark (compare the blackened chin or face of warlike personages, Zuni, Hopi). Possibly both facial painting and mask may have served to frighten the enemy or conceal identity, providing these were not merely bor-rowed traits. Note the use of turquoise (stone) in war (p. 300) and turquoise (color) in masks.

‡ A Tewa hunter who missed his rabbit changed garments with the girl who got it (Bandelier).

obscenity and one reason why the clowns have some female aspect, in dress or headdress.

I incline to think that the Koyemshi clown group got its mask from Mexico, where clown-devil masks were introduced by Spaniards, assimilating easily with the burlesque mask of Aztecs. The Koyemshi origin myth, a Zuni variant of Adam and Eve, supports the theory of Spanish-Mexican provenience of the Koyemshi mask.* A Koyemshi organization may have ante-dated the introduction of the Koyemshi mask, possibly a war scout group corresponding to the Red Eyes of Taos or the Quirana† of Keres. The special sex taboo imposed on Koyemshi point to a sometime war character, which among the Gomaiowish of Acoma is still conspicuous.

Whatever the history of the mask and, in particular, the police or bogey mask, and whatever the history of the bogey independently of mask,‡ the use of bogey as a guard for peach orchards (Zuni, Santo Domingo) or a police for bridge-building (Santo Domingo) is an invention, the application of an old ele-ment to a novel situation, the Spaniards having introduced peach trees and bridges. A similar invention is the inclusion of peach models or models of silver or gold coins or of the domestic ani-mals among the prayer-images of winter solstice ceremonial.

Innovations are constantly occurring in the kachina cult, which is very hospitable to novelties: new impersonations, new dances, new songs, new details of costume§ or array. Typical is

* In Zuni tradition, kachina masks were invented by Father Koyemshi, who also proposed having the Kachina society (Stevenson 2:34, 47). The other clown society, the Ne'wekwe, not only have charge of burlesque masks but they are represented by Ne'wekwe kachina to whom they lend their sticks of office (Bunzel 5:1080–82).

† Note resemblance of Cochiti Quirana mask to Koyemshi mask (Dumarest, Pl. VI, Fig. 4). Note, too, that the groups from which Koyemshi are recruited are warlike groups.

‡ The predatory, cannibalistic, cave-dwelling giant appears to be an old, old concept. His blood is used for ritual pigment at Taos, and his footprints were left in the rocks.

§ Just as women now wear a cotton dress with long sleeves under their native sleeveless dress, so do female impersonations. Long Horn and other Zuni impersonators have substituted a cotton shirt for a buckskin shirt. Shula-witsi, who formerly wore nothing, now wears a breechcloth (Bunzel 5:857, n.17).

the introduction into Zuni of the Keresan-Hopi Hilili-Eagle dance we have already discussed. A word more about the arrangement for singers made at that time. Among Keres it is customary for a choir to sing for dancers who do not sing for themselves. At Zuni it is customary for society people to sing indoors at night for single kachina, but they do not sing by day outdoors. Now what was to be done for these new Hilili kachina who did not sing? "The Kachina [society] chief did not want people without masks to come out to sing for the kachinas." So the older and heavier men of the kiva, who did not dance, were given small face masks and arrayed like society men with breechcloth, red hair plume,[36] gourd rattle, and eagle-wing feathers. Thus the new "singers" looked like kachina and behaved like society men, and no custom was breached. This was invention by combining old elements, invention forced, so to speak, by borrowing something which could not be used under old conditions and had to be accommodated, a familiar type of invention.

A similar process becomes apparent on First Mesa when Shalako is borrowed from Zuni, the most interesting case of inter-Pueblo borrowing on record. Proffered houses of entertainment are lacking, since this is part of the ceremony's yearlong character which is completely ignored, so the maternal houses of four clans become the customary houses of entertainment. There being no societies to furnish altars and choirs, Koyemsi are called upon to sing, and the houses themselves provide quasi-altars, by setting out masks, and, in the case of the Water-Corn clan house, making a meal altar (cloud and rain design) on which to place the masks,[37] the inventive clanspeople using old resources to meet a new situation.

Here is suggested one way Western ceremonialism may have grown ever more complicated or involuted, given rivalry of clans or societies. What is introduced by one clan or society or kiva other clans or societies or kivas are moved to match or equal. Traditions are elaborated, for a narrator will emphasize or magnify the part taken by his group in the general mythology. Here is involution through a kind of competition. Actually in mythology competition or trial, generally in rain-making, is described. Thus the Black Corn clan of Zuni or the Water-Corn clan of Hopi had to show what they could do before they were admitted into town. In a like competition the Wood society of Zuni made it snow in summer.

Involution occurs also through a splitting-off or budding of organization, as when Zuni Bedbug society split from Little Firebrand society, or Eagle People and Goose People from the Corn People of Isleta. In the Kachina cult involution by budding is lively. A kachina's personality is made up through the form and decoration of the mask, the mask feathers and other ornaments, body paint, details of costume, objects carried, posture, gait, behavior, and his call.[38] A change in these particulars creates a new kachina. You give Good Kachina a varicolored mouth band and three feather strings down the beard, and you get Upikyaiupona. Instead of making a change in the ancient kachina and continuing to call him by the same name, the variation is creative of a new kachina with a new name. Again a new kachina may be called for to meet a new need, as when people wanted a Buffalo kachina. All they had to do was to ask Pa'utiwa, the Kachina chief, to send them a Buffalo kachina. Buffalo was novel but as a kachina he was comfortably familiar, like a newly canonized saint from another nation. Through involution, variety or change is accomplished without a sense of change. It is change "within the constitution," not revolution, not mutation. Change by involution characterizes all the ritual arts of the Pueblo; it characterizes Pueblo ceremonialism as a whole.

In connection with changes in the get-up of kachina it has been pointed out that they occur more readily among recently introduced or borrowed kachina. As Bunzel says, variability increases in inverse ratio to the antiquity and sanctity of the impersonation.[39] The same principle applies, I surmise, to the Kachina cult as a whole in comparison with the society rain or curing cults, the older and more conservative cults. Besides, the society cults deal with smaller groups. The efflorescence of the

Kachina cult may be due in part to the inclusiveness of kachina dance groups.*

Wrangling, scrambling, or chasing for what kachina or clowns or runners are carrying appears to me to be a Hopi invention derived from the throw-away and give-away practices of clowns or kachina, especially the practice of taking corn ears or spruce from the kachina. Wrangling has a localized distribution, having spread only to Jemez with the "Hopi dance." Wrangling is a sort of secularization for the benefit of women and children. Distribution of "dolls," bows and arrows, and moccasins to the children by the kachina may have been a similar type of innovation.

Secularization, which is a form of innovation, in itself leads to innovation. Designs in ritualistic pottery such as drum or meal bowl probably change less than aesthetic designs. As Bunzel points out,[40] the religious design is a satisfactory technique for controlling the Spirits and so remains unchanged, whereas design for its own sake leads to individual expressions. I surmise that kick-ball or kick-stick racing was originally in Pueblo circles entirely ceremonial; races were run by kiva groups and, as today in Hopi theory, were barely competitive; there was no betting. When betting came in† and the ceremonial character of racing was changed or lessened, Zuni retained a race by kiva without betting, a purely ceremonial race and then introduced the ceremonial race by clan which spread to First Mesa and to Laguna.[41]

The Spanish decree of 1621 about Indian self-government resulted in so many changes among Pueblos, as among other Indian peoples, as to amount to the introduction of a new cultural complex. Not that representative government was set up —far from it—but a new agency was created as go-between for Indians and Whites, and as support for customs both Indian and White. Governor and staff became mouthpiece and executive

* Complementarily, lack of variability in Zuni pottery designs may be due to the small number of potters, Bunzel suggests.

† How did betting come in? Through Piman and Yuman (Maricopa) tribes? See pp. 823, 990, 999.

for the Chief of the Houses, the Town chief; and War captain and staff functioned similarly for the War chief. Upon these "representatives" the Fiscales were modeled, representing the *curas*. In accordance with the decree, all these representatives have remained annual officers, except at Zuni, where the term has been, as we would say, for good behavior, i.e., for an indefinite number of years, and where recently, before the pressure of the Indian Bureau for *annual elections*, the idea was expressed that the term was for life. The characteristic Pueblo idea of office is that it is lifelong, and this Zuni attitude toward their Spanish-instituted officers has been obviously one of resistance to short-term office. As Pueblo office is ever ceremonial, the royal idea of divorcing Church and State was also resisted. And so the officers were appointed by the hierarchy, and took on ritual functions such as prayer-stick-making and policing against witches and against intruders upon the ceremonial life.

As the new functionaries were used by Pueblo ceremonialists to protect their ways, so they were used by the *cura* to protect *his* ways. In some pueblos the Fiscales or church officers proper look after burials, formerly they enforced church attendance. The Governor enforces the marriage rules of the Church, punishing adultery or mating without authorization by the Church, and the Governor and War captains were given charge of All Souls' Day, of the saint's-day dances and the dances of Christmas, Eastertide, and Kings' Day.

Whether or not the decree of 1621 ever went into effect during the half-century of missionary occupation among Hopi is not known; at any rate, there were no lasting effects, unless the Second Mesa idea of rotation in office dates back to that period by way of Awatobi and Mishongnovi. More probably the idea was suggested by recent Zuni contacts. At any rate, a certain degree of inventiveness was called for at Shumopovi because of paucity of eligible men.* In 1920 there were but three adult

---

* Several chiefs were killed by a Spanish punitive expedition (? Martinez) twenty years after the friar was hanged and burned at the Shumopovi Mission (? 1680), according to Second Mesa tradition (Nequatewa, 46 ff.). Then the people moved up the mesa, and the principle of rotation in chiefly office was initiated.

males in the Kachina-Parrot clan to whom four major chieftaincies belonged: winter solstice, Powamu, Singers, and Agave. The way out was to have the Agave chieftaincy refilled every four years from the society membership and to have the Singers chieftaincy rotate between the Kachina-Parrot men every four years.[42]

An invention also mothered by necessity is to be seen in hairfeather ritual. Unless initiation is postponed until after school years and after the hair that has been so ruthlessly cut in school has grown long again, how fasten the hair feather indispensable at initiation or at any society assemblage? Dorsey describes such a situation at the Snake assemblage at Mishongnovi where it was suggested that the closely cropped boy of eight tie the string through the hole in his ear lobe (as is done sometimes on kachina masks), and then, when it was seen that the boy's ears had not been pierced, that the feather be tied around his neck.[43] Little inventions of this kind must have been frequent in contact with White people, little necessary acts of adjustment.

DISINTEGRATION

Borrowed elements not well integrated into the ceremonial life readily lapse, in a kind of abortion. The Poshwïmkya and Yayatü societies borrowed by Hopi from Keres came to that kind of an end,[44] possibly the Lightning society at Zuni which was obviously copied from the Laguna Shiwanna society,* possibly the Kwirana society among Tewa. Clanship is disappearing from Tewa towns, where clans are merely names and do not control marriage choices. I have the impression that jugglery, another borrowed element, is much less practiced, say at Zuni or Cochiti,† than formerly. (The Franciscan Fathers report [1910] that jugglery is lapsing among Navaho because of ridicule by the younger generation.)

War cults may have been largely borrowed, when nomads

---

* Itself a makeshift for the lapsed Flint society. The incipient Zuni society (Stevenson 2:413–14) may have met resistance from the Rain society of the West which has lightning ritual, at least today (Benedict 3:II, 108–9).

† A jugglery order is mentioned by Dumarest (p. 188) but not by Goldfrank.

made fighting necessary, and this may be one reason why the cults have lapsed so easily. The surcease of intertribal war or raiding of course contributed of itself to the passing of the war society or to its transformation. How this would happen appears very directly at Zuni. Only to save himself after taking a scalp would a man wish or consent to be initiated into the Bow priesthood or war society. When scalping ceased, initiations ceased. By 1921 the society membership had decreased from fifteen in 1896 to four. In 1921 for an initiation a scalp was improvised—from the barber shop, opined Nick, the satirist—and a new member was acquired; but even this accretion was an old man, an unbalanced man, Loco Joe.

At Acoma a simpler method had been followed when the war society was dying out—the scalps were put away "in the hills," the usual way of disposing of fetishes which are very dangerous to those ignorant of the proper ritual. From Laguna the scalps have also disappeared and from several other towns,* which means that scalp rituals or ceremonials have lapsed. Annual war ceremonies or dances in which the scalp did not figure have also lapsed or been much curtailed.

The elimination of war undoubtedly affected the clown societies. The Red Paint people of Taos and the Kashale of Acoma had to get dancers out for the Scalp dance. Red Paint people and Acoma Kashale have become extinct.

The society homologous with the Red Paint people, the Kurena (Kwirana) society, has also been lapsing among Tewa and Keres. One outcome of the lapsing of Kwirana at Sia and possibly at Laguna has been the disappearance of whipping ritual from the kachina initiation. This ritual was conducted by Kwirana.† Kachina organization in general at Sia and Laguna suffered disintegration through loss of the Kwirana.

Clown groups have been still further worn down by European-

---

* Walpi, Zuni, Isleta, San Felipe, Santo Domingo, Jemez, San Juan, Taos, and Picurís are the towns where scalps are known to be kept.

† As once possibly at Cochiti, since the betrayer of "secrets" or the rebel against dancing was "stood in the circle" *in the room of the Quirana* (Dumarest, 197, 201).

American attitudes toward the "obscene" in their play and medicine. "People don't like to eat their stew" (Zuni, Ne'-wekwe). The very idea of becoming Koshare may make a man sick (San Felipe).* Since the public use of excrement has lapsed, possibly its medicinal value has been discredited, and this cure for dysentery has gone out. (With more wells or fly screens there may be less dysentery.) The lapse of a kachina group is much less significant, to be sure, than that of a society medicine, but the unpopularity of the Mahedinasha kachina at Zuni may be put down to school-taught attitudes; these kachina disturbed people at stool.[45]

With increase of the non-Indian population, the larger game animals—elk and mountain sheep, deer and antelope—greatly diminished or became extinct, and this of course lessened the importance of the Hunt chief or society. In Keresan and Tewan towns the group has become virtually extinct.† In the rabbit hunts, war captains officiate, also the clown societies, but to what extent as substitutes is problematic. The clown groups in their role as scouts may have had an original hunt function. The major function of the Chraik'ats[i] chieftaincy associated with the Keresan Town chief was to increase the food supply, through game and wild plants (through crops, too). This once important office has either lapsed or been curtailed, at Santo Domingo, Sia, and Acoma, into a sort of stewardship.[46]

Offices, kiva or other offices, are lapsing or remaining unfilled at Zuni. No kiva has its full quota of five or six officers; Muhewa has only one manager (*wo'le*).[47] Special kiva impersonators are hard to secure. In 1890 two Rain chieftaincies had lapsed.[48] In all the Rain chieftaincies there should be, according to Zuni

---

* White 3:18, n. 35. The man was to be initiated by trespass; he blundered upon an assemblage. He lay around at home for days, not eating or speaking. Unfortunately, specific reasons for his despair were not given.

† The Hunt chief of the Tewa town of San Ildefonso, Florentino Vigil, joined the one surviving Hunt society man at the Keresan town of Cochiti. Vigil had also joined or at least been allowed to visit Cochiti Giant and Koshairi assemblages (Goldfrank 3:43, n. 16). Here is intertribal affiliation based on the practice of inviting out-of-town professionals (see p. 604) but carried farther because of society extremities.

theory, a woman member, presumably a kinswoman of the chief. For several decades these female memberships have been lapsing, including the important female membership in the Town chieftaincy,* which indicates or causes a loosening of the relation between Rain chieftaincy or society and clanship or lineage. This in turn may weaken both the ties of clanship or lineage and the social position of Zuni women.

One of the reasons currently alleged for the lapsing of female membership is that a man resents the continence taboo of his wife.[49] This is an inroad on the Zuni or Pueblo principle of identifying personal with community welfare. If this marital attitude is or becomes general, it is or will be a very significant factor of disintegration.

Economic changes may underlie change in the position of women in the ceremonial life just as economic factors once built up that position. If ownership of houses or lands passes in the West from women to men, all kinds of small ritualistic readjustments will follow which cumulatively will effect a larger change in women's status. In Hopiland men are taking women's place as masons† and gardeners; possibly there is less horticultural or agricultural participation by women everywhere. With what ritualistic effects? What happened at Taos or Santa Clara or Jemez after corn was taken quite generally to the mill and the economic contribution of women cut down by half or more? And what is happening today at Zuni since the introduction of a government mill? The use of a mill in Hopiland would certainly be devastating to the position of women in ceremonialism where grinding at all the crises of life, including initiation, is the women's foremost function. In fact, anything undermining the system of food exchange will be injurious to women's position. Mishongnovi hunters are complaining that girls are making no

---

* This office of Shiwanokya lapsed about 1907, when the last Shiwanokya (Rain chief woman) died. She had no daughters to succeed. In 1896 in all but one of the fourteen Rain chieftaincies there was a woman member; in 1917 there were but six women Rain chiefs (Parsons 6:242–43).

† "Some men are too particular to allow women to build house walls" (Mishongnovi, Beaglehole 3:58). Pueblo boys are taught masonry in boarding school.

return for the rabbits they get;[50] if so, in Mishongnovi as else-where, hunts with the girls will lapse. Whatever the causes, Hopi Women's societies appear to be lapsing.*

Even more serious to the prestige of Zuni chieftaincies than numerical diminution have been their quarrels, largely over American-induced conditions. The chiefs "are always scolding one another" about their calendrical dates[51] or about the secular officers. "It is a great shame that we always are grumbling about the White people's words and about the (secular) offices."[52] In 1890 the Town chief of San Felipe was charged with moderniza-tion and deposed, a procedure so novel and severe, writes Dumarest in 1896, that it aroused opposition and "is still a source of disorder."[53] When the Town chiefs of Oraibi decided about 1913 to forego being worked for by the townspeople in order to be free to own sheep and cattle and become rich like other men,[54] the already shattered ceremonial system received another blow.

The axiom of new goods, new customs—or, shall we say, dead customs—is exemplified in the introduction of store-supplied salt and the lapse of salt expeditions, with all the ritual insurance such dangerous trips required, and, at Acoma and Laguna, with the lapse of ritual function in Parrot and Pumpkin clans. The introduction of draft animals made a great many changes in custom, lessening for one thing the need of communal enterprise, e.g., on First Mesa in fetching wood or bringing in the harvest. When horses came to be used in hunting, the need of long-dis-tance running became less urgent. War raids were made on foot, to be sure, long after the introduction of horses; but, as war went out, accomplished running became less important and ritual racing began to fall off. At Zuni kick-stick races were no longer held for little boys; kick-stick races became less frequent at Acoma;† among Hopi, kick-ball circuits were much reduced, and Taos gave up its long-distance night races altogether.

* Marau has lapsed altogether on First and Third Mesas; Lakon has lapsed at Oraibi (probably at Hotavila), and Oaqöl is held irregularly, a sign of disinte-gration.

† Because, they say, men are spending much less time in kiva (White 7) or in the old town.

The introduction of the Julian calendar has been a factor of disintegration: the horizon calendar is disregarded and the priestly function of watching the sun begins to lapse;* conceptually the relation toward the sun begins to change; the habit of reckoning the passing of time by successive ceremonies is probably affected. There may have been drastic interferences with calendrical observances which were never recorded. At Isleta del Sur in 1895 dances were allowed on saint's days only, and according to a remarkable written constitution "it is the duty of the Capitán Major, aided by his subordinates, to remove from the pueblo every kind of witchcraft and belief contrary to our Holy Catholic Apostolic and Roman religion. No son of the pueblo . . . . is obliged to accept, for example, if so commanded, any sorcery or false belief."⁵⁵ Controversy is indicated, with the Catholic party winning out! Even in the comparatively non-Catholicized North the Church has undoubtedly forced changes in belief and in calendar. For one thing the Church as well as the school (see p. 1140) has opposed obscenity in farce or burlesque and has been a factor in eliminating it considerably from the play of the clowns.† At any rate, in the East there is no record of the extremes of sexual or excremental humor of the Hopi buffoon.

Yet, apart from these disintegrating factors in drama and in calendar, Catholicism has by and large enriched Pueblo religion, contributing God and the saints to the pantheon, fiestas to the calendar, candles and who knows how many other details to ritual. Very different has been the history of Protestants among the Pueblos. Protestant sects contribute nothing to Pueblo religion but dissension and apostasy. They present so sharp a

---

* "The Sun-watcher is not so important as in the old days," says a Hopi in 1929, commenting on planting dates (Forde 3:388).

† I recall that toward the close of a performance of the Hopi dance at Jemez the friars walked conspicuously through the plaza, and that later Father Barnabas, knowing that I had stayed through the "wrangling," inquired, "Was everything innocent?" For twenty years or more he had been seeing to it, I am sure, that everything should be "innocent." Of course others outside the Church have co-operated. Mrs. Stevenson saw to it that the Saiapa kachina warrior wore a breechcloth (Stevenson 2:538, n. a).

choice between the old religion and the new that they are called "crazy." Hopi converts move off the mesa and break entirely with the ceremonial life. Christian missionaries, White and Indian, who invaded the Mesas to sing and pray were given rude treatment, tossed in a blanket, or ostentatiously ignored. "Why do they come into the court?" queried Crow-Wing resentfully, as he looked through our door on the valiant proselytizers. "The chapel is for Jesus, the court is for the kachina." And for the saints, Crow-Wing would have added, had he been Catholic. In the different effects exerted by Catholics and Protestants upon Pueblo culture there is considerable evidence against the theory that the "folkness" of a culture, i.e., its integrity and homogeneity, is not dependent upon the historical source of its component elements.[56] Protestantism as it combines with modernized economy (or sometimes with the "crimes" of civilization)* may not only break down the old culture very rapidly but impede the general tendency to social integration or unity.

With the conversion to Protestantism of Shalïko, the woman chief of the Marau society, that society lapsed altogether at Walpi.† (As Snake clan mother and medicine brewer, Shalïko‡ was an important person also in the Snake-Antelope ceremony,

---

* One of the leading "Christians" at Oraibi is now serving a penitentiary sentence for rape—to the satisfaction of conservatives (White).

† Even prior to Shalïko's conversion, in 1903, the male chief of Marau at Oraibi went Protestant. The chieftaincy continued in his Lizard clan family (Voth 8:11, n. 1), but for how long the ceremony was continued is not known. It is not performed today at Oraibi or Hotavila.

The Marau society holds its own at Mishongnovi, but in 1934 the woman chief was absent at Gallup when the smoke talk was due, to the dismay of the hierarchy (Beaglehole 3:23, n. 5) who well knew that such dereliction did not occur in the old days.

‡ If Shalïko's account of the introduction of Marau is credible, here is an instance of how a borrowed society lapses easily. She told Fewkes that her maternal ancestor (? old, old uncle) saved the life of a Marau woman chief of Awatobi when that town of (Christian) witches was destroyed at the request of Tapolo, its chief, the condition being that the Marau woman would teach her songs and initiate Walpi women (Bloom, 206 n. 41). Voth opines that the songs, which are mostly unintelligible, are from the eastern pueblos (via Awatobi which may have been a Keresan-*singing* pueblo; compare p. 239, n.†). There are Marau songs about Paiyatemu, the Keresan Sun Youth.

and the Snakes must have been imperiled by her apostasy.)[57] At Oraibi, Protestantism coupled with Americanization in general did break up the Snake-Antelope groups, for after prolonged dissension* in 1906 the Antelope society removed with other conservatives and founded Hotavila. Although the Snake society chief went along, some Snake altar properties† were left behind at Oraibi (Kennard). The Snakes decided to carry on at Oraibi, and in 1908 held their ceremony. In the public performance in which Snakes and Antelopes dance together, Snakes were substituted in the Antelope dance line; and a curious innovation was introduced of presenting snakes to the lookers-on to hold (Lowie). Five biennial performances were held, then in 1916 the altar was taken to Hotavila, and a complete Snake-Antelope ceremony was held there (Kennard).

The quarrel at Oraibi was about sending the children to school, about wearing American clothes (and no doubt about cutting the boys' hair), about using American farming implements, about redividing the land, and about living off the mesa, in houses below. As early as 1883 Cushing found Oraibi chiefs making charges of witchcraft against one another, a sure sign of feud. School trouble started in 1888, when there was a Wüwüchim initiation for Shumopovi and Shipaulovi‡ and the chiefs refused to send the boys to the Keam's Canyon boarding school, hiding them from Walpi and Navaho police. Antischool factions developed in all the towns of Second Mesa[58] and in Oraibi, where two Town chiefs came to be recognized,§ the hereditary chief

* From 1890 on, no pro-American or progressive member took part in the Snake-Antelope ceremonies, except that in 1900 one young progressive went into the Antelope kiva. The smoke assemblage was not held in the house of the Town chief, a progressive, but in kiva (Voth 3:273, 276).

† The Snake chief was not possessed of a *tiponi*; only War god images stood on the altar.

‡ Possibly Shipaulovi has held no Wüwüchim ceremony of its own because it has been considered an "innocent" town, a place of sanctuary (Nequatewa, 46), a refuge house, *waki* as it was once called (Voth 5:61), and Wüwüchim is ceremony for war.

§ This was not the first disruptive row or split chieftaincy at Oraibi (see pp. 862, n.*; 1092, n.*).

who was pro-American and a chief chosen by the "Hostiles." In 1891 a military "punitive" expedition was sent against Oraibi, and five "chiefs" were taken prisoners to Fort Wingate, where they cultivated the gardens of the American officers and on their return called themselves war chiefs.[59] In 1897 the Hostiles or conservatives held independent winter solstice ceremonial in Chief kiva, placing their own altar. The regulars objected to this to the point of calling upon the missionary and the Agent to intervene![60] In 1897 ten kivas were co-operating in the regular ceremony, but by 1899 only four kivas—distressful years! There was trouble, too, in Shipaulovi, for in 1899 the Hostiles there moved away to Shumopovi, a more sympathetic town.*

Although winter solstice harmony was shattered in Oraibi and no Wüwüchim ceremony in its long initiatory form had been held for many years even prior to 1899,[61] and although the conservative Powamu society was so depleted that it had to initiate an old man in order to get a Kachina Father,[62] the feud at Oraibi did not come to a head until 1906, when the conservative party were pushed out† of Oraibi to found a new town—Hotavila, about six miles distant. (Pakavi was settled a little later by the less irreconcilable of the two groups of Hotavila.) Oraibi was left a wreck in several ways: beams were removed from houses so that many of them fell in, leaving a very ruinous, ramshackle-looking town; and ceremony-holding maternal families carried away with them their religious beams—altars, songs, and prayers. Besides the Antelopes, there departed to Hotavila the Oaqöl

* At least until 1906, when trouble started during Powamu by Hostiles refusing to plant their kiva beans at the time the other kiva members planted theirs (Nequatewa, 64), just as Santa Clara feudists at one time refused to work on the road or on the ditch together.

† Literally. Their leader, Yukioma of the Coyote-Firewood-Masauwü clan cut a line on a rock saying that he would have to be pushed across this line before his people would agree to leave Oraibi. The push or glorified football line kept up for hours. "Every once in a while the pressure would be so great that old Yukioma would rise up in the air. Just as soon as he was pushed over the line, he said, 'It is done, I have passed my mark,' and all at once they dropped him" (Nequatewa, 67). Yukioma belonged to the clan of Masauwü against whom, we recall, lines of exclusion are drawn on the death trail. Yukioma was applying the old pattern of trail lines of exclusion to a fresh situation.

chiefs (their altar left in Oraibi), the Blue Flutes,* and the Horns.† The Agave society chief died in 1906 and left no successor; by 1901 the society was already shattered.‡ Chiefs of Singers and of Wüwüchim§ moved down to New Oraibi. The altar of the Drab Flute was burned in 1925 together with the Horn altar, the chief having died and the successor in his family having become a Protestant (Kennard).

Apostasy through Protestant Americanization occurred at Laguna even earlier than at Oraibi. In 1851 a Baptist missionary from Cincinnati settled at Laguna and built schoolroom and chapel. He stayed ten years. A Presbyterian missionary arrived in 1875 and also stayed ten years.[63] Whatever disintegrating influence these missionaries may have had was reinforced through miscegenation. Three White men married Laguna women and reared large families. A Protestant-American-Kurena-Shikani party got control, and in 1880 the conservatives abandoned the town for Mesita and Isleta. With the loss of its Town chief, its kivas, and several of its societies Laguna ceremonial was maimed almost beyond recovery. Only its reinvigorated Kachina cult has kept Laguna in the old circle of ceremonial life.‖

The Kachina cult which was marginal among Tewa has not

---

* They did not participate in Flute ritual in January, 1901. The preceding month the winter solstice ceremony was not held in their kiva, Blue Flute kiva, which has been Chief kiva, but in Pongovi kiva, now called Chief kiva (Dorsey and Voth 1:10, 11).

† The chief died in 1925, and his successor within the Bow clan, a Protestant, living in New Oraibi, below the mesa, obtained the altar from Hotavila and burned it publicly. Then at Hotavila a Badger clansman made a new altar and is now performing the ceremony (Kennard).
Meanwhile at Oraibi, after the split, a new altar was made, but in time when the new chief fell sick he let the ceremony lapse, persuaded that it was "too dangerous for him" (Parsons 52:372–73).

‡ See Voth 9:Pls. LI and LIV for altar pictures before (1897) and after the withdrawal of one chief and members: one corn-ear fetish instead of two, two chief's jugs instead of four, no longevity crooks. Inferably one corn-ear fetish was taken to Hotavila where the society was established (Kennard).

§ They did not participate in the ceremony of 1900 (Dorsey and Voth 1:10).

‖ This may hold also for Oraibi as the Powamu and Kachina group are still intact. But Oraibi also preserves its Town chieftaincy. New Oraibi below the mesa and Pakavi, both "progressive" settlements, also dance kachina.

served Santa Clara or San Ildefonso against disintegration; it was merely one source of the division that has wracked San Ildefonso for over a decade and Santa Clara for over a century.*

* In 1701 a townsman called Francisco Canjuebe began to buy up land from Spanish grantees outside the communal town grant. In 1744 Roque Canjuebe, being rich in cattle and horses, resented the "continual public works" and asked for a separate grant of land in exchange for fields nearer town. This petition was granted when Canjuebe presented a certificate that he was an instructed Catholic. Now there grew up a hamlet of families who worked on the ditch but on no other public works, and who were not obliged to dance (Aitken, 385 ff.). Obviously a Catholic party. (Note in this connection that about 1776 a Santa Clara man called Antonio the Twin, an apostate from Catholicism, took refuge in Hopiland, presumably in Hano. His people went after him and urged him so ardently to return that the "Moqui" would have killed them had not the twin vowed that they had come only to see him, not to take him down (Thomas, 162).

Although Roque Canjuebe's grandchildren won the land suit brought by the town in 1815 (but compare Twitchell I, 371), and denounced the "customs" as diabolical rites, their families drifted back into town and became the political core of the renegade Winter People. The feud went on until in 1894 the conservative Summer People secured the power from American authority to appoint the Governor and War captain, and have continued to make these appointments, although at times (1924——) the Winter People have appointed their own Governor and War captain (Parsons 49:106). In 1897 charges of human sacrifice and of "things that cannot be said" were made before a lawyer in Santa Fé by the Winter People! And by 1910 the feud was very acute, although the Winter People had so far conformed to the customs in 1906 as to choose a Winter Town chief, José Manuel Naranjo, brother of Francisco Naranjo, the outstanding leader of the schism. The Summer People, still outraged by the withdrawal of ceremonial co-operation, declared that the selection of the Winter chief was invalid, *as it had been done without the concurrence of the War captain* (see p. 1146, n.‡), and that Naranjo should be called out to work on the ditch like any other layman (Aitken). In 1926 the two moieties would not even work on the ditch or build roads or dig wells together. Nor would they look on at a dance by the other moiety ("class"); "they won't even peep outside," said a Nambé visitor.

Unfortunately, not living in Santa Clara, I was not familiar enough with the moiety alignment in 1926 to check up well on personal affiliations and I would note here that in "The Social Organization of the Tewa" there are several errors, e.g., Pedro Baca, the short-haired solitary peyote-eater who worked out, was not Summer but Winter, in the minority group, like the Peyote boys of Taos.

My chief informant was a Winter woman and her Canjuebe (Cahete) genealogy (Genealogy III) shows well-marked clan patriliny, a support for the theory that patriliny was Spanish-derived, together with independance in land-holding and "instruction" in Catholicism. A marked degree of moiety endogamy at Santa Clara was a secondary consequence; but a tendency to descent of moiety chieftaincy patrilineally may be quite Indian; it occurs at Taos.

The feud alignment at San Ildefonso is reported by Whitman not to be by moiety. One factor of disintegration in this town is the diminution of the Winter moiety to three households, since the fatal influenza of 1916.

The history of these quarrels between progressives and conservatives has still to be written in full, but we may surmise that within the nonconformist Canjuebe family, who fought for a separate grant of land and the right to dance only when they chose to, there was some Spanish-Mexican intermarriage, also that in recent years the "Frenchman" called Dozier who married into Santa Clara, and his *métif* (half-breed) descendants played a part in the separatism of the progressive Winter People. At Santa Clara and Laguna we get hints of something of the cultural breakdown which fur-traders and their *métif* employees accomplished among northern tribes.

At Zuni no recent Indian-White marriages* have been noted except that of Margaret Lewis, a woman of mixed blood from Oklahoma;† but for thirty years or more a Protestant mission has conducted a school, given Christmas presents, and made claim to one convert. It would be of interest to learn why Protestantism has been so negligible at Zuni as compared with Laguna or Hopi towns.‡

Yet Zuni has not been without some of the disintegrating effects of Americanization. Since Naiuchi was jailed in 1896 for persecuting a witch the violence of witch-baiting has abated. Although the War chiefs have not relaxed their vigilance and

---

* At the Rebellion two Spanish women (? captives) were married to Zuni and bore children, and no doubt Spanish exiles to Zuni mated with Zuni women.

† Mrs. Lewis is unusually sympathetic toward the native culture, but she remains American and as schoolteacher or as wife of the Governor who was chosen by the chiefs because of his wife, or as mother and grandmother of young Zuni, she has been an important factor in Americanization. For example, although her first house, an adobe house, was built by her husband and his connections, when she built her second house, a larger stone house, she paid day wages to a Zuni mason and carpenter at a time when working for wages was very unusual. (The Shalako kachina plan for housebuilding was not followed for either house.)

‡ For the social psychologist what more interesting study than biography of Hopi Protestants, conversion from ritualism? To what? I have never talked with a devout Protestant Pueblo, but I surmise that he would express conceptual values surprising to missionaries, like Talasnömtiwa of Oraibi who included prayer-sticks to "God" and to "Jesus" among his offerings because once when he was very sick they made him well (Voth 9:131).

charges of witchcraft are still made, particularly during epidemic, and suspects are nagged into confession, they are not tortured physically or killed. Any check on the witchcraft nexus would undermine the curing societies. These societies have been diminished indeed in membership, at Zuni, the only place where we have chronological records. Another indication of diminution at Zuni has been the change in selecting Koyemshi clowns. They can still be drawn from Big Firebrand society, but not from the shrunken Ne'wekwe and Cactus societies.[64]

It is difficult to learn how influential American doctor or visiting nurse may have been, but the American school system has visibly affected the ceremonial life in various particulars in all the towns. It is a factor in the calendar, making of Saturday and Sunday* favorite dance days in order that the schoolchildren may be at hand. The Acoma kachina initiation is held nowadays in summer, instead of late winter, to make the children available. The prepuberty and puberty headdressing and corn-grinding observances for a Mishongnovi girl no longer take place at the summer solstice or at first menstruation, but are adjusted likewise to school terms.[65] For like reason initiation has been postponed everywhere to a later age, thereby rendering it less impressive. At Zuni and at Taos serious conflicts between school attendance and initiation requirements have occurred. It has been customary at Zuni to complete the initiation of the boys into the Kachina society during the Shalako ceremony, and for this reason and because it is a time of making presents to the younger children and of having them enjoy the dances, the Christmas school vacation was held at the beginning of December or if need be earlier. As yet Agent and schoolteachers have been kept from regularizing the Christmas date (see p. 1078, n.*), but Zuni curing societies who hold their initiations at various times during the winter have undoubtedly postponed initiations of children of school age (and so weakened their hold on initiates), just as in Hopi towns the age of initiation into Wüwüchim

---

* Sunday is now the favored race day at Zuni for the spring kick-stick races, but this is due to the economic week that is coming in with the wage system.

was advanced, after futile fighting against boarding-school police.* Taos stands up for itself far more unitedly and vigorously than feud-torn Hopiland or timid-hearted Zuni, and, when the prolonged and continuous initiation of its boys was imperiled, the case was appealed to Washington, and the Indians won.

In other ways the school has been more successfully undermining the ceremony. The self-consciousness shown by the younger generation toward their cults, more particularly in matters that schoolteachers would consider "superstitious" or obscene, are largely acquired, I believe, at school. Stephen noted an increase of self-consciousness in the girl dancers, although the younger girls still concentrated on the dancing or posturing in itself and not on any effect they made as individuals, attempting as gaudy a display in clothes as possible but "as naïvely as pheasant or turkey gobbler might spread his tail."[66] Antonio Mirabal of Taos is said to be ashamed to sing when he assists his doctoring uncle, for which people laugh at him.† Undoubtedly, clowning has been greatly modified in recent years by the new-found sense of shame; as noted, membership in clown societies has diminished. There has been rebellion by younger men against dancing kachina, as at San Ildefonso.‡

Schoolteachers or their circles are not generally well enough informed about Indian "superstitions" to be dangerous to them, directly; but indirectly, particularly through language, they are influential. The Kaiser who sent "germs" to America was merely a witch, but the notion of germ will affect the notion of *chisto* (Sp., *hechizado*, bewitched), what the witch sends into the body. Luck (Sp., *suerte*) is translation or mistranslation for power or

* The Powamu whipping of the children used to be held outdoors in the daytime. By 1921 it was being held in kiva at night (Parsons 40:50), presumably to preclude observation and interference by the Indian Bureau.

† Clash here for Antonio. Does it make him whip the harder when he is serving as Lieutenant-Governor? In other connections he has given evidence of being a fighter.

‡ This was in 1926. It is not known whether they are still dancing kachina at San Ildefonso, but the "round house" is not used; Winter people burned it out (Dr. Whitman, personal communication).

blessing, and the new English term will come to influence the old Indian concept. A virgin field for the social psychologist who is a linguist and will study teachers as well as pupils!

Boarding-school experience has tended to break down marriage rules, whether of clan exogamy or of town endogamy, and so shaken control by the elders and indirectly their ceremonial prestige. Anything that damages gerontocracy is disintegrating to Pueblo culture. Broken rules by the juniors are bad enough, but in the complicated ceremonial life there are always new rules to be made, and only the seniors have the knowledge or interest or sense of responsibility to make a new rule in accordance with an old rule, preserving cultural integrity.

No doubt many of the older men have been philosophically aware in one way or another of this situation, but the major overt opposition to the boarding school has been economic: not only does the school cut under the apprenticeship system in economic training but it deprives the household of economic help and so is as objectionable to Pueblos as a child labor law is to Catholics. Stephen writes of a Hano woman who wanted her daughter home from Lawrence, Kansas, to help grind and cook and carry water for the large family. "The girl would be much more profitably employed at home," comments Stephen, "than dawdling as a pauper at the school in the grasshopper region."[67] Years later Crow-Wing cites a flagrant case of a boarding-school girl who was not allowed to stay home to look after the younger children when their mother died, and there was nobody else to take care of them. "We were all very sorry for the children, but the Agent wouldn't help."[68] Pueblo and particularly Hopi economic life is so integrated with religion that anything hurtful to the economy tends also to be hurtful to religion.

Of like indirect effect has been the call to labor among Americans. Such economic activity may keep people from meeting their ceremonial obligations, as in the case of the Taos girls who continue to work in the hotel of Don Fernando de Taos during the month when all Taos people are required to live within the walls of the pueblo. Santo Domingo conservatives recognize the danger of working out—it must have become apparent early in

Spanish days—and they object to men as well as girls leaving town for work.[69]

The wage system produces new economic needs as well as means of satisfying them, even illicitly, through commercializing ceremonial. Ceremonial pottery and other ceremonial paraphernalia are being sold. At the annual fairs or shows of Gallup, Albuquerque, and Santa Fé, men dance for personal gain. Kachina dancing is still ruled out, but any day an entering wedge may be made by presenting masked dancers like the Navaho dancers* who are not strictly kachina.† Kachina pictures are made by Hopi artists for sale. The kachina dolls of Jemez may be bought at Santa Clara, where there is a clever exploitation of the tourist's curiosity about the esoteric. In one Santa Clara house a back room has been made to look like a kiva, with wall designs, and sight-seers are charged twenty-five cents admission. The house belongs to the Kossa who works at the Pueblo show-place near Colorado Springs, where, no doubt, he conceived this showman's idea. But when he tells the tourists that they are being admitted to his "kiva" because of recent drought or town misfortune he is indulging in his characteristic Kossa humor; he is talking backward, as is Kossa old man of San Ildefonso who dances to entertain tourists or lies to anthropologists.

Pueblo arts are ritual arts, their motivation is religious. If this motivation lapses, the arts will lapse; for the only substitute motivation in sight is commercial gain. In commercial art the buyer controls, which means, when the artist belongs to another culture, a very rapid disintegration of traditional art forms. Then, too, the substitution of foreign materials for native materials may be disintegrating. Twenty years ago at Zuni glass containers were displacing pottery meal bowls of ritualistic

---

* Already Navaho themselves are dancing Yeibichai, although without masks, at Gallup.

† Prestige as well as profit attaches to dancing for White people. This may affect the selection of dances within the pueblo. The Eagle dance is spreading from town to town because, I am guessing, it is danced in a hotel in Santa Fé.

Have tourist swarms or Snake dances by White men affected the prestige or performance of the Snake-Antelope ceremony?

design. In the nineties Hopi were substituting a box from the store for their gourd resonator in notched-stick-playing.* The gourd was whitened and painted with cloud design; the box was undecorated. As containers for ritual feathers paper boxes have replaced the oblong wooden boxes sometimes carved with ritual designs.† Aniline dyes were introduced in the nineties; with trade dyes the rituals of fetching, grinding, or applying pigments, always more or less proprietary, are bound to lapse, and the power vesting in pigments to disappear. Parrot feathers, important for fetish or mask or dancer's array, have become very scarce, possibly because it is easier or cheaper to use dyed chicken feathers than to trade for parrot feathers or to keep live birds. When cotton or other local yields of nature are substituted for by commercial supplies, the ritual of gathering lapses, and animistic theory is undermined. Cotton Woman, for example, will cease to be named in prayer. Any irrigation system independent of rainfall will be fatal to the prestige of the kachina. "Why dance kachina when you have only to open a sluice gate?" young men of the most conservative pueblo of the East are beginning to ask (White),‡ just as years ago Hopi asked, "Why practice running, when you have a horse?"

The introduction of commercial motivation, through wages or price system, has already been disintegrating to Pueblo patterns of behavior. Tsiwema, who was for many years the only authentic medicine man at Laguna, charged high fees for his treatments or medicines, although the townspeople grumbled. Tsiwema had a monopoly, but even so the idea of making definite charges must have come to him from outside, perhaps from

* Before this, sheep scapula had been substituted for deer scapula, as, in the leg rattle, sheep or goat hoofs were substituted for antelope hoofs, substitutions insignificant for art and probably for ritual.

† These boxes were no doubt post-Spanish. The pristine container may have been an agave stalk (Bartlett 1:39–40).

‡ Compare the Havasupai attitude about not depositing prayer-sticks in the cornfield, Hopi fashion. "We have a creek to irrigate with. Hopi have none and have to pray for rain all the time" (Spier 2:286). Sound utilitarians also!

Navaho,* perhaps from Americans. Did he not see the secular officers being paid fifty cents a day while in council,[70] an extraordinary arrangement? The stipulated fee has become familiar in Acoma. Formerly when an Acoman asked the Town chief for an allotment of land he would give the chief a blanket or buckskin or some meal. Nowadays the chief asks for the fee, "like the priest at baptism."[71] In the East we hear now and again of a man appointed to office running away. This is probably not a very recent form of behavior, for reluctance to take office has often been noticed; but running away, I surmise, occurs more frequently than formerly. It is merely a question of time when the communal system of work, sacerdotal and secular, will break down completely before the encroachment of the system of fees and wages. Recently, employment for pay† by the Federal government must have been hastening this outcome,‡ an ironical situation for administrators who prize and would preserve Pueblo solidarity.

SUBSTITUTION

Disintegration is often combated by Pueblos through what is probably a quite general sociological method of substitution. Functions of an extinct group may be transferred to another group or undertaken by another group or by persons called upon to fill temporarily the lapsed offices. The curing society of eastern Tewa, the Bear doctors, has lapsed at Hano, but at the

* In very marked contrast to Navaho doctor, the Hopi doctor takes whatever gifts are offered without a single comment. It is considered ill-mannered to discuss gifts or their value before him (Stephen 4:859).

† Even employment without pay may suggest changes. Around Second Mesa, road-building has been carried on in the old way, by a working-party, and again in the old way the workers have been fed, by the Agent, but in eating his canned delicacies why should the old etiquette of eating lightly be followed, the Agent has never heard of it? (Beaglehole 3:31). A telling little illustration of how in new cultural contacts "manners" may be lost.

‡ Unfortunately, during the last five years, observations have not been recorded, such as Dr. Underhill's on the "economic revolution" among Papago, in which she notes the very rapid change from a barter to a money economy, from the family unit to the individual, and, given the rise in the standard of living, from an economy of abundance to one of scarcity.

winter solstice ceremony a Bear man exorcises, a Bear *clansman*. "The Bear clan man is supposed to be Bear himself and Bear gets rid of bad things."[72] Obviously, the association between Bear and medicine has been transferred from society to clan. In Santo Domingo and San Felipe when the War society lapsed, its function as custodian of scalps was taken over by the Flint society or by the Town chief who was a Flint shaman—the Flint society had war associations.[73] At the last and final Scalp ceremony of Acoma, who should perform the adoptive head-washing (aspersing) ritual for the Scalps but the church sacristan![74] The sacristan baptizes the living, so why not the dead? Indeed, he may asperse the dead townsman, so why not the dead enemy? Substitution works on the basis of resemblance, more or less logically.

In several Keresan towns and in Jemez, men are *made* temporary scalp-taker or clown or even shaman, Opi or Koshare or Cheani. They may be "caught" in the "ash house" of the clowns or they may be asked to serve with a cigarette (Acoma, Santo Domingo). At Isleta they *make* an "aunt" if the clown they have made has no "aunt"; at Laguna they may even make a man the required kind of clansman when an office has to be filled by a certain clan.[75] Certain roles in the Flute ceremony of Walpi should be filled by Bear clansmen; but for many years there has been but a single Bear clansman at Walpi—Kotka. Kotka therefore appoints men to fill the other Bear roles. In the Zuni Scalp dance of 1921 there were not enough girl dancers, dedicated Shake girls, so some were *made* for the occasion.

To be sure, this method of substitution may be based in some cases on a practice which is differently motivated, for the use of substitutes occurs when the originals are still available. At Zuni there are a number of kachina masks, notably Koyemshi, Salimobia, and Shulawitsi, which are not the *real* masks; their use has no grave consequences. At Jemez and elsewhere warriors are *made* for the occasion, although a warrior society still exists. We recall that Walpi warriors did not dance in public lest they cause windstorm. Possibly fictitious warriors were *made* for a dance just as masks were made, so "nothing would happen."* Then, too, in borrowed performance persons might have to be "made." This explains the making of clowns and of "aunts" in Isleta maskless kachina dance and in the hunt with girls which are borrowed from Keres. The organization of Plains war dances is singularly obscure, but it appears to be of a temporary character.[76] Possibly the temporary character of war-dance personages among eastern Pueblos reflects this Plains trait.

Some lapsed offices among Pueblos are permanently provided for. Just as another lineage within the clan will be a substitute among Hopi, so another medicine society will substitute among Keres. At Acoma it was the function of Kaʙina society to set the altar for the Town chief, but in 1926 the last Kaʙina died; so the Flint society was called upon to set the altar.[77] And Flint society took over the Kaʙina function of whipping in-going War captains.† When the Hunt society lapsed at Cochiti, the Shikame took over some of its functions, assisted by Kurena and War captains.[78] With the extinction of War chief and society the secular officers, Spanish-made alcalde and constabulary, i.e., the "war captains," took on some of the old functions—representation of the War gods, appointment or installation of the Town chief,‡ prayer-stick-making and depositing (Acoma, Laguna),§ initiating kachina dances, and guarding dances and society assemblages. The lapse of the Hunt chieftaincy and of the Bow chieftaincy among Keres left hunt management also to the War

* The same idea is expressed in the taboo on Coyote clansmen impersonating their clan patron, Masauwü, god of death. They would cause death (see p. 866, n.‡).

† White 7. The last surviving Kaʙina had used a Flint man as assistant.

‡ At Santa Clara, San Felipe, and Santo Domingo (White 4:36). Without this history the appointment of a lifelong chief, the paramount chief, by annual officers would be very anomalous. There is at Santo Domingo still another detail of substitution, i.e., calling a war captain who has served four times "mother," as the War chief or Under chief was called elsewhere.

§ There being no Town chief at Laguna, the War captains are said even to take solar observations at the winter solstice (Parsons 14:184). However, this may be explained in another way, since at Acoma the War chief watched the sun (Stirling). Solar observations by War chief may have been customary among western Keres.

captains. Conversely, among Tewa the lapse of the War chieftaincy left the Hunt chief in charge of the Scalps and responsible for appointing to chiefly office or installing in office (San Juan).*

The most conspicuous case of substitution I know of is the passing of the Town chieftaincy of Walpi from the Bear clan to the Horn clan, as dramatized in the Flute ceremony. This type of substitution must have been common enough in Hopi society where the life of a ceremony is dependent upon the life of clan or lineage. When a lineage dies out, there must be another lineage to hand on the ceremony. Such exigency is one of the factors of the composite or flexible character of Hopi clans. Now the Bear clan has a number of "other names" and on Second and Third mesas some of these names refer to lineage groups to any one of whom the Town chieftaincy might be passed on.† It was only when all such groups failed at Walpi, we may suppose, that a crisis was reached and the chieftaincy had to be transferred to a different clan, with a dramatic warrant inserted into the Flute ceremony, the Pueblo way of amending the Constitution. Another transference occurred at Walpi in connection with the Squash or Sorrow-making clan that had two society chieftancies, Wüwüchim and Drab Flute. Sometime before 1880 the clan became extinct, the Drab Flute chieftaincy and ceremony lapsed, but the Wüwüchim chieftaincy passed to a "child of the clan," a Mustard clansman. The Wüwüchim chieftaincy remained in the Mustard clan for several decades, then the lineage in charge died out. No other lineage in the Mustard clan wanted to take on the chieftaincy, and so it was offered to anyone who wanted it. A Snake-Lizard man volunteered, getting the field that went with the office.[79]

* There is also the possibility that Pike, Mountain Lion, was always War chief, and that he has taken over the duties of a Hunt chief.

† During the Oraibi feud the Bluebird people associated with the Bear people claimed an equal right to the Town chieftaincy. Now all Bear or affiliated Bear lineages are near extinction at Oraibi, just as at Walpi. What is Oraibi going to do? Hotavila reconstructed by substitution, even with altars destroyed. In 1932 all chieftaincies were functioning excepting Drab Flute, Marau, and one of the other Women's societies, and a complete Wüwüchim ceremony was performed (Kennard). This remarkable ceremonial reconstruction should be studied in detail.

Substitution occurs in ritual. The place of Emergence in Zuni tradition was too far away for pilgrimage, so Kachina town was established within easy distance, for men and kachina. Similarly, to preclude having to make a trip to a distant shrine, Hopi will call a shrine near town by the name of the far shrine.[80] In Stephen's day women were buried in their white wedding mantle; thirty years later Crow-Wing reports that, when "the breath has come out to go to another world," the white mantle is merely hung outside, on the house wall, for four days.[81] Today Shipaulovi mourners rub a bit of yucca root over a few strands of hair,[82] inferably in lieu of washing the hair. Possibly fumigating the effects of the dead or throwing bits from the effects on the house fire, as is done at modernizing Laguna, or giving a few threads to the doctor for his spirit animal (Zuni) instead of a piece of cloth (Hopi),[83] all have been substitutes for destroying or giving away property of value. In throw-away dances presents may be thrown by arrangement into the hands of a relative. Traditionally, the Acoma kachina should denude himself of everything but his mask for the benefit of onlookers; actually the kachina strips, but he gets his valuables into the hands of one who will return them.

When ritual materials become scarce, substitutes are found. Dyed chicken feathers or, at Oraibi,[84] red chat feathers are substituted for the ever rare parrot feathers. Buffalo pelt is substituted for bear pelt or vice versa,[85] or sheep's wool serves for buffalo hair. Zuni masks may be made of cowhide instead of buffalo hide or buckskin. At Jemez, antelope dance pelts have been improvised of painted cotton,[86] just as at Walpi, when buckskin became scarce, native cotton cloth was substituted in making Water Serpent images.[87]

Substitution occurs in the conceptual character of ritual or ceremonial, another purpose or objective may come to be adopted. The change in the objective of the Snake-Antelope ceremony, from controlling the enemy to controlling rainfall, is a conspicuous and certain instance. From fighting raiders, war societies have turned their attention to fighting witches. Pushing a pebble under the foot along a rutted course, which is a rite of exorcism at Acoma, becomes an omen of convalescence at Laguna and a race omen at Zuni. I have suggested that kachina ceremonial was once not all for rain as it is today. Zuni Shalako, we have observed, is not only a hunt ceremony but a kachina war chief ceremony for fertility and longevity, and possibly kachina initiation, the second initiation during Shalako, was originally tribal initiation into war, and Zuni kiva-kachina groups were war groups or war-dance societies, corresponding more closely than they do today to Hopi Wüwüchim societies which still retain their war character.

IN RELATION TO PATTERN

The Pueblos are house- and town-dwellers and deeply attached to their houses and towns, yet individuals or even households move readily from one room or house into another, groups will leave one town to settle in another, or the whole population will abandon their town and resettle. Rooms, houses, towns, old or new, are all so much alike that the removal may not be felt as much of a change. Everything of value can be carried along, clothes, jewels, and implements, and all the tangible and intangible things people "live by"—fetishes and altars, songs, prayers, and the traditions. There are few if any monuments to leave behind, no ties that cannot be readily renewed. New shrines can be easily built; the abandoned town will merely figure in the tradition as one more place where they stopped a while before moving on and to which they would occasionally return with prayer-sticks, presumably for the dead who once lived there and still linger about. Here again is that mobility within steadfast design which we noted in the ceremonial life and which underlies Pueblo attitudes in general, the way of involution.

From this point of view the great number of Pueblo ruins, also the very rapid development of the big building phase, the rise of the towns of the Pueblo III period, are easily explicable. Involution is capable of being a very rapid process; culture blossoms quickly through involution, witness at Zuni, let us say, the increase of curing societies or the efflorescence of the Kachina cult, witness the age of Pericles, witness our own "age of machinery."

Once the urge to involute is arrested, the desire to elaborate design or to reapply it, decadence of a sort sets in; but, as long as people are working at or playing with their cultural patterns, their way of life appears integrated, sincere, and vital. That is why Pueblos still show a greater cultural vitality than other North American Indians, or why the culture of Western Pueblos appears more intact than that of the Easterners.

There is nothing in contemporary Pueblo culture to suggest that houses were ever deserted because of the dead. In early days there were even house burials. Fear of the dead and the will to forget them as individuals are extreme, but the dead have to remove from the living, not the living from the dead. A small amount of personal property is destroyed at death but not property which, accumulated, releases energy to meet novel circumstances or to innovate. From this point of view the destruction of property at death (or let us say in war) is ever a highly conservative factor. Property has to be restored, and that necessity directs energy along customary lines. When Pueblos took to dispatching mere samples to the dead or to fumigating the effects instead of destroying them, they facilitated other changes. (Just as Navaho have done by not killing a man's sheep at his death.)* Pueblos fear the dead, but whether they fear them less than do their semimigratory neighbors, Navaho and Apache, or neighboring Shoshonean or Yuman tribes, or whether they are more adept in social fictions, by remaining comparatively sedentary and by accumulating property Pueblos have released energy for elaborating their social organization and their ritual arts.

In the opinion of various North American populations there must be a measure to accumulating property which leads to personal distinction and away from communal service or solidarity. Hence the potlatch, the very widespread practice of contributing to ceremonial or family feasts or of "throwing away" goods, whether "coppers" or dimes or "foundations" to establish respect or status. Potlatch does not occur spectacularly among

---

* On the ground that sheep were got from the Whites and so Navaho rules do not apply (Reichard 1:157). Yet a horse is killed. Apache kill sheep as well as horses.

Pueblos, but it occurs continuously in one form or another, from sprinkling corn meal on a kachina to throwing gifts by kachina or war dancers. From every household contributions of goods or services are ever being requisitioned. Failure to contribute involves loss of standing or personal accidents and misfortunes. Besides, any conspicuous accumulation of proprety would arouse envy, and envious witches would be after you or, like my Zuni friend who owned a fortune in turquoise, you yourself would be suspected of witchcraft. Change dependent upon private capital has been out of the question. Were a flour mill owned by a Pueblo, let us say, at least by a western Pueblo, and tolerated by the town, it would be not only a factor but a sign of thoroughgoing change of attitude. On the other hand, a mill owned and operated by the town and free to all (as is a thrasher at Santa Ana) would indicate no change in town spirit, although it would involve minor changes in conduct of ceremonial and probably a major change in the position of women.

But even throw-away or food exchange keeps goods within the pueblo, within the human circle. There is not much actual destruction of property for the gods. Corn meal or food offerings are the greatest outlay, and this is reduced to a minimum by the theory of magical increase or, as in the East, by merely cutting down on the offering and sweeping your hand to the directions with little or nothing in it. On the whole, the bargain with all the gods, not alone the dead, is greatly to the advantage of their petitioners—if the gods keep the bargain. When a Zuni Wood society man sprinkles corn meal on the prayer-sticks he deposits monthly, he prays for no mean return:

> This day, my fathers,
> Taking your plume wand,
> Your prayer-meal,
> With your waters,
> Your seeds,
> Your riches,
> Your long life,
> Your old age,
> With all your good fortune
> You will bless us.[88]

Stress upon longevity is prominent in Pueblo prayers, almost as if people were aware that longevity is both an outcome and a factor of their culture. With enough material stability and physical comfort to grow old in, people do survive to old age, and my guess is that only through old people could such intricate conceptual or ceremonial organization develop. Almost it requires a sixth sense, exclaims Stephen, "it is more than a man's life can compass." Ritualism is an old age art, at least for an unlettered culture. Economic goods are shared with younger people to a considerable extent, but "what we live by," as Pueblos say, spiritual capital, is retained in the hands and minds of the old people.

Ritual is not owned or developed by youth but much must be learned in youth from seniors. Pueblo children have had many teachers, from the grandmother of the War Brothers to the ceremonial father given every boy, from the oldest "aunt" to the youngest "uncle," from masked dancers, bogeys, or clowns to chiefs who sermonize or relate the traditions or plan children's races and dances and horrendous dramatizations to shock the young into belief. Without old people to take considerable responsibility in educating the young in all kinds of ways as well as in respect for the old people's say-so, Pueblo culture could never have been so successfully "handed." To this, too, the intimate household life has contributed, and all its ways of teaching by example, through apprenticing. Through the old people in and out of the household, character standards are set: not only submissiveness and conformity but industry, thrift, moderation, endurance, concentration, persistence, and self-control, traits necessary to survival in as exacting an environment as the semiarid Southwest, traits emphasized again and again in ceremonial, but never as explicitly as by old Lina of Zuni: "Much you work. Your children will eat. Your granddaughters, your grandsons want for nothing. Therefore even though I am tired, I have planted. Therefore I am not lazy. I have toiled hard in all things. . . . . If one speaks kindly to one's child, he will listen, and so he will prosper. Therefore I always talk to my children, so that we may live together kindly."[89]

Peace in the household and peace abroad are favorable conditions for the Pueblo way of life. In a raiding or fighting culture such as that of Plains tribes there is little or no place for the old, and women count comparatively little. Pueblos experienced a long period free from war, we may infer from their ancient smallhouse clusters which were scattered over a large area. During that period gerontocracy and the favorable status of women may have become established. Even when wars of self-defense became inevitable, no great prestige was enjoyed by the warrior and success depended upon the prayers of the old men who stayed home. Furthermore, heads or scalps were put in charge of old men or women and given communal functions. Booty was distributed. Inferably hunting rules not only about the behavior of stay-at-homes but about the distribution of game were applied to war campaigns or parties.

These are all general considerations on the Pueblo patterns of life as related to change, yet they are fundamental and at any point in the discussion they could be made specific. What of the mental habits we enumerated as conspicuous among Pueblos at the outset of this study—how do these bear upon change? Certain fears—fear of ridicule, fear of what seems dangerous because unconventional or unfamiliar (although this is more fear of what clashes with the familiar than fear of the unfamiliar per se)—are obviously strongly conservative factors, and they are felt frequently in Pueblo society, certainly as frequently as in our own society. The Pueblo sense of burlesque, perhaps like humor anywhere, is another support to conventional or prescriptive conduct, and to home manners against foreign. However, burlesque draws attention to the foreign or unconventional and may loosen up opinion on the possibility of variation; Pueblo clowns are indeed dangerous and in more ways than one; enforcers of standards, yet they are potentially destroyers, quasi-individualists, quasi-witches.

Reliance on omen or dream, on familiar orientation or on favored numerals, on resemblance for interpreting causality gives a manifold and vital sense of assurance more necessary to individual or social welfare perhaps than rationality, but of course such reliance does not aid rationality. Preconceptions of number, color, or form, and all ideas of sympathetic magic or reasoning from analogy hinder direct or full observation, narrow selectiveness, and, like so many of our own captions, obstruct increase of knowledge and the kind of reasoning which is favorable to new rational adaptations.

Reasoning or thinking by analogy clutters up the mind and precludes fruitful observations,* yet it may lead to new conceptual relationships and is very favorable to the growth of ritual, giving warrant both for established rites which may not need it and for ritual innovations which do need it. For example, any running rite, say wrangling, might be easily introduced into any pueblo as an expression of mimetic magic. It is largely because of the vitality of all kinds of sympathetic magic that Pueblo ritualism has been vigorous, adaptive, or receptive to innovations.

Pueblos are ingenious in acculturation indeed largely because they think so freely by analogy and are adept in applying all the mental procedure of sympathetic magic to something novel. The best illustration I know is in the adoption of the metal knife, so plainly superior to the stone knife that it is tempting to use it even for ritual work. Yet how can an outlandish implement be used when the Arrowpoint boys of the color-directions have to be asked in prayer to cut the wood for prayer-sticks (Acoma)? By making the first cut on the tree with the stone knife[90] and assuming that the power extends to the work of the metal knife; contagious magic, if not a case of much from little! Similarly, Hopi will use an American knife for cutting prayer-sticks, but the stick must be rubbed over or the point sharpened with a stone.[91]

Thinking by analogy is also an aid to rationalizing and reinter-

---

* Let me cite a recent instance at Taos, along the line of giving a dog a bad name. In 1899 an American student paid a long visit to the Mirabal family and then wrote a book about the town which revealed no ceremonial secrets; the Mirabals had guarded them scrupulously. But, ever since, the family has been charged with giving information, and the charge has just been revived in connection with "Taos Pueblo," although any scrutiny of that publication would show that the Mirabal family were innocent.

preting existing habits or ritual. Pueblos are ever expert in the conservative technique of rationalization, easily finding new reasons for their established ways or customs, or adjusting fresh motivation, a novel purpose, to "explain" ceremonial. In last resort any complex ceremonial is rendered intelligible by saying it is for rain. Catholic ritual depends on the habit of mind which accepts authority; Pueblo ritual is not without this support ("our fathers told us"; "it came up with us," *asi es costumbre*), but it depends far more on the deep-rooted Pueblo trait of feeling and thinking by analogy, perhaps a more compulsive conditioning than any secured through doctrines of infallibility.

Pueblo ritual or ceremonial has developed very largely, we have noted, through the spread or flowering of the same pattern. This involuting process seems to be related to a sense of order or gratification derived from familiar, orderly design. Change will proceed along orderly, involutional lines and whatever is disorderly, immoderate, or unamenable will be disregarded. Thus style develops in the arts, and harmony in religion or life.

Because the friars did nothing to deprive the Pueblos of all these attitudes or philosophic approaches, they not only did not undermine Pueblo religion but they enriched it with fresh content, and the attitudes they imparted converged with Pueblo attitudes requiring acceptance of authority and faith, faith in ritual, faith in priest or shaman. Only by impairing this faith or the ingrained mental habits of the Pueblos, let us say by American tradition or schooling, will Pueblo religion be gravely imperiled. A good deal of American education may be received, of course, without much risk, since in it authority, faith, and the will of God still prevail; God's will is not a disruptive substitute for the mythical fiat of Iyatiku or War God Brothers.

In conclusion, I would like to show a few snapshots on self-determination in pattern, a very speculative field of analysis, although in general it will not be disputed that a pattern or norm "determines and restricts subsequent thought and conduct";[92] that ritualism precludes mysticism; that one kind of religious concept, say metamorphosis, precludes, say possession; that one pattern or principle of social or ceremonial organization encourages or discourages another pattern or principle; or that one type lends itself to change or to stability more than does another type. Matrilocal residence probably makes for linguistic stability. Functioning by group promises more permanency than functioning by individual. Clanship is a more unstable organizing principle than moiety or than shamanistic society, a clan being directly dependent on birth and death. Ceremonial groups that are dependent on clanship will die out more readily than those recruited through, let us say, sickness. In 1932 I found the crier chief of Zuni's Kachina society worrying because in his lineage of the Badger clan there was none to qualify as his successor. We know that Walpi lost a society, Drab Flute, because the clan or lineage in charge became extinct. To be sure, clanship is most highly developed among Hopi, and theirs is the most intact of Pueblo cultures, but we may suppose that other factors, primarily isolation, are responsible for this conservation. I surmise that, once isolation is lost, cultural disintegration among Hopi will be comparatively rapid. The lapsing of societies through contacts with Protestants and through conversions is a flamboyant example.

If the kiva is, as among Hopi, primarily a clan house, then according to clan needs the kiva will bud, so to speak, like the house cluster; when the clan overflows or in part migrates, a new kiva will be built.* On the other hand, if the kiva is associated with a ceremonial moiety system as among eastern Keres, Tewa, and in a measure at Taos, or with an organized Kachina cult as at Zuni and Acoma, the number of communal houses, given no ex-

---

* The case of the Mustard clan kivas in Walpi and Sichomovi is illustrative. The maternal family house adjacent to Wikwalobi, the Mustard clan kiva of Walpi, is nowadays deserted, the family died out or moved away, all but one old man who remained chief of kiva. Most of the Mustard clanspeople live today in Sichomovi, and in that suburb one of the two kivas, Oak Mound kiva, is theirs.

Dissension may be a factor in abandoning kivas; but as Pueblos are trained against washing dirty linen in public the record of any abandoned kiva or new kiva such as the recently abandoned third kiva of San Ildefonso or the recently built kiva at Mishongnovi (Beaglehole 3:13-14) remains obscure.

traneous factors such as borrowing, will remain comparatively stable.*

We have discussed quite fully the role of loans in change but; a word more on the type of loan, on what is intrinsically borrowable. Material objects are ever easily borrowed in comparison with large psychological complexes or entire religious systems; complementarily, it may happen that religious traits cannot be borrowed when they are closely associated with manual arts involving whole techniques. Mask, prayer-stick-making, and ceremonial array in the modern Kachina cult require techniques that preclude the spread of the cult to those like Tiwa who lack the techniques. On the other hand, kachina ideology and lore can spread, even across language barriers, given one bilinguist or some common foreign language, Navaho, Spanish, English. Of course, cult tales spreading without cult are shorn of much of their meaning, although their pattern persists, to travel around the world infertilely, undynamically, "just a story."

What is the effect of the cult tale or origin myth upon cultural dynamics? Among Pueblos, as elsewhere in Indian circles, the mythical fiat of the origin myth is a co-ordinating or unifying factor for heterogeneous ceremonies or customs,[93] old or new, an excellent acculturative technique. Whatever *can* be fitted into a creation scheme acquires authenticity and some assurance of perpetuity. Where would Tennessee be without the Book of Genesis, or the Pueblos without their Emergence tradition, without feeling certain, all of them, that they were the children of Eve or Iyatiku? Loose-ended and a little bewildered, I think, even if, in accordance with Pueblo prophecy about the consequences of disbelief, the stars do not fall or an earthquake kill everybody in the world or the sun burn it up.

But the authenticity given by Pueblo Emergence myth is valid only to a certain point; once a custom has lapsed, the tradi-

* At Nambé there is only one kiva, due, presumably, to disintegration. At Cochiti in 1922 the people of Squash kiva were engaged in building for themselves a second house or kiva, larger than their old kiva, to accommodate dances (Goldfrank 3:30). There is or was a third kiva in San Ildefonso, built perhaps in imitation of Cochiti.

tion about it also tends to lapse or to be modified. Just as scalp-taking and other war practices have gone out of Pueblo life, so scalp myth and mention in myth of organization for war tend to disappear. Pueblo mythology, like most mythology, is etiological or a posteriori to custom or ritual. There is a certain amount of lag, but the tradition is kept up to date.* Modernisms are introduced, such as the saint's-day dance (Acoma) or emphasis on interpueblo trade (Santo Domingo), and rarely does anybody, like David of Zuni, notice anachronisms. (David refused once to translate references to domestic animals in Kachina town, insisting that, as they were brought in by Spaniards, they could not figure in a pre-Spanish town.) On the whole, Pueblo ceremonial or ritual, compared at least with Navaho, is independent of myth support. Let everybody forget the myth of the lost Corn Maidens, and the Molawia ceremony would go on just the same, just as in Christendom the rites of baptism and confession will go on after the dogmas of Limbo and the Fall have ceased to circulate. Ceremonial or ritual outlasts ideology or theology. It is not surprising that highly ritualized religions like Pueblo religion and Catholicism have lasted a long time.

Possession of ceremonial paraphernalia which exact careful guardianship, being potent for good or ill, is a factor for conservatism. Ritual wealth, like other forms of wealth, renders a person conservative or sets him up a conservative standard. Pueblo chiefs or "valuable" families are expected not to abandon their town, not even to visit away; like Pope or many another spiritual potentate, they must remain put, in place and in ways of life. Nor can a Pueblo who marries out like Windsor qualify as a good chief or impersonator of a god. Because "dances" or celebrations borrowed by Pueblos have no ceremonial paraphernalia is one reason why they do not as a rule last long.

Any group property is a stabilizing influence, binding together the proprietary unit and leading to all kinds of communal practices or customs. The Zuni way of placing a man by saying

---

* Variation may be hypothecated here: the Emergence myth that must account for the whole ceremonial system (Acoma and Eastern Pueblo) should be more changeable than the less explanatory Western type.

that he *came out of such and such a house*, and Zuni and Hopi lineage or clan ownership of houses, lands, springs, or fetishes are illustrations. Indeed property, more particularly houses and ritual property, seems to be the source of Hopi or Pueblo clanship, the means by which the fiction of kinship is maintained after connection by blood is lost track of. If individual male ownership emerges from current practices in clearing wasteland or building houses off the mesa,* the clan will break down, and, as suggested above, a good deal of Hopi ceremonial will lapse.

No permanent property means no trustees and therefore none to fill managerial or dance positions permanently; temporary appointments are necessary. This is a pattern of organization which obviously does not promote stability. Again and again you hear that it is hard to get people to dance, particularly the women. This is a very familiar plaint at Zuni in connection with war and harvest dances which are being celebrated infrequently, if they have not lapsed altogether. Long intervals between celebrations are in themselves disintegrating, since those who "know how" die without passing on particularized modes or methods.

From this point of view esotericism may be a peril to stability. Undoubtedly many ceremonies or rituals have lapsed from Pueblo culture because those who knew them were excessively secretive, unwilling to share their "power" or "protection." For years there has been only an acting Town chief at Isleta because there is no one left who knows how to instal a Town chief. No Wüwüchim initiation was held on First Mesa for at least eleven years, perhaps much longer, because Hani, Singers' chief, was too feeble to function, and Hani died without apprenticing his nephews. The initiation held in 1927 after Hani's death must have suffered some impairment. I don't know why Hani did not teach his nephews nor just why at Oraibi successors in two or three chieftaincies were not appointed, but the growing feeling of the elders that young men and women are too irresponsible or indifferent to intrust with esoteric knowledge or with the

---

* As yet new fields or houses may belong to their male cultivator or builder, but at his death they go theoretically to his maternal group, not to his children (Beaglehole 3:16–17; compare Zuni, Cushing 6:131–33).

masks (lest they starve them) is bound to be in itself a source of disintegration.

On the other hand, in other circumstances esotericism precludes critical comparison, conflict, or skepticism—all factors of instability. Probably no Zuni has ever been bothered because Bear of the Color-Directions lives in the west and Bear of Shipapolima lives in the east. Bear of the West figures in one type of ritual or tale, Bear of the East in another type, and comparisons are not necessary. Similarly, different destinations for the dead do not disturb the Pueblo mind. To be sure, even without esotericism, contradictions, factual or theoretical, would probably not be any more disturbing to the Pueblos than to many other peoples.

Also esotericism adds to the prestige of any group and so promotes membership. Secrets are a form of property, if they are nothing more than secrets from children or women, as kachina impersonation is or was secret. Persons who "know something" are persons of property in Pueblo opinion, and highly respectable. Many things of common knowledge, familiar flora, fauna, or minerals, if used in proprietary secret ways take on new desirable values. Common knowledge can change without loss, but esoteric knowledge must be conserved unchanged or risk a loss. We are back again in the maze of explanations about Pueblo secretiveness.

Belief that exactness in ceremonial performance is essential to efficacy is another highly conservative factor, particularly when remissness must be remedied by repetition. If the fire goes out during the twenty-day Hopi confinement, that day is not counted, that is, the day has to be repeated; similarly, if the Fire chief of the Lakon society lets her fire go out, the retreat has to be started afresh. I recall that once during the period of the winter solstice ceremony at Zuni when no light may be made outdoors, a little boy scratched a match; he had rendered his prayers worthless, and he had to replant his prayer-sticks.

Not only inefficacy but danger may result from ritualistic inexactness or ignorance; supernatural power may destroy one who does not know how to use it. This belief, which is strong among Pueblos, as among Navaho and other peoples, contributes inferably to the desire for ceremonial organization, for enduring, dependable groups, but, as already suggested, it also promotes the lapse of a ceremony or the permanent removal of fetishes once the trustee group decays. Scalps and images are put away in caves or "in the hills"; *e'towe* are left untouchable in sealed recesses or rooms; old masks are made over, which may be one reason, by the way, why masks are never found in caches or ruins.

Masking has been a very serviceable pattern for introducing or giving value to new ceremonies or dances. Itself "valuable," the mask bestows value. In the West, Eagle and Buffalo impersonations were given masks and so became more easily established. Through the mask, Navaho, Apache, Comanche, or Sioux dances or rather traits of personal appearance and behavior have all been utilized. Will the Plains dances performed without mask at Taos and by Tewa be more fugitive, or just because they are quite secular will they hold their own in towns where dancing for tourists is coming in? The use of the Plains war bonnet in these dances is a good illustration, by the way, of how secularized paraphernalia or dance modes may have a far wider spread than the ritual complex they started from.*

The hospitality of the mask cult is a factor in rendering it mobile or variable, in any one town or from town to town. Whatever is borrowed and known to be borrowed is readily altered. Moreover, when newly introduced kachina become prominent, old kachina may lapse in popularity or even disappear. The kachina come and go in popularity something like folk tales. Both tales and kachina are a changing, living lore, the kachina being often illustrative of the tales. Again kachina may lapse in one town but not in another, as in the case of the Zuni-Hopi Natashka, those house-to-house beggars who are none too gentle in representing the early monsters. On First Mesa these bogey kachina are still going strong at Powamu, but they no longer

---

* The rain or wind rhombus which becomes a toy among certain tribes (Spier 2:290–91) is another striking illustration. (It may be used as a toy even at Zuni.)

appear at Zuni,[94] where they were never as well integrated into ceremonial. On the whole, however, the kachina dance cult has been everywhere in the ascendant,* since the turn of the century, if not before. Kachina designs are used in modern textiles and pottery.

Among many peoples buying a ritual or ceremonial is an effectual way of introducing something new and establishing it. Purchase gives value. This point of view is not at all unfamiliar to the Pueblos. Throwing away prayers, as Christians or rather Protestants do, belittles or devalues them. The Catholic practices of praying in words that cannot be learned or charging for sacraments or exacting tithes express an attitude closer to the Pueblo attitude and more intelligible. It was probably a factor in establishing the Church among Pueblos. But high costs may be also a factor of disintegration, as has frequently been the case in Catholicism among Spanish Indians or probably among tribes whose shamans have been greedy for themselves or for their family. The tendency among Navaho "singers" to keep a lucrative profession within their kinship circle may account in part for the loss of much detailed knowledge of ceremonials.[95] From these points of view Pueblo ceremonial should be comparatively stable, ritual knowledge is property but fees are low, and knowledge is shared by a group not based entirely on kinship.

Memory, length or shortness of memory, we noted as a factor in acculturation. As long as the foreign provenience of a borrowed element is remembered, acculturation is incomplete. When a Pueblo says, "It came up with us," he acknowledges the observance as his very own, something that may not be changed or relinquished; when he recalls foreign derivation, he holds the observance to be less sacrosanct or effective and may overlook or slight it. Recently borrowed kachina, like Hatashuku at Zuni or the Gowawaima class of kachina at Santo Domingo, are quasi-secular, not "valuable." At the Home-going ceremony of 1893 some of the younger men of First Mesa proposed to present Zuni Hümis, but the kiva chiefs objected, saying that at such a

* Compare fashion in ceremonies among Navaho (Matt. 4:3).

critical droughty time they should hold to their own Hopi kachina.[96] One year at Zuni in the winter-dance series He'iwa kiva presented Hilili kachina, a modern dance, instead of the customary old Good Kachina; someone had a "bad dream," and the group had to dance again.[97] Possibly the home-Chakwena or the home-Mixed kachina of Zuni (similarly the home Women's society of Jemez or the home or Town Fathers of Isleta) were planned deliberately in order to meet just such opposition. No greater degree of ability in producing "social fiction" was necessary than that shown in explaining how "short-hair" Laguna Chakwena was preceded by the home-Chakwena: Zuni Chakwena went to Laguna to dance; there they learned Laguna songs and dance posture and steps which they brought back to Zuni, deciding at Zuni to cut their hair to distinguish themselves from the stay-at-home Chakwena; thus there came to be two Chakwena groups at Zuni, home-Chakwena and short-hair Chakwena.[98]

Opposition to the new kachina dance of Hilili began, we recall, about 1890. In 1917 an old man told me that Hilili had always been a Zuni dance, and there was nothing like it anywhere else. Another old man began with these statements but finally admitted that a Zuni had seen it danced at Acoma, with women and without mask (the eastern Eagle dance) and had introduced it to Zuni as a group kachina dance; the solo figure, he insisted, had always been at Zuni in the Mixed kachina dance. Obviously, like other Americans, Pueblos set great store on what is homemade and already established. The foreign or novel, being without prestige, must pass as merely a modification of something already known and used, as it often is. Better still if the foreign source can be forgotten altogether!*

The foreign source of a kachina dance is very largely remembered through its foreign song words, and this indication of borrowing holds for other celebrations or activities, as, for example,

---

* Less easily accomplished in a literate community. From this point of view the kind of education which imparts historical memory supports opposition to the new and makes for conservatism. Battles over what is or is not 100 per cent American are far from trivial.

the musical grinding-parties of Acoma. Formerly there were three corn-grinding groups, the women who used Zuni songs, the women who used Laguna songs (introduced by a Laguna woman married into Acoma), and the women who sang the Kashale songs that "were always at Acoma." With the differences in songs went different practices: the women of the Laguna group sang their own songs; in the other groups men were invited to play the flute or beat the bundle, and were paid with two meals.[99] In this case as in many others distinction in language preserves distinction in custom.

In course of time foreign words are put down as obsolete or as sacerdotal language or even as bird-taught, a token that the song or ritual or impersonation is fully acculturated. This has happened in some of the major Hopi ceremonies, notably Snake-Antelope and Marau. The Keresan reference to clown, *payatya-mu* (literally youth, i.e., Sun Youth, i.e., Koshare), is rendered *payakyamu* and described as an *underworld* term,[100] a complete alibi against foreign derivation. Even before this happens, an ingenious acculturationist may have said that the song was native, only it was the kind of song to which foreign words may be sung.

Group conceit or sense of superiority contributes to a short memory about foreign derivation, and we have noticed that Pueblos are not lacking in conceit. Foreign accretions are forgotten as soon as may be. It may be tactless to mention them. When Mrs. Stevenson learned during a Zuni Shuma'kwe ceremony that their songs were in Pima, the society chiefs were much annoyed.[101] In Taos it is well known by some people that Matachina is a Spanish dance, but I have heard others, equally well informed, disconcerted by that idea and insist with pride upon an Indian origin. Did not Montezuma visit Taos and teach his dance?

This picture of Montezuma visiting Taos and endowing it with his ceremony would be a very proper conclusion for the Taos origin myth, whatever that is. When Badger clan control in the Kachina cult was introduced into Laguna by a Badger family from Zuni only a few generations ago, the kachina origin myth was embroidered with an episode about Badger Old Woman helping to recover the imprisoned kachina. The saint's-day dance has been put into the Acoma origin myth without any mention of the saint or the slightest hint of foreign derivation: Iyatiku wanted the people to have a good time, with everybody taking part in a free, public show,* so she engaged Kashale as impresario and called it a thanksgiving dance. Enough to make Fray Juan Ramirez turn in his grave! Apostate Acoma!

* An excellent illustration, by way, for Lowie's contention that amusement per se figures in ceremonial calendars.

BIBLIOGRAPHICAL NOTES

PREFACE

1. See Kroeber 3:392.
2. Kidder 3:148; Roberts 3:31.
3. Cf. Benedict 1, and Aitken, 372–87.
4. Kroeber 1:276.
5. Parsons 39.

INTRODUCTION

1. Voth 7:49. See pp. 294–95.
2. Bunzel 1:94, Pl. XXII, 10, 11.
3. Beaglehole 2:19.
4. Voth 2:152 (n. 6). Also a sand hill near Walpi is so called (Stephen 4:1153).
5. Voth 2:119.
6. Parsons 42:147; cf. Dumarest, 147.
7. Parsons 6:290.
8. See Parsons 6:202.
9. For house census by sex, Laguna, Parsons, 33:248–49; Cochiti, Goldfrank 3:28–29; Jemez, Parsons 41:47; Tewa, Parsons 49:38–40; Tewa and Comparative, Parsons 38:338–39; Isleta, Parsons 52:234; Taos, Parsons 58:51.
10. See Parsons 38:338–39.
11. Zuni, Kroeber 2:103; Laguna, Parsons 33:250–53; Hopi, Stephen 4:1082; Forde 3:367.
12. See Parsons 52:356.
13. Parsons 40:38–40.
14. See Parsons 41:9–10.
15. Parsons 49:31–32.
16. White 4:29.
17. Bunzel 1:57, 59.
18. Cf. Parsons 52:412.
19. Hopi, Voth 2:76, 122; Zuni, Parsons 6:197; Laguna, Parsons 33:257; Jemez, Parsons 41:12, 138–39, and compare Sia, Stevenson 1:67.
20. Parsons 33:257.
21. *Ibid.*
22. Parsons 49:246–47.
23. Parsons 35:155.
24. White 5.
25. Cf. Pima, Papago, and Maricopa, Spier 3:230; Underhill 4.
26. Parsons 23:214.
27. White 7.
28. Twitchell I, 441–42; Gunn, 99–100.
29. Twitchell I, 422, 437.
30. Kidder 1:14.
31. *Ibid.*
32. See, too, Parsons 45:111–12; cf. Espinosa, A. M., 130.
33. Espinosa, A. M., 75–77.
34. Parsons 42:175–77.
35. For building ways at Zuni see Kroeber 2:194–96.
36. Kidder 1:126–27, 129; Roberts 2:10.
37. Cushing 7:168.
38. Parsons 20:108–12; Parsons 47:602.
39. Cushing, Fewkes, Parsons, 286, 291; Titiev 3; Kennard.
40. Curtis, 10; Stephen 4:1022, 1046; Beaglehole 3:70–71.
41. Hargrave, 22; 1291–99.
42. See Parsons 20:103 for a Zuni-Laguna case.
43. See Stephen 4:261 (n. 1), 944, 1085.
44. Parsons 43; Parsons 41:130–35; Parsons 47.
45. Parsons 23:209–11.
46. Dorsey and Voth 1:9.
47. Robbins, Harrington, Freire-Marreco, 108.

48. Forde 3:371; Stephen 4:XXI–XXXII.
49. Cochiti, Goldfrank, 3:29, 30; Acoma, Parsons 14:173; White 2:34.
50. Voth 2:132 (n. 3).
51. Stephen 4:135–36, 1195–97; Beaglehole 3:63 ff.; Robbins, Harrington, Freire-Marreco, 88 ff. For Zuni, Cushing 6:298 ff., 336 ff., Stevenson 2:361.
52. Robbins, Harrington, Freire-Marreco, 93.
53. Parsons 40:22.
54. Stephen 4:354.
55. Stephen 4:1035–36; Parsons 42:49; Bunzel 6:31; White 6.
56. Stevenson 3:65.
57. Robbins, Harrington, Freire-Marreco, 76.
58. Parsons 15:333.
59. Stephen 4:275, 397.
60. White 2:59.
61. Benedict 1:574–75.
62. Bunzel 6:45.
63. Beaglehole 3:29.
64. Robbins, Harrington, Freire-Marreco, 59.
65. Parsons 40:33.
66. White 7.
67. Parsons 28:90; Parsons 40:25–26 and n. 43; Beaglehole 3:80–81.
68. Parsons 42:223.
69. Bunzel 5:1043.
70. Cf. Cushing 6:518 ff.
71. Cushing 6:581–82; Beaglehole 3:27.
72. Parsons 42:122.
73. Parsons 6:270 (n. 2).
74. Parsons 42:19; cf. Cushing 6:443–44.
75. Parsons 49:17 ff.; Parsons 41:34 ff.
76. Lummis 2:218.
77. Parsons 53:48.
78. Cushing 6:591–92.
79. Beaglehole 2:21.
80. Spier 2:378.
81. Kidder 1:14.

82. Parsons 52:453.
83. Bunzel 4:669; also Bunzel 6:44.
84. Bunzel 4:669.
85. Franciscan Fathers, 460–61.
86. Parsons 20:122 (n. 4).
87. Saville, 27, 28.
88. Hodge 3:13–15.
89. Stephen 4:396, 633, 996; Beaglehole 3:84–85.
90. Spier 2:244–46.
91. Beaglehole 3:83, 85.
92. Beaglehole 3:82–83.
93. Benedict 3:II, 207–8.
94. Bunzel 6:83.
95. Robbins, Harrington, Freire-Marreco, 109; Bourke 1:529.
96. Stephen 4:1015.
97. Bunzel 5:859.
98. Compare Robbins, Harrington, Freire-Marreco, 93; Curtis, 22.
99. Robbins, Harrington, Freire-Marreco, 87.
100. Goldfrank 3:83.
101. Beaglehole 3:82.
102. Parsons 40:18.
103. For Hopi compare Stephen 4:284; Beaglehole 3:58.
104. Robbins, Harrington, Freire-Marreco, 83; Benedict 3:I, 14; Parsons 33:273; Parsons 58:18.
105. Robbins, Harrington, Freire-Marreco, 86.
106. Bunzel 6:1; see p. 193.
107. Robbins, Harrington, Freire-Marreco, 86.
108. Parsons 42:173.
109. Stephen 2:3–4.
110. Titiev 3.
111. Ibid.; Beaglehole 1:62–63.
112. Cushing (MS).
113. Voth 5:76, 95, 133; Parsons 42:243–45; Zuni, Benedict 3:I, 26, 84; II, 154.
114. Parsons 24; Parsons 40:32–35; Voth 9:147–49; Voth 1.
115. Dumarest, 147–50; Parsons 25:166–68; Parsons 49:34–35.
116. White 6.
117. Eggan.

118. Titiev 3.
119. *Ibid.*; Beaglehole 1:47.
120. Bunzel 6:96.
121. Parsons 52:236.
122. Jemez, Parsons 41:29.
123. Hopi, Voth 7:52; Taos, Parsons 58:39; Isleta, Parsons 52:213; Cochiti, Goldfrank 3:79.
124. Jemez, Parsons 41:48; Tewa, Parsons 49:30.
125. Parsons 55:51, 91; Bunzel 2:487. See pp. 497, 600.
126. Voth 7:54, 59.
127. White 7.
128. Stirling.
129. Goldfrank 3:77; Parsons 33:191; Parsons 49:17.
130. Parsons 16, 17, 22, 37; Goldfrank 3:80–82.
131. Goldfrank 3:81.
132. Titiev 3; Beaglehole 3:20.
133. Eggan.
134. Beaglehole 3:7.
135. Beaglehole 3:74.
136. Cushing 6:570, 572.
137. Harper.
138. Titiev 3.
139. Beaglehole 3:51.
140. Stephen 4:152–53.
141. Stephen 4:126, 147 (n. 2), 152; Parsons 34:21.
142. Stephen 4:364, 452, 504, 589, 937.
143. Stephen 4:363, 387.
144. Cushing 6:604–6.
145. Bunzel 5:941.
146. Spinden, 82.
147. Bunzel 6:68–69.
148. Parsons 2:343–46.
149. Laguna, Parsons 33:264; Hopi, Parsons 22:103.
150. Bunzel 6:85–88.
151. Stephen 4:243, 254.
152. White 6.
153. Harper.
154. Parsons 2:338, 339.
155. Benedict 3:I, 11 (n. 1). See pp. 185 n. †, 214, 226.
156. Bunzel 6:79.
157. White 7.
158. Parsons 33:272.
159. Stephen 4:143, 144, 146.
160. Parsons 52:407–10.
161. Bunzel 6:78.
162. Goldfrank 3:81, 82.
163. Hodge 3:84; Parsons 62:89 (n. 60).
164. Parsons 52:219.
165. Nequatewa, 58.
166. Voth 5:265.
167. Parsons 55:26; Stephen 4:22.
168. Parsons 54.
169. Eggan.
170. Beaglehole 3:72–73.
171. Oraibi, Titiev 3; Mishongnovi, Beaglehole 3:79.
172. Beaglehole 3:73–74.
173. Oraibi, Titiev 3.
174. Beaglehole 3:73.
175. White 7.
176. Forde 1, citing Freire-Marreco, 397.
177. Cf. Beaglehole 3:79.
178. Parsons 42:188.
179. Parsons 42:191–92.
180. Parsons 6:271 (n. 1).
181. Parsons 60:230–31; Stephen 4: 1067 ff.
182. Parsons 49:93 (n. 189), 279.
183. Eggan.
184. Parsons 52:310–11; cf. Bunzel 2:492; Aitken, 382.
185. Parsons 52:312.
186. Parsons 45:111, 126.
187. Parsons 42:29 ff.
188. See Stephen 4:276.
189. Bunzel 6:51.
190. Bunzel 6:44–52.
191. Parsons 63:472.
192. Bunzel 6:52.
193. Bunzel 2:480; compare Papago (Underhill 3).
194. Dumarest, 162.
195. Bunzel 2:482; compare the assurance given in myth, p. 220.
196. Bunzel 4:634.
197. Parsons 21:67 (n. 1).
198. Voth 9:101; Parsons 1:254.

199. Parsons 1:254; Parsons 52:250 (n. 45).
200. Parsons 49:65, 68; cf. Dumarest, 170.
201. Stephen 4:60, 824–25, 827; cf. Voth 9:101; Voth 5:115.
202. Stephen 4:829; Stevenson 2:316; Bunzel 2:483.
203. Parsons 1:251; Bunzel 6:218.
204. Stephen 4:151.
205. Voth 9:102.
206. Benedict 3:II, 133.
207. Bunzel 2:483.
208. Voth 9:103.
209. Stephen 4:487; Beaglehole 3:46.
210. White 5.
211. Parsons 1:251.
212. Stephen 4:824, 825, 828.
213. Parsons 1:251, 254.
214. White 7; Stirling; for Laguna, Parsons 33:217–18.
215. White 2:137, 138.
216. Dumarest, 166–70; Goldfrank 3:65, 66.
217. Dumarest, 166 (n. 5).
218. Parsons 41:50, Fig. 4; see, too, Dumarest, 169 (n. 1).
219. Parsons 52:249–50.
220. Parsons 49:63–66.
221. Voth 9:101.
222. Beaglehole 1:12.
223. Voth 2:103 n.; cf. Boas 2:65.
224. Bunzel 2:480.
225. Boas 1:200.
226. Cushing 6:412.
227. Parsons 40:17–18, 22–24.
228. Titiev 3; Benedict 3:I, 49; Stevenson 2:360; Beaglehole 3:55; Parsons 33:226; White 2:139.
229. Parsons 52:336.
230. See p. 54.
231. Parsons 6:307–12.
232. Benedict 3:II, 84–85.
233. Parsons 52:455–56.
234. Bunzel 5:932–33.
235. Parsons 42:39–43.
236. Goldfrank 3:68.
237. Parsons 40:29 (n. 44).
238. Cushing 5:32–33.

239. Parsons 11:254.
240. Parsons 42:39–43.
241. Goldfrank 3:85; Laguna in Isleta, Parsons 52:338; Hopi, Beaglehole 2:5–6.
242. Beaglehole 2:10.
243. Parsons 52:373–74.
244. Parsons 52:369.
245. Beaglehole 3:29, 60.
246. Beaglehole 3:61 (n. 4); Parsons 12:38.
247. Stevenson 1:134 (n. 1).
248. Parsons 42:18–19.
249. Parsons 40:102.
250. Voth 7:49.
251. Voth 4:8; cf. for First Mesa, Parsons 40:103, 107.
252. Stephen 4:744, also 437 (n. 1), 779–80, 811–12.
253. Bunzel 6:55.
254. Beaglehole 2:6.
255. Goldfrank 3:88; cf. Parsons 52:338.
256. Voth 3:293.
257. Parsons 14:180.
258. Benedict 2:115.
259. Parsons 52:452.
260. Dumarest, 166.
261. Beaglehole 3:34.
262. Nequatewa, 53.
263. Bunzel 6:102.
264. Parsons 52:247.
265. Parsons 58:68.
266. Goldfrank 3:85.
267. Stephen 4:387.
268. Beaglehole 2:5; also 10.
269. Stephen 4:341 (n. 1).
270. Cf. Dumarest, 166.
271. Cf. p. 793.
272. Robbins, Harrington, Freire-Marreco, 82.
273. Parsons 40:89, 93.
274. Parsons 40:48.
275. Goldfrank 3:68, 92–93.
276. Beaglehole 3:15.
277. Stephen 4:482.
278. Beaglehole 3:59.
279. Goldfrank 3:85; cf. Parsons 52:338.

280. Benedict 3:I, 90, 230; II, 205 (n. 1); Cushing 6:94.
281. Goldfrank 3:78, 79.
282. Fewkes 8:272.
283. Parsons 22:104 n.; Beaglehole 3:57.
284. Parsons 14:176.
285. Harper; cf. Parsons 41:29.
286. Voth 7:51.
287. Parsons 52:213.
288. Voth 7:48.
289. See p. 321.
290. Goldfrank 3:76.
291. Cf. Parsons 41:29.
292. White 2:134-35.
293. Stirling.
294. Parsons 40:75, 77.
295. Benedict 3:I, 28.
296. Stevenson 1:143; Parsons 42: 22 ff.
297. Dumarest, 168; Goldfrank 3:66.
298. Parsons 42:88.
299. Harper.
300. Voth 5:163.
301. Benedict 3:I, 14.
302. Stevenson 3:606 (n. a).
303. Cf. Parsons 6:229-30.
304. Cf. Parsons 20:114.
305. From an unpublished part of his Notes on Cochiti.
306. Harper.
307. Benedict 3:I, 44.
308. Benedict 3:I, 240 (n. 2).
309. Beaglehole 2:18.
310. Parsons 40:73.
311. Stirling.
312. Benedict 2:7.
313. Benedict 3:I, 136, 144-45, 160.
314. Sia, Stevenson 1:57.
315. Parsons 42:15.
316. Benedict 3:I, 6.
317. Cf. Boas 2:109.
318. Bunzel 2:502.
319. Stephen 4:90, 500.
320. Stephen 4:826, 828.
321. Voth 3:311 (n. 5).
322. Parsons 11:236-38.
323. Parsons 42:223.
324. Parsons 6:274-75.
325. Voth 2:105.
326. White 7.
327. See p. 249.
328. Parsons 42:175-76.
329. Fewkes 1:39 (n. 2).
330. Parsons 42:227 ff.
331. Benedict 3:I, 5, 182.
332. Dumarest, 185 (n. 3).
333. Lummis 2:235-36.
334. Stephen 4:279.
335. Bunzel 5:947.
336. Robbins, Harrington, Freire-Marreco, 29.
337. Parsons 40:102.
338. Bunzel 6:44.
339. Dorsey and Voth 2:236.
340. Parsons 36:23.
341. Nequatewa, 65.
342. Bunzel 2:480; Aitken 382.
343. Beaglehole 3:29.
344. Stephen 4:995, 1035-36; Beaglehole 3:51; for San Juan, see Parsons 42:49-50.
345. Parsons 40:54-55.
346. White 3:15.
347. Goldfrank 3:31.
348. Stephen 4:414. For Mishongnovi, Beaglehole 3:13, 30.
349. Benedict 3:II, 199.
350. Bunzel 5:1037.

CHAPTER I

1. For society censuses at Santo Domingo, Cochiti, Jemez, Isleta, and among Tewa see White 4: 58-59, 64 ff.; Goldfrank 3:115-17; Parsons 41:64 ff.; Parsons 52:260 ff.; Parsons 49:118 ff.; for Zuni and Hopi censuses see Kroeber 2:155-56; Parsons 15.
2. Cf. Benedict 3:II, 38-39.
3. Cf. Dorsey and Voth 1:40; Voth 2:109 n.
4. Benedict 3:II, 159 (n. 2).
5. Bunzel 5:1009.
6. See pp. 750-51.
7. White 3:39; White 5.
8. White 4:107, 111.
9. White 2:74, 86.

10. Parsons 49:204.
11. Parsons 42:192.
12. Benedict 3:II, 109.
13. Parsons 15:334; Parsons 55:16.
14. Parsons 36:19.
15. See pp. 612, 1101, n.*.
16. White 3:12 (n. 24).
17. White 3:12 (n. 23).
18. See p. 166.
19. Wallis 1:6.
20. Stephen 4:728.
21. Bunzel 5:1068.
22. Titiev 3.
23. *Ibid.*
24. See p. 309.
25. Bunzel 2:512; Bunzel 6:54.
26. Cushing 1:39, Pls. I–VIII; Stirling.
27. Cochiti, Goldfrank 3:85; Parsons 52:337, 338.
28. Stirling; White 5.
29. Boas 2:28–29, 71; White 4:37; Dumarest, 197.
30. Parsons 49:133, 137.
31. See Parsons 30:184. See pp. 561, 609 ff., 1101, n.*.
32. Stephen 4:138.
33. Tewa, Parsons 49:123–29; Keres, White 2:111–12, White 3:18, White 4:131–32, White 5; Goldfrank 3:52–53; Zuni, Kroeber 2:157; Hopi, Stephen 4:158, 360, 364 (trespass not indicated); Parsons 55:10.
34. Ne'wekwe, Zuni, Stevenson 2:34–35; Singers, Wüwüchim, Hopi, Parsons 30:185–87.
35. Parsons and Beals.
36. Laguna, Parsons 20:123–24, 125; Cochiti, Goldfrank 3:365; Dumarest, 191; Taos, Parsons 58:75.
37. Goldfrank 3:45–46.
38. Bunzel 2:513.
39. White 4:54, 61; White 3:18; Goldfrank 3:43; White 1:606–8.
40. Parsons 41:69.
41. Parsons 41:64; Parsons 49:118 ff., 205–7.
42. Bunzel 6:36.

43. Stevenson 2:387.
44. For the Zuni prayer said at this time see Bunzel 4:792–95.
45. Bunzel 4:791–92; also Benedict 3:I, 188–89.
46. White 1:608; Stevenson 2:415.
47. White 1:614.
48. White 1:615.
49. Dumarest, 208; White 1:609–10; and pp. 711–12, 713, 728–29.
50. Parsons 45:106–7, 125; Parsons 52:242, 243, 430–31; Dumarest, 163.
51. Stevenson 2:65.
52. Bunzel 5:886.
53. Bunzel 2:522–23, 879 ff.; Bunzel 5:934.
54. Dumarest, 177.
55. Stephen 3:372–73.
56. White 8.
57. Bunzel 2:518–19; Bunzel 5:876–77.
58. White 2:71; White 7.
59. Goldfrank 3:10, 26.
60. White 3:14.
61. Zuni, Kroeber 2:197. Cf. Cochiti, Goldfrank 3:30; Jemez, Parsons 41:14; Tewa, Parsons 49: lists of households.
62. Fewkes 15.
63. Parsons 40:26.
64. Stirling.
65. Parsons 6:267 (n. 1).
66. Parsons 6:272. See pp. 597–98.
67. Stirling.
68. Cushing 6:133–52.
69. For details about the secular officers see Zuni, Parsons 6:264 ff.; Acoma, White 2:52–55, 60; San Felipe, White 3:19–21; Cochiti, Goldfrank 3:24–27; Dumarest, 200–202; Sia, Stevenson 1:16–19; Santo Domingo, White 4:38 ff.; Tewa, Parsons 49:102–7; Taos, Parsons 35:71ff; Isleta, Parsons 52:250 ff.
70. See pp. 412–13.
71. Bunzel 6:18.
72. Parsons 40:116.

73. Parsons 40:101.
74. Bunzel 6:55.
75. Voth 3:273.
76. Stephen 4:744.
77. Parsons 45:107–8, 110.
78. Parsons 56:51; compare Stevenson 2:393 for the impeachment of a Pekwin.
79. Stephen 4:59–60, 139, 203, 951, 952, 1020.
80. Parsons 52:365.
81. Parsons 31:488. See pp. 893, 904.
82. Stephen 4:950.
83. Bunzel 6:35.
84. White 2:42, 46; White 7; Parsons 14:173.
85. White 7; Goldfrank 3:40; White 3:14; White 4:35.
86. Goldfrank 3:94, Cushing 6:123.
87. Forde 3:376.
88. Beaglehole 3:38.
89. Parsons 40:112–13, 115.
90. Bunzel 6:70.
91. Beaglehole 3:28.
92. Parsons 40:111; Beaglehole 3:47–48.
93. Stephen 4:998, 1001.
94. Goldfrank 3:9.
95. Parsons 42:168.
96. Bunzel 2:503.
97. Parsons 53:47.
98. Kroeber 2:153 ff.
99. Parsons 55:22.
100. Voth 8:58.
101. Parsons 55:21.
102. Parsons 55:22.
103. Parsons 55:38; Parsons 33:212–13.
104. Beaglehole 3:13, 14; Stephen 4:XLIII.
105. Parsons 40:69.
106. Goldfrank 3:40.
107. Stirling.
108. Goldfrank 3:65.
109. Parsons 33:217.
110. Parsons 20:129.
111. Voth 9:102.
112. Voth 8:31; Stephen 4:709.
113. Bunzel 6:23.
114. Parsons 49:68.
115. Bunzel 4:656.
116. Goldfrank 3:35; Dumarest, 190, 192.
117. Parsons 52:308.
118. See p. 527; see also pp. 435–36.
119. Dumarest, 175–76.
120. Parsons 52:328.
121. Stephen 4:995.
122. White 4:51.
123. White 7.
124. Stevenson 2:Pl. XCIII.
125. Shungopovi, Cushing, Fewkes, Parsons, 297; Taos, Parsons 58:79; see p. 1136.
126. Bunzel 2:502.
127. Dumarest, 178.
128. Stephen 4:780.
129. Benedict 3:II, 153.
130. Benedict 3:II, 160.

CHAPTER II

1. Bunzel 6:249.
2. Parsons 20:87 (n. 2).
3. Dumarest, 174; cf. Zuni, Bunzel 2:483.
4. Bunzel 6:133.
5. Stephen 4:826.
6. Parsons 49:64.
7. Bunzel 6:193.
8. Voth 5:117.
9. Voth 5:116.
10. Parsons 40:77 (n. 124).
11. For Zuni, Bunzel 2:513 (n. 42), Bunzel 4:808; Tewa, Parsons 49:268; Acoma, White 2:66; Isleta, Parsons 52:344.
12. Dumarest, 182.
13. Stephen 4:333, also 592.
14. Stephen 4:XLII, 316, 318; Parsons 49:268.
15. For Santo Domingo, White 4:175.
16. Bunzel 2:521–22.
17. Voth 2:91–92.
18. White 2:69–70; Dumarest, 173; Goldfrank 3:35.
19. Parsons 52:332.
20. Bunzel 6:196–98.

21. Bunzel 4:756.
22. Bunzel 6:94.
23. Voth 5:57.
24. See p. 759, n.*, also Parsons 42: 187.
25. Bunzel 5:1036.
26. Cushing 4:Fig. 1; compare pp. 218, 626.
27. Parsons 49:265.
28. Beaglehole 3:34.
29. Parsons 52:390 ff.; Harrington and Roberts, 312 ff.
30. White 5.
31. Parsons 41:126.
32. Beaglehole 3:34.
33. Stephen 4:9.
34. Parsons 42:85.
35. Boas 2:56.
36. Parsons 65; Parsons 58:108.
37. Robbins, Harrington, Freire-Marreco, 50; Parsons 42:59–61.
38. Parsons 49:265–66; Parsons 41: 126.
39. Stevenson 2:Pl. CII.
40. Bunzel 4:685, 808.
41. Stevenson 1:39.
42. For Zuni compare Stevenson 2:20.
43. Nequatewa, 26.
44. Stephen 4:83, 94, 150, 151, 637, 676, 704, 994–95.
45. Voth 5:127 ff.
46. Stephen 4:307 (n. 1).
47. Benedict 3:I, 312–13.
48. Titiev 3; Stephen 4:307 (n. 1), 700.
49. Stephen 4:Fig. 499.
50. Cushing 1:Pl. X, Stevenson 2, altar plates *passim*.
51. Titiev 3.
52. Bunzel 6:133.
53. White 7.
54. Cushing 6:433; Stirling.
55. Goldfrank 3:86.
56. Parsons 20:127 (n. 3); Stirling; Parsons 49:250.
57. Cushing 1:18.
58. Bunzel 6:246–48; also Bunzel 2: 482.

59. Voth 3:338 (n. 2).
60. Stephen 4:860 (n. 1).
61. Boas 2:12, 74–76.
62. Goldfrank 3:44.
63. See p. 239; also Stephen 4:137–38.
64. Parsons 33:218.
65. Isleta, Parsons 52:316, 447, 448; cf. White 4:130.
66. Roberts 1:123, Fig. 27, Pl. 61b; Kidder and Guernsey, 196, Fig. 96, Pls. 93, 94.
67. Stephen 4:96.
68. Stephen 4:Fig. 33.
69. Stephen 4:744–45.
70. Acoma, White 5; Sia, Stevenson 1:26, 36, 69.
71. Dorsey and Voth 2:205.
72. Voth 3:350 (n. 2).
73. Boas 2:59.
74. Benedict 3:I, 229.
75. Stephen 4:707.
76. White 2:48; Stephen 4:745.
77. White 4:39 (n. 16).
78. Titiev 1:252.
79. Espinosa, A. M., 101.
80. Parsons 49:250–52.
81. Stephen 4:598, Fig. 333.
82. Titiev 3.
83. Beaglehole 3:59, 64.
84. Bunzel 4:804.
85. Titiev 1:253.
86. Stevenson 3:87; Bunzel 4:803 (n. 40). See Voth 3:349–51, for Hurü'ing Woman, the Hopi being of hard substances: shells, corals, turquoise.
87. Parsons 42:51 ff.
88. Stirling.
89. Titiev 3; Stevenson 2:507.
90. Parsons 4:169; Benedict 3:I, 34–38; II, 139.
91. Stevenson 2:570.
92. Parsons 52:227–29.
93. Stephen 4:448; for Zuni Yucca kachina, Cushing 6:239–41.
94. Stevenson 2:Pl. CVIa; Bunzel 6:184; Parsons 20:127–28, Parsons 52:338; Goldfrank 3:86; Stevenson 1:120.

95. Beaglehole 2:17.
96. Bunzel 2:483.
97. Beaglehole 3:35.
98. Stevenson 2:580.
99. Bunzel 6:187, 192.
100. Stephen 4:307.
101. Parsons 42:195.
102. Voth 2:123 n.
103. Parsons 20:115; Boas 2:16.
104. Stephen 4:793.
105. Taos, Parsons 65; Tewa, Parsons
     42:80–81; Espinosa, A. M., 97–
     101; Sia, White 5; Acoma, White
     2:139; Laguna, Boas 2:17 ff.;
     Zuni, Benedict 3:I, 43–49, 272–
     73; Aztec, Sahagún (a), 97.
106. Parsons 12:259.
107. Tewa, Parsons 42:108 ff.; Sia,
     Stevenson 1:65–67; Laguna, Par-
     sons 20:115; Cochiti, Dumarest
     228–31; Zuni, Parsons 12:261–
     63.
108. Bunzel 6:249.
109. Parsons 42:191.
110. Parsons 20:101, Fig. 13.
111. Parsons 42:222, 225.
112. Benedict 3:I, 98.
113. Bunzel 5:926 ff.
114. White 2:168–69.
115. Bunzel 2:498 (n. 24).
116. Bunzel 5:1014.
117. Parsons 42:250 ff.
118. Parsons 42:28–29.
119. Stevenson 1:85.
120. Stephen 4:499, 502.
121. Parsons 11:236–38.
122. Voth 2:82.
123. Voth 2:135.
124. Voth 5:119.
125. Quite literally. See Titiev 3.
126. Stephen 4:703.
127. Benedict 3:II, 138.
128. Voth 2:81.
129. Cochiti, Goldfrank 3:79; Isleta,
     Parsons 52:213; Tewa, Parsons
     37:148; Taos, Parsons 58:39.
130. Parsons 40:14 (n. 8).
131. Cushing 7:166.

CHAPTER III

1. Oraibi, Cushing 7:165, 166;
   Zuni, Cushing 6:33; Taos, Parsons 58:111.
2. Boas 2:26–27.
3. Parsons 49:251; Wallis 1:10.
4. Cushing 7:168.
5. Bunzel 6:254.
6. Bunzel 2:489.
7. See p. 241.
8. Bunzel 2:487.
9. Stevenson 3:87.
10. Oraibi, Cushing 7:166; Walpi,
    Curtis, XII, 83, 89–90.
11. Stirling.
12. Bunzel 2:487.
13. Bunzel 6:225.
14. Bunzel 2:487.
15. White 7.
16. Bunzel 6:53.
17. Boas 2:26–27, also 69–70.
18. Stephen 4:826, 829.
19. Voth 5:109–19.
20. Voth 5:109.
21. Compare Stevenson 2:79.
22. Bunzel 4:601.
23. Compare Benedict 3:I, 62–68,
    289; Isleta, Lummis 3:79–81.
24. Compare Santo Domingo tale
    variant (White 4:187 ff.).
25. From Parsons 42:169–75 (Wal-
    pi); Stephen 2 (Walpi 2); Wallis
    1:2–17 (Shumopovi); Cushing 7
    (Oraibi 1); Voth 5 (Oraibi 2).
26. White 5.
27. Boas 2:13–16.
28. Boas 2:11; Benedict 2:5.
29. White 2:154–56; Parsons 8:191–
    92.
30. Parsons 41:136–39.
31. Parsons 52:360–61.
32. Parsons 52:362.
33. Parsons 52:366–68.
34. Parsons 52:368–72.
35. Parsons 52:372–73.

CHAPTER IV

1. Hopi, Stephen 4: Index, Prayer-
   stick(s); Solberg; Zuni, Laguna,

Parsons 13; Jemez, Parsons 41:100–106, Figs. 4, 11–13. For Southwest and Mexico, pp. 995 ff., 1010, 1012, 1022, and for general distribution, Spier 2: 290.

2. Bunzel 5:845.
3. Parsons 6:321.
4. Bunzel 6:82.
5. White 2:127.
6. Compare Parsons 6:305; White 2:127.
7. White 2:32; compare Boas 2:213.
8. Stephen 4:239, 793.
9. Beaglehole 3:58.
10. Voth 2:76 (n. 122).
11. Stevenson 1:121.
12. Stevenson 3:145.
13. Stirling.
14. Stephen 4:68, 90.
15. Stephen 4:90; Fewkes 11:490; Solberg, 52.
16. Stevenson 3:96.
17. Bunzel 5:860.
18. Compare Cushing 4:9.
19. Voth 2:83 n.
20. Goldfrank 3:66 (n. 33).
21. Boas 2:70.
22. Bunzel 5:863 (n. 22).
23. *Ibid.*
24. Stevenson 3:91; Stevenson 2:433, Fig. 29.
25. Stirling.
26. Stevenson 3:88.
27. Stephen 4:510.
28. Dorsey and Voth 2:235.
29. See p. 000.
30. Stephen 4:311.
31. Compare Voth 3:280–81.
32. Stephen 4:524.
33. Stephen 4:75, 104, 311, 675, etc.
34. White 3:Pl. 2a.
35. Stevenson 1:Pl. XIa. See too, for Hopi, pp. 564–65.
36. Compare the rings of the Sia and Navaho (Stevenson 1:74, 92; Matthews 4:67).
37. Fewkes 8:Pl. XX.
38. Stirling; Voth 2:152; compare Cushing 4:3.
39. White 2:126.
40. Bunzel 2:484; Bunzel 4:799.
41. Bunzel 6:240.
42. Voth 2:73 n.
43. Dorsey and Voth 1:260 n.
44. Santo Domingo, White 4:91; Isleta, Parsons 52:320.
45. Bunzel 6:186.
46. Stephen 4:512.
47. See pp. 313, 558, 691.
48. See pp. 420, 565.
49. See p. 694.
50. Voth 2:76–77, Pl. XLVI.
51. Voth 3:313.
52. Parsons 40:95; Stephen 4:60.
53. Wallis 1:21.
54. Stirling.
55. Stevenson 2:183.
56. Voth 9:101–2; Voth 5:119.
57. Voth 8:29.
58. Stevenson 2:59; compare Hopi spring cleaning (Beaglehole 3:30).
59. Stevenson 2:427.
60. Cushing 6:464.
61. Bunzel 5:1000.
62. Fewkes 9:701; Voth 9:108.
63. Parsons 42:266, 269–70.
64. Stevenson 2:412.
65. Parsons 11:236 ff.; Parsons 6:325–26.
66. Cushing 6:412.
67. Stephen 4:875, 877, Fig. 64a.
68. Dorsey and Voth 1:57.
69. White 5.
70. Titiev 3.
71. Voth 2:75, 86; Voth 4:9.
72. Voth 4:13–14.
73. Stephen 4:1024.
74. Stephen 4:501.
75. Voth 9:103.
76. Stephen 4:827; compare Voth 2:103 n.
77. Voth 8:53, 54–55.
78. Dumarest, 172.
79. Parsons 49:238.
80. White 4:163, Fig. 48.

81. White 3:37.
82. Stevenson 2:21.
83. See pp. 420, 581, 584.
84. White 2:47.
85. Compare Robbins, Harrington, Freire-Marreco, 87.
86. Luxán, 99.
87. Stephen 4:264–65.
88. White 6.
89. Voth 3:297.
90. Beaglehole 2:13.
91. Robbins, Harrington, Freire-Marreco, 87.
92. Parsons 58:102.
93. Parsons 52:320; Parsons 58:102; Robbins, Harrington, Freire-Marreco, 87.
94. Bunzel 5:910.
95. Stevenson 2:100, 504.
96. Parsons 6:207.
97. Voth 3:347.
98. Stevenson 2:577; compare Parsons 49:253.
99. Stephen 4:153–54; White 7.
100. Stephen 4:379.
101. Compare Stevenson 2:127.
102. White 4:121, 122.
103. Parsons 58:97; Parsons 64.
104. Parsons 53:49; compare Bunzel 6:183.
105. White 6.
106. Cushing 6:162.
107. Boas 2:10, 70.
108. Stephen 4:75, 164, Figs. 56, 96, 102; Voth 2:78.
109. Parsons 52:361.
110. White 4:53; White 7.
111. Stephen 4:499, 502.
112. Bunzel 4:671, 673.
113. Bunzel 2:491.
114. Parsons 52:219.
115. Voth 2:80.
116. Parsons 20:99 (n. 4).
117. Boas 2:71.
118. Beaglehole 2:8.
119. Stevenson 2:161 (n. a).
120. Hodge 1:231.
121. Stevenson 2:172.
122. Goldfrank 3:65.
123. Parsons 52:330.
124. Acoma, Stirling.
125. Hodge 3:12.
126. Roberts 1:160–61.
127. Voth 2:86; Stephen 4:499.
128. Voth 2:111.
129. Voth 4:15.
130. Goldfrank 3:73, 74.
131. Beaglehole 3:40.
132. Boas 2:212–13.
133. Voth 2:77.
134. Beaglehole 3:6.
135. Beaglehole 3:30.
136. Bunzel 4:702.
137. Goldfrank 3:71.
138. Bunzel 6:14.
139. Voth 5:119.
140. Bunzel 6:218–19.
141. Bunzel 5:1043; Stevenson 2:91; Bourke 2:119.
142. White 2:125; Bunzel 2:498.
143. Kennard.
144. Robbins, Harrington, Freire-Marreco, 95.
145. Parsons 52:300.
146. Stephen 4:487.
147. Stevenson 1:123.
148. White 3:13.
149. Bunzel 2:498.
150. Voth 3:289.
151. Stephen 4:499, 528.
152. Cushing 6:433; Goldfrank 3:86 White 6.
153. Stevenson 2:92.
154. Stevenson 1:118.
155. Voth (Catalogue note on collection in the American Museum of Natural History, New York City).
156. Parsons 41:102; Parsons 14:62; Voth 2:77 n., Pl. XLVI.
157. Cushing 4:Figs. 6–8. See shrine in American Museum of Natural History, New York City.
158. Parsons 40:n. 70.
159. White 7.
160. Parsons 13:Pl. II; Stevenson 2: Pls. LXXXVIII, LXXXIX.
161. Parsons 49:238 ff., Pls. 41, 42.

162. Stephen 4:1014; Parsons Zuni MS.
163. Forde 1:395, Fig. 10; Beaglehole 3:39; also Dorsey and Voth 2: Pl. CIV.
164. Stevenson 2:232–33, Pl. XLVII.
165. Parsons 49: Fig. 16.
166. Hodge 3:67.
167. Nelson, 70–71, Fig. 10.
168. Bunzel 5:934; Parsons 42:187.
169. Dorsey and Voth 2: Pl. LXXIX.
170. Stephen 4:483.
171. Stevenson 2:508.
172. Parsons 52:331; compare Laguna, Parsons 33:257; Jemez, Parsons 41:139 (n. 1).
173. Stephen 4:355; cf. Parsons 58:97.
174. Voth 2: Pl. LIII.
175. Stephen 4:784.
176. Goldfrank 3:67.
177. Forde 3:396, quoting Freire-Marreco; compare Cushing 6: 162–64 for the Zuni farmer's prayer in the same circumstances.
178. Beaglehole 3:39.
179. Bunzel 4:621.
180. Bunzel 6:183.
181. Goldfrank 3:87.
182. Goldfrank 2:193.
183. Boas 2:213.
184. Bunzel 4:668.
185. Bunzel 4:712.
186. Bunzel 4:617.
187. Bunzel 4:618.
188. Voth 8:21, 28; also Voth 4:8.
189. Voth 3:277–78.
190. Voth 3:319–21.
191. See Cushing 6:146.
192. Bunzel 4:617.
193. Bunzel 4:616.
194. Bunzel 2:493.
195. Bunzel 2:494.
196. *Ibid.*
197. *Ibid.*
198. Bunzel 1:24.
199. Dorsey and Voth 2:230 ff.
200. Stephen 4:260.
201. Voth 7: Pl. LVII; Voth 6: Pl. XI.
202. Beaglehole 3:57.

203. Bunzel 5:980, 991.
204. Stephen 4:236.
205. White 7.
206. Stirling. Uncertain whether this ceremonial is observed today.
207. Parsons 41:76.
208. Voth 2:121.
209. Stephen 4:1141 (Huhiyan).
210. Bunzel 5:1015.
211. Stephen 4:515.
212. Beaglehole 3:44.
213. Bunzel 2:497.
214. Dumarest, 231–32.
215. Voth 2:129.
216. Dumarest, 166.
217. Benedict 3:I, 216; Stevenson 2:441.
218. Stephen 1:828.
219. Stephen 4:800.
220. Voth 9:116.
221. Stevenson 1:40 n. and Pl. IX; White 4:161; White 8.
222. Robbins, Harrington, Freire-Marreco, 88.
223. Goldfrank 3:66–67.
224. Stirling.
225. White 3:43.
226. Compare p. 250.
227. Stevenson 2:598 (n. *a*).
228. Stephen 4:911.
229. Stephen 4:417.
230. Voth 3:303–4.
231. Stevenson 2:26.
232. Compare Stevenson 3:88; Bunzel 2:490.
233. Voth 2: Pl. LVII.
234. Voth 2:112.
235. Stevenson 1:17, 40; White 5.
236. Dorsey and Voth 1:26 n.; also Stephen 4:27, 967.
237. Goldfrank 3:54.
238. Stevenson 2: Pl. XVII.
239. Dorsey and Voth 1:18, Pl. VI.
240. White 2:46, 129, Fig. 4*c*.
241. Dumarest, 199.
242. White 4:40; White 3:15; Parsons 62:155.
243. Stevenson 1:105.

244. See Parsons 49:Pl. 26; Parsons 41:Pl. 9a.
245. White 2:104.
246. Stephen 4:92.
247. Voth 4:27 (n. 2).
248. Stephen 4:Fig. 80; Parsons 34: Fig. 2.
249. Stevenson 2:Pl. XXXIX; Voth 8:Pl. XVIII.
250. Parsons 52:278, Fig. 16.
251. Parsons 20:Fig. 19.
252. Stephen 4:739, 838, Figs. 396, 493; Voth 8:34, Pl. V.
253. Roberts 1:Pl. 55d, e; compare Zuni, Stevenson 2:Pl. CVIII (Wood society altar).
254. Stephen 4:119 (n. 1).
255. Goldfrank 3:71.
256. Voth 8:34, Pl. V; Dorsey and Voth 1:Pl. I.
257. Stephen 4:285.
258. Stephen 4:9.
259. Bourke 1:551, Fig. 435.
260. Compare Stevenson 2:287.
261. Parsons 49:13.
262. Voth 2:Pl. LIII.
263. White 2:134, 135; Laguna, Parsons 33:193.
264. Compare Isleta, Parsons 52:452.
265. Gunn, 190–91.
266. Hodge 1:227–31; Parsons 56:53.
267. Stephen 4:137.
268. Parsons 11:241–42.
269. Parsons 59:555.
270. Voth 2:Pl. LIII.
271. Stephen 4:745, Figs. 70, 332, Pl. XVII.
272. Stephen 4:Figs. 70, 332, 365; Stevenson 2:Pl. XXXIV.
273. Dorsey and Voth 2:209–10; Voth 3:304, Pl. CLXIII.
274. Stephen 4:707, 745; see Glossary.
275. Parsons 20:118, Fig. 19.
276. Goldfrank 3:70.
277. White 3:12, 45, Fig. 13.
278. Parsons 49:128, 252.
279. White 3:44, Fig. 13.
280. Stevenson 2:428–29.
281. Stevenson 2:Pl. XLVIII.

282. Roberts 1:Pl. 60, Fig. 34.
283. Lummis 1:135, 146, 149.
284. Zuni, Cushing 1:33 ff.; Laguna, Boas 2:296.
285. Goldfrank 3:70.
286. Cushing 1:39, also Pls. I–XI.
287. Stevenson 2:432; Cushing 1: 14–15; Cushing 6:33.
288. Goldfrank 3:70.
289. Stephen 4:9, Figs. 2, 3.
290. White 4:35.
291. Voth 5:250, 256.
292. Voth 3:287.
293. Voth 2:86.
294. Voth 8:Pl. XXXII.
295. Stephen 4:94, Figs. 22, 30, 62, 67.
296. Dumarest, Fig. 31.
297. Stephen 4:70.
298. White 3:31; White 4:112–13.
299. Bunzel 5:857.
300. Bunzel 5:1026.
301. Bunzel 5:851.
302. Bunzel 5:860.
303. Bunzel 5:852.
304. Bunzel 5:1014.
305. Bunzel 5:1003, 1006–7.
306. Bunzel 5:1080.
307. Stephen 4:XLIII, 395, 515, 523, Glossary (kü'ïtü).
308. Bunzel 5:853.
309. Bunzel 5:849.
310. Bunzel 5:989.
311. White 3:29.
312. White 4:112.
313. Stevenson 1:117.
314. Bunzel 5:845.
315. Bunzel 5:853.
316. Bunzel 5:931–34.
317. Zuni, Stevenson 2:Pls. XIII, XIV; Hopi, Stephen 4:Figs. 169–71; Tewa (F.M.), Stephen 4: Fig. 204; Jemez, Parsons 41:78, 125; Isleta, Parsons 52:Fig. 14.
318. Stevenson 2:101.
319. Stephen 4:Fig. 428.
320. Parsons 41:Pl. 10.
321. Goldfrank 3:46; White 4:150–51, Fig. 42; White 7.
322. Stephen 4:221, 991.

323. Stephen 4:17, 18, 19, 20, 25, 27, 28.
324. Fewkes 4:15.
325. Laguna, Santo Domingo (White 3:615).
326. Voth 2:83.
327. White 7.
328. White 4: 60 (n. 56).
329. White 3:13.
330. Parsons 42:232. (This tale was told by a Hano man.)
331. Titiev 3; see too Parsons 42:232.
332. Stephen 4:1006.
333. White 5; Stevenson 2: Pl. CXXX.
334. Parsons 49:138.
335. Bunzel 4:679, 680, 686.
336. Stephen 4:97; compare Shipaulovi, Voth 5:57, 60.
337. White 4: 60 (n. 56).
338. Bunzel 4:681.
339. Bunzel 6:248 ff.
340. Stephen 4:370.
341. Voth 2:Pl. XLII.
342. Voth 2:Pl. XLVII.
343. Fewkes 6:268, Pls. I, II; Fewkes 7:Pls. I, II; Stephen 4:791, Figs. 425, 426.
344. Fewkes 7:247.
345. Stevenson 2:545.
346. Stephen 4:592-94, 837, 884-85, Fig. 454, Pls. XVII, XVIII, XX, XXIII; Stevenson 2:507; see pp. 661-62.
347. Stephen 4:837.
348. Stevenson 2:169.
349. Voth 3:287.
350. Voth 8:35; Stephen 4:1075.
351. Parsons 52:311, 315.
352. Parsons 52:315.
353. Stephen 4:238.
354. Stephen 4:Figs. 143-46, Pls. V-VII.
355. Steward 1:199, Fig. 90, Map 24. Note out-and-out Pueblo design in southern Nevada.
356. Steward 1:Pls. 81, 82 (southern Utah), Fig. 74*b* (pictograph, central Arizona, ? Apache, compare

Grandfather mask of Isleta); Hopi, Stephen 4:498, 507-9, 513, 518; Fewkes 4:Pls. I, II; Acoma, White 2:Fig. 6.
357. Stephen 4:Figs. 499, 502, 503.
358. Steward 1:155; Kidder and Guernsey, Fig. 96, Pl. 94; Roberts 1:Pl. 61. Resemblances between the petroglyphs of the Kayenta region and the Village of the Great Kivas near Nutria, east of Zuni, are very striking.
359. Oraibi, Titiev 1:245-46; Zuni, Stevenson 2:40, Pls. VI*b*, VII (?).
360. Stephen 4:1087 (?); Cushing 6:153.
361. Kroeber 2:178, Fig. 1.
362. Parsons 40:Fig. 8; Kroeber 2:178.
363. White 2:139.
364. Stephen 3:69, 71.
365. Cushing, Fewkes, and Parsons, 266; Wallis 1:16.
366. Stevenson 2:Pl. CXI.
367. Voth 2:Pl. XLVII.
368. Haury, Pl. XXXIII.
369. See Mimbres pottery from southwest New Mexico (Kidder 1: Pl. 45*b*).
370. Hano, Parsons 40:Fig. 11; Walpi, Stephen 4:Fig. 193; Oraibi, Voth 2:111, 114, 115; Zuni, Stevenson 2:Pls. CVIII, CXXV.
371. Lowie 3:179; Stephen 4:Fig. 520.
372. Stephen 4:87.
373. Stephen 2:67.
374. Stephen 4:Figs. 83, 84.
375. Cushing 6:155.
376. Dumarest, Fig. 30.
377. Bunzel 6:257.
378. Voth 8:76.
379. Bunzel 2:499; Stephen 4:835, 870; Dumarest, 155 (n. 1).
380. White 2:46.
381. Fewkes 13:354.
382. Stephen 4:17 ff., 963.
383. Boas 2:297.

384. Robbins, Harrington, Freire-Marreco, 88.
385. Tesuque and San Juan, Parsons 49:253; Cochiti, Goldfrank 3:63; Isleta, Parsons 52:Fig. 17.
386. Fewkes 8:268, 272.
387. See p. 254.
388. Voth 2:Pl. LIII and note.
389. See pp. 375, 445, 556, 558, 569.
390. Voth 2:103 n.; Voth 3:311 (n. 5).
391. Voth 8:51.
392. Robbins, Harrington, Freire-Marreco, 88.
393. Stephen 4:394, 824, 826.
394. White 2:87.
395. Dumarest, 197, 201.
396. Parsons 52:313.
397. White 5.
398. Boas 2:29.
399. Stevenson 2:544.
400. Stephen 4:86, 90; Voth 2:75; Voth 8:19, 24; Dorsey and Voth 1:17 n.
401. Bunzel 2:502.
402. Beaglehole 2:22.
403. Beaglehole 3:54, 55.
404. Bunzel 1:20, 23.
405. Bunzel 6:33.
406. Isleta, Parsons 52:285, 367; Picurís, Harrington and Roberts, *passim;* Taos, Parsons 64, *passim.*
407. Stirling.
408. Bunzel 4:713.
409. Boas 2:296, also 13.
410. Voth 3:297.
411. Goldfrank 3:297.
412. Bunzel 4:713, 762.
413. *Omawtapi.* Voth 2:Pl. XL; Voth 4:15; Stephen 4:Fig. 369.
414. Voth 2:87–88.
415. White 7.
416. Bourke 1:509.
417. Voth 3:346.
418. Goldfrank 3:62, 72.
419. Voth 2:108–9; Voth 3:319–21; Titiev 3.
420. Stephen 4:430.
421. Dorsey and Voth 2:233.
422. Stephen 4:760, 771, 842.
423. Stephen 4:514, 918.
424. Voth 4:46.
425. In Flute ceremony, see p. 707.
426. Voth 2:112–13.
427. Stephen 4:290.
428. Stephen 4:705.
429. Bunzel 6:8.
430. Voth 2:119.
431. Stephen 4:457.
432. Cushing 5:204, 205.
433. Bunzel 4:782.
434. Bunzel 2:292.
435. For its distribution in the Southwest, Basin, and Plains, see Spier 2:290–91.
436. Stephen 4:637–38, 718.
437. Stevenson 2:246.
438. Stephen 4:600, 775, Figs. 348, 416; see Index, "Whizzer."
439. Stevenson 2:177, Pl. XXXV.
440. Stephen 4:87, Figs. 61, 67, 182.
441. Voth 3:321, 322, 327, 328, Pl. CLXV.
442. Stirling.
443. Parsons 49:205.
444. Voth 9:Pl. XLVIII.
445. Voth 8:36, Pl. XII. In Oraibi as kachina.
446. Stephen 4:217.
447. Stephen 4:19, 980 ff., Fig. 488.
448. Voth 8:59, Pl. XVII.
449. Stephen 4:24.
450. Voth 2:78, 80.
451. Parsons 29:176; Parsons 41:122; compare San Juan, Espinosa, A. M., 101.
452. Stephen 4:154.
453. Bunzel 2:496–97.
454. Cushing 6:383 ff., compare Stevenson 2:239.
455. Parsons 29:195 ff.
456. Bloom, 215.
457. Bunzel 1:84, Pl. IX.
458. Bunzel 2:496.
459. Bunzel 5:947.
460. Stirling; see Parsons 14:163.
461. Bunzel 5:1026 (n. 9), 1027.
462. Stephen 4:10, 17 ff., 514.
463. Stephen 4:10 (n. 3), 17 ff., 707,

708, 718, Fig. 6; Voth 3:334, Pl. CLXXXIII.
464. Parsons 36:21–22.
465. Voth 3:330–31, Pl. CLXXIX A.
466. Stephen 4:86, Fig. 62.
467. For its widespread distribution, Spier 2:291.
468. Stephen 4:326, 572, 897, also Index, "Notched Stick(s)."
469. Stephen 4:408.
470. Voth 3:333 (n. 3).
471. Voth 3:337 (n. 3).
472. Bunzel 5:1012.
473. Stephen 4:Fig. 29.
474. Beaglehole 3:70.
475. Voth 4:23.
476. White 5.
477. Bunzel 4:681.
478. Bunzel 2:498.
479. Voth 2:158.
480. Boas 2:66.
481. Stevenson 2:535 (Shuma'kwe).
482. Goldfrank 3:72; White 4:143.
483. Compare Stevenson 2:226.
484. See p. 319.
485. Goldfrank 3:106.
486. Robbins, Harrington, Freire-Marreco, 95.
487. Stephen 4:505.
488. Zuni, Parsons 36:24; Acoma, Parsons 14:167; Cochiti, Goldfrank 3:111.
489. Goldfrank 3:54.
490. Parsons 49:166; Robbins, Harrington, Freire-Marreco, 97.
491. Robbins, Harrington, Freire-Marreco, 98.
492. Goldfrank 2:191, 194–95; compare Boas 2:299–300.
493. Stephen 4:369, 475, 549.
494. Stephen 4:383, 506, 575.
495. Morris, Fig. 31a.
496. Stephen 4:360.
497. Stephen 4:128.
498. Parsons 52:315; Stevenson 2:544.
499. Beaglehole 3:60; Parsons 16:38.
500. Benedict 3:22, 36, 38, 49; Stevenson 2:80.
501. Benedict 3:I, 189 (n. 1).
502. Parsons 52:214 (newborn infant), 218 (protective poker).
503. Stevenson 2:544 and passim.
504. Bunzel 2:497.
505. Voth 8:23.
506. Fewkes 10:67.
507. Spinden, 98.
508. Stephen 4:780, quoting the Flute society chief; compare Parsons 40:86.
509. Stephen 4:780.
510. Parsons 40:59.
511. White 4:91.
512. Stephen 4:272.
513. Parsons 40:89, 93.
514. Beaglehole 3:46.
515. Parsons 40:107; Dorsey and Voth 2:254–55; Beaglehole 3:48; Voth 3:Pls. CLXXIII, CLXXIV.
516. Stephen 4:263.
517. Beaglehole 2:5.
518. Parsons 15:333 (n. 3).
519. Bunzel 5:868, 990.
520. Parsons 58:91, Pl. 13 B; Voth 3:306.
521. Voth 5:260; Voth 3:345.
522. Stephen 4:853.
523. Stephen 4:489, 708.
524. Stephen 4:701.
525. Stephen 4:806.
526. White 2:101.
527. Voth 3:287–88; Stephen 4: Glossary, hüzrü'nkwa.
528. Voth 5:260.
529. Stephen 4:133.
530. Stirling; White 3:2a.
531. Stirling.
532. Stephen 4:1005.
533. Stevenson 2:Fig. 30.
534. Keech, R. A. Personal communication.
535. Stevenson 2:272.
536. Voth 3:306.
537. Goldfrank 3:93.
538. Bunzel 5:871.
539. Stirling; see Parsons 13:Pl. III.
540. Stirling.
541. Spinden, 113.

542. Bunzel 2:495.
543. Parsons 40:121 (n. 185).
544. Stephen 4:58, 80.
545. Parsons 42:240.
546. Stevenson 2:463; Parsons 40:16.
547. Isleta, Parsons 52:321.
548. Parsons 42:170.
549. Cushing 7:168.
550. Parsons 40:122 (n. 187).
551. Stephen 4:92.
552. Voth 8:70–88.
553. Bunzel 2:494.
554. Stephen 4:106.
555. See p. 834.
556. Hano, Parsons 40:121 (n. 185); Oraibi, Voth 4:44.
557. Voth 2:134.
558. Spinden, 58.
559. Stephen 4:372.
560. Bunzel 6:25.
561. Stirling.
562. Stevenson 1:123.
563. Stirling.
564. Voth 4:26.
565. Voth 4:39.
566. *Ibid.*
567. Voth 4:43.
568. Voth 2:143.
569. Bunzel 5:890, 891.
570. White 4:97–99. I have taken some liberties with the free translations.
571. Stirling. Sung by Duck kachina.
572. Stirling.
573. Spinden, 95.
574. Bunzel 5:890.
575. Bunzel 5:889, 1019.
576. Bunzel 5:1023.
577. Stevenson 2:384.
578. Parsons 58:12; Bunzel 2:491.
579. Isleta, Parsons 52:312; Zuni, Benedict 3:II, 35.
580. Stephen 4:863 (n. 1).
581. Beaglehole 3:35.
582. Stevenson 2:530.
583. Voth 3:338 (n. 2).
584. Parsons 40:46 (n. 75).
585. Voth 3:279; Stephen 4; Index, "Honey."

586. Stevenson 2:599 (n. *a*); compare p. 32, n. * and p. 1058.
587. Stephen 4:98.
588. Goldfrank 3:73.
589. White 4:60 (n. 56).
590. Benedict 3:I, 206; Parsons 10: 379–80.
591. Stephen 4:53; Voth 4:20.
592. Dorsey and Voth 1:25–26, 48.
593. Voth 3:334.
594. Voth 2:80.
595. Stevenson 1:113.
596. Voth 3:286.
597. Bunzel 5:874.
598. Parsons 58:106.
599. Stevenson 2:137.
600. Handy, 467.
601. Stevenson 2:114.
602. Stevenson 2:533.
603. Boas 2:11.
604. Stirling.
605. Dumarest, 197.
606. Stevenson 2:239.
607. Bunzel 5:866.
608. Stevenson 2:133.
609. Stevenson 2:420, 427, 540.
610. Stevenson 2:577–78, also 170; Cushing 6:122.
611. Stephen 4:942.
612. Goldfrank 3:68.
613. Stevenson 1:120.
614. Goldfrank 3:68.
615. Stevenson 2:327.
616. Goldfrank 3:86.
617. Cushing 6:417, 433; also 592 for inhaling the breath of an expiring rabbit.
618. Bunzel 5:894.
619. Voth 2:76.
620. Fewkes 12:51.
621. Parsons 42:13, 115.
622. Stevenson 1:34.
623. Voth 5:264.
624. Voth 5:166; compare Navaho (Goddard 5:177).
625. Parsons 42:67.
626. See pp. 711–12, 713, 728–29.
627. Dorsey and Voth 1:22 n.
628. Benedict 3:II, 76.

629. White 2:23.
630. Dorsey and Voth 1:25.
631. Voth 3:310; cf. Stevenson 2:505.
632. Parsons 20:125.
633. Robbins, Harrington, Freire-Marreco, 97–98.
634. Harper.
635. Stevenson 2:587.
636. Bunzel 4:681.
637. Bunzel 6:93–94.
638. Benedict 3:II, 118–19, 145 ff.
639. Benedict 3:II, 39.
640. Benedict 3:II, 109.
641. Voth 3:346.
642. Benedict 3:II, 163.
643. Bunzel 2:502.
644. White 2:111.
645. White 5.
646. Goldfrank 3:56, 104.
647. Stevenson 1:118.
648. Beaglehole 2:5.
649. Beaglehole 3:52, 53.
650. Parsons 52:373–74.
651. Stephen 4:488.
652. Stephen 4:156 (n. 3).
653. Bunzel 6:95.
654. Voth 7:50.
655. Acoma, White 5; San Felipe, White, 3:48; Cochiti, Dumarest, 205.
656. Bunzel 6:20.
657. Parsons 42:16.
658. Bunzel 6:17, 18.
659. Bunzel 6:19.
660. Voth 8:25.
661. Bunzel 4:632.
662. Bunzel 6:94.
663. Beaglehole 3:I, 53; White 2:139; Goldfrank 3:9; Benedict 2:7.
664. Beaglehole 2:5.
665. Stephen 4:588, 614, 622.
666. Parsons 42:67–68.
667. Bunzel 2:494.
668. Haile, 13.
669. Bunzel 5:971(n. 54).
670. Steward 2:76.
671. Stirling.
672. Stevenson 1:107.

673. Bunzel 5:981.
674. Bunzel 4:679.
675. Stephen 4:437 (n. 1).
676. Benedict 3:I, 22, 34, 35, 36, 38, 40, 41.
677. Cf. Bunzel 2:504.
678. Voth 4:16, 24 (n. 1).
679. Dorsey and Voth 2:193.
680. See pp. 677, 805, 810–11.
681. Goldfrank 2:190, 191.
682. See p. 805.
683. Cushing 6:620.
684. Cushing 6:48–49.
685. Stevenson 2:537; Parsons 53:3.
686. White 5.
687. Stephen 4:1008, 1010.
688. Stephen 4:1008.
689. Stevenson 2:503, 506.
690. Stevenson 2:542.
691. White 5.
692. Dumarest, 188; for stick-swallowing at Laguna, Parsons 20:109 (n. 3).
693. White 2:114–16.
694. Stevenson 2:Fig. CIX.
695. Parsons 41:66–67.
696. See pp. 695 ff.
697. Parsons 52:313.
698. Parsons 52:412.
699. Parsons 42:89; also pp. 234–35.
700. Beaglehole 3:70–71.
701. Benavides, n. 55.
702. Bunzel 5:970.
703. Bunzel 6:72; cf. Stevenson 2:507.
704. Stevenson 2:462.
705. Beaglehole 3:53.
706. Titiev 3, also 1:254; Beaglehole 3:38.
707. Beaglehole 3:44 (n. 9).
708. Bunzel 4:831.
709. Bunzel 6:34.
710. Compare Lummis 2:218.
711. Parsons 49:138.
712. Benedict 3:I, 98, 104.
713. Beaglehole 3:35.
714. Stephen 4:806.
715. Goldfrank 3:62.
716. Stephen 4:584–85.

717. White 3:12–13.
718. Dumarest, 193.
719. White 3:48; Parsons 20:122.
720. Stevenson 2:530.
721. Parsons 33:Figs. 21, 22. Fig. 20 shows a steep rutted incline north of Laguna, but information is lacking.
722. Stephen 4:680 (n. 1).
723. Titiev 3.
724. Parsons 52:313, 319–20.
725. White 2:110; compare Cochiti, Dumarest, 156–57; Goldfrank 3:63–64; San Felipe, White 3: 47; Santo Domingo, White 4: 127; Sia, White 5; Isleta, Parsons 52:310, 312.
726. Stevenson 2:385, 415; p. 716.
727. Parsons 52:310, 314, 340.
728. Parsons 52:309, Fig. 15.
729. Parsons 52:316; Lummis 3:176; compare Scholes 2:220 (Report, 1631, to Inquisition).
730. From Parsons 42:45–47.
731. For witch's doll, Nambé, Parsons 49:305; Cochiti, Goldfrank 3:64 and Dumarest, 165.
732. Boas 2:289.
733. Stevenson 1:86.
734. Parsons 33:277.
735. White 5; Bunzel 2:506.
736. Stirling.
737. Fewkes 9:702; Mishongnovi, Beaglehole 2:20–21.
738. Wallis 1:7.
739. White 5.
740. See Voth 5:180.
741. Bunzel 6:72–73.
742. Beaglehole 3:74.
743. Stephen 4:310.
744. Cochiti, Goldfrank 3:104; Sia, Stevenson 1:40 (n. 1), 116; San Felipe, White 3:36; Santo Domingo, White 4:94.
745. Cushing 6:619–20.
746. Benedict 3:I, 99. See p. 824.
747. Stirling.
748. Parsons 33:219 (n. 3).
749. Voth 8:30.

750. White 1:607.
751. Benedict 3:I, 117.
752. Stephen 4:371, 386.
753. Parsons 1:247.
754. Voth 3:348; compare Voth 2: 109; Voth 4:44.
755. Stephen 4:58, 81.
756. Voth 8:67.
757. Stevenson 1:106.
758. Parsons 49:13.
759. White 2:111.
760. Stephen 4:149.
761. Stevenson 2:217, 581, 586, 589, 604.
762. Cushing 3:441.
763. Fewkes 2:93, 102, 103.
764. Parsons 40:100 (n. 155).
765. Stevenson 2:323.
766. Boas 2:27–28.
767. Bunzel 6:94, 95.
768. Parsons 42:29.
769. Parsons 52:276; compare Lummis 3:94 (n. 1).
770. Dumarest, 166.
771. See p. 669.
772. Voth 2:109.
773. Cushing 6:576–77.
774. Stephen 4:371 (n. 2); Beaglehole 3:60.
775. Stevenson 2:492.
776. Stephen 4:881.
777. Beaglehole 2:10, 11.
778. Beaglehole 2:6; Parsons 40:14 (n. 8).
779. Stevenson 2:240.
780. See White 7 for bibliographical note on this method of "trapping."
781. Parsons 40:14 (n. 8.)
782. Stevenson 1:134.
783. Goldfrank 3:66.
784. Dorsey and Voth 1:45.
785. Voth 3:312–13.
786. Goldfrank 3:90.
787. Voth 8:44, 53; Stephen 4:879.
788. Zuni, Parsons 6:270 (n. 2); Hopi, Stephen 4:862, Fig. 464; Keres, White 2:108–9, 111; White 3:46; White 4:125; Stevenson 1:75;

Dumarest, 158; Parsons 20:121;
Tewa, Parsons 49:119; Taos,
Parsons 58:58.
789. Stevenson 2:493; White 2:119;
Isleta, Parsons 52:312.
790. Goldfrank 3:95.
791. Benedict 3:II, 208 (n. 1).
792. Parsons 33:219 (n. 1).
793. Beaglehole 2:7, 11.
794. Beaglehole 3:30.
795. White 2:48–49.
796. White 5.
797. Parsons 49:121, Fig. 2.
798. Goldfrank 3:53, 56, 68; White 5.
799. Stevenson 2:437.
800. Stevenson 2:99 ff.; Parsons 6:
156; Bunzel 5:979–80; Bunzel
2:518.
801. Bunzel 5:852; see p. 342, n. ‡.
802. Stephen 4:201–2.
803. White 2:71–75.
804. Bunzel 5:875.
805. Stevenson 2:155.
806. Stephen 4:201, 428, 458, 459,
550.
807. Bunzel 5:1000.
808. Bunzel 6:87.
809. Stephen 4:462; Parsons 40:89
(n. 139); Parsons 40:94.
810. Goldfrank 3:106.
811. Parsons 7:89.
812. Parsons 52:365.
813. Dumarest, 200–202.
814. White 6.
815. Ibid.
816. Bunzel 2:491.
817. Stephen 4:198.
818. Parsons 55:93 (n. 34).
819. Stephen 4:47 (n. 2).
820. Voth 2:75, Pl. XLII.
821. Stephen 4:Figs. 34, 37.
822. Voth 2:Pls. XXXVII, XLVII.
823. Stephen 4:Fig. 330.
824. Bunzel 4:783.
825. Voth 8:45.
826. Voth 2:131 (n. 3).
827. Stephen 4:546.
828. Titiev 3.
829. Compare Bunzel 2:501.

830. Stephen 4:989–90.
831. White 4:51.
832. Voth 2:76.
833. Parsons 40:95 (n. 147).
834. Voth 2:154 (n. 2).
835. White 7.
836. Parsons 40:16.
837. Parsons 40:95.
838. Parsons 40:45 (n. 73).
839. Stephen 4:279.
840. Stephen 4:47 (n. 2).
841. Stephen 4:704.
842. Newcomb and Reichard, 24.
843. Bunzel 2:492.
844. Voth 3:311.

CHAPTER V

1. Stephen 4:134; Beaglehole 3:26.
2. Stephen 4:197–98, 202, 210.
3. White 2:98.
4. Parsons 40:87–89, 91, 93; Parsons 55:59–60; Fewkes 2:259;
Stephen 4:389, 390, Map 12.
5. Beaglehole 3:38.
6. Cushing 6:174.
7. Forde 3:363.
8. Beaglehole 3:23.
9. Parsons 40:101; Titiev 3.
10. Goldfrank 2:188.
11. White 2:71.
12. Parsons 34:21.
13. Bunzel 2:538 (n. 87).
14. Cushing 6:155; Parsons 6:296;
Parsons 20:112 (n. 3).
15. Stephen 4:12 ff.
16. Stephen 4:94–96.
17. Stephen 4:287 ff.; Parsons 40:
53, 55 ff.
18. Forde 3:361.
19. Curtis, XII, 177–79; Stephen 4:
994–95.
20. Voth 9:107, 108; Stephen 4:540,
568–69.
21. Oraibi (Voth 3:274); Mishongnovi (Dorsey and Voth 2:172–
73); Walpi (Stephen 4:577).
22. Parsons 40:101–2.
23. Voth 3:275, 276.
24. See p. 816 for Walpi Snake race.

25. Voth 3:318 ff., 336.
26. Voth 1:Pl. CLXXXIII, 330, 334 ff.
27. Stevenson 2:115–16.
28. Stevenson 2:126.
29. Stevenson 2:126–27.
30. See Stevenson 2:66–89; Bunzel 5:976–77.
31. See pp. 758–61.
32. Bunzel 5:950–51.
33. White 5.
34. See White 3.
35. See pp. 834–36.
36. Parsons 49:205. For Christmas Basket dance see *ibid.*, p. 187.
37. Goldfrank 3:72.
38. Goldfrank 3:73.
39. See pp. 790–91.
40. Goldfrank 3:74–75.
41. White 2:127.
42. Stirling.
43. *Ibid.*
44. Parsons 41.
45. From Parsons 52:288 ff.; Parsons 25:160–65.

CHAPTER VI

1. Parsons 55:63.
2. Said at Oraibi (Titiev 3).
3. White 4:134, 135.
4. Parsons 40:94–95. Stephen makes no mention of any summer solstice ritual.
5. From Dorsey and Voth 1. Observations of 1893, 1897, 1899, and 1900, but principally 1897. Soyala in short form, not in any year of initiations.
6. Stephen 4:3 (n. 5.).
7. Titiev 3.
8. *Ibid.*
9. From Stevenson 2:109–41; Bunzel 2:534–37.
10. Bunzel 5:912.
11. From Parsons 52:290–300.
12. From Parsons 41.
13. Stephen 4:70.
14. Bunzel 6:20–21.
15. Parsons 49:114–17, 227–29.

16. From White 2.
17. See Parsons 59:555–56.
18. Goldfrank 3:39–40.
19. Parsons 6:264–77.
20. See Voth 3:297.
21. Bunzel 4:795.
22. Parsons 52:315–16.
23. Stephen 4:973; Titiev 3.
24. Parsons 55:51.
25. Stephen 4:702–94; compare Voth 3:298 ff.
26. Voth 4:22.
27. Beaglehole 2:14–16; compare Parsons 40:24.
28. Stephen 4:793; compare *ibid.*, pp. 843–44.
29. Voth 3:300.
30. From Stephen 4:960 ff.; compare for 1920 and for noninitiatory form, Parsons 30.
31. See Fewkes 7:Pl. III.
32. See pp. 227, n.*; 231 ff.; also Parsons 36:28 ff.
33. Hopi, Howina (not described); Laguna, Ahina, Parsons 20:123–24; San Felipe, White 3:52–53; Acoma, see pp. 649–54; Tewa, Powinshare and Ti'ishare, Parsons 49:189–91.
34. Titiev 3.
35. Dorsey and Voth 2:234.
36. Bunzel 4:676.
37. Bunzel 4:678–80.
38. Bunzel 4:683.
39. Bunzel 4:686.
40. Bunzel 4:686–89.
41. Bunzel 5:864 (n. 23).
42. See pp. 649 ff.
43. From Parsons 52; compare Lummis 1:111–30.
44. From Parsons 58:21–22.
45. From Stevenson 2:205–17; compare Bunzel 6:71–73.
46. From Parsons 14.
47. Stephen 4:719 ff.; compare Walpi, Stephen 4:577–767; Mishongnovi, Dorsey and Voth 2; Oraibi, Voth 3.
48. Stevenson 2:180–204.

49. Parsons 49:187–89, 191–92.
50. From Stephen 4:884–929.
51. From Parsons 41:81–87.
52. White 5.
53. Bunzel 4:643; 1:504–5.
54. From Stevenson 1:76 ff.
55. Bunzel 4:657–58.
56. Verified in Kroeber 2:159.
57. From Stephen 4:768–817.
58. Fewkes 6:Pl. I; Fewkes 7:249.
59. See p. 871.
60. Lowie 1:610.
61. Boas 2:58, 65.
62. From Dumarest, 154–61.
63. From Stevenson 1:97 ff. For a brushing and sucking cure for ant sickness by a single shaman at Isleta, Parsons 52:443–45.
64. From Stephen 4:857–63.
65. From Parsons 52:445–48.
66. Bunzel 4:792–93.
67. Stevenson 2:486.
68. Bunzel 4:796–801.
69. Stevenson 2:487–90.
70. From White 5.
71. From Parsons 52:339–40; for annual curing or exorcism of fields, village, and people see p. 546; see also pp. 718–21.
72. Bunzel 5:1046.
73. Bunzel 5:1028.
74. Bunzel 5:1045, 1064.
75. Bunzel 5:1016.
76. Bunzel 5:871.
77. Bunzel 5:1051.
78. Fine grains of quartz sphalerite and galena, a ground concentrate of zinc ore (Bunzel 5:861).
79. Bunzel 5:868.
80. Bunzel 5:863.
81. *Ibid.*
82. See p. 124; Voth 6:84; Parsons 40:99 (n. 151); Parsons 41:116, 124.
83. Bunzel 5:873–74.
84. Stephen 4:448 ff., 505, 506, 507.
85. Bunzel 5:1077.
86. Bunzel 5:1064.
87. Bunzel 5:1075.

88. See p. 1163; also Bunzel 5:1022–23.
89. Stephen 4:490.
90. Bunzel 5:863.
91. Parsons 49:179 ff.
92. White 4:99.
93. Parsons 41:87–93.
94. White 4:107.
95. Goldfrank 3:108, 109.
96. Beaglehole 3:45–46.
97. From Parsons 29:171 ff.
98. Bunzel 5:1014.
99. From Parsons 55:93–97.
100. From Bunzel 4:690–781; 4:941–45, 952–57; Parsons 6:183–215; compare Bunzel 6:13–17. For the remarkable kachina masks and the gigantesque Shalako figures see Stevenson 2:Pls. LI, LVII, LXI–LXIV.
101. Bunzel 4:760–61.
102. Compare Stevenson 2:244.
103. Bunzel 4:718.
104. White 2:88–94.
105. From White 2:94–96.
106. From Stephen 4:493 ff.
107. Dictated by a Hano townsman; compare Stephen 4:374 ff.
108. From Parsons 40:53, 55–59; compare Stephen 4:287 ff.; Fewkes 12:40–54.
109. Parsons 33:179 ff.
110. Spinden, 97.
111. From Parsons 58:90–91.
112. From Beaglehole 3:46–47; compare Stephen 4:994–95, Fig. 188; Forde 3:396–97.
113. From Goldfrank 3:93–94; compare Hopi and Tewa, First Mesa, Parsons 40:112–13, 114–15.
114. From Cushing 6:168–79, 193, 195.
115. Stephen 4:256–57; Curtis, XII, 49; Stevenson 2:477, 526.
116. Zuni, Parsons 29:184; Santo Domingo, White 4:115; (?) Hopi, Stephen 4:329–30, 367.
117. White 4:114 ff.
118. Stephen 4:256.

119. Stephen 4:458, 485; Fewkes 3; Parsons 42:225–26; Parsons 40: 89–90; compare Jemez, Parsons 41:76.
120. Kroeber 2:177, Fig. 1.
121. Parsons 5:396.
122. Stephen 4:4, 33, 286, 982–84, 994, 997, 1002–3; Beaglehole 2:14.
123. Parsons 29:191.
124. From Stephen 4:169 ff.
125. From Stephen 4:169 ff., 506 ff.
126. From Stephen 4:383–85.
127. From Stephen 4:385.
128. From Parsons 6:232.
129. From Parsons 49; compare Dumarest, 185–86.
130. See Parsons 41:95; Lummis 1: 269, 277–80.
131. Parsons 41:92.
132. From White 4:149–54; compare Zingg on Huichol carnival celebration.
133. From Parsons 52:321–24.
134. From Stephen 4:458–59.
135. From Stephen 4:652, 657–59, 705–6, 708–9.
136. From Stephen 4:851–52.
137. From Stephen 4:261–83.
138. From Parsons 56; compare Benedict 3:I, 96–116.
139. Voth 2:152–53.
140. From White 4:144–48.
141. Stephen 4:1006, 1024.
142. Parsons 49:195.
143. From Parsons 34; compare Stephen 4:124–30; Fewkes 12:30–31, 92–93.
144. From Parsons 49:199–204.
145. Spinden, 102.
146. Parsons 58:93–94.
147. Parsons 58:87.
148. For Keres see White 2:102–6 (Acoma); Goldfrank 2 (Laguna and Paguate); Parsons 32 (Santa Ana); Lummis 1:253–70 (Cochiti); White 4:159–60 (Santo Domingo); for Tewa, Parsons 49: 192–94, Pls. 23–27. The dance at Zuni (Satechi, the saint arrives) or among the Hopi (Butterfly dance) has not been fully described; but for Zuni see Bunzel 6:25–26. See pp. 843–44 for Taos.
149. From Parsons 41:96–100.
150. White 7.
151. White 5.
152. Titiev 3.
153. From Dumarest, 170–72; compare Goldfrank 3:74–75.
154. From Parsons 49:236–37.
155. From Bunzel 4:621–23; Parsons 9.

CHAPTER VII

1. Bloom, 197 (n. 37); Bancroft, 221–22.
2. Forde 3:376, Map 4.
3. Voth 2:91–92.
4. Dorsey and Voth 2:253.
5. Parsons 40:104.
6. Parsons 55:9 ff.
7. Stephen 1:212.
8. Hodge 3:52, 54, 116 (n. 114).
9. Hodge 3:23, 24.
10. Hodge 3:64, 75.
11. Hodge 3:83.
12. Stevenson 2:283–86.
13. Stevenson 2:Pl. XXXVI.
14. Bunzel 6:55.
15. Bunzel 6:37.
16. Bunzel 6:19.
17. Stevenson 2:217 ff.
18. Stevenson 2:47.
19. Stevenson 2:552.
20. *Ibid.*
21. Stevenson 2:411, 416, 441.
22. Bunzel 5:1043.
23. Parsons 56:49.
24. From White 2 and White 7.
25. See Parsons 14:165 ff.
26. White 7.
27. See White 4:16.
28. Bloom, 170.
29. Parsons 33:260–64.
30. Parsons 33:271.
31. Cf. Santo Domingo, White 4: 167.

32. White 4.
33. Redfield, 178.
34. Dumarest, 148 (n. 1).
35. Parsons 31:487.
36. White 5.
37. Thomas, 100.
38. From Parsons 41.
39. Thomas, 100.
40. Bloom, 159, 166, 171.
41. From Parsons 49.
42. Thomas, 95.
43. Parsons 42:169–74.
44. Parsons 40:116.
45. Bloom, 192 ff.
46. Census taken by A. M. Stephen, cited by Fewkes 5:166.
47. Stephen 4:1084.
48. Compare Stephen 4:XLV.
49. Parsons 40:121–22.
50. See Stephen 4:Figs. 24, 25; Parsons 40:Fig. 11; Fewkes 8:Pls. XVIII, XIX.
51. Stephen 4:393.
52. Stephen 4:182–83.
53. Stephen 4:576.
54. Stephen 4:133; see p. 182.
55. From Parsons 52 and Parsons 25 and recently acquired unpublished material.
56. Whorf and Trager, 615.
57. Thomas, 102, quoting Morfi (1782).
58. Parsons 52:Pl. 17.
59. Parsons 21:63.
60. Parsons 58.
61. Handbook, Taos.
62. Twitchell, I, 430.
63. Bancroft, 432 ff.

CHAPTER VIII

1. Stevenson 2:495, 498; White 4:178; see pp. 604 ff.
2. Parsons 60.
3. Parsons 41:Figs. 8, 17.
4. Lowie 1:603.
5. Stephen 4:679.
6. Bunzel 4:626, 706.
7. Stephen 4:679, 713 (n. 1).
8. Parsons 49:199.

9. Bunzel 5:1074.
10. Compare Bunzel 5:901, 1032.
11. Stevenson 2:531.
12. Stevenson 2:496–97, 498, 500.
13. See pp. 423, 733.
14. See Stephen 4:147 (n. 2).
15. Parsons 49:195–96.
16. See pp. 715 ff.
17. Stephen 4:675, 679, 707, 713-14, 718, 745.
18. White 7.
19. Stephen 4:814.
20. Dumarest, 188.
21. Bunzel 5:1022.
22. Parsons 8; White 2:154–56.
23. White 7; compare Parsons 33:222.
24. Parsons 40:93; Stirling.
25. Stephen 4:Fig. 30.
26. See pp. 226, 636; also Benedict 3:II, 207.
27. Parsons 47:604.
28. White 4:3; White 7.
29. White 4:78–79.
30. Sapir; Whorf and Trager.
31. Kroeber 4:411 ff.
32. Strong 1:7–12.
33. Strong 1:19–21.
34. Strong 1:35–37.
35. Forde 2:120.
36. Strong 2; Drucker.
37. Strong 1:48, 50, 52–54; Strong 2:339 ff.; Kroeber 4:413.
38. Beals, 192.
39. Spier 3:155, 181, 182, 184, 185, 186.
40. Spier 3:143, 145, 231, 232, 239, 244, 251, 280, 283, 284, 286, 290–91, 298, 322, 332, 335.
41. Spier 3:243–44, 310, 312, 314, 329.
42. Drucker.
43. Forde 2:94, 95, 96, 109, 128, 132, 137, 138, 165–66, 194, 225, 226, 228.
44. Forde, 2:97, 106. See p. 34.
45. See pp. 339, n. §, 1072–73; Stephen 4:XXVI.
46. See Index.

47. Underhill 3: In general, all Papago references unless otherwise indicated are from Underhill.
48. Underhill 4.
49. Parsons 46.
50. Underhill 2:13, 15, 18, 21, 27, 32, 35, 60; Underhill 4.
51. Mason; Underhill 2:59–60; Underhill 4.
52. Davis.
53. Underhill 1.
54. See Bennett and Zingg for all references.
55. Underhill 3.
56. Preuss and Lumholtz were early students; in 1932, Dr. Beals and I worked for three broken weeks with Cora and Huichol travelers in Tepic; Dr. Kleinberg visited the Huicholes for several weeks in 1933, and Dr. Zingg spent a year among them (1934–35). The following summary is drawn from all these sources without always distinguishing them. It is a mere sketch of comparative work urgently needed.
57. Zingg, Kleinberg.
58. Zingg.
59. Lumholtz.
60. Parsons 40:52 (n. 86).
61. Parsons and Beals.
62. Hodge 3:66–67.
63. The Zuni parallel was pointed out to me by Dr. Bunzel.
64. Sahagún (b) Book XI; chap. iv.
65. Sahagún (b) Book XI, chap. v; Saville, Pl. XXXVI.
66. Parsons 20:122.
67. Parsons 57:613.
68. Sahagún (a), 95.
69. Sahagún (b), Book XII, chap. iv.
70. Sahagún (a), 146–47, and Codex Florentino (Sahagún), Pl. V.
71. Thompson 240, citing Gomara.
72. Bunzel 5:1080–82.
73. Thompson, 239, 240, citing Gomara.

74. Thompson, 240, citing Torquemada.
75. Sahagún (a), 107, 147.
76. Bourke 1:524 citing Torquemada.
77. Sahagún (a), 124–25.
78. Sahagún (a), 66.
79. Sahagún (a), 81.
80. Sahagún (a), 56, 93–94, 148.
81. Sahagún (a), 65, 138.
82. Sahagún (b), 454–58.
83. Sahagún (a), 41.
84. Sahagún (a), 197.
85. Sahagún (a), 124.
86. Sahagún (a), 97.
87. Sahagún (a), 26.
88. Sahagún (a), 97.
89. Forde 3:Fig. 3.
90. Stephen 4:Figs. 83, 84.
91. Sahagún (a), 35, 36, 53, 64.
92. Sahagún (a), 148.
93. Sahagún (a), 35; Parsons 41:123; Bunzel 5:845.
94. Compare Zapoteca, Parsons 62:518 (n. 78).
95. Sahagún (a), 118.
96. Sahagún (b), Book V, Appens. XIX, XXVII.
97. Sahagún (a), 96.
98. Sahagún (a), 158, 244; Book IV, chap. xxxvi.
99. Sahagún (a), 41.
100. Sahagún (a), 40.
101. Sahagún (a), 39, 70.
102. Sahagún (a), 157.
103. Sahagún (a), 82.
104. Parsons 62:122 (n. 130), citing Brinton; I find no reference to insect medicine in Sahagún, though, as noted, insects are impersonated.
105. Sahagún, 147, Codex Florentino, Pl. V.
106. Sahagún (a), 90.
107. Sahagún (a), 25.
108. Sahagún (a), 44, 126.
109. Sahagún (a), 73.
110. Sahagún (a), 61.
111. Sahagún (a), 191.

112. Parsons and Beals, 512.
113. Hodge in Benavides, 227.
114. Benavides, 12 ff.; Bandelier 1:79 ff.; Bancroft, 82.
115. Roberts 2:14–15.
116. See pp. 1095–96.
117. Bancroft, 276–77.
118. Twitchell, II, 227, 228.
119. Stephen 4:709.
120. Linton, 422.
121. Stephen 4:537, 543.
122. Smith, 441, 443.
123. Smith, 439, 445.
124. Kurz, 213 (Crow).
125. Smith, 449, 450.
126. Parsons 58:21.
127. Spier 2:255–56.
128. Kurz, 104; cf. Matthews 4:37.
129. Compare Parsons 50:104, 108–9.
130. Kurz, 262.
131. Parsons 51:646, 653.
132. Parsons 51:651 ff.
133. Gilmore, 29–32.
134. Lowie 2:676, 677.
135. Lowie 2:650, 660, 663–64, 666, 668, 669, 672, 673–75, 676.
136. Kelly, 138, and see Kelly for all Chemehuevi references. References to Northern Paiute are from Lowie, Kelly, or Steward.
137. Stephen 4:169, 463 ff.
138. Hodge 3:31.
139. Stephen 4:XXVII.
140. Stephen 4:940, 952, 1046.
141. Goddard 5:131–32.
142. Parsons 42:172.
143. Haile, 18, 44, 77; compare Sia, Stevenson 1:42.
144. Newcomb and Reichard, 39.
145. Newcomb and Reichard, 48, 61.
146. Stephen 4:701–4.
147. Hill, 14.
148. Newcomb and Reichard, 23.
149. Hill, 18.
150. Stephen 4:XXVIII, 223 (n. 1), 930.
151. Stephen 4:180–81 and Glossary.
152. Franciscan Fathers, 498–500; Matthews 4:117–18.
153. Haile, 147.
154. Goddard 5:130–31, 136, 137, 138.
155. Goddard 5:171, 172.
156. Hill, 11; Wallis 2.
157. Franciscan Fathers, 461.
158. White 2:96.
159. Stephen 4:99.
160. Haile, 43, 272.
161. Matthews 1:440–41.
162. Newcomb and Reichard, 7.
163. Matthews 4:6, 67; Matthews 3: 39, 40, 42–43.
164. Matthews 1:419; Matthews 4: 75.
165. Matthews 1:425, 426; Matthews 4:57.
166. Reichard 1:158, Newcomb and Reichard, 11.
167. Matthews 4:69, Fig. 9; Matthews 1:453.
168. Haile, 32, 197.
169. Newcomb and Reichard, 23.
170. Matthews 1:419.
171. Matthews 1:422; Newcomb and Reichard, 11, 22, 69 ff.
172. Goddard 5:177.
173. Matthews 1:430; Matthews 4: 99, 108.
174. Haile, 63; Matthews 4:91.
175. Matthews 1:437; Matthews 4: 58.
176. Matthews 1:425.
177. Ibid.
178. Newcomb and Reichard, 22.
179. Matthews 4:91; Haile, 62.
180. Franciscan Fathers, 372; compare Matthews 4:94; Newcomb and Reichard, 23.
181. Goddard 5:146, 161; Matthews 1:420, 442.
182. Goddard 5:136.
183. Wyman 2.
184. Newcomb and Reichard, 14.
185. Reichard 2:109.
186. Haile, 13.
187. Haile, 239.
188. Compare Lummis 1:83–89.
189. Cochiti, Dumarest, 195–96;

Tewa, Parsons 42:166–67; Taos, Parsons 58:25.
190. Parsons 4.
191. Parsons 41:71.
192. Dumarest, 195–96.
193. Parsons 49:116.
194. Parsons 49:63.
195. Opler 2:212.
196. Cushing 6:608; Goodwin (personal communication).
197. Goodwin 2:24–25, 26.
198. Goddard 4:124, 132–33; Goodwin 3.
199. Spier 2:290; Bourke 1:502.
200. Goodwin 2:36.
201. Opler 2:221.
202. Goodwin 1:398, 399, 406, and personal communication.
203. Goodwin 3; compare Bourke 1:504.
204. Goodwin 2:34.
205. Goddard 4:123, 124, 129.
206. Goodwin 2:28, 30, 32, 33.
207. Goodwin 2:33.
208. Twitchell, II, 269.
209. Parsons 52:338; Opler 3:18.
210. Opler 5.
211. Bourke 1:465–66.
212. Opler 3:17, 23, 24, 31, 34, 37; Opler 1:65.
213. Hackett, 98–99; Twitchell, see below.
214. Hackett, 98–99.
215. Voth 5:129–30.
216. Voth 7:52.
217. Dumarest, 143; confinement fire and smoke against witchcraft.
218. Michel, 54–55.
219. Luxán, 79.
220. Luxán, 89.
221. Espinosa, A. M., 101.
222. White 4:114 ff.
223. Twitchell, II, 255.
224. Scholes 1:108.
225. Parsons 58:94.
226. Parsons 14:169.
227. White 2:71.
228. Dumarest, 161 (n. 2), 172–73.
229. Compare Parsons 62:529–30.
230. Scholes 1:105.
231. Stevenson 1:463.
232. Parsons 6:242 (n. 3).
233. Bunzel 5:1050–51; Beaglehole 3:53.

CHAPTER IX

1. Parsons 60:231.
2. See p. 5.
3. Stephen 4:1067 (n. 7).
4. Dumarest, 192.
5. Parsons 20:115; Boas 2:13 ff.
6. See pp. 258, 265.
7. Opler 4:149 ff.
8. Wyman 1:239, 243.
9. Parsons 4:169.
10. Stevenson 2:122–23.
11. Parsons 1:218–19.
12. Stephen 4:996–97.
13. Compare Reichard 1:7–8.
14. White 2:67.
15. Stephen 4:416 (n. 1), 430–31.
16. Bunzel 5:1067–68.
17. Stirling.
18. Parsons 49:225–26, 305.
19. Dumarest, 162.
20. See p. 424.
21. Cochiti, Goldfrank 3:64; Laguna, Parsons 20:121–22; Nambé, Parsons 49:225–26.
22. Hodge 3:75.
23. Hodge 3:67.
24. Parsons 62:286, 298.
25. Parsons 52:373–74, 374–75.
26. Parsons 62:94 (n. 67).
27. White 4:41.
28. Fewkes 10:65.
29. See Index Bell(s), Candle(s), Wheat.
30. Beaglehole 2:17.
31. Dorsey and Voth 2:227.
32. Voth 2:76 n., 86.
33. Stephen 4:697.
34. Stephen 4:354.
35. Voth 3:303 (n. 2).
36. Bunzel 5:1068.
37. Stephen 4:Figs. 237–40; Fewkes 12:28–29.
38. Bunzel 5:856.

39. Bunzel 5:856–57.
40. Bunzel 1:85.
41. Parsons 33:219.
42. Cushing, Fewkes, Parsons, 296–98.
43. Dorsey and Voth 2:195–96.
44. Stephen 4: Index, Poboshwĭmkya and Ya'yatü society.
45. Bunzel 5:1057–58; Parsons 6:243.
46. White 7; White 5; White 4:37.
47. Bunzel 5:877.
48. Stevenson 2:165, 168 (n. a).
49. Bunzel 2:543–44.
50. Beaglehole 2:13.
51. See p. 514.
52. Bunzel 6:55–56.
53. Dumarest, 196.
54. Forde 1:376, quoting Freire-Marreco.
55. Fewkes 10:64.
56. Redfield, 180.
57. Stephen 4:1120–21.
58. Nequatewa, 60 ff.
59. Cushing, Fewkes, Parsons, 267, 277–82; Stephen 4:37.
60. Dorsey and Voth 1:11, 43.
61. Dorsey and Voth 1:10.
62. Voth 2:90.
63. Gunn, 93, 97; Parsons 52:413.
64. Bunzel 5:949.
65. Beaglehole 3:73–74.
66. Stephen 4:126, 910.
67. Stephen 4:133.
68. Parsons 40:64.
69. Compare White 4:23; for Zuni, Parsons 6:246.
70. Gunn, 102.
71. White 7.
72. Parsons 40:121 (n. 185).
73. White 4:60 (n. 56); White 3:12 (n. 23), 13.
74. White 2:98.
75. Parsons 33:222, 278–79.
76. Smith, 450.
77. White 2:107 (n. 94).
78. Goldfrank 3:47, 84 ff.
79. Stephen 4:108, 958–59; Parsons 30:179–80.
80. Voth 8:51 (n. 1).
81. Parsons 40:77 (n. 124).
82. Beaglehole 1:12–13.
83. Bunzel 4:792; Stephen 4:859; Beaglehole 3:21.
84. Dorsey and Voth 1:38.
85. Bunzel 5:1074; Parsons 49:202.
86. Keech, R. A. (personal communication).
87. Stephen 4:301.
88. Bunzel 4:627.
89. Bunzel 6:8, 9.
90. Stirling; cf. Navaho, Matthews 4:99.
91. Stephen 4:651, 881; see also 848–49.
92. Lowie 1:619.
93. Lowie 1:624.
94. Cushing 6:624–26; Parsons 6:153; Bunzel 5:935–36, Pl. 22b.
95. Haile, 14.
96. Stephen 4:520.
97. Parsons 29:Note 10 (p. 199).
98. Bunzel 5:1022–23.
99. White 7.
100. Stephen 4:332.
101. Stevenson 2:545 (n. a).

BIBLIOGRAPHY

AITKEN, BARBARA. "Temperament in Native American Religion," *Journal of the Royal Anthropological Institute*, LX (1930), 363–87. *See* Robbins, Harrington, Freire-Marreco (Aitken).

BANCROFT, H. H. *History of Arizona and New Mexico*, in *Works*, Vol. XVII. San Francisco, 1889.

BANDELIER, A. F.
1. *Final Report*. "Papers of the Archaeological Institute of America: American Series," Vol. III. Cambridge, Mass., 1890.
2. "An Outline of the Documentary History of the Zuñi Tribe," *Journal of American Ethnology and Archaeology*, Vol. III (1892).
3. "The Montezuma of the Pueblo Indians," *American Anthropologist*, V (1892), 319 ff.

BARTLETT, K.
1. *The Material Culture of Pueblo II in the San Francisco Mountains, Arizona*. "Museum of Northern Arizona Bull.," No. 7. Flagstaff, Ariz., 1934.
2. "Hopi History," *Museum Notes of the Museum of Northern Arizona*, Vol. VIII, No. 7 (1936).

BEAGLEHOLE, ERNEST.
1. (WITH PEARL BEAGLEHOLE). *Hopi of the Second Mesa*. "American Anthropological Association Memoirs," Vol. XLIV. Menasha, Wis., 1935.
2. *Hopi Hunting and Hunting Ritual*. "Yale University Publications in Anthropology," No. 4. New Haven, 1936.
3. *Notes on Hopi Economic Life*. "Yale University Publications in Anthropology," No. 15. New Haven, 1937.

BEALS, RALPH L. *The Comparative Ethnology of Northern Mexico before 1750*, Ibero-Americana, No. II. Berkeley, 1932.

BENAVIDES. *The Memorial of Fray Alonso de Benavides 1630*, trans. MRS. E. E. AYER; annotated by F. W. HODGE. Chicago, 1916.

BENEDICT, RUTH.
1. "Psychological Types in the Cultures of the Southwest," *Proceedings of the Twenty-third International Congress of Americanists* (1928), pp. 572–81.
2. *Tales of the Cochiti Indians*. "Bureau of American Ethnology Bull.," No. 98. Washington, 1931.
3. *Zuni Mythology*. "Columbia University Contributions to Anthropology," Vol. XXI. New York, 1935.

BENNETT, WENDELL C., and ZINGG, ROBERT M. *The Tarahumara.* "University of Chicago Publications in Anthropology." Chicago, 1935.

BLOOM, L. B. "A Campaign against the Moqui Pueblos," *New Mexico Historical Review,* VI (1931), 158–226.

BOAS, FRANZ.
    1. *The Mind of Primitive Man.* New York, 1911.
    2. *Keresan Texts.* "American Ethnological Society Publications," Vol. VIII, Part I. New York, 1928.

BOURKE, J. G.
    1. "Medicine Men of the Apache," *Ninth Annual Report of the Bureau of American Ethnology.* Washington, 1887–88.
    2. "Bourke on the Southwest [*Journal,* ed. L. B. Bloom]," *New Mexico Historical Review,* XI (1936), 77–122, 188–207.

BRAND, D. D., HAWLEY, F. M., HIBBEN, F. C. "Tseh So, a Small House Ruin, Chaco Canyon, N.M.," *University of New Mexico Bulletin,* Vol. II, No. 2 (1937).

BREW, J. O. "The First Two Seasons at Awatovi," *American Antiquity,* III (1937), 122–37.

BUNZEL, RUTH L.
    1. *The Pueblo Potter.* New York, 1929.
    2. "Introduction to Zuñi Ceremonialism," *Forty-seventh Annual Report of the Bureau of American Ethnology.* Washington, 1929–30.
    3. "Zuñi Origin Myths," *ibid.*
    4. "Zuñi Ritual Poetry," *ibid.*
    5. "Zuñi Katcinas," *ibid.*
    6. *Zuni Texts.* "American Ethnological Society Publications," Vol. XV. New York, 1933.

CHILAM BALAM. *The Book of Chilam Balam of Chumayel,* ed. RALPH L. ROYS. Washington: Carnegie Institution of Washington, 1933.

CURTIS, EDWARD S. *The North American Indian,* Vols. I and XII. Seattle, Wash., 1907 and 1922.

CUSHING, FRANK HAMILTON.
    1. "Zuñi Fetiches," *Second Annual Report of the Bureau of Ethnology.* Washington, 1880.
    2. "My Adventures in Zuñi," *Century Magazine,* N.S., Vol. III (1882).
    3. "Outlines of Zuñi Creation Myths," *Thirteenth Annual Report of the Bureau of Ethnology.* Washington, 1891–92.
    4. "Katalog einer Sammlung von Idolen, Fetischen und priesterlichen Ausrüstungsgegenständen der Zuñi oder Ashiwi Indianer von Neu-Mexiko (U.S. Amerika)," *Veröffentlichungen aus dem Königlichen Museum für Völkerkunde,* Vol. IV, Part I (1895).
    5. *Zuñi Folk Tales.* New York and London, 1901.

6. *Zuñi Breadstuff.* "Indian Notes and Monographs," Vol. VIII. New York: Museum of the American Indian, Heye Foundation, 1920.

7. "Origin Myth from Oraibi," *Journal of American Folk-Lore,* XXXVI (1923), 163–70.

CUSHING, F. H.; FEWKES, J. W.; PARSONS, E. C. "Contributions to Hopi History," *American Anthropologist,* XXIV (1922), 253–98.

DAVIS, E. H. *The Papago Ceremony of Vikíta.* "Indian Notes and Monographs," Vol. III, No. 4. New York: Museum of the American Indian, Heye Foundation, 1920.

DE LAGUNA, FREDERICA. "Indian Masks from the Lower Yukon," *American Anthropologist,* XXXVIII (1936), 569–85.

DORSEY, G. A., and VOTH, H. R.
  1. *The Oraibi Soyal Ceremony.* "Field Columbian Museum Pub. 55, Anthropological Series," Vol. III, No. 1. Chicago, 1901.
  2. *The Mishongnovi Ceremonies of the Snake and Antelope Fraternities.* "Field Columbian Museum Pub. 66, Anthropological Series," Vol. III, No. 3. Chicago, 1902.

DRUCKER, PHILIP. "Culture Elements Distributions: V. Southern California," *Anthropological Records,* Vol. I, No. 1 (1937).

DUMAREST, NOËL. *Notes on Cochiti, New Mexico.* "American Anthropological Association Memoirs," Vol. VI, No. 3. Lancaster, Pa., 1919.

EGGAN, FRED. "Hopi" (MS).

ESPINOSA, AURELIO M. "Pueblo Indian Folk Tales," *Journal of American Folk-Lore,* XLIX (1936), 69–133.

ESPINOSA, JOSÉ M. *Spanish Folk-Tales from New Mexico.* "American Folk-Lore Society Memoirs," No. 30. New York, 1937.

FEWKES, J. W.
  1. "The Ceremonial Circuit among the Village Indians of Northeastern Arizona," *Journal of American Folk-Lore,* V (1892), 33–42.
  2. "A Few Summer Ceremonials at the Tusayan Pueblos," *Journal of American Ethnology and Archaeology,* Vol. II, Part I (1892).
  3. "The Wa-wac-ka-tci-na: A Tusayan Foot Race," *Bulletin of the Essex Institute,* XXIV (1892), 113–33.
  4. "A Few Tusayan Pictographs," *American Anthropologist,* V (1892), 9–26.
  5. "The Kinship of a Tanoan-speaking Community in Tusayan," *ibid.,* VII (1894), 162–67.
  6. "The Oraibi Flute Altar," *Journal of American Folk-Lore,* VIII (1895), 265–82.
  7. "The Micoñinovi Flute Altars," *ibid.,* IX (1896), 241–55.

8. "Winter Solstice Altars at Hano," *American Anthropologist*, I (1899), 251–76.
9. "Property-Right in Eagles among the Hopi," *ibid.*, II (1900), 690–707.
10. "The Pueblo Settlements near El Paso, Texas," *ibid.*, IV (1902), 57–75.
11. "Minor Hopi Festivals," *ibid.*, pp. 482–511.
12. "Hopi Katcinas," *Twenty-first Annual Report of the Bureau of American Ethnology*. Washington, 1903.
13. "Hopi Shrines near the East Mesa, Arizona," *American Anthropologist*, VIII (1906), 346–75.
14. "The Butterfly in Hopi Myth and Ritual," *ibid.*, XII (1910), 576–94.
15. "The Relation of Sun Temple, a New Type of Ruin Lately Excavated in the Mesa Verde National Park, to Prehistoric 'Towers,' " *Journal of the Washington Academy of Sciences*, VI (1916), 212–21.

FORDE, C. DARYLL.
1. "A Creation Myth from Acoma," *Folk-Lore*, XLI (1930), 359–87.
2. "Ethnography of the Yuma Indians," *University of California Publications in American Archaeology and Ethnology*, XXVIII, No. 4 (1931), 83–278.
3. "Hopi Agriculture and Land Ownership," *Journal of the Royal Anthropological Institute*, LXI (1931), 357–405.

FRANCISCAN FATHERS. *An Ethnologic Dictionary of the Navaho Language*. Saint Michaels, Ariz.: Franciscan Fathers, 1910.

GILMORE, M. R. *Arikara Account of the Origin of Tobacco and Catching of Eagles*, "Indian Notes and Monographs," Vol. VI, pp. 26–33. New York: Museum of the American Indian, Heye Foundation, 1929.

GLADWIN, H. S., HAURY, E. W., SAYLES, E. B., GLADWIN, N. *Excavations at Snaketown*. "Medallion Papers," No. XXV. Gila Pueblo, Globe, Ariz., 1937.

GODDARD, P. E.
1. "Gotal, a Mescallero Apache Ceremony," *Putnam Anniversary Volume*, pp. 385–94. New York, 1909.
2. "Apache Masked Dancers," *Anthropological Essays: Holmes Anniversary Volume*. Washington, 1916.
3. *Myths and Tales from the San Carlos Apache*. "Anthropological Papers of the American Museum of Natural History," Vol. XXIV, Part I. New York, 1918.
4. *Myths and Tales from the White Mountain Apache*. "Anthropological Papers of the American Museum of Natural History," Vol. XXIV, Part II. New York, 1919.

5. *Navajo Texts.* "Anthropological Papers of the American Museum of Natural History," Vol. XXXIV, Part I. New York, 1933.

GOLDFRANK, ESTHER SCHIFF.
  1. "A Note on Twins," *American Anthropologist*, XXIII (1921), 387–88.
  2. "Notes on Two Pueblo Feasts," *ibid.*, XXV (1923), 188–96.
  3. *The Social and Ceremonial Organization of Cochiti.* "American Anthropological Association Memoirs," Vol. XXXIII. Menasha, 1927.

GOODWIN, GRENVILLE.
  1. "The Characteristics and Functions of Clan in a Southern Athapascan Culture," *American Anthropologist*, XXXIX (1937), 394–407.
  2. "White Mountain Apache Religion," *ibid.*, XL (1938), 24–37.
  3. *Western Apache Folklore.* "American Folk-Lore Society Memoirs," No. 33. New York, 1938.

GUNN, J. M. *Schat-Chen.* Albuquerque, 1917.

HACKETT, C. W. "The Revolt of the Pueblo Indians of New Mexico in 1680," *Quarterly of the Texas State Historical Association*, XV (1911), 93–147.

HAILE, FATHER BERARD. *Origin Legend of the Navaho Enemy Way.* "Yale University Publications in Anthropology," No. 17. New Haven, 1938.

HAMMOND, G. P. "Oñate and the Founding of New Mexico," *New Mexico Historical Review*, I (1926), 42 ff., 156 ff., 292 ff.

HANDY, EDWARD S. "Zuñi Tales," *Journal of American Folk-Lore*, XXXI (1918), 451–71.

HARGRAVE, LYNDON L. *The Jeddito Valley and the First Pueblo Towns in Arizona To Be Visited by Europeans.* "Museum Notes of the Museum of Northern Arizona," Vol. VIII, No. 4. Flagstaff, 1935.

HARPER, BLANCHE. "The Jemez Child" (MS).

HARRINGTON, J. P. "The Ethnogeography of the Tewa Indians," *Twenty-ninth Annual Report of the Bureau of American Ethnology.* Washington, 1907–8.

HARRINGTON, J. P., and ROBERTS, HELEN H. "Picurís Children's Stories with Texts and Songs," *Forty-third Annual Report of the Bureau of American Ethnology.* Washington, 1925–26.

HAURY, E. W. *The Canyon Creek Ruin and the Cliff Dwellings of the Sierra Ancha.* "Medallion Papers," No. XIV. Gila Pueblo, Globe, Ariz., 1934.

HERZOG, G. "A Comparison of Pueblo and Pima Musical Styles," *Journal of American Folk-Lore*, XLIX (1936), 283–417.

HILL, W. W. *Navaho Warfare.* "Yale University Publications in Anthropology," No. 5. New Haven, 1936.

HODGE, F. W.
  1. "A Zuñi Foot-Race," *American Anthropologist*, III (1890), 227-31.
  2. *Hawikuh Bonework*. "Indian Notes and Monographs," Vol. III, No. 3. New York: Museum of the American Indian, Heye Foundation, 1920.
  3. *History of Hawikuh, New Mexico*. Los Angeles, 1937.
HOUGH, W.
  1. *Antiquities of the Upper Gila and Salt River Valleys in Arizona and New Mexico*. "Bureau of American Ethnology Bull.," No. 35. Washington, 1907.
  2. *Culture of the Ancient Pueblos of the Upper Gila Region, New Mexico and Arizona*. "Smithsonian Institute Bull.," No. 87. Washington, 1914.
  3. "The Sio Shalako at the First Mesa, July 9, 1916," *American Anthropologist*, XIX (1917), 410-15.
HRDLIČKA, A. "The Pueblos," *American Journal of Physical Anthropology*, XX (1935), 235-460.
KELLY, ISABEL T. "Chemehuevi Shamanism," *Essays in Anthropology in Honor of Alfred Louis Kroeber*, pp. 129-42. Berkeley, 1936.
KIDDER, A. V.
  1. *An Introduction to the Study of Southwestern Archaeology*. Andover: Phillips Academy, 1924.
  2. *The Pottery of Pecos*. Andover: Phillips Academy and Carnegie Institution of Washington, 1931.
  3. "Speculations on New World Prehistory," *Essays in Anthropology in Honor of Alfred Louis Kroeber*, pp. 143-52. Berkeley, 1936.
KIDDER, A. V., and GUERNSEY, S. J. *Archaeological Explorations in Northeastern Arizona*. "Bureau of American Ethnology Bull.," No. 65. Washington, 1919.
KROEBER, A. L.
  1. "Thoughts on Zuñi Religion," *Holmes Anniversary Volume*, pp. 269-77. Washington, 1916.
  2. *Zuñi Kin and Clan*. "Anthropological Papers of the American Museum of Natural History," Vol. XVIII, Part II. New York, 1917.
  3. "Native Culture of the Southwest," *University of California Publications in American Archaeology and Ethnology*, XXIII (1928), 375-98.
  4. "The Patwin and Their Neighbors," *ibid.*, Vol. XXIX (1932).
KURZ, RUDOLPH FRIEDERICH. *Journal* [trans. Myrtis Jarrell; ed. J. N. B. Hewitt]. "Bureau of American Ethnology Bull.," No. 115. Washington, 1937.
LINTON, RALPH. "The Comanche Sun Dance," *American Anthropologist*, XXXVII (1935), 420-28

LOWIE, R. H.
1. "Ceremonialism in North America," *American Anthropologist*, XVI (1914), 602–31.
2. *Societies of the Arikara Indians*. "Anthropological Papers of the American Museum of Natural History," Vol. XI, Part 8. New York, 1915.
3. "A Women's Ceremony among the Hopi," *Natural History*, XXV (1925), 178–83.
4. *Notes on Hopi Clans*. "Anthropological Papers of the American Museum of Natural History," Vol. XXX, Part 6. New York, 1929.
5. *Hopi Kinship*. "Anthropological Papers of the American Museum of Natural History," Vol. XXX, Part 7. New York, 1929.
6. "Cultural Anthropology: A Science," *American Journal of Sociology*, XLII (1936), 301–20.
LUMHOLTZ, C. *Unknown Mexico*. New York, 1902.
LUMMIS, C. F.
1. *The Land of Poco Tiempo*. New York, 1897.
2. *Some Strange Corners of Our Country*. New York, 1908.
3. *Pueblo Indian Folk-Stories*. New York, 1910.
LUXÁN, DIEGO PEREZ DE. *Journal. Expedition into New Mexico Made by Antonio de Espéjo, 1582–1583*, trans. HAMMOND and REY. Los Angeles: Quivira Society, 1929.
MASON, J. ALDEN. "The Papago Harvest Festival," *American Anthropologist*, XXII (1920), 13–25.
MATTHEWS, WASHINGTON.
1. "The Mountain Chant: A Navajo Ceremony," *Fifth Annual Report of the Bureau of American Ethnology*. Washington, 1883–84.
2. "Navaho Gambling Songs," *American Anthropologist*, II (1889), 1–9.
3. *Navaho Legends*. "American Folk-Lore Society Memoirs," Vol. V. New York, 1897.
4. *The Night Chant: A Navaho Ceremony*. "American Museum of Natural History Memoirs," Vol. VI. Washington, 1902.
MEANS, PHILIP AINSWORTH. *Ancient Civilizations of the Andes*. New York and London, 1931.
MÉTRAUX, A. *La Religion des Tupinamba*. Paris, 1928.
MICHEL, ARTUR. "Der Bandltanz in den romanischen Ländern," *Wiener Zeitschrift für Volkskunde*, XLI (1936), 49–60.
MORGAN, WILLIAM. *Human Wolves among the Navaho*. "Yale University Publications in Anthropology," No. 11. New Haven, 1936.
MORRIS, EARL H. *The Beginnings of Pottery Making in the San Juan Area; Unfired Prototypes and the Wares of the Earliest Ceramic Period.*

"Anthropological Papers of the American Museum of Natural History," Vol. XXVIII, Part II. New York, 1927.

NELSON, N. C. *Pueblo Ruins of the Galisteo Basin, New Mexico.* "Anthropological Papers of the American Museum of Natural History," Vol. XV, Part I. New York, 1914.

NEQUATEWA, E. *Truth of a Hopi* [ed. M. R. F. Colton]. "Museum of Northern Arizona Bull.," No. 8. Flagstaff, 1936.

NEWCOMB, F. I., and REICHARD, G. A. *Sand Paintings of the Navajo Shooting Chant.* New York, 1937.

OPLER, M. E.

   1. "The Concept of Supernatural Power among the Chiricahua and Mescalero Apaches," *American Anthropologist,* XXXVII (1935), 65–70.

   2. "A Summary of Jicarilla Apache Culture," *ibid.,* XXXVIII (1936), 202–23.

   3. (CASTETTER and OPLER). *The Ethnobiology of the Chiricahua and Mescalero Apache.* Albuquerque, 1936.

   4. "The Influence of Aboriginal Pattern and White Contact on a Recently Introduced Ceremony, the Mescalero Peyote Rite," *Journal of American Folk-Lore,* XLIX (1936), 143–66.

   5. "The Sacred Clowns of the Chiricahua and Mescalero Indians," *El Palacio,* XLIV (1938), 75–79.

   6. *Myths and Tales of the Jicarilla Apache Indians.* "American Folk-Lore Society Memoirs," Vol. XXXI. New York, 1938.

PARSONS, ELSIE CLEWS.

   1. "A Few Zuñi Death Beliefs and Practices," *American Anthropologist,* XVIII (1916), 245–56.

   2. "The Zuñi A'doshlĕ and Suukĕ," *ibid.,* pp. 338–47.

   3. "The Zuñi Ła'mana," *ibid.,* pp. 521–28.

   4. "A Zuñi Detective," *Man,* XVI (1916), 168–70.

   5. "The Zuñi Mo'lawia," *Journal of American Folk-Lore,* XXIX (1916), 392–99.

   6. *Notes on Zuñi.* "American Anthropological Association Memoirs," Vol. IV, No. 3, Part I, and No. 4, Part II. Lancaster, Pa., 1917.

   7. "Ceremonial Friendship at Zuñi," *American Anthropologist,* XIX (1917), 1–8.

   8. "The Antelope Clan in Keresan Custom and Myth," *Man,* XVII (1917), 190–93.

   9. "All Souls' Day at Zuñi, Acoma and Laguna," *Journal of American Folk-Lore,* XXX (1917), 495–96.

  10. "Zuñi Conception and Pregnancy Beliefs," *Proceedings of the Nineteenth International Congress of Americanists* (1917), pp. 379–83.

11. "Pueblo-Indian Folk-Tales, Probably of Spanish Provenience," *Journal of American Folk-Lore*, XXXI (1918), 216–55.
12. "Nativity Myth at Laguna and Zuñi," *ibid.*, pp. 256–63.
13. "War God Shrines of Laguna and Zuñi," *American Anthropologist*, XX (1918), 381–405.
14. "Notes on Acoma and Laguna," *ibid.*, pp. 162–86.
15. "Census of the Shi'wanakwe Society of Zuñi," *ibid.*, XXI (1919), 329–35.
16. "Mothers and Children at Laguna," *Man*, XIX (1919), 34–38.
17. "Mothers and Children at Zuñi, New Mexico," *ibid.*, pp. 168–73.
18. "Teshlatiwa at Zuñi," *Journal of Philosophy, Psychology and Scientific Methods*, Vol. XVI (1919).
19. "Increase by Magic: A Zuñi Pattern," *American Anthropologist*, XXI (1919), 279–86.
20. *Notes on Ceremonialism at Laguna.* "Anthropological Papers of the American Museum of Natural History," Vol. XIX, Part IV. New York, 1920.
21. "Notes on Isleta, Santa Ana, and Acoma," *American Anthropologist*, XXII (1920), 56–69.
22. "Hopi Mothers and Children," *Man*, XXI (1921), 98–104.
23. "The Pueblo Indian Clan in Folk-Lore," *Journal of American Folk-Lore*, XXXIV (1921), 209–16.
24. "Getting Married on First Mesa, Arizona," *Scientific Monthly* (September, 1921), 259–65.
25. "Further Notes on Isleta," *American Anthropologist*, XXIII (1921), 149–69.
26. "Notes on Night Chant at Tuwełchedu Which Came to an End on December 6, 1920," *ibid.*, pp. 240–43.
27. "A Narrative of the Ten'a of Anvik, Alaska," *Anthropos*, XVI–XVII (1921–22), 51–71.
28. "Hidden Ball on First Mesa, Arizona," *Man*, XXII (1922), 89–91.
29. "Winter and Summer Dance Series in Zuñi in 1918," *University of California Publications in American Archaeology and Ethnology*, XVII, No. 3 (1922), 171–216.
30. "The Hopi Wöwöchim Ceremony in 1920," *American Anthropologist*, XXV (1923), 156–87.
31. "Notes on San Felipe and Santo Domingo," *ibid.*, pp. 485–94.
32. "Fiesta at Sant' Ana, New Mexico," *Scientific Monthly*, XVI (1923), 178–83.
33. *Laguna Genealogies.* "Anthropological Papers of the American Museum of Natural History," Vol. XIX, Part V. New York, 1923.

34. "The Hopi Buffalo Dance, "*Man*, XXIII (1923), 21–26.
35. "The Origin Myth of Zuñi," *Journal of American Folk-Lore*, XXXVI (1923), 135–62.
36. *The Scalp Ceremonial of Zuñi*, "American Anthropological Association Memoirs," Vol. XXXI. Menasha, 1924.
37. "Tewa Mothers and Children," *Man*, XXIV (1924), 148–51.
38. "Tewa Kin, Clan and Moiety," *American Anthropologist*, XXVI (1924), 333–39.
39. "The Religion of the Pueblo Indians," *Proceedings of the Twenty-first International Congress of Americanists* (1924), pp. 140–48.
40. *A Pueblo Indian Journal, 1920–1921.* "American Anthropological Association Memoirs," Vol. XXXII. Menasha, 1925.
41. *The Pueblo of Jemez.* Andover: Phillips Academy, 1925.
42. *Tewa Tales.* "American Folk-Lore Society Memoirs," Vol. XIX. New York, 1926.
43. "Cérémonial Tewa au Nouveau Méxique et en Arizona," *Journal de la Société des Américanistes de Paris*, N.S., XVIII (1926), 9–14.
44. "The Ceremonial Calendar at Tewa," *American Anthropologist*, XXVIII (1926), 209–29.
45. "Witchcraft among the Pueblos: Indian or Spanish," *Man*, XXVII (1927), 106–12, 125–28.
46. "Notes on the Pima, 1926," *American Anthropologist*, XXX (1928), 445–64.
47. "The Laguna Migration to Isleta," *ibid.*, pp. 602–13.
48. "Spanish Elements in the Kachina Cult of the Pueblos," *Proceedings of the Twenty-third International Congress of Americanists* (1928), pp. 582–603.
49. *The Social Organization of the Tewa of New Mexico.* "American Anthropological Association Memoirs," Vol. XXXVI. Menasha, 1929.
50. *Kaiowa Tales.* "American Folk-Lore Society Memoirs," Vol. XXII. New York, 1929.
51. "Ritual Parallels in Pueblo and Plains Cultures, with a Special Reference to the Pawnee," *American Anthropologist*, XXXI (1929), 642–54.
52. "Isleta," *Forty-seventh Annual Report of the Bureau of American Ethnology.* Washington, 1929–30.
53. "Zuñi Tales," *Journal of American Folk-Lore*, XLIII (1930), 1–58.
54. "The Kinship Nomenclature of the Pueblo Indians," *American Anthropologist*, XXXIV (1932), 377–89.
55. *Hopi and Zuñi Ceremonialism.* "American Anthropological Association Memoirs," Vol. XXXIX. Menasha, 1933.

56. "Spring Days at Zuñi, New Mexico," *Scientific Monthly*, XXXVI (1933), 49–54.
57. "Some Aztec and Pueblo Parallels," *American Anthropologist*, XXXV (1933), 611–31.
58. *Taos Pueblo.* "General Series in Anthropology," No. 2. Menasha, 1936.
59. "Early Relations between Hopi and Keres," *American Anthropologist*, XXXVIII (1936), 554–60.
60. "The House-Clan Complex of the Pueblos," *Essays in Anthropology in Honor of Alfred Louis Kroeber*, pp. 229–31. Berkeley, 1936.
61. "Riddles and Metaphors among Indian Peoples," *Journal of American Folk-Lore*, XLIX (1936), 171–74.
62. *Mitla: Town of the Souls.* "University of Chicago Publications in Anthropology." Chicago, 1936.
63. "Some Mexican *Ídolos* in Folklore," *Scientific Monthly*, XLIV (1937), 470–73.
64. "The Humpbacked Flute Player of the Southwest," *American Anthropologist*, XL (1938), 337–38.
65. "Taos Tales" (MS).

PARSONS, E. C., and BEALS, R. L. "The Sacred Clowns of the Pueblo and Mayo-Yaqui Indians," *American Anthropologist*, XXXVI (1934), 491–514.

PIKE, Z. M. *An Account of Expeditions to the Sources of the Mississippi . . . . and a Tour through the Interior Parts of New Spain.* Philadelphia, 1808.

PREUSS, K. T. *Die Nayarit Expedition*, Vol. I. Leipzig, 1912.

RADIN, PAUL. "A Sketch of the Peyote Cult of the Winnebago: A Study in Borrowing," *Journal of Religious Psychology*, VII (1914), 1–22.

RAY, VERNE F. "The Bluejay Character in the Plateau Spirit Dance," *American Anthropologist*, XXXIX (1937), 593–601.

REDFIELD, ROBERT. "The Second Epilogue to Maya History," *Hispanic American Historical Review*, XVII (1937), 170–81.

REICHARD, GLADYS A.
  1. "A Few Instances of Cultural Resistance in Southwest North America," *Atti del XXII Congresso Internaz. degli Americanisti.* Roma, 1926.
  2. *Social Life of the Navaho Indians.* New York, 1928.

"Report of John Ward, Indian Agent, Los Luceros, New Mexico, June 30, 1864," *Report of the Commissioner of Indian Affairs for the Year 1864*, pp. 190–95. Washington, 1864.

ROBBINS, W. W.; HARRINGTON, J. P.; FREIRE-MARRECO, B. *Ethno-*

botany of the Tewa Indians. "Bureau of American Ethnology Bull.,"
No. 55. Washington, 1916.

ROBERTS, FRANK, H. H., JR.
1. *The Ruins of Kiatuthlanna, Eastern Arizona.* "Bureau of American Ethnology Bull.," No. 100. Washington, 1931.
2. *The Village of the Great Kivas of the Zuñi Reservation, New Mexico.* "Bureau of American Ethnology Bull.," No. 111. Washington, 1932.
3. "Archaeology in the Southwest," *American Antiquity*, III (1937), 3–33.

RUSSELL, FRANK.
1. "An Apache Medicine Dance," *American Anthropologist*, XI (1898), 367–72.
2. "The Pima Indians," *Twenty-sixth Annual Report of the Bureau of American Ethnology.* Washington, 1905.

SAHAGÚN, BERNARDINO DE. (*a*) *A History of Ancient Mexico* [Books I–IV], trans. FANNY R. BANDELIER. Nashville, Tenn., 1932. (*b*) *Histoire générale des choses de la Nouvelle-Espagne*, trans. D. JOURDANET. Paris, 1880.

SAPIR, EDWARD. "Central and North American Languages," *Encyclopaedia Britannica*, V (14th ed., 1929), 138–41.

SAVILLE, M. H. *Turquois Mosaic Art in Ancient Mexico.* "Contributions from the Museum of the American Indian, Heye Foundation," Vol. VI. New York, 1922.

SCHOLES, F. V.
1. "Civil Government and Society in New Mexico in the Seventeenth Century," *New Mexico Historical Review*, X (1935), 71–111.
2. "The First Decade of the Inquisition in New Mexico," *ibid.*, pp. 195–241.

SELER, EDWARD. *Gesammelte Abhandlungen zur Amerikanischen Sprach- und Alterthumskunde*, Vol. V, No. 7. Berlin, 1915.

SMITH, M. W. "The War Complex of the Plains Indians," *Proceedings of the American Philosophical Society*, Vol. LXXVIII, No. 3 (1938).

SOLBERG, O. "Über die Bahos der Hopi," *Archiv für Anthropologie*, N.F., Vol. IV (1906).

SPIER, LESLIE.
1. *An Outline for a Chronology of Zuñi Ruins.* "Anthropological Papers of American Museum of Natural History," Vol. XVIII, Part III. New York, 1917.
2. *Havasupai Ethnology.* "Anthropological Papers of American Museum of Natural History," Vol. XXIX, Part III. New York, 1928.
3. *Yuman Tribes of the Gila River.* "University of Chicago Publications in Anthropology. Chicago, 1933.

4. *Cultural Relations of the Gila River and Lower Colorado Tribes.* "Yale University Publications in Anthropology," No. 3. New Haven, 1936.

SPINDEN, H. J. *Songs of the Tewa.* New York, 1933.

STARR, F. "Notes upon the Ethnography of Southern Mexico," *Proceedings of the Davenport Academy of Sciences*, Vol. VIII (1889–90).

STEPHEN, ALEXANDER M.
  1. "The Po-boc-tu among the Hopi," *American Antiquarian and Oriental Journal*, XVI (1894), 212–14.
  2. "Hopi Tales," *Journal of American Folk-Lore*, XLII (1929), 1–72.
  3. "Navaho Origin Legend," *ibid.*, XLIII (1930), 88–104.
  4. *Hopi Journal.* "Columbia University Contributions to Anthropology," Vol. XXIII. New York, 1936.

STEVENSON, M. C.
  1. "The Sia," *Eleventh Annual Report of the Bureau of American Ethnology.* Washington, 1889–90.
  2. "The Zuñi Indians," *Twenty-third Annual Report of the Bureau of American Ethnology.* Washington, 1901–2.
  3. "Ethnobotany of the Zuñi Indians," *Thirtieth Annual Report of the Bureau of American Ethnology.* Washington, 1915.

STEWARD, J. H.
  1. "Petroglyphs of California and Adjoining States," *University of California Publications in American Archaeology and Ethnology*, XXIV, No. 2 (1929), 47–238.
  2. "Notes on Hopi Ceremonies in Their Initiatory Form in 1927–1928," *American Anthropologist*, XXXIII (1931), 56–79.
  3. "Ecological Aspects of Southwestern Society," *Anthropos*, XXXII (1937), 87–104.

STIRLING, W. W. "Origin Myth of Acoma" (MS).

STRONG, WILLIAM DUNCAN.
  1. "An Analysis of Southwestern Society," *American Anthropologist*, XXIX (1927), 1–61.
  2. "Aboriginal Society in Southern California," *University of California Publications in American Archaeology and Ethnology*, Vol. XXVI (1929).

THOMAS, A. B. *Forgotten Frontiers.* Norman, Okla., 1932.

THOMPSON, J. ERIC. *Mexico before Cortez.* New York and London, 1933.

TITIEV, MISCHA.
  1. "A Hopi Salt Expedition," *American Anthropologist*, XXXIX (1937), 244–58.

2. "The Problem of Cross-Cousin Marriage among the Hopi," *ibid.*, XL (1938), 105–11.
3. "Oraibi" (MS).

TWITCHELL, R. E. *The Spanish Archives of New Mexico.* Cedar Rapids, Iowa, 1914.

UNDERHILL, RUTH MURRAY.
1. "Note on Easter Devils at Kawori'k on the Papago Reservation," *American Anthropologist*, XXXVI (1934), 515–16.
2. *The Autobiography of a Papago Woman.* "American Anthropological Association Memoirs," Vol. XLVI. Lancaster, Pa., 1936.
3. *Social Organization of the Papago Indians.* "Columbia University Contributions to Anthropology" (in press).
4. "Papago Songs and Ceremonies" (MS).

VALKENBURGH, R. VAN. "Navajo Common Law," *Museum Notes of the Museum of Northern Arizona*, IX, No. 10 (1937), 51–57.

VELARDE. "Relación [of Pimería Alta, 1716], ed. R. K. Wyllys," *New Mexico Historical Review*, VI (1931), 111–57.

VOTH, H. R.
1. "Oraibi Marriage Customs," *American Anthropologist*, II (1900), 238–346.
2. *The Oraibi Powamu Ceremony.* "Field Columbian Museum Pub. 61, Anthropological Series," Vol. III, No. 2. Chicago, 1901.
3. *The Oraibi Summer Snake Ceremony.* "Field Columbian Museum Pub. 83, Anthropological Series," Vol. III, No. 4. Chicago, 1903.
4. *The Oraibi Oa'qöl Ceremony.* "Field Columbian Museum Pub. 84, Anthropological Series," Vol. VI, No. 1. Chicago, 1903.
5. *The Traditions of the Hopi.* "Field Columbian Museum Pub. 96, Anthropological Series," Vol. VIII. Chicago, 1905.
6. *Hopi Proper Names.* "Field Columbian Museum Pub. 100, Anthropological Series," Vol. VI, No. 3. Chicago, 1905.
7. *Oraibi Natal Customs and Ceremonies.* "Field Columbian Museum Pub. 157, Anthropological Series," Vol. VI, No. 2. Chicago, 1905.
8. *The Oraibi Marau Ceremony.* "Field Museum of Natural History Pub. 156, Anthropological Series," Vol. XI, No. 1. Chicago, 1912.
9. *Brief Miscellaneous Hopi Papers.* "Field Museum of Natural History Pub. 157, Anthropological Series," Vol. XI, No. 2. Chicago, 1912.

WALLIS, W. D.
1. "Folk Tales from Shumopovi, Second Mesa," *Journal of American Folk-Lore*, XLIX (1936), 1–68.
2. "Hopi Shields" (MS).

WHITE, LESLIE A.
1. "A Comparative Study of Keresan Medicine Societies," *Proceed-*

ings of the Twenty-third International Congress of Americanists (1928), pp. 604–19.

2. "The Acoma Indians," *Forty-seventh Annual Report of the Bureau of American Ethnology*. Washington, 1929–30.
3. *The Pueblo of San Felipe*. "American Anthropological Association Memoirs," Vol. XXXVIII. Lancaster, 1932.
4. *The Pueblo of Santo Domingo, New Mexico*. "American Anthropological Association Memoirs," Vol. XLIII. Lancaster, 1935.
5. "The Pueblo of Sia" (MS).
6. "An Autobiographic Sketch of an Acoma Indian" (MS).
7. "Supplementary Data on Acoma, New Mexico" (MS).
8. "The Pueblo of Santa Ana" (MS).

WHORF, B. L., and TRAGER, G. L. "The Relationship of Uto-Aztecan and Tanoan," *American Anthropologist*, XXXIX (1937), 609–24.

WINSHIP, G. P. "The Coronado Expedition, 1540–1542. (Narrative of Castañeda.)" *Fourteenth Annual Report of the Bureau of American Ethnology*. Washington, 1896.

WISDOM, CHARLES. "The Chorti" (MS).

WUTHENAU, A. VON. "Spanish Military Chapels in Santa Fé," *New Mexico Historical Review*, X (1935), 175–94.

WYMAN, L. C.
1. "Navaho Diagnosticians," *American Anthropologist*, XXXVIII (1936), 236–46.
2. "The Female Shooting Chant: A Minor Navaho Ceremony," *ibid.*, pp. 634–53.

APPENDIX

RESEARCH DESIRABLE IN PUEBLO CULTURE, AS INDICATED IN FOREGOING COMMENTARIES

GENERAL ETHNOGRAPHY:

Town surveys of Picurís* and Sandía, and of Hopi towns of Second and Third Mesas†

Survey of contemporaneous Pueblo colonies: from Zuni, Acoma, and Laguna; the Hopi colony at Moenkopi. (For cultural processes; see below.)

Survey of (?) surviving Piro and Mansos on lower Rio Grande

Comparative study of Pueblo handicrafts and arts—in fact, of the material culture in general,‡ including land ownership and use

Comparative study of Pueblo law,§ including sanctions of all kinds

ETHNOGRAPHIC DETAILS:

Ceremonies of Second Mesa towns

Winter solstice ceremonies in Second Mesa towns, in Hotavila, in Walpi (long form), described and compared

Wüwüchim initiation ritual at Walpi‖

Kachina cults and ceremonies of Second and Third Mesas

Zuni society ceremonies

Zuni Saint's dance

In ceremonial organization of Tewa and of Taos

Distribution of games throughout Pueblos, and parallels among other Southwestern peoples

COMPARATIVE ETHNOGRAPHY:

Comparative analysis of religion of Southern Athapascans and religion of Pueblos, including Pueblo-Navaho loans and Pueblo-Apache loans (after Dr. Opler publishes his Apache data)

* A brief preliminary report is forthcoming in the *American Anthropologist*.

† Reports by Dr. Titiev for Oraibi and by Dr. Kennard for Second Mesa are promised. These will cover various subjects given below.

‡ A study in Zuni economics is promised by Dr. Ruth L. Bunzel, who suggests that similar studies in owning and using property be made among Keres and Tanoans.

§ Suggested by Dr. Bunzel.   ‖ Report promised by Dr. Kennard.

Paiute-Pueblo parallels (after Dr. Kelly publishes her Southern
    Paiute data)
Cultural functions of dreaming in the Southwest
Comparative analysis of witchcraft in the Southwest

Archeological-Ethnological:

Excavation near Acoma (bearing upon early Zuni or Hopi connec-
    tions)
Excavation extended in Antelope Valley (bearing upon early Keresan
    connections)
Excavation south of Zuni and of Acoma (bearing upon Pima-Papago
    or other southern connections)
Excavation of Piro and Tompiro towns, southeast and south
Comparison of artifacts of early Tanoans with those of other Pueblo
    tribes
Survey of kivas, round and square, ancient and modern, in relation to
    kiva dances and other kiva functions
Study of culture growth and culture lag over the whole Pueblo area
    where dendro-chronological and archeological data are available to
    indicate the comparative degrees of growth, persistence, or decline
    in different areas. Analysis of such data may lead to understanding
    the reasons for peripheral lag or for areal florescence or decadence*
Examination of Pima-Papago legendary history and identification of
    archeological sites in their territories*
Analysis of Pima-Papago culture to check assumption of relationship
    to the Hohokam*
Study of Navaho-Apache archeology to determine (*a*) time of arrival
    of the Athapascan peoples in the Southwest and their migration
    routes† and (*b*) the nature and periods of Athapascan-Pueblo con-
    tacts*
Archeological studies in the eastern peripheral region of the South-
    west and in the southwestern Great Plains to determine the rela-
    tionship between known Plains' archeological horizons, such as the
    Upper Republican culture, with datable horizons in the South-
    west proper*
Archeological studies combined with intensive ethnographic-histor-
    ical analysis, down the river valleys from the Rio Grande in New
    Mexico across Texas to determine what relationships underlie
    Southwestern and Southeastern civilization based on horticulture*

* Suggested by Dr. W. Duncan Strong.

† Study of Western Apache sites is being made by Grenville Goodwin.

LINGUISTIC-ETHNOLOGICAL

Songs, Prayers, Sermons or Speeches, and Tales, in text, in Hopi
Zuni, Keresan, Tanoan*
Dialectical analyses bearing upon migrations (Keresan, Tanoan)
Analyses of variation in language in relation to variation in culture
Comparative study of town plans and nomenclature
Myths and Tales:†
From Santo Domingo, San Felipe, Santa Ana
From Jemez
Emergence myths of Taos and Isleta, Picurís and Sandía

CULTURAL PROCESSES:

Comparison of Tewa (Tano) and Hopi of First Mesa
Comparative analysis of ceremonies of Hopi Patki (Water-Corn)
people in relation to migration
Descendants of Awatobi immigrants on Second Mesa
Miscegenation throughout Pueblo area
Intertown survey of what is known or believed about other towns
Pueblo ritual techniques as a study in early art
Current calendars from all the towns
Recent Americanization

SOCIAL PSYCHOLOGY:

Analysis in individuals of traits held to be characteristic of Pueblo
culture or of traits significant in ritual, e.g., appreciation of color
or direction
Study of variation of individuals within approximately the same cul-
ture‡
Study of personality of chiefs in West ("valuable men") compared
with chiefs in East (men of "power")
Comparative study of play and games of children, of education in
general
Biography§

* Hopi and Tanoan grammars, etc., are promised by B. L. Whorf and G. L.
Trager, and Hopi texts by E. A. Kennard.

† A concordance for the Southwest is available in manuscript in the Depart-
ment of Anthropology, Columbia University. A collection of ceremonial tales
from Zuni is promised by Dr. Ruth Benedict.

‡ Suggested by Dr. Kennard.

§ Biographical material or case histories should be used as much as possible
along several lines of proposed inquiry: economics, law, dreaming, witchcraft,
miscegenation, interpueblo knowledge or belief, Americanization, cultural
changes of all kinds (see chap. ix), as well, of course, as along the lines of social
psychology just outlined.

Note: Roman numerals refer to Parsons's preface in volume 1, which in the original edition began on p. vii. Arabic numbering has not been changed.

INDEX

733 n. †, 735, 736 n. †, 761–66, 827
n. ‡, 856, 857 n. ‡, 859 n. *, 872 n. ‡,
881–87, 906, 941 n. †, 948, 953, 956,
958, 960, 961, 965, 971, 975–76,
978–79, 983, 1005, 1015, 1072 n. †,
1074 n. *, 1077, 1082, 1083, 1087,
1089, 1108, 1117, 1129, 1131, 1145,
1146, 1148, 1165; colonies, 17;
Laguna at, 131 n. *, Hopi at,
969 n. *; parallels between Hopi
and, 538 n. §, 966 n. *, 977, 980–82;
Zuni at, 969 n. *, 970; Jemez at,
969 n. *; borrows from Zuni, 970
n. *, 979–80, 1164, from Laguna,
1164

Adolescence ceremony of girls, 25 n. *,
58, 399, 601 n. *, 934; distribution,
1039; resisted by Pueblos, 1039

Adoption, 6, 11, 30, 45; tribal, 187,
884; see also Clan, Corn groups,
Moiety

Adultery, 42, 56, 81, 96, 108 n. *, 160,
185 n. †, 236 n. ‡, 419

Agave (Mescal), 22–23, 34, 37, 1058

Agave society, 116, 124, 126, 128, 155,
159, 163–64, 177 n. ‡, 190, 216, 217,
237 n. *, 281, 322, 325, 352 n. †,
365 n. †, 379, 384, 396, 398, 501,
561, 567, 601 n. †, 606 ff., 857, 866;
sing at Emergence, 239 n. *

Age, unrecorded, 162 n. *

Aged: care of, 57, 68 n. †; esteemed,
98, 162; abuse of, 236 n. ‡; and
ritualism, 1151

Ahul kachina, 139 n. *, 505–6

Ahulani kachina, 139 n. *

Albinism, 44, 90–91, 215 n. *, 524 n. †,
672; see also White

All Saints Day, 856 n. *, 857 n. †

All Souls Day or Night, 290, 303, 388,
498, 529, 531, 533, 534–35, 544, 549,
752 n. †, 801 n. *, 856 ff., 903, 913,
931, 965–66; display of wealth, 858;
animals in corrals, 858; altar, 885–
86

Altar, 269, 353 ff., 477, 481, 565–66,

870–71; position, 98, 367, 711;
paraphernalia, 118, 171, 203, 322,
329, 353 ff., 538 n. ‡, 545, 686–87,
709, 768; meal, 123, 294, 354, 356–
57, 360, 508, 545, 565, 586, 612, 628,
687, 692, 693, 725, 877 n. * (see
also Meal painting); underground,
144 n. †, 309, 310–11, 382, 919 n. ‡;
tiles, 192, 354, 359, 705, Fig. 3; seed
corn, etc., on 247, 316, 317, 357, 403,
555, 566, 570, 590, 612, 694, 704,
739, 750, 920, 966 n. *; road-marker, 289–90, 705; of the Directions,
324, 356–57, 507, 511, 606, 656, 670,
676, 677, 678, 692, 703–4, 768, 869,
870, Pl. VII; slab or slat, 354, 356,
677, 870, 956–57, 1068 n. §, Fig. 3,
Pl. VI; setting, 357, 403–4, 477, 506,
511, 630, 704, 768; initiates shown,
358, 603, 677, 705; dismantling,
358, 477, 678, 695, 871; sand, of the
Directions, 664; vegetation on, 677,
707; Rain chieftaincy, 687, 957; re-
newal, 704; see also Sand-painting

Americanization, viii, 3, 14, 15, 66,
183 n. †, 421, 611, 631, 633, 648,
651–52, 888, 1080 ff., 1122 n. §,
1128–29, 1138 ff.; see also Loan(s)

Amulet(s), 180, 209, 283, 298, 308 n. †;
see also Arrowpoints

Anachronism(s), 40, 215 n. *, 261–62,
1090, 1158

Ana Kachina (Anakchina) (Long-hair
kachina), 138, 775, 782

Analogy, thinking by, 76, 88 ff., 156,
339 n. §, 415, 755, 820, 821, 1067;
borrowing along line of, 1060 n. *;
substitution by, 1145; effects of,
1153–55

Anawita of Walpi, 128 n. †, 606 ff.

Anger, 52, 54, 68, 75, 80, 83, 103, 250,
352, 473, 523 n. †, 721

Animal(s): powers from, 62–63, 135,
187, 189 n. *, 195, 710, 879, 931,
1055; fright from, 62 n. ‡, 191;
curers, 80, 94, 96, 189, 191, 404, 710,
722 n. †, 879, thread or corn meal

to, 94, 135; skulls or bones, 127, in
shrine, 308, 352, 909, painted, 351;
starry "Mother" of domestic, 181,
269, 336; society members called,
189 n. †, 232, 233, 515; intercessors,
206; increase by ritual, 503, 543;
transformation into, 549 (*see also*
Witches); sounds from medicine
bowl, 728

Animals, prey: as Spirits, x, 99,
133 n. *, 184, 186, 932, 964, in hunt,
x, 187, 826 n. †, 827 n. ‡; underground, 53, 214, 226; orientated by
the directions, 99, 365, 416 n. ‡,
696, Pl. IV; associated with War
gods and war, 184, 186–87; guardians, 188–89, 207, 335; medicine
plants from, 189, 404, 416; images,
304 (*see also* Figurines); prayer-
sticks for, 515, 573; *see also* Ani-
mal(s), Badger, Bear, Game animals, Mountain Lion

Animal dances, 28, 532, 533, 543,
827 ff.

Animal pelts: worn, 27, 28, 197 n. †,
840, 841, 853, by witches, 136; *see
also* Deer

Animism, xii, 55, 194 ff., 1029, 1154;
see also Ashes, Awl Man

Announcement: from the housetop,
19 n. ‡, 77, 83, 110, 123, 150, 314,
527, 571, 655, 676, 860; around
town, 110, 123, 293, 451, 593, 649,
762; from house to house, 580, 743,
767; by drum, 649

Ant(s), 45, 81; medicine, 62 n. ‡; doctor, 133, 191, 931, 944 n. ‡, 971;
cause smallpox or other eruptions
or swelling or sore throat, 191, 452,
465, 679, 713; in war, 191–92, 622,
629 n. *; offering to, 207, 298,
301 n. *; dead transform into, 216;
first people, 236; prayer-sticks or
feathers, 270, 281, 286 n. ‡, 629 n. *;
meal road for, 362, 893; associated
with the directions, 365; hill gravel
in war pouch, 401; exposure in
initiation to, 519, 622 n. †, 980

Ant society, 116, 191, 192, 362, 519,
596, 621, 622, 629 ff., 637–38,
646 ff., 745, 880, 893, 904

Antelope, 184, 244; hunt, 27, 28 n. †,
81–82, 105, 758; heads on altar or in
Snake shrine, 190, 352 n. †; horns
worn or carried, 190–91, 608, 616,
928 n. ‡; impersonated, 349, 503,
543 n. *, 834, 845; power from,
1055

Antelope clan, 119, 120, 137, 140,
146 n. §, 161, 165, 246, 248, 406,
539, 541, 762, 878, 882, 890, 976

Antelope society, 83, 153, 161, 170,
185 n. *, 190, 192, 328, 349, 367,
384, 491, 600, 865, Pl. II; Youth,
511; identified with Spider-Kaвina
society, 664 n. *, 976

Antelope Valley, 861, 971, 976, 1029

Anthropomorphism, x, 198 ff., 208,
1016, 1058; *see also* Sun

Apache, viii, 30, 34, 39, 51 n. *,
80 n. §, 87, 167 n. *, 252, 358, 360,
401 n. †, 402 n. *, 432, 471 n. †,
879 n. †, 888, 924, 962, 963, 992 n. *,
1026, 1039, 1043 n. ‡, 1045,
1049 n. *, 1053 ff., 1063 n. ‡, 1072,
1099, 1109 n. *, 1150 n. *; Jicarilla,
15 n. †, 29 n. *, 75 n. †, 227 n. *,
415 n. *, 439, 639 n. *, 650 n. †,
927 n. *, 932, 935, 937, 938, 1037,
1047, 1055 n. *, 1059, 1061, 1062,
1067 n. *, 1082 n. †, borrow from
Taos, 927 n. *, 937, 1045, 1056 n. ‡,
1057–59; White Mountain, 17 n. ‡,
23, 34, 96 n. *, 236 n. *, 243 n. §,
1059, 1060; Mescalero, 22 n. ‡,
28 n. †, 432 n. *, n. ‡, 1040, 1058,
1061–64, 1080, 1094 n. †, 1096;
Chiricahua, 28 n. †, 1058, 1061–64,
1080; dance loan from, 49, 1077;
Western, 68 n. *, 225 n. *, 296 n. §,
381 n. *, 422 n. *, 423 n. *, 456 n. †,
874, 931 n. †, 968 n. *, 991 n. †,
1040, 1056 n. ‡, 1058–60, 1062;
enemy, 108 n. *, 1030; San Carlos,
210 n. †, 1059, 1063 n. §; Lipan,
461 n. ‡, 938 n. *, 1062, 1094 n. †

leled by Pueblos, 988–89, 1025 n. §, 1026, 1055 n. ‡, 1055 n. ††

Candle(s), Pl. IX; sent into body, 64; lit for ghosts, 535, 857 n. ‡, 858, for saint, 783, 852, 1069, on graves, 549, 856; offered in hills, 932

Cane(s) or sticks of office, 59, 102, 147, 148, 149, 150, 246, 284 n. *, 325 ff., 420, 496, 567, 568, 597, 714, 756–57, 892 n. ‡, 925 n. *, 929, 956, 1021–22, 1105 n. *, 1115 n. ‡; aspersed, 148, 374, 533, 543, 545; as offering, 206, 284, 325; Lincoln, 326–27, 532, 533, 543, 545, 649, 841; meal sprinkled on, 533; see also Breathing

Canyon de Chelly, 317, 1044 n. *, 1045

Canyon Wren, 94; name for War chief or Koshare, 440 n. *, 885, 890 n. †; stuffed and carried, 885

Carnival, 18, 762 n. *

Catholicism, viii; and marriage, 42, 44, 150, 315 n. †, 482 n. *, 542, 892, 932; factor in burial, 71; rites of, 392, 475–76, 548, 549, 649, 653, 849, 851, 892, 1068–69, burlesque, 809–10, 813, 1069, 1102–3; saint's-day count, 501 n. †, 848 n. *; prayer, 529, 598, 649; flowers, 548; term for priest, 1071 n. *; acculturated, 1132, 1155; see also Aspersing, Baptism, Candle(s), Cross

Cattle, 1, 89, 110, 420, 569, 969, 1064; cowhide, 1148

Cemetery(ies), 21, 71, 74, 367–68, 480, 856, 888 n. §, 1079 n. §; see also Burial

Ceremonial room(s), 2–3, 5 n. *, 9 n. †, 580, 581, 590, 592, 595, 596, 603, 604, 627, 646, 686, 687, 692, 696, 709, 724 n. *, 834, 865, 901, 921

Chaco Canyon, 93 n. *, 360 n. *

Chakwena kachina: of Zuni, 299 n. *, 339 n. ‡, 342 n. ¶, 382, 396, 397, 420, 461, 530, 756 n. †, 795, 978, 1163; considered witches, 461 n. §, 1091;

of Laguna, 536, 889, 1091; of Cochiti, 736

Chakwena kachina Woman, 309, 328, 347, 385, 396 n. ‖, 424, 464, 500, 517, 526, 578–79, 731, 758 ff.; lies in, 526, 761

Chamahia (hoes), 194, 211, 333, 404, 975; fetishes so called, 594, 883, 976 n. ‡

Change, social, viii, xiv, 19, 967, 1085–1165

Chaparral cock: clan name, 56, 156, 291 n. *; clan, 160; in myth, 233; track, 233 n. *, 244, 356, 362, 859; feather in moccasin, 362 n. †, 624, around fetish, 592

Chapio clown, 1005 n. †, 1071; see also K'apio

Cha'vaiyo kachina, 802–3

Chiefs of the Directions, 133 n. *, 170, 172, 173, 194, 195, 235 n. *, 246, 271, 276, 289, 301, 314, 333 n. †, 349, 367, 394, 410–11, 505, 546, 598, 675 n. *, 769, 868, 871, 887, 932, 965, 1121

Chiefs of the Seasons, 172, 555, 887

Chief's stick, 163, 593, 611, 617, 619, 707, 771; kachina, 575 n. *

Chieftaincy, 42–43, 117, 144 ff.; perquisites or exemptions, 27, 150, 157–58, 164, 176, 777–78, 788, 825, 877–78, 884, 896, 1137 n. *, 1147; affected by descent, 112, 114, 120, 152, 863, 864, 912, 946; demotion, 152, 154; qualification, 154–55; risks, 167, 324–25, 1136 n. †; obligations, 167, 437, 557, 562, 573, 775 n. *; dreaming power, 452; rotation, 1126–27; see also Chraik'ats[i], Firewood, Town chieftaincy, War chief(s)

Child (children): barter, 34; mortality, 45, 318; female desired, 45; in or at dances, 48, 49 n. *, 389, 499, 828, 840, 845, 851, 853; spirits, 71, 174, 222, 236, 241, 290, 303, 318 n. †, 319, 545, 588, 589,

1100 n. *; kachina presents for, 48, 49, 50, 177, 319, 376, 506; kachina or "Grandfathers" teach morals, 412, 474–75, 518, 519; ash-smeared, 463; purified with mother, 472; not whipped, 469 n. *, 476 n. *, 602; whipped ritually, 475; kachina corn hidden from, 508; protected from corpse, 1056 n. †; *see also* Dedication of child, Education, Sun

Childbirth, 91, 190 n. †, 198, 321, 426, 465; cord, 92; doctor, 931

Chili, 18, 34, 37, 39 n. ‡, 420, 774, 787, 1064

Chimayo: sanctuary, 417; Tano at, 913 n. ‡

Chraik'ats[i] chieftaincy, 122, 127, 247, 316, 824, 825, 884, 893, 903–4; lapse, 1129

Christmastide celebration, 49, 302 n. *, 317, 373, 386, 483 n. †, 494, 498, 499, 518, 531, 532, 533, 537, 542, 543, 545, 736 n. †, 782–83, 896, 903, 931, 953

Church: officers, 71, 111, 124, 150, 475–76, 911 n. ‡, 1126; repair collective, 110; wall cloud design, 359; dancing inside, 537, 543, 545, 896; drumming at, 542; plastered, 548; men and women separated in, 649; condemns witchcraft, 1132; opposes clown obscenity, 1132

Cibola, 14 n. ‡, 29 n. §, 33, 872, 878 n. *, 991 n. †, 1079 n. §, 1113

Cigarette; *see* Tobacco

Circuit(s): counter-sunwise, 99, 249, 250, 365, 457, 557, 566, 581, 612, 628, 643, 682, 726, 797, 843, 851, 859; begins in east, 101, 262, 265, 365, 957, and ends in east, 365, 644; begins in north, 367, 406, 410, 412, 699; around Snake bower, 512; race, 534; sunwise, 755; *see also* Exorcism

Clairvoyance, 85, 450 ff., 532; by medicine bowl, 85, 190 n. *, 450, 451, 452, 539, 710, 719, 721, 728, 798, 959; through arrowpoint, 85; from

deer, 96; through plants, 196, 414; through "powder" on eyes, 927; *see also* Crystal

Clan(s): adoption, 11, 62, 80, 902, 946; mother, 20, 25 n. *, 697, 770–71, 863; head, 20 n. *, 59 n. *, 863; father's, 20, 46, 57, 435, 747, 755, 756; eponymous beings of, 56 n. *, 60, 161, 175 n. *, 188 n. ‡, 198, 208, 288, 982, 1032; kachina, 56, 60, 139, 175, 208, 325, 496, 505, 515, 574, 577 n. *; child(ren) of (paternal), 57, 60 n. †, 139, 150, 504, 527, 702–3, 743, 745, 767, 796, 1147; patrilineal, 61, 1085; fetish, 324, (?) 704, 863; race by, 534, 796, 821, 982; functions, 702–3, 746, 747, 775, 796, 832; glyphs, 359, 795; Hano, 917; lapse, 1042 n. †, 1087 n. †, 1147, 1156; *see also* Clanship, Myth(s), Name(s), Society(ies)

Clanship, 5, 45; and kivas, 9–10, 61, 141, 228 n. †, 496, 503, 574, 1156; terms, 11, 55, 56–57, 60 n. †; and migration, 16, 56, 970 n. ‡, 1041 n. ‖; exogamy, 16 n. *, 44, 61, 894, 1088; and land, 20, 61; and maternal family, 60, 703, 863, 946, 1088, 1089; organization, 60, 863; and springs or reservoirs, 61 (*see also* Springs); and eagles, 61, 510; and houses, 61, 1159 (*see also* Houses); and ceremonial organization, 61, 119, 122, 129, 137, 142, 160–61, 190, 228 n. †, 246, 343–44, 523 n. §, 527, 536, 571, 572, 574, 577, 648, 696, 697, 743, 756, 769 ff., 803 n. *, 863–64, 866, 884 n. *, 887, 980–81, 1087; conceptual functions, 161, 190, 316, 511, 696, 773, 918; post-Emergence, 210 n. †, 214, 243; regency, 607 n. *, 950; in corn-planting, 792; spread, 1085 ff.; clashes with society organization, 1087, 1089; *see also* Hospitality

Clay, x, 77; Woman, 195–96, 293, (?)558, (?)566, 983, 1097 n. *

Cloud(s): houses, 2, 94, 172–73, 199,

197 n. ‡, 321 n. †, 332; board ritual, 321 n. †, 332; given turquoise heart, 424

Creation: from epidermis, 95, 182, 211, 243 n. ‡, 246, 247; of Sun, 180, 212, 240; from soft mud world, 195, 211, 213, 229 n. †, 242; of mountains, 213, 221, 242, 244, 251, 254; of Moon, 240; of canyons through lightning, 242; by song, 244; see also Images

Crier, 19 n. ‡, 83, 110, 122 ff., 146, 152, 495, 502, 503 n. *, 505, 509, 513, 556, 557, 668, 675, 864, 949; saint's, 517

Crop failure, x, 16; see also Famine

Cross: of cemetery, 21, 368; design, 38, 1073 n. ‡, in prayer-stick, 280, 284, 1068 n. ||, 1074, in dough, 317, on corn fetish, 322; center, 490; sent to or among Hopi, 486 n. *, 915 n. †, 1073 n. §, 1074 n. †, 1105 n. *; in meal, 540, 755, 759, 792; sign of the, 598, 728, 815, 856, 1073 n. ||, 1074; in pollen within circle, 701; as hanging wooden sticks, 705, 739; on head or body against witches, 463, 711; kissed in burlesque, 809; painted on racer, 818; raised at Zuni, 873; Spanish and Indian, 1073–74; ritual without myth, 1102 n. *; see also Catholicism

Cross-cousin(s), 57 n. ‡; marriage, 58 n. ‡; in dance, 830 n. *; see also "Aunt(s)"

Crow: witch, 66 n. *, 136; feathers used by witch, 108 n. *, 136; scout, 231; omen, 447, 524 n. †; feathers for scalp effigy, 577–78; Navaho change into, 578 n. *; addressed in hidden-ball, 800; see also Kachina

Crying, 32, 47, 50, 52, 53, 54, 86, 87, 222–23, 258, 259, 260, 468, 469, 721; taboo, 712, 719; ritual, 763

Crystal(s): gazing, 135, 258, 330, 450, 532, 546, 642, 711, 713, 716, 719, 729, 886, 959; fetish, 330, 565; sun's

ray refracted by, 330, 378, 607, 704, 772, 959; pendant, 450, 959; rubbed on eyes, 450; into medicine bowl, 607, 768

Cult society, 402, 522 n. †, 745; see also Kiaklo, Masauwü, Pa'utiwa, Sayatasha

Cultivating, 19, 39

Dance(s), x, xi, 10, 59; practice, 4, 9, 438, 540, 731, 829–30, 834, 848 (see Kachina [rehearse]); couriers, 33, 735; circuit, 99, 540, 636; preparations for, 110, 111; step(s), 387, 512, 650, 684, 742, 772, 784, 833, 837, 838, 843, 853–54, 1107 n. *; posture(s), 387, 512, 631, 650, 679, 684, 772, 784, 833, 837, 843, 845, 853; domiciliary visiting in, 387–88, 545, 783; accumulative pattern in, 389; formation, 512, 648, 653, 683 ff., 732, 772, 784, 833, 837–38, 841, 843, 845, 847, 851; Snake-Antelope, 667, 674 n. †; Basket, 675; director, 741–42, 777, 778, 784; see also Buffalo, Butterfly, Child, Dancing, Deer, Kachina, Kiva(s), Throw-away, War

Dance costume, 3, 27, 29, 36, 37 n. ‡, 42 n. §, 400, 647, 648, 651–52, 664 ff., 682–83, 685, 782, 832, 836–37, 838, 840–41; see also Deer (skin garments), Kachina dancers or impersonators

Dancing, 385 ff.; kachina expected once a year, 111, 167; in field, 159; as an honor, 385–86; by Corn group, 386; by shaman(s), 388, 605, 691, 696 ff., 702, 714, 727, 739, 897; circle, 388, 503, 504, 531, 534, 543, 547, 610, 611, 616, 636, 643, 646, 648, 678, 679, 699, 866, 870, 921; alternating group, 388–89, 632, 651, 683, 754, 755, 847, 926, 980; circulatory, 505–6, 507, 590, 648, 652, 741

Dangerous, 52, 67–68, 76, 78, 79, 106–7, 108, 114, 167, 174, 180 n. *,

Masauwü, 373, 608; taboo on, 373, 546, 573, 839, 886; exposure to, 441, 646, 886, 960; Christmas, 499, 854–55; kachina emerge from, 506 (see also Sipapu); Wüwüchim, 619; All Souls, 857; by flint, 926; see also Fire drill, Hunt

Fire chief, 118, 143, 676, 678, 737, 739, 1160

Fire drill, 27–28, 608, 765

Fire society, 114, 133, 144 n. *, 148, 151, 161 n. *, 208, 246, 274, 298, 364, 382 n. §, 384 n. *, 440, 441–42, 536, 539, 544, 837, 838, 885, 886, 888, 889, 901, 904, 907, 912, 969 n. *, 975; ash medicine, 463; burlesque, 810; see also Society(ies)

Fire spirits: Old Woman, 178, 312; Boy, 758, 912, 963; see also Masauwü, Shulawitsi

Fire stick (poker): represents corpse, 72, 73; animate, 197, Poker Boys, 963, 967; guardian, 209; cast away, 459

Firewood, 25, 39, 77, 109, 519; hauled for War chiefs or Town chief, 157–58, 884, 904; collected from each house, 572, 593, 857

Fish: ancestry, 210 n. †; ceremonialists called, 210 n. †, 250, 938 n. †; wall-paintings, 210 n. †; created, 244; eaten by Tewa, 252; people turn into, 252; turn into people, 938

Five, 101, 365, 368, 445, 448, 586, 640, 957; directions, 365, 729, 957

Flint (Knife) society, 114, 120, 132, 133, 148, 246, 378, 435, 440, 441, 470, 519 n. ‡, 533, 534, 539, 544, 594, 811, 825, 885, 886 n. †, 888, 889, 895, 900, 904, 907, 912, 1146; War gods initiated into, 232–33; in myth, 232 ff.; in charge of Scalps, 350, 894, 898–99; associated with Town chief, 535, 538 n. *, 893, 898, 901; impersonate Gomaiowish kachina, 762

Flood, x, 108 n. *, 195, 214, 235, 237, 891

Flowers: worn by clowns, 683, 684, 850; given by clowns, 844

Flute: serenading, 41; at corn-grinding, 41; in ritual or ceremonial, 41, 380–81, 537, 681, 687, 691, 693, 704, 706, 707, 739, 745, 753, 780 n. †, 871, 890 n. †, Fig. 3; of War god, 537; order in society, 880; fetish, 909–10; see also Paiyatemu

Flute ceremony of Hopi, 116–17, 119, 204, 240 n. †, 285, 311, 328, 337 n. ‡, 349, 354, 359, 379, 380, 394, 397, 495, 497, 500, 505, 510, 513, 603, 703–8, 795, 1042, Fig. 3

Flute dance of Jemez, 381, 389, 675, 681–85

Flute society, 143, 146, 153, 154, 192, 193, 332–33, 384, 452, 504 n. *, 508, 513, 600, 686, 864, 977

Folk tales, 10 n. ‡, 12 n. †, 40–41, 42–43, 162, 268, 269, 376, 402 n. *, 419, 420, 424, 443, 967, 1059; localized in ruins, 17, 103; migration, 17; society, 17; season or time for, 102, 437, 583; Spanish, 1069 n. §; and kachina, 1161; see also Myths

Food: wild, 1, 22, 109, 127, 481 (see also Rocky Mountain bee plant), gathering, 508; offering(s), 8, 9 n. †, 49, 69, 70, 72, 93, 163, 171 n. *, 184, 187, 188, 195, 206, 207, 290, 301 ff., 318, 324, 329, 404, 457, 477, 482, 504, 569, 588, 627, 645, 746, 747, 752, 1100 n. *, 1106, onto fire, 302, 303, 312, 461, 529, 695, 759, 860, to church, 303, 856, 857, to fetishes eaten by ceremonialists, 779; leftovers, 19, 24, 57, 755, 814; pay in, 20, 20 n. ‡, 24, 42, 57, 109, 207, 344, 345, 390, 455, 482, 605, (?)755–56, 789, 826; meals, 23; exchange, 24–25, 26–27, 42 n. *, 59, 525; propose with, 25; denial an outrage, 26, 64–65; domiciliary begging for, 105, 302, 303, 319, 390, 529, 628,

prietor, 865, 1156 n. *; number determined by pattern, 1156–57; see also Descent, Race(s), Women

Knife-Wing (Achiyelatopa), 178, 186, 187, 204, 232, 356, 416 n. ‡, 698, 699, 701 n. †, 964, Pls. IV, VI; see also Kwatoko

K'oʙishtaiya (Kopishtaya), 177 n. †, 254, 301, 426, 576 (Zuni)

K'oʙishtaiya (kachina), 246, 305 n. *, 363–64, 369–70, 389 n. *, 428, 538, 887, 953

Kok'okshi, Good Kachina, 222, 285, 286, 340 n. †, 386, 399 n. †, 404, 409–10, 412, 520 ff., 527 ff., 736, 743 ff., 1059 n. *, Pls. X, XIII

Kokop (Coyote-Cedarwood-Masauwü) clan; see Coyote clan

Kokopelli (Kokopölö) kachina, 191 n. †, 203 n. †, 332 n. *

Kolowisi; see Water Serpent

Koshare (Kashale), 95, 120, 129–30, 132, 137, 170, 182, 213, 242 n. ‡, 246, 298, 395, 398, 401, 439, 453, 460, 464, 533, 536, 537, 542, 728 n. *, 790, 826, 885, 888, 889, 894, 898, 900, 901, 902, 1083 n. *; images, 688

Kossa, 95 n. *, 128, 129–30, 166, 252, 356, 390–91, 415 n. *, 782, 809–10, 912, 919 n. †, 920, 922

Kotka of Walpi, 607 n. *, 804, 917 n. ‡, 1145

Koyemshi (Koyemsi, Koyimsi, Gumeyoish, Gomaiowish), 4, 50, 51, 52, 62, 102, 105, 128–29, 132, 140, 152, 165, 175, 193, 213–14, 224, 229, 248, 294, 307, 318, 321, 340, 369, 377, 382, 398, 400, 412, 428, 429, 431, 435–36, 437, 438, 440, 470 n. §, 485, 515, 520, 522, 525, 527, 529, 530, 531 n. *, 577, 734, 742, 743, 745 ff., 759, 762 n. ‡, 764 n. ‡, 793, 795, 801–4, 877, 886, 931 n. †, 979, Pls. XIII, XVII; permanent impersonating groups, 129, 757 n. *; mask, 132, 340, 346, 757 n. *, 890, 1122,

1145; Old Woman, 204, 221, 341; origin myth, 221, 248 n. *, 341, 890, 1122; song, 223 n. §, in Keresan, 223 n. §; pigment, 340 n. †, 376, 395; Hopi, 507, 509, 780, 973–74; invited out, 742; games, play, jugglery, 742, 754, 755, 794, 801 ff.; Laguna, 890; change in selecting impersonators, 1139

Kurena (Quirana) society, 129, 132, 140, 166, 175–76, 346, 376 n. †, 384, 397 n. †, 398, 418, 432, 465, 469–70, 534, 536, 537, 676 n. *, 790, 887, 888, 890, 894, 898, 900, 901, 902, 904, 908 n. *, 912, 983, 986 n. *; lapse, 1128

Kwatoko, 178, 186, 187, 203, 358, 701 n. †, 964

Ky'anakwe ceremony, 141 n. *, 203, 228 n. †, 384 n. †, 978; myth of, 223 ff., 385, 390, 400, 471 n. *, 500, 529, 577, 579, 732, 759 n. *, 761 n. ‡, 875, 877–78

Lactation, 94, 95, 109

Laguna, 5 n. †, 8, 9 n. ‡, 11, 12, 15, 16, 20 n. *, 22, 22 n. †, 32, 44, 46, 53, 55, 57 n. ‡, 62, 65–66, 69, 73, 75, 78, 79, 82, 84, 87, 89, 92, 93, 95, 96, 98, 100 104, 106, 108, 109 n. *, 110, 112 n. *, 113 n. †, 115, 116, 117, 120, 126, 131 n. *, 136 n. †, 140, 146, 147 150, 152, 154, 156 n. †, 159, 160, 161, 162, 163, 165, 170–71, 172, 175 n. *, 178 n. †, 179, 180 n. †, 181, 187 n. §, 188, 189, 190 n. †, 191, 193, 194, 195, 196, 197, 201, 203, 204, 205, 207, 209, 211, 214, 233 n. ‡, 242 n. ‡, 243, 244 n. *, 248, 251 n. §, 256 n. †, 258, 272, 274, 275, 276 277, 279, 280, 281, 284, 285, 288, 293, 296, 297, 298, 299, 299 n. *, 300, 301, 302, 304, 305, 306, 307 308, 309, 311, 312, 317, 318, 319, 322, 323, 326, 330, 332, 333 n. †, 334 n. †, 335, 336, 337, 339 n. †, 340, 342, 343–44, 346, 350, 356, 361, 362, 365, 367, 371, 377, 378, 379, 380,

526, 534, 539, 543, 795, 821–24, 883–
84, 886 n. †, 903, 908, as prayer-stick,
206, (?)260 ff., 306, 884, Fig. 1; relay, 48, 62, 212, 393, 499, 547,
638 ff., 795, 913, 927, 931, 936, 958;
with kachina, 48, 141, 269, 508, 736,
795, 815; by women, 58, 796–97,
817, 870, 908, 985 n. †; for growth
or crops, 89, 158, 393, 394, 796, 817;
course, 101, 394 n. *, 819, 823–24,
958; season, 102, 547, 821; associated with Sun or Moon, 200–201,
207, 212, 821, 936, 962; by kiva,
395, 507, 817 ff., 865; loser killed,
blinded, or shorn, 424, 795; omen,
449; emesis, 456; black magic in,
487, 642, 823; overtaking, 511, 543,
795, 817, 870, 908; between kachina
and clowns, 543, 795; betting, 547,
821 ff., 962, 980, 1125; purposes,
720–21; at planting, 736; long distance, 795, 962; by salt gatherers,
1084; lapse, 1131; see also Arrow-
point(s), Clan(s), Horse(s)

Rain, x; -making, 10 n. ‡, 89, 227–28,
251, 253, 254, 386, 410, 481–82, 663,
707–8, 795, 860, and human sacrifice, 220 n. †, competition, 227–28,
234–35; checked, 63; see also Kachina, Rain chiefs, Retreat

Rainbow: Clouds or kachina travel
on, 176 n. ‡, 201, 213; spirit, 208,
411; design, 310, 340; medicine,
415; "house" in sand-painting, 662

Rain chiefs (ashiwanni) or societies,
29 n. †, 54, 68 n. †, 78, 117 n. ‡,
119 n. *, 121, 122–23, 129, 132, 136,
137 n. †, 144–45, 147, 151, 152, 156–
57, 160, 164, 170, 185 n. †, 219 n. *,
234–35, 275, 276, 277, 286, 296, 302,
303, 317, 324, 333, 344, 354, 367,
378, 387, 414, 421, 431, 437, 486,
496, 498, 514, 515, 518–19, 520,
527 ff., 571 ff., 591, 596, 629 ff., 636,
646, 687, 752, 756, 758, 876–77, 960,
1130 n. *; Big Shell, 168, 226, 331,
572; ceremony, 692 ff.; for hidden-
ball, 798

Rattle(s), 43 n. §, Fig. 3; from ka
china, 50, 253; shaman, 190 n. *,
373, 384, 385, 689; of Chakwena
Woman, 203, 224, 225, 328, 385,
424; notched bone, 383–84, 549, 698,
700–701, 733, 772, 787; gourd, 384,
385, 689, 732, 733, 773, 783, 787,
802, 829, 837, 845; scapula or hoof,
384, 540, 748 n. †, 780, 790 n. *, 796,
816, 817, 850, 1143 n. *; shell, 384,
693, 704, 848, 849; scrotum, 384,
663, 666, 982, Pl. II; turtle shell,
384–85, 420, 575 n. *, 608, 619, 666,
733, 744 n. *, 745, 773, 782, 787;
witches travel by, 385; as used by
kachina, 391, 733, 745; American
can, 837; see also Bell(s)

Rebellion, Great, 13, 15 n. †, 16,
501 n. ‡, 891, 898, 901, 903, 911,
913 n. ‡, 924, 932, 1066, 1082,
1092 n. *

Red, 99; for war, 275, 286 n. ‡, 291,
298, 299, 337; for medicine society,
286; head, clan name, 337 n. §;
orientated, 365; for Snake society
feathers, etc., 655, 658, 664, 666; for
Acoma clown group, 763; for Isleta
moiety, 787; see also Hair, Prayer-
feather(s)

Red Eyes or Red Painted People, 61,
129, 143, 265, 275, 385, 645, 929,
936–37; see also Gopher(s)

Reincarnation, 71, 290, 318 n. †, 319

Repetitiousness, 387, 477, 490, 519–20,
592, 599, 693, 1048; see also Four,
Song(s)

Resistance, 6, 19, 145, 156, 966 n. *,
1085 ff.; to schooling, 185 n. †, 1082,
1134; to tolerating witches, 185 n. †;
to American machinery, 475, 1082–
83, 1134; to dance or ceremony, 770;
to questions or riddles, 945; to
peyote, 1029, 1094 ff.; by Jicarilla
Apache, 1045 n. †; to individual
power, 1055 n. §; to making sign of
cross, 1073 n. ‖; to Americanization, 1082 ff.; to railroad, 1083; by
padres, 1083 n. §; to jugglery or

885, 899, 925 n. *, 937; shell token of, 401; hairs in bandoleer, 401, carried on branches, 885; chewing, 417, 625, 928; endowments from, 436; washing, 454, 621, 623, 625–26, 706, 894; scare or fear, 460; hitting with, 474, 600 n. *, 621, 642, 867 n. ‡, 885, 927; tallied, 519 n. ‡; associated with races, 547, 621, 962; effigy thrown down hatch, 578, 959 n. *; baptized, 885: *see also* Smoking

School: row over, 16, 59, 145, 148, 1134, 1139–40; affects calendar, 499, 1139; burlesque, 808–9, 1140; boarding, 1078 n. *, 1080, 1130 n. †, encourages mixed marriage, 1141; undermines religion, 1139–41

Scolding, 54, 153

Secretiveness, xiii, 5, 11, 52, 67, 82–83, 97, 149, 151, 168 n. *, 269, 433 ff., 491 n. *, 620, 898, 940–41, 945, 968, 1081 n. *; society, 82, 107, 253, 613; relation to witchcraft, 942 n. *; values of, 1160

Self-scratcher, 58 n. *, 1055 n. ¶

Seniority: in kinship terms, 56; in household, 109 n. ‡; in kiva or society officers, 143, 162, 894–95, 901; in qualifying for chieftaincy, 154; in clanship, 162, 246, 796, 919

Septum piercing, 876 n. *, 880 n. *

Sermon(s) or speeches, 48; by clowns or bogeys, 50–51, 518 n. †; by chiefs, 145, 468, 532, 541, 582, 590, 591, 642, 873 n. *; by Governor or officers, 149, 649, 791, 1108 n. †

Sex: division of labor by, 37–38, 39–40, 92, 484 (*see also* Women); license, 42, 58 n. †, 226 n. *, condemned, 236, 238, in war ceremonial, 621, 624, (?)647, 648, 757, at Shalako, 752 n. †, 757; determined, 90, 92, 592; in ritual, 484; distinction in ritual, 484; organs, painted on body or rock, 484–85, mock or effigy, 381, 448, 484, 615, 808, tied penis, 485, 748 n. *; not emphasized

in cosmology, 485; *see also* Copulation

Shalako: Hopi Sio, 509, 864, 972, compared with Zuni Shalako, 509 n. *, 973, 1097, 1104; Hopi home-, 972 n. *

Shalako ceremony of Zuni, 23, 42 n. †, 51, 79, 104, 149, 159, 164, 173, 175, 176, 177 n. *, 201, 205, 213, 215, 223 n. §, 270, 272 n. †, 285, 295, 302, 307 n. †, 308, 314–15, 344–45, 368, 369, 373, 381, 398 n. §, 400, 401, 420, 422, 435, 436, 437, 445, 455, 474, 479, 493, 529 ff., 539, 730, 746 ff., 757–58, 875, Pl. XIV; impersonators, 139, 160, 344, 345, 429, 471, 527, 735, 744, 746; whipping initiate at, 468; prayer-stick plantings, 518, 520, 743 (*see also* Shrine[s]); compared with All Souls, 858 n. *; parallels among Huicholes, 1015; possibly Catholic feast celebration, 1077; *see also* Pottery

Shali'ko of the Walpi Snake clan, 16, 675 ff., 1133–34

Shaman(s): conducts infant naming, 46; defined, 62 n. *; transforms, 62–63, 238 n. *; funerary functions, 72–73, 272, 886; eagle feathers, 73, 190 n. *, 372, 373, 391, 400, 420, 539, 604, 606, 648, 687, 689, 711, 713, 737, Pl. IX, leading by, 605, 718; distinguished at burial, 74, 162–63; make sick, 154, 238; compete, 244, 440 n. *; necklace(s), 401; abstinence, 431 (*see also* Abstinence, Continence, Fasting); display powers, 440 ff., 604; traits, 960; *see also* Doctoring

Sheep, 1, 23, 30, 1076; herding, 1, 39, 47, 109, 443, 1064 n. †; killed for festivity, 30, 57, 141, 244, 703, 779; raiding, 31, 32; in trade, 34, 35, important, 1082; owning, 47, 863; bones in firing, 89; dipping and shearing, 109, 150; notice of work-party, 109 n. ‡; prayer-feathers, 570; wool for buffalo hair, 1148

916 n. †, 924, 958, 962, 1026, 1071, 1092–93; anomalous, 101

Tlaxcala, 378 n. †, 1018 n. †, 1069 n. §

Tobacco, 18, 481; offering, present or pay, 78, 80, 247, 282 n. †, 297, 298, 350, 538, 595, 767, 813, compulsive or demanding, 80, 165, 244, 256, 282 n. †, 298, 371, 413 n. *, 486, 642, 785 n. §, 813, 814, refused, 763; chief, 118, 161, 556, 560, 561; ritual cigarette, 297, 298, 366, 371, 595, 623–24, 739, 759, of invitation, 297, 298, 520, 541, 553, 629, 646, 647, 737, 742, 798, 839–40, 897, 1108; in feather-stoppered cane, 297, 839; in reeds of fetish, 323; for dead, 535; see also Honey

Tobacco clan, 161, 705, 773, 864

Towa, 923, 924

Town: solidarity, xiv, 6–7, 8, 9; "middle," 8, 9, 479; plan, 9; foreigners excluded from, 45; permission to leave, 145; meeting, 145, 147, 148 n. †; prayer-feather or prayer-stick roots of, 255, 272, 479; meal design, 479

Town chieftaincy, 114, 118 ff., 256, 776, 876, 949; functions, 6–7, 20, 52, 100–101, 116, 122, 125, 142, 147, 150, 159, 169 n. †, 182, 246, 294, 350, 374, 508, 527, 532, 533, 545, 546, 547, 548, 580, 589, 595, 638, 681, 727, 743, 851, 852, 882, 898–99, 909, 926–27; and land, 19, 122, 882; perquisites, 27, 155 n. *, 157, 164, 363, 495, 588, 743, 788, 825; dual, 61, 120, 195, 197, 250; witchcraft in, 66 n. *, 256 n. §; installation into, 118, 120, 596–97, 882, 902–3, 912, by War captain or chief, 899, 902, 1137 n. *, 1146, see 128, 912; and clanship, 119–20, 142, 246, 368, 882, 909, 918 n. †, 949; and society, 120, 146, 535, 790, 882, 893, 898, 949; and clowns, 120, 129, 901; and kachina, 122, 127, 140, 141, 142, 246, 470, 882, 898, 913, 925; taboos, 122,

152, 155, 157, 475, 904, 1131; harvesting for, 131, 157–58, 363, 534, 544, 790–91, 893, 898, 901, 903, 904, 909, 920 n. *; qualifications, 155, 162, 250; planting for, 157–58, 495, 534, 790, 893, 898, 901, 903, 904, 909; post-Emergence, 210 n. ‡, 246; pre-Emergence, 239 n. *; paraphernalia, 260, 325

Trade, 1, 10–11, 12, 17, 23, 33–37, 80, 129, 445, 847, 953, 991, 1030, 1039, 1057, 1059, 1082, 1100; taboo on, 72, 152, 167, 515, 527, 573

Transvestite(s), 38 n. †, 53, 65, 90, 354 n. †; kachina, 224, 540, 765

Trapping, 27, 28, 197, 1118

Traveler(s): patron, 184; "watcher" for, 189; Spirit, 201–2; prayer-sticks for, 271; puts down prayer-feathers, 290; report by, 370; on caravans to Mexico, 1064 n. †; see also Exorcism

Tribe: homogeneity of, 10; fighting within, 11–16, 898, 905

Tsatiselu of Zuni, 48, 134, 154, 368, 414 n. ‡, 416, 529 n. *, 624 n. *, 1053, 1098

Ts'awele of Zuni, 149, 154, 597, 599, 629 ff., 635, 875 n. *

Tsiwema or José of Laguna, 8, 32, 421, 536, 888, 889, 1143–44, Pl. I

Tü'inoa of Walpi, 155, 157, 917 n. ‡

Tungwup kachina, 203, 503, 506, 768

Turkey(s): as food, 22, 244; sacrifice, 28 n. ‡; domesticated, 29, 932; bread in shape of, 50; burned by sun, 241 n. *; hairs in prayer-stick, 277; given Conquistadores, 881, 903

Turkey feather(s): cloak or blanket, 29, 94, 280 n. †, on prayer-stick, 94, 280, 282; as hair charm, 92; shed for fetish, 247; on prayer-stick, 275, 280, 281, 666, 955, 1113, Fig. 1; in prayer-feather, 290–91, 581, 584, Fig. 1; associated with clowns and dead, 398, 535, 856; for whole bird, 489; worn by scalpers, 645; on head